AIA

Professional 2 Level

ETHICS AND PROFESSIONAL PRACTICE

LEARNING & PRACTICE WORKBOOK

In this edition

- A **user-friendly format** for easy navigation
- **Exam-centred topic coverage**, directly linked to AIA's syllabus
- **Exam focus points** showing you what the examiner will want you to do
- Regular **fast forward** summaries emphasising the key points in each chapter
- **Questions** and **quick quizzes** to test your understanding
- **Practice question bank** containing exam-standard questions with answers
- **Exam question bank** containing recent exam standard questions with answers
- **1 Mock exam** for real exam practice
- **A full index**

FOR EXAMS FROM MAY 2025

Second edition August 2024
ISBN 9781 0355 2582 9
eISBN 9781 0355 2610 9

British Library Cataloguing-in-Publication Data
A catalogue record for this book
is available from the British Library

Published by
BPP Learning Media Ltd
BPP House, Aldine Place
142-144 Uxbridge Road
London W12 8AA

learningmedia.bpp.com

Printed in the United Kingdom

> Your learning materials, published by BPP Learning Media Ltd, are printed on paper obtained from traceable sustainable sources.

All rights reserved. No part of this publication may be reproduced, stored in a retrieval system or transmitted in any form or by any means, electronic, mechanical, photocopying, recording or otherwise, without the prior written permission of BPP Learning Media.

The contents of this book are intended as a guide and not professional advice. Although every effort has been made to ensure that the contents of this book are correct at the time of going to press, BPP Learning Media makes no warranty that the information in this book is accurate or complete and accept no liability for any loss or damage suffered by any person acting or refraining from acting as a result of the material in this book.

We are grateful to the Association of International Accountants for permission to reproduce past examination questions. The suggested solutions in the exam answer bank have been prepared by BPP Learning Media Ltd.

BPP Learning Media is grateful to the IASB for permission to reproduce extracts from IFRS® Accounting Standards, IAS® Standards, SIC and IFRIC. This publication contains copyright © material and trademarks of the IFRS Foundation®. All rights reserved. Used under license from the IFRS Foundation®. Reproduction and use rights are strictly limited. For more information about the IFRS Foundation and rights to use its material please visit www.IFRS.org.

Disclaimer: To the extent permitted by applicable law the Board and the IFRS Foundation expressly disclaims all liability howsoever arising from this publication or any translation thereof whether in contract, tort or otherwise (including, but not limited to, liability for any negligent act or omission) to any person in respect of any claims or losses of any nature including direct, indirect, incidental or consequential loss, punitive damages, penalties or costs.

Information contained in this publication does not constitute advice and should not be substituted for the services of an appropriately qualified professional.

©
BPP Learning Media Ltd
2024

A note about copyright

Dear Customer

What does the little © mean and why does it matter?

Your market-leading BPP books, course materials and e-learning materials do not write and update themselves. People write them on their own behalf or as employees of an organisation that invests in this activity. Copyright law protects their livelihoods. It does so by creating rights over the use of the content.

Breach of copyright is a form of theft – as well as being a criminal offence in some jurisdictions, it is potentially a serious breach of professional ethics.

With current technology, things might seem a bit hazy but, basically, without the express permission of BPP Learning Media:

- Photocopying our materials is a breach of copyright
- Scanning, ripcasting or conversion of our digital materials into different file formats, uploading them to Facebook or e-mailing them to your friends is a breach of copyright

You can, of course, sell your books, in the form in which you have bought them – once you have finished with them. (Is this fair to your fellow students? We update for a reason.) Please note the e-products are sold on a single user licence basis: we do not supply 'unlock' codes to people who have bought them secondhand.

And what about outside the UK? BPP Learning Media strives to make our materials available at prices students can afford by local printing arrangements, pricing policies and partnerships which are clearly listed on our website. A tiny minority ignore this and indulge in criminal activity by illegally photocopying our material or supporting organisations that do. If they act illegally and unethically in one area, can you really trust them?

Copyright © IFRS Foundation

All rights reserved. Reproduction and use rights are strictly limited. No part of this publication may be translated, reprinted or reproduced or utilised in any form either in whole or in part or by any electronic, mechanical or other means, now known or hereafter invented, including photocopying and recording, or in any information storage and retrieval system, without prior permission in writing from the IFRS Foundation. Contact the IFRS Foundation for further details.

The IFRS Foundation logo, the IASB logo, the IFRS for SMEs logo, the "Hexagon Device", "IFRS Foundation", "eIFRS", "IAS", "IASB", "IFRS for SMEs", "IASs", "IFRS", "IFRSs", "International Accounting Standards" and "International Financial Reporting Standards", "IFRIC" "SIC" and "IFRS Taxonomy" are **Trade Marks** of the IFRS Foundation.

Further details of the Trade Marks including details of countries where the Trade Marks are registered or applied for are available from the Licensor on request.

Contents

Page

Introduction

> The introduction pages contain lots of valuable advice and information. They include tips on studying for and passing the exam, also the content of the syllabus and what has been examined.

How the BPP Learning Media Learning & Practice Workbook can help you pass – Help yourself study for your AIA exams – Syllabus – Command words and learning outcomes – The exam paper

Part A The nature and importance of ethical theory and decision making
1   Ethical theories 3
2   Stakeholder theory and ethical decision making 35

Part B Codes, guidance and standards
3   Ethical codes, guidance and standards 73
4   Application of ethical codes 121

Part C The professional accountant
5   Ethics and the professional accountant 145
6   Ethics and the professional accountant: Other aspects 175

Part D Governance and self-regulation
7   Governance and self-regulation for accountants and auditors 209
8   Global governance and corporate social responsibility (CSR) 227
9   Ethics and sustainability 267

Practice question bank 287
Practice answer bank 297
Exam question bank 325
Exam answer bank 347
Mock exam 391
Bibliography 409
Index 415

How the BPP Learning Media Learning & Practice Workbook can help you pass

> It provides you with the knowledge and understanding, skills and application techniques that you need to be successful in your exams

This Learning & Practice Workbook has been targeted at the **Ethics and Professional Practice** syllabus.

- It is **comprehensive**. It covers the syllabus content. No more, no less.
- It is written at the **right level**. Each Chapter is written with AIA's syllabus in mind.
- It is aimed at the **exam**. We have taken account of recent exams, guidance the examiner has given and the assessment methodology.

> It allows you to study in the way that best suits your learning style and the time you have available, by following your personal Study Plan (see page vii)

You may be studying at home on your own or you may be attending a course. You may like to read every word, or you may prefer to do a fast read through and learn through doing practice questions the rest of the time. However you study, you will find the BPP Learning Media Learning & Practice Workbook meets your needs in designing and following your personal Study Plan.

Help yourself study for your AIA exams

Exams for professional bodies such as AIA are very different from those you have taken at college or university. You will be under **greater time pressure before** the exam – as you may be combining your study with work. Here are some hints and tips.

The right approach

1 **Develop the right attitude**

Believe in yourself	Yes, there is a lot to learn. But thousands have succeeded before and you can too.
Remember why you're doing it	You are studying for a good reason: to advance your career.

2 **Focus on the exam**

Read through the Syllabus	This tells you what you are expected to know and is supplemented by **Exam focus points** in the text.
Study the Exam module section	Past modules are likely to be good guides to what you should expect in the exam.

3 **The right method**

See the whole picture	Keeping in mind how all the detail you need to know fits into the whole picture will help you understand it better. • The **Introduction** of each chapter puts the material in context. • The **Syllabus content** and **Exam focus points** show you what you need to **grasp**.
Use your own words	To absorb the information (and to practise your written communication skills), you need to **put it into your own words**. • **Take notes**. • Answer the **questions** in each chapter. • Draw **mind maps**. • Try '**teaching**' **a subject** to a colleague or friend.
Give yourself cues to jog your memory	The Learning & Practice Workbook uses **bold** to **highlight key points**. • Try **colour coding** with a highlighter pen. • Write **key points** on cards.

4 **The right recap**

Review, review, review	Regularly reviewing a topic in summary form can **fix it in your memory**. The Learning & Practice Workbook helps you review in many ways. • **Chapter roundups** summarise the 'Fast forward' key points in each Chapter. Use them to recap each study session. • The **Quick quiz** actively tests your grasp of the essentials. • Go through the **Examples** in each chapter a second or third time.

Developing your personal Study Plan

BPP recommends that you follow a study plan. Planning and sticking to the plan are key elements of learning successfully.

Step 1 **How do you learn?**

What types of intelligence do you display when learning? You might be advised to brush up on certain study skills before launching into this Learning & Practice Workbook but refer to the 'tackling your studies' section below which will help.

Step 2 **What do you prefer to do first?**

If you prefer to get to grips with a theory before seeing how it is applied, we suggest you concentrate first on the explanations we give in each chapter before looking at the examples and case studies. If you prefer to see first how things work in practice, read through the detail in each chapter, and concentrate on the examples and case studies, before supplementing your understanding by reading the detail.

Step 3 **How much time do you have?**

Work out the time you have available per week, given the following:

- The standard you have set yourself
- The other exam(s) you are sitting
- Practical matters such as work, travel, exercise, sleep and social life

Note your time available in box A.   A [Hours   ]

Step 4 **Allocate your time**

- Take the time you have available per week for this Learning & Practice Workbook shown in box A, multiply it by the number of weeks available and insert the result in box B.   B [   ]

- Divide the figure in box B by the number of Chapters in this text and insert the result in box C.   C [   ]

Remember that this is only a rough guide. Some of the chapters in this book are longer and more complicated than others, and you will find some subjects easier to understand than others.

Step 5 **Implement**

Set about studying each chapter in the time shown in box C, following the key study steps in the order suggested by your particular learning style.

This is your personal **Study Plan**. You should try to combine it with the study sequence outlined below. You may want to modify the sequence to adapt it to your **personal style**.

Tackling your studies

The best way to approach this Learning & Practice Workbook is to tackle the chapters in order. Taking into account your individual learning style, you could follow this sequence for each chapter.

Key study steps	Activity
Step 1 Topic list	This topic list helps you navigate each chapter; each numbered topic is a numbered section in the chapter.
Step 2 Introduction	This sets your objectives for study by giving you the big picture in terms of the context of the chapter. The content is referenced to the syllabus, and Exam guidance shows how the topic is likely to be examined. The Introduction tells you **why** the topics covered in the chapter need to be studied.
Step 3 Fast forward	Fast forward boxes give you a quick summary of the content of each of the main chapter sections. They are listed together in the roundup at the end of each chapter to help you review each chapter quickly.
Step 4 Explanations	Proceed methodically through each chapter, particularly focusing on areas highlighted as significant in the chapter introduction, or areas that are frequently examined.
Step 5 Key terms and Exam focus points	• Key terms are definitions of important concepts that you really need to know and understand before the exam. • Exam focus points highlight areas or topics that may be examined.
Step 6 Note taking	Take brief notes if you wish. Don't copy out too much. Remember that being able to record something yourself is a sign of being able to understand it. Your notes can be in whatever format you find most helpful; lists, diagrams, mind maps.
Step 7 Examples	Work through the examples very carefully as they illustrate key knowledge and techniques.
Step 8 Case studies	Study each one and try to add flesh to them from your own experience. They are designed to show how the topics you are studying come alive in the real world.
Step 9 Questions	Attempt each one, as they will illustrate how well you've understood what you've read.
Step 10 Answers	Check yours against ours, and make sure you understand any discrepancies.
Step 11 Chapter roundup	Review the roundup carefully, to make sure you have grasped the significance of all the important points in the chapter.
Step 12 Quick quiz	Use the Quick quiz to check how much you have remembered of the topics covered and to practise questions in a variety of formats.
Step 13 Question practice	Attempt the Quick quiz suggested at the very end of each chapter. These are designed for you to confirm some of the key concepts covered. Some of these questions are designed to cover more than one topic area to develop your ability to apply syllabus learning. You are then ready to attempt the questions related to this chapter which are contained in the question bank at the end of this Learning & Practice Workbook.

AIA Achieve Academy

AIA provides an interactive course of study, AIA Achieve Academy, which offers students the tools, resources and learning environment to study for the exams. The study tools include a course of study e-book, marked practice questions, a marked mock exam module and feedback and technical advice via an e-Tutor. Contact the Study Support team at: Achieve@aiaworldwide.com

Moving on...

When you are ready to start revising, you should still refer back to this Learning & Practice Workbook.

- As a source of **reference** (you should find the index particularly helpful for this)
- As a way to review (the Fast forwards, Exam focus points, Chapter roundups and Quick quizzes help you here)

PQ Qualification Syllabus

The assessment requirements in the AIA exams at the Foundation, Professional 1 and 2 stages reflect a progression of cognitive levels which successful students are expected to demonstrate in satisfying each stage of the qualification. The levels progress from an emphasis on 'knowledge and comprehension' at the Foundation stage, to a predominance of 'application and analysis' at the subsequent Professional 1 and 2 stages and incorporate 'synthesis and evaluation' at the Professional 2 stage.

Indicative weightings for the cognitive levels at each stage of the qualification are defined in the following table.

Stage of qualification	Cognitive levels of learning*			Associated learning outcomes
	Knowledge and comprehension	Application and Analysis	Synthesis and evaluation	
Foundation Level	90%	10%	0%	Outcomes consistent with the International Education Standards Board (IAESB) standards
Professional 1 Level	50%	50%	0%	
Professional 2 Level	10%	70%	20%	

*The cognitive levels of learning are associated with the following:

'Knowledge and comprehension' refer to

The acquisition of concepts, ideas, terms, facts, practices and techniques in accounting and related disciplines and understanding of how they relate to the conduct, management, reporting and assessment of the activities of business and other organisations.

'Application and analysis' refer to

The ability to apply knowledge and comprehension to actual circumstances and situations and to identify constituent components involved (concepts, ideas, terms, facts, practices, and techniques) and the relationship between these elements.

'Synthesis and evaluation' refer to

The ability to bring together a variety of components in order to form a coherent whole, and to form judgements about the application of and value of those components in a particular context or for a particular purpose.

Professional 2 Level Syllabus

Ethics and Professional Practice

Ethical issues arise in all settings where professional accountants work, whether in business, professional public practice, government and public services or charitable sectors. Although consideration of ethical dimensions is integrated into two Professional 1 and all modules at the Professional 2 Level, it is also considered important that ethics and related aspects of professional practice are examined separately in order that candidates demonstrate an appropriate level of understanding, learning and competency in the importance of, and application of, ethics to the work of a professional accountant. This module provides the basis for that knowledge to be developed and tested into a skill.

The module reflects learning outcomes which are consistent with proficiency at the Advanced Level under IES 4 *Professional Values, Ethics and Attitudes*.

In designing the syllabus and the related examination modules AIA has employed 'intended learning outcomes' as the means to communicate expectations to potential students and stakeholders and to inform the specification requirements to be tested in the assessment of students.

The use of learning outcomes:

- Is consistent with what is commonly acknowledged as good practice in the higher education sector; and
- Is consistent with the approach embodied in International Accounting Education Standards.

At the Professional 2 Levels, students are expected to demonstrate that they are able to achieve the following:

Intended Learning Outcomes[1] – Description of expectations	
Professional 2 Level	At the Professional 2 Level students are expected to demonstrate that they: - Can critically evaluate current issues and developments relevant to accounting and related practices; - Are able to integrate knowledge, understanding and technical ability from different areas of accounting and related practices to analyse situations, make judgements and recommend actions; - Understand fundamental principles and concepts underpinning accounting and related practices in organisations and can discuss the conceptual rationale that provides the basis for those practices; - Understand the role of accounting and related practices within the financial and governance context of organisations; - Are able to apply relevant regulations and standards in accounting, auditing, law and taxation; - Know and can execute basic recording and measurement techniques relevant to accounting, management and assurance; and - Are able to analyse financial information and interpret it for the purpose of supporting decision making.

---

[1] The description of the levels of proficiency supports the IAESBs use of learning outcomes in its International Education Standards (IESs) 2, 3, and 4.

Relationship to Qualification Structure

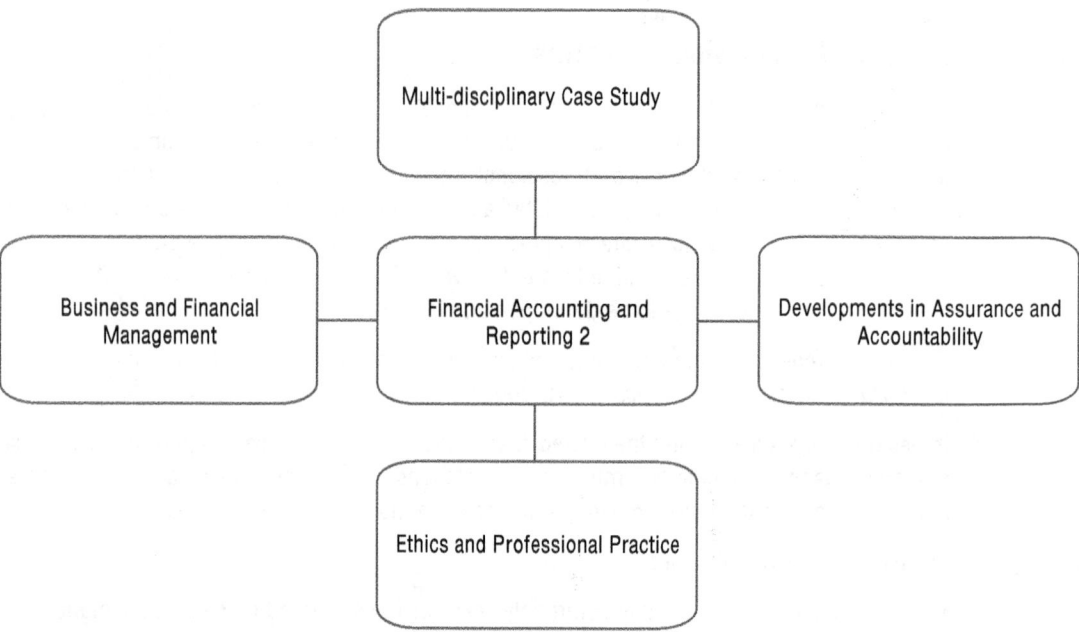

Aims

The aim of this module is to develop and examine the candidate's:

- Understanding of the importance of ethical behaviour in professional accounting and business
- Understanding of the nature of ethical challenges that can commonly arise in professional and business contexts and the ethical implications of alternative courses of action
- Ability to apply approaches to identify, analyse and resolve ethical dilemmas
- Ability to apply relevant codes and standards which provide guidance on ethics for the professional accountant
- Understanding of the responsibility of the professional accountant to the business community, the environment and wider society

This includes understanding the nature and context of ethical decision making in business, and the ability to identify ethical issues, analyse the ethical implications of alternative actions and make recommendations.

Ethics and Professional Practice Learning Outcomes

In order to successfully complete this paper, candidates will demonstrate that they are able to:

- Appraise different ethical theories and use them to assess practical aspects of business and accounting decision-making. **(Learning Outcome 1)**
- Assess appropriate and relevant ethical guidance and standards, such as the International Federation of Accountants Code of Ethics (adopted by AIA) and the Ethical Standard for Auditors issued by the Financial Reporting Council. **(Learning Outcome 2)**
- Critically analyse, using different ethical perspectives, the ethical dimensions that arise in connection with aspects of business and public practice particularly relevant to accounting and auditing with due regard to the account's responsibility towards the environment and wider society. **(Learning Outcome 3)**
- Evaluate ethical scenarios, including threats, safeguards and implications, in order to recommend courses of action and make choices that are consistent with relevant guidance and that reflect standards of ethical behaviour that are appropriate for a professional accountant. **(Learning Outcome 4)**

INTRODUCTION

Syllabus

Syllabus

1. **The Nature and Importance of Ethical Theory and Decision Making (Learning Outcomes 1 and 4)**

   Topic Weighting 25%

   - Absolutism and Relativism
   - Cognitivism and Non-Cognitivism
   - Consequentialism
   - Deontology/Utilitarianism
   - Kantism
   - Application of ethical theory
   - Stakeholder theory

2. **Codes, Guidance and Standards (Learning Outcomes 2 and 4)**

   Topic Weighting 25%

   - Review of relevant ethical codes
   - Role of ethical codes
   - Conflict between ethical codes
   - Application of codes

3. **The Professional Accountant (Learning Outcomes 3 and 4)**

   Topic Weighting 25%

   - Creative Accounting
   - Tax Planning, Avoidance and Evasion
   - Whistleblowing
   - Fraud, Bribery and Money Laundering
   - Public Sector Accounting

4. **Governance and Self-Regulation (Learning Outcomes 3 and 4)**

   Topic Weighting 25%

   - Accounting Regulation
   - Auditor Independence
   - Corporate Governance
   - Social Responsibility
   - Ethics and Sustainability

Structure of the Module

Assessment is by a three-hour 15-minute examination (including 15 minutes reading time) consisting of four compulsory questions, carrying 25 marks per question.

Relationship to Qualification Structure

Ethical behaviour is a relevant consideration in relation to all areas of the work of a professional accountant. As such, this module sits alongside other modules in the Professional levels that develop knowledge and technical skill in specific areas of practice such as financial reporting, managerial accounting and taxation. Those areas may be drawn on to provide the context for consideration of ethical dimensions of practice in this module.

Ethics

This module is constructed specifically to develop and assess professional ethics, and the coverage of the module is consistent with the relevant learning outcomes in IES 4 *Professional Values, Ethics and Attitudes*.

The Code can be accessed via the AIA website at www.aiaworldwide.com.

Recommended reading

This reading list is recommended and not essential for your studies.

You can purchase any of the books listed quickly and easily on the AIA website www.aiaworldwide.com/books

AIA Magazine – International Accountant

ISSN: 14655144

AIA Learning and Practice Workbooks

Ethics and Professional Practice

Publisher: BPP Learning Media

ISBN: 9781509732159

Accounting Ethics – Foundations of Business Ethics (3rd Edition)

Authors: Duska, RF, Duska, BS and Kury, KW

Publisher: Wiley Blackwell

ISBN: 9781119118787

Moral Philosophy: A Contemporary Introduction (2018)

Author: DeNicola, DR

Publisher: Broadview Press

Isbn: 9781554813544

The Audit Process: Principles, Practice and Cases, (7th Edition)

Authors: Gray, I, Manson S and Crawford, L

Publisher: Cengage Leaning

ISBN: 9781473760189

Auditing (12th Edition)

Authors: Millichamp, A and Taylor, J

Publisher: Cengage Leaning

ISBN: 9781473778993

Command words

The following list contains active command words appropriate for use at the Professional 2 level of the AIA qualification. Reference to the command words is essential to understanding how the assessment is applied in AIA exams.

Cognitive Levels of Learning	Command Words	Definitions
Professional 2 Synthesis and Evaluation 20% Application and Analysis 70% Knowledge and Comprehension 10%	Appraise	Assess the worth, value, or quality of
	Assess	Determine the strength, weakness and significance of
	Calculate/ Compute	Select the appropriate method and techniques and apply your knowledge and understandings to work out and show how figures were arrived at
	Critically Analyse	Examine in detail using arguments for and against, and develop a view
	Develop	Elaborate or expand in detail
	Evaluate	Determine the value in light of arguments for and against
	Integrate	Combine information and/or standards and theory from different accounting disciplines or different parts of the case study to provide holistic professional recommendations or conclusions
	Justify	Demonstrate the correctness of an action, claim or conduct
	Prepare	To make or get ready for use
	Recommend	Advise the appropriate action in terms the recipient will understand
	Report	Give an account of the results of the investigation

The nature and importance of ethical theory and decision making

Ethical theories

Topic list	Syllabus reference
1 An introduction to ethics	LO 1, LO 4
2 Absolutism and relativism	LO 1, LO 4
3 Cognitivism and non-cognitivism	LO 1, LO 4
4 Consequentialism	LO 1, LO 4
5 Deontological ethics: Kant	LO 1, LO 4
6 Virtue and common good	LO 1, LO 4
7 Application of ethical theories examples	LO 1, LO 4
8 Influences on ethics	LO 1, LO 4

Introduction

In this chapter we consider ethical theories, focusing in particular on philosophical approaches to ethics.

Ethics is a complex area in which no single consensus position exists.

In this chapter, we consider some of the principal positions that have been taken by ethical theorists over the years.

A major debate in ethical theory is whether ethics can be determined by **objective, universal principles**. How important the **consequences of actions** should be in determining an ethical position is also a significant issue.

1 An introduction to ethics

In this chapter you will encounter various philosophical, academic terms. We have to use this terminology, as the examination team will use it in questions. However, provided that you focus on certain basic issues, you will be able to negotiate this chapter successfully.

1.1 Do ethics change over time and place?

One viewpoint is that ethics do vary between time and place. Slavery, for example, is now regarded as wrong, whereas in Roman times slavery was acceptable. The view that ethics vary between different ages and different communities is known as **ethical relativism** and is related to a non-cognitivist view of meta-ethics.

The opposing view is that ethics are unchanging over time and place. Some courses of action are always right, others are always wrong. A simple example would be saying that it is always wrong to steal or to kill. The view that there are certain unchanging ethical rules is known as **ethical absolutism** and is related to the cognitivist view of meta-ethics.

1.2 Should you consider the consequences of your actions when making ethical decisions?

One view is that society is best served by everyone following certain ethical rules and obeying them no matter what the results are. The argument is that people will undermine society if they disobey ethical rules, even if they do so with the intention of avoiding adverse consequences. This viewpoint, known as **deontological ethics**, was developed by Immanuel Kant.

The opposing viewpoint is that you cannot divorce an action from its consequences and, when taking ethical decisions, you must take account of what the consequences will be. This viewpoint is known as **teleological ethics**. If you take this viewpoint, it implies that you have to define the best possible consequences. The different variations of the teleological viewpoint try to do this.

1.3 What thought processes do people use when making ethical decisions?

What the theories are aiming to do is to complete the following sentence.

'You should act ethically because ... '

The work of Kohlberg has supplied various examples of thought processes, depending on the degree of ethical development of the individual.

- People who are less ethically developed may think: 'You should act ethically because you'll be punished if you do not.'
- People who have more advanced ethical development may think: 'You should act ethically because your country's laws say you should.'
- People at the highest level of ethical development may think: 'You should act ethically because it's always right to do so, no matter what the consequences and costs are to you personally.'

Question | Ethical issues

Briefly explain the main ethical issues that are involved in the following situations.

(a) Dealing with a repressive authoritarian government abroad
(b) An aggressive advertising campaign
(c) Employee redundancies
(d) Payments or gifts to officials who have the power to help or hinder the payees' operations

Answer

(a) Dealing with unpleasantly authoritarian governments can be supported on the grounds that it **contributes to economic growth and prosperity** and all the benefits they bring to society in both the home country and the overseas country. This is a consequentialist argument. It can also be opposed on consequentialist grounds as **contributing to the continuation of the regime**, and on deontological grounds as **fundamentally repugnant**.

(b) Honesty in advertising is an important problem. Many products are promoted exclusively on image. Deliberately creating the impression that purchasing a particular product will enhance the happiness, success and sex appeal of the buyer can be attacked as **dishonest**. It can be defended on the grounds that the supplier is actually **selling a fantasy or dream** rather than a physical article.

(c) Dealings with employees are coloured by the **opposing views of corporate responsibility and individual rights**. The idea of a job as property to be defended has now disappeared from labour relations in many countries, but corporate decisions that lead to redundancies are still deplored. This is because of the obvious **impact of sudden unemployment on aspirations and living standards**, even when the employment market is buoyant. Nevertheless, businesses have to consider the cost of employing labour as well as its productive capacity.

(d) The main problems with payments or gifts to officials are making distinction between those that should never be made, and those that can be made in certain cultural circumstances.

   (i) **Extortion**. Foreign officials have been known to threaten companies with the complete closure of their local operations unless suitable payments are made.

   (ii) **Bribery**. This is payment for services to which a company is not legally entitled. There are some fine distinctions to be drawn. For example, some managers regard political contributions as bribery.

   (iii) **Grease money**. Multinational companies are sometimes unable to obtain services to which they are legally entitled because of deliberate stalling by local officials. Cash payments to the right people may then be enough to oil the machinery of bureaucracy.

   (iv) **Gifts**. In some cultures (such as Japan) gifts are regarded as an essential part of civilised negotiation, even in circumstances where to Western eyes they might appear ethically dubious. Managers operating in such a culture may feel at liberty to adopt the local customs.

1.4 Role of ethical theory

FAST FORWARD

A key debate in ethical theory is whether ethics can be determined by **objective, universal principles**. How important the **consequences of actions** should be in determining an ethical position is also a significant issue.

Ethics is concerned with right and wrong and how conduct should be judged to be good or bad. It is about how lives should be lived and, in particular, how people should **behave towards one another**. It is therefore relevant to all forms of human activity.

Business life is a fruitful source of ethical dilemmas because a large part of its purpose is **material gain**, the making of profit. Success in business requires a constant, avid search for potential advantage over others and businesspeople are under pressure to do whatever yields such advantage. Conflict is therefore a constant theme, with questions arising about how far it is ethical to go in the pursuit of one's own material interests.

It is important to understand that, if ethics is applicable to corporate behaviour at all, it must therefore be a fundamental aspect of the **mission**, since everything the organisation does flows from that. Managers responsible for strategic decision-making cannot avoid responsibility for their organisation's ethical standing. They should consciously apply ethical rules to all their decisions in order to filter out potentially undesirable developments. The question is, however, which ethical rules should be obeyed; those that always apply or those that hold only in certain circumstances?

Ethical assumptions underpin all business activity as well as guiding behaviour. The continued existence of capitalism makes certain assumptions about the 'good life' and the relationship between public and private gain, for example. Accountancy is claimed not to be a value-neutral profession. It establishes and follows rules for the protection of shareholder wealth and the reporting of the performance of capital investment. Accordingly, especially in the private sector, accounting can be seen as a servant of capital, making the implicit assumptions about morality that capitalism does.

This chapter covers several ethical theories which humanity has developed over many centuries.

- Absolutism and Relativism
- Cognitivism and Non-cognitivism
- Consequentialism (also known as Teleology) (utilitarianism and egoism aspects)
- Deontological ethics: Kant
- Virtue and Common Good

2 Absolutism and Relativism

2.1 Absolutism

Key term

> **Absolutism** is the view that there is an unchanging set of ethical principles that will apply in all situations, at all times and in all societies.

Absolutist approaches to ethics are built on the principle that **objective, universally applicable moral truths** exist and can be known. There is one set of moral rules that are always true. There are various methods of establishing these.

(a) **Religions** are based on the concept of universally applicable principles.

(b) **Law** can be a source of reference for establishing principles. However, ethics and law are not the same thing. Law must be free from ambiguity. Unlike law, though, ethics can quite reasonably be an arena for debate, about both the principles involved and their application in specific rules.

(c) **Natural law** approaches to ethics are based on the idea that a set of objective or 'natural' moral rules exists, and we can come to know what they are. In terms of business ethics, the natural law approach deals mostly with **rights and duties**. Where there is a right, there is also a duty to respect that right. For those concerned with business ethics there are undeniable implications for behaviour towards individuals. Unfortunately, the implications about duties can only be as clear as the rights themselves and there are wide areas in which disagreement about rights persists.

(d) **Deontological approaches** (see below).

Many absolutists would accept that some ethical truths may differ between different cultures. However, they would also believe in certain basic truths that should be common to all cultures (for example 'thou shalt not kill').

2.1.1 Strengths of absolutism

(a) Fundamentally, the statement that **absolute truth does not exist** is **flawed**. If it does not exist, then the statement that it does not exist cannot be true.

(b) Absolutism lays down certain unambiguous rules that people are able to follow, knowing that their **actions are right**.

2.1.2 Criticisms of absolutism

(a) Absolutist ethics **fail to consider the fluid nature of societal norms** and changes in moral understanding over time. For instance, slavery was once widely accepted and is now universally condemned, highlighting the potential rigidity of absolute moral positions.

(b) The **basis for absolutist ethics is unclear and contentious**. Should these principles stem from religion, natural law, human nature, or something else entirely? Any chosen source is subject to human interpretation, leading to multiple, often conflicting, perspectives on the same issue and making universal consensus unattainable.

(c) Absolutism **struggles to address conflicts** between two absolute moral positions. For example, if lying is absolutely wrong, is it still impermissible to lie to protect an innocent life? These scenarios highlight the potential limitations of strict absolutist viewpoints.

2.1.3 Application of absolutism in business

Absolutism posits the existence of unchanging ethical principles applicable in all situations and societies. In business, this theory provides a framework for establishing moral guidelines that transcend cultural boundaries by applying objective moral rules; natural law approaches in business ethics emphasise rights and duties. Businesses are expected to uphold these rights and fulfil corresponding duties, regardless of cultural differences.

2.2 Relativism

Key term

> **Relativism** is the view that a **wide variety of acceptable ethical beliefs and practices** exist. The ethics that are most appropriate in a given situation will depend on the conditions at that time.

The relativist approach suggests that all moral statements are essentially subjective and arise from the culture, belief, or emotion of the speaker. This is direct contrast to absolutism which states there is only one set of moral rules which are always true.

The view that right and wrong are culturally determined is called **ethical relativism** or **moral relativism**. Ethical rules will differ in different periods within the same society and will differ between different societies. Acceptance of ethical relativism implies that a society should not impose moral imperatives strictly, since it accepts that different ethical and belief systems are acceptable.

This is clearly a matter of significance in the context of international business. Managers encountering cultural norms of behaviour that differ significantly from their own may be puzzled to know what rules to follow.

Question

Morality

What can be said about the morality of a society that allows abortion within certain time limits in certain circumstances, or which allows immigration if immigrants fulfil certain requirements (eg if they will benefit the local economy)?

Answer

The suggested treatment of these issues suggests that the society is a non-cognitivist, ethically relative society. Banning abortion would be one sign of an ethically absolute society.

2.2.1 Strengths of relativism

(a) Relativism highlights how ethical positions depend on **what people observe** and biases due to the limits of their perception.

(b) Relativism also highlights differences in **cultural beliefs**. For example, all cultures may say that it is wrong to kill innocents, but different cultures may have different beliefs about who innocents actually are.

(c) The philosopher Bernard Crick argued that differing absolutist beliefs result in **moral conflict** between people. (Relativist) ethics should act to resolve such conflicts.

(d) In the global economy, where companies conduct businesses in many different countries and cultures, adopting a relativist approach presumes **more flexibility** and therefore greater success.

2.2.2 Criticisms of relativism

(a) Put simply, strong relativism is based on a **fundamental contradiction**. The statement that 'All statements are relative' is itself an absolute, non-relative statement. However, it is possible to argue that some universal truths (certain laws of physics) exist but deny other supposedly objective truths.

(b) A common criticism of relativism, particularly by religious leaders, is that it leads to a **philosophy of 'anything goes'**, denying the existence of morality and permitting activities that are harmful to others.

(c) Alternatively, some critics have argued for the existence of **natural moral laws** (discussed below). These are not necessarily religious laws. The atheist scientist Richard Dawkins has argued in favour of natural laws.

(d) Ideas such as **objectivity and final truth** do have value – consider for example the ethical principle that we shall discuss later for accountants to be objective.

(e) If it's valid to say that everyone's differing opinions are **right**, then it's equally valid to say that **everyone's differing opinions are wrong**.

2.2.3 Application of relativism in business

Relativism acknowledges the diversity of acceptable ethical beliefs and practices, emphasising context-dependent morality in business settings.

Subjectivity of Morality: Relativism asserts that moral statements are subjective and culturally determined and discourages imposing moral imperatives strictly, advocating for acceptance of diverse ethical systems. Business ethics vary across societies and time periods, reflecting differing cultural norms and values.

Therefore, managers navigating international business encounters must be cognisant of cultural norms and adapt ethical behaviour accordingly. Relativism prompts businesses to tailor ethical practices to accommodate diverse cultural perspectives, fostering cross-cultural understanding and collaboration. It also highlights the complexity of ethical decision-making in global business contexts, where conflicting cultural values may challenge universal moral principles.

3 Cognitivism and non-cognitivism

Key term

Cognitivism is the view that moral statements express beliefs which may be true or false and are in this sense similar to non-moral statements. Non-cognitivism is the inverse of this belief: moral statements are not truth statements, but express non-cognitive attitudes.

Ethical theory in the Anglo-American philosophical tradition tends to think of ethics in terms of language, so that discussion centres on the status of 'statements' or 'sentences' that have to do with ethics. Ethical theorists can then be seen as thinking about moral statements or sentences, ie those which concern whether something is right or wrong, such as the statement "X should not kill Y".

The contrast between cognitivism and non-cognitivism centres on the question of whether moral claims involve knowledge and are therefore cognitive.

3.1 Non-cognitivism

Key term

> **Non-cognitivism** is the view that moral statements do not involve knowledge and are therefore different from ordinary truth-statements.

A non-cognitivist may therefore claim that a statement such as "killing animals is wrong" is different in kind from a statement such as "the glass is on the table". The latter is a statement about a factual state of affairs and may be considered to be true (if the glass is indeed on the table) or false (if it is not). The non-cognitivist would see moral statements as not containing knowledge (cognitions) in this way.

The non-cognitivist may claim that moral statements have their origin in non-cognitive states of mind, such as those associated with emotions. Non-cognitivism is therefore related to **relativism**, which understands moral statements to have validity only in relation to cultural norms, beliefs, and practices. Thus, moral statements are understood as basically subjective, arising from the culture, belief, or emotion of the speaker.

Non-cognitivists may therefore understand the differences that exist between the rules of behaviour prevailing in different cultures as determinative of the validity of moral statements. Therefore, it is claimed that ethical rules will differ between periods of the same society and will differ between societies. Ethical relativists sometimes claim that moral imperatives should not be imposed strictly, since the moral statements on which they are based are not valid absolutely in the same way as ordinary truth-statements.

This is clearly a matter of significance in the context of international business. Managers encountering cultural norms of behaviour that differ significantly from their own may be puzzled to know what rules to follow.

3.2 Strengths and weaknesses of non-cognitivism

3.2.1 Strengths of non-cognitivism

(a) Non-cognitivism highlights how ethical positions depend on **what people observe** and biases due to the limits of their perception.

(b) Non-cognitivism also highlights differences in **cultural beliefs**. For example, all cultures may say that it is wrong to kill innocents, but different cultures may have different beliefs about who innocents actually are.

(c) The philosopher Bernard Crick argued that differing absolutist beliefs result in **moral conflict** between people. Non-cognitivist ethics should act to resolve such conflicts.

(d) In the global economy, where companies conduct businesses in many different countries and cultures, adopting a non-cognitivist approach presumes **more flexibility** and therefore greater success.

3.2.2 Criticisms of non-cognitivism

(a) Non-cognitivism may be criticised on the grounds that it leads to a **philosophy of 'anything goes'**, denying the existence of morality and permitting activities that are harmful to others.

(b) Alternatively, some critics have argued for the existence of **natural moral laws** (such as Immanuel Kant, discussed below). These are not necessarily religious laws. The atheist scientist Richard Dawkins has argued in favour of natural laws.

(c) Ideas such as **objectivity and final truth** do have value – consider for example the ethical principle, which we shall discuss later, for accountants to be objective.

(d) If it's valid to say that everyone's differing opinions are **right**, then it's equally valid to say that **everyone's differing opinions are wrong**.

3.2.3 Application of non-cognitivism in business

Non-cognitivism suggests that moral statements do not involve knowledge and are subjective expressions of emotions or cultural norms. In the realm of business, this theory highlights the challenges managers face when navigating diverse cultural landscapes. When operating in international markets with varying ethical norms, managers may encounter situations where their own moral compass conflicts with local practices. For instance, a Western manager accustomed to strict environmental regulations might find themselves at odds with business practices in a developing country where environmental concerns are less prioritised. Non-cognitivism reminds us that ethical relativism is prevalent in global business, urging managers to approach ethical dilemmas with cultural sensitivity and an understanding of subjective moral frameworks.

3.3 Cognitivism

Cognitivists argue that moral statements are fundamentally similar to factual statements. For instance, the moral statement "X should not kill Y" is viewed as describing an objective fact, much like the statement "the glass is on the table." According to cognitivism, moral statements possess an objective validity akin to factual claims, independent of subjective desires or cultural norms. Thus, a statement like "X should not kill Y" can be considered objectively true regardless of X's personal wishes or the societal norms around them (eg a soldier's actions in war). Cognitivists, similar to absolutists, assert the existence of universally applicable moral truths, suggesting that moral statements hold validity irrespective of time or context. Various ethical theories fall under the umbrella of cognitivism.

Moral cognitivism, which has similarities to the absolutist approach to ethics, affirms the existence of **objective, universally applicable moral truths** that can be known. Moral statements may be valid or invalid, irrespective of time or place.

A number of different approaches to ethics could be categorised as cognitivist, as follows.

(a) Many religions assert the existence of objective moral truths, which they claim are universally applicable across all contexts.

(b) While the law can serve as a reference point for establishing ethical guidelines, it is distinct from morality. Laws are often clear-cut, whereas ethics involves debate and interpretation, allowing for discussion about both overarching principles and their specific applications.

(c) Natural law ethics propose that a set of inherent moral rules exists universally, not derived from societal customs. In business ethics, this approach emphasises rights and corresponding duties. However, the clarity of these duties depends on the understanding and recognition of those rights.

(d) **Deontological approaches** (see section 4 of this chapter). Many moral cognitivists would accept that some ethical truths may differ between different cultures. However, they would also believe in certain basic truths that should be common to all cultures (for example 'thou shall not kill').

Question — Morality

What can be said about the morality of a society that allows immigration if immigrants fulfil certain requirements (eg if they will benefit the local economy)?

Answer

The suggested treatment of these issues suggests that the society is a non-cognitivist, ethically relative society. Banning immigration wholesale, regardless of circumstances, would be one sign of an ethically absolute society.

3.4 Strengths and weaknesses of cognitivism

3.4.1 Strengths of cognitivism

(a) Moral cognitivism lays down certain rules that people are able to follow, knowing that their **actions are ethically correct**.

3.4.2 Criticisms of cognitivism

(a) Cognitivist ethics takes **no account of evolving cultural norms** within society and the development of 'advances' in morality; for example, development of the belief that slavery is wrong.

(b) From **what source** should cognitive moral statements ethics be derived? Should it be religion, universal laws, human nature? Whatever source is used, it is then possibly subject to human interpretation with the result that different views may exist on the same issue and there will never be universal agreement.

(c) What happens when **two valid moral positions** appear **incompatible**? For example, is it permissible to tell a lie in order to save an innocent life?

3.4.3 Application of cognitivism in business

Cognitivism posits that moral statements express beliefs and involve cognitive processes similar to factual statements. In business, this theory underpins the notion of universal ethical principles that transcend cultural boundaries. For example, the belief that honesty and transparency are essential virtues in business dealings reflects a cognitivist perspective. Cognitivism provides a framework for establishing ethical codes of conduct within organisations that are not contingent on subjective interpretations or cultural relativism. Moreover, it emphasises the importance of objective moral truths in guiding business decisions, such as respecting human rights and upholding integrity in corporate governance.

4 Consequentialism (Teleology)

Consequentialism is sometimes also known as the teleological approach to ethics (from the Greek *telos*, meaning purpose, objective or aim). This approach may be contrasted with the deontological approach (from the Greek *deontos*, meaning duty). It is possible to think about the difference between these approaches in terms of the relation between the self (or subject) and the world (or object). Deontology understands ethics in terms of the subject's actions, focusing in effect on whether the subject, or self, acts from a good intention; consequentialism understands ethics in terms of the objective effect of actions, focusing on whether the consequences of the action are good. It should be borne in mind that this distinction is separate from that between cognitivist and non-cognitivist approaches, although it is possible to see some points of contact between the theories.

There are two main versions of consequentialist ethics:

- Utilitarianism – what is best for the greatest number
- Egoism – what is best for me

4.1 Consequentialist ethics: utilitarianism

The teleological approach to ethics is to make moral judgements about courses of action by reference to their **outcomes or consequences**. Right or wrong becomes a question of **benefit or harm** rather than observance of universal principles.

Key term

> **Utilitarianism** can be summed up in the **'greatest good'** principle – 'greatest happiness of the greatest number'.

This says that when deciding on a course of action we should choose the one that is likely to result in the greatest good for the greatest number of people. It therefore contrasts sharply with any absolute or universal notion of morality. The 'right' or 'wrong' can **vary between situations and over time** according to the greatest happiness of the greatest number.

Utilitarianism underlies the assumption that the **operation of the free market in a capitalist economy** produces the **best possible consequences**. Free markets, it is argued, create wealth, leading to higher tax revenue; in a mixed economy this can then pay for greater social welfare expenditures.

4.1.1 Problems with utilitarianism

There is an immediate problem here, which is how we are to define what is good for people. Jeremy Bentham, a philosopher who wrote on utilitarianism, considered that **happiness** was the measure of good and that actions should therefore be judged in terms of their potential for promoting happiness or relieving unhappiness. Others have suggested that longer lists of harmful and beneficial things should be applied.

The utilitarian approach may also be questioned for its potential effect on minorities. A situation in which a large majority achieved great happiness at the expense of creating misery among a small minority would satisfy the 'greatest good' principle. It could not, however, be regarded as ethically desirable.

However, utilitarianism can be a useful guide to conduct. It has been used to derive wide-ranging rules and can be applied to help us make judgements about individual, unique problems.

4.1.2 Application of utilitarianism in business

Utilitarianism, a consequentialist ethical theory, guides business decisions by focusing on outcomes and maximising the overall happiness or well-being of stakeholders. In business, this translates to actions that result in the greatest good for the greatest number of people. For example, when making strategic decisions about product pricing, a utilitarian approach would consider not only maximising profits but also ensuring fair pricing that benefits consumers and society as a whole. Similarly, in corporate social responsibility initiatives, companies may prioritise projects that have the most significant positive impact on the community, even if they entail short-term costs for the business.

Utilitarianism also influences corporate governance practices, encouraging transparency and accountability to stakeholders. By prioritising the well-being of all affected parties, including employees, customers, shareholders, and the broader community, businesses can build trust and reputation, leading to long-term success.

Case Study

A connected problem lies in outcomes that may in fact be beneficial but are not recognised as such. The **structural adjustment programmes** provided by the International Monetary Fund (IMF) are a case in point. They are designed to align a country's economic incentives so that, by improving trade and public finances, they meet an objective, such as debt repayment. The IMF might argue, therefore, that the pain and dislocation suffered are short-term difficulties for long-term wellbeing. Critics of IMF structural adjustment programmes might suggest the opposite; that they are designed to remove money from the very poorest. The rights of the poor are more important than those of bondholders and to insist on repayment is unethical.

4.2 Consequentialist ethics: egoism

Key term

Egoism states that an act is ethically justified if decision makers freely decide to pursue their own short-term desires or long-term interests. The object to all ethical decisions is the self.

Adam Smith claimed that an egoistic pursuit of individual self-interest produced a desired outcome for society through **free competition and perfect information** operating in the marketplace. Producers of goods for example have to offer value for money, since competition means that customers will buy from competitors if they don't. Egoism can also link in with enlightened self-interest, such as a business investing in good facilities for its workforce to keep them content and hence maintain their loyalty.

4.2.1 Criticisms of egoism

One criticism of egoism is that it makes short-term selfish desires equivalent to longer-term, more beneficial interests. A modified view would give most validity to exercising those short-term desires that were in long-term interests. A more serious criticism has been that the markets do not function perfectly, and that some participants can benefit themselves at the expense of others and also the wider environment – hence the debate on sustainability. Most fundamentally egoism is argued to be the **ethics of the thief** as well as the short-termist.

4.2.2 Application of egoism in business

Egoism, another form of consequentialism, asserts that ethical decisions should prioritise the self-interest of decision-makers. In business, egoism may manifest in actions aimed at maximising individual or corporate profit without necessarily considering the broader societal impact. For instance, a company may engage in aggressive marketing tactics to increase sales, even if it means exploiting consumer vulnerabilities or disregarding ethical marketing standards.

However, criticisms of egoism highlight its potential short-sightedness and disregard for the well-being of others. Businesses that solely prioritise self-interest risk damaging relationships with stakeholders and facing backlash from consumers and regulatory authorities. Therefore, while pursuing self-interest is inherent in business, ethical egoism encourages companies to balance their interests with broader societal welfare to ensure sustainable success.

4.3 Consequentialist ethics: pluralism

Key term

> **Pluralism** is the view there may exist several valid views of a moral situation.

Pluralism acknowledges the existence of diverse and sometimes conflicting moral perspectives. It is based on the recognition that different individuals and cultures may hold varying beliefs about what is morally right or wrong. Unlike absolutism, which asserts the existence of universal moral truths, or relativism, which suggests that morality is entirely subjective, pluralism seeks a middle ground. It accepts that while different views on morality may exist, it is often possible to find common ground or reach a consensus in certain situations.

Pluralism emphasises the importance of morality as a social phenomenon. It suggests that our ethical beliefs and practices are shaped by social interactions and cultural contexts. Recognising this social dimension of morality is crucial for establishing rules and arrangements that enable us to live together harmoniously.

A key aspect of pluralism is its focus on finding common ground among different moral perspectives. This involves identifying shared values and principles that can serve as the basis for ethical decision-making.

In the context of business, a pluralist approach is particularly valuable. Businesses operate in increasingly globalised environments where they encounter a wide range of cultural norms, ethical standards, and stakeholder expectations. A pluralist viewpoint helps businesses navigate these complexities by encouraging them to understand and respect diverse perspectives. This approach is essential for establishing a course of action that is ethically sound and socially acceptable.

- **Inclusive Decision-Making:** Pluralism promotes inclusive decision-making processes where the views of all stakeholders are considered. This can lead to more ethical and sustainable business practices.
- **Conflict resolution:** In situations where ethical conflicts arise, a pluralist approach facilitates dialogue and negotiation, aiming for solutions that accommodate the legitimate interests of different parties.
- **Ethical innovation:** By integrating diverse perspectives, businesses can innovate ethically, finding creative ways to address complex problems that single-perspective approaches might overlook.

In practical terms, applying a pluralist approach in business ethics involves several steps:

- **Stakeholder engagement:** Actively engage with all stakeholders to understand their ethical perspectives and concerns.
- **Dialogue and negotiation:** Facilitate open and respectful dialogue to negotiate ethical solutions that consider the interests of all parties.
- **Shared Ethical frameworks:** Develop shared ethical frameworks that reflect common values and principles, providing a basis for consistent and fair decision-making.
- **Continuous learning:** Encourage continuous learning and adaptation, recognising that ethical standards and social expectations can evolve over time.

By embracing pluralism, businesses can better navigate ethical complexities, promote social harmony, and achieve sustainable success. This approach not only enhances the ethical integrity of business practices but also strengthens relationships with stakeholders and contributes to the broader social good.

However, a warning, ethical consensus may not always be possible, and this is a key message of this section of the text. Irreconcilable ethical disputes tend to arise when absolutists argue with relativists, or if you have a deontological viewpoint opposed to a teleological viewpoint. For example during the recent debate in the UK about embryology, deontological arguments on the sanctity of life were opposed to teleological arguments about the scientific benefits of experimentation on embryos.

4.3.1 Application of pluralism in business

Pluralism acknowledges the existence of multiple valid ethical perspectives and emphasises the importance of considering diverse viewpoints in business decision-making. In a globalised world, where businesses operate across cultures and value systems, pluralism encourages organisations to navigate ethical dilemmas with sensitivity and inclusivity.

In business, pluralism promotes ethical dialogue and collaboration, allowing stakeholders with different moral frameworks to contribute to decision-making processes. By recognising and respecting diverse perspectives, businesses can cultivate a culture of ethical awareness and inclusivity, leading to more sustainable and socially responsible outcomes.

However, pluralism also highlights the challenges of reconciling conflicting ethical viewpoints, particularly in contentious issues such as corporate governance, environmental sustainability, and labour practices. Nonetheless, by embracing pluralism, businesses can foster innovation and resilience by harnessing the collective wisdom of diverse stakeholders.

5 Deontological ethics: Kant

Key term

> **Deontology** is concerned with the application of absolute, universal ethical principles in order to arrive at rules of conduct, the word deontology being derived from the Greek for 'duty'.

Deontology lays down **criteria** by which actions may be judged in advance; the outcomes of the actions are not relevant. The definitive treatment of deontological ethics is found in the work of the 18th century German philosopher, Immanuel Kant.

Kant's approach to ethics is based on the idea that facts themselves are neutral. They are what is; they do not give us any indication of what should be. If we make moral judgements about facts, the criteria by which we judge are separate from the facts themselves. Kant suggested that the criteria come from within us and are based on a **sense of what is right**, an intuitive awareness of the nature of good.

Kant spoke of motivation to act in terms of 'imperatives'.

A **hypothetical imperative** lays down a course of action to achieve a certain result. For instance, if I wish to watch a play in a theatre, I must purchase a ticket.

A **categorical imperative**, however, defines a course of action in terms of acting in accordance with **moral duty** without reference to outcomes, desire, or motive. For Kant, moral conduct is defined by categorical imperatives. We must act in certain ways because it is right to do so – right conduct is an **end in itself**.

Kant arrived at three formulations of the categorical imperative. These were published at different times and do overlap.

Note: The term maxim means an expression of a general rule of conduct.

(a) **Principle of Consistency**

This principle may be stated as: 'So act that the maxim of your will could hold as a principle establishing universal law.'

This is close to the common-sense maxim called the **golden rule** found in many religious texts, for example, the bible:

> 'In everything do to others what you would have them do to you, for this sums up the Law and the Prophets.' (Matthew 7:12)

The difference between Kant's views and the golden rule is that, under the golden rule, one could inflict harm on others if one was happy for the same harm to be inflicted on oneself. However, Kant would argue that certain actions were universally right or wrong irrespective of the personal, societal, or cultural conditions.

Kant went on to suggest that this imperative meant that we have a duty not to act by maxims that result in logical contradictions. Theft of property for example implies that it is permissible to steal, but also implies the existence of property. However, if theft is allowed there can be no property, a logical contradiction. Kant also argued that we should act only by maxims that we believe should be universal maxims. Therefore, if we only helped others when there was advantage for ourselves, no one would give help to others where it did not help them personally.

(b) **Principle of Human Dignity**

This principle may be stated as: 'Do not treat people simply as means to an end but as an end in themselves.'

The point of this rule is that it distinguishes between **people** and **objects**. We use objects as means to achieve an end. A chair is for sitting on, for instance. People are different.

We regard people differently from the way we regard objects, since they have unique intellects, feelings, motivations, and so on of their own. Treating them as objects denies their rationality and therefore rational action.

Note, however, that this does not preclude us from using people as means to an end as long as we, at the same time, recognise their right to be treated as distinct beings. Clearly, organisations and even society itself could not function if we could not make use of other people's services.

(c) **Principle of Autonomy**

This principle may be stated as: 'Act as though you were through your maxims a law-making member of the kingdom of ends.'

Autonomous human beings are not subject to any particular interest and are therefore only subject to the laws which they make for themselves. However, they must regard those laws as binding on others, or they would not be universal and would not be laws at all.

5.1 Criticisms of Kant

(a) **Contradictions**

Critics have pointed out a dualism in Kant's views. He sees humans as part of nature whose actions can be explained in terms of natural causes. Yet Kant also argues that human beings are **capable of self-determination** with full freedom of action and in particular an ability to act in accordance with the principles of duty. Man is therefore capable in effect of rising above nature, which appears to conflict with the view that man is a natural animal.

(b) **Consequences**

It is argued that you cannot take actions in a vacuum and must have regard for their **consequences**. The Swiss philosopher Benjamin Constant put forward the 'enquiring murderer' argument. If you agree with Kant and hold that truth telling must be universal, then one must, if asked, tell a known murderer the location of his prey. Kant's response was that lying to a murderer denied the murderer's rationality, and hence denied the possibility of there being free rational action at all. In addition, Kant pointed out that we cannot always know what the consequences of our actions would be.

(c) **Self-reform**

Kierkegaard argued that whatever their expectations of others, **people failed to apply Kant's duties** to themselves, either by not exercising laws morally or not punishing themselves if they morally transgressed.

5.2 Application of deontology in business

Kant's principle of consistency, akin to the golden rule, guides businesses to act in a way that their actions could be universalised as a moral law. For instance, a company that manufactures and markets its products should ensure that its advertising practices are truthful and transparent. Kant would argue that if a company deceives customers through false advertising, it is treating them merely as means to increase profits, violating the principle of consistency.

Furthermore, Kantian ethics urge businesses to avoid logical contradictions in their actions. For example, a company cannot advocate for environmental conservation while simultaneously engaging in practices that harm the environment. By aligning their actions with universal moral maxims, businesses can uphold the principle of consistency and maintain ethical integrity.

Also, Kant's principle of human dignity emphasises the inherent value and autonomy of individuals. In business, this principle requires companies to respect the dignity and rights of all stakeholders, including employees, customers, suppliers, and communities. For instance, businesses should ensure fair treatment and equal opportunities for employees, refrain from exploitation or discrimination, and uphold human rights standards throughout their supply chains.

Moreover, Kantian ethics caution against treating individuals solely as means to achieve corporate goals. For example, businesses should not manipulate or coerce employees into working overtime without adequate compensation, as this would violate their autonomy and dignity. By recognising the intrinsic worth of each person, businesses can foster a culture of respect and dignity in the workplace.

Kant's principle of autonomy posits that individuals, as rational beings, have the capacity to legislate moral laws for themselves. In the business context, this principle underscores the importance of ethical decision-making guided by rational deliberation and to trust and respect for the moral autonomy of stakeholders. For instance, companies should involve employees in decision-making processes, seek their input on matters affecting their work environment, and empower them to voice their concerns without fear of reprisal.

Furthermore, Kantian ethics advocate for businesses to uphold the rule of law and abide by ethical standards even in the absence of external enforcement. By acting as moral agents responsible for their actions, businesses can contribute to a culture of integrity and trust in the marketplace.

6 Virtue and Common Good

For the final section on ethical theory, we consider two more approaches to ethics: virtue ethics, and the common good.

6.1 Virtue ethics

Key term

> **Virtue ethics** is the ancient approach which focuses on the virtues of character rather than on moral actions.

The term 'virtue ethics' refers the approach to ethics that is associated with classical Greek philosophy, most notably Plato and Aristotle. This approach was the touchpoint for ethical thinking in the West until the period associated with the Enlightenment in the 18th and 19th centuries. It was the subject of a major revival in the 20th century, associated with the Scottish philosopher Alisdair MacIntyre.

The virtue approach to ethics has a different starting point from the previous approaches. Where both deontologists and utilitarians alike consider ethical dilemmas and ethical acts in isolation, under virtue ethics the ethical act is seen as part of the person who performs it. This is in line with the ancient theory of substance, articulated most fully by Aristotle, in which qualities which may be 'predicated' or said of something – such as a good act – are understood as being part of the nature of the thing itself (in this case, the person performing the act).

Connected to this, Aristotle understood ethics as being composed not of isolated questions about what would be the right thing to do in a given situation, but rather as the study of the kinds of people we as human beings ought to be. The starting point for virtue ethics, then, is the concept of the Good. The Good is understood to be the aim (*telos*) of human life, so that the study of ethics is not a study of ethical decision making in different circumstances, but rather the consideration of how human beings can best live their lives. There is thus a basic connection between what is right and what is pleasurable; both are seen as part of the Good.

The very approach to ethics that is characterised by the consideration of the 'right' way of acting in a given situation is largely foreign to virtue ethics. An ethical thinker in this tradition would be more likely to consider how best to act in accordance with one's own nature (one's substance, what one *is*) than what the 'best' thing would be in objective terms. This represents a challenge to any approach that understands ethics to be something that is somehow added onto something else; for Aristotle, by contrast, ethics has to do with the pursuit of pleasure itself, since pleasure is a part of the Good.

6.1.1 The common good

Common good theorists advocate the pursuit of what is good for the whole of society over the good of private individuals.

The concept of the common good has a long history; it dates back at least to Aristotle (c. 384 BCE to 322 BCE), who in his *Politics* described good constitutions as being for the common good ('common interest'), as opposed to merely being in the interest of rulers.

There is, however, a significant degree of debate regarding how this 'common good' is to be achieved. This can be illustrated by comparing three different views. For **Aristotle**, the end or aim (*telos*) of an individual life is to flourish, which is the same thing as the good. Aristotle considers that for this to happen for a whole community (nation or city-state) is naturally greater than for it to happen for one individual alone. Thus, Aristotle does not envisage a significant tension between the individual and the community but posits instead the idea of a common good that is attainable by a community and yet shared by that community's individual members.

Contrast this view with that of Jean-Jacques **Rousseau**, for whom conflict is an ever-present risk to social cohesion. As a result of this, political authority is only legitimate for Rousseau where it stems from the '**general will**' and is aimed toward the common good. Power which does not aim at the common good is understood by Rousseau as contrary to the 'social contract' and therefore inhibitive of society's ability to function. Rousseau therefore might agree with Aristotle that society's aim should be the common good but would perhaps go further in stating that the individual good should be subordinated to the 'general will' in order to bring this about. Where for Aristotle there was no real tension between the individual and common goods, for Rousseau this tension is acute – and the common good should prevail.

Finally, **Adam Smith** takes an altogether different view of the issue. Smith is known as an advocate of the free market, on the grounds that where the market is able to operate freely, the pursuit of an individual's own self-interest leads them to co-operate with others by selling goods (or labour) on the market. Thus, for Smith, the common good does not consist of a good set apart from individuals but is instead attained specifically through the individual's pursuit of their own individual interest. Smith therefore advocates the expansion of the market and the restriction of the public sphere, on the grounds that a free market produces both individual and common goods.

The issue is complex, however, because the individual operating in the market does not simply pursue their own pleasure, but rather their self-interest. This means that under the market, the individual addresses themselves not to their own need, but to the need of the other (of their customer); they therefore operate in a way that resembles the traditional 'golden rule' of ethics, whereby the individual directs their activity towards the good of the other. Smith does not therefore hold simply that the pursuit

of individual interests magically results in the common good, but rather that the market imposes a discipline upon individuals which gives rise to the common good.

6.2 Criticisms of virtue ethics

Virtue ethics may be criticised on several grounds.

(a) **No definitive set of virtues**

If construed in very general terms then the notions of virtue or of the good are unlikely to be controversial. However, it is as one tries to be more specific that difficulties can arise. There is no consensus among ethical theorists working in this tradition about exactly what the principal virtues should be.

Aristotle, for example, proposed nine virtues (wisdom, prudence, justice, fortitude, courage, liberality, magnificence, magnanimity, temperance), but it is hard to see whether they stand on a systematic basis.

(b) **Not a guide to action**

By focusing on a person's character, it is claimed that virtue ethics fails to provide sufficient guidance regarding what the right actions would be in certain situations. Antagonists of virtue ethics may argue that it simply avoids the difficult problems involved with deciding between the possible actions in different situations.

7 Application of ethical theories examples

Question — Application of ethical theories: Example 1

When SynTech was shortlisted for a crucial contract to develop a satellite communication system for a foreign nation, it was dependent on paying a facilitation fee to an official in the telecommunications ministry. Although this was an unconventional request, it was made very clear that SynTech would not secure the $5 billion contract, spanning 10 years, unless the relatively modest sum of $2.5 million was paid immediately, representing 0.05% of the contract value.

In recent months, SynTech had experienced a significant slowdown in business activity within the technology sector, and the company was on the brink of announcing around 500 staff layoffs. Therefore, the prospect of securing this contract was a significant relief to the board of SynTech, as it would secure many hundreds of jobs. However, only the chief executive officer (CEO) and the operations director were aware of the facilitation fee.

Given the highly sensitive nature of the situation, it was decided that no formal record of the board meeting discussions would be kept. This approach aimed to promote a candid exchange of views and encourage all directors to express their opinions openly.

CEO Michael Harrison presented the dilemma to the board, emphasising that without this contract, there would be no way to safeguard jobs. The finance director, Laura Kim, expressed her personal discomfort with the idea of paying a facilitation fee, which she equated to a 'bribe.' As a professional accountant bound by a strict code of ethics prohibiting such payments, Laura Kim said she could not endorse the payment under any circumstances.

On the other hand, HR director David Lee took a more pragmatic view. While acknowledging that any form of corruption was utterly deplorable, he pointed out that it was a reality in many countries. He argued that if the board of SynTech decided against making the payment and thus forfeited the contract, a competitor would likely seize the opportunity make the payment to win the business. The consequence would be a disservice to both employees and shareholders, who would undoubtedly experience a decline in shareholder value. David Lee contended that difficult decisions are sometimes necessary in business for the greater good and recommended that the payment to the official be made.

1: ETHICAL THEORIES

Required

Compare the ethical theories of relativism, absolutism, deontology, and teleology (consequentialism), and explain the significance of individual or personal differences in guiding ethical behaviour under each approach in a given scenario such as the situation at SynTech and analyse which of the approaches have been adopted by Laura Kim and David Lee.

Answer

Relativism

Relativism suggests that there are no absolute moral standards and that what is right or wrong depends on the circumstances and the individuals involved. It acknowledges that different people, influenced by their psychological, cultural, and moral backgrounds, will have different perspectives on what is ethical.

- Relativism allows for flexibility in moral judgments based on individual beliefs and circumstances.
- At SynTech, the HR director, David Lee, exemplifies a relativist approach. He views the facilitation fee as a necessary evil to secure jobs and maintain shareholder value, disregarding the inherent wrong of paying a bribe.

Absolutism

Absolutism holds that certain actions are intrinsically right or wrong, regardless of context or consequences. Ethical decisions should be guided by universal principles that do not vary with individual perspectives.

- Absolutism insists on a consistent adherence to moral rules, without exception.
- The finance director, Laura Kim, demonstrates an absolutist stance. She refuses to sanction the facilitation fee under any circumstances, adhering strictly to her professional ethical code that prohibits bribery.

Deontology

Deontological ethics focus on the inherent morality of actions themselves, rather than their outcomes. This approach emphasises duty and rule-based decision-making.

- Deontological ethics require adherence to established rules and principles, independent of the consequences.
- Laura Kim's refusal to approve the facilitation fee aligns with deontological ethics. She prioritises her duty to follow established ethical rules which in society deems bribery to be moral bad over the potential benefits of securing the contract.

Teleology (Consequentialism)

Teleology, or consequentialism, evaluates the morality of actions based on their outcomes. The primary consideration is the end result and whether it produces the greatest good for the greatest number.

- Teleological ethics are flexible, focusing on the consequences of actions rather than strict adherence to rules.
- David Lee's support for paying the facilitation fee reflects a teleological approach. He considers the potential positive outcomes—saving jobs and securing shareholder value—as justifying the payment, despite its unethical nature. Particularly, as the payment represents 0.05% of the contract value and will secure many hundreds of jobs.

In conclusion

Individual backgrounds and personal ethical beliefs significantly influence ethical decision-making.

For instance, Laura Kim's professional training and ethical code lead her to an absolutist and deontological stance. In contrast, David Lee's pragmatic approach, possibly influenced by his responsibility for employee welfare, aligns with relativist and teleological ethics.

David Lee adopts a teleological and relativist approach, prioritising the consequences and context of the decision to justify the facilitation fee. Laura Kim adheres to absolutist and deontological principles, focusing on the intrinsic wrongness of bribery and the need to follow ethical rules, irrespective of the potential outcomes.

Question — Application of ethical theories: Example 2

PlantMed is a prominent international pharmaceutical company renowned for its pioneering research into developing treatments for various tropical diseases. The nature of its business necessitates ongoing and substantial financial investment in research and development, for which its shareholders expect significant returns. Recently, PlantMed has discovered a rare plant native to the Amazon basin that shows immense potential in reversing the effects of dementia, a condition affecting millions of people worldwide each year.

However, the properties of this plant cannot be synthesized in a laboratory. To cultivate the plant in the commercial quantities required, extensive harvesting is necessary, impacting hundreds of thousands of square miles of the Amazon rainforest. This large-scale deforestation would negatively affect indigenous populations, displace animal life, and disrupt other plant species in the region.

Answer

(i) **Relativism**

Relativism posits that moral judgments are not absolute but depend on the context and the individual's cultural and personal perspective.

- From a relativist viewpoint, the decision to cultivate the plant for dementia treatment could be justified if one considers the immense potential benefits for millions of dementia patients worldwide. However, it would also be essential to consider the perspectives of the indigenous people and environmentalists who view the preservation of the Amason as paramount.

- Relativism acknowledges that different stakeholders, including PlantMed, the affected indigenous communities, and environmental activists, will have varying views on the ethicality of deforestation for medicinal purposes. Thus, the decision must respect the diverse moral landscapes of all parties involved.

(ii) **Absolutism**

Absolutism holds that certain actions are intrinsically right or wrong, regardless of context or consequences.

- Under an absolutist approach, the large-scale deforestation and displacement of indigenous populations and wildlife would be inherently wrong. Absolutism would argue that the environmental and social harm caused by deforestation cannot be justified by the potential medical benefits, as ethical principles must be upheld universally.

- An absolutist would likely condemn PlantMed's proposed actions, asserting that the negative environmental and social impacts are unacceptable, irrespective of the potential health benefits. The destruction of ecosystems and the violation of indigenous rights are deemed wrong without exception.

(iii) **Deontology**

Deontology focuses on adherence to ethical duties and rules, evaluating the morality of actions based on whether they conform to established principles.

- A deontological perspective would emphasise PlantMed's duty to respect the rights of indigenous peoples and the intrinsic value of preserving natural ecosystems. The potential benefits of dementia treatment would be secondary to the ethical obligation to prevent harm to the Amason rainforest and its inhabitants.

- PlantMed's actions would be deemed unethical by deontologists because they violate the principle of not causing harm to others, regardless of the potential positive outcomes for dementia patients. Deontological ethics prioritise duty and rules over consequences.

(iv) **Teleology (Consequentialism)**

Teleology, or consequentialism, assesses the morality of actions based on their outcomes, focusing on achieving the greatest good for the greatest number.

- A teleological approach would weigh the potential benefits of reversing dementia against the environmental and social costs of deforestation. If the overall benefits, such as improved health for millions of people, outweigh the negative impacts, the action could be considered ethical.

- From this perspective, PlantMed's decision could be justified if the health benefits significantly surpass the environmental and social damages. However, this approach also demands that PlantMed takes measures to mitigate the negative impacts as much as possible. A teleologist would argue for a balance between the benefits of the treatment and the conservation of the rainforest.

(v) **Virtue**

Virtue ethics emphasises the character and virtues of the moral agent rather than specific actions or consequences.

- Virtue ethics would consider whether PlantMed's decision reflects virtues such as compassion, responsibility, and respect for both human life and the environment. A virtuous company would seek a balanced approach that promotes human health while minimising harm to the environment and respecting the rights of indigenous peoples.

- PlantMed's decision would be evaluated based on whether it aligns with virtuous principles, such as showing respect for nature and empathy for affected communities. A virtuous approach might involve seeking alternative methods to utilise the plant without extensive deforestation or finding ways to sustainably harvest the plant.

(vi) **The common good**

The common good approach focuses on actions that benefit society as a whole, promoting overall well-being and harmony.

- From the perspective of the common good, PlantMed's actions should aim to balance the health benefits of the dementia treatment with the preservation of the Amason rainforest, which is crucial for global environmental health and the well-being of indigenous communities.

- PlantMed would need to consider how to achieve a solution that maximises overall societal benefits, such as investing in sustainable harvesting practices or supporting conservation efforts alongside the cultivation of the plant. This approach advocates for decisions that contribute to the welfare of all stakeholders involved.

Summary

Applying these ethical theories to PlantMed's dilemma highlights the complexity of balancing significant health benefits with the environmental and social costs of deforestation. Each approach offers a different lens through which to evaluate the ethical implications of PlantMed's decision, emphasising the need for a nuanced and considerate response to this multifaceted ethical challenge. The decision-making process must take into account the diverse ethical perspectives and strive for a solution that respects both the medical needs of dementia patients and the environmental and social integrity of the Amason region.

8 Influences on ethics

FAST FORWARD

Ethical decision making is influenced by **individual and situational factors**.

Individual factors include **age and gender, beliefs, education, and employment**, how much **control** individuals believe they have over their own situation and their **personal integrity**.

Situational factors include **the systems of reward, authority** and **bureaucracy, work roles, organisational factors**, and the **national and cultural contexts**.

The work of **Lawrence Kohlberg**, a ground-breaking psychologist from the USA, is of particular interest and can be grouped within the category of 'individual factors'. Inspired by the earlier work of Jean Piaget, who developed a general theory of human developmental stages, Kohlberg wrote about the 'stages of moral development'. Kohlberg is important because he provides an analysis of the psychological processes that in his view underpin ethical decision making. Kohlberg's developmental framework concerns the individual's degree of **ethical maturity**, ie the extent to which they are able to make their own ethical decisions.

8.1 The cultural context of ethics and corporate social responsibility

Models of ethical decision making divide the cultural factors that influence decision making into two categories.

- **Individual** – the characteristics of the individual making the decision
- **Situational** – the features of the context which determine whether the individual will make an ethical or unethical decision

The problem with identifying these factors is that it is difficult to break them down individually since many of them are interdependent. In addition, evidence on the importance of **individual factors** seems to come mainly from the **US**, whereas information on **situational factors** seems mainly to come from **Europe**. This arguably reflects an American focus on individual economic participants, whereas European attention is more focused on the design of economic institutions and how they function morally and promote moral behaviour in others.

8.1.1 Individual influences

A significant body of research exists into the factors that influence individuals' ethical decision making. Some of this is summarised below.

8.1.2 Age and gender

Although some evidence suggests that the ways in which men and women respond to ethical dilemmas may differ, empirical studies do not clearly show whether men or women can be considered as more ethical. Similarly, although different age groups have been influenced by different experiences, again empirical evidence does not suggest that certain age groups are more moral than others.

8.1.3 National and cultural beliefs

By contrast, national and cultural beliefs seem to have a significant effect on ethical beliefs, shaping what individuals regard as acceptable business ethical issues. The social psychologist Geert Hofstede has indicated that significant differences lie in the following four areas.

(a) **Individualism/collectivism** – the extent to which the culture emphasises the autonomous individual as opposed to group and community goals

(b) **Power distance** – how much acceptance there is in the society of the unequal distribution of power, and the perceived gap between juniors and seniors in a society or social structure (eg children/parents, students/teachers, citizens/legislators)

Hickson and Pugh describe power distance as how removed subordinates feel from superiors in a social meaning of the word distance. In a high-power distance culture, inequality is accepted, whereas in a low-power distance culture, inequalities and overt status symbols are minimised and subordinates expect to be consulted and to share decisions with approachable managers.

(c) **Uncertainty avoidance** – individuals' preferences for certainties, rules, and absolute truths

(d) **Masculinity/femininity** – or the extent to which money and possessions are valued against people and relationships

These factors may influence how an individual tackles an ethical problem, alone (in an individualist culture) or in consultation (in a collectivist situation). Other influences might be on how individuals respond to ethically questionable directives from their superiors. In power distance cultures, where hierarchy is respected, commands are less likely to be questioned (I was only obeying orders). Globalisation may weaken the influence of national factors, although there is often a close connection between the local culture and a particular geographical region.

8.1.4 Education and employment

By contrast, globalisation might be expected to strengthen the influence of education and employment. There do appear to be some differences in ethical decision making between those with different educational and professional experiences.

8.1.5 Psychological factors

Psychological factors are concerned with the ways in which people think and therefore **decide what is the morally right or wrong course of action**. Discussion has centred on **cognitive moral development** and **locus of control**.

8.1.6 Locus of control

The locus of control is **how much influence individuals believe** they have over the course of their own lives. Individuals with a high internal locus believe that they can shape their own lives significantly, whereas those with external locus believe that their lives will be shaped by circumstances or luck. This distinction suggests that those with an internal locus will take more responsibility for their actions and are more likely to consider the moral consequences of what they do. However, research does not clearly indicate whether this is true in practice. This may also link into attitudes towards risk and what can be done to deal with risk.

8.1.7 Personal integrity

Integrity can be defined as adhering to moral principles or values. Its ethical consequences are potentially very significant, for example, in deciding whether to **whistleblow** on questionable practice at work despite pressure from colleagues or superiors or negative consequences of doing so. However, evidence of its importance is limited because strangely it has not been included in many ethical decision models.

8.1.8 Moral imagination

Moral imagination is the level of awareness individuals have about the variety of moral consequences of what they do, and how creatively they reflect on ethical dilemmas. The consequences of having a wide moral imagination could be an ability to see beyond the conventional organisational responses to moral difficulties and formulate different solutions. Again, there is little research on this subject, but differing levels of moral imagination would seem to be a plausible reason why individuals with the same work background view moral problems in different ways.

8.2 Kohlberg's theory of moral development

Kohlberg's cognitive moral development theories concern the thought processes people go through when making ethical decisions.

Kohlberg breaks the ethical development of individuals into three levels, with two stages within each level. Although these levels are meant to relate to an individual's experience, in fact all three levels can be related to ethical behaviour. They show the **reasoning process** of individuals. It is possible that individuals at different levels will make the same moral decisions, but they will do so as a result of different reasoning processes. Kohlberg emphasises **how** the decision is reached, not **what** is decided.

8.2.1 Level 1 Pre-conventional (rewards/punishment/self-interest)

The decisions individuals make on ethical matters will have nothing to do with the ethical issues involved, but instead will depend on the personal advantage or disadvantage to the individual.

Stage 1 Punishment-obedience orientation

Individuals will see ethical decisions in terms of the rewards and punishments that will result.

- How will I be rewarded if I do this?
- What punishment will I suffer if I do this?

Stage 2 Instrumental-relativist orientation

Individuals will see ethical decisions in the more complex terms of acting in their own best interests. They will see the decision in terms of the deals they can make and whether these deals are fair for them. For example, it can mean helping others when others appear overworked, but in return expecting others to help them when the situation is reversed.

8.2.2 Level 2 Conventional

Stage 3 Good boy/nice girl orientation

This stage can be defined as individuals learning to live up to what is **expected** of them by their **immediate circle** (friends, workmates, or even close competitors). This can work both ways in a business context. An individual might feel pressurised into staying out for a long lunch because everybody else in his team does. On the other hand, individuals may feel they have to be at work by a certain time because everybody else is, even if it is earlier than their prescribed hours.

Stage 4 Law and order orientation

Individuals are seen as operating on a higher stage within this level if they operate in line with the rules laid down by society or what society believes to be socially or culturally acceptable. This implies looking at what society in general wants, rather than just the opinion of those around them. It certainly means **complying with the law** but it does not just mean that. Directors may, for example, decide to offer better terms to overseas workers because of the activities of pressure groups campaigning against 'sweatshop labour'. Many business managers appear to think with Level 2 reasoning, as do many accountants. Arguably, Stage 4 reasoning underlies most behaviour by accountants, as they comply with financial reporting and corporate governance requirements.

8.2.3 Level 3 Post-conventional

The most advanced level relates to individual development towards making their **own ethical decisions** in terms of what they believe to be right, not just acquiescing in what others believe to be right.

Stage 5 Social contract orientation

On the lower stage, what individuals believe to be right is in terms of the **basic values** of their society, including ideas of mutual self-interest and the welfare of others. This differs from Stage 4 in that individuals act **according to their own interpretation** of what the basic values are, rather than being influenced by the rules of society or the interpretations of others in society.

Stage 6 Universal ethical principle

On the higher stage, individuals base their decisions on **wider universal ethical principles**, such as justice, equity or rights, and Kant's framework. It also means respecting the demands of individuals' consciences. Business decisions made on these grounds could be disclosed on grounds of right to know that is not compelled by law, or stopping purchasing from suppliers who test products on animals, on the grounds that animals' right to be free from suffering should be respected. We must stress here that using Stage 6 reasoning may involve a personal cost, since it may mean failing to comply with existing social norms and regulations as they are seen as unethical.

8.2.4 Criticisms of Kohlberg

Kohlberg argued that the higher the stage, the more ethical a decision was. However, Kohlberg's work has been criticised for:

(a) **Biased sample**

Critics have claimed that Kohlberg's sample is too **narrowly founded** on the typical abstract principles of American males such as fairness, impartiality, rights, and the maintenance of rules. Carol Gilligan, one of Kohlberg's former students, argued that women tend to use an ethic of care with a focus on empathy, harmony and interdependent relationships in ethical decision making.

(b) **Own values**

Kohlberg has also been criticised for basing the **framework on his own value judgements**. Critics argue that the framework values rights and justice above other bases of morality, such as social consequences or the need to achieve peaceful resolutions to conflict or problems.

(c) **Influences on acceptability**

Kohlberg's argument that the **acceptability of a solution** depends on the method of reasoning has been questioned. The stage of moral development reached here would also appear to be significant.

(d) **Method of reasoning**

Critics have also questioned the assumption that moral action is **primarily decided by formal reasoning**. Social intuitionists argue that people make moral judgements in real life without necessarily considering concerns such as fairness, law, human rights, and abstract values. The judgements they make to solve a problem in real life may be different to those if given the same problem as a theoretical problem.

(e) **Assuming individual development**

This is perhaps the most serious criticism of Kohlberg: that individuals do not necessarily progress during their lives and, even if they do progress, it may only be in certain situations. They may use different methods of moral reasoning inside and outside the workplace.

Question — Kohlberg's framework

Lowfloat Airlines has been under pressure from its institutional shareholders to cut costs and boost margins. Its Board issued an internal memo to all budget holders with a demand to 'seek all possible cost reductions'. The memo is strongly worded and, among other things, encourages budget holders 'to push back the boundaries, innovate, and to think the unthinkable'.

Traditionally, a major area of cost had been aeroplane maintenance. Aircraft are constructed largely from aluminium, which is notoriously difficult to weld. In order to overcome this problem, the manufacturers of aircraft resorted to the use of aluminium composite rivets to hold the super-structure together. However, due to the molecular properties of the aluminium used, and the extremes of temperature that planes are exposed to in-flight, these rivets fatigue very quickly. Failure to replace rivets has been attributed as the cause of many of the crashes suffered by Russian airlines in the past few years.

Many aviation authorities lay down strict rules on the replacement of aircraft rivets because the reliability of the aircraft is severely compromised if rivets remain on the aircraft beyond a set number of flying hours. The rivets are very expensive due to the price of the raw materials and the fact that they must be stored in freezers prior to fitting to maintain the integrity of the composite. As such, all rivets produced by aerospace manufacturers are colour-coded in line with an international agreement so that once a rivet is past its replacement date it can be easily identified and replaced during maintenance checks.

In order to cut costs, senior managers in the engineering department are recommending that maintenance staff paint over the heads of rivets that are approaching the end of their recommended life. It is the view of the maintenance managers that rules governing rivet use are too strict and that it is perfectly safe to extend their use by two to three years.

At the board meeting the following opinions were expressed.

(a) We should find out whether and how our competitors are cutting maintenance.

(b) We should not trade human lives off against shareholder value.

(c) Passengers travel with us on the assumption that we are providing a safe form of transport.

(d) We should weigh up the penalties we might suffer if we are discovered against the very high costs of our current maintenance schedule.

(e) We have an obligation to meet the aircraft industries' regulations.

(f) We should find out the chances of being grounded if the aviation regulators discover what we have done.

Required

Identify the levels and stages of moral development from Kohlberg's framework that are demonstrated by the six contributions made at the meeting.

Answer

Pre-conventional

Stage 1

(f) The decision is seen solely in terms of how Lowfloat will be punished if its deception is discovered.

Stage 2

(d) This shows a more sophisticated view of economic self-interest with the costs of different options being weighed up.

Conventional

Stage 3

(a) This argument is based on Lowfloat doing what its peers are doing. Peers can include competitors, so the director is arguing that Lowfloat should behave in a way that is normal for the industry.

Stage 4

(e) This argument grounds ethical compliance as obeying aircraft industry regulations. It differs from Stage 3 in that it sees decisions in terms of best practice as defined by regulation; what Lowfloat and its competitors should be doing rather than what they are doing.

Post-conventional

Stage 5

(c) This is based on the underlying ideas of how society operates and what is expected of business. Passengers, when paying Lowfloat, have the expectation that Lowfloat will be able to convey them

safely. If they do not have that expectation of airlines, then the whole business model would be undermined.

Stage 6

(b) This is based on the absolute ethical view that it is always wrong to give economic considerations priority over human safety. Lowfloat should spend whatever it takes to ensure that passengers are conveyed safely.

8.3 Situational influences

The reason for considering situational influences on moral decision making is that individuals appear to have 'multiple ethical selves' – they make different decisions in different circumstances. These circumstances might include **issue-related factors** (the nature of the issue and how it is viewed in the organisation) and **context-related factors** (the expectations and demands that will be placed on people working in an organisation).

8.4 Issue-related factors

8.4.1 Moral intensity

Thomas Jones, an ethics, and management theorist, proposed a list of six criteria that decision makers will use to decide how ethically significant an issue was and, therefore, what they should do.

- **Magnitude of consequences** – the harms or the benefits that will result
- **Social consequences** – the degree of general agreement about the problem
- **Probability of effect** – the probability of the harms or benefits actually happening
- **Temporal immediacy** – the speed with which the consequences are likely to occur; if they are likely to take years, the moral intensity may be lower
- **Proximity** – the feelings of nearness that the decision-maker has for those who will suffer the impacts of the ethical decision
- **Concentration of effect** – whether some people will suffer greatly or many people will suffer lightly

Research suggests that moral intensity is significant but has to be seen in the context of how an issue is perceived in an organisation.

8.4.2 Moral framing

Moral framing sets the context for how issues are **perceived** in organisations. Language is very important. Using words such as fairness and honesty is likely to trigger moral thinking. However, managers may be reluctant to frame issues in moral terms, seeing it as promoting disharmony, distorting decision making and suggesting that they are not practical. Instead, issues are more likely to be discussed in terms of **rational corporate self-interest** (acting in a way that reduces costs and increases benefits for the corporation or company).

8.5 Context-related factors

8.5.1 Systems of reward

Reward mechanisms have obvious potential consequences for ethical behaviour. This works both ways. Basing awards on sales values achieved may encourage questionable selling practices. Failing to reward ethical behaviour (or worse still, penalising whistleblowers or other staff who act ethically) will not encourage an ethical culture.

Sadly, a majority of studies in this area seem to indicate that there is a significant link between the rewarding of unethical behaviour and its continuation (for example Kerr, 2014).

8.5.2 Authority

There are various ways in which managers may encourage ethical behaviour, for example, by **direct instructions** to subordinates and by setting subordinates **targets** that are so challenging that they can only be achieved through taking unethical shortcuts. Failing to act can be as bad as acting, for example, failing to prevent bullying. Studies suggest that many employees perceive their managers as lacking ethical integrity and that this may in turn affect other aspects of the organisation (Davis & Rothstein, 2006).

8.5.3 Bureaucracy

Key term

> **Bureaucracy** is a system characterised by detailed rules and procedures, impersonal hierarchical relations, and a fixed division of tasks.

Bureaucracy underpins the authority and reward system and may have a number of impacts on individuals' reactions to ethical decision making.

- **Suppression of moral autonomy** – individual ethical beliefs tend to be overridden by the rules and roles of the bureaucracy
- **Instrumental morality** – seeing morality in terms of following procedures rather than focusing on the moral substance of the goals themselves
- **Distancing** individuals from the consequences of what they do
- **Denial of moral status** – that ultimately individuals are resources for carrying out the organisation's will rather than autonomous moral beings

8.5.4 Work roles

Education and experience build up expectations of how people in particular roles will act. Strong evidence suggests that the expectations staff have about the roles that they adopt in work will override the individual ethics that may influence their decisions in other contexts.

8.5.5 Organisation field

Key term

> An **organisational field** is a community of organisations with a common 'meaning system' and whose participants interact more frequently with one another than those outside the field.

Organisations within an organisation field tend to share a common business environment, such as a common system of training or regulation. This means that they tend to cohere round common norms and values.

Within an organisational field, a **recipe** is a common set of assumptions about organisational purposes and how to manage organisations. If the recipe is followed, it means that organisations within the organisational field can provide consistent standards for consumers, for example. However, it can also mean that managers within the field cannot appreciate the lessons that could be learned from organisations outside the field and, therefore, transition outside the field may be difficult.

Case Study

An example would be a private sector manager joining a public service organisation and having to get used to different traditions and mechanisms; for example, having to build consensus into the decision-making process.

The result of being in an organisational field can be a desire to achieve **legitimacy** – meeting the **expectations** that those in the same organisational field have in terms of the assumptions, behaviour and strategies that will be pursued.

8.5.6 Organisational culture

Key term

> **Organisational culture** is the "basic assumptions and beliefs that are shared by members of an organisation, that operate unconsciously and define in a basic taken-for-granted fashion an organisation's view of itself and its environment." (Schein (1992) *Organisational Culture and Leadership*)

Organisational culture relates to ways of acting, talking, thinking, and evaluating. It can include shared:

- **values** that often have 'official' status being connected to the organisation's mission statement but which can be vague (acting in the interests of the community);
- **beliefs** that are more specific than assumptions but represent aspects of an organisation that are talked about, for example, using 'ethical suppliers';
- **behaviours** – the ways in which people within the organisation and the organisation itself operate, including work routines and symbolic gestures; and
- **taken for granted assumptions**, which are at the core of the organisation's culture which people find difficult to explain but are central to the organisation; the **paradigm** represents the common assumptions and collective experience that an organisation must have to function meaningfully.

Organisational culture may be different from (may conflict with) the official rules of the bureaucracy. Unsurprisingly, it has been identified as a key element in decisions of what is morally right or wrong, as employees become conditioned by it into particular attitudes to ethical decision making.

In addition to the main organisational culture, there may also be **distinct subcultures** that are often dependent on the way the organisation is structured, for example function or division subcultures.

8.5.7 National and cultural context

In an organisational context, this is the **nation** in which the ethical decision is made rather than the nationality of the decision maker. If someone spends a certain length of time working in another country, their views of ethical issues may be shaped by the norms of that other country, for example on sexual harassment. Globalisation may complicate the position on this.

Case Study

In May 2009, revelations about the size and nature of MPs' expense claims rocked politics in the UK. The controversy could be viewed from several ethical viewpoints. The controversy certainly illustrated most of Kohlberg's stages of reasoning.

Pre-conventional Stage 2. The idea of deals in MPs' own interests was illustrated by one argument used to defend the system. The argument was that a generous expenses system had been introduced to compensate MPs for the failure to grant them politically unpopular salary rises. Labour MP Harry Cohen stated that the former Conservative minister John Moore had told MPs 'Go out boys and spend it' when he introduced a big uprating of the allowance in the 1980s to head off a pay revolt by backbench Tories.

Conventional Stage 3. Some MPs and their supporters claimed that they were being unfairly singled out: 'He has only done what everyone else has done, so I don't blame him for that.'

Conventional Stage 4. The argument used by many MPs was that their claims were within the rules that Parliament had approved and were granted by the UK Parliament's Fees Office. This, for example, was the argument used by Labour politician John Prescott to justify expenditure on the fitting of mock Tudor beams to the front of his constituency home in Hull. 'Every expense was within the rules of the House of Commons on claiming expenses at the time.'

Post-conventional Stage 5. An argument used by many critics was that, in a time of recession, MPs should not be using taxpayers' money to fund large expense claims. 'He has claimed the maximum amount and I find that morally shocking. The constituency he represents is extremely deprived in parts.'

Post-conventional Stage 6. Some critics went further, arguing that MPs enjoyed a position of trust. They should not abuse this by claiming for categories of expenses that were not entirely necessary to carry out their duties. 'It's not a question of what the rules were. If he and others cannot and did not see what they were doing as morally wrong, then it's time to move aside.'

Chapter roundup

- Below are brief explanations of each ethical theory covered in this chapter:
- **Absolutism:** The belief that there are objective and universal moral principles that apply to all situations.
- **Relativism:** The idea that moral principles are subjective and context-dependent, varying based on cultural, societal, or individual perspectives.
- **Cognitivism:** The view that moral sentences express propositions that can be evaluated as true or false based on facts or reasoning.
- **Non-cognitivism:** The belief that moral sentences do not express propositions and therefore cannot be true or false; they are expressions of emotion, preference, or attitude.
- **Consequentialism (Utilitarianism):** The ethical theory that judges the morality of an action based on its outcomes or consequences, seeking to maximize overall happiness or utility.
- **Consequentialism (Egoism):** The ethical theory that states an action is ethically justified if it serves the self-interest of the decision-maker, focusing on maximizing personal benefit.
- **Deontological ethics (Kant):** The ethical theory that emphasizes moral duty and the intention behind actions rather than their consequences, based on universal moral principles.
- **Virtue:** The ethical theory that emphasizes the development of virtuous character traits, such as honesty, courage, and compassion, as the key to ethical behaviour.
- **Common Good:** The ethical principle advocating for actions that benefit the well-being and interests of society as a whole, rather than individual interests.
- Ethical decision making is influenced by **individual and situational factors**.
- **Individual factors** include **age and gender, beliefs, education, and employment**, how much **control** individuals believe they have over their own situation and their **personal integrity**.
- **Situational factors** include **the systems of reward, authority** and **bureaucracy, work roles, organisational factors**, and the **national and cultural contexts**.
- The work of Lawrence **Kohlberg**, a ground-breaking psychologist from the USA, is of particular interest and can be grouped within the category of 'individual factors'. Inspired by the earlier work of Jean Piaget, who developed a general theory of human developmental stages, Kohlberg wrote about the 'stages of moral development'. Kohlberg is important because he provides an analysis of the psychological processes that in his view underpin ethical decision making. Kohlberg's developmental framework concerns the individual's degree of **ethical maturity**, ie the extent to which they are able to make their own ethical decisions.

Quick Quiz

1. Which view of ethics states that moral sentences involve predications which may be true or false?

    A   Non-cognitivism
    B   Cognitivism
    C   Consequentialism
    D   Deontology

2. Fill in the blank:

    The .... approach to ethics is to make moral judgements about courses of action by reference to their outcomes or consequences.

3. In what areas of national and cultural beliefs has Hofstede identified significant differences?

4. At which stage of the Kohlberg model do individuals make their own ethical decisions in terms of what they believe to be right, not just acquiescing in what others believe to be right?

    A   Pre-conventional
    B   Conventional
    C   Post-conventional

5. Fill in the blank:

    The .... is the amount of influence individuals believe they have over the course of their own lives.

6. What are the six criteria that Jones suggests will be used to determine how significant an ethical issue is?

7. How does absolutism differ from relativism in its approach to ethical decision-making?

8. Explain how cognitivism and non-cognitivism differ in their understanding of moral sentences.

9. Provide an example of a business decision that would be evaluated differently under a consequentialist ethical framework.

10. How does Kant's deontological ethics differ from consequentialism in terms of determining the morality of actions?

11. Describe how virtue ethics focuses on the character of individuals rather than their actions.

12. What is the central principle of the common good approach to ethics, and how does it apply to business decision-making?

Answers to Quick Quiz

1. B   Cognitivism

2. Teleological or consequentialist

3.
    - Individualism vs collectivism
    - Acceptance of unequal distribution of power and status
    - How much individuals wish to avoid uncertainties
    - Masculinity vs femininity, money and possessions vs people and relationships

4. C   Post-conventional

5. Locus of control

6.
    - Magnitude of consequences
    - Social consequences
    - Probability of effect
    - Temporal immediacy
    - Proximity
    - Concentration of effect

7. Absolutism asserts that there are objective and universal moral principles, while Relativism argues that moral principles are subjective and vary based on cultural, societal, or individual perspectives.

8. Cognitivism holds that moral sentences have truth value and can be evaluated as true or false based on facts or reasoning, whereas Non-cognitivism argues that moral sentences do not express propositions and therefore cannot be true or false.

9. A business decision that focuses solely on maximising profits without considering its impact on the environment or society would be evaluated differently under a consequentialist framework. Consequentialism would assess the decision based on its outcomes, weighing the benefits and harms to all stakeholders.

10. Kant's deontological ethics emphasises moral duty and the intention behind actions rather than their consequences. Unlike consequentialism, which evaluates actions based on their outcomes, Kantian ethics considers actions intrinsically right or wrong based on whether they adhere to universal moral principles, such as the categorical imperative.

11. Virtue ethics focuses on cultivating virtuous character traits, such as honesty, courage, and compassion, rather than prescribing specific rules or actions. It emphasises the development of moral character and the pursuit of excellence in being rather than doing.

12. The central principle of the Common Good approach to ethics is the pursuit of what benefits the whole of society rather than individual interests. In business decision-making, this means considering the impact of actions on all stakeholders, including employees, customers, communities, and the environment, and striving for outcomes that promote the well-being of society as a whole.

Stakeholder theory and ethical decision making

Topic list	Syllabus reference
1 Stakeholder theory	LO 1, LO 4
2 Application of ethical theory	LO 1, LO 4

Introduction

This chapter focuses on ethical decision making, considering the question of to whom a company is ethically bound in the context of stakeholder theory, before moving on to cover the application of ethical theory in more general terms.

1 Stakeholder theory

FAST FORWARD

In legal terms, companies are the property of their owners and can, in principle, do whatever they decide to do in the interests of their owners, disregarding the needs or interests of others. Notwithstanding this, however, it has been claimed that the various others who are affected by the company should also be taken into account when it makes decisions. These others are the **stakeholders**.

1.1 Stakeholders

Key term

Stakeholders are any entity (person, group or possibly non-human entity) that can **affect** or **be affected by** the achievements of an organisation's objectives. It is a **bi-directional** relationship. Each stakeholder group has different **expectations** about what it wants and different **claims** on the organisation.

1.1.1 Stakeholder claims

Before considering stakeholder theory as such, we will look first at the nature of the claims made on companies by stakeholders.

The definition above highlights the important point for both business ethics and strategy: that stakeholders do more than merely exist; they also have claims on an organisation. Some stakeholders want to influence what the organisation does. Others are mainly concerned with how the organisation affects them and may want to increase or decrease this effect. However, there is the problem that some stakeholders do not know that they have a claim against the organisation, or know that they have a claim but do not know what it is.

A useful distinction can be drawn between direct and indirect stakeholder claims:

(a) Stakeholders who make **direct claims** do so with their own voice and generally do so clearly. Normally stakeholders with direct claims themselves communicate with the company.

(b) Stakeholders who have **indirect claims** are generally unable to make the claims themselves because they are for some reason inarticulate or voiceless. Although they cannot express their claim directly to the organisation, this does not necessarily invalidate their claim. Stakeholders may lack power because they have no significance for the organisation, have no physical voice (animals and plants), are remote from the organisation (suppliers based in other countries) or are future generations.

We shall discuss further the issue of the relative legitimacy of stakeholder claims and direct and indirect stakeholders later in this section.

1.1.2 Importance of recognition of stakeholder claims

Knowledge of who stakeholders are and what claims they make is a vital part of an organisation's **risk assessment**, since the **claims** made by the stakeholder can affect the achievement of objectives. Stakeholders also have **influences** over the organisation. It is important to identify what these are and how significant they are, since it may determine the organisation's decision if it has to decide between competing stakeholder claims. We discuss the assessment of the influence of stakeholders in terms of their power and interest below. An organisation also needs to know where likely **areas of conflict and tension between stakeholders** may arise.

1.1.3 Misinterpretation of stakeholder claims

As we shall see later in this chapter, the **assessment of stakeholder claims** is potentially a difficult, subjective process. Organisations may also **misinterpret** the claims that stakeholders have or are making. This can mean that organisations take wrong or unnecessary actions, or fail to take the right actions, to deal with stakeholder concerns. It also may distort organisational priorities. There is possibly also an increased chance of **conflict** between the organisation and some stakeholders, as stakeholders who have strong grounds for feeling that their concerns are not being addressed properly can take action.

1.2 Stockholder theory (shareholder theory)

The theory that focuses on the interests of shareholders is known as 'stockholder' theory, since it is mostly discussed in American literature (where shares are often referred to as 'stocks').

Stockholder theory states that shareholders alone have a legitimate claim to influence over the company. It uses agency theory to argue that shareholders (as principals) own the company. Hence directors as agents have a moral and legal duty only to take account of shareholders' interests. As it is assumed that shareholders wish to maximise their returns, then directors' sole duty is to pursue profit maximisation.

The economist Milton Freidman was a forceful advocate of this viewpoint. Friedman claimed that managers are responsible to the company's owners who generally aim to make as much money as possible. However, if managers act in line with their social responsibilities, then, logically, they have to act in some ways that are not directly in the interests of the owners and they will spend money for purposes other than those that are in those owners' interests. This problem will be particularly acute where the interests of the owners are opposed to those of the stakeholders in question, for example, where employees request a pay rise. In this case, managers who take into account stakeholders would not be acting properly as agents of the company's owners (ie of the shareholders). Instead they would be in effect raising taxes – limits on the shareholders' private appropriation of resources – and deciding how these taxes should be spent, which Friedman claims to be the proper function of government, not of companies.

1.3 Problems with the stockholder view

Modern corporations have been seen as **so powerful, socially, economically and politically**, that **unrestrained use of their power** will inevitably **damage other people's rights**. For example, they may blight an entire community by closing a major factory, inflicting long-term unemployment on a large proportion of the local workforce. They may use their purchasing power or market share to impose unequal contracts on suppliers and customers alike. They may exercise undesirable influence over government through their investment decisions. There is also the argument that corporations exist within society and are **dependent on it for the resources** they use. Some of these resources are obtained by direct contracts with suppliers but others are not, being provided by government expenditure or being part of the wider community.

1.4 Stakeholder theory

Stakeholder theory proposes **corporate accountability** to a broad range of stakeholders. It is based on companies being so large, and their impact on society being so significant, that they cannot just be responsible to their shareholders. There is a moral case for a business knowing how its decisions affect people both inside and outside the organisation. Stakeholders should also be seen not as just existing, but as **making legitimate demands** on an organisation. The relationship should be seen as a **two-way** relationship. There is much debate about which demands are legitimate, as we shall discuss below.

What stakeholders want from an organisation will vary. Some will actively seek to influence what the organisation does and others may be concerned with limiting the effects of the organisation's activities on themselves.

Relations with stakeholders can also vary. Possible relationships can include conflict, support, regular dialogue or joint enterprise.

Case Study — Animals

To what extent do you believe that animals should be considered as stakeholders? This is more than just a hypothetical question.

(a) Vegetarians do not eat meat because they believe that eating meat is wrong. Animals are ends in themselves, and do not exist just for our pleasure.

(b) Some anti-vivisection campaigners, such as The Body Shop, a cosmetics retailer, state they are against 'animal testing'.

(c) Even if animals are to be eaten, some cultures require them to be treated well, according to humane standards, as animals are capable of suffering.

(d) The moral status of particular species of animals varies from **culture** to **culture**. Pigs are 'unclean' in Judaism and Islam. Beef is forbidden to Hindus. British people do not eat 'horse', although horses are eaten in other European countries. Similarly, eating dogs is perfectly acceptable in some cultures, but is totally unacceptable elsewhere. Guinea pigs are a food staple in the Andean countries, but are school pets in Britain. In some cultures, insects are eaten, in others, not.

(e) How would your views differ if you believed, as is the case in some religions, that animals contain the reincarnated souls of dead people?

(f) How would your view change if you believed that, like humans, some animal species are able to 'learn', exhibit altruistic behaviour, and that our sense of right and wrong results from evolutionary adaptation of the social behaviour patterns of our primate ancestors? (de Waal, 2001)

1.5 Instrumental vs normative views of stakeholders

Thomas Donaldson and Lee Preston were leading figures in the development of stakeholder theory. They suggested that there are two principal types of motivation for organisations responding to stakeholder concerns: the instrumental view and the normative view.

1.5.1 Instrumental view of stakeholders

In this view, stakeholders are not valuable in themselves, but should be taken into account by a business which aims to act in the interests of shareholders. Thus stakeholders are important, but only 'instrumentally' so – as a means to the end of increasing value for shareholders. This view could be considered a refinement of the traditional 'stockholder theory' – the refinement being that it may be in the interests of shareholders for the business to take other stakeholders into account.

This reflects the view that organisations have **mainly economic responsibilities** (plus the legal responsibilities that they have to fulfil in order to keep trading). In this viewpoint, fulfilment of responsibilities towards stakeholders is desirable because it contributes to companies maximising their profits or fulfilling other objectives, such as gaining market share and meeting legal or stock exchange requirements. Therefore a business does not have any moral standpoint of its own. It merely reflects whatever the concerns are of the stakeholders it cannot afford to upset, such as customers looking for green companies or talented employees looking for pleasant working environments. The organisation is using shareholders **instrumentally** to pursue other objectives.

1.5.2 Normative view of stakeholders

In this view, stakeholders are seen as valuable in themselves. The normative view of stakeholders does not treat stakeholders as merely existing in some state of neutrality, but instead evaluates them positively. Stakeholders are seen as the end – not the means – of the company's actions.

This is based on the idea that organisations have moral duties towards stakeholders. Thus accommodating stakeholder concerns is an end in itself. This suggests the existence of **ethical and philanthropic responsibilities** as well as economic and legal responsibilities and organisations focusing on being **altruistic**.

The normative view is related to some of the ideas of the German philosopher, Immanuel Kant. Kant argued for the existence of **civil duties** that are important in maintaining and increasing the net good in society. Duties include the **moral duty to take account of the concerns and opinions** of others. Not to do so will result in breakdown of social cohesion, leading to everyone being morally worse off, and possibly losing out economically as well.

Variations on the normative view have arisen in recent years, such as Michael Porter's notion of 'Creating shared value'. This view regards the interests of shareholders and stakeholders as mutually dependent, so that the pursuit of a company's competitiveness should also entail sharing value with communities.

1.6 Classifications of stakeholders

Stakeholders can be classified by their proximity to the organisation.

Stakeholder group	Members
Internal stakeholders	Employees, management
Connected stakeholders	Shareholders, customers, suppliers, lenders, trade unions, competitors
External stakeholders	The Government, local government, the public, pressure groups, opinion leaders

There are other ways of classifying stakeholders.

1.6.1 Legitimate and illegitimate stakeholders

Stakeholder group	Members
Legitimate stakeholders	Those who have valid claims on the organisation
Illegitimate stakeholders	Those whose claims on the organisation are not valid

This is possibly the most subjective distinction of all, depending as it does on views of which stakeholders should have a claim against the organisation. However, it is also the **most important**. A number of bases have been suggested for determining legitimacy.

- A contractual or exchange basis
- Different types of claim including legal, ownership or the firm being responsible for their welfare
- Stakeholders having something at risk as a result of investment in the firm or being affected by the firm's activities
- Moral grounds; that the stakeholders benefit from or are harmed by the firm, or that their rights are being violated or not respected by the firm

Ultimately how the **legitimacy of each stakeholder's claim** is viewed may well depend on the ethical and political perspective of the person judging it. The stockholder view, for example, would make the distinction solely on whether the stakeholder has an active economic relationship with the organisation. Stakeholders who might be difficult to categorise in this way include pressure groups and charities. However, others would argue for a wider definition, maybe including distant communities, other species, or future generations.

The problem of perception can result in **conflict** between stakeholders and the organisation. Stakeholder may claim legitimacy wrongly or management views of legitimacy may not be the same as stakeholders' own perceptions.

1.6.2 Direct and indirect stakeholders

Stakeholder group	Members
Direct stakeholders	Those who know they can affect or are affected by the organisation's activities – employees, major customers and suppliers
Indirect stakeholders	Those who are unaware of the claims they have on the organisation or who cannot express their claim directly – wildlife, individual customers or suppliers of a large organisation, future generations

This classification links to the discussion above about direct and indirect claims. It demonstrates a potential problem; that stakeholders who have the largest claim on an organisation may not be aware of its activities and its impact on them. A further issue is that indirect stakeholders' claims have to be interpreted by someone else in order to be directly expressed. How can we tell what future generations would say? Do environmental pressure groups fairly interpret the needs of the natural environment?

1.6.3 Recognised and unrecognised stakeholders

Stakeholder group	Members
Recognised stakeholders	Those whose interests and views managers consider when deciding on strategy
Unrecognised stakeholders	Those whose claims are not taken into account in the organisation's decision making – these may be the same as illegitimate stakeholders

These categories refer to whether a stakeholder is recognised by management, which is distinct from whether that stakeholder is legitimate.

1.6.4 Narrow and wide stakeholders

Stakeholder group	Members
Narrow stakeholders	Those most affected by the organisation's strategy – shareholders, managers, employees, suppliers, dependent customers
Wide stakeholders	Those less affected by the organisation's strategy – government, less dependent customers, the wider community

One implication of this classification might appear to be that organisations should pay most attention to narrow stakeholders, less to wider stakeholders.

1.6.5 Primary and secondary stakeholders

Stakeholder group	Members
Primary stakeholders	Those without whose participation the organisation will have difficulty continuing as a going concern, such as shareholders, customers, suppliers and government (tax and legislation)
Secondary stakeholders	Those whose loss of participation will not affect the company's continued existence, such as broad communities (and perhaps management)

Clearly an organisation **must** keep its primary stakeholders happy. The distinction between this classification and the narrow-wide classification is that the narrow-wide classification is based on how much the **organisation affects** the stakeholder. The primary-secondary classification is based on how much the **stakeholders affect the organisation**.

1.6.6 Active and passive stakeholders

Stakeholder group	Members
Active stakeholders	Those who seek to participate in the organisation's activities. Active stakeholders include managers, employees and institutional shareholders, but may also include other groups that are not part of the organisation's structure, such as regulators or pressure groups
Passive stakeholders	Those who do not seek to participate in policy making, such as most shareholders, local communities and government

Passive stakeholders may nevertheless still be interested and powerful. If corporate governance arrangements are to develop, there may be a need for powerful passive shareholders to take a more active role. Hence, as we shall see below, there has been emphasis on institutional shareholders who own a large part of listed companies' shares actively using their power as major shareholders to promote better corporate governance.

1.6.7 Voluntary and involuntary stakeholders

Stakeholder group	Members
Voluntary stakeholders	Those who engage with the organisation of their own free will and choice, and who can detach themselves from the relationship – management, employees, customers, suppliers, shareholders and pressure groups
Involuntary stakeholders	Those whose involvement with the organisation is imposed and who cannot themselves choose to withdraw from the relationship – regulators, government, local communities, neighbours, the natural world, future generations

1.6.8 Known and unknown stakeholders

Stakeholder group	Members
Known stakeholders	Those whose existence is known to the organisation
Unknown stakeholders	Those whose existence is unknown to the organisation (undiscovered species, communities in proximity to overseas suppliers)

This distinction is important if you argue that an organisation should seek out all possible stakeholders before a decision is taken. The implication of this view is that the organisation should aim for its policies to have **minimal impact**.

1.7 Assessing the relative importance of stakeholder interests

Apart from the problem of taking different stakeholder interests into account, an organisation also faces the problem of **weighing shareholder interests** when considering future strategy. How, for example, do you compare the interest of a major shareholder with the interest of a local resident coping with the noise and smell from the company's factory?

When formulating and evaluating financial strategies, it is important to bear in mind the organisation's stakeholders. These are people or groups who have an interest in the organisation's activities. Depending on the precise relationship between the organisation and the stakeholder group, the success of the financial strategy can be affected significantly by the stakeholder group.

The various groups of internal and external stakeholders of an organisation will have diverse goals. They will exercise different levels of influence on the organisation and, in some cases, will affect the organisation's financial strategy. For example, an organisation's lenders have significant legal rights that have to be fulfilled by an organisation. Failure on the company's part to satisfy their obligations in relation to this powerful stakeholder group could lead to the company being liquidated.

A summary of typical stakeholders is provided in the following diagram.

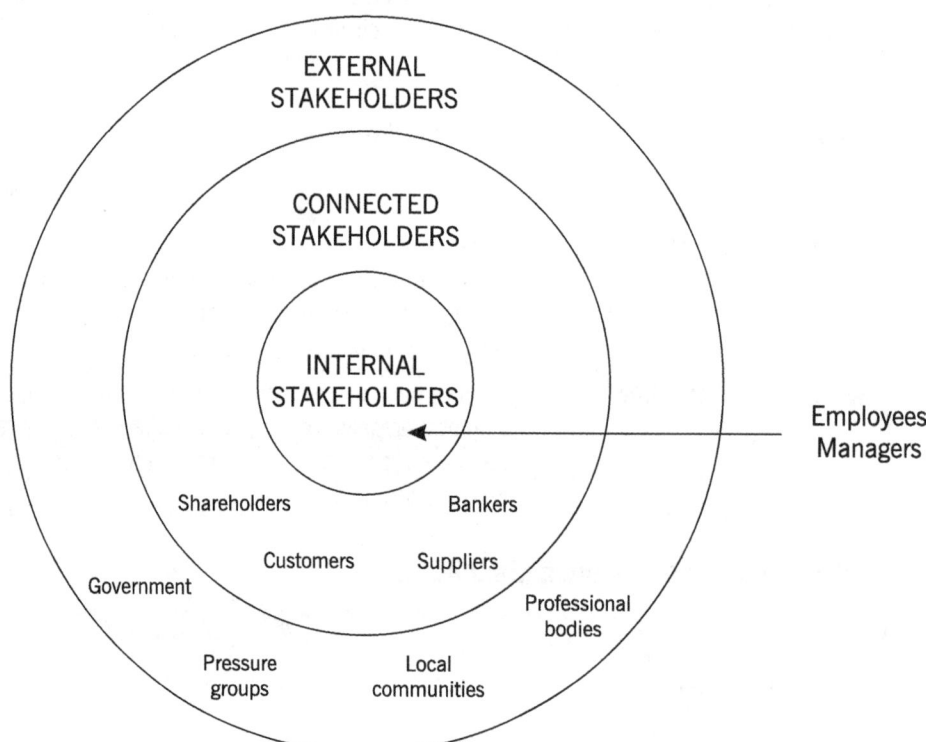

The following table is a summary of wider stakeholder objectives:

Stakeholder goals	
Shareholders	Providers of risk capital, aim to maximise wealth
Suppliers	Often other businesses, aim to be paid full amount by date agreed, but want to continue long-term trading relationship, and so may accept later payment
Long-term lenders	Wish to receive payments of interest and capital on loan by due date for repayment
Employees	Maximise rewards paid to them in salaries and benefits, also prefer continuity in employment
Government	Political and economic objectives such as sustained economic growth and high employment
Community	Wish to have a good 'corporate neighbour'. Source of stable employment and income for the local community. Economic regeneration
Management	Maximising their own rewards, safeguarding career prospects

The actions of stakeholder groups in pursuit of their various goals can exert influence on strategy. The **greater** the **power** of the **stakeholder**, the greater their influence will be.

Many managers acknowledge that the interests of some stakeholder groups (eg themselves and employees) should be recognised and provided for, even if this means that the interests of shareholders might be adversely affected. Not all stakeholder group interests can be given specific attention in the decisions of management, but those stakeholders for whom management recognises and accepts a responsibility are referred to as **constituents** of the firm.

All organisations have a range of stakeholders or stakeholder groups. Some stakeholders may be relatively passive or lack influence. However, some organisations have stakeholders whose influence can be disruptive of the achievement of strategic goals.

1.8 Stakeholder objectives

The **stakeholder view** is particularly important in the business context, where shareholders own the business but employees, customers and government also have particularly strong claims to having their interests considered.

1.8.1 Stakeholder objectives

The following are some examples of stakeholders' objectives. These examples are not intended to be comprehensive, more to demonstrate why organisations are driven to improve business performance, adapt to external markets or innovate and diversify.

(a) **Employees and managers**

    (i) Job security (over and above legal protection)
    (ii) Good conditions of work (above minimum safety standards)
    (iii) Job satisfaction
    (iv) Career development and relevant training
    (v) Personal achievement

(b) **Customers**

    (i) Products of a certain quality at a reasonable price
    (ii) Products that should last a certain number of years
    (iii) A product or service that specifically meets customer needs
    (iv) A product or service which is new, innovative or provides a seamless customer experience

(c) **Suppliers**: Regular orders in return for reliable delivery and good service

(d) **Shareholders**: Long-term wealth enhancement within acceptable risk levels

(e) **Providers of loan capital (stockholders):** Reliable payment of interest and capital repayments due and maintenance of the value of any security

(f) **Society as a whole**

    (i) Control environmental pollution, reduce energy consumption and increase usage of renewable resources
    (ii) Provide fair wages, employment rights and conditions, training and advancement opportunities
    (iii) Provide a regular source of tax to profits
    (iv) Financial assistance to charities, sports and community activities
    (v) Co-operate with government in identifying and preventing health hazards

Organisations which communicate with the different stakeholder group will understand the specific expectations on business performance and this often helps management to pursue an optimal strategy for the organisation.

It is suggested that modern corporations are so powerful, socially, economically and politically, that unrestrained use of their power will inevitably damage other people's rights. For example, they may blight an entire community by closing a major facility, thus enforcing long-term unemployment on a large proportion of the local workforce.

However, organisations are now much more cautious about how there are perceived and as a response some organisations invest in corporate communications departments specifically to manage brand image and perception, media briefings, press statements and direct communications with stakeholders.

The exercise of corporate social responsibility (CSR) constrains the organisation to act at all times as a good citizen.

1.8.2 Stakeholder risks

Each group of stakeholders will react to the severity of the risk it faces, for example, employees will strike if they fear their employment rights are being threatened. Organisations can analyse the various risks to stakeholders to understand and respond to likely stakeholder reactions.

Stakeholder	Risk (Interests to defend)	Stakeholder response to risk
Internal		
Managers and employees (eg restructuring, relocation)	<ul><li>Jobs/careers</li><li>Money</li><li>Promotion</li><li>Benefits</li><li>Satisfaction</li></ul>	<ul><li>Pursuit of systems goals rather than shareholder interests</li><li>Industrial action</li><li>Negative power to impede implementation</li><li>Refusal to relocate</li><li>Resignation</li></ul>
Connected		
Shareholders (corporate strategy)	<ul><li>Increase in shareholder wealth, measured by profitability, P/E ratios, market capitalisation, dividends and yield</li><li>Risk</li></ul>	<ul><li>Sell shares (eg to predator) or replace management</li></ul>
Bankers (cash flows)	<ul><li>Security of loan</li><li>Adherence to loan agreements</li></ul>	<ul><li>Denial of credit</li><li>Higher interest charges</li><li>Receivership</li></ul>
Suppliers (purchase strategy)	<ul><li>Profitable sales</li><li>Payment for goods</li><li>Long-term relationship</li></ul>	<ul><li>Refusal of credit</li><li>Court action</li><li>Wind down relationships</li></ul>
Customers (product market strategy)	<ul><li>Goods as promised</li><li>Future benefits</li></ul>	<ul><li>Buy elsewhere</li><li>Sue</li></ul>
External		
Government	<ul><li>Jobs, training, tax</li></ul>	<ul><li>Tax increases</li><li>Regulation</li><li>Legal action</li></ul>
Interest/pressure groups	<ul><li>Pollution</li><li>Rights</li><li>Other</li></ul>	<ul><li>Publicity</li><li>Direct action</li><li>Sabotage</li><li>Pressure on government</li></ul>

How stakeholders relate to the management of the company depends very much on what type of stakeholder they are (internal, connected or external), and on the level in the management hierarchy at which they are able to apply pressure. Clearly a company's management will respond differently to the demands of, say, its shareholders and the community at large.

The way in which the relationship between company and stakeholders is conducted is a function of the parties' relative stakeholder bargaining strength and the philosophy underlying each party's objectives.

Stakeholders' bargaining strength can be shown by means of a spectrum as illustrated in the following diagram.

Company's conduct of relationship	Weak			Stakeholders' bargaining strength			Strong
	Command/ dictated by company	Consultation and consideration of stakeholders' views	Negotiation	Participation and acceptance of stakeholders' views	Democratic voting by stakeholders	Command/ dictated by stakeholders	

Illustration of stakeholders' bargaining strength

The relative stakeholder bargaining strength exerted by each of the various stakeholder groups can shape strategic decisions made by its management as well as the overall strategic direction of an organisation as they seek to meet the various stakeholder needs.

For example, stakeholders such as shareholders or governments impose specific targets for the organisation to achieve. For example, a 5% rise in the share price or dividend or a 2% reduction in CO_2 emissions.

Without ethical safeguards in place and under pressure to meet performance targets, organisations can make decisions and implement policies which prioritise financial performance and profitability. This can sometimes result in unethical practises which can cause harm to individuals, the environment, the community or other stakeholder groups.

Here, stakeholders perform an important role in regulating company behaviour by making clear the expectations in terms of adhering to ethical principles or responding when unethical practices become known.

1.9 Stakeholder roles and responsibilities

We have considered how stakeholders can influence the **strategy** of an organisation. Now we consider how stakeholders can affect the **performance** of an organisation. We use specific examples of stakeholder groups to show how these affect the performance of organisations.

1.9.1 Employees and management

Employees and management are internal stakeholders. They may exert considerable power over the performance of the organisation. Organisations should aim to align the interests of their staff with those of the organisation.

In other words, organisations should look at ways of motivating their employees and managers to perform better by agreeing to organisational objectives, such as:

- **Motivation for employees** to perform well comes in a variety of guises. Some will work harder and better for more money whereas others prefer benefits or promotion. Many employees rank the environment in which they work as important for their well-being and productivity.
- **Performance measurement** for managers is usually designed so that by attaining targets set by the organisation, they earn rewards. These targets can be negotiated or imposed depending on the culture of the organisation. The rewards are linked to the attainment of the targets using various means.
- **Simple bonuses** can be paid on the achievement of a target return or profit.
- **Share options** can be granted whereby the reward is linked to the growth in the share price of the organisation. Thus, on the exercise of the option, and receipt of the shares, any growth in the share price from the date of grant is realised by the employee if they sell the shares or earn income from dividends on shares received.

However, there is a danger of dysfunctional behaviour where individuals concentrate on attaining just the measure that leads to the reward to the exclusion of other activities. There is also a risk of the measure being manipulated so that it is achieved, whatever the consequences. A good example of this manipulation is return on capital employed (ROCE) where the return can be improved by retaining older written down assets thereby keeping the capital employed figure low. This may not be the optimum replacement policy for assets but will improve the measure of ROCE.

1.9.2 Shareholders

Shareholders represent a class of connected stakeholder, which provides funds for investment. They often take a short-term view of their involvement in an organisation.

Shareholders can be influential stakeholders, encouraging management to improve performance, by their decision to hold or sell shares.

Institutional shareholders often have significant holdings in companies. They usually hold shares for capital growth or their revenue stream, so they tend to monitor performance closely and dispose of under-performing shares. They can be a strong influence on the decisions made by the organisation in which they hold their shares.

Profit-making organisations tend to focus on financial performance in general and on the interests of shareholders in particular.

The traditional argument for this is that shareholders are the legal owners, the company belongs to them and so their interests are paramount. This means:

(a) Maximising shareholder wealth is a long-term goal for an organisation; inevitably managers must decide between what funds they want to disburse now and what funds need to be maintained in the business to ensure the prospects of long-term profitability.

(b) Shareholders own the business, and so the directors of the company have a duty to safeguard their interests.

(c) What the shareholders require as a return is used to judge the validity of investment projects.

(d) Shareholders assess the quality of management by how well the business performs financially.

(e) Shareholders are the principal source of capital investment in an organisation. They provide funds on share issues or permit managers to retain profits for investment.

A company's senior management should remain aware of who its major shareholders are, and it will often help to retain shareholders' support if the chairman or the managing director meets occasionally with the major shareholders, to exchange views.

(a) The company's management might learn about shareholders' preferences for either high dividends or high retained earnings for profit growth and capital gain.

(b) For public companies, changes in shareholdings might help to explain recent share price movements.

(c) The company's management should be able to learn about shareholders' attitudes to both risk and gearing. If a company is planning a new investment, its management might have to consider the relative merits of seeking equity finance or debt finance, and shareholders' attitudes would be worth knowing about before the decision is taken.

(d) Management might need to know its shareholders in the event of an unwelcome takeover bid from another company, to identify key shareholders whose views on the takeover bid might be crucial to the final outcome.

1.9.3 Consumer groups

Consumer groups are a connected group representing consumers' interests. They exist to ensure that products give good value. They promote safeguards for consumers against unethical business practice.

Consumerism reflects the increased importance and power of consumers. It appears in organised consumer groups, and the recognition by producers that consumer satisfaction is the key to long-term profitability.

1.9.4 Suppliers

Suppliers are a connected group of stakeholders. They can influence the cost and quality of goods and services. Suppliers can directly influence the performance of an organisation through the quality of the goods and services that they supply to an organisation. Poor quality goods will affect the saleability of the product to the customer, depressing sales and revenues.

The prices that suppliers charge will also affect the profitability of the end product if margins are eroded.

Organisations have developed a number of strategies for controlling price and quality from their suppliers. The best known of these is just-in-time that commits suppliers to supply on-demand zero-defect parts. If an organisation has confidence in its supplier, a long-term relationship will be established.

1.9.5 Government

Government is an external stakeholder group. Central government sets the regulatory framework in which organisations operate. Local government has devolved powers and can raise local revenues from business.

Question — Identifying stakeholders

You work as a senior advisor to the board of a large, listed organisation that operates in the construction industry. The services offered range from homebuilding to large civil engineering projects, such as bridges and dams, and can be undertaken for central and local government bodies as well as other profit-making companies. All projects are carried out by staff who require formal accreditation by their professional body.

Required

Draft a list of stakeholders for the board and briefly explain the nature of each stakeholder's claim.

Answer

The list of stakeholders is likely to include the following (with their claims in brackets)

- **Shareholders** who require a return on their investment – (this is a direct claim because they are in contact with the organisation already)
- **Lenders** who require their loans to be serviced in full and on time (also direct)
- **Customers** who require good quality projects to be completed (also direct)
- **Suppliers** who require being paid on time (also direct)
- **Employees** who require good working conditions and being paid on time (also direct)
- **The general public** who requires no adverse effects from the organisation and its projects, such as safe housing, reliable infrastructure (direct/indirect)
- **The government** which requires tax to be paid on corporate profits and other expenses, plus the ideal of maximising employment levels in the economy (probably also direct)

- **Professional bodies** which require the organisation's accreditation process to be robust to maintain their reputation (also direct)
- **Flora and fauna** whose natural environment is affected by civil engineering projects being built (they require a clean, unspoilt environment to live in, but their claims are indirect because they did not ask to be affected by the organisation's projects)
- **People living near a construction project**, whether housing or some other kind, who require a quiet, clean and safe environment in which to live but who may be adversely affected by either the construction process or the finished asset (again, likely to be indirect)

1.10 Assessing stakeholder power and interest – Mendelow matrix

One way of weighing stakeholder interests is to look at the **power** they exert and the **level of interest** they have in its activities.

Mendelow classifies stakeholders on a matrix whose axes are **power** held and likelihood of showing an **interest** in the organisation's activities. These factors will help define the type of relationship the organisation should seek with its stakeholders and how it should view their concerns. Mendelow's matrix represents a continuum, a map for plotting the relative influence of stakeholders. Stakeholders in the bottom right of the continuum are more significant because they combine the highest power and influence.

	Level of interest Low	Level of interest High
Power Low	A	B
Power High	C	D

- **Stakeholders with high levels of power and interest are key players.** An organisation's strategy must be acceptable, and they need to be managed closely. An example of a key player could be a major customer. These stakeholders are grouped in Section A.
- **Stakeholders with a high power, but low interest, must be treated with care.** Although they are currently passive, they are capable of becoming key players if their level of interest increases. Therefore, they need to be kept satisfied. Large institutional shareholders could be an example of this type of stakeholder: with increasing levels of shareholder activism in recent years also demonstrating their potential to move from 'keep satisfied' to 'key players'. These stakeholders are grouped in Section C.
- **Stakeholders with low power and high interest must be kept informed.** These stakeholders have little ability to influence strategy in their own right, but their views could be important in influencing more powerful stakeholders: perhaps by lobbying, for example. They should therefore be kept informed. These stakeholders are grouped in Section B.
- **Stakeholders with low power and low interest require** minimal effort. These stakeholders are grouped in Section A.

Stakeholder analysis is used to assess the significance of stakeholder groups. This in turn has implications for the organisation.

- The framework of **corporate governance** should recognise stakeholders' levels of interest and power.
- It may be appropriate to seek to **reposition** certain stakeholders and discourage others from repositioning themselves, depending on their attitudes.
- Key **blockers** and **facilitators** of change must be identified.

Stakeholder analysis can also be used to establish **political priorities**. A map of the current position can be compared with a map of a desired future state. This will indicate critical shifts that must be pursued.

Stakeholder analysis, also referred to as stakeholder mapping, demonstrates that different stakeholders can have varying degrees of influence on the management and strategy of an organisation. Specific groups of stakeholders are motivated by different aims. In the next section, we will look at the role of the management accountant in helping management to analyse the different needs and provide management with analysis to support business performance and meet specific performance targets.

We can look in detail at the stakeholder groups that not only have an **interest** in an organisation but also have **power** over it.

The external coalition	The internal coalition
• Owners (who hold legal title) • Associates (suppliers, customers, trading partners) • Employee associations (unions, professional bodies) • Public (government, media)	• The chief executive and board at the strategic apex • Line managers • Operators • Support staff • Ideology (ie culture and formal and informal power structures)

Each of these stakeholder groups has three basic choices:

1. **Loyalty.** Stakeholders can follow decisions and/or do as they are told.

2. **Exit.** Stakeholders can exit by selling their shares or getting a new job, for example.

3. **Voice.** Stakeholders can stay and try to change the system. Those who choose voice are those who can, to varying degrees, influence the organisation. Influence implies a degree of power and willingness to exercise it.

Existing structures and systems can channel stakeholder influence.

- They are the location of power, giving groups of people varying degrees of influence over strategic choices.
- They are conduits of information, which shape strategic decisions.
- They limit choices or give some options priority over others. These may be physical or ethical constraints over what is possible.
- They embody culture.
- They determine the successful implementation of strategy.
- The firm has different degrees of dependency on various stakeholder groups. A company with a cash flow crisis will be more beholden to its bankers than one with regular cash surpluses.

Different stakeholders will have their own views as to strategy. As some groups have negative stakeholder power, in other words power to impede or disrupt the decision, their likely response might be considered.

Strategic options pose varying degrees of risk to the **interests** of the different stakeholders. It is possible that they may respond in such a way as to reduce the attractiveness of the proposed strategy.

Question — Stakeholder analysis

BA Pensions are one of the largest institutional investors in the country. Its investment strategy has traditionally been to own a minor shareholding in each of the top 200 companies listed on the various global stock exchanges. The BA Pensions investment is typically between 2% and 10% of each company and it manages funds for over one million pension fund members.

BA Pensions has always believed itself to be socially responsible. As part of its CSR strategy, BA Pensions recently purchased 100% of the shares in a residential construction company, Good Housing, which it owns as a direct holding and does not include in its managed funds. Good Housing, in turn, owns a large amount of land suitable for future low-cost housing development. The BA Pensions website reported that the reason for this purchase was to address the board's concerns over a shortage of affordable housing in the country which BA Pensions feels they can help to address by having outright ownership of Good Housing. BA Pensions reported it hopes that Good Housing will create many hundreds of new low-cost homes each year in the countries where it operates.

Good Housing wants to build a large estate of new homes in the town of Brompton, and the local council of Brompton is considering whether to grant the required building permission.

The nearby University of Brompton strongly opposes it because it believes that the new houses will ruin what is considered to be a panoramic view from the university campus which helps it to recruit staff and students to the university.

Both Brompton council and the University of Brompton have money invested as clients with BA Pensions, but the university has a substantially smaller investment in the fund than the local government authority. The council also owns shares in BA Pensions, meaning that it is both an investor in funds and a BA Pensions shareholder.

Required

Apply stakeholder analysis to consider the power, interest and need of each stakeholder in this scenario.

Answer

BA Pensions (low power, low interest)

BA Pensions needs to maximise its returns to investors, and therefore its decisions are driven by financial returns. However, as an ethical investor BA Pensions is also keen to support investments which have a positive impact on communities and on the environment.

BA pensions is unable to control the outcome of permission for the new housing development as it does not possess housing regulatory powers. Also, BA Pensions has many investments, and therefore if its fund managers cannot meet the investment achievements, they will sell their investment holdings and invest in something similar. BA Pensions has low power as the council does not have an interest in the financial returns of BA Pensions.

Brompton Council (high power, high interest)

Brompton Council exists as an elected public sector organisation to meet the needs of local residents. Therefore, a need for local housing is likely to influence their decision making although this will be balanced by ethical, environmental and social factors.

Brompton Council has a higher power than the university because of its ability to grant or withhold planning consent. This is a power devolved from central government, although it is usually required that local consultation be entered into before final approval is granted. It also has more power as it is also a shareholder of BA Pensions, and possibly some influence as an investor in BA Pensions.

As an external stakeholder, being an authority interested in the construction of low-cost housing and both a client and a shareholder of BA Pensions, there are considerable conflict issues. It has a social obligation to see the development approved, as this will allow lower-cost housing to be built, but this is potentially in conflict with concern for the profitability of the BA Pensions company in which it holds shares.

The council must balance the claims of a number of stakeholders when taking decisions of this type, including, but not limited to, the economic interests of BA Pensions. However, the council is likely to use its high power and prioritise the social value of the new housing development for the local community.

University of Brompton (low power, high interest)

The University of Brompton needs to provide an effective and attractive learning environment to attract new students.

The university has less power over the planning decision because it has no statutory power, it is not a shareholder in BA Pensions directly and has a lesser investment in BA Pensions than the local authority. It is likely that the views of such an important local institution would be taken into account, however, because a successful university is important in the development of the town.

The university is of the opinion that the new houses will reduce the views over the countryside that are currently enjoyed. This environmental argument may influence the council's decision.

Stakeholder mapping is used to assess the significance of stakeholders. This in turn has implications for the organisation.

(a) The framework of corporate governance and the direction and control of the business should recognise **stakeholders' levels** of **interest** and **power**.

(b) Companies may try to **reposition** certain stakeholders and discourage others from repositioning themselves, depending on their attitudes.

(c) Key **blockers** and **facilitators** of change must be identified.

(d) Stakeholder mapping can also be used to establish **future priorities**.

1.10.1 Using Mendelow's approach to analyse stakeholders

Power means who can exercise **most influence** over a particular decision (though the power may not be used). These include those who **actively participate** in decision making (normally directors, senior managers) or those whose views are **regularly consulted** on important decisions (major shareholders). It can also, in a negative sense, mean those who have the right of veto over major decisions (creditors with a charge on major business assets can prevent those assets being sold to raise money). Stakeholders may be more influential if their power is combined with:

- **Legitimacy**: the company perceives the stakeholders' claims to be valid
- **Urgency**: whether the stakeholder claim requires immediate action

Level of interest reflects the **effort** stakeholders put in to attempting to participate in the organisation's activities, whether they succeed or not. It also reflects the amount of knowledge stakeholders have about what the organisation is doing.

Question — Mendelow's matrix

Goaway Hotels is a chain of hotels based in one country. 90% of its shares are held by members of the family of the founder of the Goaway group. None of the family members is a director of the company. Over the last few years, the family has been quite happy with the steady level of dividends that their investment has generated. Directors are encouraged to achieve high profits by means of a remuneration package with potentially very large profit-related bonuses.

The directors of Goaway Hotels currently wish to take significant steps to increase profits. The area they are focusing on at present is labour costs. Over the last couple of years, many of the workers they have recruited have been economic migrants from another country, the East Asian People's Republic (EAPR). The EAPR workers are paid around 30% of the salary of indigenous workers, and receive fewer benefits. However, these employment terms are considerably better than those that the workers would receive in the EAPR. Goaway Hotels has been able to fill its vacancies easily from this source, and the workers from the EAPR that Goaway has recruited have mostly stayed with the company. The board has been considering imposing tougher employment contracts on home country workers, perhaps letting the number of dismissals and staff turnover of home country workers increase significantly.

In Goaway Hotels' home country, there had been a long period of rule by a government that wished to boost business and thus relaxed labour laws to encourage more flexible working. However, a year ago the opposition party finally won power, having pledged in their manifesto to tighten labour laws to give more rights to home country employees. Since their election, the new government has brought in the promised labour legislation, and there have already been successful injunctions obtained, preventing companies from imposing less favourable employment terms on their employees.

An international chain of hotels has recently approached various members of the founding family with an offer for their shares. The international chain is well known for its aggressive approach to employee relations and the high demands it makes on its managers. Local employment laws allow some renegotiation of employment terms if companies are taken over.

Required

Using Mendelow's matrix, analyse the importance of the following stakeholders to the decision to change the employment terms of home country's workers in Goaway Hotels.

(a) The board of directors
(b) The founding family shareholders
(c) The trade unions to which the home country workers belong
(d) Migrant workers

Answer

Remember that we are talking about one specific decision so we need to focus on that decision.

The board of directors

Power: Low, surprisingly perhaps. However, the new employment legislation appears to limit significantly directors' freedom to reduce labour costs by changing contractual terms. The directors also have little say over the decision of shareholders to sell shares. (This demonstrates that you cannot take anyone's role for granted.)

Level of interest: High, as this is a major decision, integral to the directors' plans for the future of the Goaway hotel chain. It may also have a significant effect on their remuneration.

Shareholders

Power: High, because the shareholders are currently in a position to sell their shares if they feel that they have received a good offer. If they do, unions and employees may find that the international company is able to take a much tougher approach.

Level of interest: Low, as none of them participate actively in Goaway's decision making. Their main concern is whether to continue to take dividends or realise a capital gain from their investment.

Trade unions

Power: High, because they have the economic power to take legal action to prevent Goaway from changing their members' employment terms.

Level of interest: High, because they wish to protect their members.

Migrant workers

Power: Low, because replacement workers can be recruited easily from the home country.

Level of interest: Low. The migrant workers seem quite happy with their current employment terms, even though these are not as favourable as the home country's workers.

1.10.2 Problems with stakeholder mapping

There are, however, a number of issues with Mendelow's approach:

(a) It can be **very difficult to measure each stakeholder's power and influence**.

(b) The map is **not static**. Changing circumstances may mean stakeholders' positions move around the map. For example, stakeholders with a lot of interest but not much power may improve their position by combining with other stakeholders with similar views.

(c) The map is based on the idea that **strategic positioning**, rather than moral or ethical concerns, should govern an organisation's attitude to its stakeholders.

(d) If there are a number of key players, and their views are in conflict, it can be very difficult to resolve the situation, hence there may be **uncertainties** over the organisation's future direction.

(e) Mendelow's matrix considers power and influence but fails to take **legitimacy** into account. Legitimacy is a distinct concept from power. For example, minority shareholders in a company controlled by a strong majority may not have much power, but law in most countries recognises that they have legitimate rights which the company must respect. Mitchell, Agle and Wood (1997) argue that legitimacy is a desirable social goal, dependent on more than the perception of individual stakeholders.

1.11 Reconciling viewpoints of different stakeholders

Michael Jensen (2002) has argued that **enlightened long-term value maximisation** offers the best and fairest method of reconciling the competing interests of stakeholders. Enlightened long-term value maximisation means pursuing profit maximisation, but with regard to **business ethics** and the **social consequences of the organisation's actions**. Jensen argued that the problem with traditional stakeholder theory is that it gave no indication of how to trade off competing interests. Lacking measurable targets, managers are therefore left unaccountable for their actions; if targets have to do with long-term value maximisation, on the other hand, then Jensen claims that this will tend to include the interests of stakeholders.

> **FAST FORWARD**
>
> Different groups of stakeholders have different objectives which can lead to conflicts between competing groups. By understanding the different stakeholders and their needs and goals, an organisation can determine strategies to resolve stakeholder conflicts which may prevent the organisation from achieving its strategic objectives.

Where companies are poorly governed and where they fail to properly meet their social responsibilities, then it is their stakeholders who will be affected by this. In recent years, the spotlight has fallen on wealth inequality and climate change as areas in which companies are failing.

Since 1978, it has been reported that executive pay has risen over 1,000%, while average pay has risen by only 12%. On average, CEOs make 278 times the pay of the average worker. Critics have pointed out the 'pernicious effects' that inequality like this has on societies, such as the erosion of social trust, and higher levels of anxiety and ill health. Companies usually try to defend high levels of CEO pay in terms of its motivational effect on the CEOs themselves, and the need to pay salaries in line with CEO's market expectations. Questions may be asked about whether these arguments are supported by evidence or are specious in nature.

Climate change is a key problem facing modern societies and provides a good illustration of the difficulties involved with governing a privately-owned corporation whose actions affect society as a whole. Most carbon emissions (the drivers of climate change) are made by private companies; these affect the whole of society, but the benefits of these carbon-intensive activities are reaped only by specific parties (eg customers, employees, shareholders). Stakeholder theory therefore provides a useful perspective on the issue – if society as a whole is considered a stakeholder, then it is argued that companies ought to take into account their impact on the environment if they are to be responsible corporate citizens.

Stakeholder theory itself has been covered in some detail earlier in this text. In this section, we will now move to consider some real-life examples of companies and their relationships with their stakeholders.

Case Study — Tesco

Tesco is a British supermarket chain which is listed on the London Stock Exchange and which has it head office in Welwyn Garden City in the UK. Tesco began as a collection of market stalls, with its first shop opening in 1931. Initially a retailer of food only, it diversified in the 1990s into the selling of books, clothing, electronics, petrol and even financial services. Tesco's 2019 financial statements report group sales of £57bn and an operating cash inflow of £2,502m (Tesco, 2020).

The principal internal stakeholders of Tesco are its management and employees. As of 2019, Tesco reported having 450,000 employees worldwide working in over 6,800 shops (Tesco, 2020). Tesco's governance structure involves a board and an executive committee.

Tesco PLC, the parent company of the group, reports the following major shareholders, who are therefore key stakeholders for the company (Tesco, 2020):

BlackRock, Inc.	6.64%
Norges Bank	4.03%
Schroders plc	4.99%

A key area of **conflict** in the past has been between investors' need for financial returns and Tesco executives' desire for large pay packages. In 2018, for example, the investor group Pirc (which represents pension funds, asset managers and banks) claimed that the Tesco chief executive's pay was too high, at 267 times that of the average Tesco supermarket worker (This is Money, 2018).

Key external stakeholders include customers and suppliers, and the company also has relationships with creditors, competitors, pressure groups, local communities, and the government.

Tesco is the largest UK supermarket, with a market share of approximately 27% (Kantar, 2020) in a market that might be described as oligopolistic. Its principal **competitors** are Sainsbury's, Asda, Morrisons, Aldi and the Co-op. Its relations with its competitors were the subject of some controversy when, in 2007, it was fined by the Office of Fair Trading (OFT) after it was found that the major UK supermarkets were acting as a cartel to fix prices. This is a good example of the way Tesco sought to manage its relationships with competitors in the interest of delivering value to one stakeholder group (shareholders) at the expense of another (consumers). This suggests that, at least at the time of this offence, Tesco was operating in line with something like either the stockholder or the instrumental theory of stakeholder relations. Further, considering Tesco's competitor relations in the light of Mendelow's stakeholder matrix, one might place Tesco's competitors in Segment C, having high power but low levels of interest.

Considering its **supplier relationships**, Tesco has been accused in the past of being too tough on suppliers. It has claimed that this was necessary in order to deliver value to another stakeholder group, its customers, although it is likely that the desire to create value for shareholders was the key motivation. In the wake of a 2015 investigation by the Groceries Code Adjudicator which found that Tesco had pressurised suppliers unreasonably, Tesco has in recent years promoted the idea of 'partnership' with its suppliers (Produce Business UK, 2016). Using Mendelow's matrix to interpret these events, it could be said that Tesco had formerly considered suppliers to have a low level of power but a high level of interest, placing them in Segment B. In the wake of the investigation, Tesco appears to have changed how it deals with its suppliers, but it is not certain whether their position as stakeholders has changed as such – so that they are deemed to have more power, for example – or whether Tesco has simply responded to the demands of a different stakeholder in the form of the industry regulator.

Various **pressure groups** have sought to influence Tesco over the years. For instance; protestors have objected to Tesco's sale of goods from Israel; animal rights protestors opposed Tesco's practice of selling battery eggs to customers in Asia (Tesco responded by committing to end the practice); anti-racist organisations (such as the magazine *Searchlight*) have opposed the sale of anti-semitic books in Tesco shops; and local residents' organisations have at times opposed the opening of new Tesco stores in their areas.

Case Study — BP

BP plc (BP) is a large multinational oil and gas company whose headquarters are in London. It is the world's 12th largest company by turnover and has oil reserves of nearly 20bn barrels as of 2018 (BP, 2018).

BP says that its stakeholders "are the many individuals and organisations who are affected in some way by BP's activities – whether it is in our role as an energy provider, an employer or as a business that helps boost local economies through jobs and revenue." (BP, 2020)

It lists six major groups of stakeholders:

- Employees
- Investors
- Communities
- Non-governmental organisations (NGOs)
- Governments
- Contractors and suppliers

To this list ought to be appended the company's management and its customers.

BP has around 73,000 **employees** around the world, in relation to whom BP says that it is committed to creating a "positive and empowering work environment". It conducts surveys to understand what employees want. In 2018, BP interpreted the survey results as meaning that employees wanted more efficient processes and has concentrated its efforts on this.

Contractors are important to BP's business, making up over half of the hours worked for the company. BP's approach here is to make requirements of contractors in order to ensure that their work is of sufficient quality.

Regarding **investors**, BP seeks to balance the need to provide short-term returns (ie dividend payments) with the need to retain funds for longer-term investment. As is the case at many companies of its kind, BP has been the subject of investor protests at the levels of **executive pay** and, in 2019, shareholders forced its chief executive Bob Dudley to take a 40% cut in pay (taking home just over $14m in 2019). This is a key area of stakeholder conflict, and one that the company does not appear to be managing effectively.

Communities have been an area of focus for BP in the years following the Deepwater Horizon oil spill in 2010. BP says that it listens to community complaints and engages with communities in an open and constructive way.

BP says that it "often consults" with **NGOs** and met with them in 2018. This is a key point of conflict, given the concerns that exist within civil society about climate change, and the impact that oil and gas companies such as BP have on the environment.

In relation to **governments**, a key issue is BP's international tax arrangements, and the practice of making payments to governments in exchange for development rights. BP says that it "supports transparency" in this area.

1.12 Managing stakeholder conflict

FAST FORWARD

The fundamental objective of any organisation should be the maximisation of shareholders' wealth. In its purest sense, this means pursuing the maximum amount of profit from the organisation's operations. A threat to this objective is conflicting shareholder objectives.

Organisations must consider that the interests of managers and owners may conflict so areas of conflict can be effectively managed. Shareholder wealth may be maximised by reducing the local workforce or changing the nature of the work done due to new technology being available. This would be perceived as a conflict with the goals of employees.

1.12.1 Separation of ownership from control

In most modern organisations the owners do not actually manage the company. Whilst the equity shareholders own the company, the day-to-day operations are managed on their behalf by the board of directors.

The directors and managers within the organisation have their own personal goals that may conflict with those of the shareholders. The problem that shareholders have is that they are seen as being passive stakeholders – that is, they do not (and are not expected to) contribute to business decisions that affect the company.

Whilst managers are privy to privileged information about the company, shareholders have to rely on publicly available details such as annual reports and press articles, a situation known as information asymmetry. As a result, managers are very much left to their own devices when making business decisions.

The relationship between management and shareholders is sometimes referred to as an agency relationship, in which managers act as agents for the shareholders. Here, there is separation of ownership from management is sometimes characterised as the 'agency problem' which is where shareholder conflict arises as a difference between the interests of managers and those of owners.

For example, if managers hold none or very little of the equity shares of the company they work for, what is to stop them from working inefficiently, not bothering to look for profitable new investment opportunities, or giving themselves high salaries and perks?

The goal of agency theory is to find governance structures and control mechanisms that minimise the problem caused by the separation of ownership and control. In that sense agency theory is the cornerstone of the theory of corporate governance. More specifically agency theory tries to find means for the owners to control the managers in such a way that the managers will operate in the interest of the shareholders.

Examples of conflicts of interest between managers and shareholders include:

- **Short-termism:** There is evidence that in many companies the primary driver of decision-making has been to increase share prices and hence managerial rewards in the short term. The longer-term benefits of investment in research and development may be ignored in the short-term drive to cut costs and increase profits thus jeopardising the long-term prospects of the company.

- **Sales maximisation:** This strategy is often employed by managers to increase market share and therefore the importance of the company within its sector. An increase in importance for the company will mean greater status for management but will not necessarily be in the best interests of the shareholders.

- **Overpriced acquisitions:** Takeovers is another manifestation of the non-alignment of the interests of shareholders and managers. Managers have motives other than shareholder value maximisation and may choose to acquire another business to seek growth and status.

- **Resistance to takeovers:** The management of a company may tend to resist takeovers if they feel that their position is threatened even if in doing so shareholder value is also reduced.

- **Relationships:** Many companies' pursuit of short-term cost reduction may lead to difficult relationships with their wider stakeholders. Relationships with suppliers may be disrupted by demands for major improvements in terms and in reduction of prices. Employees may be made redundant in a drive to reduce costs and customers may be able to buy fewer product lines and have to face less favourable terms. These policies may aid short-term profits, but in the long-term suppliers and employees are able to take full advantage of market conditions and move to other companies, and customers can shop elsewhere or over the internet.

- **Avoiding risk:** In order to maximise shareholder wealth in the long-term a company needs to evolve which means some risk must be taken. When managers' attitudes are conservative and risk-averse they are seeking the easiest path. Risk-averse managers seeks to avoid conflict or change because of the disruption it could cause. However, this may not be in the best interests of the shareholders.

- **Dividend policy:** Managers may decide to maintain high dividend pay-outs in order to avoid resistance from the shareholders. This is not necessarily the best thing for shareholder wealth maximisation in the long-term as it may be better to invest in new technology so that new products can be made, or existing products made more effectively and efficiently.

1.12.2 Conflict between stakeholders

Although we discussed the conflict between managers and owners, there are other areas of potential conflict between managers, owners and other stakeholders who provide capital, namely the debt holders.

The relationship between the long-term creditors of a company, the management and the shareholders of a company encompasses the following factors:

- Management may decide to raise finance for a company by taking out long-term or medium-term loans.
- Investors who provide debt finance will rely on the company's management to generate enough net cash inflows to make interest payments on time, and eventually to repay loans. Long-term creditors will often take security for their loan, perhaps in the form of a fixed charge over an asset (such as a mortgage on a building). Debentures are also often subject to certain restrictive covenants, which restrict the company's rights to borrow more money until the debentures have been repaid.
- The money that is provided by long-term creditors will be invested to earn profits, and the profits (in excess of what is needed to pay interest on the borrowing) will provide extra dividends or retained profits for the shareholders of the company. In other words, shareholders will expect to increase their wealth using creditors' money.

Sometimes the needs of shareholders and debtholders may conflict:

- Managers may be tempted to take risky decisions using debtholders' money to finance them, knowing that the benefits of these decisions will accrue to the shareholders. If the projects go badly and the company fails, the debtholders may suffer a greater loss than the equity shareholders.
- In many jurisdictions there are rules limiting the proportion of company assets that can be paid out as dividends. However, it may still be possible to pay out lawfully considerable sums as dividends, enough to jeopardise the company's future and hence the amounts that the debtholders have advanced, should trading results turn bad in the near future.
- Shareholders and managers may wish to prolong the company's life as long as possible, whereas debtholders may wish to safeguard the amount loaned and realise their security as soon as the company appears to be getting into difficulties.
- Managers may attempt to undermine the position of debtholders by seeking further loan capital, committing the company to an increased interest burden and hence greater risk of insolvency. The additional loan capital may also have superior claims on the company's assets to the original amounts borrowed.

1.12.3 Strategies to manage stakeholder conflict

We will now show how ensuring goal congruence and enforcing corporate governance best practice can help manage conflict between different groups of stakeholders.

- **Reward systems:** Agency theory sees employees of businesses, including managers, as individuals, each with their own objectives. Within a department of a business, there are departmental objectives. Goal congruence between managers, directors and shareholders may be better dealt with by giving managers some profit-related pay, or by providing incentives which are related to profits or share price.

    Examples of such remuneration incentives are:

    - **Profit-related/economic value-added pay**

        Pay or bonuses related to the size of profits or economic value added

    - **Rewarding managers with shares**

        This might be done when a private company 'goes public' and managers are invited to subscribe for shares in the company at an attractive offer price. This means that directors and employees, as well as shareholders, have a stake in the long-term profitability of an organisation.

    - **Executive share options plans**

        In a share option scheme, selected employees are given a number of share options, each of which gives the holder the right after a certain date to subscribe for shares in the company at a fixed price. The value of an option will increase if the company is successful, and its share price goes up.

- **Separation of roles and corporate governance:** Complying with corporate governance principles ensured that not too much power accrues to a single individual within an organisation which increases the risk of disagreement between a chief executive offers and the board of directors, the company shareholders and the employees. Also, the adoption of a corporate governance framework of decision making will restrict the power of managers and increase the role of independent non-executive directors in key decisions.
- **Negotiation:** Stakeholder conflict between shareholders and directors can be resolved by negotiating contracts that allow the principal to control the agent in such a way to ensure that the agent will operate in the interests of the principal. Also, a board of directors may schedule regular investors updates which allow key investors to voice their concerns and to provide feedback on strategic decisions made by a board of directors. Differences of opinion between a company and its customers or suppliers can also be resolved by negotiation of contractual terms, price or deliverables.
- **Self-regulation:** A voluntary code of conduct is a statement by an organisation of the standards by which it seeks to do business. Codes are usually developed by a trade association and individual members incorporate the code into the dealings they have with their customers. Organisations in some business sectors self-regulate their dealings by voluntary codes of conduct. Voluntary codes usually include a mechanism for resolving disputes through arbitration.

1.13 Enhancing stakeholder engagement

Key term

> **Stakeholder engagement:** Stakeholder engagement is the process of involving all parties affected by a company's operations in its decision-making processes.

Each stakeholder group has different expectations about what it wants and different claims on the organisation, and therefore, it is essential that organisations engage in active dialogue, assess these diverse needs, and implement strategies that balance these interests while aligning with their ethical and corporate responsibilities.

Integrating sustainability into business practice requires a robust framework of corporate accountability and proactive stakeholder engagement.

Organisations that embrace these principles not only enhance their reputations and build trust but also drive long-term sustainable value for all stakeholders. By doing so, they contribute to a more sustainable and equitable world, addressing critical global challenges such as climate change, social inequality, and environmental degradation.

1.13.1 Donaldson and Preston's stakeholder engagement theory

According to Donaldson and Preston's stakeholder engagement theory, businesses have a duty to consider the interests of all their stakeholders, not just shareholders and argue that organisations have a responsibility to balance the needs and expectations of these diverse groups of stakeholders to achieve sustainability. (Source: Donaldson, T., & Preston, L. E. (1995). "The Stakeholder Theory of the Corporation: Concepts, Evidence, and Implications." Academy of Management Review, 20(1), 65-91.)

Donaldson and Preston (1995) theory to stakeholder engagement is divided into three interrelated perspectives:

Perspectives of stakeholder engagement	Description
Normative approach	The **normative approach** asserts that considering stakeholders' interests is inherently the right thing to do. It is based on ethical principles and the intrinsic value of treating all stakeholders with respect and fairness.
Descriptive Approach	The **descriptive approach** describes how companies actually operate, showing that businesses naturally interact with various stakeholders and that these interactions influence corporate behaviour.

| Instrumental Approach | The **instrumental approach** perspective suggests that attending to stakeholders' interests can lead to better business outcomes, such as increased loyalty, improved reputation, and long-term profitability. |

1.13.2 Enhancing stakeholder engagement

Effective stakeholder engagement enhances corporate accountability by ensuring that boards of directors take stakeholder expectations and feedback seriously which means a company's actions are much more likely to align with stakeholder needs and wider societal values.

Conversely, implementing corporate accountability practices encourages the drivers for organisations to invest in meaningful stakeholder engagement.

Therefore, organisations require a methodology to achieve effective stakeholder engagement. Donaldson and Preston (1995) theory of stakeholder engagement recommends the following three stages.

1. **Identify key stakeholders**

    Organisations must recognise the diverse groups affected by their actions, including employees, customers, suppliers, local communities, and investors.

2. **Deploy stakeholder engagement strategies**

    Effective stakeholder engagement involves open communication, transparency, and responsiveness. Organisations use various methods such as surveys, public consultations, and social media platforms to engage with stakeholders.

3. **Integrate stakeholder feedback to organisation's strategic and operational objectives**

    Organisations should evaluate then incorporate feedback from stakeholders into their strategic planning and operations.

2 Application of ethical theory

Ethical theories were discussed in Chapter 1 and the different approaches to stakeholders were explored previously. When it comes to applying ethical theories, there is help at hand in the form of some decision making frameworks to help deal with concrete ethical dilemmas. Two key models are:

- The American Accounting Association model
- Tucker's five question model

FAST FORWARD

In a situation involving ethical issues, there will often be practical steps that should be taken. Any actions should be justified on the basis of an analysis of the situation, and will often involve striking a compromise between different interests and considerations.

As a starting point, applying ethical theory will involve the following.

- Analysis of the situation
- Identifying the ethical issues
- Considering the alternative options
- Stating the best course of action based on the steps above
- Justifying your recommendations

The analysis of 'ethical issues' is a key point here and forms a link to the ethical theories discussed in Chapter 1. It might be possible to see a dilemma from the perspectives of different theories so that one might, for example, elucidate a utilitarian perspective on an issue and then contrast this with a Kantian perspective. One might consider the various stakeholders who would be affected by a decision, and the different views of how they should be treated.

It is important to bear in mind that when it comes to ethics, there is frequently no single right answer, but rather a multiplicity of views with many shades of grey between them. What matters then is the quality of your discussion and the extent to which you are able to weigh the differing aspects of a decision against one another. The watchword of ethics is complexity.

PART A THE NATURE AND IMPORTANCE OF ETHICAL THEORY AND DECISION MAKING

2.1 American Accounting Association (AAA) model

The AAA model was set out in a report by Langenderfer and Rockness back in 1990. They recommended a seven-step model.

Step	Question	Approach to use in answers
1	**What are the facts of the case?**	The aim is to show clearly what is at issue. A brief summary should suffice, maybe just one sentence.
2	**What are the ethical issues in the case?**	These should be based on the facts.
3	**What are the norms, principles and values related to the case?**	This means placing the decision in its social, ethical and professional behaviour context, including considering professional codes of ethics or social expectations of the profession. Use the terminology of the ethical guidelines (for example, fairness, bias and influence) when discussing objectivity. Do not be afraid to use the term justice if that is most appropriate.
4	**What are the alternative courses of action?**	State each course without making reference at this stage to the norms, principles and values. To generate ideas, consider the issue from the points of view of the 'guilty' party and the organisation.
5	**What is the best course of action that is consistent with the norms, principles and values identified in Step 3?**	Combine Steps 3 and 4 to see which options accord with the norms and which do not.
6	**What are the consequences of each possible course of action?**	This is to ensure that each of the outcomes is unambiguous.
7	**What is the decision?**	This is based on the analysis in Steps 1-6.

 Question   AAA model

Cadge is a clothing manufacturer based in Europe that supplies various large retail groups. Over the last two years, it has suffered falls in profits due to the loss of a couple of large contracts and a general fall in demand for its clothes. Industry opinion is that Cadge has failed to innovate sufficiently in its clothing designs.

A few days ago, an unknown factory owner based outside Europe contacted Cadge's design director out of the blue. He introduced himself only as 'Mr Sim' and offered to sell – for what appeared to be a reasonable sum of money – the season's new up and coming designs belonging to one of Cadge's key competitors who was using Sim's factories to manufacture its goods. If these designs could be purchased by Cadge and launched onto the market before the competition could launch theirs, Cadge's profitability for the coming year could significantly increase.

Required

Analyse, using the American Accounting Association model, the decision of whether to accept Mr Sim's offer.

Answer

What are the facts of the case?

The facts are that the company has been offered some designs that appear to have been stolen.

What are the ethical issues in the case?

The ethical issue is whether to gain a business advantage by using designs that belong to someone else.

What are the norms, principles and values related to the case?

Accepting the offer is likely to be illegal in Cadge's home country or illegal under international design protection laws. Even if the action could be justified as legal, it would demonstrate a lack of honesty and integrity if Cadge used designs that belonged to someone else whom it had not paid.

What are the alternative courses of action?

1   Reject Mr Sim's offer.
2   Accept Mr Sim's offer, pay Mr Sim money and use the designs.

What is the best course of action that is consistent with the norms, principles and values identified in Step 3?

The best course of action is Option 1, as accepting the designs would be dishonest. The directors would need to decide whether to have no further dealings with Mr Sim, or to whistleblow on him to the competitors.

What are the consequences of each possible course of action?

1   Cadge will not be able to gain a competitive advantage.
2   Cadge may be able to gain a temporary advantage, but the consequences if the transaction is discovered could be severe. Cadge's customers are likely to view this activity unfavourably and this could jeopardise existing contracts. The board may come under pressure from other shareholders who find this behaviour unacceptable.

What is the decision?

The ethical decision in Option 1, to refuse Mr Sim's offer.

As you can see from this example, it is not always necessary to bring philosophical theories of ethics into practical questions. The important thing is to adopt a logical approach to forming a judgment about the best decision in each situation.

2.2 Tucker's five question model

Tucker's model is conceptually different from the AAA model, and needs to be applied carefully to each situation. The model can be used to determine the most ethical outcome in a particular situation, generally an ethical problem for business. It focuses on five key questions that should be asked of a response to an ethical dilemma:

- Profitable?
- Legal?
- Fair?
- Right?
- Sustainable?

Not all of Tucker's criteria will be relevant in every situation. In addition, there are complications with each criterion.

Is the decision:	
Profitable?	Compared with what? Use of profitability as criteria also implies the Tucker model may be more useful for business decisions than for individuals' moral dilemmas.
Legal?	This obviously depends on the jurisdiction(s) involved.
Fair?	In whose perspective? There is a need to consider who stakeholders are and the impact of the decision on them.

Right?	This depends on the ethical position; in particular the distinction between deontological and teleological approaches to whether account should be taken of the consequences of the transaction is significant.
Sustainable?	Is the decision environmentally sound, or sustainable in other ways (eg the long-term success of the company)?

Question — Tucker's five question model

Refuse Recycling (RR) is a large recycling company, which collects waste and recycles a large variety of products. Its most profitable product for recycling is glass, although it also collects other materials including plastics. Most of the plastics it collects are under local government contracts for domestic waste collection and recycling. Because RR lacks facilities and expertise in the recycling of plastics, the plastic waste it collects is sorted by item/type and transported long distances to specialised plastic recycling plants operated by other recycling companies.

For some time now the board of RR has been concerned about reduced margins. As a result of a study initiated by the finance director, the company has established that the collection and recycling of plastics is proving unprofitable. Transportation costs have been extremely high, as many recycling operators have not been accepting plastics collected by RR in the hope that this would make the contracts less profitable for RR. They believed this would increase their own chances of winning future tenders.

The chairman of RR recently called a board meeting to examine the terms of the company's existing contracts with local governments for domestic waste collection and recycling. At this meeting, the finance director stated that, though he felt strongly about the value of recycling to society as a whole, he also felt that RR simply should not continue to perform unprofitable activities if there was 'a way out'.

On examining the contracts, the board discovered that several specified an overall percentage of material collected that must be recycled of 70% (others specified 80%). Based on the volumes of paper, glass, metal and plastics collected over the past year, the board decided that in some locations RR could meet a contractual obligation of 70% without recycling any plastics at all. Plastic collected under these '70% contracts' could simply be dumped at landfill sites, with significant savings from reduced sorting and transport costs. Some board members had reservations about implementing this policy, but were swayed by the strength of the finance director's reasoning.

The dumping of plastics is about to start. Although the board of RR feels the company's actions do not breach the terms of their contracts, it was decided that the vehicles involved in the dumping process would not carry the RR name.

Required

Analyse the board's decision to dump plastics at landfill sites, using Tucker's five question model.

Answer

Using Tucker's five question model, we have to ask, is the decision:

Profitable

The main justification for the decision is to **increase short-term profitability** and if the finance director's figures are correct, that aim has been achieved. However, the effect on long-term profitability may be very different if what RR has done becomes public. A recycling company, even one operating in a commercial environment, must be seen as **caring about the environment** if it is to attract and retain customers. Some local government customers may try to cancel existing contracts on the grounds that RR is not abiding by the spirit of these contracts. In any case local government agencies are likely to be unwilling to renew contracts and RR may be unable to win other new contracts.

Legal

Clearly RR is using **legal landfill sites**. Assuming the board has interpreted the contracts correctly, the company has not breached the strict legal terms of the contract even if it has possibly breached the spirit. Transporting the waste in unmarked vans may be questionable legally though.

Fair

If the view is taken that the customers are vital stakeholders, then what RR is doing is unfair to them, as they may have made **claims** about the support, they are giving to recycling which are unintentionally misleading. Any loss of reputation that local authorities suffer in the fallout that follows discovery of what RR has done may be particularly serious, as it may impact on re-election chances of local councillors. The only mitigation for RR under this heading is that the problem has arisen because of other recycling operators refusing to take RR's waste. They too appear to be putting their commercial interests ahead of the objective of supporting recycling.

Right

The fact that the waste is being **transported in unmarked vans** is effectively an admission by the board that what they are doing is indefensible on moral grounds. Any mitigation may be based on other criteria, that RR is acting within the law and doing its best for its shareholders, but it is nearly impossible to defend the actions on these grounds.

Sustainable

This is potentially the easiest criterion of them all, as what RR is doing appears to be going against environmental best practice. Apart from anything else, RR's ability to continue doing this depends on the **availability of landfill sites**. In some countries they are running out. The only environmental justification is that by using the landfill sites, RR is cutting down the miles plastics are transported, and is reducing its carbon footprint to that extent.

Question — Kohlberg and Tucker

How would different people operating at each of Kohlberg's levels of ethical reasoning view Tucker's criteria? (Kohlberg's three levels are pre-conventional, conventional and post-conventional, which we covered in Chapter 1 of this workbook.)

Answer

Here are some suggestions, although it should be borne in mind that this is not a definitive answer.

	Pre-conventional	**Conventional**	**Post-conventional**
Profitable	A very important criteria, as the pre-conventional level is based on the idea of rewards for self.	Profitability may be seen as quite important depending on the local ethos – very important if the decision maker works in a major financial centre for example. Decision makers will also be influenced by any local requirements in company law to seek profit maximisation.	Surprisingly perhaps, this could be a very important criterion. Equally it could have no importance if the decision maker believes it goes against other concepts. Those holding the pristine capitalist viewpoint would argue that companies have a moral duty to make profits to reward the shareholders whose finance underwrites their existence. Use of monies for other purposes is effectively theft of

PART A   THE NATURE AND IMPORTANCE OF ETHICAL THEORY AND DECISION MAKING

	Pre-conventional	Conventional	Post-conventional
			shareholders' funds under this stance.
Legal	The pre-conventional level will be more concerned with the consequences of breaking the law than its content.	At the higher conventional level, this will be seen as all-important. At the lower level, it may depend on the views of local society, some societies having a more relaxed view to certain laws than others.	Strangely, obedience to the law may not be seen as so significant at this level. This is because post-conventional viewpoint may see the law as inadequately defining ethics and thus decision makers need to go beyond it. Alternatively, some laws may be seen as immoral (for example, requiring the decision maker to swear allegiance to a cause with which they disagree).
Fair	The concept of fairness is likely to be interpreted as confined to fairness to the decision maker alone.	Fairness may be significant if it means fairness to others in society whose approval is sought, or fairness is a concept enshrined in law.	Fairness may well be a key ethical concept, but fairness to whom may be a difficult issue, dependent on who are seen as legitimate stakeholders.
Right	The consequences of being caught doing wrong are more likely to be an issue than whether the decision is actually right.	The decision maker will see what is right as significant, but they will see right as defined by others in their local society or right as enshrined in law. The decision maker may not be able to supply their own definition of what is right.	Right will always be important for post-conventional decision makers. Remember though the distinction between the two levels at this stage. Right may be as defined by the decision maker's society's ethics or it may be outside society's ethics.
Sustainable	Again the consequences for the decision maker rather than anyone else will be paramount.	This depends on how sustainability is viewed in the decision maker's local environment, or the importance given to it in law. The campaigns conducted by many organisations internally to improve sustainability awareness are perhaps an acknowledgement that many of their employees are taking decisions at this level. Thus the organisations are trying to change the ethos to make employees behave in a more socially responsible way.	Sustainability may well be a key ethical concept for post-conventional decision makers, although what sustainability means exactly may cause problems.

2.2.1 Weaknesses of answers

Possibly the most **common fault** of students' answers to questions on ethics is that they include large **amounts of unanalysed detail copied out from the question scenarios** in their answers. This is unlikely to earn marks.

Other things to avoid doing include:

Paraphrasing the question	This does not add anything.
Regurgitating the Ethical Guidelines	As in other areas of the exam, you may not get any credit unless you apply relevant knowledge.
Failing to make a decision or failing to recommend action if asked	The examination team may ask you to consider different viewpoints, but if you are asked to advise or recommend you must do so.
Justifying your decision merely by saying 'This should be done because it's ethical'	That will not convince the marker. Stronger justification will be necessary.

2.3 The problem

The exam may present you with a scenario, typically containing an array of detail of which much is potentially relevant. The problem, however, will be one or other of two basic types.

(a) **A wishes B to do C which is in breach of D**

where A = a situation, person, group of people, institution or the like
B = you/an accountant, the person with the ethical dilemma
C = acting, or refraining from acting, in a certain way
D = an ethical principle

(b) Alternatively, the problem may be that A has done C, B has become aware of it and D requires some kind of response from B.

2.4 Example: the problem

An accountant joined a manufacturing company as its finance director. The company had acquired land on which it built industrial units. The finance director discovered that, before they had started at the company, one of the units had been sold and the selling price was significantly larger than the amount which appeared in the company's records. The difference had been siphoned off to another company – one in which their boss, the managing director, was a major shareholder. Furthermore, the managing director had kept their relationship with the second company a secret from the rest of the board.

The finance director confronted the managing director and asked them to reveal their position to the board. However, the managing director refused to disclose their position to anyone else. The secret profits on the sale of the unit had been used, they said, to reward the people who had secured the sale. Without their help, they added, the company would be in a worse position financially.

The finance director then told the managing director that unless they reported to the board, they would have to inform the board members themselves. The managing director still refused. The finance director disclosed the full position to the board.

The problem is of the **second basic type**. **B** is of course the easiest party to identify. Here it is the **finance director**. **A** is clear, as well; it is the **managing director**. **C** is the **managing director's breach of their directorial duties** regarding related party transactions not to obtain any personal advantage from their position of director without the consent of the company for whatever gain or profit they have obtained. **D** is the **principle that requires B not to be a party to an illegal act**. (Note that we distinguish between ethical and legal obligations. B has legal obligations as a director of the company. They have ethical obligations not to ignore their legal obligations. In **this** case, the two amount to the same thing.)

2.5 Relationships

You may have a feeling that the resolution of the problem described above is just too easy, and you would be right. This is because A, B, C and D are either people, or else situations involving people, who stand in certain relationships to each other.

A may be B's boss, B's subordinate, B's equal in the organisational hierarchy, B's husband, B's friend.

B may be new to the organisation, or well established and waiting for promotion, or ignorant of some knowledge relevant to the situation that A possesses or that the people affected by C possess.

C or D, as already indicated, may involve some person(s) with whom B or A have a relationship – for example, the action may be to misrepresent something to a senior manager who controls the fate of B or A (or both) in the organisation.

Question — Relationships

Identify the relationships in the scenario above. What are the possible problems arising from these relationships?

Answer

The MD is the finance director's boss. They are also a member of the board and longer established as such than B, the finance director.

In outline, the problems arising are that **by acting ethically the finance director will alienate the MD**. Even if the problem were to be resolved, the episode would sour all future dealings between these two parties. Also, **the board may not be sympathetic to the accusations of a newcomer**. The finance director may find that they are ignored or even dismissed.

Relationships should never be permitted to affect ethical judgement. If you knew that your best friend at work had committed a major fraud, for example, **integrity** would demand that **as a last resort** you would have to bring it to the attention of somebody in authority. But note that this is only as a last resort. Try to imagine what you would do in practice in this situation.

Surely your **first course** of action would be to try to **persuade your friend** that what they had done was wrong, and that they themselves had an ethical responsibility to own up. Your **second option**, if this failed, might be to try to get **somebody** (perhaps somebody outside the organisation) that you knew could **exert pressure** on your friend to persuade them to own up.

There is obviously a limit to how far you can take this. The important point is that just because you are dealing with a situation that involves ethical issues, this **does not mean that all the normal principles of good human relations and good management have to be suspended**. In fact, this is the time when such business principles are most important.

2.6 Consequences

Actions have consequences and the consequences are quite likely to have their own ethical implications (remember the teleological approach we covered in Chapter 1).

In the example given above, we can identify the following further issues.

(a) The MD's secret transaction appears to have been made in order to secure the sale of an asset, the proceeds of which are helping to prop up the company financially. Disclosure of the truth behind the sale may mean that the company is pursued for compensation by the buyer of the site. The **survival of the company** as a whole may be jeopardised.

(b) If the truth behind the transaction becomes public knowledge this could be highly damaging for the company's **reputation**, even if it can show that only one person was involved.

(c) The board may simply rubber stamp the MD's actions and so the finance director may still find that they are expected to be party to dishonesty. (This assumes that the **company as a whole is amoral** in its approach to ethical issues. In fact the MD's refusal to disclose the matter to the board suggests otherwise.)

In the last case, we are back to square one. In the first two cases, the finance director has to consider the ethicality or otherwise of taking action that could lead to the collapse of the company, extensive redundancies, unpaid creditors and shareholders, and so on.

2.7 Actions

In spite of the difficulties, your aim will usually be to reach a satisfactory resolution to the problem. **The actions that you recommend** will often include the following:

(a) **Informal discussions** with the parties involved

(b) **Further investigation** to establish the full facts of the matter. What extra information is needed?

(c) The **tightening up of controls or the introduction of new ones**, if the situation arose due to laxity in this area; this will often be the case and the principles of professional competence and due care and of technical standards will usually be relevant

(d) **Attention to organisational matters** such as changes in the management structure, improving communication channels, attempting to change attitudes

Question — Cunning plan

Your finance director has asked you to join a team planning a takeover of one of your company's suppliers. An old school friend works as an accountant for the company concerned. The finance director knows this, and has asked you to try and find out 'anything that might help the takeover succeed, but it must remain secret'.

Answer

There are three issues here. Firstly you have a **conflict of interest** as the finance director wants you to keep the takeover a secret, but you probably feel that you should tell your friend what is happening as it may affect their job.

Second, the finance director is asking you to deceive your friend. Deception is unprofessional behaviour and will break your ethical guidelines. Therefore the situation is presenting you with **two conflicting demands**. It is worth remembering that no employer should ask you to break your ethical rules.

Finally, the request to break your own ethical guidelines constitutes **unprofessional behaviour** by the finance director. You should consider reporting them to the relevant body.

Chapter roundup

- In legal terms, companies are the property of their owners and can, in principle, do whatever they decide to do in the interests of their owners, disregarding the needs or interests of others. Notwithstanding this, however, it has been claimed that the various others who are affected by the company should also be taken into account when it makes decisions. These others are the **stakeholders**.

- Different groups of stakeholders have different objectives which can lead to conflicts between competing groups. By understanding the different stakeholders and their needs and goals, an organisation can determine strategies to resolve stakeholder conflicts which may prevent the organisation from achieving its strategic objectives.

- The fundamental objective of any organisation should be the maximisation of shareholders' wealth. In its purest sense, this means pursuing the maximum amount of profit from the organisation's operations. A threat to this objective is conflicting shareholder objectives.

- In a situation involving ethical issues, there will often be practical steps that should be taken. Any actions should be justified on the basis of an analysis of the situation, and will often involve striking a compromise between different interests and considerations.

Quick Quiz

1. What is the key tenet of the stockholder theory?
2. How may stakeholders with direct and indirect claims be distinguished?
3. Donaldson and Preston put forward two main views of stakeholders; name and briefly describe each of these views.
4. What are the seven stages of the AAA model?
5. What are the five questions in the Tucker model?

Answers to Quick Quiz

1. Stockholder theory states that shareholders (stockholders) have the sole legitimate claim to influence the company, and that the influence of other stakeholders should be reduced.

2. Stakeholders with direct claims are able to express and pursue their claims directly with the company; those with indirect claims do not do this. An example of a stakeholder with a direct claim may be an employee represented by a trade union; such a stakeholder would have an indirect claim if they were unable to express this to the company, for example, as a result of fear of repercussions for their livelihood.

3. Donaldson and Preston distinguished the instrumental from the normative view of stakeholders. The instrumental view regards stakeholders as intrinsically worthless, but as in need of consideration if the company is to deliver profit to its shareholders. The normative view sees stakeholders as valuable in themselves, and holds that the company has a moral duty to take them into account in its actions.

4.
   - What are the facts of the case?
   - What are the ethical issues in the case?
   - What are the norms, principles and values related to the case?
   - What are the alternative courses of action?
   - What is the best course of action that is consistent with the norms, principles and values identified in Step 3?
   - What are the consequences of each possible course of action?
   - What is the decision?

5. Is the decision:
   - Profitable?
   - Legal?
   - Fair?
   - Right?
   - Sustainable?

Codes, guidance and standards

Ethical codes, guidance and ethics standards

Topic list	Syllabus reference
1 Role of company ethical codes	LO 2, LO 4
2 Code of ethics for professional accountants	LO 2, LO 4
3 Review of relevant ethical codes	LO 2, LO 4
4 Confidentiality	LO 2, LO 4
5 Accepting new appointments: Accountants in practice	LO 2, LO 4
6 Safeguarding auditor independence	LO 2, LO 4

Introduction

In this chapter, we continue to move from the theoretical consideration of ethics to its application.

The focus is first on the overall purpose and role of ethical codes, be they codes of ethics created by an organisation to govern its operations or professional codes, such as the IESBA *International Code of Ethics for Professional Accountants*.

We then move on to consider the detailed provisions of the IESBA *Code of Ethics* for accountants in business and accountants in practice.

The final section considers how the IESBA Code of Ethics and FRC Ethical standards safeguard the independence of auditors.

PART B   CODES, GUIDANCE AND STANDARDS

1 Role of ethical codes

There are two main types of ethical code that aim to influence the behaviour of AIA members: corporate codes of ethics, and professional codes of ethics. In this section, we cover each of these in turn.

1.1 Corporate codes of ethics

FAST FORWARD Organisations have responded to pressure to be seen to act ethically by publishing **ethical codes**, setting out their **values and responsibilities** towards stakeholders.

In order for the companies to demonstrate their commitment to ethics, they will often publish ethical codes, showing what they value and their responsibilities to the stakeholders with which they are involved. There is usually a series of statements to show their ethics values and how they behave towards their stakeholders. The code of ethics is an important internal control where it is communicated to its employees and compliance monitored and enforced, as employees are less likely to behave in an unethical manner.

1.2 Corporate codes and corporate culture

Question — Code of ethics

Here are some extracts from an article that appeared in the UK *Financial Times*.

> 'Each company needs its own type of code: to reflect the national culture, the sector culture, and the exact nature of its own structure.
>
> The nature of the codes is changing. NatWest's code, for example, tries to do much more than simply set out a list of virtues. Its programme involves not only the production of a code, but a dedicated effort to teach ethics, and a system by which the code can be audited and monitored.
>
> For example, it has installed a 'hot-line' and its operation is monitored by internal auditors. The board of NatWest wanted it to be confidential – within the confines of legal and regulatory requirements – and the anonymity of 'whistle-blowers' has been strictly maintained.
>
> The code contains relevant and straightforward advice. For example: "In recognising that we are a competitive business, we believe in fair and open competition and, therefore, obtaining information about competitors by deception is unacceptable. Similarly, making disparaging comments about competitors invariably invites disrespect from customers and should be avoided." Or: "Employment with NatWest must never be used in an attempt to influence public officials or customers for personal gain or benefit."
>
> Jonathan Bye, manager of public policy at NatWest, said the bank is continually looking at ways of refreshing the code and measuring its effectiveness.'

How would you suggest that the effectiveness of a company's policy on ethics could be measured?

Answer

Some ideas that you might think through are:

- Training effectiveness measures
- How breaches of the code are dealt with
- Activity in the ethics office
- Public perceptions of the company

Try to flesh them out and think of some other ideas. The previous extract should suggest some.

1.3 Company code of ethics

An **ethical code** typically contains a **series of statements setting out the organisation's values and explaining how it sees its responsibilities towards stakeholders**.

Codes of corporate ethics normally have the following features:

- They **focus on regulating individual employee behaviour**.
- They are **formal documents**.
- They **cover specific areas** such as gifts, anti-competitive behaviour, and so on.
- Employees may be **asked to sign** that they will comply.
- They may be **developed from third-party codes** (eg regulators) or use third parties for monitoring.
- They tend to **mix moral with technical imperatives**.
- Sometimes they do **little more than describe current practices**.
- They can be used to **shift responsibility** (from senior managers to operational staff).

1.3.1 Benefits of a code of ethics

(a) **Establishment of organisation's values**

Ethical codes form part of the organisation's **underlying environment**. They develop and promote values that are linked to the organisation's mission statement. The ethical code will mirror the company's mission and values statements. Hence, they are connected to the company's underlying environment.

(b) **Promotion of stakeholder responsibilities**

Codes also demonstrate whom the organisation regards as **important stakeholders**. They show what action should be taken to maintain good **stakeholder relationships** (such as keeping them fully informed). They can show external stakeholders that they are dealing with people who **do business fairly**. Drafting parts of the code to comply with customer wishes demonstrates that businesses are **responsive to customers**.

(c) **Control of individuals' behaviour**

By **promoting or prohibiting certain actions**, ethical codes form part of the human resources mechanisms by which employee behaviour is controlled.

All staff should be aware of the importance of the ethical code and it should be referred to when employee actions are questioned.

All employees will be made aware of the code of ethics and its importance for their actions on behalf of the company. The employees will be aware that there will be consequences of not following the code of ethics. If an issue arises then the code will be referred to and used to judge the employee's behaviour. Any sanctions in the code can be used.

Once employee are trained up on the ethical code and have signed it off, then they will be aware that they are required to meet the code.

(d) **Promotion of business objectives**

Codes can be an important element in a company's strategic positioning. Taking a **strong stance on responsibility and ethics** and earning a good ethical reputation can enhance appeal to consumers in the same way as producing the right products of good quality can.

(e) **Conveying values to stakeholders**

The code is a **communications device**, not only acting to communicate between partners and staff, but also increasing the transparency of the organisation's dealings with its stakeholders.

Stakeholders of the company will be made aware of what the company is expecting ethically and hence will be aware that they should also follow the same code. For example, if the company has parts of its code dealing with environmental issues, then a supplier of the company that knows the code will be aware that they should also be taking care of the environment. If the supplier is damaging the environment when it produces or supplies goods to the company then that will have an impact on the company, potentially meaning the company does not meet its code. This will require good communication, honesty and transparency from the company as well as the supplier.

1.3.2 Commonly included content in a company code of ethics

A code of ethics can contain many elements, dependent on the business that a company is involved in. Some of the most common codes of ethics contain the following:

- The company and its staff are always expected to behave ethically.
- Employees are key to the company's ethical policy. Only employees that are committed to the company's ethical policies will be employed; their behaviour will be monitored and there will be consequences for any breach of the policy.
- The customers of the company are essential for the future success of the company and will always be treated well. If there is a customer complaint, then the company will listen carefully and respond when there has been an ethical breach.
- The company and its employees will always follow the laws of the countries it operates in and also the standards that are in place it its industry, from the guidelines that the industry has put into place on ethical behaviour.
- The company is committed to treating its suppliers with respect in their relationship. That will involve any contracts entered into with the supplier, the pricing of the supplier's products, making sure that the supplier is paid on time. The company will require suppliers to behave ethically with respect to their staff and the environment as well as how they act towards the company.
- The company will make sure that it is behaving properly to any competitors and the markets that it operates in. It will not gain competitive advantage by entering into questionable payments or favours. The company believes in open and fair markets.
- The company will do its best to protect the environment and help protect against climate change and depletion of nature. It will try to be efficient in its use of natural resources at all times. If there are opportunities to help the environment the company will do so.
- The company will look more broadly at the direct stakeholders it has as well as the wider population of the countries it trades in. As well as meeting government requirements it will also try to help in raising education attainment, health outcomes, safety in the wider community. It will do whatever it can to encourage diversity and help level up poorer parts of the countries. It will try to be a good corporate citizen, wherever possible giving charitable donations, and contributing to education, culture and local affairs.

Example

Polestar (Nasdaq: PSNY) is the Swedish electric performance car brand determined to improve society by using design and technology to accelerate the shift to sustainable mobility. Headquartered in Gothenburg, Sweden, its cars are available online in 27 markets globally across North America, Europe and Asia Pacific including Singapore.

Polestars code of ethics can be viewed here, which guides its employees in manufacturing and selling operations.

https://www.polestar.com/en-sg/legal/ethics/

1.3.1 Example of code of ethics

Typical statements in a corporate code
• The company conducts all its business on **ethical principles** and expects staff to do likewise.
• **Employees** are seen as the most important component of the company and are expected to work on a basis of trust, respect, honesty, fairness, decency and equality. The company will only employ people who follow its ethical ideals.

Typical statements in a corporate code
• **Customers** should be treated courteously and politely at all times, and the company should always respond promptly to customer needs by listening, understanding and then performing to the customer requirements.
• The company is dedicated to complying **with legal or regulatory standards** of the industry, and employees are expected to do likewise.
• The company's relationship with **suppliers and subcontractors** must be based on mutual respect. The company therefore has responsibilities including ensuring fairness and truthfulness in all its dealings with suppliers including pricing and licensing, fostering long-term stability in the supplier relationship, paying suppliers on time and in accordance with agreed terms of trade and preferring suppliers and subcontractors whose employment practices respect human dignity.
• The company has a responsibility to: foster open markets for trade and investment, promote **competitive behaviour** that is socially and environmentally beneficial and demonstrates mutual respect among competitors, and refrain from either seeking or participating in questionable payments or favours to secure competitive advantages.
• A business should protect and, where possible, improve **the environment**, promote sustainable development and prevent the wasteful use of natural resources.
• The company has a responsibility in **the community** to: respect human rights and democratic institutions, and promote them wherever practicable, recognise government's legitimate obligation to the society at large and support public policies and practices that promote human development through harmonious relations between business and other segments of society, collaborate with those forces in the community dedicated to raising standards of health, education, workplace safety and economic wellbeing, respect the integrity of local cultures, and be a good corporate citizen through charitable donations, educational and cultural contributions and employee participation in community and civic affairs.

Question — Employee behaviour

How can an organisation influence employee behaviour towards ethical issues?

Answer

Here are some suggestions.

- Recruitment and selection policies and procedures
- Induction and training
- Objectives and reward schemes
- Ethical codes
- Threat of ethical audit

1.4 The impact of codes of conduct

A code of conduct can set out the company's expectations, and in principle a code such as that outlined above addresses many of the problems that the organisations may experience. However, **merely issuing a code is not enough**.

(a) The **commitment of senior management** to the code needs to be real, and it needs to be very clearly communicated to all staff. Staff need to be persuaded that expectations really have changed.

(b) Measures need to be taken to **discourage previous behaviours** that conflict with the code.

(c) **Staff need to understand** that it is in the **organisation's best interests** to change behaviour and become committed to the same ideals.

(d) Some employees – including very able ones – may find it very difficult to buy into a code that they **perceive may limit their own earnings** and/or restrict their freedom to do their job.

(e) In addition to a general statement of ethical conduct, **more detailed statements** (codes of practice) will be needed to set out formal procedures that must be followed.

Case Study

The Co-operative bank pursues ethical policies through its banking and insurance divisions. Both are founded on the assumption that investors have no say in, and do not know how, other banks invest their money. The Co-operative bank on the other hand consults its customers.

The banking division's ethical policy has two sides to it. It seeks to encourage certain businesses or organisations, or certain business practices. For example, it supports charities, credit unions and community finance initiatives. It also supports businesses involved in recycling, renewable energy and sustainable natural products. On the other hand, it will not invest in businesses or practices that operate in areas of concern to customers. These include currency speculation, tobacco product manufacture, irresponsible marketing practices in developing countries, unsustainable harvesting of natural resources and animal testing of cosmetic or household products.

Co-operative Insurance's ethical engagement policy is based on using its influence as a corporate shareholder to change companies from the inside. It has asked companies to seek modifications to the working conditions of factory workers and encouraged oil and energy companies to pursue biofuels with long-term potential for sustainable production. It focuses in particular on corporate governance practices such as directors' pay, board appointments and treatment of employees.

1.5 Problems with codes of conduct

1.5.1 Inflexibility

Inflexible rules may not be practical. One example would be a **prohibition on accepting gifts from customers**. A simple prohibition that would be quite acceptable in a Western context would not work in other cultures, where non-acceptance might be seen as insulting.

1.5.2 Clarity

It is difficult to achieve **completely unambiguous wording**.

1.5.3 Irrelevance

Surveys suggest that ethical codes are often perceived as irrelevant for the following reasons:

(a) They fail to say anything about the sort of **ethical problems that employees encounter**.

(b) Other people in the organisation **pay no attention** to them.

(c) They are **inconsistent with the prevailing organisational culture**.

(d) Senior managers' behaviour is **not seen as promoting ethical codes**. Senior managers rarely blatantly fail to comply; rather they appear out of touch on ethics because they are too busy or unwilling to take responsibility.

1.6 Identity and values guidance

Corporate ethical codes are often **rather legalistic documents**, consisting largely of prohibitions on specific undesirable actions such as the acceptance of gifts from suppliers. More general guidance with an emphasis on principles may be more appropriate.

Identity and values programmes describe corporate values without specifying in detail what they mean. Rather than highlighting compliance with negatives they **promote positive values** about the company and form part of its culture. (Compliance programmes are about limiting legal and public relations disasters.) Even so, they need to be integrated with a company's values and leadership.

1.7 Other measures

To be effective, ethical guidance needs to be accompanied by **positive attempts to foster guiding values, aspirations and patterns of thinking that support ethically sound behaviour** – in short a **change of culture**.

Increasingly, organisations are responding to this challenge by devising **ethics training programmes** for the entire workforce, instituting comprehensive **procedures for reporting and investigating ethical concerns** within the company, or even setting up an **ethics office** or department to supervise the new measures.

Case Study

'The view from the trenches'

Badaracco and Webb (1995) carried out in-depth interviews with 30 recent Harvard MBA graduates. They found that unethical behaviour appeared to be widespread in the middle layers of business organisations.

> '... in many cases, young managers received explicit instructions from their middle-manager bosses or felt strong organisational pressures to do things that they believed were sleazy, unethical, or sometimes illegal.'

However, these young managers categorised only a few of their superiors as fundamentally unethical. Most were basically decent but were themselves pushed into requiring unethical behaviour by four strong organisational pressures.

(a) Performance outcomes are what really count.
(b) Loyalty is very important.
(c) Do not break the law.
(d) Do not over-invest in ethical behaviour.

The outcome of these pressures was a firm impression that ethical conduct was a handicap and a willingness to evade ethical imperatives an advantage in career progression.

2 Code of ethics for professional accountants

FAST FORWARD

> In addition to following any corporate code of ethics, a member of the AIA is bound by the International Ethics Standards Board for Accountants (IESBA) *International Code of Ethics for Professional Accountants* (IESBA *Code*), which the AIA has adopted. Professional codes of ethics such as these apply to the **individual behaviour** of professionals. The IESBA *Code* is based on principles, supplemented by guidance on **threats and safeguards**.

The existence of this ethical guidance for AIA members demonstrates that the accountancy profession is structured according to a particular view of the profession's responsibilities to **stakeholders** (as considered in general terms in the previous chapter). It is held that **accountants have a duty to act ethically**, which is distinct from, for example, acting solely to increase the profitability of their firm (in the interests of shareholders).

The principles of the *Code of Ethics* (given below) focus on the professional accountant's commitment to honesty, and their duty to remain independent of anything that may significantly compromise that commitment. It is instructive to consider what alternative views might be formed of the profession; from a pristine capitalist perspective, for instance, such a view of the accountant's independence could be

considered unjust since it could mean prioritising ethical independence over the delivery of returns to the accountancy firm's owners. At the other extreme, the Marxist critic might consider the very commitment to impartiality itself to be unethical, since the accountant's ethical duty is confined to the consideration of whether existing laws and regulations have been properly applied, laws which for the Marxist merely enact the liberal ideology of the bourgeois class in general, and its antagonism to the collective interests of the working class. The *Code of Ethics* appears to adopt a middle ground position, wherein the accountant is understood to be personally independent, not bound to consider the underlying justice of laws or regulations, but with an ethical duty that extends beyond the service of the interests of capital as such.

2.1 International Code of Ethics for accountants

The primary International *Code of Ethics* for accountants is issued by the International Federation of Accountants (IFAC).

As previously mentioned, the International Ethics Standards Board for Accountants (IESBA) is an independent standard-setting board under the International Federation of Accountants (IFAC) and is responsible for developing and maintaining the *Code of Ethics (Code of Ethics)* for professional accountants globally.

The IFAC *Code of Ethics* comprises several sections, and one of the primary sections is the *Code of Ethics* for Professional Accountants issued by IESBA (IESBA *Code*) which establishes ethical requirements specifically for firms of professional accountants. A professional firm of accountants may not apply less stringent standards than those stated in the IESBA *Code*.

The IESBA *Code* is designed to be globally applicable and provides guidance for all professional accountants, regardless of their specific roles or jurisdictions. The objective of setting the IESBA *Code* is to harmonise ethical standards and practices on a global basis. Public trust in the accountancy profession can only be enhanced when it is made mandatory for professional accountants to observe and follow strict regulations and ethics codes throughout the world.

The IESBA *Code* covers areas such as independence, confidentiality, objectivity, professional competence and professional behaviour in the context of providing professional accountancy advice and engagements.

The following main principles of the IESBA *Code* are explained in the following sections:
- Professional conduct and compliance with IESBA *Code*
- Five fundamental principles to ensure ethical conduct
- Conceptual framework to guide ethical decision making
- Conceptual framework to help manage ethical dilemmas

The IESBA *Code of Ethics* for Professional Accountants can be found here:

https://www.ethicsboard.org/iesba-code

2.1.1 Professional conduct and compliance with IESBA *Code*

Accountants are required to demonstrate professional conduct and comply with the IESBA *Code* and other applicable standards and regulations. They should promote ethical conduct within the profession and take appropriate action if they become aware of any breaches of ethical requirements.

Also, public interest comes first which means that an accountant should not be thinking about themselves immediately when making ethical decisions but taking a far wider view, to see who is affected by the decision and what the consequences are.

2.1.2 Five fundamental principles to ensure ethical conduct

In order to assist an accountant with ethical decision making, IESBA *Code* sets down five fundamental principles in order to assist professional accountants with ethical decision making and ensure ethical conduct is applied.

The five fundamental principles which professional accountants should be guided by when making ethical decisions are as follows:

1. **Integrity:** Accountants should be straightforward and honest in all professional and business relationships. They should maintain their integrity and avoid any behaviour that could compromise their professional judgment.

2. **Objectivity:** Accountants should not allow bias, conflicts of interest, or undue influence of others to compromise their professional judgment. They should provide unbiased and independent advice and ensure their decisions are based on relevant and reliable information.

3. **Professional competence and due care:** Accountants should continuously maintain and develop their professional knowledge and skills to provide high-quality services. They should perform their duties with diligence, competence, and due care, considering the relevant technical and professional standards.

4. **Confidentiality:** Accountants should respect the confidentiality of information acquired during their professional engagements. They should not disclose such information unless there is a legal or professional obligation to do so, or when authorised by the client.

5. **Professional behaviour:** Accountants should comply with relevant laws, regulations, and avoid any conduct that might discredit the profession. They should act in a manner consistent with the good reputation of the profession and demonstrate a commitment to professionalism.

2.1.3 Conceptual framework to guide ethical decision making

Additionally, the IESBA *Code* has introduced a conceptual framework which aims to guide and assist professional accountants with ethical decision making.

Section 120 of the IESBA *Code* outlines the conceptual framework for professional accountants to apply in ethical decision-making. It provides guidance on how to identify, evaluate and address ethical issues encountered in their professional roles. It serves as a structured approach for accountants to navigate ethical dilemmas, ensuring they uphold integrity, objectivity, professional competence, confidentiality and professional behaviour in their professional practice.

Additionally, the conceptual framework requires accountants to exercise professional scepticism by having an inquiring mind, exercising professional judgement and applying the third-party test when dealing with ethical threats to the five fundamental principles.

- **Having an inquiring mind.** Accountants are encouraged to possess an inquisitive mindset, which involves actively seeking out relevant information and questioning assumptions. An attitude of professional scepticism helps in identifying potential ethical issues and understanding the context in which they arise. Accountants should critically assess the information and evidence obtained and remain alert to any potential misstatements, contradictions or other irregularities and ask probing questions to investigate further.

- **Exercising professional judgement.** Accountants are expected to exercise professional judgement when faced with ethical dilemmas. Professional judgement involves the application of training, knowledge, skills and experience commensurate with the facts and circumstances, taking into account the scope and nature of the professional activities being undertaken, and the relationships involved. Professional judgement is required when applying the conceptual framework in order to make informed decisions to ensure compliance with the five fundamental ethical principles. This includes making a judgement regarding the need to consult with others with the relevant expertise and experience and ensure the professional accountants own preconceptions and bias do not influence their decision making.

- **Reasoned and informed third-party test.** Accountants should assess their ethical decisions using a reasoned and informed third-party test. This means considering how a reasonable and informed third party, possessing all relevant information, would view the decision. The objective of this test is to confirm that a third party with the same information would come to the same view. This test helps ensure objectivity and accountability in ethical decision-making processes.

2.1.4 Conceptual framework to help manage ethical dilemmas

The IESBA *Code* conceptual framework on ethics provides a structured approach for accountants to analyse and respond to ethical issues. It emphasises the importance of identifying and addressing threats, applying safeguards and exercising professional judgment to ensure ethical behaviour and maintain public trust in the accounting profession.

The conceptual framework to help manage ethical dilemmas is split into six parts:

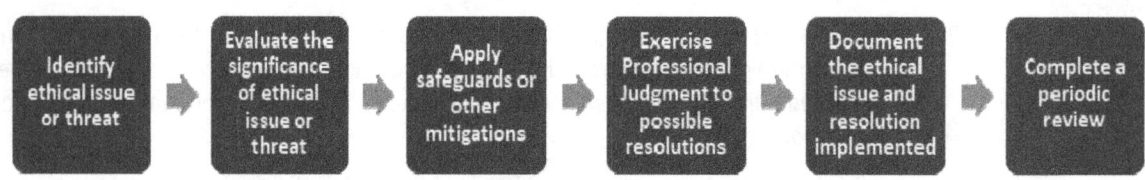

Each component is explained as follows:

1. **Identify ethics risks or threats:** Accountants should identify and evaluate any threats that may compromise compliance with the fundamental principles of the IFAC *Code* of Ethics. These threats can arise from various sources, such as self-interest, self-review, advocacy, familiarity, or intimidation.

2. **Evaluate the significance of ethical risks or threats:** Accountants should assess the significance of the identified threats. They need to determine whether the threats are at a level where they would impair their compliance with the fundamental principles. If the threats are considered significant, appropriate safeguards should be applied to mitigate or eliminate them.

3. **Apply safeguards or other mitigations:** Safeguards are measures designed to reduce threats to an acceptable level. Accountants should identify and apply safeguards that are relevant and available in the circumstances. These safeguards can be categorised into three groups: (a) safeguards created by the profession, legislation, or regulation; (b) safeguards in the work environment; and (c) safeguards in the individual's own ethical mindset.

4. **Exercise professional judgment when evaluating possible resolutions:** Accountants should exercise professional judgment when applying the conceptual framework. This requires considering all relevant facts and circumstances and using ethical reasoning to arrive at an appropriate resolution.

5. **Document the ethical issue and resolution implemented:** Accountants should document the ethical issue they encountered, and the safeguards applied to address it. This documentation helps in demonstrating compliance with the ethical requirements and provides an audit trail for future reference.

6. **Complete a periodic review:** Accountants should periodically review and evaluate the effectiveness of the safeguards implemented. They need to ensure that the safeguards remain relevant and sufficient to address the threats to compliance with the fundamental principles.

2.1.5 Advantages of professional codes of ethics

(a) Codes represent a clear statement that **professionals** are expected to act in the public interest, and act as a **benchmark** against which behaviour can be judged. They should thus enhance public confidence in the professions.

(b) Codes emphasise the importance of professionals **considering ethical issues actively** and seeking to comply, rather than only being concerned with avoiding what is forbidden.

(c) The IESBA *Code* states that it can be **applied internationally**. Local differences are not significant.

(d) Codes can include detailed guidance, which should **assist ethical decision making**.

(e) Codes can include **explicit prohibitions,** if necessary.

(f) Codes prescribe **minimum standards of behaviour** that are expected.

2.1.6 Disadvantages of professional codes of ethics

(a) Professional codes, with their **identification of many different situations**, can lose focus on key issues.

(b) Evidence suggests that some treat codes as a set of rules to be **complied with and 'box-ticked'**.

(c) **International codes** such as the IESBA *Code* cannot fully capture **regional variations in beliefs and practice**.

(d) The value of international codes may be limited by their not being legally enforceable around the world.

(e) **Illustrative examples** can be interpreted mistakenly as rules to follow in similar circumstances.

(f) Giving a lot of illustrative examples in codes may give the impression that ethical considerations are **primarily important** only when accountants are facing decisions illustrated in the codes. They may **downplay the importance of acting ethically** when facing decisions that are not clearly covered in the codes.

2.2 Advantages and disadvantages of professional codes of ethics

The IESBA suggests that the sheer variety of threats to compliance with the fundamental principles mean that no guidance can cover every situation where there is a potential threat.

2.2.1 Advantages of principles-based guidance

The IESBA suggests that requiring use of a principles-based conceptual framework rather than a set of specific rules is in the public interest for the following reasons.

(a) It places the onus on the professional to **consider actively** relevant issues in a given situation, rather than just agreeing action with a checklist of forbidden items. It also requires them to **demonstrate** that a responsible conclusion has been reached about ethical issues.

(b) It **prevents professionals from interpreting legalistic requirements narrowly** to get around the ethical requirements. There is an extent to which rules engender deception, whereas principles encourage compliance.

(c) It **allows for variations** that are found in every **individual situation**. Each situation is likely to be different.

(d) It can accommodate a **rapidly changing environment**, such as the one in which auditors operate.

(e) It can include **examples** to illustrate how the principles are applied.

2.2.2 Disadvantages of principles-based guidance

(a) As ethical codes cannot include all circumstances and dilemmas, accountants need a very good understanding of the **underlying principles**.

(b) A principles-based code can be difficult to enforce legally unless the breach of the code is blatant. Most are therefore **voluntary** and perhaps therefore less effective.

2.3 What is independence?

A professional accountant must be, and be seen to be, independent. What is required for this to be the case?

Key terms

> **Independence of mind.** The state of mind that permits the expression of a conclusion without being affected by influences that compromise professional judgment, allowing an individual to act with integrity, and exercise objectivity and professional scepticism. (IESBA *Code*: para. 120.12 A1)
>
> **Independence in appearance.** The avoidance of facts and circumstances that are so significant that a reasonable and informed third party would be likely to conclude that a firm's or an audit or assurance team member's integrity, objectivity or professional scepticism has been compromised. (IESBA *Code*: para. 120.12 A1)
>
> **Professional scepticism.** An attitude that includes a questioning mind, being alert to conditions which may indicate possible misstatement due to error or fraud, and a critical assessment of audit evidence. (ISA 200: para. 13(m))

The degree of independence required is less stringent for a firm providing a low-level assurance engagement to a non-audit client than for a reasonable assurance external audit. This is summarised in the following table:

Who must be independent within the firm?			
	Audit	**Non-audit, general use**	**Non-audit, restricted use**
Audit client	The assurance team, the firm and the network firm must all be independent of the client.		
Non-audit assurance client	N/A	The assurance team and the firm must be independent of the client.	The assurance team and the firm must have no material financial interest in the client.

2.3.1 When must the assurance provider be independent?

The team and the firm should be independent **during the period of the engagement**.

For a **recurring audit**, independence may only cease on **termination of the contract** between the parties.

FAST FORWARD

> The IESBA *Code* gives examples of a number of situations where independence might be threatened and suggests safeguards to independence.

2.4 A dilemma: independence vs effectiveness

Auditor and accountant independence is rarely a matter of clear questions with black and white answers. It is not just an issue of whether the 'rules' say that an engagement should be accepted or declined ('yes or no'), but rather of the auditor exercising proper judgment in the complex circumstances of an actual engagement.

The basic dilemma is this. The auditor must be independent of the client in order to express their own opinion on whether the client's financial statements give a true and fair view. However, the auditor must also place some trust in the client if the audit is to be conducted effectively, as they will need to rely on anything from the accounting systems and controls to explanations provided by management.

It is between the two extremes of this dilemma that the concept of 'professional scepticism' attempts to place itself:

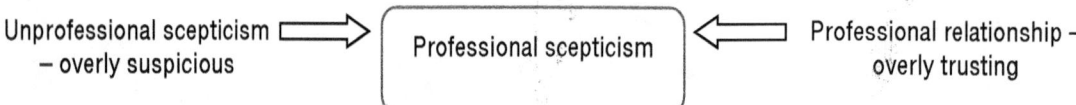

If the accountant is **too** sceptical about everything the client does or says, then it will be impossible for them to conduct the engagement effectively. At the extreme, this would mean checking every transaction in the financial statements without accepting any internal records or documents at all as genuine. More practically, a breakdown in trust would mean that the engagement would be conducted less efficiently: if the accountant must assume that management is not at all competent or trustworthy, then it will be very difficult for them to work with management at all. This would take more time and would make the engagement much more costly. Some degree of trust is therefore essential to the effective and professional conduct of any engagement.

On the other hand, if the accountant is not sceptical enough then the quality of the work is likely to suffer. The accountant may easily be deceived in the case of fraud or may mistakenly place too much trust in the validity of evidence and explanations provided by the client. This links with the question of independence generally, and the risk that the audit is not conducted with professional competence and due care as a result of a lack of scepticism.

In the end, the accountant must balance being sceptical with being trusting, and the concept of 'professional scepticism' is an attempt to convey this. It has also been said elsewhere that the accountant should 'trust but verify' what the client tells them.

2.5 Ethical threats to compliance with the fundamental principles for accountants in practice

The IESBA fundamental ethical principles are designed to ensure that the accountant acts in the public interest and meets the expectations of society. The following table is a reminder of the five principles.

Fundamental principles	
Integrity	To be straightforward and honest in all professional and business relationships.
Objectivity	Not to compromise professional or business judgments because of bias, conflict of interest or undue influence of others.
Professional Competence and Due Care	To: (i) Attain and maintain professional knowledge and skill at the level required to ensure that a client or employing organisation receives competent professional service, based on current technical and professional standards and relevant legislation; and (ii) Act diligently and in accordance with applicable technical and professional standards.
Confidentiality	To respect the confidentiality of information acquired as a result of professional and business relationships.
Professional Behaviour	To comply with relevant laws and regulations and avoid any conduct that the professional accountant knows or should know might discredit the profession.

The IESBA *Code* set out guidance to ensure independence at professional firms by addressing the five threats to independence. These are self-interest, self-review, advocacy, familiarity and intimidation which are explored further here.

2.5.1 Self-Interest threat

This threat occurs when a professional accountant's financial or other personal interests could compromise their objectivity and independence. It could arise when the accountant has a significant financial interest in a client or stands to benefit personally from a particular outcome.

Example: A professional accountant owns a significant number of shares in a client company. This ownership interest could potentially bias the accountant's objectivity and independence when providing auditing services to the client.

2.5.2 Self-Review threat

This threat arises when a professional accountant is involved in the preparation of the same subject matter or significant judgments as part of their assurance work. It can impair objectivity as reviewing one's own work may lead to a biased assessment.

Example: An accountant is responsible for preparing financial statements for a client and is subsequently asked to perform an audit on those same financial statements. The accountant's involvement in the preparation of the statements may compromise their ability to independently review and evaluate the information.

2.5.3 Advocacy threat

Advocacy threat occurs when a professional accountant promotes or defends a client's position or opinion to the extent that it compromises their objectivity. It may arise when the accountant aggressively advocates for the client's interests, potentially compromising their professional judgment.

Example: An accountant is a strong advocate for a client's proposed accounting treatment that has significant financial implications. The accountant's strong advocacy for the client's position may compromise their objectivity and independence when evaluating the appropriateness of the treatment.

2.5.4 Familiarity threat

This threat arises when a professional accountant becomes too close or excessively sympathetic to the interests of a client. It can impair objectivity and independence if personal or long-standing relationships create a bias or compromise independent judgment.

Example: A professional accountant has a close personal relationship with a client's management team. The accountant's personal relationship may create a bias or undue influence that compromises their objectivity and independence when making professional judgements or decisions related to the client.

2.5.5 Intimidation threat

Intimidation threat occurs when a professional accountant feels unduly pressured or influenced by others to act contrary to their professional judgment. This threat may arise if the accountant fears negative consequences or retaliation for taking a particular position or expressing an independent opinion.

Example: A professional accountant feels pressured by a client's management to alter audit findings or conclusions to avoid potential negative consequences, such as the loss of future engagements. The fear of retaliation or negative repercussions from the client may influence the accountant's independence and objectivity.

As noted in the IESBA *Code*, the threats to independence listed above are also threats to compliance with the five fundamental principles (integrity, objectivity, professional competence and due care, confidentiality and professional behaviour).

IESBA *Code* emphasises that it is essential for professional accountants to be aware of these threats to independence and take appropriate measures to address them. These measures often involve applying safeguards, such as establishing ethical policies and procedures, maintaining a robust ethical culture within the firm, and ensuring effective oversight and review processes.

By recognising and managing these threats, accountants can uphold their independence and maintain public trust in their professional judgment and the integrity of financial information they provide.

IESBA *Code* principles and conceptual framework are adopted in EP 100 *Code* of Professional Conduct and Ethics

As we shall see in the next section, these threats are particularly relevant in the context of threats to independence.

2.6 Ethical safeguards for accountants in practice

The IESBA *Code* contains separate guidance for accountants in business and in public practice, together with specific requirements in relation to auditors, all of which are covered in this chapter.

The IESBA identifies two general categories of ethical safeguard:

- Safeguards created by the profession, legislation or regulation
- Safeguards within the assurance client/the firm's own systems and procedures

2.6.1 Examples of ethical safeguards created by the profession, legislation or regulation

- Educational training and experience requirements for entry into the profession
- Continuing professional development requirements
- Corporate governance regulations
- Professional standards
- Professional or regulatory monitoring and disciplinary procedures

The International Federation of Accountants (IFAC) issues ethical standards (via IESBA), and quality control standards and auditing standards (via the International Auditing and Assurance Standards Board), that work together to ensure independence is safeguarded and quality audits are carried out.

2.6.2 Examples of ethical safeguards in the firm's own systems and procedures

If a professional accountant works for an accountancy practice, the firm should have the following safeguards in place in relation to the firm.

- The firm's leadership stressing **compliance with fundamental principles**
- Leadership of the firm establishing the expectation that **employees will act in the public interest**
- **Quality control policies and procedures**
- Documented policies on **identification and evaluation of threats** and **identification and application of safeguards**
- Documented policies covering **independence threats and safeguards** in relation to assurance engagements
- Documented internal procedures requiring **compliance with fundamental principles**
- Policies and procedures enabling **identification of interests and relationships between the firm's team** and **clients**
- Policies and procedures to **manage reliance on revenue from a single client**
- Using **different teams for non-assurance work**
- Prohibiting individuals who are not team members from **influencing the outcome of the engagement**
- **Timely communication of policies and procedures** and appropriate training and education
- Designating a senior manager to be **responsible for overseeing quality control**
- Advising staff of **independence requirements** in relation to specific clients
- **Disciplinary measures**
- **Promotion of communication** by staff to senior management of any ethical compliance issue that concerns them

There should also be safeguards relating to specific assignments, such as:

- Involving an additional professional accountant to review the work done or otherwise advise as necessary
- Consulting an independent third party, such as a committee of independent directors, a professional regulatory body or another professional accountant

- Rotating senior personnel
- Discussing ethical issues with those in charge of client governance
- Disclosing to those charged with governance the nature of services provided and extent of fees charged
- Involving another firm to perform or re-perform part of the engagement
- Rotating senior assurance team personnel

The specific safeguards that should be put in place will depend on the type of threat they are intended to mitigate; the specific guidance on safeguards is therefore discussed later in this chapter, when we discuss the specific threats that can arise.

2.6.3 Examples of ethical safeguards in the firm's own systems and procedures

The fundamental principles of the *Code of Ethics* for Professional Accountants apply to all professional assignments.

The provision of non-assurance services will often result in the assurance team obtaining information on the client's business and operations that is helpful in relation to the audit engagement. The greater the knowledge of the assurance client's business, the better the assurance team will understand procedures and controls, and the business and financial risks, but at the same time the provision of such services may create threats to the independence of the firm by threatening its objectivity.

Consequently, it is necessary to evaluate the significance of any threat created by the provision of such services. In some cases, it may be possible to eliminate or reduce the threat created by application of safeguards. In other cases, no safeguards are available to reduce the threat to an acceptable level.

Some consideration to the threat to each of the fundamental ethical principles for professional accountants are set out in the following table.

Integrity	Accountants may be working in an environment and dealing with individuals who are dishonest and lack integrity. If there is any risk that their own integrity may be compromised they should decline or withdraw from the assignment.
Objectivity	Any perceived threats to objectivity will undermine the credibility of the accountant's opinion or findings
Professional competence and due care	Assignments may require very specialised skills, for example, where evidence gathering requires specific IT skills. A firm should consider very carefully whether they have adequate skills and resources before accepting the assignment.
Confidentiality	Accountants will often be working for one party in a situation, possibly a dispute, and have access to very sensitive information. Subject, of course, to legal rules of disclosure in court cases, it is clearly essential to maintain the strictest confidentiality.
Professional behaviour	Fraud cases and other situations such as takeover disputes can be very much in the public eye. Any lapse in the professionalism could do serious damage to the reputation of the profession as a whole.

2.7 Ethical safeguards for accountants in business

The safeguards created by the profession, legislation or regulation also apply to accountants in business.

2.7.1 Ethical safeguards in the workplace for accountants in business

- The employer's oversight systems
- The employer's ethics and conduct programmes
- Recruitment procedures
- Strong internal controls
- Appropriate disciplinary processes

- Leadership that stresses ethics
- Policies and procedures that promote and monitor employee performance
- Timely communication of the employer's policies and procedures to all employees
- Training and education of employees
- Whistleblowing provisions
- Consultation with another professional accountant

In other words, a strong control environment.

However, if these safeguards are ineffective, the professional accountant may have to seek legal advice or resign.

3 Review of relevant ethical codes

In this section, we consider the detailed guidance given for professional accountants in business and professional accountants in public practice in the IESBA *Code* of Ethics.

3.1 Independence for accountants in business

This section applies to accountants working in what is sometimes known as 'industry', usually in finance departments but not limited to this – the guidance applies to AIA members working in any business role.

In addition to giving general guidance regarding principles, threats and safeguards, the IESBA *Code* is specific about the requirements that apply to accountants working in business. This guidance is necessary because qualified accountants have a duty to act in the public interest and are expected to be independent. The guidance applies irrespective of the professional accountant's job role or the legal form of the relationship between the professional accountant and their employing organisation.

The accountant in business may face a variety of difficulties including conflicts between professional sufficient expertise, financial interests or inducements. Ethical guidance stresses that a professional accountant should normally support the legitimate and ethical obligations established by the employer. However he may be pressurised to act in ways that threaten compliance with the fundamental principles. These include:

- Acting contrary to law, regulation, technical or professional standards
- Aiding unethical or illegal earnings management strategies
- Misleading auditors or regulators
- Issuing or being associated with a report that misrepresents the facts

The IESBA *Code* aims to strike a balance between the accountant's duty to their employer, and their duty to be independent:

> A professional accountant has a responsibility to further the legitimate objectives of the accountant's employing organisation. The *Code* does not seek to hinder accountants from fulfilling that responsibility but addresses circumstances in which compliance with the fundamental principles might be compromised.
>
> (IESBA *Code*: para 200.5 A1)

The following steps should then be taken by an accountant in business where there is a potential threat to independence:

Step 1   Identify threats

Step 2   Evaluate threats

Step 3   Address threats

Step 4   Consider communicating with those charged with governance

Step 1: Identify threats

The accountant should consider if there is a threat to independence. The *Code* gives the following examples of where threats to compliance with the fundamental principles that might arise for accountants in business (IESBA *Code*: para. 200.6 A1).

Self-interest threats	• A professional accountant holding a financial interest in, or receiving a loan or guarantee from, the employing organisation
	• A professional accountant participating in incentive compensation arrangements offered by the employing organisation
	• A professional accountant having access to corporate assets for personal use
	• A professional accountant being offered a gift or special treatment from a supplier of the employing organisation
Self-review Threats	• A professional accountant determining the appropriate accounting treatment for a business combination after performing the feasibility study supporting the purchase decision
Advocacy Threats	• A professional accountant having the opportunity to manipulate information in a prospectus in order to obtain favourable financing
Familiarity Threats	• A professional accountant being responsible for the financial reporting of the employing organisation when an immediate or close family member employed by the organisation makes decisions that affect the financial reporting of the organisation
	• A professional accountant having a long association with individuals influencing business decisions
Intimidation Threats	• A professional accountant or immediate or close family member facing the threat of dismissal or replacement over a disagreement about: – The application of an accounting principle; or – The way in which financial information is to be reported.
	• An individual attempting to influence the decision-making process of the professional accountant, for example with regard to the awarding of contracts or the application of an accounting principle

Step 2: Evaluating threats

The severity of the threat should be evaluated. This might be affect by the environment that the accountant is working in, for example where there is a strong ethical culture then the threat is likely to be less severe (IESBA *Code*: para. 200.7 A3).

Step 3: Addressing threats

Where the threat is assessed as severe (so that the threat to compliance with the fundamental ethical principles is not at an 'acceptable level'), then the accountant must take action. Actions in relation to specific threats that can arise are discussed below.

If it is not possible to take appropriate actions to mitigate the threats, then the accountant should dissociate themselves from the matter. They should withdraw from the specific project, and in extreme cases may need to resign from the employing organisation (IESBA *Code*: para. 200.8 A2).

Step 4: Consider communicating with those charged with governance

If the accountant faces these problems he should obtain advice from inside the employer, the professional body or lawyers, or use the formal procedures within the organisation.

3.1.1 Conflicts of interest

A conflict of interest may exist where:

- There is a conflict between the parties for whom the professional accountant performs work
- The professional accountant's interests conflict with a party they are working for

In general, a professional accountant shall not allow a conflict of interest to compromise professional or business judgment (IESBA *Code*: para. R210.4).

Examples of circumstances that might create a conflict of interest include:

- Serving in a management position for two organisations and acquiring confidential information from one organisation that might be used to the advantage or disadvantage of the other organisation
- Undertaking a professional activity for each of two parties in a partnership, where both parties are employing the accountant to assist them to dissolve their partnership
- Preparing financial information for certain members of management of the accountant's employing organisation who are seeking to undertake a management buy-out

When **evaluating the threat**, its severity is increased with the directness of the connection between the accountant's work and the matter giving rise to the conflict.

Safeguards include:

- Restructuring or segregating certain responsibilities and duties
- Obtaining appropriate oversight, eg acting under the supervision of an executive or non-executive director (IESBA *Code*: para. 210.7 A3)

Generally, it is necessary to **disclose the conflict of interest to the relevant parties and obtain their consent** before proceeding (IESBA *Code*: para. 210.8 A1).

3.1.2 Preparation and presentation of information

Professional accountants prepare information for stakeholders (ie parties who have a stake in that information). These may include management, investors or regulatory bodies.

As well as complying with financial reporting standards, the professional accountant in business should aim to prepare information that describes clearly the nature of the business transactions, classifies and records information in a timely and proper manner and represents the facts accurately.

The accountant must (IESBA *Code:* para. R220.4):

(a) Prepare or present the information in accordance with a relevant reporting framework, where applicable;

(b) Prepare or present the information in a manner that is intended **neither to mislead nor to influence outcomes** inappropriately;

(c) Exercise professional judgment to:

   (i) **Represent the facts accurately and completely** in all material respects;
   (ii) **Clearly describe** the **true** nature of business transactions or activities; and
   (iii) Classify and record information in a **timely** and proper manner; and

(d) **Not omit** anything with the intention of rendering the information misleading or of influencing outcomes inappropriately.

This is the case even where relying on the work of others (ie where the accountant is responsible for that work).

A difficulty arises where the presentation of information requires the exercise of **professional judgment**. The *Code* states that:

> The professional accountant shall not exercise [...] discretion with the intention of misleading others or influencing contractual or regulatory outcomes inappropriately.
>
> (IESBA *Code:* para. R220.5)

Where the accountant knows or believes information is misleading, they take steps to resolve the issue. The accountant should not be associated with misleading information, and may need to seek legal advice or report to the appropriate authorities.

Actions to resolve the potential to mislead include discussing the matter with their supervisor or with management, whistleblowing, or consulting with a third party such as the AIA. If the matter is not resolved, the accountant must dissociate themselves from the information.

3.1.3 Acting with sufficient expertise

In order to implement the principle of professional competence and due care, the accountant must not intentionally mislead others about their expertise or experience (IESBA *Code:* para. R230.3).

Ethical guidance stresses that the professional accountant should only undertake tasks for which he has sufficient specific training or experience. Certain pressures may threaten the ability of the professional accountant to perform duties with appropriate competence and due care:

- Lack of time
- Lack of information
- Insufficient training, experience or education
- Inadequate resources

Whether this is a significant threat will depend on the other people the accountant is working with, his seniority and the level of supervision over his work. If the problem is serious, the accountant should take steps to remedy the situation including obtaining training, ensuring time is available and consulting. Refusal to perform duties is the last resort.

Safeguards include:

- Obtaining assistance or training from someone with the necessary expertise
- Ensuring that there is adequate time available for performing the relevant duties

If the threat to professional competence and due care cannot be sufficiently mitigated then the accountant should **decline the work**.

3.1.4 Financial interests linked to financial reporting and decision making

Ethical guidance highlights financial interests as a self-interest threat to objectivity and confidentiality. In particular the temptation to manipulate price-sensitive information in order to gain financially is stressed. Financial interests may include shares, profit-related bonuses or share options.

This threat can be countered by the individual consulting with superiors and disclosing all relevant information. Having a remuneration committee composed of independent non-executive directors determining the remuneration packages of executive directors can help resolve the problems at senior levels.

Where a professional accountant has a financial interest in the outcome of work done on financial reporting (or decision making), then there is a self-interest threat. Common examples of this include:

- Eligibility for a profit-related bonus where the accountant's work might affect the amount of the bonus
- Holding share options where the accountant's work might affect the value of the shares

The professional accountant must not manipulate information or use confidential information for personal gain or for the financial gain of others (IESBA *Code:* para. R240.3).

The extent of the self-interest threat should be evaluated. This will depend on:

- The materiality of the interest to the individual.
- The extent of policies and procedures relating to the interest (eg whether senior management remuneration is determined by an independent committee).

3.1.5 Inducements, including gifts and hospitality

An inducement is something that is used to influence someone's behaviour. The *Code* recognises that this can take a variety of forms: an inducement can be an 'object, situation, or action'.

Ethical guidance highlights the possibility that accountants may be offered inducements to influence actions or decisions, encourage illegal behaviour or obtain confidential information.

Examples of inducements include:

- Gifts
- Hospitality
- Entertainment
- Political or charitable donations
- Appeals to friendship and loyalty
- Employment or other commercial opportunities
- Preferential treatment, rights or privileges   (IESBA *Code:* para. 250.4 A1)

Where an inducement is prohibited by laws or regulations, the professional accountant must obtain an understanding of these – so that ignorance is not a defence for breaching such laws or regulations. An example of this would be the Bribery Act 2010, which applies to UK citizens whether they are acting in the UK or overseas.

The professional accountant **must not offer or accept an inducement with intention to improperly influence behaviour** (IESBA *Code:* para. R250.7-8).

Where the threat is assessed to be severe, it should be considered whether safeguards might reduce it to an acceptable level. These could include:

- Informing senior management of the inducement
- Amending or terminating business with the offeror   (IESBA *Code:* para. 250.10 A2)

Where there is **no intent to influence behaviour** and the value is **trivial and inconsequential**, any threats created will be at an acceptable level (IESBA *Code:* para. 250.11 A2).

Finally, the *Code* notes that inducements giving rise to threats may not only be offered to/by the professional accountant, but to/by their immediate or close family members too. Where this happens, the accountant should advise them not to offer or accept the inducement.

3.2 Responding to non-compliance with laws and regulations (NOCLAR)

3.2.1 What is NOCLAR?

Non-Compliance with Laws And Regulations (NOCLAR) is defined by IESCA as comprising acts of omission or commission, intentional or unintentional, committed by a client, or by those charged with governance, by management or by other individuals working for or under the direction of a client which are contrary to the prevailing laws and recommendations.

NOCLAR covers both:

- Any act of non-compliance with laws or regulations
- Suspected acts of non-compliance with laws and regulations

NOCLAR relates to acts or suspected acts carried out by (IESBA *Code:* para. 260.5 A1):

- Employees of the entity
- The management of the entity
- Those charged with governance (TCWG)
- Third parties under the control of the entity

The laws and regulations that are most likely to be affected by a NOCLAR discovered by, or disclosed to, a professional accountant are those that cover areas such as:

- Money laundering, terrorist financing and proceeds of crime
- Fraud, bribery and corruption
- Securities markets and trading
- Banking and other products and services
- Data protection

- Tax and pension liabilities and payments
- Environmental protection
- Health and safety
- Employment

3.2.2 Responsibility for compliance with regulations and law

It is the responsibility of the client's management, with the oversight of those charged with governance, to ensure that the client's business activities are conducted in accordance with laws and regulations. Non-compliance may result in consequences for the organisation such as fines or litigation. The impact of these may have a material effect on its financial statements and may also negatively affect investors, creditors, employees or the general public. (IESBA *Code:* para. R260.8)

3.2.3 The professional accountant's responsibility and response to NOCLAR

The professional accountant is not responsible for preventing and detecting all NOCLAR; rather, this is the responsibility of the employing organisation's management.

The professional accountant's responsibility begins where they become aware of NOCLAR. For example, during the course of their work, a professional accountant may discover acts, or suspected acts, of non-compliance with laws and regulations (NOCLAR). These acts may have a direct effect on the employing organisation's financial statements, or it may have an indirect but fundamental effect.

This puts the professional accountant in a difficult position as they have an ethical responsibility not to ignore the matter, but it is also likely to be a difficult and stressful situation for the PA who also must comply with the fundamental principle of confidentiality.

The purpose of the NOCLAR pronouncement is to provide guidance to professional accountants in dealing with non-compliance or suspected non-compliance with laws and regulations and in determining how best to act in the public interest.

In responding to a NOCLAR, the aims of a professional accountant should be:

- To comply with the fundamental principles of integrity and professional behaviour whilst taking into account the public interest.

  Rather than hiding behind their duty of confidentiality, the professional accountant must act to dissuade others from NOCLAR and should be ready to take any further action necessary in the public interest (such as reporting to the authorities).

- For the entity, to correct the NOCLAR and take action to remediate or prevent its occurrence where it is still suspected.

In some jurisdictions, there may be regulations that require accountants to make reports of NOCLAR. Where these requirements are stricter than those of the *Code*, they should be complied with.

The NOCLAR guidance prescribes an approach that should be taken by professional accountants when responding to a NOCLAR.

Where a professional accountant becomes aware of a matter then the professional accountant must take timely steps to understand the nature of the matter and the potential harm to the interests of the entity, investors, creditors, employees or the general public.

3.2.4 Specific responsibilities of the professional accountant re: NOCLAR

The specific responsibilities of the professional accountant to NOCLAR when acting in different capacities are set out below.

Senior professional accountants in business responsibilities to NOCLAR

A senior professional accountant – ie a company director or senior manager – is subject to a greater expectation of acting in the public interest. However, their responsibility is not in principle different from other professional accountants – they are not responsible for preventing or detecting it as such. The requirements for senior professional accountants who become aware of NOCLAR are set out in (IESBA *Code:* para. R260.12-20) as follows.

1. Becoming aware and understanding the matter

Where a senior professional accountant becomes aware of NOCLAR, however, they must obtain a thorough understanding of the matter. IESBA *Code:* para. R260.12 requires the professional accountant to understand:

(a) The nature of the non-compliance or suspected non-compliance and the circumstances in which it has occurred or might occur;

(b) The application of the relevant laws and regulations to the circumstances; and

(c) An assessment of the potential consequences to the employing organisation, investors, creditors, employees or the wider public.

2. Discuss the matter

IESBA *Code:* para. R260.12 requires the NOCLAR to be discussed with the accountant's immediate superior.

If the superior is involved in the matter then it should be reported to the next higher level of authority (IESBA *Code:* para. R260.13).

3. Address the matter

IESBA *Code:* para. R260.14 then requires the senior professional accountant to take the following steps to address the matter:

- Have the matter communicated to TCWG;
- Comply with applicable laws and regulations (including eg anti-money laundering regulations);
- Have the consequences of the NOCLAR rectified, remediated or mitigated;
- Reduce the risk of re-occurrence; and
- Seek to deter NOCLAR if it has not yet occurred.

4. Determine if further action is needed

IESBA *Code:* para. R260.16-17 suggests the senior professional account to consider in assessing the appropriateness of the response of the senior professional accountant's superiors, if any, and those charged with governance include whether:

(a) The response is timely.

(b) They have taken or authorized appropriate action to seek to rectify, remediate or mitigate the consequences of the non-compliance, or to avert the non-compliance if it has not yet occurred.

(c) The matter has been disclosed to an appropriate authority where appropriate and, if so, whether the disclosure appears adequate.

The accountant should also consider disclosing the matter to the organisation's auditor.

In light of the response of the senior professional accountant's superiors, if any, and those charged with governance, the accountant shall determine if further action is needed in the public interest.

The determination of whether further action is needed, and the nature and extent of it, will depend on various factors, including:

- The legal and regulatory framework.
- The urgency of the situation.
- The pervasiveness of the matter throughout the employing organisation.
- Whether the senior professional accountant continues to have confidence in the integrity of the accountant's superiors and those charged with governance.
- Whether the non-compliance or suspected non-compliance is likely to recur.
- Whether there is credible evidence of actual or potential substantial harm to the interests of the employing organisation, investors, creditors, employees or the general public.

5. Seek advice

As assessment of the matter might involve complex analysis and judgments, the senior professional accountant might consider it necessary to seek advice, eg internally in the organisation, from the AIA, or from legal counsel.

6. Determining whether to disclose the matter to an appropriate authority

IESBA *Code:* para. R260.20 considers the necessity to disclose of the matter where the purpose of making disclosure is to enable an appropriate authority to cause the matter to be investigated and action to be taken in the public interest.

NOCLAR makes it clear that this disclosure **will not be considered as a breach of confidentiality** and will be viewed as an act of good faith in the public interest.

The determination of whether to make such a disclosure depends in particular on the nature and extent of the actual or potential harm that is or might be caused by the matter to investors, creditors, employees or the general public.

For example, the senior professional accountant might determine that disclosure of the matter to an appropriate authority is an appropriate course of action if:

- The employing organisation is engaged in bribery (for example, of local or foreign government officials for purposes of securing large contracts).
- The employing organisation is regulated and the matter is of such significance as to threaten its license to operate.
- The employing organisation is listed on a securities exchange and the matter might result in adverse consequences to the fair and orderly market in the employing organisation's securities or pose a systemic risk to the financial markets.
- It is likely that the employing organisation would sell products that are harmful to public health or safety.
- The employing organisation is promoting a scheme to its clients to assist them in evading taxes.

In deciding whether to disclose the NOCLAR, the extent of the harm caused should be taken into account. The accountant should take care to avoid 'tipping off' in line with the Money Laundering Regulations.

Professional accountants (not 'senior') responsibilities to NOCLAR

A professional accountant who is not a 'senior professional accountant' must also obtain an understanding of NOCLAR (once they become aware of it), but this understanding need not be as thorough as for a senior professional accountant, ie they need not obtain an understanding of laws and regulations beyond that which they need for their job role.

If, in the course of carrying out professional activities, a professional accountant becomes aware of information concerning non-compliance or suspected non-compliance, the accountant shall seek to obtain an understanding of the matter. This understanding shall include the nature of the non-compliance or suspected non-compliance and the circumstances in which it has occurred or might occur. (IESBA *Code:* para. R260.24)

The professional accountant should inform their immediate superior of any NOCLAR, or the next higher level of authority where the superior is involved in the NOCLAR. External disclosure of the NOCLAR is only necessary in 'exceptional circumstances' (IESBA *Code:* para. R260.26).

3.3 Pressure to breach the fundamental principles

Pressure to breach the fundamental principles creates an intimidation threat.

The *Code* requires professional accountants neither to allow pressure to result in a breach of the principles, nor to place pressure on others that may result in them breaching the principles (IESBA *Code:* para. R270.3).

Pressure might be explicit or implicit and might come from:

- Within the employing organisation, eg from a colleague or superior;
- An external individual, eg a vendor, customer or lender; or
- Internal or external targets and expectations. (IESBA *Code:* para. 270.3 A1)

Examples of specific pressures include:

- Pressure to report misleading financial results to meet investor, analyst or lender expectations
- Pressure from colleagues to misstate income, expenditure or rates of return to bias decision making on capital projects and acquisitions
- Pressure from superiors to perform a task without sufficient skills or training or within unrealistic deadlines
- Pressure from others, either internal or external to the employing organisation, to offer inducements to influence inappropriately the judgment or decision-making process of an individual or organisation

3.4 Independence for accountants in public practice

This section focuses on the guidance for accountants working in public practice, found in Part 3 of the IESBA Code *of Ethics*. The guidance here is distinct from the specific independence requirements that are applicable to audit and to review engagements. This area could be thought of as occupying a middle ground between accountants in business and auditors, since it has to do with the accountancy firm as a business, dealing with clients.

> **FAST FORWARD**
>
> Threats to the independence of accountants in practice include the **self-interest**, **self-review**, **advocacy**, **familiarity** and **intimidation** threats.
>
> Accountants in practice may face **conflicts of interest** between their own and clients' interests, or between the interests of different clients.

3.5 Independence

Independence is most important for accountants acting as auditors and assurance providers for the following reasons.

(a) **Reliability of financial information**

Corporate governance reports have highlighted **reliability of financial information** as a key aspect of corporate governance. Shareholders and other stakeholders need a trustworthy record of **directors' stewardship** to be able to make decisions about the company. Assurance provided by independent auditors is a key quality control on the reliability of information.

(b) **Credibility of financial information**

An unqualified report by independent external auditors on the accounts should give them more **credibility**, enhancing the appeal of the company to investors. It should represent the views of independent experts, who are not motivated by personal interests to give a favourable opinion on the annual report.

(c) **Value for money of audit work**

Audit fees should be set on the basis of charging for the work **necessary to gain sufficient audit assurance**. A lack of independence here seems to mean important audit work may not be done, and the shareholders are not receiving value for the audit fees.

(d) **Threats to professional standards**

A lack of independence may lead to a failure to **fulfil professional requirements** to obtain enough evidence to form the basis of an audit opinion. Failure by auditors to do this **undermines the credibility of the accountancy profession** and the standards it enforces.

4 Confidentiality

Key term

> **Confidentiality:** To **respect the confidentiality of information** acquired as a result of professional and business relationships. (IESBA *Code:* para. 110.1 A1)

The following are points that relate to confidentiality in general.

- Do **not** disclose information acquired, ie respect the principle of confidentiality (IESBA *Code:* para. R114.1).
- Information **may be disclosed** in certain circumstances, eg where it is required by law (see below) (IESBA *Code:* para. 114.1 A1).

In exchange for this duty of confidence owed by the auditor to the client, the client must agree to disclose in full all information relevant to the engagement. The professional accountant must make the client aware of the duty of confidentiality, and of the fact that it can be overridden where there is a right or duty to disclose.

Maintaining confidentiality means avoiding **inadvertent disclosure** as much as intentional disclosure (IESBA *Code:* para. R114.1). For instance, information must not be disclosed unintentionally when socialising. The *Code* also notes that the **duty of confidentiality continues even after the end of the relationship with the client** (IESBA *Code:* para. R114.2).

4.1 Exceptions to the rule of confidentiality

Binding though the duty of confidence is, there are nevertheless exceptions to it. The *Code* identifies three general circumstances where disclosure may be appropriate.

- Disclosure is permitted by law and is authorised by the client.
- Disclosure is required by law (eg for legal proceedings).
- There is a professional duty or right to disclose (eg to comply with a quality review by a professional body such as AIA; to respond to an investigation by a regulatory body; to protect the professional accountant's interests in legal proceedings; to comply with technical and professional standards, including ethics requirements).

(IESBA *Code:* para. 114.1 A1)

A key area in which confidentiality may be breached is where there is non-compliance with laws or regulations. This is discussed in detail in section 4.1.7 below.

4.1.1 Specific guidance: conflicts of interest

A professional accountant shall not allow a conflict of interest to compromise professional or business judgment. (IESBA *Code:* para. R310.4)

There are two kinds of conflict of interest:

- Conflicts between the interests of different clients
- Conflicts between members' and clients' interests

(IESBA *Code:* para. 310.2)

Audit firms should take reasonable steps to identify circumstances that could pose a conflict of interest.

Examples of conflicts of interest
Using **confidential information** obtained during an audit to help another client to acquire the audit client
Advising **two clients at the same time** who are competing to acquire the same company
Providing **services to both a vendor and a purchaser** in relation to the same transaction
Representing **two clients who are in a legal dispute** with each other (eg during divorce proceedings)

(IESBA *Code:* para. 310.4 A1)

The *Code* emphasises the importance of considering potential conflicts of interest **before accepting a new client** (IESBA *Code:* para. R310.5). An issue here is first **identifying that there is a conflict** – it may be that, for example, the engagement partner for a new client is not aware that there is a conflict because they do not know all of the firm's other clients. It is therefore necessary to have an **effective conflict identification process** (IESBA *Code:* para. 310.5 A1–2).

As with all threats, **safeguards** should be applied if necessary. If safeguards would not be enough, then the engagement should be declined or discontinued.

Examples of safeguards
Disclosure of the nature of the conflict of interest (and related safeguards) to clients affected, to **obtain their consent** to the professional accountant performing the services
Mechanisms to **prevent unauthorised disclosure of confidential information**, such as: • Separate engagement teams • Creating separate areas of practice for specialty functions within the firm • Establishing policies and procedures to limit access to client files
Review of safeguards by a senior individual not involved with the engagement(s)
External **review** by a professional accountant
Consulting with third parties, such as a professional body, legal counsel or another professional accountant

(IESBA *Code:* para. 310.9-13)

Disclosure is the key safeguard here. If the **client refuses** to give consent, then the engagement giving rise to the conflict should be discontinued.

5 Accountants in practice: Accepting new engagements

This section deals with accepting new engagements or making changes to the terms of existing engagements. Accountants in practice are faced with the risk of taking on clients who are involved with illegal activities; doing so may threaten the accountant's integrity or professional behaviour.

The threat is from 'client involvement in illegal activities, dishonesty, questionable financial reporting practices or other unethical behaviour' (IESBA *Code:* para. 320.3 A1).

Broadly speaking, the difficulties created by clients of this nature make the accountant's work more difficult, creating a self-interest threat to the principle of professional competence and due care. The key safeguards are:

- Assigning sufficient engagement personnel with the necessary competencies.
- Agreeing on a realistic time frame for the performance of the engagement.
- Using experts where necessary.   (IESBA *Code:* para. 320.3 A5)

Changes to a professional appointment may carry threats, particularly where the accountant:

- Is asked by a potential client **to replace another accountant**;
- Considers tendering for an engagement held by another accountant; or
- Considers undertaking work that is complementary or additional to that of another accountant.

In this situation, it is possible that the potential client wants to change accountants because their previous accountant did not go along with their unethical practices. Taking on such a client would clearly create significant threats to independence.

The principal **safeguards** here are:

- Making contact with the previous accountant, for example to find out whether there is any information that they should be aware of before accepting the engagement
- Obtaining information from other sources, eg from third parties, or from background investigations of the client's senior management (IESBA *Code:* para. 320.4 A4)

The *Code* seeks to provide guidelines for the communication between the previous and the proposed accountant. The **proposed accountant** should write to the predecessor accountant to ask for all information to be made available for them to decide whether to accept the appointment. If they receive no satisfactory reply, then they must write again, using a recorded delivery service, stating that they will assume that there are no matters they need to be aware of.

When they receive a communication from the proposed accountant, then the **predecessor accountant** should:

(a) Comply with relevant laws and regulations governing the request; and
(b) Provide any information honestly and unambiguously.   (IESBA *Code:* para. R320.7)

There may be an issue with the principle of confidentiality: if the client has given the proposed accountant permission to discuss the client, then they should do so. If they have not given permission then the predecessor accountant should inform the proposed accountant of this.

For **recurring engagements**, the professional accountant should periodically review whether to continue with the engagement (IESBA *Code:* para. R320.9).

5.1 Second opinions

There is nothing to stop a company director talking to a second firm of accountants about treatments of matters in the financial statements. Providing a second opinion to an entity that is not an existing client might create a self-interest threat.

However, the firm being asked for a second opinion should **be very careful**, because it is possible that the opinion they form could be incorrect anyway if the director has not given them all the relevant information. For that reason, firms giving a second opinion should ensure that they seek permission to communicate with the existing auditor and they are appraised of all the facts (IESBA *Code:* para. 321.3 A3).

If permission is not given, the second auditors should consider whether they can reasonably act in such circumstances (IESBA *Code:* para. R321.4).

5.2 Fees and other types of remuneration

The level and nature of fees and remuneration can create a self-interest threat.

In principle, an accountant can quote whatever fee they like. The *Code* focuses on the issue of low fees, and what is sometimes called 'lowballing': the practice of quoting a fee that is judged to be lower than the existing accountant's fee, in order to obtain the work. The accountant may then intend to increase the fee in future years. The issue in this situation is simply whether the fees are large enough to allow sufficient work to be done on the engagement; if they are too low then corners may be cut in order to reduce costs.

Note that the guidance regarding audit fees is different from these general points and is covered in the section dealing with independence for auditors.

Contingent fees

Contingent fees are likely to create threats in certain circumstances, but do not pose a problem when used for certain **non-assurance services** (IESBA *Code:* para. 330.4 A1).

Factors that are relevant in evaluating threats include:

- The nature of the engagement (generally, the less subjectivity or judgment involved, the better)
- The range of possible fee amounts
- The basis for determining the fee
- Disclosure to users of the work performed and the fee basis
- Quality control policies and procedures
- Whether an independent third party is to review the work
- Whether the level of the fee is set by an independent third party (eg a regulatory body)

Safeguards include:

- Independent quality review of the engagement; and
- Obtaining an advance written agreement with the client on the basis of the fee.

Referral fees or commissions

A referral fee may create a self-interest threat, for example where the accountant receives a fee from a seller of accounting software for recommending that software to clients.

Safeguards include disclosing the existence of such a fee to the client or obtaining the client's agreement for such an arrangement.

5.3 Inducements, including gifts and hospitality

Offering or accepting inducements might create a self-interest, familiarity or intimidation threat.

The guidance in this area for professional accountants in public practice is fundamentally similar to that for professional accountants in business, which was covered earlier in this chapter.

In summary, the professional accountant in public practice should obtain an understanding of laws and regulations in this area. However, inducements that are not illegal may still create ethical threats.

The main difficulty arises where the inducement is not innocent, ie there is 'intent to improperly influence behaviour': where the inducement is a bribe. The professional accountant must not offer and must not accept any such inducement (IESBA *Code:* paras. R340.7-8).

Safeguards include:

- Informing senior management of the firm or TCWG of the client regarding the offer
- Amending or terminating the business relationship with the client

As with accountants in business, the *Code* also gives guidance on inducements given or received by close family members: the rules on inducements apply to these people too, so one cannot use as a defence the fact that a bribe was actually given by one's spouse.

5.4 Custody of client assets

A professional accountant must not hold a client's money or assets unless this is permitted by law (IESBA *Code:* para. R350.3).

There is a risk that the accountant could be used to launder money, ie to help a client to conceal the source of illegal funds (even inadvertently). In order to prevent this they should:

(a) Make inquiries about the source of the assets; and
(b) Consider related legal and regulatory obligations.   (IESBA *Code:* para. R350.4)

Great care must be taken with money that belongs to a client. As a rule, any client monies should be held in a separate bank account. The *Code* requirements are to:

(a) Comply with the laws and regulations relevant to holding and accounting for the assets;
(b) Keep the assets separately from personal or firm assets;
(c) Use the assets only for the purpose for which they are intended; and
(d) Be ready at all times to account for the assets and any income, dividends, or gains generated, to any individuals entitled to that accounting.   (IESBA *Code:* para. R350.5)

5.5 Responding to illegal acts/non-compliance with laws and regulations

When a professional accountant in public practice is faced with NOCLAR, their objectives should be:

- To comply with the principles of integrity and professional behaviour;
- By alerting management or TCWG, to seek to:
  - Enable them to rectify, remediate or mitigate the consequences of the identified or suspected non-compliance; or
  - Deter the commission of non-compliance where it has not yet occurred; and
- To take such further action as may be needed in the public interest.

(IESBA *Code:* para. 360.4)

The laws and regulations covered by the framework are those which either directly affect the financial statements, or which are fundamental to the client's business. For example, law dealing with:

- Fraud, corruption and bribery
- Money laundering, terrorist financing and proceeds of crime
- Securities markets and trading
- Banking
- Data protection
- Tax and pension liabilities and payments
- Environmental protection
- Public health and safety

(IESBA *Code:* para. 360.5 A2)

Outside the scope are: matters which are clearly inconsequential; personal misconduct unrelated to a client's business; and acts of non-compliance committed by someone other than the client.

Management is responsible for ensuring that the business complies with laws and regulations, and to address any non-compliance (IESBA *Code:* para. 360.8 A1).

If the accountant discovers non-compliance, they first **obtain an understanding** of the matter (IESBA *Code:* para. R360.10). The issue should be **discussed with management**/TCWG (IESBA *Code:* para. R360.11).

The accountant should advise management/TCWG to:

- **Rectify** the situation
- **Deter** further non-compliance
- **Disclose** the non-compliance to the appropriate authority

(IESBA *Code:* para. R360.14)

Then the accountant must assess whether management's response is appropriate, taking into account whether:

- The response is **timely;**
- The non-compliance has already been investigated;
- Action has been taken to **remedy** it;
- Action has been taken to **deter** it;
- Steps have been taken to **prevent re-occurrence**; and
- The non-compliance has been **disclosed.**

(IESBA *Code:* para. 360.19 A1)

The accountant then **decides whether further action is needed in the public interest**. This essentially depends on the urgency and seriousness of the matter, and how likely it is to re-occur. The accountant should also consider whether this affects their assessment of **management's integrity** (IESBA *Code:* para. R360.20).

Further action might include:

- **Disclosing** the matter to the relevant authorities
- **Withdrawing** from the engagement

(IESBA *Code:* para. R360.21 A1)

Disclosure would be made if the matter is serious; examples include: if the entity is engaged in bribery; if this would threaten any licences to operate; or if products sold by the entity could be harmful to the public (IESBA *Code:* para. 360.25 A2).

The accountant must also keep **documentation** of this process.

5.6 Advertising

The latest IESBA Code gives only general guidance on advertising, covering the matter as part of its considerations on the fundamental principle of professional behaviour.

Adverts must not bring the profession into disrepute. The following are specifically prohibited:

- Making exaggerated claims for the services offered, or the accountant's qualifications or experience
- Making disparaging references or unsubstantiated comparisons to others

(IESBA *Code:* para. R115.2)

This means that adverts should be relatively straightforward and factual and should avoid exaggeration. Comparisons with competitors should be avoided.

Adverts must not suggest that the accountant will compromise their independence; thus an advert should not promise an auditor's report with an unmodified opinion or promise to reduce a client's tax bill.

Where there is doubt about the appropriateness of an advert or of marketing material, the accountant should consult with the AIA.

6 Safeguarding auditor independence

In this long section, we discuss the independence standards to which auditors are held. The syllabus for this AIA exam requires knowledge of the IESBA Code *of Ethics* (which the AIA has adopted), a substantial part of which is devoted to auditor independence.

The IESBA Code *of Ethics* is an internationally recognised standard on many which national or professional codes of ethics are based. The IESBA Code *of Ethics* can be accessed here.

https://www.ethicsboard.org/iesba-code

The syllabus also includes the FRC *Ethical Standard for Auditors* (FRC ES) which was revised in 2024 and can be accessed here.

The FRC ES applies to statutory auditors in the UK, and in many places its requirements are more stringent than those of the IESBA Code. Both sources of guidance are discussed in this section.

https://media.frc.org.uk/documents/Revised_Ethical_Standard_2024.pdf

This section considers the following threats to auditor independence and safeguards or other requirements which auditors should follow.

1. Self-interest threat
2. Self-review threat
3. Advocacy threat
4. Familiarity threat
5. Intimidation threat

This section then closes with a summary of the FRC Ethical Standard Section 6 provisions available for audits of small entities.

6.1 Self-interest threat

The IESBA *Code of Ethics* highlights a great number of areas in which a self-interest threat might arise.

6.1.1 Financial interests

Key term

> **Financial interest:** Exists where an audit firm has a financial interest in a client's affairs – for example, the audit firm owns shares in the client, or is a trustee of a trust that holds shares in the client.

A financial interest in a client constitutes a substantial self-interest threat. According to the IESBA Code, the parties listed below are not allowed to own a direct financial interest or an indirect material financial interest in an audit client.

- The firm
- A member of the audit team or any immediate family member
- Any other partner in the same office (or their immediate family)
- Other partners/managers who provide non-audit services to the audit client

(IESBA *Code:* para. R510.4)

If these hold a **direct** financial interest, then **no safeguards would be sufficient**.

For members of the audit team, if the interest is **not direct** (eg is held by an employee's pension scheme) or is **not material** (so the client cannot exercise significant influence over the auditor), then the following **safeguards** may be relevant:

- Disposing of the interest
- Removing the individual from the team if required
- Using an independent partner to review work carried out if necessary

Such matters will involve judgment on the part of the partners making decisions about such matters. For example, what constitutes a material interest? A small percentage stake in a company might be material to its owner. How does the firm judge the closeness of a relationship between staff and their families? In other words, what does 'immediate' mean in this context?

Audit firms should have quality control procedures requiring staff to disclose their relevant financial interests and those of their close family members. They should also foster a culture of voluntary disclosure on an ongoing basis so that any potential problems are identified on a timely basis.

(IESBA *Code:* para. 510.10)

In the UK, such matters should be resolved in consultation with the ethics partner (FRC ES: para. 2.15).

6.1.2 Loans and guarantees

The advice on loans and guarantees falls into two categories:

- The client is a bank or other similar institution
- Other situations

If a lending institution client lends an **immaterial amount** to an audit firm or member of the audit team on **normal commercial terms**, there is **no threat** to independence. If the loan were material, it would be necessary to apply safeguards to bring the self-interest threat to an acceptable level. A suitable safeguard is likely to be an independent review (by a partner from another office in the firm) (IESBA *Code:* para. 511.5 A3).

Loans to members of the audit team from a bank or other lending institution client are likely to be material to the individual but, provided that they are on normal commercial terms, these do not constitute a threat to independence.

An audit firm or individual on the audit team should not enter into any loan or guarantee arrangement with a client that is not a bank or similar institution (IESBA *Code:* para. R511.5).

The firm or audit team member **must not make a material loan to a client** (IESBA *Code:* para. R511.4). This rule is important because overdue fees from a previous audit could be construed to be a loan and must therefore be settled before an audit begins.

6.1.3 Business relationships

Examples of when an audit firm and an audit client have an inappropriately close business relationship include:

- Having a material financial interest in a joint venture with the assurance client
- Arrangements to combine one or more services or products of the firm with one or more services or products of the assurance client and to market the package with reference to both parties
- Distribution or marketing arrangements under which the firm acts as distributor or marketer of the assurance client's products or services or vice versa

(IESBA *Code:* para. 520.3 A2)

Again, it will be necessary for the partners to judge the materiality of the interest and therefore its significance. However, **unless the interest is clearly insignificant, an assurance provider should not participate in such a venture with an assurance client**. Appropriate safeguards are therefore to end the assurance provision or to terminate the (other) business relationship.

If an individual member of an audit team has such an interest, they should be removed from the audit team. However, if the firm or a member (and immediate family of the member) of the audit team has an interest in an entity when the client or its officers also has an interest in that entity, the threat might not be so great (IESBA *Code:* para. R520.5).

Generally speaking, **purchasing goods and services from an assurance client on an arm's length basis does not constitute a threat to independence**. If there are a substantial number of such transactions, there may be a threat to independence and safeguards may be necessary (IESBA *Code:* para. 520.6 A1).

In the UK, the term '**inconsequential**' is used instead of 'insignificant' (FRC ES: para. 2.26).

6.1.4 Serving as a director or officer of an audit client

A partner or employee of an assurance firm should not serve as a director or officer of an assurance client (IESBA *Code:* para. R523.3; FRC ES: para. 2.53).

It may be acceptable for a partner or an employee of an assurance firm to perform the role of company secretary for an assurance client, if:

- The role is essentially administrative, with no managerial decision making; and
- This practice is specifically permitted under local law and professional rules.

(IESBA *Code:* para. R523.4).

Although a partner or employee cannot serve on a client's board, it is possible for them to attend board meetings. This is common practice, and moreover, may be necessary if there are issues that need to be raised with management.

6.1.5 Compensation and evaluation policies

There is a self-interest threat when a member of the audit team is evaluated on selling non-assurance services to the client. The significance of the threat depends on:

- The proportion of the individual's compensation or performance evaluation that is based on the sale of such services

- The role of the individual on the audit team
- Whether promotion decisions are influenced by the sale of such services

(IESBA *Code:* para. 411.3 A1)

In the UK, performance criteria and remuneration of staff shall not depend on the selling of non-audit services. Remuneration should be set to provide sufficient performance incentives to ensure engagement quality (FRC ES: para. 4.35).

The firm should either revise the compensation plan or evaluation process or put in place appropriate safeguards. Safeguards include:

- Revising the compensation plan or evaluation process for that individual;
- Reviewing their work; or
- Removing the member from the audit team.

(IESBA *Code:* para. 411.3 A2–3)

A key audit partner shall not be evaluated based on their success in selling non-assurance services to their audit client (IESBA *Code:* para. R411.4).

Key term

> The **key audit partner** is the:
>
> - Engagement partner
> - Individual responsible for the engagement quality control review
> - Other audit partners on the engagement team, if any, **who make key decisions or judgments on significant matters with respect to the audit** of the financial statements on which the firm will express an opinion. Depending upon the circumstances and the role of the individuals on the audit, 'other audit partners' may include, for example, audit partners responsible for significant subsidiaries or divisions.
>
> (IESBA *Code:* Glossary)

6.1.6 Gifts and hospitality

Unless the value of the gift/hospitality is **trivial and inconsequential**, a firm or a member of an assurance team should not accept it (IESBA *Code:* para. R420.3; FRC ES: para. 4.40).

6.1.7 Overdue fees

In a situation where there are overdue fees, the auditor runs the risk of, in effect, making a loan to a client, whereupon the guidance above becomes relevant. If the previous year's fees remain unpaid when the current year's auditor's report is to be signed, then safeguards should be applied such as a pre-issuance review of the audit or obtaining partial payment of overdue fees (IESBA *Code:* para. 410.7 A2).

Audit firms should guard against fees building up and being significant by discussing the issues with TCWG, and, if necessary, the possibility of resigning if overdue fees are not paid.

6.1.8 Contingent fees

Key term

> **Contingent fee:** A fee calculated on a predetermined basis relating to the outcome of a transaction or the result of the services performed. A fee that is established by a court or other public authority is not a contingent fee. (IESBA *Code:* para. 410.9 A1)

A firm shall not enter into a contingent fee arrangement in respect of an audit. For **any assurance engagements provided to audit clients**, unless immaterial or unconnected to the audit, a contingent fee would still carry a threat so great that no safeguards could reduce it to an acceptable level (IESBA *Code:* para. R410.10–11).

For non-assurance engagements (eg tax services), where the client is **not an audit client**, the significance of the threat depends on:

- The range of possible fee amounts;
- Whether an appropriate authority determines the outcome of the matter on which the contingent fee will be determined;
- Disclosure of the work and the nature of the fees charged to intended users;
- The nature of the service; and
- The effect of the event or transaction on the subject matter information.

(IESBA *Code:* para. R410.12 A2)

Possible safeguards include:

- Having a **professional accountant review** the relevant assurance work or otherwise advise as necessary; or
- Obtaining advance written agreement with the client on the basis of remuneration.

(IESBA *Code:* para. 410.12 A3)

6.1.9 Fees – relative size

In the UK, the key point about fees is that the partner must allow the team enough time to perform the engagement in line with auditing standards, irrespective of the fees charged (FRC ES: para. 4.1).

Audit fees should not be influenced or determined by the provision of non-audit services to the audited entity (FRC ES: para. 4.3). The audit fee should reflect the **time spent** and the **skills and experience** of the personnel performing the audit.

When a firm receives a high proportion of its fee income from just one audit client, there is **a self-interest** or **intimidation threat**, as the firm will be concerned about losing the client. A high percentage fee income does not by itself create an insurmountable threat. This depends on the following:

- The **operating structure** of the **firm**
- Whether the **firm** is well-established or **new**
- The **significance of the client** to the firm

(IESBA *Code:* para. 410.3 A2)

In the UK, the total fee income received from non-audit services from any one client can be **no more than 70% of total fees** – or more precisely, 70% of the average of the fees paid in the last three consecutive financial years (FRC ES: para. 4.15). This requirement results from the EU Audit Regulation. This means that the **maximum ratio** of non-audit: audit fees is 70:30.

Further, the total fees received by the whole audit firm from non-audit services must not exceed 70% of the firm's total fees (ie at least 30% of the firm's income must be from audit fees).

Possible safeguards include **reducing** the **dependence** on the client (eg by increasing the client base) (IESBA *Code:* para. 410.3 A3).

It is not just a matter of the audit firm actually **being** independent in terms of fees, but also of it being **seen to be independent by the public**. It is as much about public perception as reality.

The *Code* also states that a threat may be created where an individual partner or office's **percentage fees from one client** is high – this can be summarised as follows:

Public interest entities	If fees from one client regularly make up 5–10% of total fees, the ethics partner should be consulted (and TCWG of the client) to determine whether safeguards are required.	If fees regularly exceed 10% for one client, the firm shall **either resign or not stand for reappointment**, as appropriate.
Non-public interest entities	If fees from one client regularly make up 10–15% of total fees, the ethics partner should be consulted (and TCWG) to determine whether safeguards are required.	If fees regularly exceed 15% for one client, the firm shall **either resign or not stand for reappointment**, as appropriate.

(Adapted from FRC ES: paras. 4.23-4.34)

6.1.10 Lowballing

When a firm quotes a significantly lower fee level for an assurance service than would have been charged by the predecessor firm, there is a significant **self-interest threat**. If the firm's tender is successful, the firm must apply safeguards such as:

- Maintaining records such that the firm is able to demonstrate that appropriate staff and time are spent on the engagement
- Complying with all applicable assurance standards, guidelines and quality control procedures

6.1.11 Recruitment services

As well as creating a **self-interest threat** by taking on work regardless of the ethical consequences, the audit firm should not provide a service which would involve the firm **taking responsibility** for the appointment of any director or employee of the audit client (FRC ES: para. 5.85).

For a **listed company** the audit firm should not provide a recruitment service in relation to a key management position, as a **familiarity threat** may arise in this situation (FRC ES: paras. 5.111–112).

The firm should also not provide advice on the level of remuneration of any directors or employees of the company (FRC ES: para. 5.86).

6.2 Self-review threat

The key area in which there is likely to be a self-review threat is where an audit firm provides non-assurance services to an audit client (providing multiple services). There is a great deal of guidance in the IESBA Code about the various other services that accountancy firms might provide to their clients, and these are dealt with later in this text.

For auditors in the UK, the FRC *Ethical Standard* has a decisive say on which non-audit services an auditor can provide to an audit client. The 2019 revision of the FRC ES brought with it an approach whereby **auditors of public interest entities are only allowed to provide services included on the ES list**. If a service is not on the list then it cannot be provided.

Auditors of public interest entities may therefore provide the following services only (to their audit clients):

Audit related services

This is work carried out by members of the engagement team that is closely related to the audit work.

These include:

- Reporting required by law or regulation to be provided by the auditor
- Reviews of interim financial information
- Reporting on regulatory returns

Only the services specified by the FRC ES may be described as audit-related in communications with those charged with governance.

6.2.1 Provision of non-audit and assurance related services

The provision of non-assurance services by an audit and assurance firm will often result in the audit team obtaining information on the client's business and operations that is helpful in relation to the audit engagement.

The greater the knowledge of the assurance client's business, the better the audit team will understand procedures and controls, and the business and financial risks, but at the same time the provision of such services may create threats to the independence of the firm by threatening its objectivity.

Consequently, it is necessary to evaluate the significance of any threat created by the provision of non-assurance services by accountants in practice who also provide audit and assurance services to the same client.

In some cases, it may be possible to eliminate or reduce the threat created by application of safeguards. In other cases, no safeguards are available to reduce the threat to an acceptable level.

Where providing assurance services, professional accountants are not allowed to:
- Authorise, execute or consummate a transaction
- Determine which recommendations should be implemented
- Report in a management capacity to those charged with governance

Therefore, where external auditors are providing a non-assurance service, external auditors should not:
- Audit their own work
- Make management decisions for the company
- Create a mutuality of interest, or
- Find themselves in the role of advocate for the company.

To respond to the threat to independence from providing non-assurance services, the audit and assurance firm can put in place the following safeguards:

- Ensuring non assurance team staff are used for these roles
- Involving an independent professional accountant to advise
- Quality control policies on what staff are and are not allowed to do for clients
- Making appropriate disclosures to those charged with governance
- Resigning from the assurance engagement

The non-audit services discussed in the remainder of this section may therefore only be provided to audit clients which are not public interest entities.

6.2.2 Preparing accounting records and financial statements

There is clearly a significant risk of a self-review threat if a firm prepares accounting records and financial statements and then audits them.

On the other hand, auditors routinely assist management with the preparation of financial statements and give advice about accounting treatments and journal entries.

Therefore, assurance firms must analyse the risks arising and put safeguards in place to ensure that the risk is at an acceptable level. If this can be done, then **these services may be provided**.

Examples of the kinds of 'routine or mechanical' services **which may be provided** include:

- Preparing payroll calculations or reports for approval and payment by the client
- Recording recurring transactions for which amounts are easily determinable from source documents or originating data
- Calculating depreciation on non-current assets (property, plant and equipment) when the client determines the accounting policy and estimates of useful life and residual values
- Posting transactions coded by the client to the general ledger or client-approved entries to the trial balance
- Preparing the financial statements based on information in the client-approved trial balance and preparing the related notes based on client-approved records

(IESBA *Code:* para. 601.4 A1)

For audit clients that are **not public interest entities**, assurance firms are only **allowed** to provide services of a routine or mechanical nature and must consider any threats arising from these services, applying **safeguards** such as using staff members other than audit team members to carry out the work and an independent review (IESBA *Code:* para. R601.5, 601.5 A1).

6.2.3 Valuation services

The audit firm should **not** undertake an engagement to **provide a valuation** to (FRC ES: para. 5.56):

(a) An audited entity that is **a UK listed company** or a significant affiliate of such an entity, where the valuation would have a material effect on the listed company's financial statements, either separately or in aggregate with other valuations provided; or

(b) Any other audited UK entity, **where the valuation would both involve a significant degree of subjective judgment** and have a **material effect** on the financial statements, either separately or in aggregate with other valuations provided.

The principal threats are the **self-review threat** and the **management threat** (FRC ES: para. 5.53).

The audit firm should not provide actuarial services to a listed company (or a significant affiliate of a listed company) unless it is satisfied that the valuation has no significant effect on the company's financial statements. For any other client, actuarial services should not be provided unless the firm is satisfied that either all significant judgments, including assumptions, are made by informed management, or the valuation has no material effect on the financial statements (FRC ES: para. 5.62).

6.2.4 Taxation services

In principle, tax services may be provided to audit clients, but they may give rise to self-interest, self-review, management and advocacy threats. As with other professional services, it is necessary to evaluate the significance of any threat created by the provision of taxation services. In some cases, it may be possible to eliminate or reduce the threat created by application of safeguards, such as the creation of a separate and independent team to carry out taxation services.

In the UK there are some specific circumstances where **tax service may not be provided**:

(a) Where the audit engagement partner has, or ought to have, **reasonable doubt** as to whether the **related accounting treatment** involved is based on well-established interpretations or is **appropriate**, having regard to the requirement for the financial statements to give a true and fair view (FRC ES: para. 5.71)

(b) Where the engagement would involve the audit firm undertaking a **management role** (FRC ES: para. 5.72)

(c) In the case of a **listed client**, where **current or deferred tax calculations** are to be **used when preparing accounting entries** that are **material** to the financial statements (FRC ES: para. 5.75)

(d) Where this would involve acting as an **advocate** for the client before an appeals tribunal or court **on a material issue**, or one that is dependent on an audit judgment (FRC ES: para. 5.79)

6.2.5 Internal audit services

An audit firm must not undertake internal audit work for any audit client, whether listed or otherwise, where undertaking an audit or assurance engagement. (FRC ES: para. 5.45)

6.2.6 Temporary audit firm employee secondments

The seconding of employees by a professional firm to an audit client may create a self-review threat when the individual is in a position to influence the preparation of the financial statements. In practice, such assistance may be given but only on the understanding that the audit firm's personnel will not be involved in making management decisions or exercising any authority.

The audit client should acknowledge its responsibility for supervising the activities of the assignee and the audit firm should ensure that the individual is not given responsibility for auditing any function that he or she performed during the temporary staff assignment.

6.2.7 Legal services

'Legal services' are defined as any services for which the person providing the services must have the required legal training to practice law. The provision of legal services by a firm to an entity that is an audit client may create both self-review and advocacy threats.

An audit firm shall not provide legal services to an entity relevant to an engagement, where this would involve acting as the General Counsel of that entity, or a solicitor formally nominated to represent the entity in the resolution of a dispute or litigation (FRC ES: para. 5.87).

As always, the threats to independence need to be considered depending on the nature of the service to be provided, whether the service provider is separate from the audit team and the materiality of any matter in relation to the entity's financial statements. Acting for an audit client in the resolution of a dispute when the amounts involved are material in relation to the financial statements would create advocacy and self-review threats so significant that no safeguard could reduce the threat to an acceptable level. Therefore, the firm should not perform this type of service for an audit client.

6.2.8 Provision of corporate finance

The range of services encompassed by the term 'corporate finance services' is wide. FRC ES: para. 5.92 includes the following examples.

- To identify possible purchasers for parts of the entity's business and provide advisory services in the course of such sales;
- To identify possible 'targets' for the entity to acquire;
- To advise the entity on how to fund its financing requirements;
- To act as sponsor on admission to listing on the London Stock Exchange, or as Nominated Advisor on the admission of the entity on the Alternative Investment Market (AIM); or
- To act as financial adviser to entity offerors or offerees in connection with public takeovers.

Certain aspects of corporate finance will create self-review threats that cannot be reduced to an acceptable level by safeguards. Therefore, assurance firms are not allowed to promote, deal in or underwrite an assurance client's shares. They are also not allowed to commit an assurance client to the terms of a transaction or consummate a transaction on the client's behalf.

Other corporate finance services, such as assisting a client in defining corporate strategies, assisting in identifying possible sources of capital and providing structuring advice may be acceptable providing that safeguards are in place, such as using different teams of staff, and ensuring no management decisions are taken on behalf of the client.

Corporate finance covers a range of activity but the main threats are the **self-review**, **management** and **advocacy threats** (FRC ES: para. 5.89).

The engagement partner needs to ensure that appropriate safeguards are applied. For example (FRC ES: para. 5.95):

- The corporate finance advice is provided by partners and staff who have no involvement in the engagement
- Any advice provided is reviewed by an independent corporate finance partner within the firm
- External independent advice on the corporate finance work is obtained
- A partner who is not involved in the engagement reviews the engagement work performed in relation to the subject matter of the corporate finance services provided to ensure that such engagement work has been properly and effectively reviewed and assessed in the context of the engagement

There are certain circumstances where the corporate finance work should **not** be undertaken. These include:

- Where the engagement would involve the audit firm taking responsibility for dealing in, underwriting or promoting shares or providing advice on investments in such shares, debt or other financial instruments; or
- Where the partner doubts the appropriateness of an accounting treatment related to the advice provided.

6.2.9 Loan staff assignments

In the UK, a firm shall not enter into an agreement with an entity relevant to an engagement to provide any partner or employee ('**loan staff**') to work for a temporary period as if that individual were an employee of any such entity or its affiliates (a 'loan staff assignment').

There are a few exceptions to this ban:

- In respect of staff employed by a UK national audit agency, in a role with no management responsibilities;
- When the role to be filled in an entity relevant to an engagement has no line management or management responsibilities;
- For a period of no longer than three months; and
- Where the service to be provided would not be prohibited by this Ethical Standard (FRC ES: para. 2.36)

6.2.10 IT Services

In the UK, the audit firm should not undertake an engagement to design, provide or implement **information technology systems** for an audited entity where (FRC ES: para. 5.52):

(a) 'The systems concerned would be important to any significant part of the accounting system... or to the production of the financial statements... (and) the **persons conducting the engagement would place significant reliance on them as part of the audit** of the financial statements...'

(b) '...for the purposes of the IT services, the audit firm would undertake part of the **role of management**.'

The principle threats are the **self-review threat** and the **management threat** (FRC ES: para. 5.49).

6.2.11 Recruitment and Remuneration Services

(FRC ES: para. 5.89) An audit firm shall not provide recruitment services to an entity relevant to an engagement, that would involve the firm taking responsibility for, or advising on the appointment of any director or employee of the entity, or a significant affiliate of such an entity, where the firm is undertaking an engagement. (FRC ES: para. 5.89). Examples include:

- Searching for or seeking out candidates
- Undertaking reference checks of prospective candidates
- Acting as a negotiator on the entity's behalf
- Recommending the person to be appointed

6.2.12 General other services

The audit firm might sell a variety of other services to audit clients, such as restructuring services, litigation support or recruitment services. The audit firm should not accept such work if relevant matters might have a **material impact** on the financial statements or where the audit firm takes managerial responsibility.

The specific rules on providing other non-assurance services can be found in Section 5 of the FRC revised ethical standard 2024.

https://media.frc.org.uk/documents/Revised_Ethical_Standard_2024.pdf

6.3 Advocacy threat

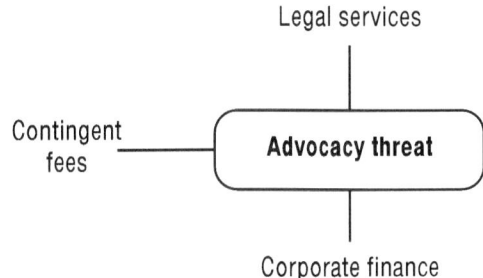

An advocacy threat arises in certain situations where the assurance firm is in a position of taking the client's part in a dispute or somehow acting as their advocate. The most obvious instances of this would be when a firm offers legal services to a client and, say, defends them in a legal case or provides evidence on their behalf as an expert witness. An advocacy threat might also arise if the firm carries out corporate finance work for the client – for example, if the audit firm is involved in advice on debt reconstruction and negotiated with the bank on the client's behalf.

As with the other threats above, the firm has to appraise the risk and apply safeguards as necessary. Relevant safeguards might be using different departments in the firm to carry out the work and making disclosures to the audit committee. Remember, the ultimate option is always to withdraw from an engagement if the risk to independence is too high.

6.4 Familiarity threat

A familiarity threat arises where independence is jeopardised by the audit firm and its staff becoming overly familiar with the client and its staff. There is a substantial risk of loss of professional scepticism in such circumstances.

We have already discussed some examples of when this risk arises, because very often, a familiarity threat arises in conjunction with a self-interest threat.

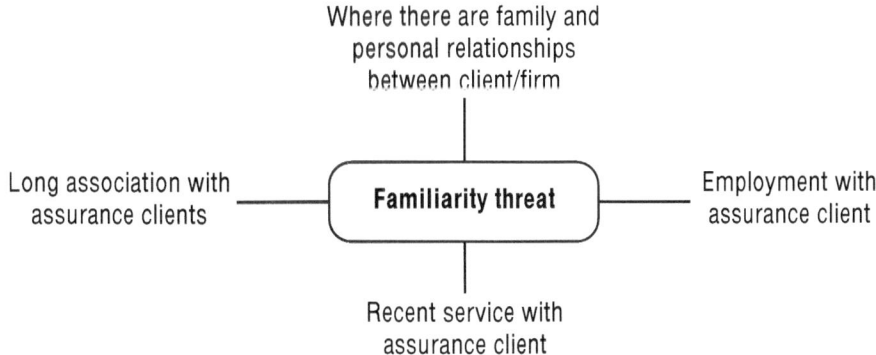

6.4.1 Long association of senior personnel with audit clients

Having an audit client for a **long period of time may create a familiarity threat** to independence. The severity of the threat depends on such factors as:

- The length of the relationship between the individual and the client (especially if this extends over employment at more than one firm);
- How long the individual has been on the audit team and the nature of the roles performed;
- The extent of any supervision and review of the individual by senior personnel;

- The extent of the individual's influence over the outcome of the audit;
- The closeness of any personal relationship between the individual and anyone in a responsible position at the client; and
- The nature, frequency and extent of interaction between the individual and anyone in a responsible position at the client.

Other factors can be relevant here, such as the client's accounting and reporting framework or its senior management personnel, including any recent changes.

(IESBA *Code:* para. 540.3 A3)

Possible **safeguards** include:

- **Rotating** the **individual** off the **audit team** or **changing** the nature of their **role** or **tasks**;
- Having a **professional accountant** who was not a member of the audit team **review** the work of the senior personnel; or
- **Regular** independent **internal or external quality reviews** of the engagement.

(IESBA *Code:* para. 540.3 A6)

In the UK, where audit engagement partners, key audit partners and staff in senior positions have a long association with the audit, safeguards should be applied. **Where they cannot be applied, the audit firm should either resign or not stand for reappointment** (FRC ES: paras. 3.1–3.2).

Safeguards include:

- Appointing a new partner (with no previous involvement)
- **Rotating the audit partner** and other senior members of the audit team after a predetermined number of years
- Involving an **additional partner**
- Applying **independent internal quality reviews**

(FRC ES: para. 3.5)

Once an audit partner has held the role for a continuous period of ten years, careful consideration should be given to whether objectivity would have the appearance of being impaired (FRC ES: para. 3.6).

Public interest entities

The rules for **public interest entities** are stricter. The Companies Act 2006 s. 490 *et seq.* requires public interest entities to change their auditor at least every **ten years**.

The firm must establish policies to ensure that:

(a) No one shall act as **audit engagement partner** for more than **five years**.

(b) Anyone who has acted as the audit engagement partner for a period of five years shall **not** subsequently **participate in the audit** engagement until a **further period of five years** has elapsed.

(c) On completing their rotation, the engagement partner shall not have significant or frequent interaction with management/TCWG until the cooling off period has elapsed.

(FRC ES: para. 3.10)

However, there may be circumstances in which it is necessary to be **flexible** about rotation. If **the client's audit committee** decides that flexibility is necessary to safeguard the quality of the audit, then the audit engagement partner may continue in the role for **two more years**, making **seven years in total** (FRC ES: para. 3.15).

This might happen for example where:

(a) Substantial change has recently been made or will soon be made to the nature or structure of the audited entity's business

(b) There are unexpected changes in the senior management of the audited entity

(c) The firm, having taken all reasonable succession planning steps, has no other partners with the necessary knowledge and experience who are able to take over as engagement partner

Alternative **safeguards** should be applied, such as expanded review by an engagement quality control reviewer.

Where **senior staff** have been involved on an audit for a continuous period of longer than **seven years** the audit engagement partner should **review** the **safeguards** put in place.

In addition, a key partner involved in the audit should not act for more than **seven years**. If the engagement partner becomes a key partner, the total for their combined roles must not exceed seven years.

Engagement quality control reviewers

The ES specifies the following rules for **engagement quality control reviewers' total** (FRC ES: para. 3.19).

(a) No one should act as the engagement quality control reviewer for a continuous period of longer than **seven years**.

(b) Where the engagement quality control reviewer becomes the audit engagement partner, the combined service in these two positions should not exceed seven years.

(c) People who have held these positions for seven years (continuously or in aggregate) should not return to them for at least five years.

6.4.2 Recent service with an audit client

An individual may have recently worked for an audit client. If they worked for the client **during the period audited**, then they **cannot be on the audit team** if they:

- Had served as a **director** or officer of the audit client; or
- Were an employee in a position to exert **significant influence** over the accounting records (or financial statements).

(IESBA *Code:* para. R522.3)

If one of the above individuals did not work for the client during the period being audited (ie they left the client before that), then a threat is created. The firm should consider the threat and apply appropriate safeguards, eg obtaining a quality control review of the individual's work on the audit (IESBA *Code:* paras. 522.4 A1–3).

6.4.3 Employment with an audit client

It is possible that staff might transfer between an assurance firm and a client, or that negotiations or interviews to facilitate such a move might take place. Both situations are a threat to independence:

- An audit staff member might be motivated by a desire to impress a future possible employer (objectivity is therefore affected – self-interest threat).
- A former partner turned finance director may have too much knowledge of the audit firm's systems and procedures (familiarity threat).

In general, there may be **self-interest, familiarity** and **intimidation threats** when a member of the audit team joins an audit client. A **'significant connection'** still **remains** between the audit firm and the former employee/partner where:

- The individual is entitled to benefits from the audit firm (unless fixed and predetermined, and not material to the firm)
- Any amount owed to the individual is not material to the firm
- The individual continues to participate in the audit firm's business or professional activities

(IESBA *Code:* para. R524.4)

Any familiarity or intimidation threat depends on the following:

- The **position** the individual has taken at the client
- Any **involvement** the individual will have **with the audit team**
- The **length of time** since the individual was a member of the audit team or partner of the firm
- The **former position** of the individual **within the audit team or firm**; for example, whether the individual was responsible for maintaining regular contact with the client's management or TCWG

(IESBA *Code:* para. 524.4 A3)

Safeguards could include:

- **Modifying** the **audit plan**;
- **Assigning individuals** to the audit team **who have sufficient experience** in relation to the individual who has joined the client; or
- Having an independent professional accountant **review** the work of the former member of the audit team.

(IESBA *Code:* para. 524.4 A4)

Should an audit team member be pursuing employment with an audit client, they should inform the firm of this as soon as possible. Safeguards to address the self-interest threat presented here are to remove the individual from the audit team, and to review their work for any indication of bias (IESBA *Code:* para. R524.5).

If the **audit client** is a **public interest entity**, then 'cooling off' periods are required. The IESBA Code states that **when a key audit partner joins such a client**, either as a director or as an employee with significant influence on the financial statements, the client must have issued audited financial statements covering at least 12 months before the employment can begin. The partner in question must also not have been a member of the audit team in relation to those audited financial statements (IESBA *Code:* para. R524.6).

In the case of a **senior or managing partner joining an audit client**, **12 months** must have passed (ie there is no requirement for audited financial statements to have been issued) (IESBA *Code:* para. R524.7).

A firm, partner or member of staff cannot become an officer (director) of an audit client, a member of a board subcommittee of an audit client, or in such a position in any entity holding more than 20% voting rights in the client (FRC ES: para. 2.53).

Where a former director or employee of a client joins the audit firm, then they cannot be involved in the audit of that entity for **two years** (FRC ES: para. 2.57).

6.4.4 Family and personal relationships

Key terms

> **Immediate family:** A spouse (or equivalent) or dependant.
>
> **Close family:** A parent, child or sibling who is not an immediate family member.
>
> (IESBA *Code:* Glossary)

Family or close personal relationships between assurance firm staff and client staff could seriously threaten independence. Each situation has to be evaluated individually.

When an **immediate family member** of someone on the audit team is a director, an officer, or an employee who is in a position to exert direct and significant influence over the financial statements, then the individual should be **removed from the audit team** (IESBA *Code:* para. R521.5). Otherwise, safeguards should be applied, such as either removal from the audit team or restructuring someone's role in the firm so they are not dealing with matters under the family member's responsibility (IESBA *Code:* paras. 521.4 A3–4).

If the person is only a **'close' family member** (but not an 'immediate' family member), then the threat is evaluated and the same safeguards can be applied (IESBA *Code:* paras. 521.6 A3–4).

If the relationship is not a family relationship but is still close (eg friendship), then the threat is evaluated and safeguards applied (IESBA *Code:* para. R521.7).

A firm should have quality control policies and procedures under which staff should disclose whether a close family member employed by the client is promoted within the client company. If a firm inadvertently violates the rules concerning family and personal relationships, then they should apply additional safeguards, such as undertaking a quality control review of the audit or discussing the matter with the audit committee of the client, if there is one.

In the UK, a firm shall establish **policies and procedures** that require:

(a) Partners and professional staff members to **report to the firm any persons** closely associated with them, any close family who are not a person closely associated with them, and other personal relationships, where any of those persons is **involved with an entity relevant to an engagement of the firm**, where the partner or professional staff member considers that the relationship might create a threat to integrity or objectivity or may compromise independence

(b) **The relevant engagement partners to be notified** promptly of any information reported by partners and other professional staff members as required by paragraph (a)

(FRC ES: para. 2.62)

6.5 Intimidation threat

An intimidation threat arises when members of the assurance team have reason to be intimidated by client staff.

These are also examples of self-interest threats, largely because intimidation may only arise significantly when the assurance firm has something to lose.

6.5.1 Actual and threatened litigation

There may be an intimidation threat when the client threatens to sue, or indeed sues, the audit firm for work that has been done previously. The firm is then faced with the risk of losing the client, bad publicity and the possibility that they will be found to have been negligent, which will lead to further problems. This could lead to the firm being under pressure to produce an unmodified auditor's report when they have been modified in the past, for example.

Generally, audit firms should seek to avoid such situations arising. If they do arise, factors to consider are:

- The materiality of the litigation
- Whether the litigation relates to a prior audit engagement

(IESBA *Code:* para. 430.3 A2)

The following safeguards could be considered:

- Removing the individual from the audit team
- Having a professional review the work performed

(IESBA *Code:* paras. 430.3 A3-4)

In the UK, where litigation between the audited entity and the audit firm is already in progress or is probable, the audit firm shall either not continue or should not accept the engagement (FRC ES: para. 4.44-4.46).

6.5.2 Second opinions

Another way that auditors can suffer an intimidation threat is when the audit client is unhappy with a proposed audit opinion and seeks a **second opinion** from a different firm of auditors.

In such a circumstance, the second audit firm **will not be able to give a formal audit opinion** on the financial statements – only an appointed auditor can do that. However, the problem is that if a different firm of auditors indicates to someone else's audit client that a different audit opinion might be acceptable, the appointed auditor may feel under pressure to change the audit opinion. In effect, a self-interest threat arises, as the existing auditor may feel that they will lose next year's audit if they do not change this year's opinion.

Given that second opinions can cause independence issues for the existing auditors, audit firms should generally take great care if asked to provide one anyway. Increasingly, new accounting standards do not give a choice of accounting treatments, meaning that second opinions might be less called for.

6.6 FRC Ethical Standard Section 6 provisions available for audits of small entities

The FRC is aware that a limited number of the requirements in sections 1 to 5 of the Ethical Standard are difficult for certain audit firms to comply with, particularly when auditing a small entity, and accepts that certain dispensations are appropriate to facilitate the cost-effective audit of the financial statements of small entities. As a result the *Provisions Available for Audits of Small Entities* (FRC ES Section 6) were issued.

The less stringent requirements of this section can be used to the advantage of the audits of small companies as defined by the Companies Act 2006, as well as certain other types of entity (FRC ES: para. 6.4).

Section 6 provides alternative provisions for auditors of small entities to apply in respect of the threats arising from economic dependence, and where tax or accounting services are provided. It allows the option of taking advantage of exemptions from certain requirements in sections 1-5. Where an audit firm takes advantage of the exemptions within this standard, it is required to disclose in the auditor's report the fact that the firm has applied section 6.

3: ETHICAL CODES, GUIDANCE AND ETHICS STANDARDS

Chapter roundup

- Organisations have responded to pressure to be seen to act ethically by publishing **ethical codes**, setting out their **values and responsibilities** towards stakeholders.

- In addition to following any corporate code of ethics, a member of the AIA is bound by the International Ethics Standards Board for Accountants (IESBA) *International* Code *of Ethics for Professional Accountants* (IESBA Code), which the AIA has adopted. Professional codes of ethics such as these apply to the **individual behaviour** of professionals. The IESBA Code is based on principles, supplemented by guidance on **threats and safeguards**.

- The IESBA Code gives examples of a number of situations where independence might be threatened and suggests safeguards to independence.

- Threats to the independence of accountants in practice include the **self-interest**, **self-review**, **advocacy**, **familiarity** and **intimidation** threats.

  Accountants in practice may face **conflicts of interest** between their own and clients' interests, or between the interests of different clients.

Quick quiz

1. What does an organisation's ethical code usually contain?

2. What are the main contents of the IESBA Code *of Ethics*?

3. Which of the following is not an advantage of a principles-based ethical code?

    A   It prevents narrow, legalistic interpretations
    B   It can accommodate a rapidly changing environment
    C   The illustrative examples provided can be followed in all similar situations
    D   It prescribes minimum expected standards of behaviour

4. Fill in the blank:

    ……………………………… means to be straightforward and honest in all professional and business relationships.

5. According to the IESBA Code *of Ethics*, what should professional accountants consider when attempting to resolve ethical issues?

6. Give four examples of a familiarity threat.

7. A firm that is sued by a client must resign from engagement with that client.

    True ☐

    False ☐

8. Fill in the blank:

    ……………………………… is the collective wellbeing of the community of people and interests that the accountant serves.

Answers to quick quiz

1. A statement of the organisation's values and an explanation of its responsibilities towards its stakeholders

2. - An acceptance by the accountancy profession of the responsibility to act in the public interest
   - Fundamental principles of ethics
   - Conceptual framework, requiring accountants to address threats to compliance and apply safeguards

3. C   Although the examples may be good guides for conduct in many instances, circumstances will vary, so they should not be seen as totally prescriptive.

4. Integrity

5. - The facts
   - The ethical issues involved
   - Related fundamental principles
   - Established internal procedures
   - Alternative courses of action, considering the consequences of each

6. - Family and personal relationships between the client and the firm
   - Long association with assurance client
   - Employment with assurance client
   - Recent service with assurance client

7. False. Not necessarily. Other safeguards can be used (disclosure to the audit committee, removing certain individuals from the team, involving an additional professional accountant on the team to review work). However, resignation may be required in the end.

8. The public interest

Application of ethical codes

Topic list	Syllabus reference
1 Application of codes	LO 2, LO 4
2 Conflicts in application of ethical principles	LO 2, LO 4
3 A practical approach for addressing ethical dilemmas in business	LO 2, LO 4

Introduction

In this chapter, we examine the issues and conflicts involved when applying ethical codes to real life situations. This chapter provides a framework to practically resolve ethical dilemmas which may arise in professional practice or in business.

PART B CODES, GUIDANCE AND STANDARDS

1 Application of codes

> **FAST FORWARD**
>
> Applying ethical codes requires judgment to translate general principles into particular actions.

The application of ethical guidance is not simply a question of applying rules, although it is the case that professional accountants must still operate within applicable laws and regulations. Central to the application of the fundamental principles is the use of professional judgment.

The IESBA *Code* states that professional judgment involves the application of training, knowledge, skill and experience (IESBA *Code*: para. 120.5 A1). In relation to undertaking professional activities, the exercise of professional judgment is required when applying the conceptual framework to make informed decisions about the courses of actions available, and to determine whether such decisions are appropriate in the circumstances. The requirement for the accountant to exercise professional judgment is not, of course, limited to deciding how to act in line with ethical principles. It is a fundamental aspect of the work of the accountant, whether they work in industry or in practice. Connected to this is the attribute of professional scepticism. These two terms are defined for auditors by the IAASB's International Standards on Auditing; these terms have a meaning and an importance for AIA members, however, that goes beyond the work of the auditor alone. Here is a definition of professional judgment:

> The application of relevant training, knowledge and experience, within the context provided by auditing, accounting and ethical standards, in making informed decisions about the courses of action that are appropriate in the circumstances of the audit engagement.
>
> (FRC *Glossary of Terms (Auditing and Ethics)*)

Professional judgment and professional scepticism could be thought of as applications of the ethical principles in the context of the actual work of the professional accountant.

1.1 Role of professionalism in ethics

> **FAST FORWARD**
>
> By virtue of the knowledge, skill and guidance which unpin professionalism, means a professional is more likely to make considered, rationale and ethical choices.

Key terms

> **Profession:** A profession is based on a body of theory and skills, adherence to a common code of values and conduct, and acceptance of a duty to society as a whole. In return for accepting a duty to society, members of a profession are allowed privileges, for example being able to practise certain activities or to use a title.
>
> **Professionalism:** Professionalism means avoiding actions that bring discredit on the accountancy profession.

The knowledge and professional skills of a professional are acquired by a structured training process, validated by examination and maintained through continuing professional education.

A set of values often underpin the professional's actions. For example the medical profession is underpinned by the principle of the sanctity of life. A professional's common code of values and conduct should be independently administered by a governing body.

Possessing professional skills and values will enhance the weight of a professional's judgement as these are what the professional holds himself out to have by virtue of calling himself an accountant (for example) and belonging to a professional institute.

Professionalism can also be considered as a state of mind, a concern to take action in the public interest and sometimes to lead public opinion, for example in developing guidance on reporting.

Therefore, being a professional in itself should lead to more considered and ethical choices.

1.2 Professional accountants and the public interest

Key term

> **Public interest:** Public interest is considered to be the collective well-being of the community of people and institutions the professional accountant serves.

(IESBA *Code* 100.1) says it is the distinguishing mark of the accountancy profession is its acceptance of the responsibility to act in the public interest.

This means an accountant's responsibility is not exclusively to satisfy the needs of an individual client or employer but also includes the public interest. This responsibility extends to client, lenders, governments, employers, employees, investors, the business and financial community and to society at large, as often the work of a professional accountant consists of supplying information that society needs.

The fundamental ethical requirement of professional behaviour imposes an obligation on professional accountants to act in the public interest. Therefore, professional accountant should comply with relevant laws and regulations and avoid any action that may bring discredit to the profession.

This means professional accountants are obligated to be behave ethically and to make or influence ethical decisions, due to their responsibility to act in the public interest.

1.3 Emotional intelligence impact on ethics

Emotional intelligence, or Emotional Quotient (EQ), refers to the ability of an individual to monitor their own emotions as well as the emotions of others, to distinguish between and label different emotions correctly, and to use emotional information to guide your thinking and behaviour and influence others (Goleman, 1995; Mayor and Salovey, 1990).

The concept of EQ was popularised by Daniel Goleman (1995) who states that EQ consists of five components or elements:

1. Self-awareness
2. Self-regulation
3. Motivation
4. Empathy
5. Social skills

Humans are, by nature, highly emotional and as such many of the decisions we make will be based on, or influenced by, emotion.

Developing a high level of EQ can, therefore, play a key role in helping individuals make decisions when an ethical dilemma presents itself.

Many poor ethical decisions are not intentional, they arise due to decisions made based on the wrong values, such as increased revenue, or the wrong emotions, such as fear or anxiety.

Understanding the emotions that are driving a decision can therefore help decision makers to make better, well thought out choices and may make them less susceptible to making decisions that result in ethical failure.

The five components of the EQ model can be applied to an ethical dilemma as follows.

1. **Self-awareness**
   - Understanding your own emotions about the decision and the impact that your decision is likely to have on those that will be impacted can help you to view the decision with a well-rounded perspective.
   - Being aware of your own strengths and limitations can help in more accurately assessing the decision and determining the likely outcome.

2. **Self-regulation**
   - An ability to regulate your own emotions can help you to remove disruptive emotions from the decision process and avoid making impulsive decisions.

- Helps individuals to retain integrity and morality in decision making by looking at the dilemma logically.
- Can assist in the ability to keep an open mind.

3. **Motivation**
   - Understanding the motivation that is driving you to make a particular decision can help to determine if the decision is, in fact, ethical or if it is being driven by disruptive emotions, such as greed.
   - Self-motivated individuals are also more likely to strive for excellence in their work, which may make them more perceptive of, and thus able to avoid, potential ethical issues that could arise.

4. **Empathy**
   - The concept of empathy, an ability to put yourself in the place of others, is a key skill in terms of facing ethical dilemmas. More empathic individuals are more likely to know and understand the full consequences of decisions, and therefore are less likely to make poor ethical decisions.
   - Empathy can also relate to political awareness, meaning the individual has the ability to read and understand the emotional currents of groups and any power relationships that may be in place. Factors such as these are likely to influence key decisions being taken by an organisation.

5. **Social skills**
   - Key social skills that will play a role in ethical decision making include, conflict management, leadership skills, communication, collaboration and co-operation, and team working. All of these can lead an individual to make better decisions, influence others towards the right decision, and communicate clearly to drive the decision in an ethical direction.

The digital age presents huge potential for ethical failures due to the ability to quickly and widely transfer information and the fast, impulsive decisions that may be made as a result.

For example, consider the many cases where high profile individuals and organisations post unethical or unacceptable messages on social media and are left to face the consequences in the public arena. Reputation can be very quickly damaged as the message will be quickly circulated to a potentially worldwide audience. Damage control is more difficult as the message cannot be quickly stopped before it becomes widely known. Even is an ethical message on social media is deleted, a screenshot or response to it from others will continue to be shared.

Decisions such as these are impulsive and based heavily on the emotion of the individual in the moment. Only when that moment has passed, does the individual logically think through the decision, by which time it is too late.

Therefore, developing a higher EQ can help to combat this and lead individuals towards making more considered, rational and ethical choices.

1.4 Ethical codes and Kohlberg's guidance

FAST FORWARD — A principles-based code of ethics may be thought of in terms of Kohlberg's levels, as distinct from external rules that must be adhered to.

One key aim of a principles-based ethical code is in effect to move subjects to **levels of reasoning** as defined in Kohlberg's framework (which was discussed in Chapter 1). The principles are meant to provide ideals towards which ethical decisions should aspire. The emphasis in the code that the examples given are not a comprehensive list of every situation that could be affected by the code indicates the expectation that the code is aiming beyond giving examples of common situations in which individuals follow set behaviour. It is aiming to encourage individuals to make their own ethical judgments.

1.4.1 Raising and dealing with ethical dilemmas

As we have seen in this topic, there are a number of possible options available for accountants wishing to raise ethical issues, for example:

- Discussions within their own organisation (eg with a manager or director)
- Via a helpline or whistleblower line
- With their accountancy body (eg the AIA)

However, it is important that the approach an accountant takes is consistent with the *Code of Ethics*. The following diagram suggests an approach for dealing with, and resolving, ethical dilemmas.

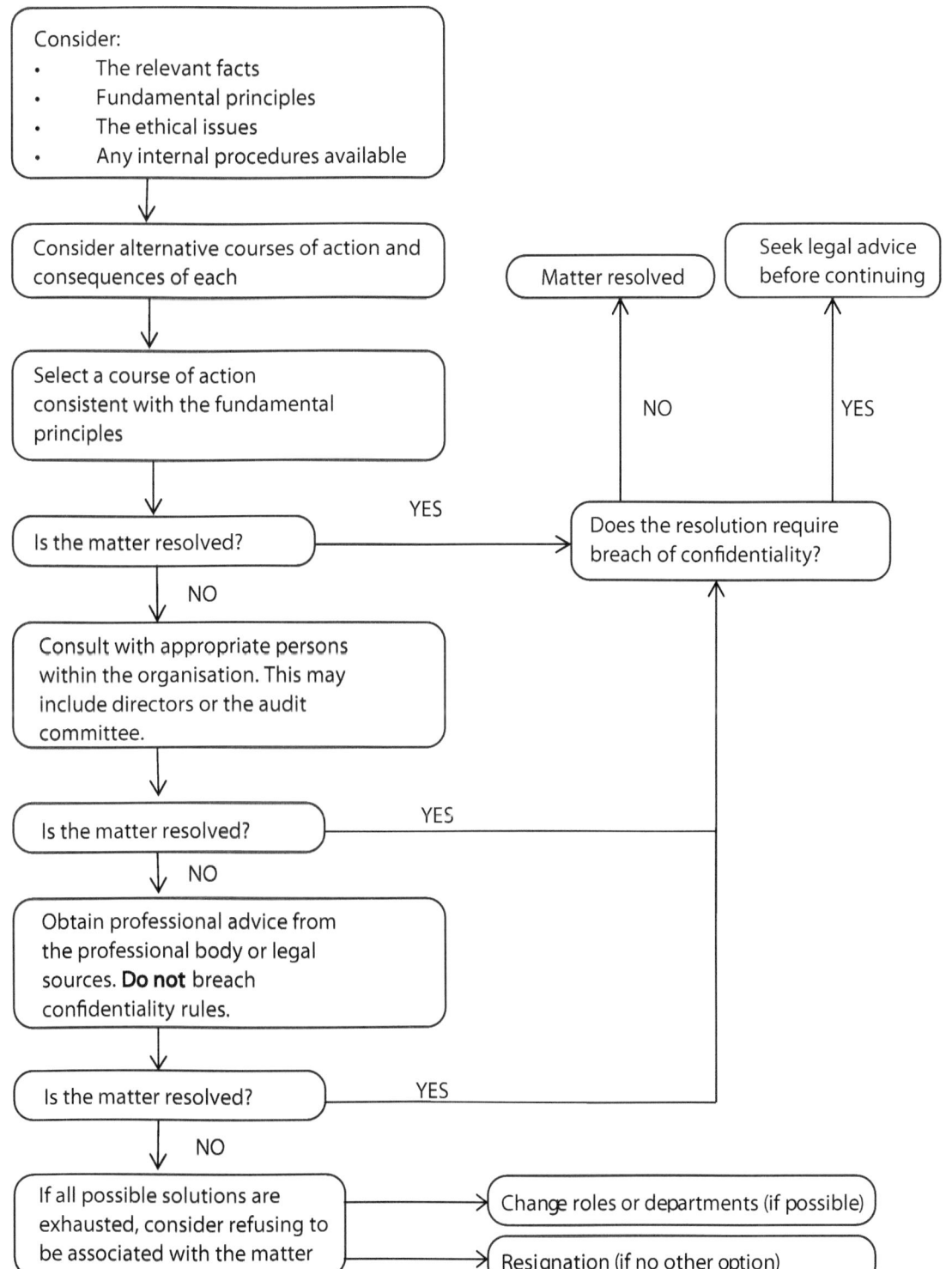

At all stages, it is recommended that members document the substance of the issue and all discussions and decisions made.

Question
Potential conflict of interest

Siddiqui & Co is a statutory auditor operating in the UK. Its client, Jones Co, has requested that in addition to auditing the financial statements, it will also perform valuations of certain non-current assets included in the financial statements.

How should Siddiqui & Co respond to this request?

Answer

Using the approach given above, Siddiqui & Co should first establish the facts. An audit client has asked it to perform a valuation service in relation to items that are included within the financial statements.

The ethical issue is that this gives rise to a self-review threat on the audit because Siddiqui & Co would need to obtain audit evidence in relation to these assets. It may put too much faith in valuations that it has itself performed, leading to insufficient or inappropriate evidence being obtained. It may also fail properly to apply professional scepticism.

The fundamental principle being threated here is the auditor's objectivity.

It may be possible to apply safeguards to reduce the threat to an acceptable level. These could include having the valuation performed by staff not on the audit team and subjecting this part of the audit to additional review by an independent professional accountant.

Alternatively, if it is not possible sufficiently to reduce the threat arising, then the engagement to perform the valuation should not be undertaken.

2 Conflicts in application of ethical principles

FAST FORWARD — Ethical conflict may arise when several principles need to be applied to a situation.

Ethical conflict is part of the effort to apply ethical principles to the complexities of the situations that occur in the actual life of a professional accountant. The conflict can take on different forms, from the simple conflict between the accountant's ethical duty and for instance their self-interest, to the difficulty of deciding on the best course of action in situations where there may be multiple possible good actions.

The IESBA *Code of Ethics* states that firms should have established policies to resolve conflict and should follow those established policies. These internal policies act as a guide to the accountant's judgment and should not override the accountant's duty to act ethically.

Professional accountants should consider:

- The relevant facts
- The ethical issues involved
- Which fundamental principles are threatened
- Established internal (firm) procedures
- Alternative courses of action

2.1 The problem

As we have seen, the IESBA *Code* is principles-based. The application of these principles requires a degree of **judgment**. As a result of this judgmental aspect, it is possible to have **more than one 'right answer' in a given situation** – more than one reasonable judgment of how the fundamental ethical principles should be applied.

Contrast this to the situation with a rules-based code of ethics. There, applying the rules strictly should result in only one possible outcome. It might not be an outcome that is ethical, eg because it is a result of a loophole, but it will be the only correct outcome (assuming that the rules themselves are not ambiguous). By contrast, a principles-based code may allow for several outcomes that are equally 'correct'.

It should be borne in mind, however, that the principles-based approach is not intended to be less rigorous than a rules-based one. Indeed, it could be seen as more rigorous because it requires an inward discipline in the form of obedience to principles, rather than mere adherence to external rules. This would preclude the very attitude that rules-based codes can promote, namely, seeing ethics as a series of external requirements to be circumvented, rather than as a set of principles to be applied.

Similarly, the adoption of a principles-based approach does not mean that the accountant can pick and choose which provisions of the code to observe; they cannot use their discretion as such. Rather they must use their professional judgment to arrive at the most faithful application of the fundamental principles in each situation, using the specific guidance given in the *Code* as guidelines for the application of this judgment. The *Code* distinguishes 'requirements' (denoted by the letter 'R' at the start of the relevant paragraph) from ordinary guidance; requirements refer to the basic range that the accountant's judgment regarding the principles *must* fall within – the guidance then provides further help on how to apply the principles.

There may be conflict between different ethical principles. The aim here must be to use judgment to resolve the conflict, or to try to balance the principles involved.

Question — Audit fees

Long & Co receives audit fees, from a listed client, which constitute 14.5% of its total recurring fee income for the year.

The company Code of Ethics applicable in Long & Co's jurisdiction sets the acceptable threshold for fee income in situations such as this at 15%.

State the different approaches that would be taken depending on whether the applicable Code of Ethics were rules- or principles-based.

Answer

When applying a rules-based code, this situation would not present a problem because the 15% threshold has not been breached.

A principles-based code, on the other hand, may allow this situation in principle because the 15% threshold has not been breached. It may also, however, require Long & Co to consider whether any fundamental principles – such as integrity or objectivity, in the case of the IESBA *Code of Ethics* – have been threatened, even though the threshold has not been breached. Therefore, it may still be necessary to apply safeguards to reduce the threat to an appropriate level.

2.2 Matters to consider

The resolution process should include consideration of:

- Relevant facts – Do I have all the relevant facts (eg an organisation's policy and procedures)?
- Relevant parties – Who is affected by the ethical issue (eg shareholders, employees, employers, the public)?
- Ethical issues involved – What kinds of issues are these? Would they affect the profession's reputation (eg professional ethical issues, personal ethical issues)?

- Fundamental principles related to the matter in question – What are the threats? Refer to ethical code.
- Established internal procedures – Are there procedures for dealing with this sort of situation (eg discuss with your supervisor, or firm's legal department)?
- Alternative courses of action – Have all the consequences been evaluated? Consider laws and regulations, long-term consequences, public consequences.

(adapted from ICAEW 2016b)

2.2.1 Unresolved conflict

If the matter is unresolved, the member should consult with other appropriate persons within the firm. They may then wish to obtain advice from the AIA or legal advisers. If after exhausting all relevant possibilities, the ethical conflict remains unresolved, members should consider withdrawing from the engagement team, a specific assignment, or to resign altogether from the engagement.

Consider the following example.

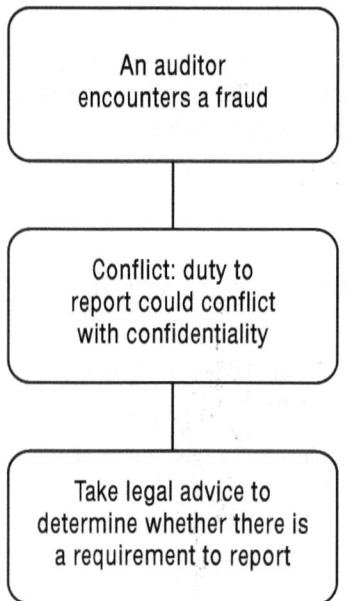

3 A practical approach for addressing ethical dilemmas in business

It is essential for a board of directors to be equipped to promptly address any ethical issues that may arise in the course of business and apply IESBA ethical principles to do the 'right thing' for all stakeholders.

However, the course of action is not always clear.

This section provides a framework for professional accountants to apply to business scenarios containing ethical dilemmas, enabling them to formulate solutions that address identified problems.

In the exam for this module, candidates may be presented with an ethical dilemma and are advised to apply the framework outlined in this section to structure their evaluation of the issues presented and suggested solutions.

3.1 Types of ethical dilemmas

Ethical dilemmas emerge when an issue arises which involves:

- A breach of the law or regulation. For example, failure to disclose directors' remuneration so shareholders are unable to fully evaluate the directors' performance. Also, health and safety at work is an important issue for employees and there is legislation that should be complied with.

- A breach of a company's own ethical code. For example, a company states it will treat all employees fairly, then denies a certain individual the opportunity to apply for promotion. Also, if a company has a code mentioning diversity in the workplace but does not follow the code.

- Close personal relationships between the parties involved in an ethical issue. For example, a director awards a supplier contract to the company of a family member, foregoing company policy to follow supplier selection procedures. Also, a politician that a director went to school with could be approached to help a company get an advantage in the awarding of a government contract.

- Actions causing harm to a stakeholder.
    - Harm may be physical. For example, the release of toxic pollutants from a manufacturing plant into the water supply resulting in health issues for local residents.
    - Harm may be financial. For example, a very low pay below a living wage or directors awarding themselves excessive rewards whilst reducing the payment of dividends to shareholders.
    - Harm may be to an individual's mental wellbeing. For example, discrimination targeted against particular individuals in the workplace. Also, bullying in the workplace will have a negative effect on the individual being bullied.

- There is a lack of equality or fairness in a company's actions (eg a company fails to pay a supplier on time resulting in working capital issues for that supplier). Another example could be that the company pays more to men than women for doing the same job or treats one stakeholder favourably compared to another in the case of winding a company up.

- There is a breach of fiduciary duty by the directors to its shareholders. This could be a lack of board meeting resulting in a failure to focus on strategy or implement a sufficient system of internal control, or failure to identify and control a specific business risk which has now occurred. Another example is selling company assets below market value to repay debt, rather than make efforts to find another solution to resolve this.

- There is a breach of business trust or integrity by individuals within an organisation. For example, shareholders are provided with misleading information in investor reports. Also, a company might manipulate its financial reporting dates so that it can make each part of its business look better when they come to produce their accounts.

3.2 Examples of ethical dilemmas

Fairness and Equity: Dilemmas involving questions of fairness, equal treatment, and the distribution of resources or opportunities among different individuals or groups. For example, in a company, two employees with similar qualifications and experience apply for a promotion. However, due to a personal connection between the candidate and interviewer, one employee receives the promotion over the other, despite the other employee being equally or more deserving. The decision-maker faces an ethical dilemma of ensuring fairness and equal treatment in the promotion process.

Whistleblowing: Situations where individuals must decide whether to report unethical or illegal activities within their organisation, weighing potential personal and professional consequences. For example, an employee discovers that their company participates in fraudulent activities, manipulating financial records to inflate profits. The employee faces an ethical dilemma of whether to report the misconduct, weighing the potential personal and professional consequences, such as retaliation, loss of job security, or damage to their reputation.

Social Responsibility: Dilemmas concerning the responsibility of individuals or organisations towards society, the environment, or the welfare of stakeholders beyond financial considerations. For example, a manufacturing company produces and sells paint products that contribute to anti-social behaviour in the form of graffiti. The management faces an ethical dilemma between maximising profits and taking responsibility to restrict sales or product use to minimise the anti-social impact.

Cultural or Value Differences: Ethical dilemmas arising from differences in cultural norms, values, or ethical standards, especially in a global or multicultural context. For example, an international company with branches in different countries has a diverse workforce representing various cultures and religions. The company decides to implement a dress code policy that mandates specific attire, including prohibiting religious symbols or attire that are important to certain employees' religious practices. This decision creates an ethical dilemma as it infringes upon employees' freedom of religious expression and cultural identity, potentially leading to discrimination and a hostile work environment. The company must navigate the clash between its desire for a unified dress code and the need to respect and accommodate cultural and religious diversity within the organisation.

Physical harm: A person is physically injured, or their health is impaired as a result of an organisation's activities. For example, a medical professional discovers that a colleague is providing substandard care to patients, potentially endangering their lives. They face a dilemma of whether to report their colleague, knowing that it could have personal and professional consequences.

Harm to well-being: A person's mental health is impaired as a result of behaviour or company policy. For example, despite being aware of workplace bullying or harassment involving influential employees, a manager hesitates to intervene. The manager observes concerning behaviours between one employee and another, even though the company has anti-bullying policies in place. However, due to concerns about potential repercussions on their own professional relationships, the manager is reluctant to act. This situation presents a dilemma for the manager, who must weigh the well-being of employees against the risk to their own professional standing. However, it is important to note that choosing not to act in such circumstances is considered unethical, as it results in harm to the employee involved.

Financial harm: Company actions and activities lead to consequential financial harm on customers, suppliers, employees or shareholders, which could have been avoided if the company had operated ethically. For example, upon discovering financial irregularities within their organisation, an accountant is confronted with a dilemma. The accountant is apprehensive about reporting the irregularities due to concerns that it might result in layoffs or even the financial collapse of the company, thereby causing harm to employees and stakeholders. This ethical dilemma arises from balancing the importance of financial integrity against the potential adverse consequences. However, it is essential to recognise that by choosing not to take any action, the accountant risks further harm to employees and shareholders. Disclosure of the irregularities can facilitate timely intervention and resolution, minimising the overall impact on those affected.

Harm to the environment: Company actions and activities lead to pollution of the environment or biodiversity, for example, an executive in a manufacturing company is aware that their production practices contribute to significant environmental pollution to a local river where it is more cost effective to release untreated chemical waste rather than dispose of it safely. Here, the executive faces an ethical dilemma between prioritising profit and mitigating harm to the environment and public health.

These examples illustrate how ethical dilemmas can arise in different contexts, involving physical harm, harm to well-being, financial harm, and harm to the environment. Ethical decision-making requires careful consideration of the potential consequences and the ethical principles and values at stake.

3.3 Framework for addressing ethical dilemmas in business

The following framework is a practical approach for resolving ethical dilemmas in business.

(1) Identify the ethical dilemma
(2) Consider if existing safeguard or other mitigations are in place
(3) Evaluate the ethical dilemma
(4) Recommend a solution
(5) Justify your solution

The following sections explain each component of the suggested framework in more detail.

3.3.1 Identify the ethical dilemma

In an exam scenario, there will be indications that something has happened. Consider the effect on the stakeholders in the material.

Some examples of the issue that may have arisen are:

- **Harm:** company activities cause harm to the environment, harm to health or well-being of individuals or due to unfairness
- **Manipulation**: alteration to mislead or create a false impression to others
- **Omission**: deliberately missing out a key piece of information to distort the picture
- **Confidentiality**: inappropriately disclosing privileged information such as leaving confidential business information accidentally in a public place
- **Conflict of interest**: an additional situation to the one being considered that causes apparent or actual bias to be introduced and objectivity to be impaired

The question that arises is whether it is necessary to raise the alarm to the appropriate authority externally or within the organisation.

There is also the question of fact versus speculation. Is there evidence confirming unethical behaviours have taken place, or is it unconfirmed, for example if it has been raised in a letter to the company or discussed in a newspaper article or media report? In some cases, it is necessary to advise that an organisation performs a full investigation to confirm the facts and circumstances.

Additionally, where relevant, the following five IESBA fundamental principles of ethical conduct can be applied to understand if there is further evidence of unethical behaviour.

1. Integrity
2. Objectivity
3. Professional competence and due care
4. Confidentiality
5. Professional behaviour

There may well be more than one ethical principle that has been breached by the issue that has arisen, though a single issue is enough to raise the alarm.

Make sure that you know IESBA's five fundamental principles of ethical conduct (listed above) so that you can apply them to the situation faced and use specific principles to explain why certain behaviour is unethical and must be stopped or prevented.

A reminder, the IESBA Code of Ethics for Professional Accountants can be found here:

https://www.ethicsboard.org/iesba-code

In identifying the ethical dilemma, it is very important to use your analysis to explain why the observed behaviour is unethical. For example, a decision not to invest in replacement machinery is creating a higher risk of personal injury for employees in the workplace. This neglect by the directors reflects a failure to fulfil their duty of care towards employees, as they knowingly prioritise cost savings over compliance with health and safety standards.

3.3.2 Consider if existing safeguards or other mitigations are in place

When considering an ethical dilemma, it is crucial to first evaluate and consider existing safeguards or mitigations before implementing a new solution, as existing internal controls or other mitigations may already be in place, which have failed. This approach is important for several reasons:

- **Efficiency and Effectiveness:** Existing safeguards or mitigations have already been established and implemented to address ethical concerns and mitigate risks. By reviewing and using these measures, you can save time and resources, as they are already in place and designed to address specific ethical challenges.

- **Evaluation of Adequacy:** Assessing existing safeguards allows you to determine their effectiveness and adequacy in addressing the ethical dilemma at hand. You can evaluate whether the current measures sufficiently address the specific ethical concerns or if any gaps or weaknesses exist.
- **Utilisation of Established Best Practices:** Existing safeguards often reflect established best practices and lessons learned from previous ethical dilemmas or industry standards. By considering these measures, you can leverage the knowledge and experiences gained from previous ethical challenges, increasing the likelihood of finding effective solutions.
- **Consistency and Continuity:** Utilising existing safeguards promotes consistency and continuity in ethical decision making. It ensures that ethical principles and values are consistently applied across the organisation or profession, fostering a culture of ethics and integrity.
- **Avoiding Redundancy or Duplication:** Before implementing a new solution, considering existing safeguards helps prevent redundant or duplicative efforts. It ensures that resources are used efficiently and that solutions are streamlined rather than creating unnecessary complexity or overlap.

By first considering existing safeguards or mitigations, you can leverage the established measures, evaluate their adequacy, and build upon the knowledge and experiences gained. This approach promotes efficient use of resources, consistency, and effectiveness in addressing ethical dilemmas while ensuring that resources are used wisely, and trust is maintained.

The purpose of applying safeguards or other mitigations when evaluating an ethical dilemma is to minimise or eliminate the potential risks and negative consequences associated with the dilemma. Safeguards are measures or actions taken to protect against ethical lapses, conflicts of interest, or compromised ethical decision making.

3.3.3 Evaluate the ethical dilemma

The next step in addressing an ethical dilemma involves evaluating its significance within the broader context of who is affected, the organisation, its operating environment and its stakeholders.

This evaluation entails considering factors such as the size of the dilemma, its potential consequences, and the reactions of key stakeholders, including the general public, shareholders, employees, suppliers, and customers. It may be beneficial to quantify the potential impact using various metrics, such as financial implications or changes in product demand.

Conducting a thorough evaluation allows for a comprehensive understanding of the ethical dilemma's implications. It helps determine the urgency and importance of taking action to resolve the dilemma, as well as the potential benefits and risks associated with different courses of action. Additionally, the evaluation provides insights into preventing the re-occurrence of similar ethical dilemmas in the future.

By assessing the ethical dilemma's significance, an organisation can determine the need for immediate action and develop a well-informed strategy for resolution. This may involve implementing measures to rectify the situation, addressing any harm caused, and preventing similar incidents from happening again. Conversely, the evaluation may reveal that no immediate action is required, but it is important to document the reasons for this decision to maintain transparency and accountability.

In summary, evaluating the ethical dilemma's significance enables organisations to make informed decisions about the appropriate actions to take. It ensures that the organisation addresses the issue responsibly and ethically, either by resolving the dilemma and preventing its re-occurrence or by providing valid justifications for not taking immediate action.

3.3.4 Recommend a solution

What will help resolve the ethical dilemma so that those that have been adversely affected by it are helped to mitigate or remove any impact?

Give a solution based on the facts provided. Here, it is worth stating any next steps if there are other possibilities if that solution does not work.

Also, think about a solution which:

(1) Stops the unethical behaviour, if currently happening, by taking clear and decisive actions. Be clear actions should be immediate, where this is practical.

(2) It may be necessary to issue a press release which responds to negative publicity or comments in the media regarding the unethical practices noted. It is important in such a statement to acknowledge that a company will:

- Fully investigate the circumstances and take full corrective action
- Apologise to the general public and to the company's stakeholders for the organisation's behaviour falling short of their expectations in this instance
- Reassure the public and stakeholders that this was an isolated occurrence (where this is true)

(3) Aim to prevent future reoccurrence by:

- Reviewing all other business activities for evidence of similar unethical activities
- Strengthening the internal controls environment and implement new controls to address the specific unethical behaviours noted
- Considering implementing or extending the organisation's own code of ethics to specifically prohibit the unethical behaviour noted and to provide further guidance to employees, so it is clear the unethical behaviour evidence is unacceptable in this organisation

Solutions to ethical dilemmas are unique to each situation, but the following themes can help to provide feasible and commercially viable solutions for an organisation.

- **Protecting integrity:** Solutions to maintain the integrity of individuals, organisations, and the decision-making process by reducing the likelihood of unethical behaviour or compromised judgments. These could involve training, supervision, authorisation, redistribution or transparency of decision-making, require disclosure, due diligence, documenting and recording or seeking professional third-party advice.

- **Minimising harm:** Safeguards aim to minimise the harm caused to stakeholders, including employees, clients, customers, and the public, by preventing or mitigating the negative impact of ethical dilemmas.

- **Promoting compliance:** Safeguards ensure compliance with applicable laws, regulations, and ethical standards, helping individuals and organisations fulfil their legal and professional obligations.

- **Enhancing transparency:** Decision-makers can enhance the transparency and accountability of their actions, ensuring that ethical decisions are made openly and justifiably.

- **Preserving trust:** Actions which preserve trust in individuals, organisations, and the profession as a whole. It demonstrates a commitment to ethical behaviour and responsible decision-making, fostering trust among stakeholders. This could involve new appointments, such as an independent ethics committee, or a compliance officer.

- **Damage limitation:** Implementing measures to minimise the extent of harm or negative consequences resulting from unethical behaviour or ethical dilemmas. This may include taking prompt action to rectify any harm caused, providing restitution, or implementing strategies to mitigate the impact.

- **Zero tolerance:** In some instances, such as bribery or other corruption, bullying and intimidation, it may be necessary to remove the root cause of the issue and terminate the employment of employees involved, or cease trading with specific suppliers.

- **Ensuring no re-occurrence:** Taking steps to prevent the recurrence of unethical behaviour or similar ethical dilemmas in the future. This involves identifying the root causes or contributing factors and implementing corrective actions or preventive measures to address those underlying issues.

- **Improve prevention of unethical behaviour:** Implementing measures and strategies to proactively prevent unethical behaviour from occurring. This may include establishing strong ethical frameworks, promoting ethical awareness and education, fostering an ethical organisational culture, and encouraging ethical decision-making at all levels.

- **Improve detection of unethical behaviour:** Enhancing mechanisms and systems to identify and detect unethical behaviour or ethical lapses promptly. This may involve implementing robust internal controls, whistle blower hotlines or reporting channels, regular monitoring, and audits to identify and address any instances of unethical behaviour effectively.

Going through the following checklist will help you to determine the scale of the appropriate solution for a given situation and whether more than one action is required. For example, there may be different immediate and longer-term actions.

- Consider if there are any relevant legal or compliance issues and ascertain all the parties affected by the dilemma.
- Are the facts of the issue confirmed? Or is further investigation required?
- Is information relevant to the ethical dilemma already in the public domain?
- Consider if the organisation's reputation is at risk. Also, consider if external stakeholders may perceive the dilemma differently to the board of directors and senior management
- Consider if legal advice is required
- Consider if it is necessary to disclose the issue to the relevant authorities, for example, in the case of theft.

3.3.5 Justify your solution

Make sure that there is a logical explanation dealing with the issue that has occurred and the people involved on both sides of the issue. In doing so:

(1) Explain the negative impacts and consequence which will be avoided by addressing the unethical behaviour.

(2) Explain the benefits to the company's stakeholders on the company's reputation and sustainability by addressing unethical behaviours.

The following three examples will help you to develop your approach for dealing with ethical dilemmas.

Question — Ethical dilemma I

A company called ICount Ltd has had its draft financial statements prepared for the latest year. Profits have dropped substantially, and this has a consequent effect on the statement of cash flows.

The directors of ICount Ltd are concerned about this and want to reduce the impact that the knowledge of this will have on its investors. They believe the problem was down to issues that one of its main customers was facing and that the economy in general had suffered over the year, so hopefully this will be a short-term problem. Results had picked up a bit in the last months of the financial year.

There are other consequences of the poor results that will be reported based on the draft accounts. These include:

- Poor bonuses awarded to the directors
- A breach of the terms of the loan covenants that the company has on its main loans
- A strong drop in market confidence, with negative consequences over time

The directors have approached the chief financial accountant of the company to tell her to adjust the financial statements by including some of the operating expenses as extraordinary items in the financial statements, to mitigate the effect on the reporting of the results by keeping the reported operating profit at a better level.

Required

Create a response to the ethical dilemma below using the following framework.

(1) Identify the ethical dilemma
(2) Consider if existing safeguard or other mitigations are in place
(3) Evaluate the ethical dilemma
(4) Recommend a solution
(5) Justify your solution

Answer

(1) Ethical dilemma

The ethical dilemma in this scenario is the directive given by the directors of ICount Ltd to the chief financial accountant, requesting her to adjust the financial statements by categorizing some operating expenses as extraordinary items. The purpose is to mitigate the impact of the poor results on the reporting of operating profit, with the aim of reducing the consequences on investors, such as poor bonuses, breach of loan covenants, and loss of market confidence.

There is an undoubted manipulation of the company's accounts if the chief financial accountant tries to make the accounts look better than they are. There is a conflict of interest for the chief financial accountant as she will want to keep the directors happy but will not want the financial accounts to be manipulated and be wrong. If she is unable to persuade the directors that the financial results should be correctly reported, then she may eventually have to raise the alarm or resign.

If the financial accounts are manipulated then this means they are misleading and a lack of integrity has been displayed by the directors which is a breach of IESBA's fundamental concept.

There is also a problem with objectivity as the chief financial accountant will have let bias, conflict of interest or the influence of others override her professional judgment. This is made worse if she would benefit from the performance-related pay as she would stand to gain from the situation herself.

There would be a breach of professional behaviour if normal operating expenses are categorised as extraordinary. Hence, there is a lot wrong with the course of action that the directors are suggesting and this places a lot of pressure on the chief financial accountant.

(2) Existing Safeguards or mitigations

The first step is for the accountant to consider if any existing safeguards or mitigations are in place within ICount Ltd's financial reporting framework. This may include established accounting standards, regulatory requirements, internal controls, and governance policies that govern the preparation and presentation of financial statements. As the directors are seeking to override existing internal controls then it is unlikely there are mitigations in place. This is because a lack of integrity and professional judgement displayed by the directors in this situation has not prevented the request being made.

(3) Evaluation of the ethical dilemma

It is wrong to manipulate accounts as this may mislead investors and other stakeholders. It is also a breach of the directors fiduciary duty to the company shareholders, as the directors are agents for the owner of the business, not the owners themselves in many cases.

An accountant is under an obligation to make sure financial accounts are correct and to report to others if not. The potential impact of the issue is severe, as this could impact the auditor's report and individuals may also be culpable of committing fraud. This is a severe situation for an accountant, dishonesty in financial reporting is wrong. There will be legal issues once the matter is revealed to the relevant authorities and the chief financial accountant is under an ultimate obligation to do this.

(4) Recommendation for a solution

Based on the evaluation, the recommended solution would be to adhere to the principles of transparency, accuracy, and compliance with accounting standards. The financial statements should reflect the true financial position and performance of the company, without deliberately misclassifying expenses as extraordinary items to manipulate the reported operating profit.

Therefore, the accountant should first try to persuade the directors to do the right thing and explain that the consequences of not doing so are likely to be far more severe for them and their company, even threatening its existence in the end. Accounting standards exist to be complied with. The accountant is also advised to seek legal advice, though her accountancy training should have made it obvious that manipulation of financial accounts is wrong.

Therefore, the recommended solution is for the financial accounts not to breach the accounting rules, which would be wrong. If the directors have a problem with this, then the accountant would probably have to resign and also have to report the issue to the company's auditors as well. Informing the relevant financial reporting body may well be necessary if the directors continue with their approach.

(5) Explanation of your choice

Choosing to maintain integrity in the financial reporting process is crucial for the long-term sustainability and trustworthiness of ICount Ltd. By accurately reflecting the company's financial situation, investors and other stakeholders can make informed decisions based on reliable information. Adjusting the financial statements to artificially improve operating profit would compromise transparency, mislead stakeholders, and potentially violate accounting standards and legal requirements.

Furthermore, it is important to address the underlying issues that led to the poor financial results. The directors should focus on analysing the causes, addressing them appropriately, and communicating a clear plan for improvement to investors and other stakeholders. This approach promotes accountability, fosters trust, and enables the company to work towards genuine and sustainable growth.

Question — Ethical dilemma II

In a recent meeting, the CFO of Pursuit plc, a UK listed company, briefed its financial controller on the latest strategic development initiative of the Chair and CEO to diversifying the company's business by seeking out new acquisition opportunities.

A company has been identified as the target and the CFO has asked the financial controller to hastily prepare a review report on the target company for the upcoming board meeting held in two weeks' time. The financial controller explained his concern about insufficient time to conduct thorough due diligence checks of the target company. In response, the CFO told the financial controller to not worry and focus on 'generating a positive report' for the acquisition. The CFO asked the financial controller to be creative where information is limited and 'fill in the gaps using your professional knowledge where necessary.'

The CFO said the deal is a good one as the target company as it is owned by the Chair's family and the CEO is fully in the picture and therefore, we should get a low price as the Chair has promised the CEO share options worth S$1 million for closing the deal. The CFO also said that the financial controller will have excellent career prospects that come with a pay rise and promotion if he can show to the CFO that he is on the company's side on this with a pay rise and promotion.

Required

Analyse the ethical issues in this situation to evaluate and recommend a response to the CFO's request.

Answer

1. Identify the ethical dilemma

The CFO has asked the controller to provide a favourable report on an acquisition target, but accurate due diligence information is incomplete. Based on the information available there is concern the acquisition target is overpriced but it is owned by the Chair's family. The CFO promises financial and career rewards if the accountant provides a favourable report to facilitate the deal.

2. Consider if existing safeguard or other mitigations are in place

As the Chair, CEO and CFO are seeking to override existing internal controls in this situation then it is unlikely there are mitigations in place as integrity and professional judgement of the Chair, CEO and CFO has not prevented in the request being made to the accountant to falsify the report.

3. Evaluate the ethical dilemma

Integrity: It would be dishonest for the accountant to prepare a report which is known to be inaccurate, especially if doing so were for personal gain. The CFO is attempting to persuade the accountant to prepare misleading financial information for the Board meeting. As a result, the other directors may be misled by the financial information and make a wrong decision.

Objectivity: The fact that the acquisition target is owned by the Chair's family represents a conflict of interest. By concealing the fact that the acquisition is a connected transaction, the Chair has put his own interests above those of the company. In fact, the CFO and Chair owe a fiduciary duty to the shareholders, including a duty to act in good faith and in the best interest of his company, which will breached due to the potential for personal gain. Also, the accountant has been offered an inducement of pay rise and a potential promotion for closing the deal which is a self-interest threat to objectivity.

Professional competence and due care: Should the accountant agreed to prepare a favourable report without considering all the relevant information, then the accountant has failed to exercise due care. The accountant cannot demonstrate professional competence and due care if gaps are filled in the report without conducting a thorough due diligence. In fact, as a professional accountant in business, the accountant has a guardian role to ensure the due diligence report provides a fair evaluation on the target company for the Board's thorough consideration.

Professional behaviour: There is a potential non-compliance with the laws and regulations and hence a breach of this key fundamental principle. As the target company is owned by the Chair's family, the acquisition may be considered as a connected transaction according to the UK listing rules and therefore should be disclosed in an announcement to the public, circulars to the shareholders and annual report, and conditional on shareholders' approval. If the accountant accepts the pay rise and promotion from the Chair for facilitating the acquisition, then this may be evidence of bribery.

Financial harm: The shareholders of the target company could receive a lower price for its sale due to deception and manipulation and/or falsification on a report which is likely to be influential during price negotiations. This is unfair to those affected, as some will make a personal gain at the expense of affected shareholders.

4. Recommend a solution

The accountant should not blindly follow the instructions of the CFO or succumb to the ill-intended pressures imposed by the Chair, CEO and CFO. Therefore, the accountant should arrange a meeting with the presence of the Chair, CEO and CFO and explain to them their unwillingness to prepare a review report which they believe to contain inaccurate information. This is because the principle of integrity requires a professional accountant not to be associated with information which they believe to be false or misleading. If the Chair, CEO and CFO choose not to heed this advice, then the audit committee should be involved or consult a relevant professional body or seek legal advice before taking a further step.

PART B CODES, GUIDANCE AND STANDARDS

5. **Justify your solution**

   The severity of the request is high and it is likely to be illegal. Therefore, it is crucial that the professional accountant refuses to comply and, if necessary, choose to resign to protect their integrity.

Question   Ethical dilemma III

City Fitness Ltd (CFL) is a small private company operating in the fitness sector. It provides training space and equipment to its members through its network of fitness centres. The business was founded 30 years ago to take advantage of the growing interest in health and fitness at that time, which has grown ever since.

The CEO and all four board members are AIA-qualified accountants as they met while undergoing training and left public practice to set up the company.

The buildings that house its fitness centres are all owned by CFL and are extremely popular with local office workers, who visit the centres early in the morning, at lunchtimes and after work. The Board of CFL have been aware for some time that these buildings (along with other CFL centres) need refurbishment and minor structural improvements but have never been regarded as unsafe by the Board.

Last year, a formal building condition survey report on the condition of one particular building was provided by a company which occupies the adjacent building. This report highlighted some structural problems with the neighbour's building which is attached to the fitness centre and constructed by the same building developer.

The report advised CFL to vacate the fitness centre until a full building survey could be undertaken to investigate if the building faults observed in the neighbouring company building are also present in the CFL building where the fitness centre is located. The CEO decided not to take any action as he could see no evidence of any building problems himself. The rest of the Board agreed, as the fitness centre concerned had the highest number of visits per week of any of its branches, and so it was important that it was kept open for members.

Last week, part of the ceiling collapsed in the centre, hurting one arm of a member who was using a rowing machine and required minor hospital treatment. The neighbouring business has used social media to point out that CFL was warned previously.

Required

The Board should demonstrate adherence to the IESBA five fundamental ethical principles. The principles of integrity, objectivity, professional competence and due care, and professional behaviour are all relevant here.

(a) Evaluate the situation using the IESBA fundamental ethical principles.

(b) Discuss how to proceed to resolve the ethical dilemmas in the scenario.

Answer

(a) **Integrity**

The principle of integrity involves being straightforward and honest in all professional and business relationships. Integrity also implies fair dealing and truthfulness. The CEO was faced with a dilemma: should the CEO be open and honest about the issue raised in the report or choose not to act on information provided in good faith by a neighbouring company?

The CEO and CFL Board have a responsibility to be straightforward and honest with their customers about the information contained in the report. By keeping important information out of the public domain, they knowingly put gym members at risk of physical harm. The CEO's behaviour

in complying with the decision not to act upon the information has also brought his integrity as an AIA-qualified accountant into question. The decision not to address problems with the building earlier and close the gym until a survey and remedial building work had been completed meant the CEO put commercial interests ahead of member safety.

Objectivity

The principle of objectivity means that bias, conflict of interest or undue influence should not be allowed to override professional or business judgement. In addition, relationships that may impair objectivity should be avoided. The CEO contravened this principle by relying on his own non-expert observations rather than considering the findings of an independent building report and implementing a building survey on behalf of CFL to confirm the facts.

Professional competence and due care

The principle of professional competence and due care implies the need to act diligently and in accordance with professional standards. The CEO and the other board directors have contravened this principle because they did not take appropriate action when the building report was originally received from the neighbouring company concerning possible damage to the building. It could be argued that the CEO and the CFL Board failed to carry out their collective duties diligently or to exercise professional competence, even though there was no firm evidence that there was a safety issue.

The CEO and the Board have an obligation to act diligently on behalf of employees, shareholders, customers and the general public. All board members have a responsibility to conduct themselves in a manner consistent with the reputation of CFL and the standards expected of an AIA-qualified accountant. It is clear that the Board have failed to provide due care in protecting their members and the general public from concerns regarding the building's safety.

Professional behaviour

This is the requirement to comply with laws and regulations and avoid actions that discredit the individual's profession. By deciding to keep the report private, the Board could be covering up negligence that has potentially been committed by failing to act upon information received.

This may potentially result in court action, and it would be up to the courts to decide. Given the ceiling has collapsed, then a claim for damages from the injured party should be expected. The Board are advised to provide for legal expenses and take legal advice which results from their inaction to address the issue.

(b) **Identify the ethical dilemma:**

A member was hurt and required hospital treatment following a partial collapse of a ceiling in one of the gym sites operated by the CFL. This event could have been foreseen as the CFL was pre-warned in a building report from a neighbouring occupant that the building where the gym operates was potentially hazardous. No remedial building work was completed as the report was ignored by the CEO and the Board.

Evaluate the ethical dilemma:

On receiving a formal building report from the neighbouring company, the CEO and board of CFL failed in its duty of care to protect its gym members.

CFL was warned by a neighbouring business of potential structural issues in the report, and the CEO and board chose to ignore the contents of this report to keep a popular gym site open. The CEO relied on his own observation of the building and could see nothing wrong. However, the CEO is not a building inspector and is not professionally competent to make that judgement.

As a result, members were put in physical harm's way, which is unethical. The CEO acted without due care of CFL's customers, which is a serious lapse in integrity.

Recommend a solution:

It is recommended that a full independent review of the building is undertaken by an expert building surveyor and CFL's compliance with health and safety regulations should be reviewed independently by an industry expert.

CFL should undergo remedial building works as soon as possible for any defects noted. Where defects are noted, the correct action is to close the sites, as CFL has a duty to protect the safety of its members.

CFL needs to consider providing compensation to the injured member, and at the very least cover any medical bills. Justify your solution: performing a review of every site for health and safety concerns is a minimum action where the safety of its customers and employees is at stake.

The CFL Board must take urgent measures to ensure this does not happen again due to the danger this exposed CFL gym members to. Therefore, the CFL Board is advised to complete a full business risk analysis in light of this issue and perform a full building inspection of all CFL fitness centres in case there are other structural building problems which have been overlooked or ignored.

The CFL Board must evaluate very carefully its decision not to close the affected site when it was first informed of a potential structural problem with the building. Also, the CFL Board must be ready to adopt new internal controls and ethical principles to prevent similar events occurring.

4: APPLICATION OF ETHICAL CODES

Chapter Roundup

- Applying ethical codes requires judgement to translate general principles into particular actions.
- A principles-based code of ethics may be thought of in terms of Kohlberg's levels, as distinct from external rules that must be adhered to.
- Ethical conflict may arise when several principles need to be applied to a situation.
- Developing a practical approach to responding to ethical dilemmas provides a framework to demonstrate application of the IESBA five fundamental principles, rationale to consider potential solutions and make a recommendation, with justifications, to decision makers for implementation.

Quick Quiz

1. Fill in the blanks:

    The IESBA *Code of Ethics* states that professional judgement involves the application of ………….., ………….., ………….. and ………….. .

2. "Where an auditor encounters a fraud at a client, they should immediately report it to the relevant authorities."

    True ☐

    False ☐

3. "A principles-based code allows an accountant to decide which principles to apply."

    Briefly discuss this statement.

4. State the definition of the principle of confidentiality from IESBA *Code of Ethics*.

5. If a professional accountant cannot resolve an ethical conflict in relation to an engagement, what should they do?

Answers to Quick Quiz

1. The IESBA *Code of Ethics* states that professional judgment involves the application of **training**, **knowledge**, **skill** and **experience**.

2. False. The auditor should consider whether there is a legal duty to report, as well as whether there are any reasons why a report should not be made (eg anti-money laundering regulations).

3. A principles-based code requires an accountant to exercise their professional judgment in the application of the principles. This means that they will decide which principles are most relevant to a given situation, however, this decision will need to be based on a thorough consideration of the guidance given in the code itself. Any decision made in applying the principles is therefore not an arbitrary decision and should embody those principles themselves.

4. To respect the confidentiality of information acquired as a result of professional and business relationships.

5. The professional accountant should decline the engagement if it is a prospective engagement, or if the engagement has already begun then should resign from it where this is possible in line with the laws and regulations applicable in their jurisdiction.

The professional accountant

Ethics and the professional accountant

Topic list	Syllabus reference
1 Creative accounting	LO 3, LO 4
2 Revenue recognition	LO 3, LO 4
3 How much to disclose to the finance director	LO 3, LO 4
4 Fraud and fraudulent disclosures	LO 3, LO 4
5 Pressure from management	LO 3, LO 4
6 Omission of financial records	LO 3, LO 4
7 Timing differences	LO 3, LO 4
8 Concealed liabilities and expenses	LO 3, LO 4
9 Asset valuation	LO 3, LO 4

Introduction

In this chapter, we will consider the **ethical dimensions** that arise in connection with various aspects of business and public practice relevant to accounting and auditing. In terms of the Ethics and Professional Practice syllabus, we will look at how important it is for **professional accountants** to behave in an ethical manner before considering some of the ethical **challenges** they might face, and how they should **respond** to them.

1 Creative accounting

1.1 The accountant's personality

Key term

> **Creative accounting** happens because an organisation's financial position and/or performance is not what the organisation wants it to be.

The **traditional view** of the accountant is that of a **straightforward** and **uncomplicated** individual: while not always prone to humour, there are a number of jokes that refer to accountants not being the most dynamic or attractive members of society. There are other views, perhaps that the accountant can be easily led into producing information that has strayed from the true and fair view that financial statements are meant to illustrate. The fact that this perception exists, albeit in humour, must have some foundation: even the term **creative accounting** is a **euphemism** that attempts to add a degree of professionalism to what can ultimately only be described as **fraud**.

Where do such perceptions come from? The typical **personality traits** displayed by accountants might help us to understand why we need to have so many codes of ethics to guide our behaviour. The Swiss psychologist **Carl Jung** (1875-1961) devised a series of **personality types** that provided four scales that attempt to categorise individuals and their personality:

Jung's personality types

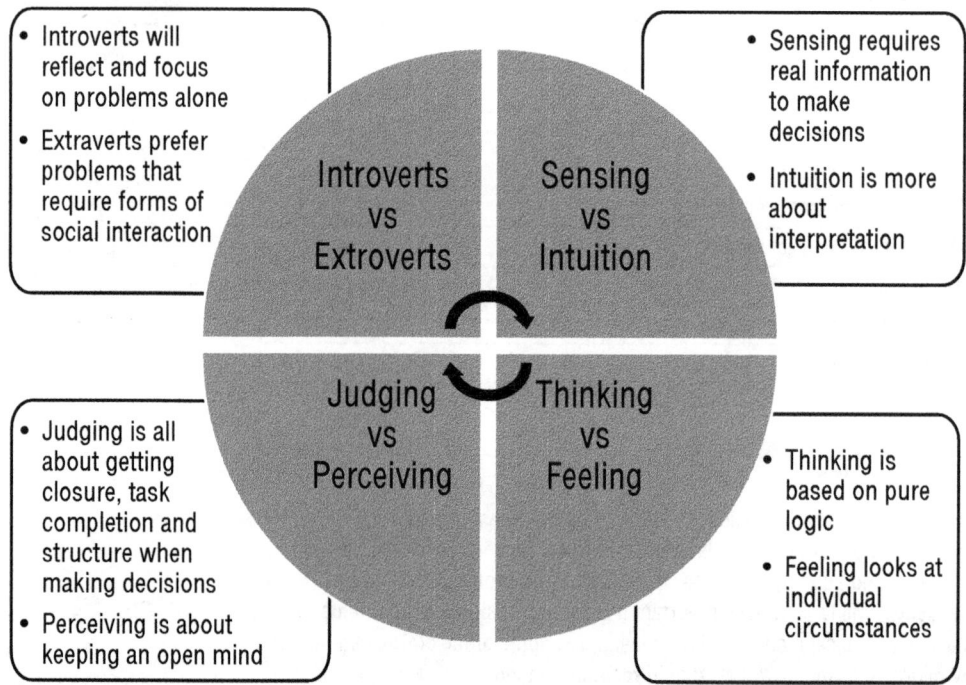

In 1923, Jung's research was applied by **Isabel Myers** (1897-1980) and her mother **Katharine Briggs** (1875-1968) to eventually develop the **Myers-Briggs Type Indicator** which uses a questionnaire and, depending on the answers given, categorises the subject into one of 16 types based on where they sit on each of the four scales.

According to analysis carried out by the **Australian Bureau of Statistics** in 2016 (cited by Morgan, 2016) there are **six** of these 16 types that are **most likely to apply to accountants** – in four out of these six types, accountants were most likely to display **extraversion**, **sensing** and **feeling**, while in five out of the six, accountants were most likely to **judge**. What does this tell us about the type of person that an accountant really is?

- It suggests someone who requires **social stimulation**, **action** and **achievement**, using **information** to reach decisions **not interpretation**.
- They are less likely to be purely logical and will instead look at **specific circumstances**.
- Overwhelmingly, they will seek **closure** and **task completion**, favouring **structure** and **decision making** over keeping their choices open.

These results may surprise you – however, they do point to a more **complex** personality and therefore someone who would definitely **benefit** from guidance when presented with difficult choices. Perhaps the idea of **creative accounting** is not quite so fanciful now if these personality types are to be believed.

There are **many illustrations of creative accounting** which we will cover in subsequent sections of this chapter. For now, let's consider the **basic ethical expectations** for professional accountants that should stop such practices in their tracks. You already know about the **fundamental ethical principles** and how the **conceptual framework** illustrates the sorts of threats that could exist: let us add to this by looking at some other areas where professional accountants need to consider what it means to do the right thing.

1.1 - *IESBA Exposure Draft – Proposed Revisions to the Code to Promote the Role and Mindset Expected of Professional Accountants (2019)*

You should already be aware of the importance of **professional scepticism** as a key part of the approach used by **auditors**. Over recent years, the International Federation of Accountants (IFAC) and its various committees have considered whether the term professional scepticism should be **applied to all accountants, not just auditors**. Having concluded that the term professional scepticism should continue as something that relates to auditors, IESBA issued this exposure draft to seek feedback from stakeholders on **how to communicate the desired role and mindset expected of professional accountants within an ethical framework** that all accountants would use.

The exposure draft contains edited sections of the **IESBA *International Code of Ethics for Professional Accountants (including International Independence Standards)*** which suggest the following **amendments**:

- Reinforcement that professional accountants should behave in an ethical manner to serve the **public interest**.
- **Objectivity** should promote the positive display of judgement without being compromised by various forms of bias, conflict of interest or undue influence or reliance.
- **Professional behaviour** should include **acting in the public interest**.
- **Integrity** should include the **bravery** to do the right thing even **under pressure** or facing an **ethical dilemma**. It stresses the determination required to be able to stand one's ground and **challenge** those when required.
- When applying the IESBA *Code*, professional accountants should maintain an **inquiring mind** (mirroring the professional scepticism displayed by auditors).
- Staying alert to the risk of both **conscious and unconscious bias** when assessing ethical situations (such as **anchoring bias** that uses an initial assumption to build a hypothesis around; **availability bias** which prioritises facts that are easily available; **selective perception** which only focuses on one person's view; **overconfidence** in one's own viewpoint and even **groupthink** where new, individual viewpoints are discouraged by the existing norms found in larger organisations).

The need to serve the **public interest** and the ethical nature of the profession (plus the somewhat **complex nature of their personalities**) means that accountants are at risk of **losing credibility** if they are **not honest**. Professional accountants will have been **educated** in school, and probably some form college or university as well. When you consider what they have also learned in their **professional exams** and in their **employment**, plus the fact that they have a **code of ethics** to apply to any situations they might face in real life, they should obviously **know** when bad things are happening. However, this chapter will try to explain the **tough choices** that accountants might face, why they might **choose the wrong course of action** and what they can do **to address this**.

Question: Characteristics of a professional accountant

You work for a professional accountancy institute and are designing a promotional campaign for careers advisors who work in schools and colleges.

Required

List the top five personality characteristics that you think a professional accountant should possess.

Answer

It is unlikely that there could ever be a definitive response here, but here are some of the key things that professional accountants should probably be:

- Honest
- Fair
- Competent
- Sceptical
- Adaptable
- Patient
- Brave
- Open-minded

Did you come up with anything not on this list? Would they be more important than any of these suggestions?

If you missed any of these characteristics, can you see why they would be considered in this context?

2 Revenue recognition

2.1 Revenue

In most profit-making companies, the **largest financial amounts** will probably relate to revenue (certainly in their statements of profit or loss) so it seems logical to start our journey through creative accounting here. Thinking purely quantitatively, if revenue is significant in size, it will not need much variation for this amount to become material. However, we know that **external audits** are usually conducted on a **risk basis**, prioritising the **most material items** for **more detailed testing**, so the greater the sums involved, the higher the scrutiny that revenue will be under.

In simple terms, profits could be boosted by **recognising more revenue than the company should actually receive**, whether deliberately or by accident. This could occur in a number of ways:

Inconsistent cut-off dates when producing the financial statements that extend the reporting period at the beginning and/or end of the financial year (this can be exacerbated when revenue relates to items bought in **different parts of the world** and the time taken to **transport** the goods is uncertain)

Recognising revenues that are processed by the company, but which actually relate to **third parties** using the company's sales system (such as vendors that sell their products via online marketplaces)

Inventing revenue, such as retail outlets that no longer exist, recognising **gains** such as interest as revenue or recording revenues from activities that **never existed**

Overstatement of revenues either by making unrealistic estimates or by including amounts that are unlikely to be recovered (discussed later on in this chapter)

Duplication of revenues by including the same amounts more than once

Misstatement of sales taxes which would inflate the amount of revenue recognised from legitimate sales

2.2 IFRS 15 Revenue from Contracts with Customers

Although it was issued in 2014 and could be adopted from that time onwards, IFRS 15 only became **effective** for reporting periods that started on or after 1 January 2018 and puts the onus on the accountant to **prove** that certain **conditions** have been met in order for revenue to be legitimately **recognised**. These conditions are referred to as **performance obligations** and the standard stipulates that only revenue in accordance with the **terms** of the sales **contract** is recognised once the associated performance obligation has been **satisfied**. The previous accounting standards in place were less specific about what you could recognise and when you could recognise it, meaning that their replacement by IFRS 15 had become essential, especially when you consider the **complexity** of revenue streams for many modern companies. However, having the right standard in place still does not guarantee that your revenue will not be misstated in some way.

Question

Revenue analysis

Consider a mobile phone service provider that sells a variety of products and services to its customers.

Required

(a) List as many different types of revenue as you can think of that would apply to this provider.
(b) How would each of these revenue streams differ in the way they are accounted for?

Answer

(a) Types of revenue	(b) Differences between them
Handset	Either charged in a one-off payment or spread across the length of the contract (usually more than one accounting period)
Line rental	Often charged on a monthly basis and may include a set amount of calls, messages and data (discounts might apply in the early months as an incentive)

(a) Types of revenue	(b) Differences between them
SIM card only fees	Again, these are usually charged on a monthly basis
Call charges	These may not be charged separately unless they go above a certain threshold or relate to exceptional activity (such as calls to specific types of number)
Data usage	Likely to be included in line rental up to a certain amount, payable thereafter based on activity
Charity donations	Usually passed on to the charity concerned but still needs to be disaggregated from other charges
Insurance	May not always be charged but will relate to the handset and may need to be passed on to a third party if not an in-house provision
Additional products (such as tablets or headphones)	The cost of these may be spread across a number of months and could include a finance charge
Additional services (such as streaming services)	These may again be discounted in the early months of a contract but will need to be passed on to the service provider in line with their agreement
Separate revenue for corporate customers	These could include some or all of the items discussed above but may be handled by a separate part of the company, aggregated by company, charged at different amounts, etc

Despite each of these revenue streams being **accounted for** differently by the mobile phone service provider, they are likely to be **collected** together in one sum, usually taken directly from the customer's bank account by direct debit. This will mean the service provider will need to have a **separate system** for each of these **complex** and **unique** revenue streams which is then **aggregated** for the purpose of billing and then **disaggregated** once payment has been received. Clearly, not every company will operate in the same way, but this does illustrate the challenge faced by professional accountants when either deliberate or accidental misstatement of material revenue is possible.

Case Study

What do you buy people for Christmas? In recent years, there has been an increase in the popularity of buying **gift cards** with pre-loaded sums of money that can be exchanged for goods and services at a multitude of retailers. Crockett (2020) cites evidence that estimates between 10% and 20% of the balances on these cards **never gets spent**. Although this money stays as a **contract liability** (also known as deferred income) on a retailer's statement of financial position, it can at some point in the future be recognised as income (known as **breakage income**) if the retailer can demonstrate that it will never get spent. This offers the professional accountant an interesting opportunity: as long as the **estimates** of breakage income are not overstated, this could be legitimately recognised. The key issue for accountants is the **reasonableness** of this estimation process, which presents yet another ethical challenge (source: The economics of unused gift cards, January 2020, The Hustle online).

2.3 Aggressive earnings management

It is important to note at this point that recognising revenue which does not meet performance obligations **might not automatically be fraudulent**. The **complexity** and **volume** of transactions may mean that the professional accountant makes an **honest mistake** which leads to misstatement of revenue in some capacity. Remember though that **professional competence and due care** is still one of the fundamental ethical principles, so accidental misstatement is still a matter of ethics.

What happens if a professional accountant or someone in a position of authority within management goes rogue and decides that they will **deliberately** misstate revenue? It is worth pointing out at this stage that revenues could be manipulated so **less is recognised than should be** – usually this would be in an attempt to **reduce corporate taxes** – however, this is discussed in more detail in Chapter 6 so we will not consider the ethics of this any further here.

Let us assume a professional accountant decides to recognise revenue inappropriately, using some or all of the techniques we discussed earlier. Once there is **intent**, and the amounts involved are **material**, this is going to be something that the **external auditor** will be interested in, as it represents **fraud**, which is part of the auditor's responsibilities (non-material fraud identified by the auditors would also be reported to those charged with governance, but only if it emerges during the course of the audit).

In the wake of the **credit crunch** of 2007, the **financial crisis** of 2008 and the resulting **economic downturn** experienced across much of the global economy, there was still **pressure from investors** for companies to report the best results they could. Understandably, this presented many professional accountants with an unwelcome choice: either **obey**, and risk losing their licence to operate in the public interest by adopting creative accounting techniques to inflate performance and position or **tell the truth** and **present a more pessimistic view**, putting the financial support of the company in jeopardy as investors switch to what they perceive to be a less risky bet. Sometimes (and this threat has perhaps always existed) this pressure can cause a company to lose its way.

Case Study

UK grocer Tesco was investigated in 2014 following allegations of aggressive earnings management which saw them manipulate their profits by over £250 million using two separate activities:

- Recognising revenues from suppliers that it had not yet received – these related to rebates that the supplier would pay Tesco if their product was placed in a more advantageous position on the shelves of its stores
- Withholding sums of money payable to suppliers in an attempt to suppress their costs

These activities were uncovered by the company's external auditors and led to criminal prosecutions of three directors and an investigation by the Serious Fraud Office (SFO) in the UK. Although no convictions were secured, Tesco admitted its part in these misstatements and agreed to pay a fine of £129 million to the SFO. Having already admitted to the UK stock exchange that it had presented misleading information to the market in 2014, Tesco also agreed with the UK Financial Conduct Authority to fund a compensation scheme for investors who had been adversely affected by these events. The Tesco board said it would take appropriate steps to prevent similar cases of misstatement in the future, although subsequent restructures have seemingly focused on more commercial issues than anything related to financial reporting. The pressures that Tesco faced in 2014 still exist to this day (competition from low-cost supermarkets and increasing downward pressure on costs) meaning it is likely that the same challenges they faced in 2014 will continue for the foreseeable future.

3 How much to disclose to the finance director

Within this section, we will cover situations where employees may **choose to withhold information** that the company's finance director (FD) should be aware of but which they may not know anything about. There may be a number of **reasons** for this which will be considered from the perspective of a member of the finance department who works for the FD.

In essence, this is as much an **operational** issue as it is ethical – how much information should be passed up the line to the FD in a typical finance department? A lot of this will depend on the **role** that you are employed for. Contact between financial controller, chief accountant and FD will tend to be of a more strategic nature, focusing on high level data and less structured decision making. The lower down the organisation a professional accountant is employed, the less contact they will have with the FD, unless it has a very flat or lean structure.

Unless you are given **specific instructions** for all of the tasks you are required to perform, there is a risk that **assumptions** will be made regarding this kind of contact with the FD which could create a problem.

> The professional accountant might assume that **the FD knows everything** going on in the business so does not need to be told anything, meaning **critical information may be ignored**.

> By contrast, there may be a perception that the FD is so far up the organisation, **they do not know anything** so should be told everything, **swamping them with unnecessary detail**.

Without good management and clear communication protocols, the relationship between the FD and other professional accountants could become **dysfunctional**.

A stronger **ethical dimension** emerges when a choice has to be made about whether to pass on information to the FD or to keep it secret. A professional accountant may seek to demonstrate that they can cope with the **demands of the role**, no matter how **stressful** or **impossible** these appear to be. While this displays an admirable personal quality, it could also lead to work **being done poorly or not at all**: hiding this fact from the FD and others may result in **problems** that the organisation struggles to cope with. It is questionable whether this is behaving in the public interest.

Adding further intrigue to this, what if the professional accountant feels a strong desire to **impress** the FD and decides to adopt **creative accounting practices** that make the company look better but which are actually illegal or unethical. Contrast this with the **fear** of losing your job if the company's **results** are **not as expected** (whether this is your fault or not) so you choose not to inform the FD of this and find ways of reporting an artificially improved position instead. In both of these situations, there has clearly been a significant **failure** in ethical leadership by the organisation (and perhaps in your own moral compass too) so again we go back to the procedural to ensure professional accountants at all levels are aware of their ethical responsibilities.

Various pieces of **legislation** exist to advise company directors of their responsibilities: for example, in the UK, sections 175 and 177 of the Companies Act (2006) contain lists of duties that relate to **conflicts of interest** that directors should disclose regarding matters such as employment, property and transactions with other organisations and individuals from outside of the company. It is possible that a professional accountant might discover that the FD has failed to make such a disclosure and is then faced with an **ethical dilemma** over whether or not to escalate this matter. We will discuss this later in relation to the topic of **whistleblowing** in the next chapter, but it seems likely that keeping this quiet is the wrong thing to do.

5: ETHICS AND THE PROFESSIONAL ACCOUNTANT

Question — Matters for attention

You work in the finance department of a large bank. Here is a list of tasks that you have performed in the last week:

- Successfully completed your month-end reconciliations without issue
- Responded to a query from the company's legal team about the identity of a new client
- Responded to all queries from the bank's operations team about the previous month's management accounts
- Attended a 1:1 interview with your line manager about the new salary scheme being introduced

Required

Identify which of the matters from your list of tasks that you should bring to the attention of the finance director.

Answer

You should consider raising this issue with the finance director:

- Responded to a query from the company's legal team about the identity of a new client

This is because it could have wider implications for the company and yourself: identity is one of the issues required when considering money laundering (crucial as you work in a bank).

4 Fraud and fraudulent disclosures

4.1 Fraud

Key term

Fraud is defined as "An intentional act by one or more individuals among management, those charged with governance, employees, or third parties, involving the use of deception to obtain an unjust or illegal advantage" (FRC (2017), ISA (UK) 240 (revised): para. 11a)

Occasionally one or more employees may decide to **act dishonestly** and commit fraud.

Fraud is a criminal offence, but employees (or individuals from outside the organisation) may see an opportunity for personal gain. An organisation may be exposed to small amounts of fraud, but there may also be occasions when losses due to fraud could be very high.

4.1.1 Types of fraud

The following are all examples of fraud.

Type of fraud	Explanation
Ghost employees	Maintaining fictitious employees on the payroll and making regular salary payments to them.
Collusion with a supplier or customer	There may be collusion with a supplier to claim payments for fictitious deliveries of goods. Or there may be collusion with a customer in which deliveries to the customer are not recorded.
Over-stating expenses	Making claims for non-existent expenses or over-claiming expenses, such as claiming for first-class air travel when the individual travelled economy class.

PART C THE PROFESSIONAL ACCOUNTANT

False financial reporting	Senior management may deliberately produce misleading financial statements in order to earn a large annual bonus and to deceive shareholders.
Misstating time spent on client work	Over-stating time spent on working for a client is a fraud against the client, who will be charged for the time.
Unauthorised use of company resources	This is a form of theft of company resources.

4.1.2 Why does fraud occur? Cressey's Fraud Triangle

To address fraud in an organisation, it is useful to understand where it comes from and how it occurs. In 1973, **Donald Cressey** explained that fraud was likely to occur if **three conditions** were present. This is known as the Cressey's Fraud Triangle which is displayed below.

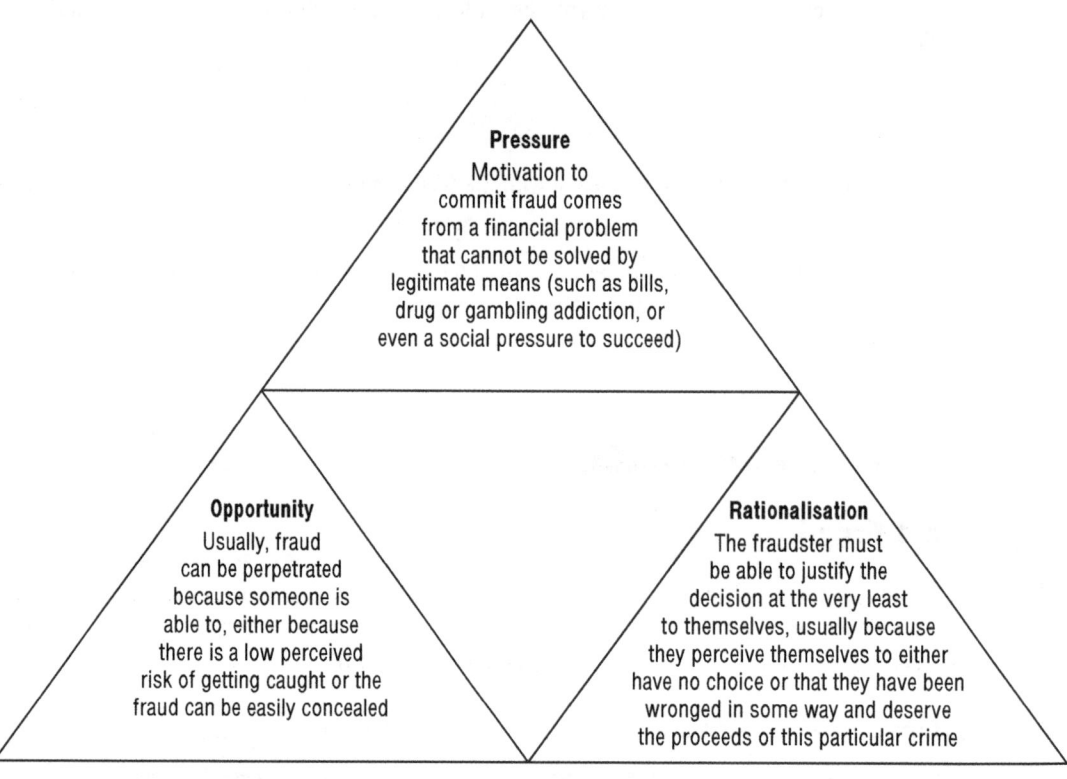

(Cressey's Fraud Triangle, 1973: p.30)

Knowing that fraud is usually a **product** of these three conditions means that an organisation can focus on each one when considering both prevention and detection. For example:

- **Pressure** – are staff likely to be affected by **external factors**, such as blackmail, addiction or extortion?
- **Opportunity** – are assets likely to be **vulnerable** (and are any of our **controls poor**)?
- **Rationalisation** – are staff **disenfranchised** or desperate enough to commit fraud, and do our recruitment procedures always check **employee references** for any previous fraudulent behaviour

Question — Fraud

Example of fraud triangle

Jane, a senior accountant at XYZ Corp., has been with the company for several years. Recently, she has been facing significant financial pressure due to unexpected medical bills and personal debt.

Jane begins to embezzle funds by writing checks to fictitious vendors and manipulating the accounting records to cover her tracks. Over time, she diverts significant sums of money to pay off her personal debts and cover her medical expenses.

The fraud is eventually detected during an internal audit, leading to Jane's termination and legal action. XYZ Corp. implements stronger internal controls, segregates accounting duties, and provides ethics training to prevent future incidents.

Required
Apply Cressey's Fraud Triangle to analyse why this fraud occurred.

Answer

(1) **Pressure**

- **Financial Pressure:** Jane is struggling with mounting medical bills and personal debt, creating a sense of urgency to find additional funds.
- **Work-Related Pressure:** Facing constant stress from her financial problems, Jane feels pressured to find a solution quickly to avoid further personal and financial turmoil.

(2) **Opportunity**

- **Weak Internal Controls**: XYZ Corp. lacks robust internal controls, allowing Jane to have unsupervised access to financial records and the authority to approve transactions.
- **Poor Segregation of Duties**: Jane handles both recording transactions and reconciling bank statements, creating an opportunity to conceal fraudulent activities.

(3) **Rationalization**

- **Justification:** Jane believes she is underpaid and deserves additional compensation for her hard work.
- **Entitlement:** She rationalizes her actions by thinking, "I will repay the money once my financial situation improves."
- **Minimization of Harm:** Jane convinces herself that the company is large and profitable, so a small amount taken will not be missed or cause significant harm.

4.1.3 Factors preventing controls from mitigating fraud risk

Management also needs to understand the factors that may prevent controls from operating properly.

(a) Controls will not function well if there is a **lack of emphasis on compliance** or a **lack of understanding** of why the controls are required, how they should operate and who should be operating them.

(b) **Staff problems** such as understaffing, poor-quality staff or poorly motivated staff can prevent the effective operation of controls.

(c) **Changes in senior personnel** can lead to a lack of effective supervision or management.

(d) **Emphasis on the autonomy of operational managers** may lead to controls being bypassed.

4.1.4 Fraud prevention policies and controls

The following fraud prevention policies and controls are recommended.

PART C THE PROFESSIONAL ACCOUNTANT

(a) **A strong ethics policy ('tone at the top')**. Some companies have formal codes of ethics which employees are required to sign covering areas such as gifts from customers. Management can also ensure that they set 'a good example'.

(b) **Personnel controls** may reduce the risk of fraud by recruiting suitable people to work for the organisation.

(c) **Training and raising risk awareness** are important. Fraud awareness education should therefore be an integral part of training, particularly for managers and staff in high-risk areas such as procurement.

Specific prevention controls should be implemented in areas of the business where a high risk of fraud has been identified.

(a) **Segregation of duties** may be a key control in fraud prevention although it may not prevent fraud when there is collusion.

(b) **Appropriate documentation** should be required for all transactions.

(c) **Limitation controls** should be applied, such as only allowing staff to choose suppliers from an approved list.

(d) **Authorisation and access controls** are controls that require authorisation for certain actions or that limit access to high-security areas of operation, such as limiting access to the computer network by means of passwords.

(e) Policies should be clearly communicated and certain actions should be **prohibited**, such as leaving a computer terminal without logging off.

Question — Controls to address potential fraud

Required

Suggest suitable controls to prevent the following fraudulent activities.

Suitable controls

(a) **Ghost employees**
(b) **Collusion with third parties**
(c) **Inflating expense claims**
(d) **Stealing assets**
(e) **Manipulation of financial statements (F/S)**

Answer

To effectively prevent various fraudulent activities, implementing suitable controls is crucial. Here are specific controls for each type of fraud mentioned:

(a) **Ghost Employees**

- **Regular Payroll Audits** - Conduct periodic audits of the payroll to ensure that all employees listed are legitimate and active.

- **Segregation of Duties** - Separate the responsibilities of hiring, payroll processing, and distributing pay checks to minimise the risk of fraudulent entries.

- **Employee Verification** - Use employee identification numbers and regularly update employee records with photos, contact information, and other identifying details.

- **Physical Checks** - Perform regular, unannounced physical headcounts to match with payroll records.

(b) **Collusion with Third Parties**
- **Vendor Management Controls** – Implement a robust vendor approval process, including background checks and regular reviews of vendor relationships.
- **Segregation of Duties** – Ensure that no single employee has control over the entire procurement process from vendor selection to payment authorisation.
- **Conflict of Interest Policies** – Require employees to disclose any potential conflicts of interest and regularly review these disclosures.
- **Audit Trails** – Maintain detailed records of all transactions and approvals to facilitate audits and investigations.

(c) **Inflating Expense Claims**
- **Detailed Expense Policies** – Establish clear, detailed policies for allowable expenses and require detailed documentation for all claims.
- **Approval Hierarchy** – Implement a multi-level approval process for expense claims, ensuring that claims are reviewed by multiple parties.
- **Periodic Audits** – Conduct random and regular audits of expense claims to identify and address any discrepancies.
- **Automated Expense Management Systems** – Use software to track and manage expense claims, which can flag unusual or excessive claims automatically.

(d) **Stealing Assets**
- **Inventory Controls** – Implement regular inventory checks and maintain accurate, real-time records of all assets.
- **Access Controls** – Restrict access to physical and digital assets to authorised personnel only.
- **Surveillance Systems** – Install surveillance cameras in key areas to monitor asset movement and deter theft.
- **Asset Tagging and Tracking** – Use asset tags and tracking systems to monitor the location and condition of valuable assets.

(e) **Manipulation of Financial Statements**
- **Internal and External Audits** – Conduct regular internal and external audits to verify the accuracy and completeness of financial statements.
- **Segregation of Duties** – Ensure that different individuals are responsible for preparing, reviewing, and approving financial statements.
- **Automated Controls** – Use financial software with built-in checks and balances to detect anomalies and enforce compliance with accounting standards.
- **Whistleblower Policies** – Encourage employees to report suspicious activities by establishing a confidential whistleblower program.

4.2 Fraudulent disclosures in accounts

Small companies

In the UK, there are conditions that apply to small companies regarding the format of **financial information** required to be **submitted to Companies House**. Such information is then available for

analysis by current and prospective investors, as well as other stakeholders such as regulators, employees, customers and suppliers. Professional accountants in public practice will be employed by small companies such as this to help with the provision of **accounting services** including advice on the submission of suitable financial information.

There are many examples of **mistakes** made by small companies, mainly because they do not employ a professional accountant, which include submitting **incomplete information** or providing information that is **not required**. This latter category does throw up an ethical conundrum.

Advice
Professional accountants may choose to **advise** their clients to submit financial information that does not give a complete view of the position and performance of the small company concerned. While this is **permitted** under the legislation, it is debatable whether it is **ethical**.

Presentation
Summarised accounts (known in the UK as **abridged accounts**) would not include any profit or loss information, or a breakdown of debtors and creditors, meaning that the corporation tax liability is not disclosed and therefore **profits** earned by the company are **not shown**.

Transparency?
The company would therefore avoid having to disclose if it has made a **loss**. While this may help it to secure funding and business from suppliers and customers, it does not work in the opposite direction and increases the risk to other stakeholders from their involvement with a company facing an uncertain future.

This approach is not technically fraudulent and may serve the professional accountant in their relationship with their client, but arguably goes against their responsibility to act in the wider **public interest**, which we know to be unethical.

Big companies

The **accounting standards** used by big companies offer plenty of scope in how specific items should be disclosed, but the size and importance of these types of entity mean that employing staff who are **not competent** in the production of their financial information (both internally and externally available) is simply **not an option**. There are also no options to file abridged accounts once you get above the small company threshold (in the UK, this is turnover of £10.2 million, gross assets of £5.1 million and an average of 50 employees) and of course, such companies will also require an **audit** to be completed which includes scrutiny of disclosures as well as financial information.

Throughout this chapter, there are examples of **creative accounting** practices that have been designed to manipulate the amounts shown within a set of financial statements, regardless of the entity's size. The same pressures to **manipulate disclosures** will apply. Here are some **examples** of the sorts of disclosures that could be subject to some kind of fraud or irregularity:

- Inconsistencies between the audited accounts and **other information** in the annual report
- Unrealistic assumptions when considering a company's **going concern** status
- Inaccurate information about **directors** and their **remuneration**
- Incomplete disclosure of **contingencies**
- Inadequate levels of detail about a company's **risks**
- Imprecise or incomplete **data** on the company's **operations**

While some of these disclosures will be subject to **audit**, those that are not will usually fall with the scope of **corporate governance** requirements (eg for a **listed entity**) or other **corporate reporting** responsibilities (eg those directly required by **legislation**). It is therefore **very unusual** to see a set of **published financial statements** containing disclosures that would be considered fraudulent or deliberately misleading (whether they were **originally drafted** with sufficient levels of disclosure before they were audited is perhaps of greater interest, but sadly, unlikely to ever be known).

However, there are cases when the information presented by a company within their **audited financial statements** may still **fall short** of the requirements of the law and accounting standards.

Case Study

In 2016, UK retailer **Sports Direct** was investigated twice by the **Financial Reporting Council** (FRC) which at the time was acting as regulator for all accounting, auditing, corporate governance and actuarial matters in the UK (at the time of writing, the FRC is due to be replaced by the Audit, Reporting and Governance Authority (ARGA). Two separate investigations were conducted which focused on different areas of **disclosure** that the FRC felt were not adequately reflected in the company's financial statements even though they had been audited:

- During the year 2014/15, there was **inadequate disclosure of the company's international operations within the strategic report** (this report is a legal requirement for most UK companies)

- During the year 2015/16, there was **inadequate disclosure** within the audited financial statements of a **related party** (a distribution company owned by John Ashley, brother of Sports Direct founder, Mike Ashley) contravening IAS 24 *Related Party Disclosures*.

In each case, the company fully complied with these investigations and **disclosed** their interactions with the FRC in a separate disclosure note within the financial statements for the year 2016/17.

Whether this disclosure gets **read** or not is another story – despite the devastating impact of the credit crunch of 2017 and financial crisis of 2018, many of the **banks** responsible for creating these conditions had openly disclosed the inherent risks from their investment business models in prior years, but these disclosures went unnoticed until it was too late.

The **message** about fraudulent disclosures seems to be that, although there is scope to be **creative** with narrative information in publicly available financial statements, **controls** in place such as **audit** and **regulatory inspection** mean that these are unlikely to be illegal and even if they do breach standards, are still likely to be spotted. However, this does not mean that **stopping them at the source** is any less important – like any other form of creative accounting, the **pressures** that might lead to this type of disclosure being made should be considered.

In 2001, the film *Ocean's Eleven* (Soderbergh, 2001) presented a complicated heist story featuring a criminal out on parole. During an interview at the start of the film to determine whether the criminal would **re-offend** if released, the parole board asked: 'Mr Ocean, what we are trying to find out here is whether there was a reason you committed this crime, or whether there was simply a reason you got caught this time.' Tackling fraudulent disclosures, like any other form of dysfunctional behaviour, requires a **complex** response, including both prevention and cure, to stand any chance of being effective.

5 Pressure from management

We mentioned the term **aggressive earnings management** in a previous section when discussing the manipulation of financial statements as a kind of self-preservation in times of economic downturn. The need to meet certain financial targets does not only apply when things are going badly though: there is always some form of pressure to deliver the best results possible when operating in a competitive environment and managers will be tasked with responding. **Where** does this pressure on management come from and how should a professional accountant under this type of pf pressure **respond**?

5.1 Sources of pressure

Let us consider various different organisations and the **external pressures** they

Listed companies are always under pressure to satisfy their investors, although this may not always be as straightforward as it seems. Shareholders do not always behave in a uniform manner, but often the expectations of **institutional investors** will dominate and lead to a strategy that the company will attempt to pursue: this is likely to be quite ambitious as stock markets are seldom patient, so there is a need to hit whatever growth or performance targets are set or suffer from adverse market reaction.

Non-listed companies may still have significant targets set either by their owners or by other investors, which could include venture-capitalists or financial institutions whose timescales for recouping their investment may create a different kind of pressure.

For **smaller businesses**, without the stock market involved, there may still be the need to service bank loans or other investors' needs.

Pressure may also come from **within** – ambitious **leaders** may decide that their organisation needs to go in a certain direction which includes targets and milestones: if these are not met, the consequences for the organisation and its employees may be significant. **Managers** may also be **incentivised** to achieve certain targets based on profit, revenue or market share in order to get their bonus.

Whatever the source of the pressure, it is likely to be felt throughout the organisation and as the financial statements are simply a representation of the organisation's position and performance in financial terms, the **professional accountant** will feel this pressure too. How will this manifest itself in **ethical** terms?

If a company is able to respond **positively** to this kind of pressure and continues to prosper, surely this will mean that professional accountants are likely to be **busy** but should otherwise not need to make any **difficult choices**? This is probably true, but when successful, it is human nature to want even more, so there may be pressure to **inflate results further** (although we will discuss how this can be used in a more clandestine manner later in this chapter).

Conversely, the organisation may **not be able to respond to this pressure** and the company **may not deliver results as expected**. The company's **going concern status** may even be in jeopardy as a result of pursuing a strategy that is inappropriate. Consequently, an **ethical dilemma** exists for the professional accountant:

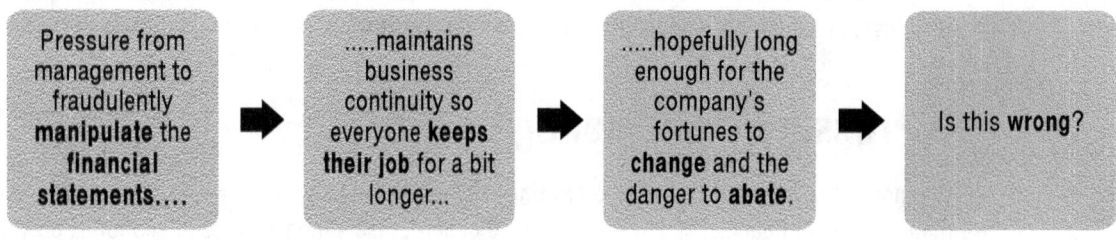

5.2 How to respond to this pressure

Clearly, to allow the publication of misleading financial information, even for the right reasons, goes against the public interest and **should not be considered** as a suitable response to the pressures encountered. Under most **corporate governance** codes, disclosure of the company's ability to continue as a **going concern** is one of the **board's key responsibilities**. Under ISA (UK) 570 (Revised June 2016) *Going Concern*, **external auditors** are also expected to robustly challenge any assertions made by directors regarding their assessment of the company's going concern status, so professional accountants should definitely **not** become involved with any measures to prolong the existence of their employing organisation inappropriately.

What about situations when the company's survival is **not in any immediate danger**, but a professional accountant is still **under pressure to manipulate the financial statements** in some way (either to meet or exceed expectations)? Clearly, the same message applies as before: it is **wrong** to deliberately manipulate the accounts of an organisation via any form of creative accounting as it goes against all **ethical guidelines** and our overall duty to serve the **public interest**.

Fortunately, this is also on the regulator's radar. We have already discussed **fraud** in general terms: however, **ISA (UK) 240** is helpful when it comes to considering how the **external auditor** should identify **evidence** of **pressure from management to manipulate the financial statements**:

- **Those charged with governance** (effectively directors) are responsible for oversight of the **controls** in place in their organisation regarding financial reporting, including an awareness of '...efforts by management to **manage earnings** in order to **influence the perceptions of analysts as to the entity's performance and profitability**' (ISA (UK) 240 (revised): para 4).

- **Auditors** are also responsible for determining the risk of material fraud in the financial statements and responding accordingly, including making an assessment of **accounting policies** that could relate to anything **subjective** or **complex** which may be an indication of **management's attempts to manage earnings** (ISA (UK) 240 (revised): para 29b).

The pressure to achieve and exceed ambitious targets is part of the **entrepreneurial spirit** that underpins all companies – the role of the professional accountant is not only to **record success or otherwise** in the achievement of these targets but also to **counsel those in senior positions** when that pressure becomes too much.

Question — Sources of pressure on professional accountant

Required

List three sources of pressure that a professional accountant may experience.

Answer

1. Pressure from investors to report artificial results
2. Pressure from management to manipulate the financial statements
3. Pressure from the professional accountant themselves to distort the truth for what they feel are the right reasons

Clearly this list could include many other sources of pressure – consider why your list may be different to this one and how your context might be unique compared with other professional accountants.

The IESBA *Code* discusses the possible intimidation that a professional accountant may face when under pressure to breach the fundamental ethical principles. They may consider factors such as the intentions of the person creating this pressure, the culture of the organisation that allows it to occur and any policies or procedures that are present in an organisation to address such pressure (IESBA *Code:* section 270).

6 Omission of financial records

There is a famous philosophical question that is posed by academics to try and understand the nature of existence and perception:

> 'If a tree falls in the middle of a forest and nobody is there to hear it, does it make any sound?'

The recurring theme of this chapter is the **temptation to manipulate financial statements** and the ethical choices faced by professional accountants in a variety of situations. Can an organisation present any position and performance it likes if it chooses to **ignore** any evidence that supports a different set of results? If the organisation **destroys** all of the evidence regarding a fraud, **is it actually a fraud and did any fraud take place**?

If we are having a **philosophical discussion**, the impact of the fraud on the financial statements (such as inflated revenues) is surely the evidence that points to its existence, so no further evidence is required and the fraud has occurred, because the financial statements would otherwise reflect events as they were without the fraud.

However, before we get ourselves tied up in knots, let's get back to the **ethics** of this – clearly, any kind of manipulation is **wrong**! What this is highlighting is the fact that accidental or deliberate omission of financial records can have a significant effect on the financial statements and ensuring the **completeness** of these records is one of the professional accountant's key duties.

One of the main types of activity that an **external auditor** will perform is **substantive testing** – ISA 330 *The Auditor's Responses to Assessed Risks* defines this as '…an audit procedure designed to detect material misstatements at the assertion level' (FRC, 2017: para. 4a). **Assertions** are the characteristics that items in the financial statements must possess in order to belong there – they include the following:

Completeness – events/transactions and assets/liabilities are not understated
Existence – assets and liabilities are not overstated
Occurrence – events and transactions are not overstated
Cut off – items have been recorded in the appropriate accounting period
Accuracy, valuation and allocation – assets or liabilities are recorded at the appropriate amount
Accuracy – a precise record of the amount recorded for an event or transaction
Classification – events/transactions and assets/liabilities are recorded in the proper accounts
Rights and obligations – any rights or obligations in respect of assets/liabilities are included
Presentation – all events/transactions and assets/liabilities are appropriately aggregated or disaggregated, clearly described and all related disclosures are relevant and understandable

(ISA (UK) 315: para. A129)

If the auditor cannot find evidence that supports any of these assertions when testing items in the financial statements, there will need to be a discussion about whether that item can still be included.

It is possible that incriminating evidence of **fraud** has not been kept – however, whether deliberate or accidental, if evidence **cannot be found** as part of an audit, it suggests either that:

1 The item **never existed/occurred** in the first place; or
2 It did exist/occur, but because it cannot be substantiated, it **cannot be included in the financial statements**.

5: ETHICS AND THE PROFESSIONAL ACCOUNTANT

Question: Omission of financial records

Required

Consider the nine assertions discussed above. Which of them will be most relevant in determining whether or not any financial records have been omitted?

Answer

Taking this in the context of an audit, there are two angles that an auditor might take when considering omission of financial records:

1. Completeness – ensuring that legitimate assets, liabilities and transactions are reflected in the financial statements (in other words, there is a record of these items in the financial statements)

2. Existence – ensuring that if an asset or a liability is included in the financial statements, it can be traced back to some form of source evidence that proves its existence (which means that if financial records relating to these assets or liabilities have been omitted, they have been overstated in the financial statements)

3. Occurrence – this is the equivalent of existence for transactions – if source evidence cannot be found, then it is possible the transaction never occurred and it too has been overstated in the financial statements

Other assertions would clarify the timing, value, classification and even ownership of items carried in the financial statements, but without evidence of either over- or under-statement the item may not appear at all.

7 Timing differences

Earlier in this chapter we discussed **revenue recognition** as a form of creative accounting and one example of this was **recognising too much income** towards the end of the year and then **posting credit notes** against this income in the next financial year. Although this will lead to a zero net effect, it does create an **imbalance** as it is recorded and presented over two accounting periods, meaning that revenue in the first year is inflated, but revenue in the next year is reduced.

In theory, if the amounts added are **consistent**, over time the effect will **cancel itself out** as credits at the start of the year will be balanced out by inflated revenues at the end of the year. It therefore begs the question **why** a professional accountant would use this as a technique for creative accounting if it was not expected to be repeated. The following **diagram** illustrates how this could work:

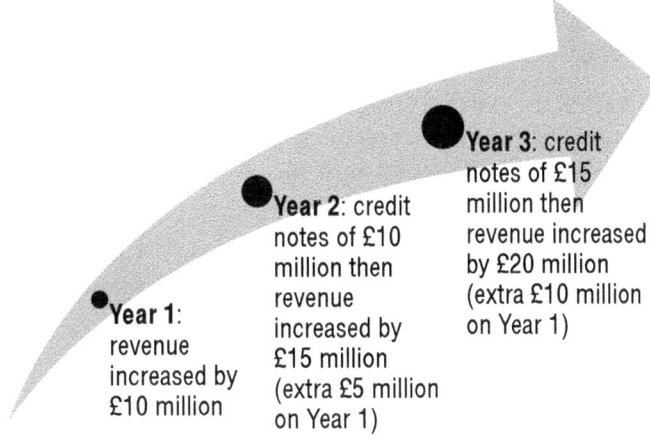

To be **effective** as a way of **consistently recording over-performance** year on year, the temporary revenue increases in each subsequent year must therefore be **bigger than in previous years**. However, unless matched in some way by an improvement in the company's actual sales activity, this approach will eventually lead to a situation where the net extra amounts of revenue recognised cannot be smoothed out and the company's **going concern status** could be under threat because, the company's financial information is so misleading, it is hard to understand where the company is actually going.

Sometimes using timing differences to one's own advantage can be **perfectly legitimate**: maintaining a program of delaying certain payments and requesting other forms of receipt earlier than required can make a company's cash balance look more healthy at a specific point in time. Other **less acceptable** examples of timing differences include manipulating the accounting treatment of certain **costs** by recognising them in different accounting periods, using **inappropriate tax bases** for depreciation of non-current assets and inappropriately adjusting the **exchange rates** used to account for overseas transactions.

Again, while some of these practices sound **unbelievable,** it does not mean they have not been tried: remember that in times of **economic hardship**, the creativity of accountants knows no limits, making it important to have **visibility** so they can be stopped **at source**.

The alternative to **prevention** is **cure** – external auditors are expected to review all material amounts when they perform tests on the financial statements, meaning that unusual transactions without any business justification should be **identified** and **questioned**. Although the quality of external auditing is a very topical issue right now, professional accountants in practice are expected to demonstrate **professional scepticism** when presented with consistently strong performance and should therefore **challenge** the companies they audit to **justify** the inclusion of anything creative.

Case Study

A famous example of manipulating transactions to exploit timing differences around reporting dates emerged in 2008 when Lehman Brothers, one of the largest investment banks in the US, filed for bankruptcy despite regularly reporting healthy financial statements. The cause of their demise was a chronic lack of liquidity from borrowing too much money to invest in property-based financial assets that were almost worthless.

In the months that followed Lehman's closure, it emerged that there had been significant financing problems for some time, but that these had been masked by creative accounting practices known as Repo-105. Under this approach, significant sales of financial instruments were recorded towards the end of each quarter and then bought back again at the start of the next, creating an artificially inflated view of the company's position and performance.

This use of Repo 105 was referred to as an example of what is known as window-dressing. However, the losses and debts eventually attributed to Lehman Brothers were in terms of hundreds of billions of US dollars, suggesting that this Repo 105 activity had been extremely successful at masking the company's true position and performance and had gone beyond the traditional view of window-dressing as a subtle way of improving a company's prospects.

In the aftermath of the events at Lehman Brothers, regulators and other stakeholders have consistently called for more visibility over the risks being taken by companies such as Lehman Brothers who are trusted to look after other people's money. However, in its Annual Economic Report of 2018, the Bank for International Settlements cited evidence suggesting that ten years after the events of Lehman Brothers, window-dressing activity using practices similar to Repo 105 is increasing.

Question — Creative accounting

Earlier in this section, it was suggested that prevention and cure are two ways of addressing the manipulation of timing differences for creative accounting.

Required

State one example for each of prevention and cure that could be used to address creative accounting in this context.

Answer

The manipulation of financial statements via timing differences could be reduced by any of the following techniques:

- **Prevention** via education of professional accountants, accounting standards and codes of ethics that discourage this type of behaviour
- **Cure** via the work of internal audit and other forms of internal control, external audits and the scrutiny of audit committees and other stakeholders

8 Concealed liabilities and expenses

8.1 A history lesson

Within this chapter, we have regularly gone back to **famous examples from history** where a certain combination of professional accountant and professional ethics has not ended well. What does this mean for our profession?

This is **good** because there are no more recent examples of this type of unethical behaviour and it soon becomes ancient history

This is **bad** because we need to keep on reminding ourselves of what can happen if we continue making the same mistakes

Sadly, there are still examples from the 21st Century where professional accountants have made the **wrong choices** for their employers and themselves so, unfortunately, it is the latter of these two suggestions.

Carillion plc (2018)
The UK construction and business services firm collapsed after it emerged that despite appearing to be financially viable, it had actually made significant losses on some of its contracts and could no longer service its debts.

Patisserie Valerie (2018)
Irregularities in the UK cafe chain's financial affairs emerged to the surprise of everyone (including its owners) including hidden overdrafts and overstated cash balances. Many branches were closed as the company was radically restructured.

Thomas Cook (2019)
The UK travel agent suddenly collapsed as it could no longer support its costly infrastructure of shops and airlines in the face of online competition. Coupled with debts it could not manage, the company failed to plan ahead for the changing world around it.

This section is looking at the practice of concealing liabilities and expenses – without **full recognition** of these items, financial statements will respectively **understate a company's obligations** and **overstate its profits**, leading to a gross misstatement of its position and performance. In the cases outlined above, the **surprise** and **shock** from finding out the true state of the company's affairs was a common thread, leading to accusations that the professional accountants involved in each case (both **preparing** and **auditing** the financial statements) **failed in their duty to act in the public interest** by holding on as long as they could before it was too late.

8.2 Big bath accounting

Key term

> **Taking a big bath** relates to a one-off adjustment put through the financial statements.

The required **accounting treatment** for a big bath will probably be a **provision** that does the following:

- DEBIT expenses
- CREDIT reserves

Taking a big bath will usually happen in either a **very good year** (so nobody will really notice it compared with the rest of the company's excellent results) or a **very bad year** (burying the cost so it gets lost among the rest of the bad news) and involves the creation of a **provision** which in reality has no function and supports no future liability other than to attempt to **distort** the company's true position and performance. The company can then release some or all of this provision in subsequent years whenever it suits by reversing the original accounting treatment in part or full, perhaps as a bail-out if making **losses** or used by management to **manipulate profits** in order to satisfy the terms of a **profit-related bonus**.

Assuming that the **professional accountant** involved in undertaking this activity **for a company** has made a **poor choice** when presented with this opportunity, the **external auditor** should still be alert to this form of creative accounting from following the various **standards** that should be applied during the external audit process:

- **IAS 37** *Provisions, Contingent Liabilities and Contingent Assets* states that a provision should only be recognised in certain situations (effectively a probable and measurable liability that relates to an entity) so any material attempts to take a big bath should be spotted and challenged by the auditor if they are doing their job properly (IFRS Foundation, IAS 37: para 10).

- **Professional scepticism**. As part of their responsibilities, external auditors are expected to review journal entries that could indicate some form of **fraud**, for example round sum entries with no business rationale that are posted to unusual accounts by staff who do not normally post journals (FRC, ISA (UK) 240: para. A43).

As we have seen elsewhere in this chapter, **prevention** is better than **cure**, but the cure should be enough to stop this spreading.

Question: Elements of financial statements

Consider the various elements that make up a typical set of financial statements.

Required

From your list, select two liabilities and two expense items and explain how they could be concealed from the financial statements and the consequences of doing this.

Answer

There are many possibilities, but here are some examples of what might happen if liabilities and expenses were concealed, and the consequences of doing this:

Liabilities	
Allowances for trade receivables	This is often a judgement made by management and will consider the collectability of sales made on credit. As the double entry for this is DEBIT expense CREDIT liability, reducing this allowance will affect expenses too. Liquidity ratios will be healthier as a result of this manipulation due to a lower denominator in the equation but ultimately non-payment of debts will catch up with a company if it runs out of cash.
Warranty provisions	Management should estimate the likely costs it will incur if it makes a commitment to either repair or replace any faulty goods or services within certain parameters (whether management provides the right amounts to meet these commitments is again up for discussion though and if warranty provisions are insufficient, it could lead to additional unexpected repair costs which will affect cash flow and/or reputation in the future)
Provisions for inventory write-downs	Inventory is supposed to be held at the lower of cost and net realisable value: for a write-down to be necessary, management will need to assess when inventory has been impaired in some way (such as obsolescence or damage) but might still choose to manipulate this amount downwards so liquidity ratios are not adversely affected by a drop in inventory amounts. This will become an issue when the company has too much inventory that it cannot sell and needs to buy more in order to maintain longer-term profitability.
Onerous lease commitments	This should be a simple case of reviewing the terms of any contracts relating to assets that still have lease payments to be made but which are not helping the business to generate suitable revenues. These may result in accounting treatment that differs from viable leases due to being considered fixed and thus ignored. Again, the cash outflow will still need to be serviced.
Bank loans and overdrafts	Misclassification of loans between current and non-current can lead to better liquidity ratios and will not affect cash flows, apart from servicing the loans and any associated bank covenants. This may provide an incomplete picture of liquidity.
Accruals	These will be another case where the double entry assists in the manipulation of both liabilities and expenses. Understating the amounts expensed will increase the provision and increase profits, but when the actual amount is due (such as a telephone bill) there may not be enough visibility of the cash required and insufficient funds may be available.

Expenses	
Corporation tax	This could appear as both an expense and a liability – given the complexity of how tax is calculated, manipulation of this is possible (although any inability to pay such tax is unlikely to be greeted favourably by the relevant authority and could lead to penalties and fines, further affecting cash flow and reputation).
Finance or depreciation charges	Frequently, the reported profit figure for a company might be EBITDA (earnings before interest, tax, depreciation and amortisation) to allow operational performance to be assessed. If expenses were misclassified as interest charges or depreciation, they could be excluded from EBITDA and a better view of the company could be reported (depreciation will be covered later in this chapter).
Amortisation of development costs	As well as the EBITDA issue discussed above, deciding on the amount of development cost that is to be recognised as an expense compared with the amount that is to be capitalised and then amortised has always been an area that is prone to manipulation, leading to misstatement in the financial statements and possible overstatement of non-current assets plus understatement of expenses.

If you struggled to find expenses such as these, it is understandable – provisions relate to probable future outflows, while expenses are more immediate and are more likely to be missed if they are not included in the financial statements. It is also likely that in each case, concealment means understatement as opposed to omission.

Case Study

It is now over 20 years old, but the story of **Enron** needs to be told here. Enron was one of the most successful companies in US corporate history, providing a variety of energy services to millions of customers and then soon adding energy trading to its portfolio of activities. Despite regularly posting profits year on year, in 2001 it emerged that the company had actually been making significant losses in its underlying operating activity, with all the losses and associated debts contained in obscure group companies that were not fully consolidated into the published group accounts, meaning the visible parts of the group looked far more healthy and profitable than the group's true position and performance. It left an enormous hole in the US economy, affecting the following stakeholders:

- Current employees who lost their job
- Former employees who lost their pensions
- Suppliers who lost business
- Customers who lost their energy supply
- Shareholders who lost their investment

The collapse of Enron eventually led to the demise of their external auditors, Arthur Andersen, for their part in perpetuating the myth that the company was doing well. It also led to criminal prosecutions and convictions for a number of high profile board members, the creation of the Sarbanes-Oxley Act in 2002 to police US corporate governance and even the release of a film called 'Enron: The Smartest Guys in the Room' in 2005 (so-called because the board members of Enron apparently believed that at its peak, whichever room they walked into, anywhere in the world, they would be the smartest guys in that room).

The Enron story still resonates today because of the sheer scale and audacity of the financial statement manipulation that occurred – although we are covering it in the context of concealed liabilities and expenses, it could apply to virtually any of the ethical dimensions we have discussed in this chapter.

9 Asset valuation

Although we have covered a number of areas of **creative accounting**, there are always going to be new ways for professional accountants to be tested in relation to their ethics. Here we will look at how various categories of **asset** could be **misrepresented** in a statement of financial position.

9.1 Non-current assets

You should be familiar with the various categories of tangible and intangible non-current assets that an organisation could present within its financial statements. In most cases, there will be a desire to show the values of **tangible non-current assets** such as land and buildings at the highest cost possible (although any change in an asset's carrying value can affect **depreciation** amounts, so adjusting the value of depreciated assets **downwards** is possible). The company could also decide that it wants to benefit from a more **targeted** approach and consider **selective revaluation** of some but not all of its tangible non-current assets.

However, the **accounting standards** in place do not allow this – for example, **IAS 16** *Property, Plant and Equipment* (IASB, 2003) contains guidance on how assets should be recognised, measured and disclosed:

- There are strict **criteria** on what can be recognised as an asset.
- **Cost** or **revaluation** can be used as a basis for measurement, but the latter must be applied consistently.
- **Depreciation** amounts must take account of an **asset's life**, which can vary over time.

Provided that any professional accountant involved in the creation of a set of audited financial statements is aware of the standards, inaccuracies in asset valuation should not occur.

For **intangible assets**, there is more scope for uncertainty over their valuation, mainly due to their complexity and subjectivity. **IAS 38** *Intangible Assets* (IASB, 2004) illustrates the variety of asset that could apply here – for example:

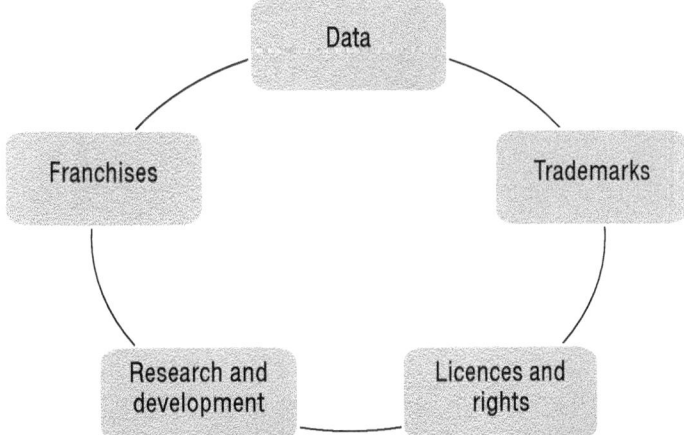

By their very nature, intangibles are at risk of being misstated, either **deliberately** or as the result of an **honest mistake**, usually due to some combination of complexity or subjectivity. For example:

- **Data** assets might include lists of important customers and their characteristics, such as those collected by a supermarket from its loyalty card, or even intellectual property for publishing companies or universities.
- **Trademarks, licences, rights** and **franchises** all have commercial aspects to them, where each could provide some form of benefit to the holder and as such has some kind of value - however, the initial recognition and ongoing monitoring of this value is also challenging (eg should the holder of a licence to operate in certain location **suddenly become the only entity to possess such a licence**, this will clearly have an impact on the value of holding that licence).

- **Research and development** bring a number of accounting challenges that auditors are usually alert to - creating a development asset means that any attributable expenditure can be **capitalised** and not expensed, meaning that **profit** is affected by the decision to capitalise on this development expenditure. This can only take place though if the criteria laid down in IAS 38 are met (such as the item under development being technically feasible, likely to be sold and having sufficient resource available to allow it to be completed). Unless challenged, an entity might treat research costs inappropriately in order to improve their performance and position.

Looking at this selection, it is clear that accounting for any kind of intangible asset brings a **risk of misstatement** which could be **material** for a set of financial statements, so at the very least, the fundamental ethical principle of **professional competence and due care** applies here, even before we come to any areas where the professional accountant could be tempted to manipulate anything.

9.2 Inventory

When it comes to the valuation of inventory, in practice, this is usually calculated as a product of **two factors**, both of which could be manipulated.

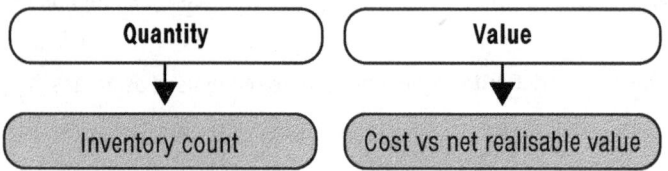

Although it may sound like a very routine process, an **inventory count** can still present problems, especially for organisations that have **significant numbers** of **different product lines** in **multiple locations** (some of which they do not own but look after for **third parties**). Leaving aside the risk of accidental errors in assessing quantity, inventory counts can also be manipulated to include **fictitious items**, either by creating inventory that does not exist or inflating the amounts of existing inventory (including overstating the values of inventory that is clearly **damaged** or **obsolete**).

Controls over inventory counts should be assessed by **external auditors** to provide assurance that the **quantity** of assets recorded and an overall view of their **condition** is reasonable when performing their audit procedures. However, **professional scepticism** should always be displayed when assessing the arrangements in place at an inventory count.

 Case Study

In 2009, three senior employees of a Welsh slate mine were convicted of fraudulently inflating the company's performance. In addition to supplying fictitious documentation to support their story, they also misled auditors during the inventory count by showing them a warehouse that contained numerous boxes of slates. The auditors only inspected those boxes that were easiest to access – however, a significant number of boxes that were not so accessible were in fact empty but the auditors recorded them as being full. This allowed the subterfuge to continue by creating an inventory quantity that supported the fictitious position supplied by the company (North Wales Live, 24 September 2009).

Once quantity is established, **value** needs to be determined. This can be manipulated using either **fictitious cost records** or **adjusting** the **net realisable value** by making unrealistic assumptions about the likely market value of inventory, thus helping to create an amount that is more in line with the figure that the company wishes to see in the financial statements. What can be more difficult is the valuation of **work in progress (WIP)** which can be **subjective** when you consider the elements that it consists of:

- **Labour** – it can be hard to allocate individual payroll costs to a specific product or contract unless there is some kind of costing system (however, this might still require some form of judgement, so fraud and/or error are still possible)

- **Materials** – as with labour, unless there is a costing system, this can include allocation errors
- **Overheads** – organisations usually struggle to allocate overheads whatever they are doing

It is worth pointing out that allocating existing costs across various items of WIP will not change the **overall amount of money spent by a company** as part of its operations, but the **manipulation of WIP** can affect how **cost of sales** is calculated, which clearly does have a **profit impact**.

9.3 Receivables

We discussed the manipulation of **allowances for trade receivables** in a previous section. Related to this is the possibility that trade receivables may be manipulated by **overstating** them in order to **increase current assets** and improve a company's **liquidity ratio**: however, as the double entry to this is the creation of additional revenues, this also falls under the remit of **creative accounting** and **revenue recognition**. Artificially inflated revenues may lead to larger receivables amounts which can be written off in subsequent years as required.

9.4 Cash and other forms of investment

A **bank statement** or **share certificate** should be sufficient to satisfy the external auditor that the cash and investments of a company can be **recognised** within the financial statements. The **assertions** that were mentioned in an earlier section would therefore be satisfied by verifying the following:

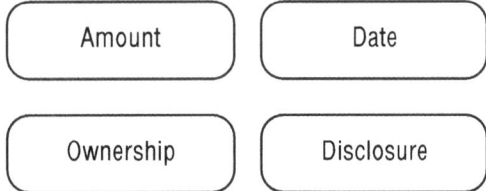

However, what about **existence**? Is it possible that the cash or shares could be a work of fiction to bolster a company experiencing financial difficulties? That would require some kind of **forged documentation** – surely no-one would ever fall for this type of fraud?

Case Study

Italian dairy company **Parmalat** grew from a small family business to become one of the largest companies in Italy, at one point owning Serie A football team, Napoli. In 2003, the company started to experience liquidity issues and soon after it was unable to settle its liabilities, going into administration because it was unable to service significant levels of debt that were approaching €15 billion.

Understandably, questions were asked about how this could have occurred, especially so soon after the Enron scandal from the US in 2001 that prompted calls for immediate action to stop such widespread corporate fraud occurring again. It emerged that the external auditors of one of Parmalat's subsidiaries had been provided with evidence of a Bank of America account which contained €4 billion: the auditors therefore concluded that the company's liquidity was not in jeopardy. As soon as Parmalat started struggling to settle its debts, the evidence supplied to substantiate the Bank of America account was declared a forgery, and the company's finances gradually unravelled. Criminal convictions, lawsuits and regulatory inspections followed – Parmalat is now part of a larger dairy company and to date, it remains Europe's largest ever corporate collapse.

Question: Creative accounting: assets

Consider the following types of asset that could be subject to some form of creative accounting:

Tangible non-current assets	
Intangible non-current assets	
Inventory	
Cash	

Required

From the following picklist of options, match each type of asset with the most appropriate form of creative accounting:

- Manipulating overheads
- Subjective valuation
- Extending the asset's life
- Forged documentation

Answer

Tangible non-current assets	Extending the asset's life (This would reduce depreciation and manipulate profits.)
Intangible non-current assets	Subjective valuation (Often intangibles are complex and subjective.)
Inventory	Manipulating overheads (This would apply if the inventory was work in progress.)
Cash	Forged documentation (Examples include a bank statement or certificate of deposit.)

Chapter roundup

- Professional accountants are very **complex** individuals and although they operate in a very tightly controlled environment, **creative accounting** is a very serious threat that requires strong guidance to ensure they continue to make the right choices.

- There are many sources of **revenue** for a company that all require very specific accounting. It is important that a professional accountant understands the **technical standards** in place to help them create accurate sets of financial statements and is **prepared** for the many **temptations** that could lead to **fraud**.

- Knowing **how much to disclose to the finance director** comes from both operational and ethical dimensions.

- **Fraud** requires certain conditions to thrive – making sure that **disclosures** do not become fraudulent requires both sticks and carrots to prohibit and discourage respectively.

- Professional accountants may be under **pressure from management** to manipulate the financial statements in some way but both preparers and auditors of financial statements can refer to standards to help them respond appropriately.

- **Accounting records** must support the financial statements and need to display certain characteristics to make sure the accounts are true and fair.

- Although there are some legitimate methods that use **timing differences** to help a company prepare its financial statements, it can be very easy to distort the company's true position and professional accountant need to be alert to these.

- There have been plenty of examples of companies in the last 20 years that have been unable to continue under their business model, despite **concealing liabilities and expenses** for some time before their ultimate demise. The lesson here seems to be that such actions will always lead to disaster at some point in the future.

- **Asset valuation** techniques can be used as a way of bolstering a company's financial security but without adherence to accounting standards they are unlikely to prove effective in the long term.

Quick quiz

1. Name two different types of bias that professional accountants might display when assessing ethical situations.
2. Suggest three examples of fraud that relate to revenue recognition.
3. State the three conditions that usually need to be present for fraud to exist.
4. What does the term 'aggressive earnings management' mean?
5. State three examples of financial statement assertions used by auditors during substantive testing.
6. What does the term 'taking a big bath' mean?
7. State two types of asset that can have their value manipulated as part of creative accounting.

Answers to quick quiz

1. Any two from:
   - Anchoring bias
   - Availability bias
   - Selective perception
   - Overconfidence in one's own viewpoint
   - Groupthink

2. Any three from:
   - Inconsistent cut-off dates
   - Inventing revenues
   - Recognising revenue due to third parties
   - Overstated revenues
   - Duplicated revenues
   - Misstated sales taxes

3. The three preconditions for fraud are:
   - Pressure to commit fraud
   - Opportunity being presented
   - Rationalisation as the right thing to do

4. Aggressive earnings management refers to the practice of manipulating financial statements to present performance and/or position that is untrue. This is either to mask poor performance or to make it look even better than it truly is.

5. Any three from the following list:
   - Completeness
   - Existence
   - Occurrence
   - Cut off
   - Accuracy, valuation and allocation
   - Accuracy
   - Classification
   - Rights and obligations
   - Presentation

6. Taking a big bath refers to the practice of creating large unique journal adjustments to create reserves that serve no purpose other than to make funds available in subsequent years for profit manipulation.

7. Any two from:
   - Trade receivables
   - Cash
   - Investments
   - Inventory
   - Tangible non-current assets
   - Intangible assets

Ethics and the professional accountant: Other aspects

Topic list	Syllabus reference
1 Tax planning, avoidance and evasion	LO 3, LO 4
2 Tax avoidance	LO 3, LO 4
3 Whistleblowing	LO 3, LO 4
4 Bribery and corruption, money laundering and financing of terrorism	LO 3, LO 4
5 Public sector accounting	LO 3, LO 4

Introduction

This chapter aims to explore some of the ethical dimensions that arise in connection with aspects of business and public practice relevant to accounting and auditing in the areas of tax, whistleblowing and public sector accounting. There are lots of examples here to illustrate what is a very dynamic series of issues, so you should be prepared to have enough to say in the event of a discursive question appearing in your exam.

1 Tax planning, avoidance and evasion

1.1 Tax planning

There is a saying:

> 'Two things in life are certain – death and taxes.'

In virtually every jurisdiction in the world, there is some form of tax that exists to **address the needs of society** and to **guide behaviour**. For example:

- Tax on the **incomes** of individuals and companies is levied to allow government to spend money on public services such as healthcare and education that benefit society as a whole.
- Tax is levied on **activities** such as smoking, drinking alcohol or even driving a specific type of car to try and limit their use because they are perceived to be harmful in some way.
- Tax can also be used to **encourage** certain activities, such as a government offering tax breaks as an incentive to film companies if they work in their country.

As economies become more sophisticated, the use of tax in both an **economic** and **political capacity** has led to it becoming a very complex area which requires **specialist knowledge** to understand and apply it. Consequently, tax planning has become a **lucrative source of income** for accountants and professional firms for many years.

Key term

> **Tax planning** is the process of legally minimising tax liabilities for individuals or organisations by operating within the tax arrangements currently in place.

This work can range from simply understanding the various elements of taxation that apply in an economy in order to provide **advice**, all the way through to supporting a tax authority (such as Her Majesty's Revenue and Customs (HMRC) in the UK) when a **dispute** over tax liabilities needs to be settled by a tribunal or a trial.

Why does tax planning require coverage in a book about **ethics**, though?

Case Study

The rise in popularity of city breaks has led to an unusual development that illustrates the sort of ethical dilemma that taxation can create. Local government councils in cities such as Edinburgh, Amsterdam and Barcelona, plus national governments in both Japan and New Zealand, consider a tourist tax to be the fairest way of getting visitors to contribute towards the inevitable cost of supporting the demands that tourism brings (such as traffic congestion, healthcare, street cleaning and policing).

However, in an industry that is not always as profitable as it would wish to be, the levy of a tourist tax could backfire and create an unnecessary financial burden on hotels and restaurants which makes them less competitive and could force them out of business, having an adverse effect on economies and the people who rely on them. Who should dominate in this debate – local government or local businesses? Is tax about raising money or moderating behaviour?

Let us consider tax planning and accountants. The IESBA *Code* has different requirements relating to tax depending on the role of the professional accountant.

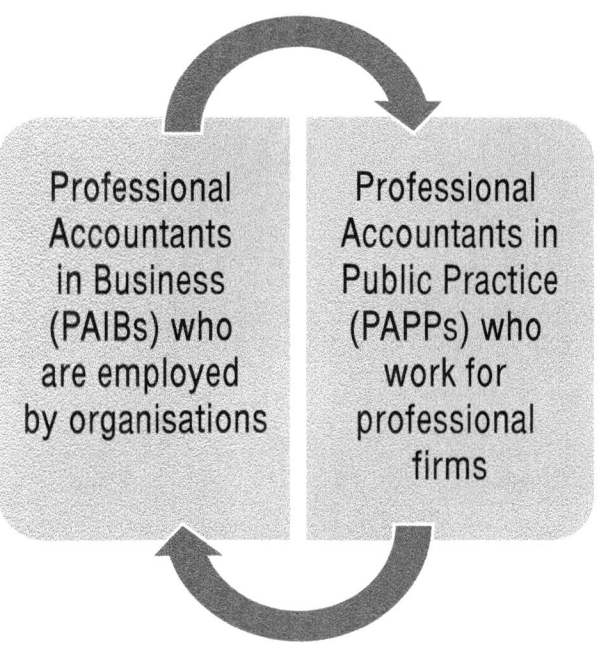

For **PAIBs**, the *Code* requires compliance with the fundamental ethical principles and application of the conceptual framework (ie threats) when preparing returns (such as tax returns) and considering non-compliance with any laws or regulations regarding tax payments and liabilities for their employing organisation.

For **PAPPs**, the *Code* identifies a broad range of tax services that might create threats to compliance with the fundamental ethical principles:

- Tax return preparation
- Tax calculations for preparing accounting entries
- Tax planning and tax advisory services
- Valuations used for taxation
- Assisting in the resolution of tax disputes (IESBA *International Code of Ethics*; para. 604.3 A1)

With the exception of tax return preparation, which is usually a more mechanical process based on historical information requiring little professional judgment, each of these activities creates threats to independence for PAPPs, usually:

- **Self-review** when the firm will audit the output of the tax service; and
- **Advocacy** when promoting the interests of an audit client in a court case or tribunal.

The *Code* requires PAPPs to consider factors such as **materiality**, **subjectivity** and **legal precedent** before deciding whether or not they can deliver tax services to a client. Many tax services can be provided to audit clients that are not **public interest entities (PIEs)** as long as suitable safeguards are applied, such as the use of separate teams to perform the audit and tax work and appropriate review of either the tax service or the audit work. In general, there are fewer tax services that auditors of PIEs can provide but, again, they require consideration before the firm is able to act.

In the UK, the **Revised Ethical Standard** (FRC, 2019) concurs with the IESBA guidance, also stating that tax services can give rise to **self-interest** threats when a firm may benefit from fee income for tax services that could compromise its independence. It also states the need for TCWG of the audited entity to act as **informed management** about the severity of such threats and to ensure the audit firm does not take on any management responsibilities.

However, **further guidance** in the IESBA *Code of Ethics* on **tax planning** is the main reason for its inclusion in this chapter. Both PAIBs and PAPPs are advised to be alert to the threat of clients or employers attempting to **evade** tax. We will discuss **tax evasion** later in this chapter, but there is another term that we need to address which we will look at next.

Question
Taxation uses

Required

List three reasons for the use of taxation within an economy.

Answer

Clearly there could be many different answers to this question, and you can expect something more focused in your exam, but for now, we would expect taxation to exist for three main reasons:

1. To raise revenues for public services
2. To discourage certain behaviours or activities
3. To encourage other behaviours or activities

1.2 Tax avoidance

To help us further understand the reasons why tax planning requires ethical guidance, we must now consider **tax avoidance**, starting with the following definition:

Key term

> **Tax avoidance** is a legal way of reducing tax liabilities for individuals and organisations.

This sounds very much like tax planning – what is the **difference** between tax planning and tax avoidance then?

Tax planning makes use of specialist expertise to examine the way that an individual or organisation operates and exists, in order to identify legal ways to reduce the tax payable to the local tax authority. Earlier, we discussed how economies aim to generate revenues for public services from both personal and corporate taxation. Within the complex tax rules that exist, there are also incentives, allowances and exemptions which encourage legal ways of minimising tax liabilities. For example:

For organisations
- Using corporate structures that create tax savings
- Treating costs as taxable allowances for small entities
- Creating gift aid for charitable organisations

For individuals
- Tax-free personal savings accounts
- Tax relief on pension contributions
- Inheritance tax allowances

Further details on tax planning activities can be found within the materials for the Taxation (UK) paper.

Tax authorities such as HMRC will generally **encourage** the use of certain activities within legitimate tax planning as they are supporting either an **economic** or **political aim** (such encouraging an individual to set aside cash for their pension, as it reduces the likely impact on public services when that individual is too old to work).

If tax planning is encouraged by HMRC, what about **tax avoidance**? Usually this is **actively challenged**, although it is still **technically legal** - however, it is perhaps best considered as not being **in the spirit** of what the law is set up to try and achieve. There is a phrase that has often been used by politicians and journalists which states:

> 'Tax is the price we pay for a civilised society.'

Whether forced to pay taxes or merely encouraged, the statement implies that paying tax is a **fair trade** for living in a civilised society, because taxes help to pay for **public services** that benefit everyone and could therefore be considered a **social responsibility**. **Tax planning** allows an **acceptable** amount of tax to be saved by the individual or organisation (in this sense, acceptable to government and society); by contrast, **tax avoidance** allows individuals or organisations to save more tax than either the government or society might wish to be saved.

Avoidance works by seeking out legal ways of reducing tax liabilities even further than the tax laws in place were intended to allow. Going back to the phrase quoted above, the implication is that paying less tax than you should is not in society's best interests and should therefore be discouraged. This is complex and difficult, as methods of legal tax avoidance are not always straightforward to identify, thus requiring the use of the same specialists who are most likely to be employed in **socially** as well as **legally acceptable** tax planning.

We will cover **examples** of techniques used as part of legal tax avoidance later in this section. We will also discuss some **famous cases** where previously unknown tax avoidance schemes have been uncovered, thus closing the legal loopholes that allowed them to exist in the first place. Given the difficulties associated with differentiating between tax planning and tax avoidance, it is at least a little clearer now why it should be seen as an area in need of ethical guidance, especially for professional accountants.

Is **tax evasion** the same as tax avoidance? In short, no – they are **fundamentally different**.

1.3 Tax evasion

What is tax evasion then?

Key term

> **Tax evasion** is reducing tax liabilities for individuals and organisations by illegal means.

For this to be separate to both tax planning and tax avoidance, there will be **no grey areas about the methods used**: they will be illegal and require fraud, theft and false accounting in order to operate. Examples of the type of activity that could be considered tax evasion are as follows:

- **Recording lower revenues** than the organisation actually receives (in the same vein, creating artificial costs that have not been incurred) both of which aim to **artificially reduce taxable profits**

- **Hiding the existence and activity of business operations to avoid paying taxes** on their proceeds (eg only using cash, which is hard to keep track of)

- Treating personal expenses in the same way as business expenses with the aim of **reducing an individual's personal tax liability**

Case Study

One of the most famous cases of tax evasion is that of US mafia boss, Al Capone. Despite being considered by many to be responsible for many deaths in the 1920s and 1930s across Chicago and other parts of the US, he was eventually convicted for tax evasion in 1931 and spent over seven years in various prisons, including the infamous island penitentiary of Alcatraz. The court ruled that he was liable for $215,000 plus interest in back taxes (the equivalent of over $3.5 million in today's money).

Question — Tax evasion

Required

For each of the following descriptions, select the most appropriate term from the picklist below.

Illegal methods of paying less tax	
Legal methods of paying less tax	
Socially acceptable methods of paying less tax	

Picklist
- Tax planning
- Tax avoidance
- Tax evasion

Answer

Illegal methods of paying less tax	Tax evasion (this is clear and obvious)
Legal methods of paying less tax	Tax avoidance (this could also refer to tax planning)
Socially acceptable methods of paying less tax	Tax planning (planning is also legal, but is more socially acceptable than avoidance, so is more relevant here)

2 Tax avoidance

In this section, we will take a closer look at some of the highest profile and most common examples of tax avoidance in recent years.

2.1 Companies

Case Study

During 2012, the **UK Public Accounts Committee**, consisting of members of parliament from different political parties, interviewed representatives from **Google**, **Starbucks** and **Amazon** amid accusations that, although each company was considered very successful in financial terms, the tax liabilities owed to HMRC from their UK operations were negligible.

It emerged that in each case, a combination of **multinational corporate structures** and **imaginative transfer pricing** between them had led to profits only being taxable in jurisdictions like the Republic of Ireland, the Netherlands and Luxembourg where the corporate rates of tax levied were much lower than in

the UK. There was no suggestion that any of this was illegal, but the chosen tax arrangements for each of these companies was considered immoral.

At around the same time, separate investigations alleged that **eBay**, **Facebook** and **Apple** had also used similar tax avoidance strategies to manage their UK tax liabilities.

Similar accusations continue to be levelled at these and other global organisations, leading to a widespread call for consumers to boycott each company. The **reputation** of each of these entities has understandably been affected: some have chosen to voluntarily pay more tax, such as Starbucks, but this has been seen by some observers as merely an empty gesture designed to placate angry customers.

Even as recently as 2019, stories continue to emerge of large organisations being able to pay no corporate tax in the UK: oil company **Royal Dutch Shell** took advantage of complicated oil rig decommissioning arrangements to pay no tax on pre-tax profits of £731 million (source: FT.com, 2019)

2.2 Individuals

Tax avoidance is not just the preserve of large companies. Individuals can also pay experts who advise them how to protect their wealth by entering into complex arrangements where small companies are used as a way of receiving revenues earned by an individual who can then access funds without being subject to traditional employment taxes. Using **incorporation** in this way is not unusual, but the extent and complexity of the arrangements used in each case has turned them into front page news from time to time.

Former UK prime minister **David Cameron**, comedian **Jimmy Carr** and musician **Gary Barlow** have all been accused of benefiting from offshore tax avoidance schemes which, while not illegal, are considered unethical and in the case of David Cameron, politically embarrassing as well, because as UK prime minister, he was simultaneously attempting to direct the anti-avoidance debate in the UK to boost tax revenues in a country ravaged by the effects of the financial crisis of 2008.

Sports stars have not been exempt from scrutiny when it comes to their tax affairs either. In 2019, English rugby union club **Saracens** were fined £5.36 million and given a 35 league point deduction for a breach of the rules associated with salary caps. This related to the use of what appeared to be tax avoidance schemes by some of the club's highest earners relating to property usage and image rights income, which allowed them to enjoy good salaries without being limited by a cap which attempted to limit the amounts paid to players across all clubs in the same competition. While not illegal, it was seen by many as unfair (coining the phrase 'financial doping') and certainly not in the spirit of fair play, both on or off the field. Since these events, the club was told it would be relegated at the end of the 2019/20 season as further punishment for non-compliance with the salary cap rules.

There have been stories of other sports stars being investigated for their personal tax arrangements – for example, in 2017, Argentina and Barcelona footballer **Lionel Messi** was convicted in Spain of a €4 million tax fraud regarding non-payment of tax on his image rights income. As is the case in Spain with prison sentences of less than two years, Messi was allowed to serve it under probation terms instead of behind bars. Although this is an example of **tax evasion**, it does show the extent of the problem faced by law makers across the world when attempting to clamp down on such practices – despite this conviction, Messi continues to be seen as role model, winning the prestigious ballon d'or award in 2019 for his footballing achievements.

2.3 Dealing with tax avoidance

There is an argument that tax avoidance is merely the **reward for innovation**, but this is not socially acceptable: the perception across the world is that not enough is done to address tax avoidance – a common thread running through all these stories is that avoidance is often perceived to be the preserve of the **wealthy** who can afford to pay for the best tax expertise, while the majority of people cannot afford such advice and therefore still have to pay tax without the opportunity to enjoy any of this innovation.

The **UK Government** has pledged to take action on anti-avoidance and in 2019 published its approach towards tackling tax avoidance, evasion and other forms of non-compliance. The following table summarises the steps currently in place in the UK.

Making tax easier to deal with by adopting digital technology to manage tax liabilities and payments
Targeting non-compliance in an appropriate manner (ie prioritising the highest areas of missing tax)
Focusing on wealthy tax payers, especially those whose residency status is in question
Actively shutting down organisations and individuals that offer tax avoidance services to clients
Pursuing opportunities where tax is not currently collected, such as online marketplaces
Actively targeting off-shore tax arrangements, such as the Paradise and Panama papers
Greater scrutiny of cross-border tax arrangements (such as those used by Google, Amazon and Starbucks)
Pursuing the hidden economy (ie the cash economy)
Targeting organised crime via anti-money laundering measures

However, despite all this, many observers still consider that not enough is being done to address the problem. Part of the reason for this may be the fact that so many tax avoidance schemes are not confined to UK shores, meaning the fight is now waged **across international borders** and requires greater co-operation between nations to stand any chance of succeeding.

Case Study

In November 2019, the European Union (EU) Code of Conduct Group (Business Taxation) published an updated list of what they refer to as non-cooperative jurisdictions for tax purposes, alongside a longer list of those jurisdictions that have committed to cooperate with the EU by implementing good tax governance principles in the areas such as transparency and fair taxation. The eight countries that were listed as non-cooperative jurisdictions were as follows:

- American Samoa
- Fiji
- Guam
- Oman
- Samoa
- Trinidad and Tobago
- US Virgin Islands
- Vanuatu

Clearly, this process of naming and shaming is designed to put pressure on jurisdictions where tax avoidance is still encouraged and it is likely that over time, this list will get even shorter.

More radical suggestions for international efforts to reduce tax avoidance have led to ideas such as having a **single or unitary system of taxation** in place across the world. While this is both logical and ideological, sadly it is probably also very impractical:

- Whose system should be adopted?
- Would everyone accept the adopted system?
- Who would regulate and monitor this new system?
- How would the new system stay aligned in the face of inevitable political and economic change?

Consequently, such a suggestion is unlikely to ever succeed. Tax is not just an **economic issue**: it is a **political issue** due to the **behavioural elements** that tax is meant to address, encouraging some activities and discouraging others, meaning **cultural** as well as legal and economic alignment would be necessary for such an idea to stand a chance of working.

Instead of targeting individuals, there have been recent examples of larger countries operating together to **target the conditions that accommodate tax avoidance and evasion** – traditional tax havens such as **Jersey**, **Lichtenstein** and **Luxembourg** are gradually being brought under increasing levels of scrutiny and the opportunities for such schemes to flourish are rapidly diminishing.

Another angle to this could be greater use of publicly **naming and shaming** individuals and organisations who avoid paying what is considered to be their fair share of tax – this is all part of the wider subject of **managing reputation**.

Allied to this is the use of **tax codes of conduct** by various organisations in an attempt to control this before it becomes legally enforceable. Examples of **best practice** include the following organisations:

- **Companies** such as Vodafone
- **Professional firms** such as Pricewaterhouse Coopers
- **Banks** such as Société Générale

Question — Addressing tax avoidance

Consider the country where you live and work. Companies and individuals will all be expected to contribute to society by paying a variety of taxes which can be optimised by means of legal and socially acceptable forms of tax planning. Tax avoidance and tax evasion are socially unacceptable and illegal respectively, but still occur.

Required

Recommend three policies that the government in your country should consider adopting in order to address tax avoidance and tax evasion.

Answer

The answers you provide will obviously be connected to where you currently live and work, so it is possible you may prioritise avoidance over evasion or vice versa. Current practices may also vary across different jurisdictions as well. However, here are some suggestions for dealing with each type of activity.

Tax avoidance	Tax evasion
Social media communications to encourage tax planning without the need for tax avoidance	More resource allocated to identifying and stopping instances of tax evasion
Greater scrutiny of existing legislation to remove as many loopholes as possible	Greater penalties for experts who are found to have assisted in tax evasion
Simplification of taxation to make avoidance less attractive	Stronger penalties for those convicted of tax evasion offences
Greater financial incentives for the use of socially acceptable tax planning	Encouraging those who actively evade tax to participate in something more socially acceptable
Pressure on professional institutes to further discourage their members from helping with tax avoidance schemes	Greater publicity for those convicted of tax evasion to discourage others from following the same path as them

You may favour one type of approach over another (such as the prioritisation of 'sticks' over 'carrots') but governments have to consider a wide range of ideas, which shows that formulating policy is not straightforward.

2.4 The future of tax

There is currently a **debate** among experts that exists in the space between two worlds that are very relevant to you as an accountant in the 21st century:

1. Tax
2. Sustainability

Key term

> **Sustainability** was defined in 1987 by what became known as the Brundtland Report as meeting '... the needs of the present without compromising the ability of future generations to meet their own needs.' (World Commission on Environment and Development, 1987)

People continue to thrive on this planet, with estimates of future **global population levels rising** exponentially, placing an inevitable **strain on the world's natural resources** which are essential to sustain this population. We have already seen that tax is used in many economies to **encourage socially acceptable behaviour**. It is easy to tax human activity such as **employment, drinking alcohol** and **smoking cigarettes** because more and more humans exist as each day goes by and this growth is unlikely to be affected by any tax strategies in force, meaning tax revenues continue to be earned by governments without necessarily affecting population growth (indeed, discouraging cigarettes and alcohol would actually increase the pressure on population growth).

The role that tax could play in encouraging environmentally sustainable behaviour is less clear cut. There are **emissions taxes** on vehicles, lower taxes on **cleaner forms of energy and transportation** and **carbon taxes** on companies that create greenhouse gases such as CO_2. However, there are **no taxes** that attempt to manage the amount of **water** of **land** used by companies and some of the **tax allowances** available to companies for their plant and machinery may even be used to **create harmful emissions** (such as the vast amounts of CO_2 created during the manufacture of cement).

What if there was a **rebalancing of the tax system** that attempted to prioritise **targeting resource usage and pollution** and **reward more imaginative uses** of people doing this, creating circular economies that embraced sustainability by focusing on renewable energy, reducing natural resource usage and recycling? There is a perception that many sustainability taxes such as landfill or carbon taxes are **not changing behaviour** and are simply being seen as an **acceptable cost** while pollution levels and resource usage remain broadly unaffected.

Clearly, this and all these other topics are merely scratching the surface of the tax debate and you will need to undertake some **ongoing research** of your own to stay on top of what is going to continue to be one of the key areas for debate by accountants worldwide.

3 Whistleblowing

You may have heard the term 'whistleblowing' used to describe one of the ways in which an accountant could raise an ethical issue that relates to a very specific set of circumstances.

Key term

> **Whistleblowing** is the disclosure by an employee of illegal or unethical practices by their employer.

Employers will have confidentiality and disclosure policies in place; however, protection is also offered to employees, ensuring they cannot be dismissed for disclosing confidential information to an external party such as the appropriate regulator.

Although most high-profile instances of whistleblowing arise where a whistleblower discloses information **externally**, whistleblowing can also be internal. When an employee reports something illegal or unethical within the organisation they work for to someone more senior in that organisation, that represents **internal whistleblowing**.

Legislation exists across the world to protect whistleblowers and to protect, in the public interest, employees who denounce illegal acts and behaviours. Provided that any disclosure they make is in good faith, whistleblowers cannot be sued for making that disclosure (even if it breaches the principle of confidentiality).

Key term

> In the UK, the relevant legislation is the **Public Interest Disclosure Act (1998)** which uses the term 'qualifying disclosure' when describing the matters that are covered by the Act:
>
> - A criminal offence
> - The breach of a legal obligation
> - A miscarriage of justice
> - A danger to the health and safety of any individual
> - Damage to the environment
> - Deliberate concealment of information tending to show any of the above five matters

For the Act to provide **protection** to the whistleblower, these disclosures can only be made to an employer or other responsible person, legal advisor, government official or other prescribed person. In some cases, whistleblowing should be made to an **appropriate authority** (eg to HMRC if an accountant has concerns about fraud, such as tax evasion). If an authority receives information which does not fall within its remit, it should forward that information on to the appropriate authority, together with the identity of the whistleblower. Disclosures are expected to be made in **good faith** and not for the purpose of any form of **personal gain**.

We have already noted that accountants have a responsibility to act in the **public interest** and part of this obligation includes reporting or disclosing unethical behaviour whenever identified. Therefore, it may be necessary for an accountant to act as a whistleblower in order to fulfil their public interest duty.

Information can be provided verbally, in writing, or through any other means. It can be provided by a single individual, or a group of people. However, before whistleblowing externally, the issue of concern should be discussed internally with management. Some large organisations may have an **audit committee** and a **senior independent director** who, among other responsibilities, will help set ethical standards and provide guidance on ethical issues. If such resources are available, they should be consulted. This may resolve the issue.

External whistleblowing should be a last resort option. Before getting to the whistleblowing stage, it is advisable to take third-party advice (eg contacting the AIA or taking legal advice). Remember, the principles of confidentiality and loyalty are important to the profession.

A recent addition to the accountant's lexicon is the term **moral courage** which generally means doing the right thing under considerable pressure when not doing it would be substantially easier. Various codes of ethics around the world are starting to make this more prominent to reflect the perceived **difficulty** that doing the right thing might require.

Case Study

Olympus is a well-established Japanese manufacturer of optical imaging, laboratory and medical equipment. In 2011, it appointed its first ever non-Japanese president, a 30-year company veteran from the UK named Michael Woodford. A few months later, Mr Woodford was also appointed chief executive. In July of that year, his attention was drawn to an article alleging that Olympus had made substantial and secret payments relating to a series of acquisitions. He attempted to find out the truth behind these allegations, but all of his enquiries were blocked by staff and fellow directors.

In October, at an emergency board meeting where Mr Woodford was not allowed to speak or vote, the board unanimously fired him as chief executive. In a press release, the company explained that Mr Woodford's removal was being due to the fact that he had 'largely diverted from the rest of the management team in regard to the management direction and method...'

PART C THE PROFESSIONAL ACCOUNTANT

Mr Woodford turned whistleblower, telling the media about the issue, and calling for the resignation of the entire board. The company denied any problems but, after extensive investigations and involvement of law enforcement authorities around the world, it was discovered that secret payments had been made to cover up losses on investments going back to the 1980s. There were many arrests and resignations. Mr Woodford received a substantial settlement from Olympus and went on to work as a speaker and consultant.

Olympus represented a spectacular failure of both internal controls and ethical standards, with senior management colluding in accounting fraud. In this situation, it was only the ethical principles of a new CEO that brought the issue to light. Most situations are not so extreme, but all organisations face risks and therefore need to find a way to manage these risks. The Olympus scandal cut its stock market valuation by 75-80%. Clearly, the penalty for poor ethics can be severe. Mr Woodford needed to display significant amounts of courage against the Olympus management (and alleged intimidation by Japanese gangsters or 'yakuza'). Organisations should support whistleblowers better than they currently do – research indicates that only 44% of employees will raise an issue at work for fear of reprisal by either management or fellow employees suggesting that companies need to work harder to support whistleblowing as a form of risk management.

BBC News, 2011: https://www.bbc.co.uk/news/business-15330870

Question — Whistleblowing

Required

Which one of the following whistleblowing claims would NOT be considered a qualifying disclosure under the UK Public Interest Disclosure Act (1998)?

- Your manager has stolen money from a colleague's purse.
- Staff have been asked to work overtime when they have completed their daily tasks.
- A director at your firm has ordered a colleague to lie under oath in order to avoid conviction.
- Staff at your firm are being forced to work in locations where there is war and civil unrest.
- You have witnessed staff from your firm knowingly disposing of hazardous materials on public land.

Answer

By definition, the option that does not meet the criteria of a qualifying disclosure is:

- Staff have been asked to work overtime when they have completed their daily tasks.

While not entirely ethical, this is unlikely to result in any of the following definitions because of being asked, not forced, to work overtime (otherwise it may be considered a breach of the employee's legal contract of employment).

Options that would be considered qualifying disclosures are shown in brackets after the relevant criterion:

- A criminal offence (*stealing money from a colleague's purse*)
- The breach of a legal obligation
- A miscarriage of justice (*asking someone to lie under oath for them*)
- A danger to the health and safety of any individual (*being forced to work in dangerous conditions*)
- Damage to the environment (*dumping hazardous materials on public land*)
- Deliberate concealment of information tending to show any of the above five matters

4 Bribery and corruption, money laundering and financing of terrorism

> **FAST FORWARD**
>
> To act as whistleblower is extremely difficult as it often requires the individual to **confront** their employer in some capacity – either an individual in a position of authority or the organisation itself in some capacity.

Accountants are often involved as they are in a position to see the financial implications of operational actions taken by an organisation and its stakeholders; due to their professional status, accountants are also expected to challenge anything they see that contravenes laws and regulations.

We have already discussed a number of actions that accountants could take which could jeopardise their compliance with the various ethical codes in place (see Chapter 5 for more details). This section will look at bribery, money laundering and other forms of corruption, where an accountant may need to act as whistleblower.

4.1 Bribery and corruption

Key term

> **Bribery:** 'Giving someone a financial or other advantage to encourage that person to perform their functions or activities improperly or to reward that person for having already done so' (UK Bribery Act, 2010).

> **FAST FORWARD**
>
> The involvement of directors and others responsible for corporate governance in bribery and corruption can **undermine the relationships of trust** on which corporate governance is based.

The involvement of directors and others responsible for corporate governance in bribery and corruption can **undermine the relationships of trust** on which corporate governance is based.

4.1.1 Bribery

The purpose of **bribery** is to **influence** the conduct of the recipient. A bribe may not be money or a tangible gift: it can be granting a privilege to the recipient; a bribe need not be paid to be effective. Sometimes a promise or undertaking may be sufficient to influence decision making and conduct. As well as the payer and the recipient of the bribe, others may be complicit if they know about the bribe and fail to report it, if they ignore signs that bribery is taking place or if they hold a position of responsibility and fail to take action to prevent bribery. Legislation such as the **UK Bribery Act (2010)** therefore makes commercial organisations liable if their employees pay bribes unless they take adequate procedures to prevent bribery.

For example, an organisation which gives a politician money to get a lucrative government contract job or to influence new government legislation is committing an act of bribery.

The UK Bribery Act creates four categories of offences:

1. Offering, promising or giving a bribe to another person;
2. Requesting or agreeing to receive or accept a bribe from another person;
3. Bribing a foreign public official; and
4. The corporate offence of failing to prevent bribery.

For example, an organisation which gives a politician money to get a lucrative government contract job or to influence new government legislation is committing an act of bribery.

An organisation will commit this offence if an 'associated person' performing services on its behalf bribes another person to obtain or retain business or gain a business advantage.

The penalties for a violation can be severe. The maximum penalty for individuals will be ten years imprisonment and/or a fine. The maximum penalty for the new corporate offence will be an unlimited fine.

Of course, there may also be damaging collateral consequences, such as director disqualifications, company debarment from public contracts and asset confiscation proceedings.

The UK Bribery Act requires organisations to implement internal controls based on six principles:

1. Proportionality
2. Top-level commitment
3. Risk assessment
4. Due diligence
5. Communication
6. Monitoring and review

Should an offence of bribery be committed by an employee, then the implementation of internal controls can limit corporate liability.

4.1.2 Examples of bribery

Type of Bribery	Brief Description
Political Bribery	A government official accepts money from a corporation in exchange for favourable legislation or regulatory decisions.
Corporate Bribery	A company offers gifts or kickbacks to foreign officials to secure contracts or gain preferential treatment in business dealings.
Judicial Bribery	A judge accepts bribes from a defendant or plaintiff to influence the outcome of a court case, such as dismissing charges or altering sentencing.
Academic Bribery	A student bribes a teacher or professor for better grades or exam scores, often through cash payments, gifts, or favours.
Healthcare Bribery	Pharmaceutical companies provide incentives or kickbacks to doctors or healthcare professionals in exchange for prescribing their drugs or medical devices over competitors'.
Supplier Bribery	A company pays bribes to its suppliers to ensure timely delivery of goods or to obtain discounts, favourable terms, or preferential treatment in procurement contracts.
Contract Bribery	A corporation offers bribes to secure government contracts, construction permits, or licenses, bypassing fair competition and regulations.

4.1.3 Bribery across borders

The extra-territorial reach of legislation such as the UK Bribery Act and the US Foreign Corrupt Practices Act (1977) (FCPA) mean that **geographical borders are no barrier to prosecution**. Those liable under each of these pieces of legislation are therefore a wide-ranging group:

- British nationals or foreign nationals ordinarily resident in the UK
- Companies which have subsidiaries in the UK
- Companies which are listed on London Stock Exchanges
- Companies which have UK agents or distributors

The **FCPA** makes it illegal to bribe foreign government officials in order to gain or retain business. The Act defines who is liable – and it is a very wide range.

- Any company that issues US-registered securities
- Any company that is required to file periodic reports with the US Securities and Exchange Commission
- Any company that undertakes business in US dollars
- Any US soil that is crossed in paying a bribe (including sending an email that passes through a US server or using the US postal service)

- Any US citizen involved anywhere

Case Study

The US financial markets regulator is the **Securities and Exchange Commission** (SEC). One of its responsibilities is to enforce the FCPA whenever any breaches are discovered. Here is a selection of recent enforcement actions to illustrate the type of activity they experience.

- **Panasonic Corporation**: The Japan-based company agreed to pay more than $143 million to resolve FCPA charges involving a lucrative consulting position it offered to a government official at a state-owned airline to induce the official to help its US subsidiary in obtaining and retaining business from the airline.

- **Credit Suisse Group AG**: Agreed to pay more than $30 million to the SEC and a $47 million criminal penalty to resolve charges that the firm obtained investment banking business in the Asia-Pacific region by corruptly influencing foreign officials in violation of the FCPA.

- **Sanofi**: Agreed to pay more than $25 million to resolve charges related to corrupt payments to win business in Kazakhstan and the Middle East.

- **Petróleo Brasileiro S.A.**: The Brazil-based oil and gas company agreed to pay $1.78 billion in a global resolution arising out of a massive bribery and bid rigging scheme.

Question — Potential bribery

You work as an audit senior in a professional services firm. One of your firm's audit clients is a company called ABPJ Ltd which produces computer software used in the security industry. While reviewing the evidence on file for the current ABPJ Ltd audit, you notice that the audit junior has flagged a series of cash payments totalling £15,000 which have been made to a prominent politician with no apparent connection to your client. There is no narrative against the entry. You remember that you have seen a recent news story about this politician who chairs the committee which agrees procurement for IT projects across the whole of government.

Required

How should you respond to this matter?

Answer

While there may be a perfectly legitimate reason for these payments, professional scepticism should alert you to the possibility that this may be a bribe to influence the procurement committee and boost the chances of ABPJ Ltd being selected as a supplier of security software to the government.

Assuming that this is a bribe, how should you respond? We know that bribery is a criminal offence, and that both ABPJ Ltd and the politician may have profited from this crime, so it is safe to assume that this could be considered the proceeds of crime and therefore the firm's money laundering procedures should be followed:

- Secure the evidence to make sure there is no way it could be tampered with (it may eventually be required as part of a criminal prosecution).

- Maintain confidentiality on this matter and avoid tipping off any of the parties involved.

- Inform your firm's money laundering reporting officer (MLRO) about your suspicions who will then decide on next steps.

4.1.4 Other forms of corruption

Key term

> **Corruption** can be defined as deviation from honest behaviour.

Bribery is an example of corruption. Other forms of corruption include the following:

- **Abuse of a system** – using a system for improper purposes
- **Bid rigging** – promising a contract in advance to one party, although other parties have been invited to bid for the contract
- **Cartel** – a secret agreement by supposedly competing producers to fix prices, quantity or market share
- **Influence peddling** – using personal influence in government or connections with persons in authority to obtain favours or preferential treatment for another, usually in return for payment

Ethical guidance points out that threats to compliance may appear to arise not only from the accountant **making or accepting the inducement** but also from the offer **having been made in the first place**. It recommends that directors or senior managers be **informed**, and disclosure may have to be made to third parties. An organisation's guidance should make it clear that managers and staff should seek guidance about and disclose any activities that are questionable. **Guidance** on whistleblowing procedures should also make clear that they extend to reporting **suspicions** of bribery and corruption. Staff should have the opportunity to make suggestions for improvement of bribery prevention procedures.

As part of their regular monitoring of **risk management**, the board should receive reports on **compliance** with internal procedures, such as **due diligence** on agents, and details about questionable behaviour that has been discovered. The UK guidance makes it clear that **monitoring** the systems designed to prevent bribery is an important element of the board's overall monitoring of internal control systems and consideration of whether systems need to be **improved** as the risk environment changes. Events that may result in changes to systems include changes of government, reports of bribery or other negative press coverage. Accountants can be involved in all of these anti-corruption activities.

Case Study

A survey by consulting firm Protiviti and the law firm Covington & Burling (2011) identified five common control weaknesses in firms that had faced legal action under the US Foreign Corrupt Practices Act (FCPA).

1. **Inadequate contract pricing review**

   Controls could not determine whether contract prices were inflated to conceal kickbacks. They could not identify when illicit commissions were disguised as legitimate business expenses and unwarranted additional fees were added to contract prices. Firms needed to introduce competitive bidding and insist on invoices showing sufficient detail.

2. **Inadequate due diligence and verification of foreign business representatives**

   Failings included inadequate risk assessments, a lack of written contracts containing FCPA compliance terms and using representatives with a previous history of dubious payments.

3. **Ineffective accounts-payable payments and review**

   Weaknesses included making inappropriate payments that were disguised as legal fees, lack of back-up for payments and paying for services that were not included in contracts.

4. **Ineffective financial account reconciliation and review**

   Documentation failed to describe transactions so that reviewers could identify problems. Issues included inflated revenues, recording of entries that were false or placed in the wrong account and payment of false invoices.

5. **Ineffective commission payment review and authority**

   Commissions were not verified and as a result, bribery payments to foreign government officials were not identified. Commissions were also paid for duties that were not assigned by the contract; misleading information was presented to internal auditors and commission payments were inflated to include bribes. There needed to be careful review of commissions, including reviewing contracts to see if agents were entitled to a commission and the amount of the commission, and determining whether the work met the contract. Payments should be made to the contract counter party and not a third party. Checks should be carried out to make sure that the payments were not made to an offshore account.

4.2 Money laundering

Accountants also need to be alert to the threat presented by a very specific form of corruption – **money laundering**. There are many definitions of the term money laundering, but in its simplest form:

Key term

> **Money laundering** is the process of converting the proceeds of crime into funds that appear to have come from legitimate activities.

Money laundering is used to describe the process by which criminals disguise the origin of the proceeds of crime by creating transactions so that cash proceeds appear to be derived from legitimate sources of business.

Money laundering is difficult for authorities to prove as it usually involves many financial transactions which are designed to integrate the proceeds of the crime into the economy, which can then be held in banks and used for any purpose.

Money laundering is illegal because it allows criminals to profit from crime and use these proceeds in the everyday economy to fund other businesses, buy property and invest on the stock market and other markets.

Most countries have passed anti-money laundering legislation which aims to deter criminals from money laundering activity due to power to seize assets and fine and imprison those found guilty of money laundering.

4.2.1 Process of money laundering

The process is usually undertaken in three stages allowing the proceeds of crime to become laundered money:

(1) **Placement** – the physical disposal of cash proceeds derived from illegal activities

(2) **Layering** – the process of creating complex layers of financial transactions designed to disguise the source of the money, confuse the audit trail and provide anonymity

(3) **Integration** – the process of creating the impression of apparent legitimacy to criminally derived wealth by connecting it to legitimate business activities

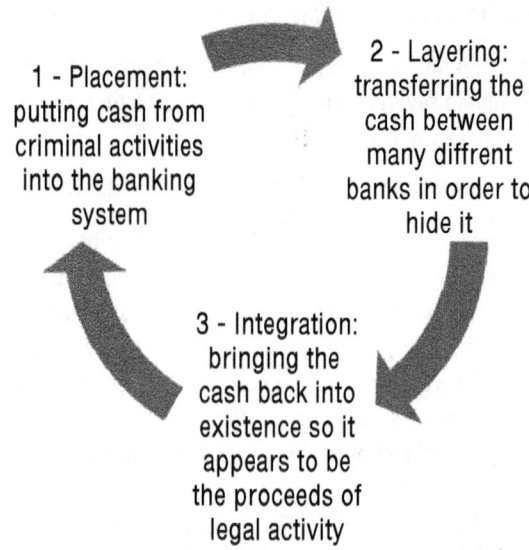

4.2.2 Anti-money laundering legislation in the UK

Relevant anti-money laundering legislation in the UK includes:

- The Terrorism Act 2000. It is a criminal offence in the UK to finance or facilitate the financing of terrorism.

- The Proceeds of Crime Act 2002. Three money laundering offences under this Act are:

    - **Section 327.** An offence is committed if a person conceals, disguises, converts, transfers, or removes from the jurisdiction property which is, or represents, the proceeds of crime which the person knows, or suspects represents the proceeds of crime.

    - **Section 328.** An offence is committed when a person enters into or becomes concerned in an arrangement which he/she knows or suspects will facilitate another person to acquire, retain, use, or control criminal property and the person knows or suspects that the property is criminal property.

    - **Section 329.** An offence is committed when a person acquires, uses, or has possession of property which he/she knows, or suspects represents the proceeds of crime.

        In the UK, The Proceeds of Crime Act 2002 requires people or organisations to submit a Suspicious Activity Report to the National Crime Agency if they know or suspect that a person is engaged in, or attempting, money laundering.

4.2.3 Controls which address the risk of money laundering

The UK Financial Conduct Authority (FCA) is the conduct regulator for 59,000 financial services firms and financial markets in the UK and the prudential supervisor for 49,000 firms, setting specific standards for 19,000 firms.

The FCA requires that firms:

- Give overall responsibility for anti-money laundering systems and controls to a director or senior manager. They should know about the money laundering risks to your firm and make sure steps are taken to mitigate those risks effectively.

- Appoint a Money Laundering Reporting Officer (MLRO), who is a focus for the firm's anti-money laundering (AML) activity. The MLRO supervises the firm's compliance with its AML obligations. If you are a sole trader with no employees, you are not subject to this requirement.

The FCA advises that some companies are at greater risk than others of breaching the laws against money laundering, such as banks. Affected companies must assess the risk of money laundering in their business and take necessary action by identifying the risks and taking measures, for example, by refusing to enter into business transactions with customers who are suspected of money laundering.

UK Money Laundering Regulations 2019 require that:

- Firms must have policies, controls and procedures to identify and scrutinise transactions which are complex or unusually large, or have unusual patterns of transactions, or which have no apparent economic or legal purpose.
- Firms must ensure that appropriate measures are taken to assess and, if necessary, mitigate any money laundering/terrorist financing ('ML/TF') risk when adopting 'new products, new business practices (including new delivery mechanisms) or new technology'.
- Firms must have group-wide policies, controls and procedures for sharing information about clients with other group companies for anti-money laundering purposes.
- Training requirements for 'relevant employees' who are capable of contributing to identifying or mitigating MT/TF risk or preventing or detecting money laundering.
- Institutions are required to engage in Customer Due Diligence, which means verifying the true identity of customers with whom they undertake transactions and undertaking ongoing Customer Due Diligence with customers with whom they have a business relationship.

UK money laundering regulations also require firms to include new additional high-risk factors when assessing the need for enhanced due diligence and seek additional information and monitoring in certain cases. These may occur where:

- There are relevant transactions between parties based in high-risk third countries.
- The customer is the beneficiary of a life insurance policy.
- The customer is a third-country national seeking residence rights or citizenship in exchange for transfers of capital, purchase of a property, governments bonds or investment in corporate entities.
- Non-face-to-face business relationships or transactions without certain safeguards, for example, as set out in regulation 28 (19) concerning electronic identification processes.
- Transactions related to oil, arms, precious metals, tobacco products, cultural artefacts, ivory or other items related to protected species, or items of archaeological, historical, cultural and religious significance, or of rare scientific value.

Money laundering regulations require organisations to make reports to UK Companies House in relation to discrepancies between information collected during customer due diligence and information on the Persons with Significant Control register.

4.2.4 Role of accountant regarding money laundering

In most jurisdictions where anti-money laundering legislation exists, accountants are singled out for **scrutiny** due to the unique role they play in helping to manage the finances of their clients. Clearly, they should act as **whistleblower** whenever money laundering is suspected (but there are some very specific things that an accountant needs to be aware of **before** this can be done, which we will look at later).

Obviously, knowingly being involved in money laundering is a crime. However, looking at the three stages above, it is possible that **an accountant could be involved** in any of these stages **but not be aware of their involvement**. Without knowing the true source of a client's income, the accountant is at risk of being considered part of the process of money laundering.

Even if there is a **suspicion** of money laundering being undertaken by a client, an accountant's role can still lead to a conflict of interest developing:

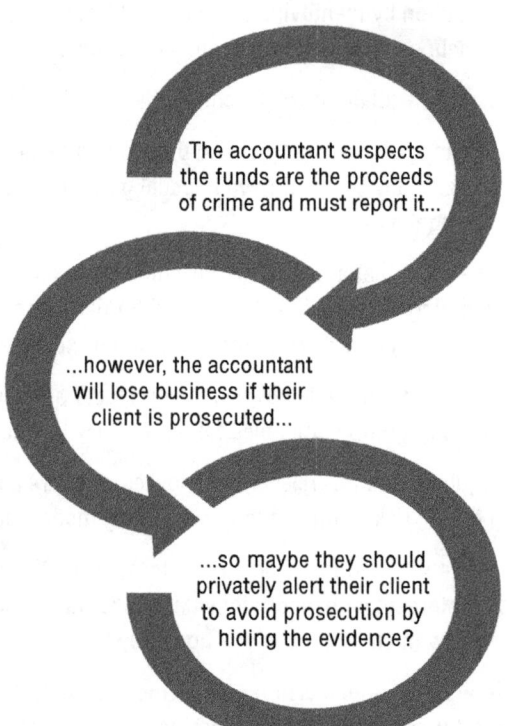

This activity is known as **tipping off** and unsurprisingly, it is also a criminal offence.

In conclusion, when it comes to whistleblowing on money laundering, clearly the accountant has a number of responsibilities that must be followed:

- Knowing the identity of your clients and the sources of their income, sometimes known as **know your client (KYC)** or **customer due diligence (CDD)**
- **Reporting any suspicions** of money laundering as soon as possible
- **Avoiding tipping off** the parties under suspicion

Usually, accountants will need to **maintain suitable records** to demonstrate their compliance with these regulations and also be required to undertake **training** on anti-money laundering procedures. They will therefore need to have procedures set up to facilitate this, including the appointment of an individual known as a **money laundering reporting officer (MLRO)** to whom any suspicions should be reported in the first instance. They would then decide whether a suspicious activity report (SAR) should be filed with the National Crime Agency (NCA).

4.2.5 Typical money laundering sanctions across the world

Below are typical money laundering sanctions for a person laundering money:

- A person convicted of the offence of money laundering is liable to penalties and imprisonment depending on the severity of the crime.
- Prohibit any transaction in relation to any account, property or investment which may have been used or which may be used in connection with the offence of money laundering.
- Property derived from an offence of money laundering can be forfeited to the state.
- The act of tipping-off, which is pre-warning suspects of impending action, is punishable under anti-money laundering legislation.
- Those suspected of money laundering can be extradited back to the country of prosecution for criminal trial.

For organisations which may knowingly or unknowingly be involved in servicing money laundering transactions then disciplinary actions that can be taken including:

- Publicly reprimanding the financial institution
- Ordering the financial institution to take any action for the purpose of remedying the contravention
- Ordering the financial institution to pay a pecuniary penalty not exceeding the greater of $10 million or three times the amount of profit gained, or costs avoided, by the financial institution as a result of the contravention

4.3 Terrorist financing

Terrorist financing is the intentional use of property or finance, either directly or indirectly, to commit a terrorist act(s)

Terrorist financing is defined by UK statute as:

(a) The provision or collection, by any means, directly or indirectly, of any property (i) with the intention that the property be used; or (ii) knowing that the property will be used, in whole or in part, to commit one or more terrorist acts (whether or not the property is actually so used);

(b) Making available any property or financial (or related) services, by any means, directly or indirectly, to or for the benefit of a person knowing that, or being reckless as to whether, the person is a terrorist or terrorist associate; or

(c) The collection of property or solicitation of financial (or related) services, by any means, directly or indirectly, for the benefit of a person knowing that, or being reckless as to whether, the person is a terrorist or terrorist associate.

4.3.1 The Financial Action Task Force

The Financial Action Task Force (FATF) was established in July 1989 by a Group of Seven (G-7) Summit in Paris, initially to examine and develop measures to combat money laundering.

The objectives of the FATF are to set international standards and promote effective implementation of legal, regulatory and operational measures for combating money laundering, terrorist financing and other related threats to the integrity of the international financial system. The FATF monitors countries' progress in implementing FATF recommendations; as well as reviews money laundering and terrorist financing techniques and counter-measures.

All FAFT members, including the UK, are required to implement a credible anti-money laundering (AML) and counter-terrorism financing (CFT) regime which would apply to designated non-financial business and professions (DNFBPs) as well as to financial institutions.

4.4 Controls on anti-money laundering and counter-terrorism finance

Some companies are at greater risk than others of breaching the laws against money laundering and terrorist financing, such as banks, solicitors and accountants. Therefore, companies may go beyond the legislation to assess their own risk to money laundering or terrorist financing in their business and take necessary action: for example, by refusing to enter into business transactions with customers who are suspected of money laundering or financing terrorism.

Controls can include:

- Give overall responsibility for anti-money laundering systems and counter terrorist financing to a director or senior manager as a specific focus. They should know about the money laundering and terrorist financing risks and have the power to make sure steps are taken to mitigate those risks effectively.

- Appoint a Money Laundering Reporting Officer (MLRO), who is a focus for the company's AML activity. The MLRO supervises the company's compliance with its AML obligations. If you are a sole trader with no employees, you are not subject to this requirement.

- Institutions are required to engage in customer due diligence, which means verifying the true identity of customers with whom they undertake transactions, and undertaking ongoing customer due diligence with customers with whom they have a business relationship. In doing so, organisations should perform the following:

    - Establishing the identity of clients.

    - Establishing effective escalation and advisory procedures to ensure that high-risk customers are appropriately identified and handled, and that staff responsibilities are clear.

    - Obtaining information where the type or level of business activity diverges from the customer's source of wealth.

    - Verifying the accuracy of the customer's declaration about the source of wealth through reliable sources such as: publicly available property registers, land registers, asset disclosure registers, company registers, past transactions (for existing customers) and other sources of information about legal and beneficial ownership.

    - Challenging the source of wealth information (where appropriate) during the new customer due diligence process.

    - Proactively following up gaps in sources of wealth information for higher-risk relationships during the course of the relationship.

    - Reviewing relationships periodically to ensure due diligence information remains current, and the risk assessment and associated controls remain appropriate.

Question — Audit client

You are an audit manager at a professional accountancy practice called XYZ Ltd and you have been assigned to manage the audit of Investo Ltd, which is a relatively new audit client.

The audit is currently being undertaken and you have observed an unusual cash transaction. One $150,000 cash transaction was noted in Investo Ltd.'s bank statements which was deposited into the company's bank account from a bank located in the Cayman Islands at the beginning of the year. The same amount was paid on the next business day to an unknown bank account with a Hong Kong bank.

The transaction is disproportionately large as the company's cash balance is $21,000 and the largest sales transaction is $1,500. Investo Ltd.'s financial accountant does not know anything about the transaction.

The Investo Ltd.'s two directors have not responded to a request to provide an explanation for the cash transaction.

Required

Advise the audit partner of XYZ Ltd on the next steps which the practice should take.

Answer

As the transaction of $150,000 is disproportionate to the client's activities and company employees do not know of its legitimate purpose or commercial rationale then there are ground for suspicion, particularly as neither of the company directors have responded to a request for further explanation.

The transaction is suspicious of a 'U-turn' transaction, where money passes from one person or company to another and then back to the original person or company. Therefore, the transaction must be treated as potential money laundering.

It is possible the transaction is legitimate, so the partner must urgently contact the company directors once again and request an explanation of the commercial rationale of the transaction. The partner must be careful not to discuss suspicions of money laundering to avoid tipping off.

In the meantime, the transaction must be treated as suspicious. The audit partner must report the transaction to the designated Money Laundering Reporting Officer ('MRLO') for the practice. The MRLO should promptly evaluate if there are suspicious circumstances that would require a suspicious transaction report to be made to relevant authorities.

If there are suspicious circumstance then the MLRO shall report all relevant details to the JFIU, without undue delay and should co-operate with any resulting investigation. In this instance, the practice is advised to resign for its role as company auditor immediately. If the MLRO determines there are insufficient grounds to report the transaction, then the MLRO should document the rationale for its decision.

As this is a relatively new audit client, the MLRO should confirm customer due diligence and a risk assessment was properly performed, including confirming the identity of the company directors. If it was not, then the MLRO should launch an internal investigation into why this did not occur in line with policy at the accountancy practice which may result in disciplinary action and recommendations for improvement to the company's anti-money laundering policy, processes, systems, controls and employee training.

4.5 Employee behaviour risk to governance

Employee behaviour can increase the probability of corporate liability or expose the company to adverse reputational or regulatory risk. Examples include:

- Negligence of duties
- Acts of crime such as theft, fraud, bribery or facilitating money laundering
- Bullying others or aggressive behaviour to others
- Overriding of company health and safety or environmental controls
- Pursuing short-termism or self-interest
- Unauthorised information sharing or insider dealing

These behaviours can have a legal and reputational impact as well as a financial one. Persistent bad behaviours can also lead to poor morale and high staff turnover.

Communication from the top of unacceptable behaviour plays an important role in setting expectations.

Employee contracts, employee codes of conduct and enforcement, recruitment controls and training all play a part in controlling this risk.

4.6 Insider dealing

Insider dealing occurs when an individual who is 'connected' to a listed company has price-sensitive information about the company and uses this information to deal in the company's shares (or advise someone else to deal in the shares) in order to make a profit or avoid a loss.

A 'connected person' includes directors of the company and professional advisors.

'Price-sensitive information' is information that the public does not yet know, but when the information becomes public knowledge, it is likely to have an impact on the share price (so that the share price is likely to go up or down by a substantial amount).

An example of price-sensitive information is information about a merger or acquisition that is not yet public knowledge.

5 Public sector accounting

5.1 Different types of organisation

FAST FORWARD

> The **private sector** comprises a variety of organisations with the principal aim, in accounting terms, of undertaking commercial activity in order to generate a profit for the individual owners or shareholders who provide the entity with capital.
>
> Although the process of accounting is fundamentally the same in any context (understanding performance and position in financial terms) the **public sector** is different from any other type of organisation because of its aims and purpose, its size, its sources of funding and the way it demonstrates its accountability. This means that the accounting information created for public sector organisations has to have a different **focus**.

Public sector organisations can **exist** at any one of **three levels**:

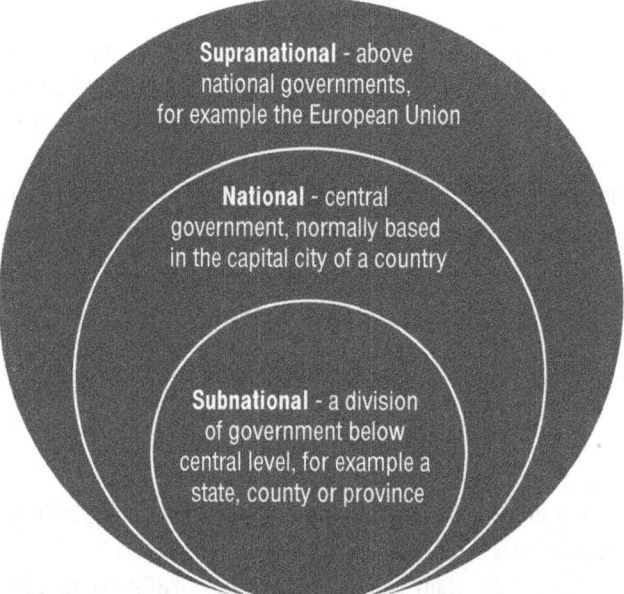

- **Supranational** - above national governments, for example the European Union
- **National** - central government, normally based in the capital city of a country
- **Subnational** - a division of government below central level, for example a state, county or province

The characteristics of a nation or state vary considerably depending on whether it is a democracy, whether it has a formal constitution and so on. The UK, for example, is a **constitutional monarchy** where the monarch is the head of state (a largely ceremonial role) and the prime minister is the head of the government. Most states require the following four **organs of state** in order to function.

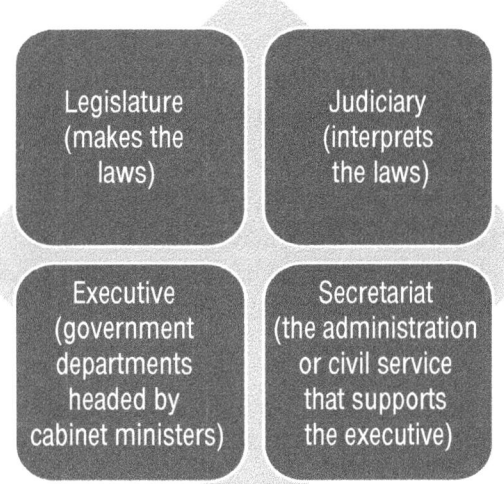

In general terms, the public sector delivers those goods and services that cannot or should not be provided by private sector companies or the business sector. The public sector provides services for the population either free of charge or for a cost. These services may be on a **national level**, such as the UK National Health Service (NHS) or on a **local level**, such as libraries or schools.

The public sector may be **funded** from local taxation, from central government grants, or from a combination of the two. Public services are administered by elected officials at national level (Members of Parliament) or at local level (local councils or municipalities).

To add further context, there are some other types of organisation that look the same as the public sector but, in reality, are often very different:

- **Charities** are organisations set up for specific not-for-profit purposes, separate from government and funded by donations.
- **Non-governmental organisations (NGOs)** and **non-departmental public bodies (NDPBs)** (sometimes referred to as **quasi-autonomous non-governmental organisations** or **QUANGOs**) are bodies set up by government to carry out functions similar to government but with non-elected executive members. The UK Cabinet Office's definition of a QUANGO is:

    '... a body which has a role in the processes of national government, but is not a government department, or part of one, and which accordingly operates to a greater or lesser extent at arm's length from Ministers.'

The following table shows the main characteristics of these types of organisation.

	Public sector	Private sector	Charities	NGOs/NDPBs
Purposes and objectives	Public service	Profit	Relief of poverty, research, etc	As defined by its owners
Performance	Central regulation	Financial reporting standards	Statement of recommended practice (SORP)	Set outcomes
Ownership	Government	Partners/shareholders	Donors	Government
Leadership	Democratically elected representatives	Board of directors	Trustees	Board members
Stakeholders	The public, central government, service users	Shareholders, regulators, taxation authorities	Service users	Government, lobby groups

Lobby groups are parties that come together with a common interest, with a view to influencing government policy. They may come under criticism if they are seen to have sufficient power to influence policy in their favour, especially if this is seen as going against the public interest.

5.2 Public sector accounting and ethics

Once you understand what is meant by a public sector organisation, it should be easier to consider the associated **ethical dimensions** that arise as part of accounting and auditing. We have already covered topics such as **fraud**, **bribery** and **corruption** elsewhere in these materials – specifically in a **public sector context**, there are plenty of examples of how these could be present:

- Tenders for lucrative national or local government **contracts** could be manipulated to ensure a specific party is successful via the payment of bribes
- Housing or health **benefits** that are targeted towards vulnerable members of society could be claimed fraudulently by parties that are not eligible by some form of deception
- **Expenses** could be deliberately diverted because controls do not exist to identify such issues (often the public sector is not sufficiently resourced to operate the most expensive systems)

One of the key differences between private and public sectors is the need to demonstrate that public money has been **used for the purposes intended** and that **value for money** has been obtained. One way of measuring this is to evaluate performance against the '**three Es**':

Economy – obtaining inputs of the appropriate quality at the lowest price available

Efficiency – delivering the service to the appropriate standard with minimum wastage (process)

Effectiveness – achieving the desired objectives as stated in the entity's performance plan (outputs)

Sometimes, the term **best value** is used to describe this approach – fundamentally, it is concerned with making the most out of finite resources, the perennial issue when considering public sector accounting.

However, despite a common methodology like this, the nature of services provided by the public sector and the way that they are funded still makes them harder to **monitor** than those in the private sector. For example, the **cost of delivering common medical procedures** such as hip replacements, cataract removal or caesarean sections may be compared by central government to help identify best practice and allow funding to be allocated locally. Depending on the favoured approach at each location, these costs could vary due to a number of reasons, such as:

- The amount of post-operative physical rehabilitation offered to patients;
- The technology in place for the procedure; and
- The cost and application of any medication used to manage pain.

However, these **cost estimates** could also **vary** due to the way that a unit cost is calculated by the accountant at each location (such as how to allocate overheads or what assumptions to make on the proportion of straightforward elective cases compared to more expensive emergency procedures and so on). Whether by accident or design, this variation in approach could lead to **different levels of funding** which could ultimately affect the viability of hospitals concerned, meaning that public sector accountants may be presented with some form of **decision** to make about what is best for their organisation (never mind the fact that the more funds go to one service, the less there is available for others).

In addition to the various ethical codes that you have met so far throughout your studies, there is also guidance that exists in the UK called **the seven principles of public life** (Committee on Standards in Public Life, 1995) that apply to anyone who works as a public office-holder and all those in sectors that deliver public service, including accountants:

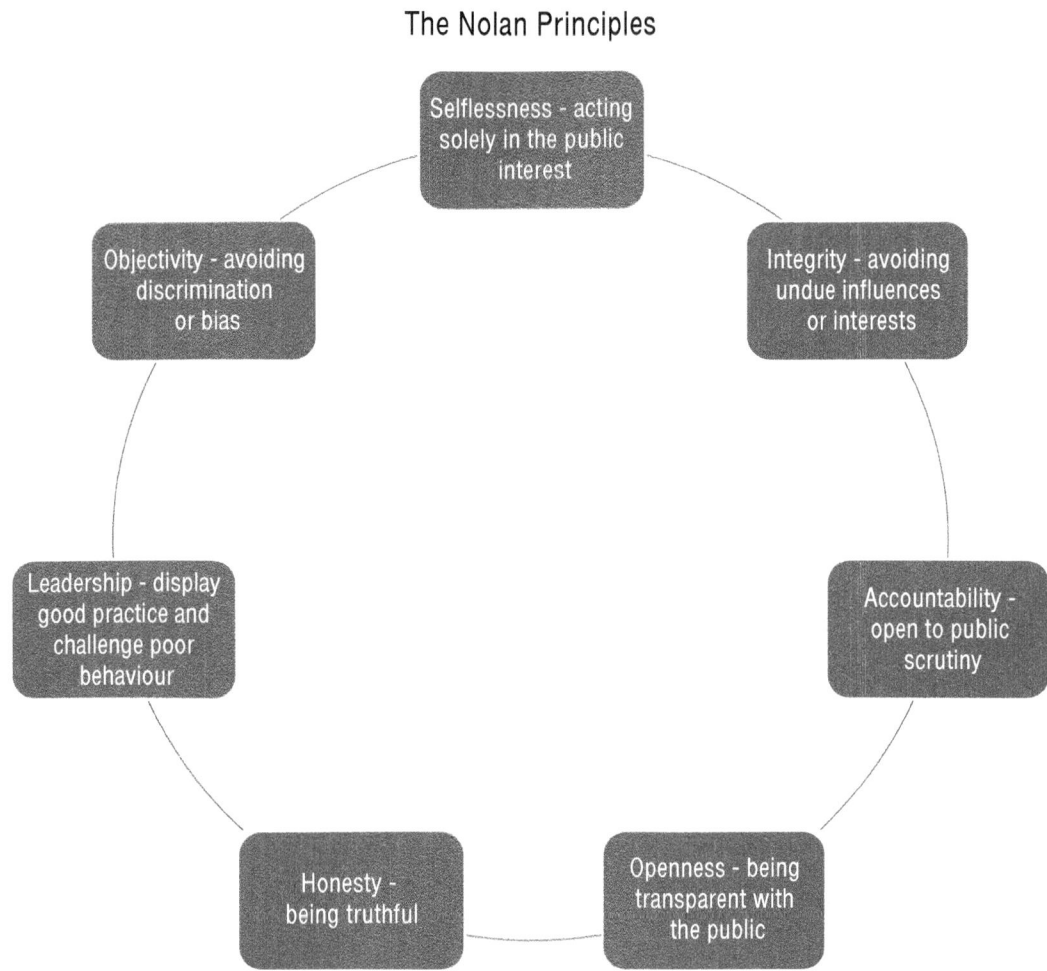

The Nolan Principles

These principles clearly overlap with what you have already learned about ethics – however, the reason they exist is to reinforce the need to operate within the social licence that is granted to anyone working in the public sector whose prime function should always be to **serve the public interest** (such as police officers, local councillors or social workers).

Public sector performance differs from that of the private sector in one other main capacity: **profit**. One of the main ethical dimensions that applies to both accountants and auditors in the **private sector** is an awareness of the threat of inflating profits for the purpose of **manipulating a company's prospects**, either on the stock market or for the benefit of other stakeholders. Such a threat is unlikely to exist in a **public sector organisation**, although the need to break-even may still lead to what we have previously seen as areas of **creative accounting** in an attempt to achieve this key objective.

It is important to remember that although working in the public sector is fundamentally ethical because it is by definition **serving the public interest**, that does not mean that working in the private sector is inherently less ethical: the same approach to doing the right thing should apply regardless of where you are employed.

5.3 Public sector financial statements

Producing a record of overall performance and position for the public sector can be quite a daunting prospect – although **size** and **complexity** will be a factor, the **maturity of systems** in place will also be important, especially if the country in question is either a developing nation or in a state of conflict. As an example of a typical developed nation, the **UK Government** publishes a set of financial statements for the whole of the UK, showing **income**, which is mostly derived from various forms of tax, and **expenditure** on areas such as social care, health, defence, transport and housing. The accounts also show **assets**, such as land, infrastructure and financial assets as well as **liabilities** that include pension liabilities, government borrowing and provisions.

Case Study

A closer look at the UK Whole of Government Accounts (WGA) for the year ended 31 March 2018 uncovers a series of unique accounting issues that would only be experienced by an accountant operating in the public sector. For example:

- One of the UK's most famous historical monuments, **Stonehenge** in Wiltshire, has been owned by the UK government since 1918 when it was given to the nation by a man called Cecil Chubb. Like many other UK-owned historical assets, it is **valued in WGA at close to zero.** (Such unique assets cannot be revalued because there is no active market to determine fair values.)

- The **timescales** that WGA use can be very different to those used by companies: for example, projections used to estimate the financial needs of the UK go as far ahead as 2068, while there are nuclear decommissioning provisions that extend the UK's liability to the year 2137.

- The sheer scale of WGA means that **materiality levels** used by the UK Comptroller and Auditor General when arriving at an audit opinion for the year ended 31 March 2018 was set at £8 billion.

Clearly, not all public sector accounting roles will operate under these kinds of conditions, but it is important to understand the **unique** nature of accounting in the public sector and the importance of using skills to deliver transparent and understandable messages to the public at large.

In addition to the WGA prepared by central government, local government councils, NHS trusts and other public sector bodies also prepare financial statements, thus allowing a more detailed picture of the public sector. These financial statements are all prepared under the **accruals concept**. However, this is not the norm across the rest of the world and has only been in place in the UK for around a decade – receipts and payments approaches are still commonplace across large parts of the world's public sector.

The **International Federation of Accountants (IFAC)** operates a member body called the **International Public Sector Accounting Standards Board (IPSASB)** which is responsible for considering the accounting, auditing and financial reporting needs within all parts of the public sector across the world. Currently, IPSASB is represented by 18 countries, including the UK, US, Canada and Australia. One of their main aims is to raise the quality of financial reporting in the public sector to match private sector information created under IFRS – this is expected to occur by worldwide implementation of their own public-sector focused **International Public Sector Accounting Standards (IPSAS)**. Although a number of high-profile organisations do use IPSAS (such as the Organisation for Economic Cooperation and Development or OECD and the North Atlantic Treaty Organisation or NATO) very few countries have adopted IPSAS for their public services.

The need for **ongoing public scrutiny** of how taxpayers' money is used has led to a wealth of information which accountants are at the forefront of producing – however, as we can see from the large variety of activities that make up our public services, finding a way to report this in straightforward terms to people without any financial expertise continues to prove challenging. **CIPFA (Chartered Institute of Public Finance and Accountancy)** in England, Northern Ireland and Wales and **LASAAC (Local Authority (Scotland) Accounts Advisory Committee)** are jointly responsible for managing this process in the UK.

Question — Auditors: public versus private sector

Explain why the roles played by accountants in the public sector and the private sector are likely to be different.

Answer

As with all discursive questions, there are many different points that could be made here, so there is no one perfect answer. However, there are some key points that would help to explain why public and private sector accountants' roles are different.

Private sector entities are usually created with the aim of making a profit. While public sector organisations still need to demonstrate the same degree of financial accountability, they exist to provide a service that supports some form of political or social need. Profit is generated by making a sale; service delivery in the public sector however is often far less easy to determine and may require complex inputs to achieve.

As a consequence of this social or political need, there is likely to be more variety in the type of activity that the public sector accountant is involved in, due to the frequency of changes in government, legislation, tastes, trends and aspirations in place within any given society.

Public sector accountants could also be exposed to much more variety in terms of scope, scale and size. Political organisations can vary from small local councils all the way to whole of government accounts, with legacy commitments to account for which the private sector will simply never need to consider.

Although private sector entities will be constrained by how much resource they have at their disposal, taking on additional debt or equity is an option to allow them the ability to change and evolve (or simply survive). Public sector entities are often constrained by fixed budgets that mean difficult decisions are sometimes necessary and services are rationed on the basis of the highest priority. Accountants may be centre stage in helping such decisions to be made.

Finally, despite the significant regulatory role played by organisations such as the Financial Reporting Council in the UK or the Securities and Exchange Commission in the US, private sector entities are never under the same scrutiny as their public sector counterparts: this is due to the fact that public sector entities are funded by taxpayers' money and as such, they will always need to demonstrate transparency and accountability for their actions which accountants are at the forefront of delivering.

Chapter roundup

- Tax is a **complex political** and **economic** issue for most countries. Accountants operating in these countries need to understand the differences between desirable **tax planning**, unethical **tax avoidance** and illegal **tax evasion**.

- Accountants also need to know about the many **ethical challenges** that tax work can present, hence its inclusion in a variety of guises within the ethical codes that exist. Fortunately, due to the many **real world examples** of where tax and ethics collide, this is not difficult to understand!

- **Whistleblowing** is where an employee makes disclosure of illegal or unethical behaviour carried out by an organisation. This is challenging because it requires moral courage to stand up to your employer and necessitates protection that comes from the law and best practice.

- Examples of situations where whistleblowing might apply include fraud, bribery, corruption and money laundering, although the latter requires some very specific actions to ensure any disclosure complies with the law.

- **Money laundering** is the process of creating transactions so that cash from criminal proceeds appears to be derived from legitimate sources.

- **The UK Bribery Act** creates four categories of offences: (1) Offering a bribe, (2) Agreeing to receive a bribe, (3) Failing to prevent bribery, and (4) Bribing a foreign public official.

- **Public sector accounting** exists in a variety of different organisations and requires very different mechanisms for both recording and reporting position and performance. Although accountants in any sector are expected to uphold the public **interest**, the link between the public sector and **public services**, as well as their means of funding, means that **accountability** and **transparency** are especially important.

- The **private sector** comprises a variety of organisations with the principal aim, in accounting terms, of undertaking commercial activity in order to generate a profit for the individual owners or shareholders who provide the entity with capital.

- Although the process of accounting is fundamentally the same in any context (understanding performance and position in financial terms) the **public sector** is different from any other type of organisation because of its aims and purpose, its size, its sources of funding and the way it demonstrates its accountability. This means that the accounting information created for public sector organisations has to have a different **focus**.

Quick quiz

1. What is the difference between tax planning, tax avoidance and tax evasion?
2. Suggest three examples of tax planning activities that an accountant might perform for one of their clients.
3. Match each of the following activities with a suitable description of what is happening from the picklist:
   - Keeping two sets of financial accounts but only submitting one of them for review by HMRC
   - Employing an accountant to determine your tax liability when you start as a self-employed builder
   - Transferring your company's income to an overseas company where the rate of corporate tax is lower than the rate of tax in the country where that income was generated

   Picklist:
   - Tax planning
   - Tax avoidance
   - Tax evasion

4. Define the term whistleblowing.
5. What are the three stages of a typical money laundering scheme?
6. List five responsibilities that apply to accountants when money laundering is concerned.
7. Describe the three Es most commonly used for evaluating public services?

Answers to Quick Quiz

1. **Tax planning** is the process of legally minimising tax liabilities for individuals or organisations by operating within the tax arrangements currently in place.

   Tax avoidance is a legal way of reducing tax liabilities for individuals and organisations.

   Tax evasion is reducing tax liabilities for individuals and organisations by illegal means.

   Although the first two sound similar, tax avoidance uses techniques that are still legal but are felt to be against the spirit of the tax legislation in place, so are often considered unethical.

2. Answers can vary, but here is a list of likely areas of tax planning:

   - Encouraging the use of pensions for employees to save for their retirement
   - Discussing the maximum amounts an individual is allowed to save in a tax-free account
   - Recommending inheritance strategies to families that allows them to pass on as much of their wealth to future generations as possible
   - Advising self-employed workers on tax-deductible expenses that can reduce their taxable profits
   - Evaluating the most appropriate way of recognising dividend income for investors
   - Identifying tax breaks for companies that wish to start investing in certain areas
   - Restructuring organisations so they can enjoy favourable tax treatments in certain jurisdictions

3.

Keeping two sets of financial accounts but only submitting one of them for review by HMRC	Tax evasion. This suggests the accounts submitted to HMRC are inaccurate, which sounds very much like fraud!
Employing an accountant to determine your tax liability when you start as a self-employed builder	Tax planning. It is quite likely that a builder will not possess the right skills to set up suitable tax planning arrangements, so this is acceptable.
Transferring your company's income to an overseas company where the rate of corporate tax is lower than the rate of tax in the country where that income was generated	Tax avoidance. Without full knowledge of the company or jurisdiction, this can never be definitive, but it sounds like legal, but unethical, tax avoidance!

4. **Whistleblowing** is the disclosure by an employee of illegal or unethical practices by his or her employer.

5. The process used in a typical money laundering scheme contains three stages:
   1. **Placement** – putting cash from criminal activities into the banking system
   2. **Layering** – transferring the cash between many different banks in order to hide it
   3. **Integration** – bringing the cash back into existence so it appears to be the proceeds of legal activity

6.
   - Undertaking training in anti-money laundering regulations
   - Maintaining records of all clients
   - Ensuring that the identity of all new clients is obtained
   - Reporting suspicions to the MLRO
   - Avoiding tipping off the potential money launderer

7.
   - Economy – obtaining inputs of the appropriate quality at the lowest price available
   - Efficiency – delivering the service to the appropriate standard with minimum wastage
   - Effectiveness – achieving the desired objectives as stated in the entity's performance plan

Governance and self-regulation

Governance and self-regulation for accountants and auditors

7

Topic list	Syllabus reference
1 Accounting regulation	LO 3, LO 4
2 Auditor independence	LO 3, LO 4
3 Conflicting clients' interests	LO 3, LO 4
4 Placing unreasonable expectations on a trainee	LO 3, LO 4

Introduction

This chapter covers the regulation of the accountancy profession, focusing on the regulatory frameworks that apply to accountants and auditors. The chapter also shows the pathway through a situation where an accountant or auditor has clients whose interests conflict, and the ethical approach to situations where trainees are made subject to unreasonable expectations.

1 Accounting regulation

International Financial Reporting Standards are a key element of accounting regulations in Europe and in other parts of the globe.

1.1 GAAP

Accounting standards take the form of Generally Accepted Accounting Principles (GAAP). This term signifies all the rules, from whatever source, which govern accounting. In individual countries, this is seen primarily as a combination of:

- National corporate law
- National accounting standards
- Local stock exchange requirements

Although those sources are the basis for the GAAP of individual countries, the concept also includes the effects of non-mandatory sources such as:

- International Financial Reporting Standards (IFRS® Standards)
- Statutory requirements in other countries

In many countries, like the UK, GAAP does not have any statutory or regulatory authority or definition, unlike other countries, such as the USA. The term is mentioned rarely in legislation, and only then in fairly limited terms.

1.2 IFRS Standards

In some jurisdictions, financial statements must be prepared on the basis of IFRS Standards. For example, in the UK, company law recognises two financial reporting frameworks – IFRS and UK and Ireland GAAP. Public listed companies are required to apply IFRS in the preparation of their consolidated financial statements but may choose between IFRS and UK and Ireland GAAP for the preparation of their individual parent financial statements. Other entities have a free choice between the two frameworks.

IFRS adopt a **fair presentation** approach to financial reporting, which is ultimately derived from the requirement in the UK for accounts to present a 'true and fair view'. This is analogous to the principles-based approach that the IESBA adopts in relation to ethics, and which the IAASB adopts for auditing standards, and is therefore distinguished from rules- or compliance-based approaches to financial reporting.

This notion of fair presentation is discussed in IAS 1 *Presentation of Financial Statements*. IAS 1 states that fair presentation means to represent fairly "…the effects of transactions and other events (…) in accordance with the definitions and recognition criteria for assets, liabilities, income and expenses as set out in the [*Conceptual*] *Framework*" (IAS 1: para. 15).

Fair presentation is achieved if IFRS are appropriately applied and additional disclosure is given when it is necessary (IAS 1: para. 15).

However, very rarely, management may come to the conclusion that complying with an IFRS requirement would be "so misleading that it would conflict with the objective of financial statements set out in the *Framework*" (IAS 1: para. 19). If so, and if local laws and regulations permit, the entity can depart from that IFRS requirement, as long it "discloses:

(a) That management has concluded that the financial statements present fairly the entity's financial position, financial performance and cash flows;

(b) That it has complied with applicable IFRSs except that it has departed from a particular requirement to achieve a fair presentation;

(c) [Full details of the departure]; and

(d) … the financial effect of the departure on each item in the financial statements that would have been reported in complying with the requirement."

(IAS 1: para. 20)

However, when local law **prohibits departure** from the requirement, then the entity should make disclosures which will reduce the perceived misleading effects of complying. These include the details of why management believe it to be misleading and adjustments showing what they believe is necessary to fairly present the information (IAS 1: para. 23).

1.3 The accountancy profession and the public interest

> Professionalism means **avoiding actions** that bring **discredit on the accountancy profession**.
>
> **Acting in the public interest** means acting for the welfare of society at large.
>
> Various commentators have argued that the **figures** accountants produce are **not neutral**, but incorporate value judgments and are in accordance with the wishes of certain viewpoints in society.

1.4 Professions and professionalism

1.4.1 Profession

The theory and skills to become a member of a professional body are acquired by an extensive structured training process, validated by examination and maintained through continuing professional education.

Values underpin the professional's actions. For example, the medical profession is underpinned by the principle of the sanctity of life. The common code of values and conduct should be independently administered by a governing body.

The skills and values **enhance the weight of a professional's judgment**. They are what the professional presents themselves as having by virtue of calling themselves an accountant (for example) and belonging to a professional institute.

In return for accepting a duty to society, members of a profession are allowed privileges, for example being able to practise certain activities or to use a title. They do not, however, have a right to receive any particular level of remuneration, although it is the case that work in a profession will tend to be well paid as a result of the barriers to entering the profession and the consequent restriction of labour supply within it.

1.4.2 Professionalism and professional behaviour

IESBA's *Code of Ethics* defines professionalism in terms of **professional behaviour**. Professional behaviour imposes an obligation on professional accountants to act in the **public interest**. They should **comply with relevant laws and regulations** and **avoid any action** that may **bring discredit to the profession**. Professional behaviour is one of the fundamental principles that we discussed earlier in this chapter, and professional behaviour in a wider sense would include compliance with the other four ethical principles.

Professionalism can also be seen as a state of mind, a concern to take action in the **public interest** and sometimes to lead public opinion, for example in developing guidance on reporting.

As we have seen, in marketing themselves and their work, professional accountants should not bring the profession into disrepute. They should avoid making exaggerated claims for their own services, qualifications and experience and should not refer to others disparagingly. Accountants may also have other professional responsibilities depending on the roles they hold, for example responsibilities as company directors.

A recent survey produced a wider definition of professionalism. The survey suggested that the most important competencies for accounting professionals were:

- Maintaining confidentiality and upholding ethical standards
- Preparing financial information
- Complying with legal and regulatory requirements
- Interpreting financial statements

- Communicating effectively
- Preparing financial statements
- Problem solving and managerial skills

Professionalism is also important when dealing with professional colleagues, particularly if the individual is a senior member of the organisation. As leaders, senior accountants should aim to work well with other team members, and deal appropriately with concerns they raise about the work they are doing. They should also look to set an example to junior staff.

It is also possible to see professionalism in terms of the attributes which professionals should demonstrate. These could include the following:

Competency. This links in with the fundamental ethical principle of professional competence and due care.

- Reliability and accountability. This means, for example, always being prepared for meetings, honouring commitments and accepting responsibility where things do not turn out as planned.
- Honesty and integrity. This means telling the truth and not compromising values, in line with the ethical principles of objectivity and integrity.
- Self-control. This means remaining calm and business-like even where others are not. This requires a degree of emotional intelligence, a key prerequisite of professionalism.
- Flexibility. Professionals adapt to the reasonable needs of their employer, for example staying a little later than contracted where this is needed (while maintaining a work-life balance).
- Respect for others. This means treating others with respect and kindness, irrespective of their seniority.
- Professional image. This includes both personal presentation (eg hair and clothing), but also includes other things, such as writing grammatically.

1.5 The public interest

Key term

> The **public interest** is considered to be the collective wellbeing of the community of people and institutions the professional accountant serves, including clients, lenders, governments, employers, employees, investors, the business and financial community and others who rely on the work of professional accountants. (IESBA)

The IESBA comments that an accountant's responsibility is not exclusively to satisfy the needs of an **individual client or employer**. It extends to society, and often consists of supplying information that society needs.

One fundamental problem with the debate about accountants acting in the public interest is the lack, in most jurisdictions, of a robust definition of what the public interest is, and of one that is backed by enforcement mechanisms. Within UK law, for example, there is no statutory definition of the public interest. As one critic, Alan Lovell, comments: "Its malleability possibly explains both its longevity and its unreliability in a court of law" (in Gowthorpe & Blake, *Ethical issues in accounting*: p63).

Critics of the view that accountants act in the public interest have focused on the alleged closeness between accountants' definition of the public interest and the profession's self-interest. Critics have claimed that accountants' insistence on self-regulation indicates where their priorities lie. Some believe that the accountancy profession has always been vulnerable to this charge. TA Lee's history of the accountancy profession in the 19th century comments: "The most obvious feature of early UK professionalisation is the pursuit by accountants and their institutions of economic self-interest in the name of a public interest".

1.6 Influence of the accountancy profession on organisations

That the influence of the accountancy profession is potentially huge can be established simply by considering all the different areas which involve accountants:

- Financial accounting and reporting
- Audit and assurance
- Management accounting
- Consultancy
- Tax services
- Public sector accounting

Accountants' advice will also be crucial in situations of change, where accountants are advising on the financial and information systems aspects of new developments.

Case Study

Accountants dominate senior business positions in many countries. The variety of involvements that accountants have within each area of their expertise is also very large. The Institute of Chartered Accountants in England and Wales' recruitment literature highlights, for example, the role of tax accountants.

"Some professionals will advise on policy for our tax system, others will write the tax law. Someone else will administer the collection of taxes for the Government. Others will act for businesses of all types who have to pay these taxes. Marketing, IT, media and publishing all need tax specialists."

Accountants therefore have a significant impact, a significant footprint, on the organisations for which they work. Is this always for the best?

Case Study

In the book *Ethical Issues in Accounting*, a chapter by Alan Lovell points out that accountants will be responsible for managing public sector organisations in as cost effective a way as possible, which may not necessarily be compatible with the service objectives of those organisations nor the codes of other professional staff who work within those organisations.

Lovell utilises Kohlberg's view of ethical hierarchy to explain how accountants effectively view other professionals. The accounting system in effect assumes that, as the other professionals do not trust the system or those who operate it, this illustrates that they have a low level of moral reasoning and therefore justifies a strict performance management system, together with anti-whistleblowing codes designed to deter employees from revealing shortcomings in patient care.

Accountants' low level of moral reasoning contrasts with the ethical codes to which doctors and nurses adhere are founded on the idea that they are their patients' advocates. This implies that they need to use a much higher level of moral reasoning.

1.7 The accountancy profession in society

At one level, the numbers included within accounts can have a number of impacts.

(a) **Mechanistic issues** are where the accounts are used to judge the performance of a company or its directors in line with a regulation or contract. Examples are company borrowing limits which are frequently defined as a multiple of share capital and reserves and directors' bonus schemes that are based on some proportion of reported profits.

(b) **Judgmental issues** are where the figures in the accounts influence the judgment of their users. The accounts may influence not just the view of investors, but governments seeking to assess what a reasonable tax burden would be and employees determining their wage claims.

1.8 Accountancy as a value-laden profession

Critics of the accountancy profession claim that the work done and the conclusions drawn by accountants are determined by a set of beliefs and values that imply a particular view of how power and wealth should be distributed in society. Accountants, it is claimed, believe that precedence should be given to the interests of suppliers of financial capital.

Many accountants would argue in response that the numbers in accounts support no cause and it is for others to draw conclusions on the figures produced. The counter argument to this is that the very idea of neutral financial information, that can be considered separately from its social content, is itself a social construct, arising in the context of the capitalist mode of production.

If pressed, accountants might argue that they are following the requirements of laws or of their clients. However, the laws may be ethically suspect and the following the requirements of clients argument does not support ideas of accountants' independence or, worse, leads to the suspicion that accountants are pursuing ethically dubious courses of action.

Even if the ends are not explicitly ethically suspect, much accounting literature does assume that accountants are producing information for individuals or corporations seeking to **maximise their personal wealth**. If this has a moral justification, it is based on the ideas of **liberal economic democracy**. These ideas are that individuals should be free to **exercise their economic choices** and are equally able to do so. No group in society dominates either economically or politically, according to these ideas. The result of the individual pursuit of economic benefit is economic efficiency, maximum profits and economic growth, and everyone within society being better off.

1.8.1 Criticisms of liberal economic democracy

Critics have claimed that the model of liberal economic democracy is far from reality and has various flaws. By providing the information that supports the present systems, accountants are complicit in perpetuating its flaws.

(a) **Lack of equality**

One significant criticism is that individuals are not equal economically and are evidently **not able to make economic choices** that will benefit themselves. The argument that people make a rational economic choice to be homeless is clearly wrong. Accountants are therefore accused of supporting those who can make economic choices and by doing so perpetuate social inequality, ensure that wealth continues to be distributed among the already wealthy, and suppress minorities and the disenfranchised and powerless.

(b) **Role of institutions**

A related criticism is that individuals do not exercise the real power but institutions – principally the **Government and corporations**. Indeed, critics point to many instances of governments acting to protect the interests of shareholders and the information rights of the financial community against less well-off groups in society.

Marxist arguments take this viewpoint to its furthest conclusion, arguing that power is held by **capital**, that capital and labour are inevitably in conflict and that the state acts to protect capital and suppress labour. Accountants too are complicit in this.

(c) **Failure to increase social welfare**

The argument that the pursuit of individual self-interest leads to maximum social welfare appears tenuous. Even if wealth is maximised, there is **no guarantee** that all aspects of **social welfare** will be **maximised**. Indeed, some aspects of social welfare, such as quality of life or health, would not seem to have an obvious link with maximising income. In addition, the maximisation of wealth does not imply that wealth will be fairly distributed. Critics have claimed that economic growth has been at the expense of a widening gap between rich and poor, both within developed countries and between developed and developing countries.

(d) **Environmental problems**

Critics such as the 'deep ecologists' have claimed that the pursuit of growth has been at the expense of **environmental degradation** and that society needs to change its priorities. By aiding the promotion of economic growth, accountants are complicit in supporting activity that harms the environment.

(e) **Ethical viewpoint**

Some critics have gone back to ethical theories (as detailed in Chapter 1) and have claimed that accountants are complicit in a version of **utilitarianism** with the economic ends justifying the means rather than another (preferable) ethical position.

Question — Liberal democracy

The accountancy profession has been described as an institution of liberal democracy.

Outline some arguments in favour of liberal democracy.

Answer

It may be claimed that liberal democracy is the political system corresponding to the market economy. Such a system places a high value on individuals (rather than on groups or communities), and involves a system of government in which politicians are elected by individuals. Similarly, economic decisions are made by the aggregation of individual actors that constitutes the market.

Since power in such a system is dispersed among individual actors, it is held that liberal democracies produce good government that is relatively free of the tyrannical domination of one individual or group. The mechanisms of representative democracy provide a means by which potential tyrants may be deposed.

Similarly, in such a system each individual is free of fetters to their ability to trade and thus to enrich themselves.

It is argued that such a system results in economic and political freedom, as well as high levels of prosperity.

1.9 Criticisms of the accountancy profession

Inevitably perhaps, it has been the critics of the accountancy profession who have been most vocal in highlighting the influence of accounting in resource allocation, seeking to demonstrate its complicity in wealth distribution and its role as the agent of capital.

1.9.1 Accountants in management accounting

In his book *The Social and Organisational Context of Management Accounting*, Tony Puxty argued that the 'received wisdom' of management accounting cannot legitimately be taken for granted.

PART D GOVERNANCE AND SELF-REGULATION

Case Study

Puxty highlighted behavioural studies of budgeting that use the phrase 'dysfunctional behaviour', meaning behaviour that is harmful to the **organisation**. But why should this be so? Is it not 'dysfunctional' from the point of view of the **manager** that they are expected to suffer the misery of having their actions constrained by budget targets? There are many other examples: what, for instance, is 'favourable' about a favourable labour rate variance, from the point of view of the workforce?

Puxty went on to show that traditional management accounting is rooted in modes of thought that are only considered to be 'common sense' for the time being. 'Common sense' he asserted, is determined by the **beliefs** and **values** of the society in which it supposedly applies. It is not common to all eras (it is relativist).

In particular, the ideas that considerations of society (of which businesses are a part and a microcosm) should take the individual as their starting point and that individuals have rights to liberty and property are fundamental to accounting, yet they only originated with philosophers like Hobbes and Locke in the 17th century.

Puxty also argues that Foucault's ideas about the way in which **regimes of power** have grown and been sustained through **disciplinary mechanisms** and the **institution of norms** for human behaviour are very relevant to the role of the accountancy profession.

Case Study

Other studies along similar lines to Puxty have attempted to show how the origins of accounting reside in the exercise of social power and how accounting is "implicated in the creation of structures of surveillance and power that permit modern management to function at a distance from the work process itself."

One study considers the development of standard costing and budgeting in the 1920s as simply one part of a general widening of the apparatus of power at this time.

"The practices that developed were intended to make the person (…) more amenable to being managed and controlled".

This should be seen in the context of other drives current at the time, such as the wide advocacy of eugenics (the sterilisation of the 'unfit' to improve the country's breeding stock) and an interest in 'mental hygiene' to be promoted by means of such methods as IQ testing.

Macintosh in *Management Accounting and Control Systems* (1994) looks at Foucault's ideas about the general principles of discipline and control that became widespread in the Western world from about 1700 onwards.

(a) The **enclosure principle**, in essence keeping people in confined spaces (at the desk, at their workstation)

(b) The **efficient body principle**, which disciplines individuals' time when they are in their confined spaces

(c) The **correct comportment principle**, disciplining behaviour through surveillance, through the imposition of norms of behaviour, and through examination

Macintosh has little difficulty in drawing parallels with management accounting – responsibility accounting, standard costing practices and performance measurement systems among the examples chosen.

1.9.2 Accountants and financial accounting

Unsurprisingly, accountants have been criticised in similar terms for the picture published financial accounts paint and the support they provide to capital markets. Prem Sikka argues that many accountants:

> '... believe that mobilising accounting and auditing practices in support of markets and financial capital (held by shareholders) is ethically acceptable but mobilising accounting to give visibility to poverty and institutionalised exploitation is somehow unethical (...) Accounting and auditing practices remain preoccupied with prioritising capital over labour (in the statement of profit or loss) and the property rights (in the statement of financial position). Most accounting books have little to say about social justice or the rights of employees.'

For example, Professor Sikka and others proposed expanding the level of disclosures in accounts in the early 1990s to include disclosures of low pay. This proposal was made at a time when the Labour party was pressing for the introduction of the minimum wage.

Sikka and others have emphasised the idea that accountancy decisions inevitably have **political consequences** and that it is difficult to see how accountants could hold positions that are not influenced by wider values. However, one criticism of their view is that accountants are not free to determine their own stance, and that instead they are constrained by politicians' attitudes expressed in legislation.

1.9.3 Accountants and taxation advice

Prem Sikka and others have also criticised accountants for being complicit in their clients paying less than their 'fair' share of tax. In some cases, accountants have been found guilty of helping clients evade tax and duly punished. However, some critics seem to suggest that accountants should not be involved in helping their clients legally avoid tax. Again, however, the question arises as to whether accountants should base their advice on the law, or on some sort of notion as to what a fair tax liability is.

1.10 Acting against the public interest

Criticism of the accountancy profession has extended to the rules that it follows. Critics have argued that the rules:

(a) Are **too passive**, allowing too great a variety of accounting treatments, and failing to impose meaningful responsibilities on auditors such as an explicit responsibility to detect and report fraud.

(b) **Emphasise the wrong principles**, giving priority to client confidentiality over disclosure in the wider public interest, and teaching accountants to follow rules rather than question them.

(c) Allow auditors to **establish a long-term, cosy relationship** with clients by the failure to require compulsory rotation of auditors and allowing auditors to provide non-audit services, rather than forcing auditors to maintain a distance.

(d) Allow the creation of **too small a number of large firms** who dominate the audit of major listed companies and therefore can effectively set the agenda as regards scope of audit work (although arguably it is only large firms that can audit the very biggest companies).

Arguably these views depend to some extent on hindsight, the implication being that, as auditors and governance structures have failed to identify corporate malpractice, there must be something wrong with the rulebook that is being followed.

However, we have seen how the fallout from the Enron case influenced the development of the stricter Sarbanes-Oxley rules in the United States. Partly, this was due to Enron appearing in a number of ways to 'tick the right boxes'. It had a good number of non-executive directors on its board with a strong range of experience, for example.

PART D GOVERNANCE AND SELF-REGULATION

Question   Stakeholders

Think about all the major activities that you are involved in if you work as an accountant. Who are the stakeholders involved? Who do you treat as the most important stakeholders? And why?

Answer

Answers will vary depending on your responsibilities. If, for example, you are involved in audit and answered 'the clients because they pay our bills', who do you mean when you say the client – the directors or shareholders? If you work in tax planning, by reducing your client's tax bill, are you contributing to society as a whole losing out through diminished tax revenues?

2 Auditor independence

FAST FORWARD

> The audit profession has a complex governance structure. UK firms are subject to public oversight from the FRC in the UK.

Corporate scandals, most prominently that of Enron in the US but more recently the furore surround the collapse of Carillion in the UK, have brought the audit profession under close scrutiny from investors, businesses, regulators and others.

There is a trend towards businesses becoming more complex and global, and firms of accountants have expanded their range of services well beyond traditional assurance and tax advice. This has led to a great deal of re-examination of regulatory and standard-setting structures both nationally and internationally in recent years.

Laws are, in many respects, a last resort in the task of ensuring that audits are conducted properly and are of a high quality. As a generalisation, laws tend to be prescriptive and dissuasive. They are external to the auditor, requiring them to act within the letter (although not necessarily the spirit) of the law in order to avoid punishment. Law is a relatively blunt instrument for regulation.

At the other extreme would be a moral code that is purely internal to the auditor's self, which the individual would adhere to, irrespective of external consequences or laws. The audit profession does not attempt to set out such a code, this being the more proper area for broader social, moral or religious authority.

Audit regulations do take the presence of external laws and internal morality as their starting points, but sit somewhere in between these two extremes. International standards are principles-based, representing a common set of principles and practices which are more flexible than statutory laws, allowing for an element of ambiguity and judgment on the part of the auditor. At the same time, however, auditing standards are not simply general statements of morality: they contain specific suggestions for the auditor to consider in specific circumstances, which are not legally binding but which provide a starting point for the auditor in a given situation.

2.1 Overview of the UK regulatory framework

The authority to give approval to carry out statutory audits in the UK is delegated to Recognised Supervisory Bodies (RSBs). An auditor must be a member of an RSB and be eligible under its own rules – so that an AIA member, awarded with the AIA RPQ, will then need to register with an RSB in order to act as a statutory auditor.

The RSBs are required by the Companies Act to have rules to ensure that persons eligible for appointment as a company auditor are either

(Companies Act 2006: sections 1212–1215):

- Individuals holding an appropriate qualification
- Firms controlled by qualified persons

2.2 International standard setting

International Standards on Auditing (ISAs) are produced by the International Auditing and Assurance Standards Board (IAASB), a technical standing committee of the International Federation of Accountants (IFAC). You should also be familiar with the International Ethics Standards Board for Accountants (IESBA), another body of IFAC and the producer of the *Code of Ethics*.

```
                    IFAC
          (International Federation of
                  Accountants)
                   /        \
                  /          \
              IAASB          IESBA
   (International Auditing and   (International Ethics Standards
    Assurance Standards Board)      Board for Accountants)

   • ISAs (International Standards   • Code of Ethics for
     on Auditing)                      Professional Accountants
   • ISQCs (International
     Standards on Quality Control)
   • ISREs (International
     Standards on Review
     Engagements)
   • ISAEs (International
     Standards on Assurance
     Engagements)
   • ISRSs (International
     Standards on Related
     Services)
```

The IAASB's *Preface to International Standards on Quality Control, Auditing, Assurance and Related Services Pronouncements* states that all the IAASB's 'engagement standards' above are 'authoritative material', which means that they must be followed in an audit that is conducted in accordance with ISAs.

The IAASB also publishes four kinds of 'non-authoritative material'.

- International Auditing Practice Notes (IAPNs) – These do not impose additional requirements on auditors, but provide them with practical assistance

- Practice Notes Relating to Other International Standards (eg in relation to ISREs, ISAEs or ISRSs)

- Staff publications, which are used to help raise awareness of new or emerging issues, and to direct attention to the relevant parts of IAASB pronouncements

- Consultation papers, which seek to generate discussion with stakeholders

Within each country, local regulations govern, to a greater or lesser degree, the practices followed in the auditing of financial or other information. Such regulations may be either of a statutory nature, or in the form of statements issued by the regulatory or professional bodies in the countries concerned.

National standards on auditing and related services published in many countries differ in form and content. The IAASB takes account of such documents and differences and, in the light of such knowledge, issues ISAs which are intended for international acceptance.

The European Union, for example, has since 2014 required ISAs (as issued by the IAASB) to be adopted at EU level. Member states may impose additional requirements on auditors, but these must not contradict EU ISAs. An example of this is the UK's FRC, whose ISAs (UK) are in some places more stringent than the IAASB's ISAs.

2.3 Public oversight internationally

The **Public Interest Oversight Board (PIOB)** exists to oversee all of IFAC's 'public interest activities,' including its standard-setting bodies such as the IAASB & IESBA. Its work involves:

- Monitoring the standard-setting boards;
- Overseeing the nomination process for membership of these boards; and
- Co-operation with national oversight authorities.

The objective of the international PIOB is to increase the confidence of investors and others that the public interest activities of IFAC are properly responsive to the public interest. The PIOB is based in Madrid, Spain, where it operates as a non-profit Spanish foundation.

Oversight within the EU is by the Committee of European Auditing Oversight Bodies (**CEAOB**), which was set up in June 2016 as a result of the EU Audit Regulation. The CEAOB acts as the framework for cooperation between European national audit authorities.

The CEAOB is made up of:

- Representatives of the national audit oversight bodies across the EU
- Representatives from national audit authorities of the European Economic Area

Additionally, the European Banking Authority (EBA) and the European Insurance and Occupational Pensions Authority (EIOPA) attend as observers.

2.4 Other examples of public oversight

An example of public oversight is the Professional Oversight team of the UK's FRC (formerly the Professional Oversight Board, or POB), which has a number of statutory responsibilities. These include:

- Independent **oversight of the regulation of statutory** auditors by the RSBs;
- Independent **supervision of Auditors General** in respect of the exercise of their function as statutory auditors; and
- The **receipt** of statutory **change of auditor notifications** from companies and statutory auditors in respect of 'major audits'.

In the US, the response to the breakdown of stock market trust caused by perceived inadequacies in corporate governance arrangements and the Enron scandal was the **Sarbanes–Oxley Act 2002.** The Act applies to all companies that are required to file periodic reports with the Securities and Exchange Commission (SEC).

The **Public Company Accounting Oversight Board (PCAOB)** is a private sector body in the US created by Sarbanes-Oxley. Its aim is to oversee the auditors of public companies. Its stated purpose is to 'protect the interests of investors and further the public interest in the preparation of informative, accurate and independent auditors' reports' (PCAOB, 2016). Its powers include setting auditing, quality control, ethics, independence and other standards relating to the preparation of auditor's reports by issuers. It also has the authority to regulate the non-audit services that audit firms can offer.

Sarbanes–Oxley has been criticised in some quarters for **not being strong enough** on certain issues, for example the selection of external auditors by the audit committee, and at the same time being overly rigid on others. Directors may be less likely to consult lawyers in the first place if they believe that legislation could override lawyer–client privilege.

In addition, it has been alleged that a Sarbanes–Oxley compliance industry has sprung up, focusing companies' attention on complying with all aspects of the legislation, irrespective of how significant they may be. This has distracted companies from **improving information flows** to the market and then allowing the market to make well-informed decisions. The Act has also done little to address the temptation provided by generous stock options to inflate profits, other than requiring possible forfeiture if financial statements are subsequently restated.

Most significantly, perhaps, there is some evidence of companies having turned away from the US stock markets and towards other markets, such as London. It was said that this was partly due to companies tiring of the **increased compliance costs** associated with Sarbanes–Oxley implementation. In addition, the nature of the **regulatory regime** may be an increasingly significant factor in listing decisions.

3 Conflicting clients' interests

The auditor may have clients whose interests conflict with one another.

Audit firms should take reasonable steps to identify circumstances that could pose a conflict of interest. Examples of this include:

- Using **confidential information** obtained during an audit to help another client to acquire the audit client
- Advising **two clients at the same time** who are competing to acquire the same company
- Providing **services to both a vendor and a purchaser** in relation to the same transaction
- Representing **two clients who are in a legal dispute** with each other (eg during divorce proceedings)

(IESBA *Code*: para. 310.4 A1)

The *Code* emphasises the importance of considering potential conflicts of interest **before accepting a new client** (IESBA *Code*: para. R310.5). An issue here is first **identifying that there is a conflict** – it may be that, for example, the engagement partner for a new client is not aware that there is a conflict because they do not know all of the firm's other clients. It is therefore necessary to have an **effective conflict identification process** (IESBA *Code*: para. 310.5 A1–2).

As with all threats, **safeguards** should be applied if necessary. If safeguards would not be enough, then the engagement should be declined or discontinued.

Examples of safeguards
Disclosure of the nature of the conflict of interest (and related safeguards) to clients affected, to **obtain their consent** to the professional accountant performing the services
Mechanisms to **prevent unauthorised disclosure of confidential information**, such as: • Separate engagement teams • Creating separate areas of practice for specialty functions within the firm • Establishing policies and procedures to limit access to client files
Review of safeguards by a senior individual not involved with the engagement(s)
External **review** by a professional accountant
Consulting with third parties, such as a professional body, legal counsel or another professional accountant

(IESBA *Code*: para. 310.9-13)

Disclosure is the key safeguard here. If the **client refuses** to give consent, then the engagement giving rise to the conflict should be discontinued.

4 Placing unreasonable expectations on a trainee

AIA students are bound by its *Code of Ethics and Professional Conduct* in exactly the same way as full members are.

Some specific issues can arise in relation to training and the expectations made of a trainee accountant, particularly where the expectations made are too high. It should be borne in mind, however, that a trainee must be exposed to a certain level of challenge if they are to acquire the skills and experience necessary for their future career as full members. It is clear, then, that a balance must be struck between challenging the student and providing them with tasks that they are able to complete; this can perhaps be encapsulated in the idea of an appropriate challenge. This should be applied consistently to the student throughout training, and underpinned by the provision of adequate resources and support to enable the trainee to meet the challenge.

Trainee accountants may be subject to special pressures that may lead them to compromise their independence. An ethical duty falls both on the trainee and on the professional accountant(s) responsible for allocating work to them. The IESBA *Code of Ethics* contains guidance that is relevant here, in section 270. This was covered in general terms in Chapter 3, so some of this material is repeated here.

The fundamental principle most under threat in this situation is that of **professional competence and due care**.

The *Code of Ethics* states that a professional accountant shall not:

- **Allow pressure from others** to result in a breach of compliance with the fundamental principles; or
- **Place pressure on others** that the accountant knows, or has reason to believe, would result in the other individuals breaching the fundamental principles.

(IESBA *Code*: para. R270.3)

The first of these points is relevant to the trainee themselves; the second is relevant to anyone allocating work to another person. This could be, for example, an audit manager deciding on the allocation of work tasks within the audit team, but it would also apply to an audit trainee giving work to a more junior trainee. Ethical duties therefore arise at both ends of the relationship, giving and receiving work.

An issue that can sometimes arise with trainees is that of **time pressure**. It is vital that sufficient allowance is made for the **additional time** that a trainee will require to complete a given task in comparison with a more senior accountant. This should be factored into a trainee's hourly rate, for example, so that there is no need for time to be written off on the grounds that the trainee was new to a task.

Question   IESBA Code of Ethics

In which of the following situations has there been a breach of the IESBA *Code of Ethics*?

1. An audit manager allocated a part-qualified trainee three hours to recalculate the depreciation charges on the non-current assets of a small company, and to vouch any additions to supporting documentation. This is the standard time allocation for such a task.

2. A part-qualified audit trainee gave a new graduate trainee the task of finding specific purchase invoices as part of the purchases cycle testing for the audit. The trainee falsified the audit working papers; this was discovered later by the audit manager, who noticed that the trainee had noted the details of sales invoices instead of purchase invoices.

3. A new purchase ledger clerk has been recruited to the finance team of a small company. At the month end it became clear that the clerk was not able to use the company's computerised accounting system, in spite of this being a core requirement of their job role.

Answer

1. No breach. This is likely to be sufficient time for a part-qualified trainee to perform this task, particularly given that this is the standard time allocation for this task, and it is usual for it to be performed by a trainee with this level of training and experience.

2. Breach. The part-qualified audit trainee has given the new graduate trainee work that they are not able to perform. They should have confirmed that the trainee understood the task they were being asked to do, and then should have provided further explanations when these were required. Similarly, the new graduate trainee should not have accepted a task that they were not in a position to complete; the falsification of audit documentation is a serious breach of the *Code of Ethics*.

3. Breach. The clerk has been allocated work that they are not able to do. This would appear to be a failure of the recruitment process, although it is not clear whether the clerk is at fault (eg for having said they could use such a computerised system when in fact they could not), or whether the recruiter simply failed to ascertain whether the clerk would be able to do the job.

Chapter roundup

- International Financial Reporting Standards are a key element of accounting regulations in Europe and in other parts of the globe.

- Professionalism means **avoiding actions** that bring **discredit on the accountancy profession**.

  Acting in the public interest means acting for the welfare of society at large.

  Various commentators have argued that the **figures** accountants produce are **not neutral**, but incorporate value judgments and are in accordance with the wishes of certain viewpoints in society.

- The audit profession has a complex governance structure. UK firms are subject to public oversight from the FRC in the UK.

Quick Quiz

1. Which of the following are included within the meaning of the term GAAP?

    A   Accounting Standards (IFRS)
    B   Auditing Standards (ISAs)
    C   Company law
    D   Stock exchange regulations

2. Is the following statement true or false?

    The IESBA takes the view that the accountant's duty to their client always overrides the need to act in the public interest.

3. "Accountancy is a value-neutral profession"

    Briefly outline some arguments for and against this position.

4. Avinesh, a full AIA member working in public practice, has asked Basia (a recent graduate and student AIA member) to prepare the group accounts for a medium-sized group of companies.

    Which fundamental principle is most under threat here?

    A   Integrity
    B   Professional integrity
    C   Professional behaviour
    D   Professional competence and due care

5. South & Co has for a long time acted as auditor to Pencil Co, but has recently been invited to tender for the audit of its rival, Crayon Co.

    What should South & Co do before tendering to mitigate any potential conflict?

Answers to Quick Quiz

1. A, C, D Auditing standards will apply to statutory auditors operating in a given jurisdiction, but they are not part of GAAP.

2. False. The IESBA has determined that the professional accountant must act in the public interest, most notably where the client has not complied with applicable laws and regulations.

3. It is claimed by some that the accountancy profession is value-neutral, because its focus is on the provision of objective, value-free financial information to users.

    Against this, it may be argued that the financial information produced by accountants is focused primarily on the needs of private capital (eg profit), rather than those of society as a whole.

4. D The professional competence and due care of both Basia and Avinesh are compromised.

5. South & Co should disclose the situation both to Pencil Co and to Crayon Co. It may tender but should only proceed with both audits with the consent of both clients.

PART D GOVERNANCE AND SELF-REGULATION

Global governance and corporate social responsibility (CSR)

Topic list	Syllabus reference
1 Corporate governance	LO 3, LO 4
2 Social responsibility	LO 3, LO 4
3 Corporate social responsibility (CSR)	LO 3, LO 4
4 Integrated Reporting	LO 3, LO 4

Introduction

A central theme of the Ethics and Professional Practice module is the importance of companies acting responsibly and ethically. Key aspects of this include corporate governance, social responsibility, and corporate social responsibility (CSR). Good corporate governance is crucial in guiding companies to operate in an ethical manner, ensuring accountability, transparency, and the overall well-being of society.

PART D GOVERNANCE AND SELF-REGULATION

1 Corporate governance

Corporate governance, the system by which organisations are directed and controlled, is based on a number of concepts, including transparency, independence, accountability and integrity.

1.1 What is corporate governance?

Key term

Corporate governance is the **system** by which organisations are directed and controlled. *(UK Corporate Governance Code)*

Corporate governance is a **set of relationships** between a company's directors, its shareholders and other stakeholders. It also provides the structure through which the objectives of the company are set, and the means of achieving those objectives and monitoring performance, are determined. (OECD 2018)

A number of comments can be made about these definitions of corporate governance.

(a) The **management, awareness, evaluation and mitigation of risk** are fundamental in all definitions of good governance. This includes the operation of an **adequate and appropriate system of control**.

(b) The notion that **overall performance is enhanced** by **good supervision** and **management** within **set best practice guidelines** underpins most definitions.

(c) Good governance provides a **framework** for an organisation to pursue its strategy in an **ethical and effective** way and **offers safeguards against misuse of resources**, human, financial, physical or intellectual.

(d) Good governance is not just about externally established codes; it also requires a willingness to **apply the spirit** as well as the letter of the law.

(e) Good corporate governance can **attract new investment** into companies, particularly in developing nations. It should mean that shareholders can **trust** those responsible for running and monitoring the company.

(f) **Accountability** is generally a major theme in all governance frameworks, including accountability not just to shareholders but also to other **stakeholders**, and accountability not just by directors but by auditors as well.

(g) Corporate governance **underpins capital market confidence in companies** and in the government/regulators/tax authorities that administer them. It helps **protect the value of shareholders' investment**.

1.1.1 History of governance

Governance focuses on ownership because ownership, and therefore financing, results in businesses being formed and expanded. Different systems of governance are seen as best practice in different countries, as we shall see later in this text. However, much of the governance debate has been seen in the context of the so-called Anglo-Saxon model where ownership and management are separate, and companies can obtain a listing on a stock exchange where their shares are bought and sold.

1.1.2 Governance in companies and non-governmental organisations

Although mostly discussed in relation to large, quoted companies, governance is an issue for all corporate bodies, commercial and not for profit, including public sector and non-governmental organisations. There are certain ways in which companies might differ from other types of organisation, such as their ownership (principals), their mission and the legal/regulatory environment within which they operate.

Public sector organisations are organisations that are **controlled by one or more parts of the state**. Their functions are often to **implement government policy** in secretarial or administration areas. Some are supervised by government departments (for example, hospitals or schools). Others are devolved bodies,

such as local authorities, nationalised companies (where the majority or all of the shares are owned by the Government), supranational bodies or non-governmental organisations.

These organisations are in the public sector because the control over a particular public service, utility or public good is seen as so important that it cannot be left to the profit-motivated sector, which may for example seek to close socially vital loss-making services, such as bus routes.

Objectives will be determined by the political leaders in line with government policy. They are likely to focus on **value for money and service delivery objectives**, possibly underpinned by legislation. The level of control may be high, leading to accusations of excess bureaucracy and cost.

In many countries, there are thousands of charities and voluntary organisations that exist to fulfil a particular purpose, maybe social, environmental, religious or humanitarian. Funds are raised to support that purpose. Charities are not owned as such but will be primarily responsible to the **donors** of funds and the **beneficiaries** (those who receive money or other aid out of the charities' resources). Charities will be subject to their own legal regime that grants privileges (for example tax concessions) but imposes requirements on how funds can be spent and the charities' assets managed.

Organisation for Economic Co-operation and Development

The Organisation for Economic Co-operation and Development (OECD) first developed its Principles of Corporate Governance in 1999 and issued revised versions in 2004 and 2015. They are non-binding principles, intended to assist governments in their efforts to evaluate and improve the legal, institutional and regulatory framework for corporate governance in their countries.

They are also intended to provide guidance for stock exchanges, investors and companies. The focus is on stock exchange listed companies, but many of the principles can also apply to private companies and state-owned organisations. The OECD principles deal mainly with governance problems that result from the separation of ownership and management of a company. Issues of ethical concern and environmental issues are also relevant, although not central to the problems of governance.

The G20/OECD Principles of Corporate Governance

In conjunction with the G20 (a group of the 20 largest advanced and emerging economies in the world) the OECD issued its revised principles in 2015 (*OECD, 2015*). They are grouped into six broad areas:

(a) Ensuring the basis for an effective corporate governance framework
(b) The rights and equitable treatment of shareholders and key ownership functions
(c) Institutional investors, stock markets, and other intermediaries
(d) The role of stakeholders in corporate governance
(e) Disclosure and transparency
(f) The responsibilities of the board

International Corporate Governance Network

The International Corporate Governance Network (ICGN) first issued its Global Governance Principles in 2005 to support the OECD principles. The ICGN principles set out the corporate governance responsibilities that boards and institutional shareholders should adhere to. The purpose was to provide practical guidance for corporate boards to use when attempting to meet the expectations of investors.

The ICGN believes that companies will only achieve value in the longer term if they manage effectively their relationships with stakeholders such as employees, customers, local communities and the environment as a whole. The most recent version of this guidance (*2017*) uses the following Global Governance Principles.

(a) Board role and responsibilities – be informed and support long-term shareholder benefit
(b) Leadership and independence – clarity and integrity for the board in order to be successful
(c) Composition and appointment – balance of skills, experience and objectivity for decisions
(d) Corporate culture – blend of corporate objectives, values and business ethics as part of strategy
(e) Risk oversight – proactive approach to managing risks as part of a changing world
(f) Remuneration – alignment of board, shareholders and strategy to create sustainable value for all
(g) Reporting and audit – internal and external reporting to maintain corporate accountability
(h) Shareholder rights – rights of all shareholders should be equal and must be protected

1.2 Corporate governance concepts

One view of governance is that it is based on a series of underlying concepts.

1.2.1 Fairness

The directors' deliberations and also the systems and values that underlie the company the company must be **balanced** by respecting the rights and views of everyone who has a legitimate interest in the it. In many jurisdictions, corporate governance guidelines reinforce legal protection for certain groups, for example minority shareholders. It should mean the company deals **even-handedly** with others.

1.2.2 Transparency

Key term

> **Transparency** means **open and clear disclosure** of relevant information to shareholders and other stakeholders, as well as not concealing information when it may affect decisions. It means open discussions and a default position of information provision rather than concealment.

Disclosure in this context obviously includes **information in the financial statements**, not just the numbers and notes to the accounts but also narrative statements such as the directors' report and the operating and financial or business review. It also includes all **voluntary disclosure**; that is, disclosure above the minimum required by law or regulation. Voluntary corporate communications include management forecasts, analysts' presentations, press releases, information placed on websites and other reports such as standalone environmental or social reports.

The main reason why transparency is so important relates to the **agency problem**, ie the potential conflict between owners and managers. Without effective disclosure, the position could be unfairly weighted towards managers since they have far more knowledge of the company's activities and financial situation than the owner/investors. Avoidance of this **information asymmetry** requires not only effective disclosure rules but also strong internal controls that ensure the information that is disclosed is **reliable**. Information also needs to be published in sufficient detail to meet the needs of shareholders/owners. Publication of abbreviated information may be counter-productive and may give the impression of concealment rather than openness.

Linked with the agency issue, publication of relevant and reliable information **reassures investors and underpins stock market confidence** in how companies are being governed and thus **significantly influences market prices**. International accounting standards and stock market regulations based on corporate governance codes require information published to be **true and fair**. Information can only fulfil this requirement if adequate disclosure is made of uncertainties and adverse events. It is therefore clear that financial data will be insufficient without supporting explanation.

Circumstances where concealment may be justified include discussions about **future strategy** (knowledge of which would benefit competitors), **confidential** issues relating to individuals, and discussions leading to an agreed position that is then made public.

Case Study

Ethics guru Chris MacDonald has raised a number of issues with the concept of transparency.

1. The requirement of transparency to check how directors (agents) are doing indicates a big problem with governance. If shareholders had complete confidence in directors, there would be no concern about transparency.

2. Transparency assumes that those who receive information are well informed but problems may arise through misinterpretation. The example quoted was a hospital executive being criticised for having the perk of expensive membership of an exclusive private club. However, if the executive was responsible for fundraising, the club would provide networking opportunities with members who could make large donations to the hospital.

3. In the context of directors' remuneration evidence suggests that full transparency can ratchet up average reward. A chief executive, seeing how much other chief executives in their sector are earning, may want their rewards to match theirs. A remuneration committee may regard the fact that its chief executive is earning below average remuneration as poor publicity for the chief executive and the company.

4. Full transparency of rewards of one type may lead to those in positions of trust to seek less visible, and perhaps more costly, rewards. For example, the 2009 scandal about excessive expenses being claimed by UK Members of Parliament was linked to the political unacceptability of increasing MPs' salaries significantly. To head off a revolt by members, the Conservative Government in the 1980s introduced a big increase in members' expense allowances, with the minister responsible allegedly telling MPs 'go out, boys, and spend it.'

1.2.3 Innovation

The concept of innovation in the approach to corporate governance recognises the fact that the needs of businesses and stakeholders can change over time. It also has an impact on how organisations respond to meeting the 'comply or explain' requirement contained in various codes of corporate governance that are currently in effect.

1.2.4 Scepticism

The UK Corporate Governance Code, under the heading of 'Leadership', encourages non-executive directors (NEDs) to adopt an air of scepticism so that they can effectively challenge management decisions in their role of scrutiny. Applying professional scepticism is also an important part of the role of auditors and audit committees. ISA 200 defines professional scepticism as: "An attitude that includes a questioning mind, being alert to conditions which may indicate possible misstatement due to error or fraud, and a critical assessment of audit evidence." This does not mean that all management decisions and evidence have to be approached with suspicion or mistrust; but rather that an open and enquiring mind must always be employed. A healthy corporate culture and environment is one that encourages and enables such scepticism to thrive.

1.2.5 Independence

Key term

> **Independence** is the avoidance of being unduly influenced by vested interests and free from any constraints that would prevent a correct course of action being taken. It is an ability to stand apart from inappropriate influences and be free of managerial capture, to be able to make the correct and uncontaminated decision on a given issue.
>
> Independence is a quality that can be possessed by individuals and is an essential component of professionalism and professional behaviour.

An important distinction generally with independence is **independence of mind and independence of appearance**.

- **Independence of mind** means providing an opinion without being affected by influences compromising judgment.
- **Independence of appearance** means avoiding situations where an informed third party could reasonably conclude that an individual's judgment would have been compromised.

Independence is an important concept in relation to directors; in particular, **freedom from conflicts of interest**. Corporate governance reports have increasingly stressed the importance of **independent non-executive directors**, directors who are not primarily employed by the company and who have very strictly controlled other links with it. They should be in a better position to **promote the interests of shareholders and other stakeholders**. Freed from pressures that could influence their activities, independent non-executive directors should be able to carry out **effective monitoring** of the company and its management in conjunction with equally independent external auditors on behalf of shareholders.

Non-executive directors' lack of links and limits on the time that they serve as non-executive directors should promote **avoidance of managerial capture** – accepting executive managers' views on trust without analysing and questioning them.

The **independence of external auditors** from their clients is also important in corporate governance. As the auditor is acting on behalf of the shareholders and **not** the client, close friendship with the client may influence the external auditor's judgment and mean that the external auditor is not effectively representing the shareholders' interests. Internal auditors also need to be **independent** of the colleagues whom they are auditing.

A complication when considering independence is that there are varying degrees of independence, lying between **total independence** (no knowledge/connection with the other party) and **zero independence** (inability to take a decision without considering the effect on the other party). In real-life situations, the two extremes are unlikely but, in most situations, independence should be as near to total independence as possible.

Question
External auditor independence

Why is the independence of external auditors so important?

Answer

(a) Shareholders and other stakeholders need a trustworthy record of directors' stewardship to be able to take decisions about the company. Assurance provided by independent auditors is a key quality control on reliability.

(b) An unqualified report by independent external auditors on the accounts should give them more credibility, enhancing the appeal of the company to investors.

(c) A lack of independence may mean that an effective audit is not done. Thus the shareholders are not receiving value for the costs of the audit.

(d) A lack of independence may lead to a failure to fulfil professional requirements. Failure to do this undermines the credibility of the accountancy profession and the standards it enforces.

1.2.6 Probity/honesty

Hopefully this should be the most self-evident of the principles. It relates to not only telling the truth but also not misleading shareholders and other stakeholders. Lack of probity includes not only obvious examples of dishonesty, such as taking bribes, but also reporting information in a slanted way that is designed to give an unfair impression.

Guidance in the UK charitable sector has defined probity in terms of receipt of gifts or hospitality by trustees. All gifts should be clearly recorded, and trustees should not accept gifts with a significant monetary value or lavish hospitality. They should certainly not accept gifts or hospitality which may seem likely to influence their decisions.

1.2.7 Responsibility

Responsibility means management accepting the credit or blame for governance decisions. It implies clear definition of the roles and responsibilities of the roles of senior management.

The King report (from South Africa) stresses that, for management to be held properly responsible, there must be a system in place that allows for **corrective action and penalising mismanagement**. Responsible management should do, when necessary, whatever it takes to set the company on the right path.

King states that the board of directors must act responsively to, and with responsibility towards, all stakeholders of the company. However, the responsibility of directors to other stakeholders, both in terms of to **whom** they are responsible and the **extent** of their responsibility, remains a key point of contention in corporate governance debates. We shall discuss the importance of stakeholders later in this chapter.

1.2.8 Corporate accountability

Key term

> **Corporate accountability:** Corporate accountability is the principle that organisations (and their directors) should act ethically and be answerable to their stakeholders for the consequences of their actions, decisions, policies and impacts on society and the environment.

Directors being answerable to shareholders have always been an important part of company law, well before the development of the corporate governance codes. For example, companies in many regimes have been required to provide **financial information** to shareholders on an **annual basis** and hold **annual general meetings**. However, particularly because of the corporate governance scandals of the last 30 years, investors have demanded greater assurance that directors are acting in their interests. This has led to the development of corporate governance codes.

Making accountability work is the responsibility of **both** parties. Directors, as we have seen, do so through the quality of information that they provide whereas shareholders do so through their willingness to **exercise their responsibility as owners**, which means using the available mechanisms to query and assess the actions of the board.

1.2.9 Public sector accountability

The accountability relationship will be different for bodies owned or run by national or central government. The nature of the relationship may be clear – that government determines objectives. How accountability is demonstrated and enforced may depend though on how coherent the objectives are. The main problem will often be where the body's main objectives are non-economic, but the government also wishes to limit the amount it spends on the body.

As with responsibility, one of the biggest debates in corporate governance is the extent of management's **accountability** towards **other stakeholders**, such as the community in which the organisation operates. This has led to a debate about the contents of accounts themselves.

In the context of public service, the UK Nolan Committee on Standards in Public Life commented that **holders of public office** are **accountable** for their decisions and actions to **the public** and must submit themselves to whatever scrutiny is appropriate for their office.

A wider issue with the extent of accountability in the public sector is the **extent of accountability towards different groups in society**. For example, politicians can be seen as being accountable to the body of taxpayers as a whole – it is their interests that parliamentary bodies have been established to represent. However, politicians are also accountable to a group within the category of taxpayers – the voters who voted for them. This raises the issue of what happens if the actions politicians take advantage their voters, but disadvantage other taxpayers.

1.2.10 Reputation

Reputation is determined by how others view a person, organisation or profession. This includes a reputation for **competence**, supplying good quality goods and services in a timely fashion, and also being managed in an orderly way. However, a **poor ethical reputation** can be as serious for an organisation as a poor reputation for competence.

The consequences of a poor reputation for an organisation can include:

- Suppliers' and customers' unwillingness to deal with the organisation for fear of being victims of sharp practice
- Inability to recruit high-quality staff
- Fall in demand because of consumer boycotts
- Increased public relations costs because of adverse stories in the media
- Increased compliance costs because of close attention from regulatory bodies or external auditors
- Loss of market value because of a fall in investor confidence

Case Study

Over the past few years, the American retail giant Wal-Mart has made efforts to improve its reputation in various ways. These have included improving its labour and healthcare records, donating to not-for-profit organisations and promoting the case that it helps economic growth and provides healthy groceries. This has partly been for strategic purposes, as the company has sought to open stores in cities in face of local hostility, due to the adverse effect on other local retailers.

Wal-Mart's attempts to portray itself as more ethical have been undermined by a recent bribery scandal.

We shall see later on in this Workbook how risks to an organisation's reputation depend on how likely other risks are to crystallise.

In the context of governance, reputation also means **personal and professional reputation**, and the **moral reputation of the accountancy profession** as a whole. All are influenced by the extent to which individuals or members of the profession demonstrate the other underlying concepts we have discussed.

1.2.11 Judgment

Judgment means the board **making decisions that enhance the prosperity** of the organisation. This means that board members must acquire a broad enough knowledge of the business and its environment to be able to provide meaningful direction to it. This has implications not only for the attention directors have to give to the organisation's affairs, but also on the way the directors are recruited and trained.

The complexities of senior management mean that the directors have to bring **multiple conceptual skills** to management that aim to maximise long-term returns. This means that corporate governance can involve balancing many competing people and resource claims against each other. Although, as we shall see, risk management is an integral part of corporate governance, corporate governance is not just about risk management.

1.2.12 Integrity

Key term

> "**Integrity** means straightforward dealing and completeness. What is required of financial reporting is that it should be honest and that it should present a balanced picture of the state of the company's affairs. The integrity of reports depends on the integrity of those who prepare and present them.' (Cadbury report)
>
> **Integrity** (means that) holders of public office should not place themselves under any financial or other obligation to outside individuals or organisations that might influence them in the performance of their official duties. *(UK Nolan Committee Standards on Public Life)*

Integrity can be taken as meaning someone of **high moral character**, who sticks to strict moral or ethical principles no matter the pressure to do otherwise. In working life, this means adhering to the highest standards of professionalism and probity. **Straightforwardness, fair dealing and honesty in relationships** with the different people and constituencies whom you meet are particularly important. Trust is vital in relationships, and belief in the integrity of those with whom you are dealing underpins this.

Integrity is an underlying principle of corporate governance. All those in agency relationships should possess and exercise absolute integrity. To fail to do so breaches the relationship of trust. The Cadbury report definition highlights the need for **personal honesty and integrity** of preparers of accounts. This implies qualities beyond a mechanical adherence to accounting or ethical regulations or guidelines. At times, accountants will have to use judgment or face financial situations which are not covered by regulations or guidance and, on these occasions, integrity is particularly important.

Integrity is an essential principle of the **corporate governance relationship**, particularly in relationship to representing shareholder interests and exercising agency. Monitoring and hence agency costs can be reduced if there is trust in the integrity of the agents. In addition, we have seen that a key aim of corporate governance is to inspire confidence in participants in the market and this significantly depends on a **public perception of competence and integrity**.

Integrity is also one of the fundamental principles discussed in the IESBA *Code of Ethics*. It provides assurance of good intentions and truthfulness to those with whom the accountant deals.

2 Social responsibility

> **FAST FORWARD**
>
> An organisation's ethical stance relates to how it **views its responsibilities** to shareholders, stakeholders, society and the environment and is intertwined with the principle of corporate accountability.
>
> Remember, corporate accountability is the principle that organisations (and their directors) should act ethically and be answerable to their stakeholders for the consequences of their actions, decisions, policies and impacts on society and the environment.

Key terms

> **Social costs:** Social costs are defined as the tangible and intangible costs and losses sustained by third parties or the general public as a result of economic activity, for example pollution by industrial effluent.
>
> **Social responsibility:** Social responsibility is the principle that organisations should act in a manner which benefits society as well as meeting strategic and financial objectives.

The primary purpose of a business organisation is to make profits, thereby increasing the wealth of its owners, the shareholders. Businesses do not, however, exist in splendid isolation; they are dependent on the society in which they operate, and they should therefore contribute to that society. Businesses make use at least in part of the infrastructure of the country or countries in which they operate, for example roads, utilities and other social goods paid for through taxation. For this reason, it can be seen as only fair that businesses are aware of their social responsibility, and their ethical reputation can depend on the extent to which they take this responsibility seriously.

By implementing corporate accountability and social responsibility principles, organisations can make a positive impact on local and global communities by addressing identified social costs.

Businesses that implement a social responsibility initiative that's in line with their values can benefit from improved reputation and increased customer loyalty.

2.1 The ethical stance

Key term

> An organisation's **ethical stance** is defined by Johnson and Scholes (2002) as the extent to which it will exceed its minimum obligation to stakeholders.

Crane and Matten (2005) and Johnson and Scholes (2002) have identified a number of key assumptions (in the form of questions) on which ethical and social responsibility stances are based.

Who is responsible for ethical conduct in business?	Is it the individual, or is control exercised socially, by governments?
Who is the key actor in business ethics?	Is it the corporation, or is it the government or other collective bodies such as trade unions?
What are the key guidelines for ethical behaviour?	Again, does it rest with the corporation in the form of corporate codes of ethics, or is the key guidance a legal framework negotiated with, or imposed on, business?
What are the key issues in business ethics?	Are they single-decision issues involving misconduct and immorality, or are they social issues surrounding the framework of business?

To whom are businesses responsible?	Should the focus be on enhancing shareholder value or on multiple stakeholders?
How should performance be measured?	Should it be measured by bottom line financial results or by pluralistic measures?
How should an ethical stance be incorporated into business activity?	Should an ethical stance be seen primarily in terms of compliance with law/corporate governance codes, or should it be actively incorporated into an organisation's mission and strategy?
How important is reputation?	Does it make any difference to financial results? Should organisations strive to have a good reputation even if doing so makes no demonstrable difference to their bottom-line profits?

Johnson and Scholes illustrate the range of possible ethical stances for organisations and individuals by giving four illustrations.

- Short-term shareholder interest
- Long-term shareholder interest
- Multiple stakeholder obligations
- Shaper of society

2.1.1 Short-term shareholder interest

An organisation or individual might limit its ethical stance to taking responsibility for **short-term shareholder interest** on the grounds that it is for **government** alone to impose wider constraints on corporate governance. This approach may not look much beyond the current financial year. This minimalist approach would accept a duty of obedience to the demands of the law but would not undertake to comply with any less substantial rules of conduct. This stance can be justified on the grounds that going beyond it can **challenge government authority**. This is an important consideration for organisations operating in developing countries.

2.1.2 Long-term shareholder interest

The longer view will look years rather than months ahead and consider the legitimacy of a claim in terms of its effect on long-term shareholder value. There are two reasons for taking a wider view of ethical responsibilities when considering the **longer-term interest of shareholders**.

(a) **Corporate image** may be enhanced by an assumption of wider responsibilities. The cost of undertaking such responsibilities may be justified as essentially promotional expenditure.

(b) The responsible exercise of corporate power may prevent a build-up of social and political **pressure for legal regulation**. Freedom of action may be preserved and the burden of regulation lightened by acceptance of ethical responsibilities.

2.1.3 Multiple stakeholder obligations

An organisation or individual might accept the **legitimacy of the expectations and/or claims of stakeholders other than shareholders** and build those expectations into its stated purposes. This would be because, without appropriate relationships with groups such as suppliers, employers and customers, the organisation would not be able to function.

The **legal rights** of stakeholders other than shareholders have to be respected. These are extensive in the UK, including wide-ranging **employment law** and **consumer protection law**, as well as the more basic legislation relating to such matters as contract and property. Where **moral entitlements** are concerned, organisations need to be practical. They should take care to establish just what expectations they are prepared to treat as **obligations**, bearing in mind their general ethical stance and degree of concern about bad publicity.

Acceptance of obligations to stakeholders implies that **measurement of the performance** must give due weight to these extra imperatives.

2.1.4 Shaper of society

It is difficult enough for a commercial organisation to accept wide responsibility to stakeholders. A **shaper of society** can be defined as an organisation whose actions should be such that they benefit society, with financial and other stakeholder interests being of a secondary nature only. The role of **shaper of society** is even more demanding than one that merely includes responsibilities toward particular stakeholders and is largely the concern of public sector organisations and charities, though some well-funded private organisations or very powerful and wealthy individuals might act in this way. The legitimacy of this approach for organisations depends on the framework of **corporate governance** and **accountability**. Where organisations are clearly set up for such a role, either by government or by private sponsors, they may pursue it. However, they must also satisfy whatever requirements for financial viability are established for them.

Case Study

Traidcraft aims to fight poverty through a wide range of trade-related activities. The company's structure is that of a trading company and a development charity working together, pioneering the development of fair trade by:

- Building lasting relationships with small-scale producers in developing countries
- Supporting people to trade out of poverty
- Working to bring about trade justice and fair business practices
- Striving to be transparent and accountable

In poorer countries, Traidcraft supports traders by providing business training, information and help in winning sales. In the UK, Traidcraft works to encourage businesses to apply corporate social responsibility and provide social accounts. It aims to persuade UK businesses to change their practices so that they have a positive impact on their suppliers.

Traidcraft's policy unit exists to campaign for changes in the rules of trade and work with business and institutions to deliver poverty-alleviating policies. The organisation has recently campaigned against European partnership agreements – agreements between European countries and their former colonies – on the grounds that these are forcing the colonies' economies to liberalise too fast. This will result in farmers and industries having to compete openly with EU corporations before they are ready, resulting in them losing markets and going out of business.

2.2 Social responsibility accounting

Social responsibility accounting is the identification, measurement and reporting of the social costs and benefits resulting from economic activities.

Why should organisations play an active social role in the society within which they function?

(a) **'The public' is a stakeholder in the business**. A business only succeeds because it is part of a wider society. Giving to charity is one way of **enhancing the reputation** of the business.

(b) **Charitable donations** and artistic **sponsorship** are a useful medium of **public relations** and can reflect well on the business.

(c) Involving managers and staff in **community activities** is good **work experience**.

(d) It helps create a **value culture** in the organisation and a sense of mission, which is good for motivation.

(e) In the long term, upholding the community's values, responding constructively to criticism and contributing towards community wellbeing might be good for business, as it **promotes the wider environment** in which businesses flourish.

(f) There is increasing **political pressure** on businesses to be socially responsible. Such activities help 'buy off' environmentalists.

2.3 Gray, Owen and Adams social responsibility stances

In their book *Accounting and Accountability* (1996), Gray, Owen, and Adams identify seven viewpoints on social responsibility.

Each of the seven stances reflects a different ethical perspective on how businesses should act in relation to society, the environment, and their various stakeholders. In the table below, each stance is explained from a business ethics perspective.

Gray, Owen and Adams Stance	Business ethics perspective
1. Pristine Capitalists	Believe the primary ethical responsibility of companies is to maximise profits within the confines of the law, with no moral obligations beyond satisfying shareholders and creditors. Pursuing other stakeholders' interests is seen as theft, diverting wealth from shareholders who legally own the company. Ethical considerations focus solely on financial outcomes.
2. Expedients	Accept that ethical considerations may align with business interests, but only when they serve to protect profitability. They acknowledge societal and moral requirements but view ethical compliance as a strategic choice to avoid reputational risks or enhance market positioning, rather than as a moral imperative.
3. Proponents of the Social Contract	Argue that businesses have a societal license to operate and should conform to society's ethical norms and values. Companies must consider the social impacts of their actions, as societal support depends on delivering benefits to society and avoiding harm, emphasising accountability to customers, employees, and communities.
4. Social Ecologists	Recognise the social and environmental footprint of business activities and argue that companies have a moral duty to address the problems they create, particularly environmental harm. They advocate for changes in business practices that go beyond societal norms to rectify issues caused by economic processes.
5. Socialists	View businesses as instruments of capitalist oppression, concentrating wealth and power in the hands of a few. They argue that ethical business practices should focus on promoting equality and remedying social imbalances, serving a broader range of stakeholders, particularly workers, and requiring changes to the capitalist framework.
6. Radical Feminists	Criticise economic and social systems for privileging masculine traits like aggression and competition over cooperation and nurturing. They argue for a cultural shift that embraces traditionally feminine values, asserting that ethical business practices must adopt these values for corporate social responsibility to be meaningful.
7. Deep Ecologists	Advocate that businesses are morally obligated to recognise that human needs are not above those of the natural world. They argue that trading off environmental health for economic objectives is fundamentally unethical, calling for a business paradigm that respects all forms of life and avoids exploiting natural resources for profit.

Question

Gray, Owen and Adams 1

Which of the seven Gray, Owen and Adams viewpoints do the following statements appear to illustrate?

Our corporate responsibility stance will appeal to our customers and ethical shareholders.	
The building of the new shopping centre should not disrupt the lives and livelihoods of the local community.	
Companies should continuously strive to reduce their environmental footprint.	
The problem with stakeholder analysis such as Mendelow's matrix is that it consistently prioritises those who provide finance over those who produce.	
Companies can never do enough to reduce their environmental footprint.	
Is there not room for the small shop as well as the supermarket?	
The business of business is business.	

Answer

Bear in mind that it would be helpful to have knowledge of the motivation of the individuals making these statements.

Our corporate responsibility stance will appeal to our customers and ethical shareholders.	**Expedient**: a very pragmatic and perhaps very common view
The building of the new shopping centre should not disrupt the lives and livelihoods of the local community.	**Social contract**: the idea that business developments should take account of the impact on the local community
Companies should continuously strive to reduce their environmental footprint.	**Social ecologist**: the difference between this view and that of the deep ecologist is the implication that this reduction should take place within the existing framework
The problem with stakeholder analysis such as Mendelow's matrix is that it consistently prioritises those who provide finance over those who produce.	**Socialist**: the idea that superiority of the capital providers or capitalists is inherently wrong
Companies can never do enough to reduce their environmental footprint.	**Deep ecologist**: the implication being that business activity as currently pursued is inherently unsustainable
Is there not room for the small shop as well as the supermarket?	**Radical feminist**: the key concept is that there is room for peaceful coexistence in the business world, rather than one type of business trying to drive another type out of business
The business of business is business.	**Pristine capitalist**: a good one-line summary of this viewpoint

2.4 Using the Gray, Owen and Adams corporate responsibility positions

You may be asked to apply Gray, Owen and Adams' corporate responsibility position to analyse or rank stakeholder concerns about an ethical issue.

Step 1: Analysing the Scenario

When examining a business scenario, identify key elements relevant to each ethical stance:

Gray, Owen and Adams Stance	Key ethical elements and approach
1. Pristine Capitalists	Focus on financial implications and actions that maximise shareholder wealth, considering other stakeholders only if they threaten financial returns.
2. Expedients	Consider societal views on corporate responsibility and show how ethical behaviour could align with business interests to avoid reputational risks and enhance profitability.
3. Proponents of the Social Contract	Look at the company's impact on the community, government stance, and relationships with stakeholders, highlighting how the business can serve various groups and reconcile interests.
4. Social Ecologists	Identify the environmental footprint and focus on the ethical responsibility of the business to address environmental and social problems caused by its activities.
5. Socialists	Assess indications of inequities where owners benefit at the expense of employees or society, suggesting changes to benefit workers and address social imbalances.
6. Radical Feminists	Examine competitive business practices that may exploit traditionally feminine values for profit and promote a cultural shift towards cooperation, fairness, and nurturing.
7. Deep Ecologists	Evaluate the business's impact on the natural environment and advocate for a re-evaluation of activities, criticising the prioritisation of economic objectives over ecological sustainability.

Step 2: Constructing your ethical analysis

Your answer will need to focus on factors that are relevant to each position.

Gray, Owen and Adams Stance	Constructing Your Ethical Analysis
Pristine Capitalists	Argue for actions that maximise shareholder wealth, considering other stakeholders only if they threaten financial returns.
Expedients	Show how ethical behaviour could align with business interests, trading off social responsibilities with economic benefits.
Proponents of the Social Contract	Highlight society's ethical norms and explore how the business can serve the interests of different groups while reconciling competing interests.
Social Ecologists	Focus on the ethical responsibility of the business to address environmental and social problems caused by its activities.

8: GLOBAL GOVERNANCE AND CORPORATE SOCIAL RESPONSIBILITY (CSR)

Gray, Owen and Adams Stance	Constructing Your Ethical Analysis
Socialists	Emphasise the ethical need for addressing inequalities, suggesting changes to benefit employees and other oppressed groups.
Radical Feminists	Discuss the ethical issues arising from competition and profit-seeking behaviours, promoting values like cooperation and fairness over traditional business practices.
Deep Ecologists	Advocate for a re-evaluation of business activities in light of their impact on the natural environment, criticising the prioritisation of human economic interests.

Question

Gray, Owen and Adams

Willmont Recruitment Services is a prominent firm of recruitment consultants based in the capital city of its home country. At the board's most recent meeting the human resources director reported several alarming trends indicating serious ethical issues within the company.

Over the past year, Willmont has experienced a significant turnover of experienced staff, particularly female employees. It has come to light that many of these female employees were pressured into taking on work during antisocial hours, despite this contradicting their original employment contracts. There have been instances where staff members were given ultimatums to accept these changes in working conditions or risk termination. Some female employees felt compelled to comply out of fear of losing their jobs, highlighting a culture of intimidation within the firm.

Furthermore, several female employees have raised complaints about unequal pay. They have discovered that they are being paid considerably less than their male colleagues for performing the same roles. The HR director has justified this discrepancy by claiming that male employees have additional responsibilities, justifying higher pay. However, investigations reveal that many of these claims are false, as the additional responsibilities cited do not exist in numerous cases. This unfair treatment has led to increasing resentment among staff, escalating absenteeism, a noticeable drop in productivity, and a concerning decline in the quality of client service.

The chief executive and the director of quality management have entered the discussion, not to address the complaints or implement fair practices, but to focus on maintaining Willmont's reputation. The company is eager to defend its "Consultant of the Year" title, which was primarily awarded for its high-quality service and client satisfaction. The chief executive and quality director received substantial bonuses for this recognition last year and are eager to secure the title again, even if it means ignoring the mistreatment of their employees. To achieve this, they have suggested covering up any internal conflicts and low staff morale to project an image of a thriving, ethically run organisation.

The situation is further complicated by the fact that Willmont operates in a country that has implemented the European Union's social chapter provisions, which mandate fair employment practices, equal pay, and employee rights. The company's actions not only violate its employees' contracts but also potentially breach national and EU laws regarding worker protection, equal pay, and workplace discrimination. Despite these violations, the company's management has shown little intention of rectifying the issues, choosing instead to focus on profit and external accolades.

Required

Evaluate this ethical issue from the seven Gray, Owen and Adams social responsibility stances.

Answer

Gray, Owen and Adams Stance	Ethical Evaluation
1. Pristine Capitalists	From this perspective, the focus would be on maximising shareholder wealth. The company's actions, including pressuring employees to work antisocial hours and prioritising the "Consultant of the Year" title, are seen as justified if they enhance profitability and shareholder returns. Employee complaints would only matter if they directly threaten the company's profits or reputation.
2. Expedients	Expedients would recognise the negative impacts of employee mistreatment on the company's reputation and productivity. To avoid reputational risk and potential legal issues, the company might need to make concessions, such as addressing pay disparities or improving working conditions. The ethical decision here is driven by maintaining profitability and market positioning.
3. Proponents of the Social Contract	This stance argues that Willmont has a societal obligation to treat its employees fairly, as there is an implicit "social contract" between the company and its workers. Ignoring employee rights, unequal pay, and poor working conditions breaches this contract, risking the company's social license to operate and the trust of the community and clients it serves.
4. Social Ecologists	Social ecologists would emphasise that the company's unethical work practices contribute to a negative social footprint. The exploitation of employees for profit and the resulting decline in their well-being contradicts the moral responsibility businesses have to promote a healthy, sustainable work environment. Willmont must change its practices to mitigate its harmful social impact.
5. Socialists	Socialists would view the situation as a clear example of capitalist oppression, where the company prioritises executive bonuses and awards over the fair treatment of workers. The gender pay disparity and job insecurity reflect structural inequalities that need to be addressed by prioritising employee welfare and challenging the existing profit-centric model.
6. Radical Feminists	Radical feminists would criticise the firm's exploitation of traditionally feminine qualities, such as nurturing and flexibility, for profit. The pay disparity and unfair treatment of female employees highlight systemic gender inequality. A fundamental cultural shift is required within Willmont to promote values like equality, cooperation, and respect for all workers, regardless of gender.
7. Deep Ecologists	While deep ecologists primarily focus on environmental ethics, they would argue that Willmont's practices reflect a broader issue of exploiting resources—human resources in this case—for economic gain. They would advocate for a re-evaluation of business values to respect the well-being of all forms of life, suggesting the company's ethical approach is flawed by prioritising profits over people.

2.5 Social and environmental effects of economic activity

FAST FORWARD

There is increasing concern about businesses' relationship with the natural environment. Businesses may suffer **significant costs** and a **loss of reputation** if problems arise.

2.5.1 Significance of environmental effects

Is there a problem and how serious is it?

Case Study

The World Wildlife Fund warned in a report published in October 2006 that current global consumption levels could result in a large-scale ecosystem collapse by the middle of the 21st century. It warned that if demand continued at the current rate, two planets' worth of resources would be needed to meet the consumption demand by 2050. The loss in biodiversity is the result of resources being consumed faster than the planet can replace them.

The report based its findings on two measures.

Living Planet Index – assessing the health of the planet's ecosystems by tracking the population of over 1,000 vertebrate species. It found that species had declined by about 30% since 1970.

The Ecological Footprint – measuring the amount of biologically productive land and water to meet the demand for food, timber and shelter and absorb the pollution from economic activity. The report found that the global footprint exceeded the world's biocapacity by 25% in 2003, which meant that the earth could no longer meet what was being demanded of it.

Case Study

Most seriously of all, there is the issue of whether business activities have contributed to climate change.

Intergovernmental Panel

The Intergovernmental Panel on Climate Change reported in February 2007. The report emphasised that global atmospheric concentrations of carbon dioxide, methane and nitrous oxide have increased markedly as a result of human activities since 1750 and now exceed pre-industrial values. The main causes are fossil-fuel usage (the most significant cause), land-use change and agriculture.

The report stated that evidence of warming of the climate system is unequivocal, as is seen from observations of increases in global average air and ocean temperatures, widespread melting of snow and ice, and rising global average sea level. Numerous changes in climate are long term. These are most likely to be due to increases in greenhouse gas concentrations.

For the next two decades, a warming of about 0.2°C is projected based on projected levels of greenhouse gas emissions. Continued greenhouse gas emissions at or above current rates would cause further warming and induce many climate changes in the 21st century that will be larger than those observed in the 20th century. These include increases in heatwaves, spells of heavy rain and intensity of tropical cyclones.

Stern report

A few months before the Intergovernmental panel report was published, a UK report was published on the costs of climate change. The report's author was Sir Nicholas Stern, former chief economist at the World Bank, and adviser to the former UK Chancellor of the Exchequer Gordon Brown who commissioned the report. The report warned of a global recession that could cut between 5% and 20% from the world's wealth later this century, unless the world invests now in the technologies needed to create a global low-carbon economy.

The effects would be on a scale similar to those associated with the two World Wars and the 1930s depression. They include huge disruption to African economies as drought hits food production, up to a billion people losing water supplies, hundreds of millions losing their homes to sea level rises and potentially big increases in damage from hurricanes.

Stern called for a global investment of about 1% per year of global GDP over the next 50 years to combat these threats. His findings contradicted past claims from economists that the world would do better adapting to climate change rather than trying to halt it. In response to the report, Gordon Brown called for industrialised countries to cut their carbon dioxide emissions by at least 30% by 2020 and by at least 60% by 2050.

World Wildlife Fund (WWF)

The World Wildlife Fund's Climate Savers programme encourages companies to reduce carbon dioxide emissions by:

- Increasing the energy efficiency of buildings and factories
- Taking advantage of recent advances in combined heat and power to increase energy efficiency and lower energy costs
- Purchasing power generated from renewable energy sources
- Integrating next-generation efficiency measures into the design of new buildings, factories and products
- Integrating energy and environmental efficiency into building, product and process design
- Optimising existing manufacturing processes
- Educating employees, customer base and supply chain to help take advantage of best practices for greenhouse gas mitigation

Examples of companies who have joined the programme include:

- Johnson & Johnson, 30% of whose total US energy use is from green power sources such as wind power, on-site solar, low-impact hydro, renewable energy sources
- IBM, whose energy-saving methods include installing motion detectors for lighting in bathrooms and copier rooms, rebalancing heating and lighting systems and resizing high purity water pumping systems in semi-conductor manufacturing lines
- Polaroid, which is upgrading and replacing compressors, chillers, boilers, hot water systems, lighting systems and motors, purchasing green power and switching to cleaner forms of fuel for on-site operations; Polaroid's Facilities organisation now requires each employee to identify energy-saving projects as part of their performance evaluation
- Nike, which offsets the majority of its business travel carbon dioxide emissions through partnerships with air carriers, rental car companies, government energy departments and the retail market
- Lafarge, the cement manufacturer which uses industrial by-products such as fly-ash from coal-fired power plants and slag from the steel industry as substitutes for raw materials that require significant energy to produce; Lafarge has also shifted some of its fuel use to waste fossil fuels (industrial waste, tyres, oils, plastic and solvents) and waste biomass (rice husks, coffee shells, animal meal)

The WWF points out the following benefits of joining Climate Savers.

- **Knowledge increase**, providing an opportunity to develop relationships with other stakeholders, business colleagues and technology experts
- **Visibility** through publicity in the WWF's literature and press reports
- **Cost advantages**, greater efficiency leading to reduction in energy costs

Climate change will be one of the most topical areas of your syllabus, so we would advise you to read and keep copies of stories on how businesses are responding to climate change.

Clearly there are concerns which need to be closely examined. Note, however, that organisations can also have **positive impacts**, for example improving the energy efficiency of their buildings.

2.6 Impact on environment of economic activities

Key term

> **Environmental footprint** is the impact that a business's activities have on the environment including its resource consumption and pollution emissions. It concerns the environmental consequences of a business's inputs and outputs.

At an individual firm or business level, environmental impact can be measured in terms of environmental costs in various areas. Much business activity takes place at some cost to the environment. A 1998 IFAC report identified several examples of impacts on the environment.

- Depletion of natural resources
- Noise and aesthetic impacts
- Residual air and water emissions
- Long-term waste disposal (exacerbated by excessive product packaging)
- Uncompensated health effects
- Change in the local quality of life (through for example the impact of tourism)

With some of these impacts, however, a business may be contributing negatively to the environment but positively in other ways. An increase in tourism will provide jobs and other economic benefits to the community but could lead to adverse effects on the environment as the roads become more crowded, or as an unintended consequence of infrastructure improvements.

Ways of assessing the impact of inputs include the **measurement of key environmental resources** used, such as energy, water, inventories and land. Measurement of the impact of outputs includes the proportion of product **recyclability, tonnes of carbon or other gases produced by company activities, waste or pollution**. A business may also be concerned with the **efficiency of its processes**, maybe carrying out a mass balance or yield calculation.

2.6.1 Direct and indirect impacts

Measures of impact can apply directly and narrowly to the organisation, or they can be applied more broadly to the indirect, associated impacts that it has. For a manufacturer, indirect measures could report on the forward and backward supply chains which it uses from sourcing its raw materials to bringing its products to market. A bank could include the environmental consequences of the activities it finances through its business loans. However, reporting of indirect measures is rare, as the other parties are primarily responsible for reporting the direct impacts that they have. Clearly it would also be particularly difficult for a bank to track the impacts of all its business borrowers.

Case Study

In 2012, Microsoft introduced an internal 'carbon fee' that holds its business units responsible for carbon emissions. In this way, Microsoft changed its behaviour by factoring carbon emissions into its internal budgetary control systems. It then actually spent the money raised internally on green power, in an effort to further reduce emissions.

In 2020, the company then went further by announcing two goals:

- Aiming to be carbon-negative by 2030
- Aiming to have removed from the environment the carbon it has emitted since its foundation in 1975

These commitments reflect the fact that Microsoft's business is significantly less carbon-intensive than those of some other large companies, however they do offer an example of corporate citizenship that is committed to helping society to achieve its goals in relation to carbon emissions.

2.7 Impact on organisation of environmental costs

In addition, a business may suffer a large number of environmental costs internally.

Direct or indirect environmental costs

- Waste management
- Remediation costs or expenses
- Compliance costs
- Permit fees
- Environmental training
- Environmentally driven research and development
- Environmentally related maintenance
- Legal costs and fines
- Environmental assurance bonds
- Environmental certification and labelling
- Natural resource inputs
- Recordkeeping and reporting

Contingent or intangible environmental costs

- Uncertain future remediation or compensation costs
- Risk posed by future regulatory changes
- Product quality
- Employee health and safety
- Environmental knowledge assets
- Sustainability of raw material inputs
- Risk of impaired assets
- Public/customer perception

Clearly, failing to take sufficient account of environmental impact can have a significant impact on the business's accounts as well as the outside world.

2.8 Social impacts of activities

Key term

> **Social footprint** is the impact of an organisation on human, social and constructed capitals (Anthro capitals). (The Center for Sustainable Organizations)

Partly because of the publicity generated by reports like the recent WWF report, there is now significant focus on the environmental impact of businesses' activities. However, corporate social responsibility does not start and end with the environment. Organisations need to consider other aspects of corporate social responsibilities.

The definition of social footprint formulated by the Center for Sustainable Organisations is measured in terms of impacts that arise from organisational activities. Sustainability entails the **maintenance and/or production of vital capitals** as required to ensure human (and non-human) well-being.

The definition concentrates on anthro capital which is created by people and can be produced at will – more can always be created. It is thus different from natural capital which humanity cannot reproduce. The focus is on providing enough resources to maintain levels of social capital.

The Center provides more details about the categories of capital given in the definition. The different types of capital are all used to take effective action and ensure their own wellbeing.

Capitals	
Human	Personal health, knowledge, skills, experience, human rights, ethical entitlements. Relied on by individuals
Social	Social networks and mutually held knowledge – relied on by collectives
Constructed	Material things such as tools, technologies, roads, utilities and infrastructures

Again, business strategies may have **positive and negative consequences** for social sustainability. A business that outsources production to a low-cost economy abroad may create new jobs and provide training and development opportunities for the employees in that country. However, it may also be

accused of exploiting those employees by paying them an insufficient wage. In addition, the jobs that may be lost in the business's home country will have adverse social consequences such as increased unemployment and the need for benefits to support the unemployed.

2.8.1 Stakeholder expectations

Pressure on organisations to widen the scope of their corporate public accountability comes from **increasing expectations of stakeholders** and knowledge about the **consequences of ignoring such pressures**.

Stakeholders in this respect include communities (particularly where operations are based), customers (product safety issues), suppliers and supply chain participants and competitors. Issues such as plant closures, pollution, job creation, sourcing, etc can have powerful **social effects** for good or ill on these stakeholders.

Case Study

These are a few examples in which consumers have been successful in applying pressure to seek changes in business practices.

(a) Consumers began boycotting Shell filling stations in large numbers, leading the company to reverse its policy on a controversial environmental subject concerning the disposal of an oil drilling platform.

(b) Pressure was applied to change the Nestlé company's practice of exploiting the market for processed milk in developing countries.

Similar campaigns have targeted Nike (alleged exploitation of overseas garment-trade workers) and McDonalds (alleged contribution to obesity and related illnesses).

2.8.2 Reputation risk

Increasingly a business must have the reputation of being a **responsible business** that enhances long-term shareholder value by addressing the needs of its **stakeholders** – employees, customers, suppliers, the community and the environment.

Case Study

In April 2008, Greenpeace protestors dressed as orangutans stormed a number of sites owned by Unilever in Europe. The protest was against the damage to Indonesian tropical rainforests by the production of palm oil, used in many Unilever products. As well as damaging the forests, the process of deforestation has resulted in large emissions of carbon dioxide and also threatened local wildlife (including orangutans).

Soon after the protest, Unilever announced that it would be drawing all the palm oil it purchased from sustainable sources within the next seven years. However, Greenpeace wanted Unilever to take tougher action, by ceasing to buy from suppliers who were breaking the law. Enquiries by Unilever embarrassingly revealed that all its Indonesian suppliers were flouting Indonesian law or sustainability standards.

Case Study

Reputation can be affected adversely even if the company has good intentions. An example was Monsanto believing that investment in genetically modified (GM) products would be seen as helping farmers in developing countries by increasing yields. However, they failed to take on board the fact that these farmers usually save seed from one crop to sow the following season. This would not be possible with GM crops.

Bad publicity portrayed Monsanto as exploiting, rather than helping, developing countries. In addition, inadequately addressed environmental concerns about the effect of GM crops on nature led to:

- A consumer boycott of GM products
- Trial crops being destroyed
- A tumbling share price

The final straw was the news that Monsanto's UK staff canteen was-GM free!

Case Study

Mining companies in Canada are carrying out social risk assessment for major projects, assessing how the local social, economic and cultural conditions may affect the project. These assessments reflect the impact that mining projects often have on environmentally and socially sensitive areas such as wildlife habitats, biodiversity points and indigenous communities. Linked issues may include poverty, conflict, political instability and human rights violations. Failure to take account of these issues may result in serious opposition, cultural conflict, delays in granting of mining rights and rejections of mining licences.

Social risk assessments aim to engage stakeholders and understand their concerns as well as assessing key social and political issues. They feed through into strategic and operational plans as well as community investment, stakeholder engagement and communication plans.

3 Corporate social responsibility (CSR)

FAST FORWARD

Corporate social responsibility (CSR) refers to the expectation in society that companies are accountable for the social and ethical effects of their actions. Some argue however that businesses already contribute enough to society via the taxes on their profits.

Corporate social responsibility is an organisation's obligation to maximise shareholder benefits whilst minimising the negative effects of its actions.

CSR is a fairly recent development brought about by pressure on companies to show an awareness of the social and ethical effects of their actions. It is not the same as ethical behaviour although the two are related.

Organisation and societal culture, politics, socio-economic priorities, governance gaps, market access and the influence of multinational companies all influence government, company and consumer attitudes all contribute to an organisations stance on corporate social responsibility.

3.1 Definition

The term corporate social responsibility (CSR) is used to describe a wide range of obligations that an organisation may feel it has towards its secondary or external stakeholders, including the society in which it operates.

If it is accepted that businesses currently do not bear the total social cost of their activities, it could be suggested that corporate social responsibility might be a way of recognising this.

Corporate social responsibility includes **economic** and **legal issues**, as well as **ethical ones**, reflecting the whole range of stakeholders who have an interest in an organisation.

3.2 Corporate citizenship

Key term

Corporate citizenship is the business strategy that shapes the values underpinning a company's mission and the choices made each day by its executives, managers and employees as they engage with society. Three core principles define the essence of corporate citizenship, and every company should apply them in a manner appropriate to its distinct needs: minimizing harm, maximizing benefit, and being accountable and responsive to stakeholders. (Boston Center for Corporate Citizenship)

Much of the debate in recent years about **corporate social responsibility** has been framed in terms of corporate citizenship, partly because of unease about using words like ethics and responsibility in the context of business decisions. Discussion of corporate citizenship also often has political undertones, with corporations acting instead of governments that cannot – or will not – act to deal effectively with problems. Commentators have also pointed to liberalisation, deregulation and privatisation placing more power in the hands of corporations and less in the hands of the state.

The general concepts of rights and responsibilities are fundamental to the debate on citizenship.

3.2.1 Rights

The rights that a corporate citizen has include **being able to take actions that are lawful and to enjoy the protection of the law**. The rights of a company include the right to **exist as a separate legal entity** and **carry on a lawful business**. Society will grant it protection under the law and will also permit it to develop and expand.

3.2.2 Responsibilities

Responsibilities are the **duties owed to society** by the citizen as a consequence of the citizen belonging to the society and enjoying rights within it. In order to enjoy the protection, the individual or organisation has to **comply with the laws** that affect it and **act in accordance with society's behavioural norms**.

Matten *et al* have suggested that there are three perspectives or corporate citizenship.

Limited view: The business's philanthropy consists of limited projects undertaken in the business's self-interest. The main stakeholder groups that the corporation engages with are local communities and employees.

Equivalent view: This is based on a wider concept of corporate social responsibility based on stakeholder theory. The corporation responds to the demands of society and focuses on balancing the interests of different stakeholders. Acting according to the business's self-interest is not the most important priority.

Extended view: This view is based round a partly voluntary, partly imposed view of active social and political citizenship. Corporations must promote citizens' rights, particularly as governments have failed to provide some of the safeguards necessary for their society's citizens and corporations are the most powerful institutions in society.

Under the extended view, organisations will promote:

- **Social rights** of citizens by provision of, for example, decent working conditions
- **Civil rights**, by intervening to promote citizens' individual rights themselves or to pressurise governments to promote citizens' rights
- **Political rights** by allowing individuals to promote their causes by using corporate power

Again the focus is on a wide range of stakeholders, with a combination of self-interest promoting corporate power (and responding to political campaigns aimed at corporations) and wider responsibility towards society.

3.2.3 Impact of the concept of corporate citizenship

Looking at the definitions, it seems that the only one that adds a **fresh perspective** to the concept of the company in society is the extended view, since it emphasises the **political role of the corporation** and therefore the importance of its **accountability**. It also provides perspectives on the organisation as a **global participant**, having to cope with different concepts of citizenship worldwide.

3.2.4 Critiques of corporate citizenship

Corporate citizenship and corporate social responsibility have been attacked for introducing concepts that are counter to good order in the free market. The underlying idea of these criticisms is that economic self-interest and allocative efficiency ensure **maximum economic growth** and therefore **maximum social welfare**.

On the other hand, other critics of corporate citizenship argue that it often tends to be restricted to what should be disclosed in the accounts that organisations themselves prepare, and that the range of concerns and stakeholders to which organisations are accountable is limited. More fundamentally, critics claim that its supporters operate and therefore acquiesce in the free market and take attention away from the need for **fundamental structural change** in economies.

Nevertheless supporters argue that corporate citizenship and corporate social responsibility reporting can be extended to illuminate **inequalities in distribution** in society and **limitations of traditional accounting methods**. Reporting has a major role in making organisations more visible and transparent.

Case Study

Scottish Power's corporate social responsibility programme has been developed from multi-stakeholder consultation. The stakeholders emphasised the need for the company to prioritise its most significant social and environmental impacts. This consultation identified 12 impacts, and Scottish Power's corporate social responsibility report detailed what had been done to address these.

(a) **Provision of energy**

Scottish Power was involved in a competition to develop carbon capture and storage. It spent £456 million in refurbishing its electrical network and committed £20 million in investment to its hydroelectric plant.

(b) **Health and safety**

The Lost-Time Accident rate fell for the fifth successive year. Its children's safety education programme won two major awards.

(c) **Customer experience**

Scottish Power achieved the highest satisfaction rating for online energy service in the market and was ranked the second UK gas supplier. Its customer base increased by 4%.

(d) **Climate change and emission to air**

Scottish Power's Green Energy Trust awarded £232,809 to 20 small renewable energy projects. It entered a contract to supply all Debenhams' properties with electricity generated from green sources and met 57% of its carbon emission reduction programme through its customer energy efficiency programme.

(e) **Waste and resource usage**

Scottish Power increased its investment in oil containment and received a Queen's Award in the Sustainable Development category.

(f) **Biodiversity**

The company took steps to allow the public to watch wildfowl. A cable pipeline was drilled below the Dovey Estuary to avoid disturbance to a Site of Special Scientific Interest.

(g) **Sites, siting and infrastructure**

Scottish Power completed connections to more renewable energy sources and implemented a programme to keep parts of its network underground in Snowdonia.

(h) **Employee experience**

The company launched two new employee share plans. Staff participated in community development programmes that provided training for young people.

(i) **Customers with special circumstances**

Scottish Power contributed £1 million to the Scottish Power Energy People Trust. It launched a new social tariff that combined low prices with energy efficiency advice and measures to take vulnerable customers out of fuel poverty.

(j) **Community**

Over 58,000 primary schoolchildren benefited from Powerwise, Scottish Power's classroom safety education programme.

(k) **Procurement**

Scottish Power developed a group-wide responsible procurement policy and spent £74 million on customer energy efficiency measures.

(l) **Economic**

Scottish Power provided employability training to 68 Skillseekers during the year.

3.3 Significance of corporate social responsibility

Businesses, particularly large ones, are subject to increasing expectations that they will exercise corporate social responsibility. Carroll's model of social responsibility suggests there are four levels of social responsibility.

3.3.1 Economic responsibilities

Companies have economic responsibilities to shareholders demanding a good return, to employees wanting fair employment conditions and customers who are seeking good-quality products at a fair price. Businesses are set up to be properly functioning economic units and so this responsibility forms the basis of all others.

3.3.2 Legal responsibilities

Since laws **codify society's moral views**, obeying those laws must be the foundation of compliance with social responsibilities. Although in all societies corporations will have a minimum of legal responsibilities, there is perhaps more emphasis on them in continental Europe than in the Anglo-American economies where the focus of discussion has been on whether many legal responsibilities constitute excessive red tape.

3.3.3 Ethical responsibilities

These are responsibilities that require corporations to act in a **fair and just way** even if the law does not compel them to do so.

3.3.4 Philanthropic responsibilities

According to Carroll, these are **desired** rather than being required of companies. They include charitable donations, contributions to local communities and providing employees with the chance to improve their own lives.

3.4 Corporate social responsibility stances

Corporate social responsibility (CSR) is concerned with the ways in which an organisation exceeds its minimum, legally required obligations to stakeholders (Johnson, Scholes and Whittington, 2007, p.146).

Therefore, CSR is more closely associated with contemporary business issues, and concerns organisations giving something back to society, and being good citizens.

In contrast to ethics, CSR is socially mediated and likely to be specific to the time and culture in which it is considered. For example, CSR could include:

- Staff development via training and education
- Equal opportunities statements
- Written anti-discrimination policies
- Commitment to reporting on CSR
- Policies for restricting the use of child labour by suppliers

- Policies on fair trade
- Commitment to the protection of the local community

However, the approaches organisations take to CSR can vary significantly, and this will influence the way organisations act, and the way they judge their performance.

> **Key term**
>
> An organisation's **CSR** or **ethical stance** is defined by Johnson and Scholes as the extent to which it will exceed its minimum obligation to stakeholders.

Crane and Matten and Johnson and Scholes have identified a number of key assumptions (in the form of questions) on which ethical and social responsibility stances are based.

Who is responsible for ethical conduct in business?	Is it the individual, or is control exercised socially, by governments?
Who is the key actor in business ethics?	Is it the corporation, or is it the Government or other collective bodies such as trade unions?
What are the key guidelines for ethical behaviour?	Again does it rest with the corporation in the form of corporate codes of ethics, or is the key guidance a legal framework negotiated with, or imposed on, business?
What are the key issues in business ethics?	Are they single-decision issues involving misconduct and immorality, or are they social issues surrounding the framework of business?
To whom are businesses responsible?	Should the focus be on enhancing shareholder value or on multiple stakeholders?
How should performance be measured?	Should it be measured by bottom line financial results or by pluralistic measures?
How should an ethical stance be incorporated into business activity?	Should an ethical stance be seen primarily in terms of compliance with law/corporate governance codes, or should it be actively incorporated into an organisation's mission and strategy?
How important is reputation?	Does it make any difference to financial results? Should organisations strive to have a good reputation even if doing so makes no demonstrable difference to their bottom line profits?

Johnson and Scholes illustrate the range of possible CSR stances for organisations and individuals by giving four illustrations.

- **Short-term shareholder interest**
- **Long-term shareholder interest**
- **Multiple stakeholder obligations**
- **Shaper of society**

3.4.1 CSR: Short-term shareholder interest

An organisation might limit its CSR stance to taking responsibility for short-term shareholder interest on the grounds that it is for government alone to impose regulations and wider constraints using a code of corporate governance. This means some organisations take a minimal approach to CSR in the short term as there is little pressure to do more.

For example, organisations may focus only on direct profit making activities and not invest in any activities which benefit local communities as there is no requirement to do so.

3.4.2 CSR: Long-term shareholder interest

In the longer term, many organisations can identity the value and benefits of investing in CSR in the longer term.

The rationale behind an 'enlightened self-interest' stance is that there can be a long-term benefit to shareholders from well-managed relationships with other stakeholders. Therefore, the justification for social action is that it makes good business sense.

There are two reasons why an organisation might take a wider view of social responsibilities when considering the **longer-term interest of shareholders**.

(a) The organisation's **corporate image** may be enhanced by an assumption of wider responsibilities. The cost of undertaking such responsibilities may be justified as essentially promotional expenditure.

(b) The responsible exercise of corporate power may prevent a build-up of social and political **pressure for legal regulation**. Freedom of action may be preserved, and the burden of regulation lightened by acceptance of social and ethical responsibilities.

3.4.3 CSR: Multiple stakeholder obligations

Organisations adopting this stance accept the **legitimacy of the expectations of stakeholders other than shareholders** and build those expectations into the organisation's stated purposes. Such organisations recognise that, without appropriate relationships with groups such as suppliers, employees and customers, they would not be able to function.

However, organisations adopting a 'multiple stakeholder obligations' stance also argue that performance should not be measured simply through the financial bottom line. They argue that the key to long-term survival is dependent on social and environmental performance as well as economic (financial) performance and, therefore, it is important to take account of the views of stakeholders with interests relating to social and environmental matters.

3.4.4 Shaper of society

Shapers of society regard financial considerations as being of secondary importance to changing society or social norms. For such organisations, ensuring that society benefits from their actions is more important than financial and other stakeholder interests.

3.5 Corporate social responsibility and corporate citizenship

Corporate citizenship refers to an organisation's responsibilities toward society. The goal of corporate citizenship is to produce higher standards of living and quality of life for the communities that surround them and still maintain profitability for stakeholders.

It involves the social responsibility of businesses and the extent to which they meet legal, ethical, economic and environmental responsibilities, as established by shareholders and other stakeholders.

The concept of corporate citizenship personalises an organisation as part of the community, so a board of directors consider the impact of business operations on the environment and socially as well as on profit and take actions which limit harm.

Corporate citizenship includes complying with best practice and being responsive to ethical concerns. An organisations reputation as a good corporate citizen may be thought to be worth the extra costs incurred in order to maximise long term sustainable strategic objectives and performance.

Corporate citizenship is growing increasingly important as investors, potential employees, customers, suppliers, banks and other stakeholders are seeking out companies that have socially responsible orientations such as their environmental, social, and governance (ESG) practices.

We can suggest that companies achieve society's expectation that they are good corporate citizens through their philanthropic responsibilities. Philanthropic means seeking to promote the welfare of others or being generous and benevolent and philanthropic examples include making charitable donations; supporting local schools, arts or sports projects; or even building educational or leisure facilities in the local communities where they operate.

However, an important point to note about philanthropic responsibilities is that, while local communities may hope that companies contribute to their wellbeing, it does not make the companies unethical if they do not. Philanthropic responsibilities may be desired by society, but companies are not obliged to make such contributions, and they should not be considered unethical just because they do not make them.

A business managed with the sole objective of maximising shareholder wealth can be run in just as ethical a fashion as one in which far wider stakeholder responsibility is assumed. On the other hand, however, there is no doubt that many large businesses have behaved irresponsibly in the past and some continue to do so.

3.6 Corporate social responsibility and strategy

As part of developing a business strategy, an organisation must determine its strategy for corporate social responsibility. To assist in the organisations sometimes carry out corporate social responsibility audits. This generally involves:

- Recognising a firm's rationale for engaging in socially responsible activity
- Identifying programmes which are congruent with the mission of the company
- Setting objectives and priorities related to this programme
- Specifying the nature and range of resources required
- Evaluating company involvement in such programmes (past, present and future)

In the USA, corporate social responsibility audits on environmental issues have increased since the Exxon Valdez catastrophe in which millions of gallons of crude oil were released into Alaskan waters. The **Valdez principles** were drafted by the Coalition for Environmentally Responsible Economics to focus attention on environmental concerns and corporate responsibility.

- Eliminate pollutants and hazardous waste
- Conserve non-renewable resources
- Market environmentally safe products and services
- Prepare for accidents and restore damaged environments
- Provide protection for employees who report environmental hazards
- Companies should appoint an environmentalist to the board of directors, name an executive for environmental affairs and develop an environmental audit of global operations

3.7 Corporate social responsibility and sustainability reporting

Consumers are increasing concerned about the impact of business activities on the environment. There has been an increase in the use of the environmental approach to market products. 'Dolphin friendly' tuna and paper products from managed forests are good examples. Companies now monitor the impact they have on the environment as part of their CSR obligations due the significant impact environmental issues can have.

Environmental impacts on business may be **direct**.

- Changes affecting costs or resource availability
- Impact on demand as **consumers demand** products which appear to be environmentally friendly
- Effect on power balances between competitors in a market
- Additional Taxes (eg landfill tax)

Also, **environmental impacts** on business may be **indirect**. Pressure for better environmental performance is coming from many quarters.

(a) **Environmental pressure groups** have increased their membership and influence dramatically.

(b) **Employees** are increasing pressure on the businesses in which they work for a number of reasons: partly for their own safety, partly in order to improve the public image of the company.

(c) **Legislation** has increased for **less pollution** from industry with greater **regulation** by government (eg recycling targets). Many countries now have laws to cover land use planning, smoke emission, water pollution and the destruction of animals and natural habitats.

(d) **Environmental risk screening** has become increasingly important. Companies in the future will become responsible for the environmental impact of their activities.

Sustainability is explored further in the next chapter

3.8 CSR Strategy

A business that has a strategy in place to demonstrate its corporate social responsibility will have a deliberate plan with specific activities identified. Examples of CSR activities might include:

- Making donations to charity
- Contributing to the activities on non-governmental organisations (NGOs)
- Supporting local good causes
- Including stakeholders in key decisions
- Managing the social and environmental impacts of the business

Having a strategy means making choices, providing funding for the CSR initiatives chosen, and monitoring the outcomes.

3.9 CSR initiatives to meet CSR strategic goals

It could be argued that CSR activities should reflect the ethos of the business, which leads to the concept of strategic CSR. When CSR activities become strategic, they are concerned with the long-term success of the business and should therefore be beneficial to the business as well as to society. The increasing prevalence of strategic CSR is linked to the development of frameworks such as the Integrated Reporting framework, which places an emphasis on the long-term success of an organisation and is covered in more detail later in this chapter.

Examples of strategic CSR initiatives might include:

- A pharmaceutical company funding the training of medical staff, in the hope that when qualified they will source drugs from that company
- A bank providing free internet training for senior customers, who might then be disposed to buying financial products
- Encouraging employees to nominate and get involved in good causes, in order to develop loyalty to the company
- Sponsoring sports teams in return for advertising space on shirts, other merchandise, and at the ground.

The decision as to whether CSR should be strategic is an ethical one. From a pristine capitalist point of view, all CSR activities should be strategic since all of a company's money should be used to benefit shareholders. On the other hand, a deep green perspective would argue that, because businesses take from society, they should give something back.

One difference between 'CSR strategy' and 'strategic CSR' is the extent to which an organisation will promote the support given to a CSR cause, making it more likely that strategic CSR will be more visible. Consequently, the ethical viewpoint most likely to support this could be that of the expedient (promoting strategic CSR in a way that benefits the organisation).

3.10 Pressures on organisations

Organisations face a number of pressures from different directions to be socially responsible.

3.10.1 Governance requirements

The South African King report emphasises the importance of **sustainability**, linking it with the value of ethics and improved ethical standards. The King report stresses that sustainability is a business opportunity to eliminate or minimise adverse consequences for the company, on the community and on the environment and to improve the impact of the company's operations on the economic life of the community. The triple bottom line (economic, social and environmental responsibilities) enables a company to be relevant to society and the natural environment.

3.10.2 Stakeholder expectations

Pressures on organisations to widen the scope of their corporate public accountability come from **increasing expectations of stakeholders** and **knowledge** about the **consequences of ignoring such pressures**. The King report stresses the importance of engagement with external stakeholders, and individual workers and stakeholders being able to communicate openly.

Stakeholders include communities (particularly where operations are based), customers (product safety issues), suppliers, supply chain participants and competitors. Issues such as plant closures, pollution, job creation and sourcing can have powerful **social effects** on these stakeholders.

3.10.3 Reputation risk

Increasingly, a business must have the reputation of being a **responsible business** that enhances long-term shareholder value by addressing the needs of its **stakeholders**.

3.11 Corporate social responsibility and stakeholders

Inevitably, discussion on corporate social responsibilities has been tied in with the stakeholder view of corporate activity, the view that as businesses benefit from the goodwill and other tangible aspects of society, that they owe it **certain duties** in return, particularly towards those affected by its activities.

As previously discussed, organisations need to identify and classify stakeholders systematically and decide on how they will respond to stakeholder claims. The Mendelow model is one method of assessing the power and interest of stakeholders.

3.11.1 Problems of dealing with stakeholders

Whatever the organisation's view of its stakeholders, certain problems in dealing with them on corporate social responsibility may have to be addressed.

(a) Collaborating with stakeholders may be **time consuming** and **expensive**.

(b) There may be **culture clashes** between the company and certain groups of stakeholders, or between the values of different groups of stakeholders with companies caught in the middle.

(c) There may be **conflict between the company and stakeholders** on certain issues when they are trying to collaborate on other issues.

(d) **Consensus** between different groups of stakeholders may be difficult or impossible to achieve, and the solution may not be economically or strategically desirable.

(e) Influential stakeholders' **independence** (and hence ability to provide necessary criticism) may be compromised if they become too closely involved with companies.

(f) Dealing with certain stakeholders (eg public sector organisations) may be complicated by their being **accountable in turn to the wider public**.

3.12 Impact of corporate social responsibility on strategy and corporate governance

Social responsibilities can impact on what companies do in a number of ways.

3.12.1 Objectives and mission statements

If the organisation publishes a mission statement to inform stakeholders of strategic objectives, **mention of social objectives** is a sign that the board believes that they have a significant impact on strategy.

3.12.2 Ethical codes of conduct

As part of their guidance to promote **good corporate behaviour** among their employees, some organisations publish a **business code of ethics**.

3.12.3 Corporate social reporting and social accounts

Organisations, as part of their reporting on operational and financial matters, report on **ethical or social conduct**. Some go further, **producing social accounts** showing quantified impacts on each of the organisation's stakeholder constituencies.

3.12.4 Corporate governance

Impacts on corporate governance could include representatives from key stakeholder groups on the board, or perhaps even a **stakeholder board of directors**. It also implies the need for a binding corporate governance code that regulates the rights of stakeholder groups.

3.13 Ownership and corporate social responsibility

Having talked about the social responsibilities of companies, we also need to consider the responsibilities of shareholders in companies. This is complicated by the nature of ownership of shares. Shareholders are not buying something tangible that they can use as they please and regulate how others use it. Instead shareholders are buying a **right to participate in risks and rewards** from a separate legal entity.

One view is that shareholders have **responsibilities arising directly out of their rights**, particularly the rights to vote in an annual general meeting. The argument is that they should use the voice they have at this meeting. If they own a large block of shares, they should make the most of the influence this gives them to ensure good corporate governance and accountability for decisions made.

A wider view is that shareholders, by buying shares in the hope of an opportunity of greater returns than they could achieve from a safe investment, also have a responsibility to society in the same way as they would be responsible for controlling tangible property that they owned. They should be insisting that those managing the company carry out a policy that is consistent with the **public welfare**. Institutional investors can help achieve this by having publicly-stated policies that they will only invest in companies that demonstrate corporate social responsibility.

One of the main problems with this view in relation to large corporations is the **wide dispersion of shareholders**. This means that shareholders with small percentage holdings have negligible influence on managers. In addition, the ease with which shareholders can **dispose of shares** on the stock markets arguably loosens their feeling of obligation in relation to their property. This then raises the question of why the speculative (and possibly short-term) interests of shareholders should prevail over the longer-term interests of other stakeholders.

In corporate governance discussions, the idea of ownership responsibilities has had a significant influence because of the importance of **institutional shareholders**. Not only do they have the level of shareholdings that can be used as a lever to pressure managers, but they themselves have **fiduciary responsibilities** as trustees on behalf of their investors.

Question — Writing a code

If you were writing a corporate governance code, would you employ a principles-based or rules-based approach?

Answer

In the end, it would depend on the society in which you lived and what you were trying to achieve in the code.

A society with an emphasis on obeying a **strict legal code** would probably be most comfortable with a governance framework that reflected this and was very much **rules-based**. Similarly, a society with an active legal profession in pursuit of any loopholes they can find probably needs some watertight rules. You would also probably prefer a governance framework that was rules-based if your objectives were **fairly narrow** if you were concerned with specific abuses rather than all-round corporate governance. In effect you would be developing a framework similar to many accounting standards, which in recent years have aimed to narrow (or eliminate) choices in accounting practice.

A society where the emphasis was on being a 'sound' corporate citizen (a good member of the Stock Exchange club, perhaps), and which focused on following best practice with limited law or regulations in support, would probably be most happy with a **principles-based approach**. You would also have to use that approach if your code covered governance best practice over a wide spectrum, since many aspects of governance cannot be easily defined in terms of following simple rules.

You may have taken the compromise position, that the code should be a combination of general principles with some specific provisions, for example requiring all listed companies to have an audit committee. The risk with doing this may be that companies focus on complying with the specific provisions, and neglect the governance areas covered by the vaguer, more general principles. However, research suggests that companies that happily comply with specific provisions in codes also have a good compliance record with the more general recommendations.

3.14 Corporate social responsibility and risk management

The Deloitte (2008) guide *The Risk Intelligent Approach to Corporate Responsibility and Sustainability* suggests that sustainability can be approached from a perspective of risk management, seeing corporate responsibility issues as providing opportunities as well as dangers. This should in turn mean that the organisation's approach to these issues is aligned and integrated with strategic initiatives in other parts of the business.

Deloitte recommends a nine-stage approach.

1	Understanding the present	This includes assessing regulatory trends, benchmarking against competitor activity, finding out what is important to stakeholders, understanding all the CSR activity currently happening in the organisation
2	Envisioning the future	This involves assessing the legacy the organisation wishes to leave. This will mean integrating CSR activities with business strategies, for example a publishing company sending its employees to libraries and schools or donating books.
3	Planning the journey	CSR issues should be prioritised using a gap analysis between current and future states, and the organisation and its competitors. Assess opportunities for action, risks of inaction and not achieving objectives.
4	Planning and building	The human resource element is vital, including example set and oversight by senior management. CSR achievements should be built into performance reviews and remuneration. Assess availability of grants and tax concessions for green behaviour. Also, consider broadening stakeholder base and organisation's ethical culture.
5	Execution	Develop in controlled fashion, enhancing governance procedures related to implementation.
6	Review and revision	Develop metrics to measure activities. Use hard data rather than impressions, though stakeholder feedback is important.
7	Reporting and communicating	A CSR development programme may mean reporting on CSR needs to be revamped. The organisation could report in accordance with various external reporting standards or produce customised report.
8	Assuring internally	Adapt measures used initially to assess CSR development to monitor how the organisation is doing. Use internal resources such as internal audit, legal, health and safety and human resources to assist in development.
9	Assuring externally	When CSR reaches a certain level, seek verification from outside the organisation of assertions in CSR report.

4 Integrated reporting

In December 2013 the International Integrated Reporting Council (IIRC) published *The International Integrated Reporting Framework*.

The aim of integrated reporting is to **demonstrate the linkage between strategy, governance and financial performance** and the **social, environmental and economic context within which the business operates**. By making these connections, businesses should be able to take more sustainable decisions, helping to ensure the effective allocation of scarce resources. Investors and other stakeholders should better understand how an organisation is really performing. In particular, they should make a meaningful assessment of the long-term viability of the organisation's business model and its strategy.

Integrated reporting should also achieve the simplification of accounts, with excessive detail being removed and critical information being highlighted.

4.1 Six capitals

Organisations use six types of capital to deliver their products or services.

Integrated reporting is designed to make visible the six capitals (resources and relationships) on which the organisation depends, how the organisation uses those capitals and its impact on them.

The six capitals are as follows:

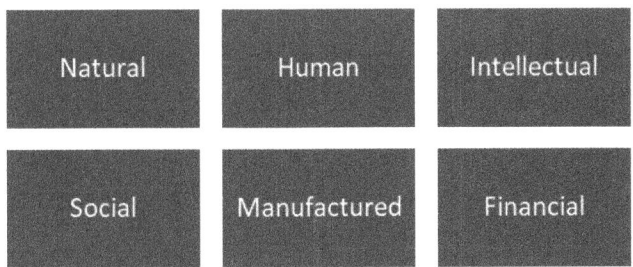

The six capitals are explained in the table below.

Financial	Funds available for use in production obtained through financing or generated through operations
Manufactured	Manufactured physical objects used in production or service provision: • Buildings • Equipment • Infrastructure
Human	Skills, experience and motivation to innovate: • Alignment and support for organisation's governance framework and ethical values • Ability to understand and implement organisation's strategies • Loyalties and motivations for improvements
Intellectual	Knowledge-based intangibles providing competitive advantage: • Patents, copyrights, software, rights and licences • Tacit knowledge, systems and protocols
Natural	Input to goods and services and what activities impact: • Water, land, minerals and forests • Biodiversity and ecosystem health

Social and relationship	Institutions and relationships within each community stakeholder group and network to enhance wellbeing: • Common values and behaviour • Key relationships • Brand and reputation • Social licence to operate

4.1.1 Examples of the six capitals

1. **Financial Capital**

   Apple, with its vast cash reserves, investments in various financial instruments, and steady income from product sales and services, Apple possesses substantial financial capital resources that fuel its operations, investments in research and development, and strategic initiatives.

2. **Manufactured Capital**

   Toyota Motor Corporation exemplifies manufactured capital through its extensive physical infrastructure, advanced manufacturing facilities, and cutting-edge technology used in vehicle production. With state-of-the-art factories, machinery, and patented manufacturing processes, Toyota relies heavily on its manufactured capital to maintain its position as a leading global automobile manufacturer.

3. **Intellectual Capital**

   Microsoft Corporation showcases intellectual capital through its vast portfolio of patents, trademarks, and copyrights, along with the expertise and skills of its employees. As a technology giant, Microsoft owns valuable intellectual property rights to software products like Windows and Office, while also leveraging the knowledge and innovation of its workforce to develop new technologies and solutions.

4. **Human Capital**

   Google demonstrates strong human capital through its highly skilled and diverse workforce, comprised of talented engineers, developers, and professionals across various fields. With a focus on employee education, training, and well-being, Google invests in nurturing its human capital to drive innovation, creativity, and productivity across its diverse range of products and services

5. **Social Capital**

   Starbucks Corporation exemplifies social capital through its extensive network of relationships with stakeholders, including employees, customers, suppliers, and communities. Through initiatives like ethical sourcing, community outreach programs, and employee welfare initiatives, Starbucks builds trust, fosters positive relationships, and earns social license to operate, enhancing its brand reputation and long-term sustainability.

6. **Natural Capital**

   The Body Shop, a cosmetics company, emphasises natural capital through its commitment to sustainable sourcing, environmental conservation, and biodiversity preservation. By using natural ingredients, supporting fair trade practices, and advocating for environmental causes, The Body Shop relies on natural capital to create eco-friendly products and contribute to the preservation of natural resources and ecosystems.

4.2 Integrated Reporting

Key term

> **Integrated reporting:** Integrated reporting is a reporting approach that aims to provide a holistic view of an organisation's performance, value creation, and impact across the six capitals.

Unlike traditional financial reporting, which focuses primarily on financial capital, integrated reporting considers the organisation's broader value creation process and its interactions with various forms of capital.

Integrated reporting encourages organisations to communicate how they create value over time by utilising and affecting the six capitals. It emphasises the interdependencies between financial, environmental, social, and governance factors and their influence on organisational performance and sustainability.

Integrated reporting is highly relevant to sustainable development as it provides a comprehensive framework for organisations to assess and communicate their sustainability performance and impact. By considering the interconnectedness of financial, environmental, social, and governance factors, integrated reporting enables organisations to:

Evaluate their contribution to sustainable development goals and objectives.

- Identify opportunities to enhance value creation while minimising negative impacts on society and the environment.
- Engage stakeholders in meaningful dialogue about sustainability issues and performance.
- Enhance transparency, accountability, and trust by providing a more complete picture of the organisation's activities and impacts.
- Explanation of the IFRS International Integrated Reporting Framework.

The International Integrated Reporting Framework (IFRS Framework) provides guidance and principles for organisations seeking to adopt integrated reporting practices. It outlines the fundamental concepts, content elements, and guiding principles of integrated reporting, helping organisations effectively communicate their value creation story.

The IFRS Framework emphasises the importance of connectivity, materiality, conciseness, and reliability in integrated reporting. It encourages organisations to tailor their reports to reflect the unique circumstances, strategies, and impacts relevant to their operations and stakeholders.

The diagram provided by the IFRS Framework illustrates the key components of integrated reporting, including the organisation's business model, governance structure, performance measures, and outcomes across the six capitals. It serves as a visual representation of how organisations can integrate financial and non-financial information to communicate their value creation process and impact on sustainable development.

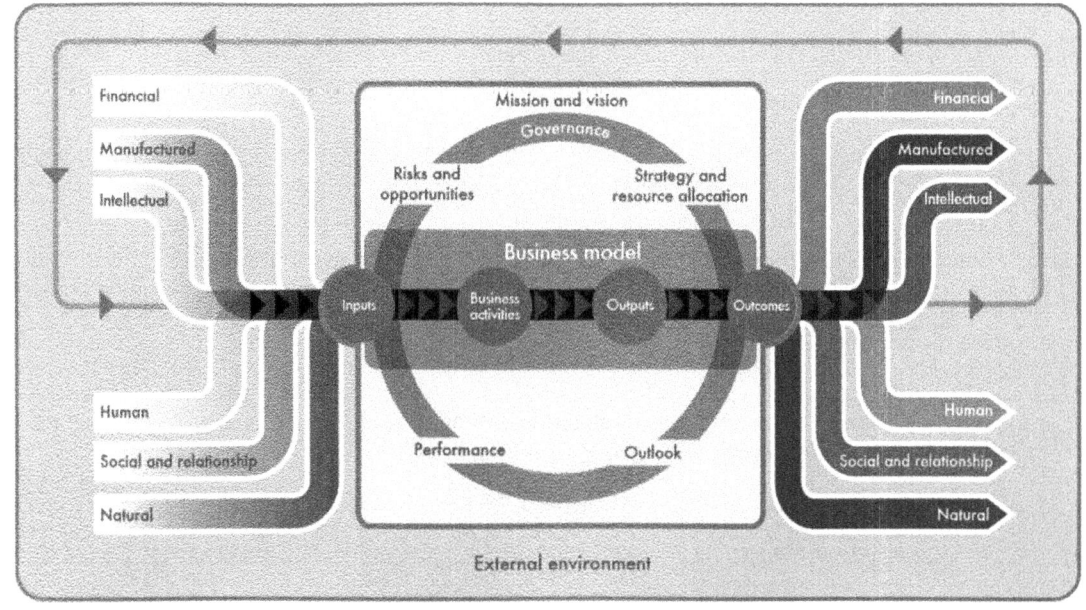

(Source: https://integratedreporting.ifrs.org/resource/international-ir-framework/)

4.2.1 Integrated reporting guiding principles

A number of guiding principles underpin the content and presentation of an integrated report.

Strategic focus and future orientation	Insights into strategy, and how it relates to organisation's ability to create value in the short, medium and long term, and how it affects the capitals
Connectivity of information	A holistic view of the combination, interrelatedness and dependencies between the factors that affect the ability to create value over time
Stakeholder relationships	The nature and quality of relationships with key stakeholders and how their legitimate needs and interests are taken into account
Materiality, conciseness, reliability and completeness	Provision of important and reliable information including all material items, both positive and negative, in a concise manner
Consistency and comparability	Consistent over time and comparable with other organisations

4.2.2 Content elements

The content elements follow on from the guiding principles.

- Organisational overview and external environment
- Governance
- Business model
- Risks and opportunities
- Strategy and resource allocation
- Performance
- Outlook
- Basis of presentation

4.2.3 Benefits of integrated reporting

The following are potential benefits of integrated reporting.

(a) **Stakeholder needs**

The information will be more in line with **investor and other stakeholder requirements**, leading to a higher level of trust from, and engagement with, stakeholders. Investors will have better information to assess ability to generate cash flows and risk opportunities. The connections made in reporting will enable investors to assess better the combined impact of the diverse factors affecting the business. This should result in better investment decisions and more effective capital allocation.

(b) **Decision making**

Having the information will enable better resource allocation decisions, enhanced risk management and better identification of opportunities.

(c) **Reputation**

Greater transparency should result in a decrease in reputation risk and lower cost of, and better access to, capital.

(d) **Harmonisation**

Integrated reporting provides a platform for standard setters and decision makers to harmonise reporting.

(e) **Stewardship**

Because of its emphasis on resources and relationships and a longer timeframe, organisations are better placed to act, and be more accountable, as stewards of common resources.

(f) **Stakeholder relationships**

The emphasis on stakeholder engagement should lead to greater consultation with stakeholder groups and dealing with their concerns.

4.2.4 Challenges of integrated reporting

There are a number of challenges of developing an effective implementing integrated reporting system.

(a) **Local regulation**

Regulations that vary between jurisdictions currently affect components of integrated reporting, and progress towards integrated reporting will happen at different speeds in different countries.

(b) **Directors' duties**

Directors' duties also vary between jurisdictions. Integrated reporting will be influenced by the users of accounts whom the directors are required to address.

(c) **Directors' liability**

Concerns about liability will need to be addressed, as directors will be reporting on the future and on evolving issues.

(d) **Confidentiality**

Organisations will need to balance the benefits of integrated reporting with the desire to avoid disclosing competitive information.

(e) **Incentives**

Integrated reporting needs to assist in overcoming focus on short-term rewards.

PART D GOVERNANCE AND SELF-REGULATION

Chapter Roundup

- **Corporate governance**, the system by which organisations are directed and controlled, is based on a number of concepts, including transparency, independence, accountability and integrity.
- **Corporate citizenship** has been used to describe how an organisation's values are shaped and the impact concepts of responsibility have on business decision making.
- An organisation's ethical stance relates to how it **views its responsibilities** to shareholders, stakeholders, society and the environment.
- There is increasing concern about businesses' relationship with the natural environment. Businesses may suffer **significant costs** and a **loss of reputation** if problems arise.
- **Sustainability** means limiting use of resources to what can be replenished.
    - The **Global Reporting Initiative** provides a framework for a **sustainability report**.
    - **Full cost accounting** is a method of accounting for all relevant costs including externalities.

Quick Quiz

1   Fill in the blank:
    .... is the business strategy that shapes the values underpinning a company's mission and the choices made each day by its executives, managers and employees as they engage with society.

2   Match the position on social responsibility with the viewpoint held.

    (a) Pristine capitalist
    (b) Expedient
    (c) Social contract proponent
    (d) Social ecologist
    (e) Socialist
    (f) Radical feminist
    (g) Deep ecologist

    (i)   Economic systems that trade off threats to the existence of species with economic imperatives are flawed.
    (ii) Businesses have to accept some social legislation and moral requirements if they are to be able to generate profits.
    (iii) Companies exist to make profits and seek economic efficiency.
    (iv) The economic framework should change from being one that promotes materialism to one that promotes equality.
    (v)   Economic processes that result in resource exhaustion, waste and pollution must be modified.
    (vi) Economic systems emphasise aggression, conflict and competition rather than co-operation and reflection.
    (vii) An organisation's survival and prosperity is based on delivery of benefits to society in general.

3   Fill in the blank:
    .... is the impact that a business's activities have on the environment, including its resource environment and pollution emissions.

4   What is sustainability in relation to a company's activities?

Answers to Quick Quiz

1. **Corporate citizenship** is the business strategy that shapes the values underpinning a company's mission and the choices made each day by its executives, managers and employees as they engage with society.

2.

Pristine capitalist	Companies exist to make profits and seek economic efficiency.
Expedient	Businesses have to accept some social legislation and moral requirements if they are to be able to generate profits.
Social contract proponent	An organisation's survival and prosperity is based on delivery of benefits to society in general.
Social ecologist	Economic processes that result in resource exhaustion, waste and pollution must be modified.
Socialist	The economic framework should change from being one that promotes materialism to one that promotes equality.
Radical feminist	Economic systems emphasise aggression, conflict and competition rather than co-operation and reflection.
Deep ecologist	Economic systems that trade off threats to the existence of species with economic imperatives are flawed.

3. **Environmental footprint** is the impact that a business's activities have on the environment, including its resource environment and pollution emissions.

4. Sustainability involves developing strategies so that the company only uses resources at a rate that allows them to be replenished (in order to ensure that they will continue to be available). At the same time the company's emissions of waste are confined to levels that do not exceed the capacity of the environment to absorb them.

Ethics and sustainability

Topic list	Syllabus reference
1 Introduction to ethics and sustainability	LO 3, LO4
2 Sustainable business practices	LO 3, LO4
3 Ethics and sustainability	LO 3, LO4

Introduction

Sustainability and ethics are closely intertwined, focusing on the responsibility to meet current needs without compromising future generations.

Ethical decision-making is central to sustainability, requiring businesses to consider the social, environmental, and economic impacts of their actions.

As sustainability challenges like climate change and social inequality become more pressing, organisations must integrate ethical principles into their strategies and operations.

This chapter explores how aligning business practices with ethical sustainability leads to long-term success and a positive societal impact.

1 Introduction to sustainability

Sustainability is a multifaceted concept aimed at improving people's lives and safeguarding the planet for future generations. Originating from the 1987 Brundtland Report, sustainable development is defined as "development that meets the needs of the present without compromising the ability of future generations to meet their own needs." This definition places a strong emphasis on ethical decision making, highlighting the responsibility to balance current economic and social development with the preservation of environmental resources for future generations.

The scope of sustainability has evolved beyond environmental concerns to encompass a wide range of interconnected issues, including wealth disparities, population growth, biodiversity loss, deteriorating air and water quality, climate change, human rights, and corruption. This expanded view recognises that sustainable development requires ethical decision-making that integrates social, environmental, and economic considerations.

In recent years, heightened awareness of Environmental, Social, and Governance (ESG) issues has prompted global stock exchanges to mandate sustainability reporting for listed companies. As a result, board directors and senior management are now expected to embed ESG and ethical considerations into their business strategies and decision-making processes. This involves making informed choices that not only enhance organisational performance but also ensure a positive impact on society and the environment.

This chapter delves into the importance of sustainable business practices, emphasising the ethical dimensions of sustainability in improving an organisation's overall performance. It explores how businesses can navigate the complexities of ethical decision-making to foster a more responsible approach to growth, ensuring that their actions align with both current needs and future aspirations.

In recent years, the concept of sustainability has gained significant traction across various sectors, from business and finance to environmental conservation and social development. The pressing challenges of climate change, resource depletion, and social inequality have underscored the urgent need for a paradigm shift towards ethical and sustainable practices on a global scale. This discussion aims to explore the critical importance of integrating ethical decision making into global sustainability efforts and the profound implications for stakeholders worldwide.

1.1 Sustainability and ESG

Environmental, Social and Governance (ESG) is referred to as the three pillars of sustainability. ESG issues derive from increasing political and stakeholder concerns on the growing adverse effect of business operations on human sustainability.

As a reminder from your previous studies, there are no standard definitions of ESG issues, however, the Principles of Responsible Investment (PRI) define ESG issues as follows.

Key terms

Environmental: These are issues relating to the quality and functioning of the natural environment and natural systems. These include biodiversity loss; greenhouse gas (GHG) emissions; climate change; renewable energy; energy efficiency; air, water or resource depletion or pollution; waste management, stratospheric ozone depletion; changes in land use; ocean acidification and changes to the nitrogen and phosphorus cycles.

Social: These are issues relating to the rights, well-being and interests of people and communities. These include human rights; labour standards in the supply chain; child, slave, and bonded labour; workplace health and safety; freedom of association and freedom of expression; human capital management and employee relations; diversity; relations with local communities; activities in conflict zones; health and access to medicine; HIV/AIDS; consumer protection; and controversial weapons.

Governance: These are issues relating to the governance of companies and other investee entities. In the listed equity context these include board structure; size; diversity; skills and independence; executive pay; shareholder rights; stakeholder interaction; disclosure of information; business ethics; bribery and corruption; internal controls; risk management; and, in general, issues dealing with the relationship between a company's management, its board, its shareholders and its other stakeholders. This category may also include matters of business strategy.

(Source: https://www.unpri.org/sustainability-issues/environmental-social-and-governance-issues)

Sustainability describes a world of thriving economies and just societies based on what nature can afford. It incorporates consideration of both the impacts and dependencies of an organisation and so includes those factors that are material both to the organisation but also to society.

Environmental, social and governance (ESG) approaches this issue through a corporate lens and considers only how these risks and opportunities affect a business and its enterprise value.

Whilst sustainability includes the concept of environmental and social limits (planetary limits and a social foundation) within which there is a safe operating space, ESG does not.

ESG focusses on enterprise value and does not include consideration of planetary limits and a social foundation, together considered the 'safe operating space' within which companies, governments and individuals can sustainably operate. Therefore, ESG is separate from the overall concept of sustainability.

Note, organisations tend to consider only how ESG related risks and opportunities affect a business and its enterprise value.

2 Sustainable business practices

In today's business environment, sustainability is a critical factor for long-term success and viability. Companies are increasingly recognising the importance of integrating sustainability into their core business practices, which involves a commitment to corporate accountability and proactive stakeholder engagement.

2.1 Corporate Accountability

Key term

Corporate accountability: Corporate accountability is the principle that companies should act ethically and be answerable to their stakeholders for their actions, decisions, policies and impacts on society and the environment.

As we learned from the previous chapter, corporate accountability extends beyond financial performance to include social and environmental dimensions, ensuring that businesses contribute positively to sustainable development.

Gray and Adams (2014) argue that sustainable business practices are essential for achieving long-term success and sustainability. Therefore, sustainable business practices are intrinsically linked to corporate accountability.

2.2 Sustainability accounting

Sustainability accounting focuses on expanding traditional accounting practices to incorporate environmental and social impacts, requiring businesses to measure and report their impacts on the environment and society as well as their financial performance.

Sustainability accounting aims to provide a more comprehensive view of an organisation's performance by including the impacts of its activities on society and the environment, alongside the traditional financial metrics.

Gray and Adams (2014) define the three components which provide a comprehensive approach to sustainability accounting: environmental accountability, social accountability, and economic accountability. Each of these is explained further below.

2.2.1 Environmental accountability

Key term

> **Environmental accountability:** Environmental accountability is how organisations take responsibility for their environmental impacts by implementing sustainable practices and reducing their ecological footprint.

An example of environmental accountability is US company Tesla, which has been at the forefront of promoting electric vehicles to reduce carbon emissions over the past decade. Also, Apple, a US computer and smart device manufacturer, has committed to using 100% recycled aluminium in its products to reduce the environmental impact of its products.

2.2.2 Social accountability

Key term

> **Social accountability:** Social accountability involves ensuring that business operations respect human rights, provide fair labour conditions, and contribute to the well-being of its employees and wider society.

An example of social accountability is US shoe manufacturer Nike's efforts to improve labour conditions in its supply chain after facing criticism for sweatshop practices. As a result, Nike regularly audits its factories and publishes detailed reports on labour conditions.

2.2.3 Economic accountability

Key term

> **Economic accountability:** Economic accountability is where companies are required, or voluntarily, demonstrate that their economic activities support sustainable development. This can include investing in local economies, supporting small businesses, and fostering inclusive growth.

An example of environmental accountability is Danone, a French multinational food-products corporation. Its operations fund the "Danone Communities" initiative which supports social businesses that address issues like malnutrition and access to clean water, creating economic opportunities in communities where access to food and clean water is challenging.

Environmental, Social and Economic accountability provide a comprehensive approach to sustainability accounting which provides transparency to stakeholders so they can fully understand the scope and impact of a company's operations and its commitment to meeting its sustainability objectives.

(Source: Gray, R., Adams, C. A., & Owen, D. (2014). "Accountability, Social Responsibility and Sustainability: Accounting for Society and the Environment." Pearson Education Limited)

2.3 Sustainable business practices

> **Sustainable value creation:** Sustainable value creation is when organisations engage with stakeholders to help identify opportunities for creating sustainable value.

By considering the needs and interests of all stakeholders, companies can create long-term value and achieve sustainable growth. This approach not only benefits the company but also contributes positively to society and the environment.

Donaldson and Preston suggest that when organisations engage with their stakeholders and uphold corporate accountability then sustainable business practices follow and an organisation's sustainability performance improves.

The following are examples of sustainable business practices.
1. Inclusive decision-making
2. Responsiveness and Responsibility
3. Transparency and reporting
4. Ethical Practices

Each of these sustainable business practices are explained further in the table below.

Sustainable business practice	Description	Example
1. Inclusive decision-making	Companies are encouraged to involve a wide range of stakeholders in their decision-making processes. This inclusivity ensures that diverse perspectives are considered, leading to more balanced and sustainable business strategies.	Ben & Jerry's actively engages with local communities and social justice organisations to guide their business practices and ensure they align with broader societal goals.
2. Responsiveness and Responsibility	Organisations that are responsive to stakeholder concerns demonstrate their commitment to accountability.	After receiving feedback from environmental groups, Coca-Cola pledged to reduce plastic waste by increasing the use of recycled materials in its packaging, showing responsiveness to stakeholder concerns.
3. Transparency and reporting	To be accountable, companies must transparently report their sustainability efforts and impacts. This includes disclosing information on environmental performance, social initiatives, and governance practices to stakeholders. Transparency in reporting and operations builds trust with stakeholders.	Nestlé applies Global Reporting Initiative (GRI) standards to provide comprehensive sustainability reports that cover various stakeholder concerns.
4. Ethical Practices	Businesses are expected to adopt ethical practices that respect stakeholder interests and promote sustainability. This includes reducing environmental footprints, ensuring fair labour practices, and contributing to community development.	Patagonia, the UK outdoor wear clothing company, ensures ethical practices by using sustainable materials in its manufacturing processes and follows fair trade labour practices as part of its code of ethics. It also donates a portion of profits to environmental causes.

Case Study

The following organisations demonstrate corporate accountability practices through their sustainability and corporate responsibility initiatives.

Ben & Jerry's (US)

Ben & Jerry's is a United States-based ice cream manufacturers and retailer. This company has developed a reputation for strong social and environmental commitments. Ben & Jerry's engages with various stakeholders, including local communities, suppliers, and customers. The company uses fair trade ingredients and supports social justice causes, demonstrating a robust model of corporate accountability and stakeholder engagement.

Starbucks (US)

Starbucks engages with its stakeholders through its ethical sourcing practices, community involvement, and environmental initiatives. The company's "Starbucks C.A.F.E. Practices" ensure that coffee is ethically sourced, benefiting farmers and promoting sustainable farming practices.

Unilever (Netherlands/UK)

Launched in 2010, Unilever's Sustainable Living Plan aimed to decouple strategic business growth from its environmental impact while increasing positive social impact. The company focuses on improving health and well-being, reducing its environmental footprint, and enhancing employee and supplier livelihoods. Unilever actively engages with various stakeholders, including customers, employees, suppliers, and communities, to realise their aims and to understand and address their concerns, and Unilever publishes detailed sustainability reports, providing transparent data on their environmental and social impact.

IKEA (Sweden)

IKEA's commitment to sustainability and ethical practices is contained in its "People & Planet Positive Strategy". IKEA's sustainability strategy aims to use resources efficiently, promote renewable energy, and contribute to a circular economy by 2030. IKEA is also known for its efforts in ensuring ethical sourcing and working conditions throughout its supply chain and it audits suppliers regularly to ensure compliance with its code of conduct. Also, the IKEA Foundation supports numerous global initiatives to improve children's education and support refugee families.

Siemens (Germany)

Siemens has committed to becoming carbon-neutral by 2030. The company focuses on energy-efficient products and solutions, contributing significantly to reducing global emissions. Siemens actively promotes diversity and inclusion within its workforce, implementing policies to ensure equal opportunities for all employees and it has implemented a robust compliance framework to prevent corruption in its business practices, such as bribery and money-laundering, which ensures ethical conduct in all business activities.

Novo Nordisk (Norway)

Novo Nordisk aims to have zero environmental impact by 2030 through initiatives like recycling and reducing waste. The company follows GRI standards for sustainability reporting, ensuring transparency in their social and environmental impact and it runs several programs to make diabetes care affordable and accessible in low- and middle-income countries.

3 Ethics and sustainability

Sustainability is closely tied to ethical principles, as it involves fulfilling present needs without jeopardising the ability of future generations to meet theirs. The ethical aspect of sustainability addresses the obligations that businesses and individuals have towards society, the environment, and the global community. This section examines the ethical roots of sustainability and how organisations can weave ethical considerations into their sustainability initiatives.

3.1 Ethical foundations of sustainability

The essence of sustainability lies in ethics, focusing on concepts such as fairness, justice, and respect for both people and the natural world. Ethical considerations in sustainability involve questions about rights, responsibilities, and the equitable use of resources. The ethical approach emphasises that development should not undermine future generations' prospects and stresses responsible management of environmental and social assets.

Ethically driven sustainability requires organisations to go beyond merely adhering to legal requirements. It involves actively striving to minimise environmental damage, enhance social welfare, and promote economic stability. This perspective covers a broad spectrum of ethical issues, from human rights and equitable labour practices to biodiversity preservation and addressing climate change.

3.2 Incorporating ethics into sustainable business practices

For businesses, integrating ethics into sustainability efforts means taking a comprehensive view that considers the social, environmental, and economic consequences of their actions. Ethical sustainable practices include:

- **Transparent reporting:** Ethical businesses are committed to transparent reporting on their sustainability efforts, providing stakeholders with clear and accurate information about their environmental, social, and governance (ESG) performance. This openness builds trust and accountability.

- **Fair labour practices:** Ensuring fair wages, safe working conditions, and respect for workers' rights are core to ethical business operations. Companies must actively work to eradicate child labour, forced labour, and exploitation within their supply chains.

- **Environmental responsibility:** Ethically sustainable companies aim to reduce their ecological footprint through responsible resource management, reducing greenhouse gas emissions, and supporting biodiversity initiatives.

- **Community engagement:** Ethical businesses engage with local communities, respecting their rights and interests. This involves considering the social implications of business activities and contributing positively to local development.

- **Ethical supply chains:** Organisations are responsible for ensuring their supply chains adhere to ethical standards, including environmental preservation, human rights, and anti-corruption practices.

3.3 Leadership and ethical application of sustainability principles

Ethical leadership plays a crucial role in embedding sustainability into an organisation's values and practices. Leaders set the standards for corporate conduct, driving the integration of ethical values into decision making and strategic planning. By prioritising sustainability and maintaining high ethical standards, leaders foster a corporate culture that supports long-term success while benefiting society and the environment.

3.4 Ethical dilemmas in sustainability

Businesses frequently encounter ethical challenges when striving to meet sustainability objectives. These challenges arise from the need to balance economic goals with social and environmental responsibilities. Ethical decision-making in such contexts requires companies to carefully weigh short-term gains against long-term impacts on society and the planet.

Ethical dilemmas in sustainability include the following examples.

3.4.1 Profit versus environmental protection

Companies may be tempted to prioritise immediate profits over environmental stewardship, potentially leading to the over-exploitation of natural resources and ecological degradation. Ethical business decisions require finding strategies that enable economic success without compromising the environment.

For example, in the Amazon rainforest, logging companies often prioritise profit by engaging in deforestation, clearing large areas of forest to make way for agricultural expansion or timber production. This practice significantly contributes to habitat destruction, biodiversity loss, and climate change. Ethical companies in this sector, however, strive to implement sustainable forestry practices, balancing economic activities with environmental conservation.

3.4.2 Lack of social equity in global operations

In global operations, businesses face varying labour standards and human rights practices. Ethical companies must navigate these differences, advocating for fair treatment and equity across all regions in which they operate, regardless of local practices or regulations.

For example, Nike faced criticism in the 1990s for poor labour conditions in its overseas factories, including low wages, excessive working hours, and unsafe working conditions. This public backlash forced the company to reassess its labour practices. In response, Nike implemented more rigorous auditing of its suppliers, established a code of conduct, and improved transparency in its supply chain operations.

3.4.3 Greenwashing

One of the most prevalent ethical dilemmas in sustainability is greenwashing – the practice of falsely portraying a company's products, services, or practices as environmentally friendly. Companies may invest more in marketing themselves as "green" rather than implementing genuine sustainable practices. This deception misleads consumers, investors, and other stakeholders, ultimately damaging trust and hindering progress toward true sustainability.

For example, Volkswagen's diesel emissions scandal in 2015 is a prominent case of greenwashing. The company marketed its diesel vehicles as environmentally friendly while secretly installing software to manipulate emissions tests. This deception allowed them to appear compliant with environmental regulations, even though their cars emitted pollutants well above the legal limits.

3.4.4 Misleading sustainability reporting

Many companies produce sustainability reports to showcase their environmental and social performance. However, sustainability reporting is not always subject to strict verification or assurance, and it is often not fully mandated. This lack of standardisation opens the door to manipulation and misrepresentation, where companies may selectively disclose information to appear more sustainable than they truly are. Ethical companies must commit to honest, transparent reporting, ensuring that their sustainability claims are accurate and verifiable.

For example, in 2019, fast-fashion retailer H&M faced accusations of misleading sustainability reporting. Critics argued that the company's "Conscious Collection" was marketed as sustainable without clear evidence of reduced environmental impact or improved labour conditions in the supply chain. The lack of transparency and verification of their claims raised concerns about greenwashing in the fashion industry.

3.4.5 Green finance avoidance or misrepresentation to green finance providers

Green finance refers to financial products and services, such as green bonds or loans, that are specifically intended to support environmentally friendly and sustainable projects. These may include investments in renewable energy, energy efficiency, pollution control, and sustainable agriculture. Despite the long-term benefits of green finance, some businesses opt for cheaper, conventional financing to minimise costs in the short term. This approach can hinder progress toward more sustainable practices and slow the transition to environmentally friendly initiatives.

In some cases, businesses may go a step further and wilfully misrepresent their sustainability credentials to secure green financing. This unethical behaviour involves providing false or exaggerated information about a company's environmental initiatives to qualify for green finance products, which could otherwise have been allocated to genuinely sustainable projects.

Ethical decision making in this context means recognising the importance of supporting green finance, even if it may not yield immediate cost savings like traditional financing. Honest engagement with green finance not only contributes to sustainability goals but also supports transparency and integrity in the financial market.

For example, a major oil company, aiming to secure green financing for its operations, might misrepresent its sustainability credentials to obtain a green bond or loan. For instance, the company might falsely claim that it has implemented extensive carbon capture technologies or is actively investing in renewable energy projects. This allows it to qualify for green finance under the guise of promoting environmentally friendly practices, despite continuing its conventional oil drilling operations. By doing so, the company not only secures lower-cost financing designated for green initiatives but also misleads investors and undermines the credibility of green finance markets. This wilful misrepresentation prioritises short-term financial gains while disregarding the long-term objectives of environmental sustainability and ethical financial practices.

3.4.6 Sustainability goals avoidance in business decisions

Organisations sometimes struggle to balance sustainability goals with green finance considerations. For instance, companies may face pressure to make investments that favour immediate financial returns over long-term environmental or social benefits. Ethical decision-making requires considering how investments and business strategies impact not only the company's financial health but also its environmental and social responsibilities.

For example, in 2020, despite mounting evidence of the detrimental environmental impact of plastics, many companies continued investing in single-use plastic production due to its cost-effectiveness. Although alternatives like biodegradable materials or recycled plastics were available, the perceived higher costs prevented widespread adoption, indicating a preference for short-term economic benefits over long-term sustainability.

These ethical dilemmas highlight the complex nature of sustainability in business. Addressing them requires a commitment to transparency, integrity, and a holistic approach that prioritises long-term welfare over short-term gains.

Question — Ethics and sustainability

EcoWave Ltd, a household cleaning product manufacturer, promotes its sustainability initiatives on its website, claiming to be a leader in environmental practices. It reports achievements like a 40% reduction in plastic packaging and a transition to "green energy" in its manufacturing. However, shareholders suspect greenwashing, citing data that EcoWave still heavily relies on single-use plastics and questioning the authenticity of its reported sustainability KPIs, which may have been manipulated to align with the company's strategic goals.

The following extracts from EcoWave Ltd's website and sustainability reports are provided.

EcoWave website extract:
"EcoWave Ltd is committed to protecting the planet. Our sustainable practices have led to a 40% reduction in plastic packaging across our product lines. By adopting renewable energy sources, we have

PART D GOVERNANCE AND SELF-REGULATION

transitioned our manufacturing facilities to run on 100% green energy, reducing our carbon footprint significantly. We believe in transparency and have incorporated eco-friendly practices at every step of our operations to ensure a healthier planet for future generations."

EcoWave Sustainability Report extract (2023):

"EcoWave has achieved a 40% decrease in plastic usage for our packaging materials compared to our 2020 baseline. This was accomplished through the integration of recycled materials and innovative packaging designs. We continue to explore options to further minimise our reliance on plastics.

As of 2023, 100% of our energy consumption at manufacturing sites is classified as 'green energy.' We have partnered with local renewable energy providers to meet our operational power requirements sustainably."

Subsequently, an internal employee has come forward with concerns about the company's sustainability claims. The whistleblower has provided the following statement.

"In reality, EcoWave is falling significantly short of its publicly declared sustainability targets. The supposed 40% reduction in plastic usage is largely overstated, as our product lines still heavily rely on single-use plastics.

The claims of using 100% green energy are also misleading; a considerable portion of our energy still comes from non-renewable sources. I have seen internal data manipulated to present a better sustainability performance than what is actually being achieved. There is pressure from management to align our reporting with the company's strategic goals, even if it means distorting the facts."

Required

(a) Review the extracts of EcoWave Ltd's website and sustainability reports to identify potential signs of greenwashing and manipulation.

(b) Explain the potential ethical implications of greenwashing and KPI manipulation on EcoWave and its stakeholders.

(c) Provide recommendations for EcoWave Ltd to enhance transparency and accuracy in its strategic disclosures and sustainability reporting.

Answer

(a) **Greenwashing indicators at EcoWave**

The website claims a "40% reduction in plastic packaging" but lacks specific details on the methodology, timeframe, and exact changes implemented. The whistleblower's statement contradicts this claim, suggesting that single-use plastics are still heavily used in EcoWave's product lines.

The report asserts that EcoWave has transitioned to "100% green energy," yet the whistleblower reveals that a significant portion of energy consumption still comes from non-renewable sources. The vague term "classified as green energy" raises questions about the criteria used for this classification and whether it accurately reflects the company's energy sources.

Both the website and report use broad, positive language such as "committed to protecting the planet" and "incorporated eco-friendly practices at every step," which are common in greenwashing practices, as they create a perception of environmental leadership without offering concrete evidence.

Potential Manipulation of KPIs at EcoWave

The sustainability report claims a "40% decrease in plastic usage" based on a 2020 baseline, but without third-party verification or a breakdown of data, it is difficult to verify this achievement. The whistleblower's statement suggests that internal data might have been manipulated to align with strategic goals, indicating potential misrepresentation.

The statement about "100% green energy" lacks transparency regarding the nature of the energy sources, partnerships with renewable providers, and the auditing processes. The whistleblower's disclosure points to internal data being adjusted to falsely present an image of full reliance on green energy.

(b) The following potential ethical implications of greenwashing and KPI manipulation on EcoWave and its stakeholders are explained as follows.

- **Misleading stakeholders.** Greenwashing and manipulation of KPIs mislead customers, investors, and other stakeholders into believing that EcoWave is more sustainable than it actually is. This undermines informed decision-making, as stakeholders may base their purchasing, investment, or partnership decisions on false information.

- **Loss of trust.** Once stakeholders become aware of the greenwashing practices, EcoWave's reputation is likely to suffer significant damage. The revelation of dishonesty can lead to a loss of trust, which may be difficult to rebuild, harming the company's brand and customer loyalty in the long term.

- **Financial and legal risks.** Misleading reporting can expose EcoWave to legal consequences, including fines or lawsuits from regulatory bodies, shareholders, and consumers. It may also affect the company's financial stability if investors withdraw support due to ethical concerns.

- **Market perception of sustainability.** Greenwashing by companies like EcoWave can erode public trust in sustainability initiatives as a whole, leading to scepticism and cynicism regarding the genuine efforts of other companies. This undermines the broader movement towards corporate responsibility and environmental stewardship.

- **Internal ethical conflict.** Employees aware of the data manipulation, like the whistleblower, may experience ethical dilemmas, which can lead to decreased morale, increased turnover, or further whistleblowing, creating a toxic work environment and internal strife within the company.

(c) The Board of EcoWave are advised to implement the following measures to enhance transparency and accuracy in its strategic disclosures and sustainability reporting and rebuild its reputation, strengthen stakeholder trust, and to genuinely work towards achieving its sustainability goals in an ethical and transparent manner.

- **Conduct independent sustainability performance data audits.** EcoWave should engage a third-party auditor to review and verify its sustainability claims, including plastic usage reduction and energy sourcing. Independent audits add credibility and transparency, assuring stakeholders of the integrity of the reported data.

- **Provide more detailed disclosure in its sustainability reporting.** The company must provide more detailed information in its reports, including the specific methodology used to calculate plastic reduction, energy usage breakdown, and the timeline for achieving these targets. Clear, quantifiable data should replace vague claims to ensure that progress is accurately represented.

- **Improve transparency in sustainability reporting.** EcoWave should adopt global reporting standards, such as the Global Reporting Initiative (GRI), to structure its sustainability disclosures. These standards emphasise transparency, consistency, and accountability, ensuring that sustainability reports offer a true reflection of the company's performance.

- **Enhance internal oversight of sustainability reporting**. Establish an internal sustainability committee that includes a cross-section of employees from different departments. This committee would oversee data collection, reporting, and alignment with sustainability targets, ensuring that sustainability efforts are not compromised by pressure from management.

- **Seek out stakeholder engagement.** EcoWave should actively involve stakeholders, including employees, customers, investors, and local communities, in reviewing its sustainability strategy and performance. Regular stakeholder meetings and open forums would foster dialogue, build trust, and ensure that the company is addressing genuine concerns.

3.5 The role of regulation and policy in ethical sustainability

Regulations and policies are fundamental in shaping how businesses approach sustainability and ethical practices. Governments, international organisations, and regulatory bodies establish rules and guidelines that compel companies to adopt more sustainable and responsible behaviours.

Policies such as the Paris Agreement, the EU Green Deal, and various national regulations set benchmarks for reducing carbon emissions, conserving natural resources, promoting human rights, and ensuring equitable labour practices.

However, the effectiveness of these regulations can vary significantly depending on regional enforcement and the scope of the policies themselves. In some regions, strict environmental and social policies are in place, while others may have more lenient or poorly enforced regulations, leading to ethical challenges for multinational companies operating across diverse regulatory landscapes. Additionally, certain companies exploit regulatory gaps or engage in lobbying efforts to weaken sustainability-related regulations, prioritising short-term profits over long-term ethical commitments.

Ethically driven businesses often recognise that compliance with the law is merely a starting point. They go further by advocating for stronger sustainability policies and embracing voluntary initiatives, such as Fair Trade standards, to demonstrate their dedication to ethical sustainability. By supporting robust regulations and voluntarily holding themselves to higher standards, companies can lead industry-wide change and foster a more responsible business environment.

3.6 Stakeholder engagement and ethical decision-making

Incorporating stakeholder engagement into decision-making is critical for promoting ethical sustainability. Stakeholders – including customers, employees, investors, suppliers, local communities, and environmental groups – bring diverse perspectives and concerns that can help shape a company's sustainability strategy.

By actively involving stakeholders in discussions and decisions, companies gain valuable insights into material issues, allowing them to address concerns and align business practices with societal values.

Effective stakeholder engagement involves more than mere consultation; it requires ongoing dialogue, transparency, and a genuine willingness to integrate stakeholder feedback into company policies and actions. For example, community involvement in environmental impact assessments can lead to more responsible land-use decisions, while employee input can help improve workplace conditions and foster a more inclusive culture.

Nevertheless, balancing conflicting stakeholder interests can be a complex ethical dilemma. Companies must navigate situations where prioritising one group's interests may not align with others. Ethical decision-making in this context means striving for solutions that maximise overall benefit while remaining true to the company's core values and long-term sustainability goals.

By placing stakeholder concerns at the forefront of their strategies, businesses can build trust, enhance their social license to operate, and contribute more positively to society.

3.7 Transparency and accountability mechanisms

Transparency and accountability are foundational to ethical sustainability, as they help build trust between companies and their stakeholders. Businesses that are open about their sustainability practices and impacts demonstrate a commitment to accountability and ethical conduct. This involves clear and comprehensive reporting on Environmental, Social, and Governance (ESG) performance, alongside robust mechanisms for third-party auditing and certification.

Sustainability reporting, using frameworks such as the Global Reporting Initiative (GRI) or integrated reporting standards, allows companies to disclose their environmental, social, and economic impacts. However, without independent verification, these reports risk becoming tools for selective disclosure or, in some cases, greenwashing. Third-party audits, certifications like ISO 14001, or Fair Trade, and assurance processes add credibility to a company's sustainability claims, offering stakeholders confidence that the business is genuinely committed to ethical practices.

Technological innovations, such as blockchain, have also emerged as powerful tools for enhancing transparency. By creating an immutable and traceable record of products and transactions, blockchain can provide unprecedented visibility into supply chains, ensuring that goods are sourced ethically and sustainably. Implementing these mechanisms not only strengthens corporate accountability but also signals a company's dedication to responsible and sustainable operations.

3.8 The impact of corporate culture on ethical sustainability

Corporate culture plays a vital role in determining a company's approach to sustainability. A culture that prioritises ethical values such as integrity, social responsibility, and environmental stewardship naturally supports the integration of sustainability into business operations. Corporate leaders are instrumental in shaping this culture, setting the tone for ethical behaviour and embedding sustainability into the organisation's vision, mission, and strategy.

Examples of companies where a strong ethical culture drives sustainability include Patagonia and Unilever. Patagonia's ethos of environmental stewardship is reflected in its use of recycled materials, commitment to fair labour practices, and advocacy for environmental causes. Unilever, through its Sustainable Living Plan, has embedded sustainability into every aspect of its business model, from product sourcing to production and distribution. These companies demonstrate that a deeply ingrained culture of ethics can influence not just internal practices but also external advocacy for systemic change.

Conversely, a corporate culture focused solely on short-term profit can impede the adoption of sustainable practices, leading to ethical lapses such as greenwashing, poor labour conditions, or environmental neglect. Thus, fostering a corporate culture that values sustainability is essential for achieving long-term success and ethical integrity. It encourages employees at all levels to take ownership of sustainable practices, driving collective action toward a more responsible business model.

3.9 Navigating the ethical landscape of sustainability

The ethical landscape of sustainability is intricate and multifaceted, requiring businesses to make challenging decisions amid competing interests and priorities. Companies must navigate the complex interplay between economic, environmental, and social factors to develop strategies that contribute to long-term well-being.

One way to navigate this landscape is by adopting ethical frameworks that guide sustainability efforts. Approaches such as utilitarianism (focusing on the greatest good for the greatest number), deontology (emphasising duties and rights), or virtue ethics (centred on moral character) provide different lenses for addressing ethical dilemmas. For example, a utilitarian approach might prioritise strategies that offer the maximum benefit to society, while a deontological stance would focus on upholding human rights and environmental responsibilities irrespective of costs.

In addition, companies must remain flexible and adaptive as societal values, technological advancements, and scientific knowledge evolve. Continuous learning, self-assessment, and stakeholder engagement are

crucial to ensure that sustainability practices remain relevant, ethical, and aligned with broader social and environmental objectives.

Ultimately, ethical sustainability is an ongoing journey that demands a balance of transparency, stakeholder engagement, strong corporate culture, and a commitment to responsible practices. By acknowledging and addressing ethical challenges, embracing regulatory guidance, and fostering an organisational culture rooted in sustainability, businesses can navigate the complex ethical landscape effectively. This proactive approach not only drives positive change within the company but also contributes to the creation of a more just, equitable, and environmentally conscious world.

Chapter roundup

- **Sustainability** means meeting current needs without compromising future generations, placing ethical decision-making at the forefront of balancing economic, social, and environmental considerations.
- The **scope of sustainability** has expanded to **include complex ethical issues** like wealth inequality, human rights, corruption, and climate change, creating new challenges for businesses.
- **Environmental, Social, and Governance (ESG) issues** highlight the ethical responsibilities businesses face in mitigating environmental damage, promoting social welfare, and ensuring good governance practices.
- Companies often encounter **ethical dilemmas in sustainability,** such as prioritising profit over environmental stewardship, requiring strategic decision making to avoid compromising ecological well-being.
- **Greenwashing is** a prevalent ethical issue whereby companies falsely market products or practices as environmentally friendly, deceiving stakeholders and undermining genuine sustainability efforts. To manage greenwashing, companies must focus on transparency, ensuring their sustainability claims are accurate, verifiable, and supported by clear evidence.
- **Misleading or manipulated sustainability reporting** is another ethical challenge, where selective disclosure of achievements can mislead investors, consumers, and other stakeholders.
- **Corporate accountability** goes beyond financial performance, requiring companies to be answerable for their environmental, social, and economic impacts, particularly when ethical conflicts arise.
- **Ethical leadership** is key to embedding sustainability values into business strategies, guiding organisations through ethical dilemmas by setting a standard for responsible conduct and transparent decision-making.
- **Incorporating stakeholder engagement** helps identify and manage ethical dilemmas by balancing the interests of diverse groups, including customers, employees, and communities, in the decision-making process.
- **Addressing ethical challenges requires transparency in reporting,** including full disclosure of both successes and areas needing improvement, to build trust and avoid accusations of selective information or greenwashing.
- **Strong corporate culture** is crucial in managing ethical dilemmas; a culture rooted in integrity and responsibility drives sustainable practices and helps prevent ethical lapses like greenwashing.
- To effectively navigate the ethical landscape, companies should **adopt ethical frameworks** which provide a basis for addressing sustainability dilemmas and aligning business practices with societal values.
- **Managing sustainability-related ethical dilemmas** is an ongoing process that involves regulatory compliance, stakeholder engagement, transparent reporting, and a commitment to long-term, ethically driven growth strategies.

Quick quiz

1. What is the core principle of sustainability?
2. What are the three pillars of ESG?
3. Name two ethical issues that sustainability addresses besides environmental concerns.
4. What is greenwashing?
5. How can companies manage the risk of greenwashing?
6. What is a common ethical dilemma companies face in sustainability?
7. What role does corporate accountability play in sustainability?
8. Why is ethical leadership important in sustainability?
9. What is the purpose of sustainability reporting?
10. How can companies ensure credibility in their sustainability reports?
11. What is the importance of stakeholder engagement in ethical decision-making?
12. What can companies do to manage ethical dilemmas in their supply chains?
13. How does corporate culture influence ethical sustainability?
14. What is the relationship between ESG and enterprise value?
15. Why is managing sustainability-related ethical dilemmas an ongoing process?

Answers to quick quiz

1. The core principle of sustainability is meeting present needs without compromising the ability of future generations to meet theirs.

2. The three pillars of ESG are Environmental, Social, and Governance.

3. Two ethical issues that sustainability addresses besides environmental concerns are wealth inequality and human rights.

4. Greenwashing is the practice of falsely marketing products or practices as environmentally friendly.

5. Companies can manage the risk of greenwashing by ensuring transparency and providing accurate, verifiable evidence of their sustainability claims.

6. A common ethical dilemma companies face in sustainability is choosing between immediate profits and long-term environmental protection.

7. Corporate accountability in sustainability involves companies being responsible for their social, environmental, and economic impacts.

8. Ethical leadership is important in sustainability because it sets the standard for responsible conduct and guides the organisation through ethical dilemmas.

9. The purpose of sustainability reporting is to disclose a company's environmental, social, and economic impacts transparently.

10. Companies can ensure credibility in their sustainability reports by adopting global standards like the GRI and involving third-party auditors.

11. Stakeholder engagement in ethical decision making helps balance diverse interests and informs decision making for more responsible practices.

12. Companies can manage ethical dilemmas in their supply chains by implementing ethical supply chain standards and actively monitoring compliance.

13. Corporate culture influences ethical sustainability because a culture rooted in integrity and responsibility promotes sustainable practices and prevents ethical lapses.

14. The relationship between ESG and enterprise value is that ESG focuses on how social, environmental, and governance risks impact a business's enterprise value.

15. Managing sustainability-related ethical dilemmas is an ongoing process because it requires continuous regulatory compliance, stakeholder engagement, and a commitment to long-term, ethically driven growth.

Practice question bank

1 Deon

Deon Co operates in a small central African republic, and was recently acquired by Dionysos Co, a firm of venture capitalists that is based in the US. A debate is taking place between Zahir Awan and Mei Chong about whether Deon should employ child labour, which is considered the norm in the country in which it operates.

Mei Chong explained that in her view, employing child labour was always ethically wrong. Zahir Awan asked whether the money that children earned by working in the relatively safe conditions at Deon was an important source of income for their families. Mei Chong said that the money was important to them but even so, it was still wrong to employ children, as it was exploitative and interfered with their education. She also said that it would alienate the European customers who bought from Deon partly on the basis that it did not take part in ethically questionable practices of this kind.

For the last few years, the government of Deon's home country has been planning to sell, for development, a large plot of land in a mostly undeveloped area of the country, about 70 kilometres east of the capital city. Media speculation feared that it would become another tourist area and this would not help local companies and local people with their housing needs. The government has launched an initiative to move people out of currently over-crowded cities to better housing elsewhere.

The government has recently finalised the sale of the land to Deon. The government has given outline planning permission for Deon's plans for the entire area, but formal government approval will still be required prior to the start of any specific construction work.

There has been a growing amount of adverse publicity concerning this development. Most of the area's few inhabitants do not like the idea that their isolation will be destroyed by new development. Environmental lobbyists are concerned that the area currently has a few endangered species of small wildlife animals, which are dependent on the existing habitat. While every effort has been made to preserve as many trees as possible, to enhance the appeal of the completed development, there will be a need to clear a large area of forest where some of the housing and the commercial office buildings area would be constructed.

Required

(a) Explain and contrast a deontological with a consequentialist based approach to business ethics.
(6 marks)

(b) Assess Mei Chong's belief that employing child labour is 'always ethically wrong' from deontological and teleological (consequentialist) ethical perspectives. **(10 marks)**

(c) Explain why the company's decision to undertake the new investment can be justified from a utilitarian perspective and discuss the criticisms of adopting this approach. **(9 marks)**

(Total = 25 marks)

2 Tyranno

Tyranno is a prominent investment bank with branch offices located in several European capitals and throughout the world. Through its network of branches, fund managers trade across the range of investment instruments, including the standard debt and equity as well as derivative instruments.

During the last year, the management of Tyranno discovered that Neville Garage, a commodities trader working in the Apotychia branch, had made a very large loss. The losses arose from Mr Garage's practice of ignoring Tyranno's trading rules and in particular the bank's limits on the types of instruments that can be traded.

Mr Garage's losses are highly material and are considered to be big enough to threaten the going concern status of the bank as a whole. Tyranno's management described Mr Garage as a 'rogue trader'. Upon investigation, it was found to be common practice in the Apotychia branch, for trading rules to be disregarded in the pursuit of short-term gains. In addition to this, Mr Garage had not only exceeded the monetary limits placed on trading but had also traded in some extremely high-risk instruments that were specifically prohibited by Tyranno's trading rules.

Questions have been raised in the national media about why Mr Garage's activities were not discovered sooner. One newspaper reported that Mr Garage had in fact been very well-regarded within Tyranno for the returns he delivered. It has been contended that Tyranno was happy not to ask questions about how Mr Garage delivered these returns until problems arose. One of Mr Garage's colleagues said of him that he was very charismatic but that he often said that he did not care for trading rules, which he described as 'bureaucracy' and 'red tape'. The colleague said that Mr Garage did not care about moral questions and had once said that he 'does what he does' for his 'own self-interest'. Tyranno's chief executive officer stated that Mr Garage had been a rogue trader who was criminally responsible for the theft of company assets.

Required

(a) (i) Explain the three levels of Kohlberg's theory. **(6 marks)**

(ii) Identify the level that Mr Garage operated at and justify your choice using evidence from the case. **(5 marks)**

(iii) Identify, with reasons, the stage of Kohlberg's moral development most appropriate for a professional bank employee such as Mr Garage as he undertakes his trading duties. **(2 marks)**

(b) Distinguish between narrow and wide stakeholders and identify three narrow stakeholders in Tyranno from information in the case. Assess the potential impact of the events described on each narrow stakeholder identified. **(12 marks)**

(Total = 25 marks)

3 Zebra

Zebra is a clothing manufacturer, based in an EU member state, with an international market for its designs. The company's regular monthly board meeting will take place in a couple of days' time. It seems likely that most of the meeting will be taken up with discussing two issues.

Factory closure

The chief executive of Zebra has received an offer from a property developer for one of its factories in its home country. The proposal is to buy the freehold and to demolish the factory to build office units. The developer is offering €3 million for the site which presently employs 150 staff. The developer wishes to exchange contracts as soon as possible but would not take possession of the site for another year. The chief executive believes that accepting the offer makes strategic and financial sense for Zebra. The developer is quite happy for the offer to be made public once contracts have been exchanged.

It will be possible to relocate all but one of the current manufacturing contracts currently being undertaken by this factory to Zebra' remaining factories in other countries over time, without undue delay. However, the one exception is by far the largest contract Zebra currently has. The customer has imposed tight time limits on this contract and will terminate it if its requirements are not met. Production on this contract must continue uninterrupted for the next six months at this factory if the customer's requirements are to be met.

The policy of Zebra is to offer either jobs elsewhere in the group or redundancy packages of 30% of current salary to staff who are affected by a factory closure. The redundancy packages are rather more generous than the statutory minimum in Zebra's home country. However, only 20% of staff, mostly at managerial level, are likely to receive offers to transfer to other parts of the group. There are no similar jobs available locally.

The chief executive is concerned that rumours may possibly soon start circulating about the offer and staff may start demanding assurances from management that their jobs are safe. The chief executive fears that if staff knew or feared that the factory will close, there would be a fall-off in output and quality, and possibly industrial action. These would seriously jeopardise Zebra' ability to fulfil the large contract.

Treatment of staff

One of the company's directors has recently returned from visiting a factory located in another European Union member state. Over the last few years this factory has performed better than any other in comparison with cost budgets and has been particularly good at keeping its labour costs under control. However, on his return from his visit, the director reported some worrying facts to the chief executive.

The factory had suffered a significant number of losses of experienced part-time female staff. Although none had been dismissed, other employees still working at the factory made serious accusations that some had been 'forced' to resign by the actions of the factory manager. Among other accusations, it was suggested that they had been pressurised to take on work outside their contractual hours, or at times when they had never in the past had to work, such as during school holidays, weekends or on late shifts.

Some had taken on the extra work in fear of losing their jobs and in the knowledge that other clothing factories locally had closed down in recent months. However, many of the other staff had found the new working arrangements impossible to fit in with their domestic situations and had reluctantly handed in their notice. To replace the staff who had left, the factory manager recruited full-time staff on flexible contracts, which required them to accept shift changes provided two weeks' notice was given to them.

Required

(a) Analyse whether to disclose the decision to close the factory to the staff working in the factory, using the American Accounting Association ethics model. **(13 marks)**

(b) Analyse whether the factory manager's treatment of his staff is ethical by applying the following three ethical theories.

   i. Absolutism
   ii. Relativism
   iii. Cognitivism
   iv. Non-cognitivism
   v. Consequentialism
   vi. Deontological ethics: Kant

(12 marks)

(Total = 25 marks)

4 Adam Tsai

Adam Tsai is a non-executive director of the National Electricity Board (NEB), the nationalised energy provider of a small east Asian state. NEB operates a number of coal-fired power stations and delivers energy through a national grid which it controls. The electricity generated is then sold to the general public by private sector electricity distribution companies.

Adam Tsai is concerned about the ethical implications of a couple of issues that were discussed at NEB's most recent board meeting which was held yesterday. As a non-executive director, he believes he has a particular responsibility to consider ethical issues carefully.

A recent report ranked NEB's home country in the top ten of its worst polluters, as measured by carbon emissions per head of population. This report has been seized upon by environmental groups who have called for a month of action during the general election campaign. They wish to highlight the environmental damage being caused by the government's environmental policies and to highlight the need to switch to alternative renewable energy technologies. As a result, Adam Tsai would like to the board of NEB to consider how to improve its current environmental impact and introduce new strategies to improve its future environment performance.

In the last few days small groups of protestors have broken through perimeter fences at two of NEB's power stations and managed to delay deliveries of coal by chaining themselves across railway tracks. There have been some reports in the press of heavy handed treatment being meted out by the security firm hired by NEB to deal with the protests. NEB's managing director has dismissed these reports, saying the protestors' solutions are impractical, they have no rights of access, and that NEB is entitled to take whatever action is required against the protestors to protect its property and maintain electricity supplies.

Required

(a) Explain how National Electricity Board (NEB) can (i) achieve environment stability by lessening the current impacts on the environment and (ii) improve its future environment performance.

(13 marks)

(b) Using Tucker's model for decision making, assess the factors that NEB's board should consider when dealing with the current protests by environmental groups. **(12 marks)**

(Total = 25 marks)

5 Rossi

(a) Describe the purposes and typical contents of a corporate code of ethics. **(7 marks)**

As the minister for finance of a south Asian republic, Thalia Peracha has stated publicly that the audit profession's work should always be judged by the effect it has on public confidence in business. She said that it was crucial that professional services such as audit and assurance were always be performed in the public interest, and that there should be no material threats to the assurer's independence. Major corporate failures continue to happen, she said, because some accountants do not understand what it is to act in the public interest. She stressed that it was important that firms should not provide more than one service to individual clients. If a firm audited a client, then, she said, it should not provide any other services to that client.

Mr Wasant Patel, a journalist who had worked in audit and assurance for many years, was in the audience. He suggested that the normal advice on threats to independence was wrong. On the contrary, in fact, the more services that a professional services firm can provide to a client the better, as it enables the firm to better understand the client and its commercial and accounting needs. Mrs Peracha disagreed, saying that his views were a good example of professional services firms not acting in the public interest.

Mr Patel said that when he was a partner at a major professional services firm, he got to know his clients very well through the multiple links that his firm had with them. He said that he knew all about their finances from providing audit and assurance services, all about their tax affairs through tax consulting and was always in a good position to provide any other advice as he had acted as a consultant on other matters for many years including advising on mergers, acquisitions, compliance, and legal issues. He became very good friends with the directors of client companies, he said. The clients, he explained, also found the relationship very helpful and the accounting firms did well financially out of it.

Another reporter in the audience argued with Mr Patel. Vinesh Mistry said that Mr Patel represented the 'very worst' of the accounting profession. He said that accounting was a 'biased and value laden' profession that served minority interests, was complicit in environmental degradation and could not serve the public interest as long as it primarily served the interests of unfettered capitalism. He said that the public interest was badly served by accounting, as it did not address poverty, animal rights or other social injustices.

Required

(b) Explain, using accounting as an example, what 'the public interest' means as used by Mrs Peracha in her speech. **(5 marks)**

This requirement concerns ethical threats. It is very important for professional accountants to be aware of ethical threats and to avoid these where possible.

Required

(c) (i) With reference to the case as appropriate, describe five types of ethical threat. **(5 marks)**
    (ii) Assess the ethical threats implied by Mr Patel's beliefs. **(8 marks)**

(Total = 25 marks)

6 Absconditum

Your firm, ABC LLP, acts as auditor and adviser to Absconditum Co, a private limited company, and to its four directors. The company is owned 50% by Lev Menshe, 25% by his wife Maria and 10% by Joseph Stal. Lev is the chief executive and Joseph is the finance director. Joseph's sister, Natalia, has recently resigned from the executive board, following a disagreement with the Capellas. Natalia has now formed her own company, Apsconditum Co, in competition with Absconditum Co.

Natalia is currently negotiating with her former co-executives the profit-related remuneration due to her and the sale of her 15% holding of shares in Absconditum to one or all of them.

Natalia has contacted you to find out Lev's current remuneration package since he refuses to disclose this to her. She has also requested that your firm should continue to act as her personal adviser and become auditor and adviser to Apsconditum.

Required

(a) Explain the importance of the role of confidentiality to the auditor-client relationship and discuss current guidance in this area. **(5 marks)**

(b) Comment on the matters that you should consider in deciding whether or not your audit firm can comply with Natalia's requests. **(10 marks)**

(c) Recommend a plan for addressing the potential conflicts of interest and maintaining professional integrity when providing advisory and audit services at ABC LLP. **(10 marks)**

(Total = 25 marks)

7 Orange Cucumber

(a) Explain the term creative accounting and suggest three reasons why it might occur. **(4 marks)**

(b) Explain the term fraud and describe, with examples, the conditions that would lead to fraud occurring. **(4 marks)**

(c) The Orange Cucumber Co is a private catering business that supplies food to pubs, restaurants, and other companies in a rural location in the north of England. The owner of company is a 62 year-old former chef who has built the business up over the last 25 years. He still works in a very hands-on way with food preparation and employs a sales manager and catering manager to help him run the company, although all company decisions are made by him. The workforce consists of 20 staff who work in the kitchens, another ten who operate the company's distribution network and a further 15 who work in head office functions such as finance and administration.

A sudden and significant decline in demand across the world has left the company in financial difficulties. Around three-quarters of staff have been made redundant and the rest have been put on temporary leave of absence at 25% of their pay. The owner has said that he deeply regrets this decision but has no choice. There are now very few business purchases as operational activity has slowed to almost nothing. The company's premises and distribution vehicles are leased, while the company's kitchen equipment is owned.

The owner expects that demand will pick up in the next three to six months and has therefore concluded that the company simply needs a temporary extension of its existing bank overdraft facility and a payment holiday on some of its loans in order to improve cashflow and provide essential breathing space during this downturn in the economy. The owner will apply to the company's bank for this financial support.

The company is exempt from audit so the bank has concluded that as part of the application for financial support, it requires forecasts of profit and cash flow, plus a summary of significant trading assumptions for the next year.

The owner has decided to create fictitious contracts that were apparently agreed before demand was affected. These have been reflected within the profit and cash flow forecasts in addition to the

activity enjoyed before demand fell away. The owner's idea is to secure temporary funding to get through the next six months then look to re-commence trading when demand picks up again and employ staff as necessary, restoring the salaries of retained staff as soon as possible.

Prior to these events, the owner had discussed retirement and selling the business as a going concern.

Required

(a) Examine the ethical dimensions that arise from the actions of the owner of The Orange Cucumber Co **(11 marks)**

(b) Advise on six ethical measures that board of The Orange Cucumber Co's could implement which will help to address its financial issues. **(6 marks)**

(Total = 25 marks)

8 Tax and public and private sector ethics

(a) Explain the reasons why tax planning, tax avoidance and tax evasion can create ethical problems for professional accountants. **(6 marks)**

(b) Chidgey Council is public sector body responsible for a number of social and political responsibilities in a suburban district of Ceeland. Like all public sector bodies in Ceeland, it is under significant financial pressure to deliver services to all its residents within the funding constraints set by national government. A recent discovery of valuable minerals on land owned by Chidgey Council has led to a proposal that it should extract these minerals in order to create wealth for the benefit of the area that it represents. The land where the majority of the mineral reserves were found is currently used by Chidgey Council for social housing providing vulnerable individuals and their families with homes. Early estimates of the reserves suggest there is an opportunity for the council to make significant profits from this discovery.

While investigating this project, Chidgey Council has approached your firm for tax advice on the set up of a company to process these minerals. The council's representatives have indicated that the council wants to minimise any tax liabilities by trading as a not-for-profit entity, although local media coverage of the situation suggests that this would not be appropriate and would not reflect the true nature of the operation. Chidgey Council has offered to pay your firm an additional fee based on any tax savings.

Required

Evaluate the request to provide services to the Council. Your answer should specifically focus on the ethical dimensions of this work. **(8 marks)**

(c) You are the financial controller of Panther plc is a small UK listed company which manufacturers bespoke parts of high-performance and luxury vehicles. The finance team has informed you of a concerning discrepancy in the performance data for the year ended 31 December 2024 used in the analysis to determine if each executive director qualified for a performance bonus based on the targets established by the nomination committee and the value of each bonus. The financial performance data in the performance bonus analysis is 12% higher than the financial data included in our reported year-end financial statements.

Panther Nominations Committee approved these executive director bonuses in April 2024 based incorrect data which was subsequently paid and included in the profit and loss statement within the audited 2024 Panther Annual Report. It would now be embarrassing to admit that directors' bonuses where approximately $2 million higher than they should have been. The Board could ignore this issue as the actual bonuses were accurately disclosed in the 2024 directors remuneration note in the annual financial statements, and no queries were raised by the audit committee or external auditor.

Required

Apply the following framework to suggest an approach for the Board of Panther plc to consider.

(1) Identify the ethical dilemma
(2) Consider if existing safeguard or other mitigations are in place
(3) Evaluate the ethical dilemma
(4) Recommend a solution
(5) Justify your solution

(11 marks)

(Total = 25 marks)

9 Douglas Drinks

Douglas Drinks is a company that operates a chain of coffee shops. It is based in Europe and has been expanding over the last few years. Its managing director considers it to have reached its maximum growth potential in its own country and should expand into other European countries. It will need substantial finance to do this and is planning to obtain a listing on its local stock exchange.

The country in which Douglas Drinks is based is not part of the European Union and has not developed its own governance code. International investors who invest on the local stock exchange and whom the board of Douglas Drinks is hoping to attract tend to favour companies who follow national guidance from major countries such as Sarbanes-Oxley, or international codes such as the Organisation for Economic Co-operation and Development principles of corporate governance and the International Corporate Governance Network report on corporate governance. Douglas Drinks's managing director wants to have a greater understanding of the reasons that have led to the development of the corporate governance codes and wants to see comparisons between different international guidance.

The managing director also believes that Douglas Drinks's competitive position may be enhanced by adopting a corporate social responsibility code.

Required

(a) Discuss the main issues that led to the development of international corporate governance codes.

(7 marks)

(b) Contrast the requirements of the Sarbanes-Oxley legislation with the Organisation for Economic Co-operation and Development principles of corporate governance and the International Corporate Governance Network report on corporate governance. **(13 marks)**

(c) Discuss the case for Douglas Drinks developing a corporate social responsibility policy. **(5 marks)**

(Total = 25 marks)

10 Imago BPO

The board of Imago BPO, a design and artwork company, was debating an agenda item on the possible adoption of a corporate code of ethics. Carol Changstein, the chief executive, and majority shareholder, was a leading supporter of the idea. She said that many of the large companies in the industry had adopted codes of ethics and that she thought it would signal the importance that Imago BPO placed on ethics. She also said that she was personally driven by high ethical values and that she wanted to express these through her work and through the company's activities and policies.

Cosmo Kraepelin, the creative director, explained that he would support the adoption of the code of ethics as long as it helped to support the company's long-term strategic objectives. He said that he could see no other reason as the company was 'not a charity' and had to maximise shareholder value above all other objectives. In particular, he was keen, as a shareholder himself, to know what the code would cost to draw up and how much it would cost to comply with it over and above existing costs.

PRACTICE QUESTION BANK

Carol argued that having a code would help to resolve some ethical issues, one of which, she suggested, was a problem the company was having over a particular image it had recently produced for a newspaper advertisement. The image was produced for an advertising client and although the client was pleased, it had offended a particular religious group because of its content and design.

When it was discovered who had produced the 'offending' image, some religious leaders criticised Imago BPO for being insensitive and offensive to their religion. For a brief time, the events were a major news story. As politicians, journalists and others debated the issues in the media, the board of Imago BPO was involved in intense discussions and faced with a dilemma as to whether or not to issue a public apology for the offence caused by the image and to ask the client to withdraw it.

Cosmo argued that having a code of ethics would not have helped in that situation, as the issue was so complicated. His view was that the company should not apologise for the image and that he did not care very much that the image offended people. He said it was bringing the company free publicity and that was good for the business. Carol said that she had sympathy for the viewpoint of the offended religious leaders. Although she disagreed with them, she understood the importance to some people of firmly-held beliefs. The board agreed that as there seemed to be arguments both ways, the decision on how the company should deal with the image should be Carol's as chief executive.

Required

(a) Analyse Carol's and Cosmo's motivations for adopting the code of ethics using the normative-instrumental forms of stakeholder theory. **(8 marks)**

(b) Assess Carol's decision on the possible apology for the 'offending' image from conventional and pre-conventional moral development perspectives. **(4 marks)**

(c) Explain and assess the factors that the board of Imago BPO might consider in deciding how to respond to the controversy over the offending image. **(10 marks)**

(d) Comment on the legitimacy of the religious group's claims on Imago BPO's activities. **(3 marks)**

(Total = 25 marks)

11 ChemXL

ChemXL plc is a global chemical manufacturer listed in the UK. The board of ChemXL plc understands that the corporation could significantly enhance its environmental, social, and governance (ESG) performance, as well as its financial performance, by implementing sustainable business practices.

To achieve this, the board acknowledges it must improve its stakeholder engagement to understand the needs of its key stakeholders, driving changes in its strategic approach to sustainability and in its operational practices.

Required

(a) Explain how implementing specific sustainable business practices at ChemXL plc will improve its environmental, social and governance sustainability performance. **(10 marks)**

(b) Recommend how ChemXL plc can improve its shareholder engagement to improve its sustainability business practices. **(9 marks)**

In one part of its operations, ChemXL legally releases contaminated water used in chemical manufacture into the local river. The contaminated water is first treated with neutralising agents and as its dilution with river water renders it harmless to humans. This has been independently proven by extensive scientific. There is no evidence of any harm to human health or drinking water contamination in the local areas. However, there is evidence of immediate harm to river life with dead fish observed in the immediate 100 metre section of the river where the contaminated water is released.

(c) Apply the ethical theories of (i) Cognitivism, (ii) Non-cognitivism and (iii) Consequentialism to evaluate if ChemXL is behaving ethically in this situation. **(6 marks)**

Practice answer bank

1 Deon

This question tests content found in Chapter 1.

(a) **Deontological**

Deontology is concerned with the **application of universal ethical principles** in order to arrive at rules of conduct. It lays down in advance conditions by which actions may be judged. The criteria for judgement are separate from the facts of the situation, and are determined on the basis of **consistency, universal application,** and **human dignity**.

Consequentialist

The consequentialist approach to ethics is to make moral judgements about ethical decisions on the **basis of their outcomes.** Right or wrong then becomes a question of **benefit or harm**. One example of a consequentialist approach is **utilitarianism** – the principle that the chosen course of action is likely to result in the greatest good.

Contrast between deontological and consequentialist approaches

The main contrast between the two approaches is that the deontological approach takes **no account of consequences**; the same ethical decision will be made in all situations no matter what the differing outcomes of the decision might be in each situation. Consequentialist ethics by contrast **depend on the consequences.**

(b) **Deontological viewpoint**

The deontological (Kantian) viewpoint would stress that a decision such as whether to employ child labour was **absolutely right or absolutely wrong**, depending upon the ethical principle(s) that was relevant. This would mean that if it is **wrong in some circumstances**, then it is **always wrong**, even if in some situations there may be some arguably favourable consequences.

Child labour

Mei Chong's viewpoint is that employment of child labour is ethically wrong by itself. This is partly based on the grounds that it exploits children as they **lack the ability to give informed consent to the terms** under which they are employed. They also do not have the physical and mental resources to cope with employment and are traditionally paid much less than adult workers doing the same jobs.

Interruption of education

Mei Chong has identified a further ethical principle, that a child's best hope in life is to receive a **proper education**. Child labour employment is therefore wrong since it denies children the chance to receive that education.

Contrary to code of ethics

In addition, Deon has been able to **establish trading relations with European customers** on the basis of an ethical code prohibiting child labour. Deciding subsequently to use child labour could be seen as wrong, since Deon would not be honouring a commitment that underpins the trading relationship.

Capitalist viewpoint

However if the pure capitalist view is taken as to what is absolutely right, then Deon has a duty to its shareholders to **maximise profits**. Taking actions for reasons other than profit maximisation is morally wrong. Here as employment of child labour is legal, then if it ensures profits are maximised by minimising labour costs, then it is the right decision to take.

Teleological viewpoint

The teleological viewpoints stresses that the **consequences** of actions should be considered when an ethical decision is made. The correct ethical decision may vary according to the **situation.** The complication is to decide which consequences are most important, and the significance of the various parties affected by the ethical decision.

Consequentialist viewpoint

A consequentialist version of the capitalist viewpoint would be that pursuit of profit maximisation by all companies **generates the maximum amount of economic wealth**. The economic wealth can be distributed so that everyone benefits.

Wages

Zahir Awan raised the issue of Deon providing opportunities for children to **earn income** to support their families. The important consequences are thus that Deon is providing the opportunity for families to **increase their standard of living.**

Better working conditions

Zahir Awan also has highlighted the issue that Deon provides **better working conditions** than any of its competitors. If therefore children will work for Deon's competitors if Deon does not employ them, then the argument is that it is better for Deon to employ them as they will be treated better there than anywhere else.

Interference with education

Use of the teleological view may mean acknowledging that employment of child labour could have adverse consequences for the children's education. However, it could be argued that these are **outweighed by the economic benefits** to children and their families, or that Deon can take steps to ensure **damage to education is minimised** by providing teaching and training itself.

(c) ### Utilitarian perspective

This means choosing the course of action that provides the greatest good for the greatest number of people.

Utilitarian justification

The government is arguing that a number of groups in society will directly benefit from this decision. These include people currently living in overcrowded cities who will enjoy **more space** if they move to the new settlement. Businesses that move will enjoy the benefits of **purpose-built office space** and a pool of employees from occupiers of the new houses. The economy as a whole could be said to benefit from the construction work given to Deon and hence the increased employment, and also because it seems that using the land for business and residential purposes is a better use economically and environmentally than using it for tourism.

Criticisms of utilitarianism

Comparison of benefits and demerits

One criticism of utilitarianism is that it is **often not possible to compare like with like**. The existing inhabitants of the region will suffer disruption and the loss of their isolated environment; does this outweigh the benefits to the incoming inhabitants and businesses.

Effect on minorities

Even if a way could be found to **compare directly the effect on existing and incoming inhabitants**, and this method demonstrated that the development fulfilled utilitarian criteria, this decision would mean effectively that the impact on the minority (the existing inhabitants) did not matter. It could be argued that the harm visited on the minority would be ethically an unacceptable price for undertaking the development.

Absolute harm

A similar viewpoint would regard the development as unacceptable because of the adverse impact on the animals and plants. A deep ecologist view would be that man's economic requirements should not prevail over the life needs of other species. Such a view would be an absolute view, and this relates to another criticism of utilitarianism, that it does not allow for **absolute ethical rules**.

What is defined as the greatest good can vary between time and place. Utilitarianism can therefore be criticised if it is felt that society's underlying values at the time are wrong, for example the promotion of material happiness above other considerations.

2 Tyranno

This question tests content found in Chapter 1.

(a) (i) **Pre-conventional**

The decisions individuals make on ethical matters will have nothing to do with the ethical issues involved but will instead depend on the **personal advantage or disadvantage to the individual**, including rewards, punishments, and deals.

Conventional

When taking ethical decisions individuals live up to what they think is **expected of them**, by their **immediate circle,** or by society as expressed in **laws or social customs.**

Post-conventional

Individuals make ethical decisions in terms of what they **believe to be right in line with higher or absolute ethical principles**, not just acquiescing in what others believe to be right.

(ii) **Pre-conventional**

Mr Garage appears to have operated at Kohlberg's pre-conventional level for the following reasons.

Lack of ethics

The colleague's claim that Mr Garage **did not care about moral questions** indicates that his decision-making was not influenced by whether a course of action was ethical.

Reward

The colleague's claim indicates instead that the decisions made were determined by how much **personal reward** they would bring him.

No pressures to act at conventional level

Mr Garage **ignored internal control systems** and did not face any pressures to act at a **conventional level,** as trading rules were not enforced in his office. Instead he was encouraged to take risks in return for a trade-off of high rewards.

(iii) **Desired level**

Mr Garage should have operated at the **Conventional level Stage 4** making decisions in accordance with the ethical norms expressed in **trading rules and internal guidance.** Stage 3 here would not be sufficient due to the possibility of office pressures to ignore the rulebook.

(b) **Distinction between narrow and wide stakeholders**

Narrow stakeholders are the stakeholders who are **most affected** by the organisation's strategy and policies, including shareholders, managers, suppliers, and important customers. **Wide stakeholders** are those who are **less affected** by the organisation's strategy, including government and the wider community.

Investors

The impact on investors' interests is that the **market price of their shares has presumably already fallen.** They now face a choice between paying out for additional shares to fund the losses made by Mr Garage, or refusing to support the rights issue and increasing the risk that the company will become insolvent and wipe out their existing investment. They will presumably wish to gain more

assurance before subscribing to the rights issue. The rights issue itself does not guarantee Tyranno's continued existence. If investors refused to subscribe to an issue that goes ahead, then their holding will be **diluted**, reducing their influence over the bank.

Employees

If Tyranno is in financial trouble, many of its employees could **lose their jobs.** Those that remain could find themselves operating under **more restrictive controls**, with **more stringent limits** being placed on their **performance-related bonuses.** Employees based in the Apotychia branch who are found to have known what was going on could **lose their licence to trade.**

Directors

Directors who are up for re-election at the next annual general meeting may find themselves being **voted out of office**. The whole board may face a **vote of no confidence** at a **general meeting**. Even if they avoid this, they may experience **increased scrutiny and intervention by investors**. This may adversely affect their **remuneration or bonuses.** Some or all of the directors may face **local legal sanctions for** making an inaccurate statement about internal control effectiveness.

3 Zebra

This question tests content found in Chapter 2.

(a) **What are the facts?**

Zebra has **received an offer** for one of its factories and it appears to be in the interests of shareholders that the board should accept the offer. However, if staff learn of the acceptance of the offer, they are likely to take industrial action and jeopardise Zebra's biggest contract.

What are the ethical issues?

The first issue is whether the factory should be closed at all. The staff in the factory are clearly adding value. They are after all working on Zebra's biggest contract. One viewpoint is that staff are key stakeholders, and the decision to close the factory wrongly prioritises shareholder interests over staff interests.

If the board decides the factory should be sold:

- Whether to disclose the sale of the factory to the staff in the absence of any pressure to do so
- If rumours start circulating and staff ask whether the factory will be closing, whether to tell staff the truth or deny the rumours

What are the norms, principles and values that relate to the case?

In most jurisdictions, companies have a general duty to act in the **interests of their shareholders**. Closing the factory would be in line with this responsibility. Zebra would be acknowledging it had **some responsibility towards its employees** by giving them a generous pay-off package.

If the offer was accepted, and the board did not come under pressure to disclose it, the situation is finely balanced. The board would generally be regarded as having a right to keep **some information confidential for commercial reasons**. The question is whether the need of staff to have this information as soon as possible so that they can start making **alternative employment arrangements overrides the board's right to keep the information confidential**. It could also be argued that failing to tell staff is itself a distortion of the truth.

If staff do start asking questions, the ethical issue then becomes not only whether the board can keep the information confidential but also whether to do so it has the **right to give staff incorrect information.**

What are the alternative courses of action?

One course would be to decline the developer's offer.

If the offer is accepted and the board does not come under any pressure to disclose the information, it could nevertheless:

- Tell staff as soon as the deal is finalised; or
- Wait six months and tell staff once the work on the large contract is finished.

If the board comes under pressure from staff because rumours are circulating, it can either:

- Maintain that the rumours are misguided or state that an offer has been received but rejected; or
- Tell staff the truth.

What is the best course of action that is consistent with the norms, principles and values that relate to the case?

The best course of action would appear to **sell the site and tell staff the truth** only when the board is **pressurised to do so**. This would certainly be in shareholders' best interests, as the factory sale would go ahead and the board would be making every effort not to jeopardise the large contract. However, if the board is pressed on the issue, it would seem most ethical for the truth to be told then.

What are the consequences of each course of action?

If the developer's offer is declined, and it becomes public knowledge that it has been declined, the board **may come under pressure from shareholders** for failing to take decisions in their best interests.

Assuming no pressure is applied, telling the employees now is most likely to jeopardise the large contract. The board may be able to **mitigate the unrest** by providing more generous redundancy packages, giving assistance in job hunting and possibly giving staff a **consultation period** to come up with an alternative business plan.

Not telling employees until after the contract is completed would mean that **production was not disrupted**. However, although staff in other factories may not wish to take industrial action, there may be a loss of trust in senior management and, hence worsening industrial relations.

Telling staff the truth when pressure is applied would also jeopardise the contract but is less likely to do so the later in the **six months the disclosure is made**. Again, the board may be able to mitigate the unrest, although the factory's staff may be less inclined to co-operate if they are angry that the board has kept the news from them.

Denying the news until after the contract is completed may lead to **legal repercussions** and certainly a loss of trust in the board by other employees.

What is the decision?

The recommendation is that the board **accept the offer** and to **tell the employees immediately**. If it is in shareholders' interest for the factory to be closed, then loss of the contract would be a necessary cost. The board would appear to be acting in good faith and doing its best to mitigate the hardship faced by its employees.

(b) (i) **Absolutism:**

From an absolutist perspective, the factory manager's treatment of staff would be deemed unethical if it violates any universally applicable moral principles, regardless of cultural or situational factors. For example, if the actions of pressuring employees to work outside their contractual hours without adequate compensation or consideration for their well-being are deemed inherently wrong, regardless of the circumstances, then the treatment would be considered unethical under absolutism.

The key here is the adherence to fixed moral principles, where certain actions are deemed inherently right or wrong, irrespective of context. In this case, if the actions of the factory manager are seen as fundamentally violating principles of fairness, respect, or autonomy, they would be judged as unethical under absolutism.

(ii) **Relativism:**

Relativism suggests that the ethicality of the factory manager's treatment of staff may vary depending on cultural or situational contexts. Under relativism, the actions may be considered ethical if they align with the norms or values of the specific culture or context in which the factory operates.

However, if the actions are inconsistent with prevailing norms or values, they may be deemed unethical. In this context, whether the treatment of staff is deemed ethical or unethical depends on whether the actions are deemed acceptable within the cultural or social norms of the community where the factory is located. Relativism allows for flexibility in ethical judgments, acknowledging that what is considered right or wrong can vary based on cultural perspectives.

(iii) **Cognitivism**

From a cognitivist perspective, the factory manager's treatment of staff can be evaluated based on whether it conforms to logically consistent moral principles that can be objectively assessed.

For example, if the treatment violates principles of fairness, respect for autonomy, or non-coercion, it would be considered unethical under cognitivism. In this case, cognitivism would focus on identifying the underlying moral principles at play, such as fairness in employment practices or respect for individual autonomy.

The ethicality of the treatment would be assessed based on whether it upholds or violates these foundational principles, regardless of situational factors.

(iv) **Non-cognitivism**

Non-cognitivism suggests that ethical statements do not express propositions that can be true or false, but rather convey emotions, attitudes, or preferences.

Therefore, evaluating the factory manager's treatment of staff from a non-cognitivist perspective would involve assessing the emotional or attitudinal response it evokes rather than determining its truth or falsity. Non-cognitivism focuses on the subjective aspects of ethics, such as personal feelings or societal attitudes towards the treatment of staff.

Whether the treatment is deemed ethical or unethical would depend on the emotional reactions it generates in individuals or groups within the community.

(v) **Consequentialism**

Consequentialism evaluates the ethicality of actions based on their outcomes or consequences. In this case, the factory manager's treatment of staff would be considered unethical if it leads to negative consequences such as employee dissatisfaction, decreased productivity, or harm to employee well-being, despite potential short-term benefits for the company's performance.

Consequentialism prioritises the overall consequences of actions, weighing the benefits against the harms. If the treatment of staff results in more negative consequences than positive outcomes, it would be deemed unethical under consequentialism, regardless of the intentions behind the actions.

(vi) **Deontological ethics (Kant)**

Deontological ethics, based on Kant's principles, focuses on moral duties and the intentions behind actions rather than their consequences. The factory manager's treatment of staff would be deemed unethical if it violates universal moral principles, such as treating employees as ends in themselves rather than merely means to an end or failing to respect their autonomy and dignity.

Kantian deontology emphasises the inherent dignity and autonomy of individuals, suggesting that ethical actions are those that respect and uphold these principles. Therefore, if the treatment of staff fails to treat them as autonomous agents or violates their dignity, it would be considered unethical under Kantian deontology.

4 Adam Tsai

This question tests content found in Chapter 2 and Chapter 9.

(a) The following considers how National Electricity Board (NEB) can improve its environmental impact in the short-term and long-term.

Achieving environmental stability by lessening the current impacts on the environment

To address the current impacts on the environment, NEB must undertake several proactive measures. Firstly, NEB can invest in upgrading its existing coal-fired power stations with advanced pollution control technologies such as electrostatic precipitators, flue gas desulphurisation systems, and selective catalytic reduction systems. These technologies can significantly reduce emissions of harmful pollutants such as sulphur dioxide (SO_2), nitrogen oxides (NO_x), and particulate matter, which would result in cleaner air and less harmful health impacts on workers and nearby communities.

NEB should prioritise the implementation of carbon capture and storage (CCS) technology to capture and store carbon dioxide (CO_2) emissions generated from its power plants. CCS involves capturing CO_2 emissions at the source, transporting it to storage sites, and securely storing it underground to prevent it from entering the atmosphere and contributing to climate change.

NEB can explore opportunities to improve energy efficiency across its operations by upgrading equipment, optimising processes, and adopting best practices for energy management. By reducing energy consumption and optimising resource utilisation, NEB can minimise its environmental footprint and enhance operational sustainability.

NEB should actively promote the use of renewable energy sources such as solar, wind, and hydroelectric power to diversify its energy portfolio and reduce reliance on fossil fuels. Investing in renewable energy infrastructure and supporting renewable energy projects can help NEB transition towards a more sustainable and environmentally friendly energy generation mix.

NEB can also work closely with suppliers of coal to lessen the impact of coal extraction from the Earth by protecting biodiversity in mining areas and restoring the environment to how it was before mining commenced once mining in a particular area ceased. Collaborating with coal suppliers to implement responsible mining practices, reforestation initiatives, and habitat restoration projects can mitigate the environmental impact of coal extraction and promote ecological sustainability.

Improving its future environmental performance

To improve its future environmental performance, NEB must adopt a comprehensive sustainability strategy that encompasses both short-term and long-term goals. NEB should develop a roadmap for transitioning towards a low-carbon economy by setting targets for reducing greenhouse gas emissions, increasing renewable energy capacity, and enhancing energy efficiency.

NEB can collaborate with environmental experts, research institutions, and government agencies to identify innovative renewal energy solutions for investment such as wind, solar, nuclear and bio-fuels. Also, NEB can research and implement best practices for environmental management across it current coal fired power stations to reduce pollution and improve power generation efficiency from raw fuels. This may involve conducting research and development initiatives to innovate new technologies for clean energy generation, energy storage, and electricity grid optimisation to reduce energy loss on transfer.

NEB should prioritise stakeholder engagement and community outreach to build trust and foster transparency regarding its environmental initiatives. By actively engaging with stakeholders, including local communities, environmental NGOs, and government agencies, NEB can gain valuable insights, address concerns, and garner support for its sustainability efforts.

NEB should implement robust monitoring, reporting, and verification (MRV) mechanisms to track its environmental performance, measure progress towards sustainability goals, and ensure compliance with environmental regulations and standards. The board can adopt a top down approach to regularly monitor key environmental indicators and report on sustainability performance, NEB can demonstrate accountability and commitment to environmental stewardship to its stakeholders and by the general public impacted by its operations.

(b) The stages of Tucker's five question model are in the decision:

Profitable

Although the nationalised corporation will be a non-profit making body, it has the duty to control its costs. The costs of combating the protestors will include:

- The **costs of security**
- The **costs of taking action** to counter the bad publicity that may be a consequence of the treatment of the protestors
- The **costs of legal action** brought by the protestors as a result of the actions of the security guards

The other issue however is whether there is any alternative to **incurring these costs**. If the protestors are determined to protest, the alternative may be disruption to the country's power supply, which is likely to be regarded as being much more important.

Legal

The legality of the security guards' action depends upon local legislation, in particular the **rights to protest, to protect property and use reasonable force**. There is also the issue of how far NEB will be held responsible for the actions of **its agent**, the security firm. Because of the issues of poor publicity and also the costs described above, NEB's board should be wary if it appears that excessive force may be being used, since this is likely to be a legally grey area.

Fair

The pressure groups may claim that they have a **legitimate right to protest**. Their case may be weakened by the fact that they can currently take **political action in the general election campaign**, although perhaps they might argue that none of the major parties fairly represents their views. However even if the board was to accept that the pressure groups are **legitimate stakeholders**, it also has a duty to consumers, who are undoubtedly also legitimate stakeholders, to **preserve the continuity of electricity supplies**. These include consumers whose livelihoods and indeed lives may be threatened by power cuts (hospital patients for example).

Right

The main ethical issues are whether it is right for the pressure group to take potentially **life-threatening action** in order to advance a cause that has fundamental long-term consequences (action against global warming). From NEB's point of view the ethical issue is whether **force** should be used against the pressure group if its actions are life-threatening; if it can be, **how much force** would be right; ultimately would it be legitimate to take action that might jeopardise the lives of the protestors.

Sustainable

Because of the general election campaign and a possible change of government, the board cannot be expected at present to make long-term decisions about switching to a **more environmentally friendly method of electricity generation**. However if the managing director's attitude is typical of the board, then the viewpoint is **not sustainable**; continued use of coal will mean supplies are eventually exhausted and there is strong scientific evidence that the emissions are having **adverse climatic effects**. Many countries are investigating alternative sources of power. Whatever the result of the general election, NEB's board has a duty to ask the new government to review energy policies.

5 Rossi

This question tests content found in Chapter 3.

(a) **Purposes of corporate code of ethics**

Establishment of organisation's values

Ethical codes form part of the organisation's underlying environment. They develop and promote values that are linked to the organisation's mission statement.

Promotion of stakeholder responsibilities

Codes also demonstrate whom the organisation regards as **important stakeholders**. They show what action should be taken to maintain good **stakeholder relationships** (such as keeping them fully informed).

Control of individuals' behaviour

By **promoting or prohibiting certain actions**, ethical codes form part of the human resources mechanisms by which employee behaviour is controlled. Ethical codes can be referred to when employee actions are questioned.

Contents of corporate code of ethics

Broad principles

Codes generally open with a wide statement stressing that it is company policy to conduct all of its business on ethical principles and it expects its employees to do likewise.

Role of employees

Codes normally stress the **core role of employees** in the organisation, often stating that they are the organisation's most important component. Because of this, the **duties of employees to follow the organisation's ethical ideals** are stressed in codes. Codes will also set out the concepts such as trust, respect, honesty, and equality to which employees are expected to commit.

Relations with other stakeholders

Relations with customers and suppliers are often highlighted since they are primary stakeholders with whom many employees deal. Codes stress the need for dealing with **customers courteously and politely** and **responding promptly** to their **needs**. They define relations with suppliers as being based on **mutual respect and truthfulness**, and stress various aspects of fair dealing including paying suppliers on time and in accordance with agreed terms of trade.

Legal and regulatory standards

Codes normally stress that it is company policy to **comply with industry legal and regulatory standards** and that employees are expected to do so. This emphasises that compliance should be regarded as **conventional behaviour.**

Fair business practices

Codes often develop wider ethical standards by stressing that the company aims to act as a good **corporate citizen in the markets** in which it operates. This is often defined as meaning being committed to open markets, promoting responsible competitive behaviour, and prohibiting actions that undermine fair markets such as seeking or participating in questionable payments or favours.

Corporate social responsibility

Ethical codes often include statements that **define the basis** of the **organisation's corporate social responsibility commitment.** This may include commitments to **promoting sustainable development** and **preventing waste of natural resources.**

(b) ### Definition

The **public interest** is the **collective wellbeing** of the community of people and institutions that the professional accountant serves, including the business and financial community and others who rely on the work of professional accountants.

Trust

Trust is a key issue in terms of the public interest as it relates to accountants. The working of capital markets depends upon **reliable financial information,** as does business decision-making affecting jobs and supply. The public has to be able to believe that accountants' opinions are given on a basis of sufficient work and that they are **unaffected by external pressures**.

Audit and assurance

Mrs Peracha is arguing that accountants who provide audit or assurance services must be able to demonstrate clearly their **detachment from the client**. They cannot do this if they are providing other services to the client.

(c) (i) ### Self-interest

Self-interest means the accountants' own interests being affected by the **success of the client,** or the **continuation of the accountant-client relationship.** An example would be a financial interest in a client.

Self-review

Self-review means the accountants auditing or reviewing work that they **themselves have prepared.** This could include auditing work that has been prepared as part of a non-audit service, something that prompts the suggestion that firms should not provide more than one service to a client.

Advocacy

Advocacy means **strongly promoting the interests of the accountants' clients** and undermining the accountants' objectivity. Accountants can be seen as acting in the client's, rather than the public, interest.

Familiarity

Familiarity means dealing with a client's affairs for a long time and developing a close relationship. This can lead to **reliance on previous knowledge** rather than a questioning approach to information supplied.

Intimidation

Intimidation means conduct of the assignment or conduct towards the client being **influenced by pressure exerted by the client.**

(ii) ### Self-interest

Mr Patel's comment about a firm providing multiple services highlights one threat to self-interest. If a firm providing audit and other services disagrees with the client over the accounts that it is auditing, it faces the risk of **not just losing the income from the audit**, but perhaps also the **much greater income from providing other services**. Mr Patel's comments highlight how well financially firms can do out of providing multiple services.

Self-review

If the accountants provide other services that materially affect the content of the accounts, then they will have to **audit figures that they themselves have prepared**, for example valuations.

Advocacy

Mr Patel mentioned providing **legal advice**. There are two problems. Firstly providing that advice could be seen as promoting the client's interests rather than the public interest. Secondly the accounts may need to contain **provision for, or disclosure about, legal actions.** This will depend on the likelihood of the success of legal action, which could in turn depend on the advice Mr Patel had given. Therefore, there is a clear possibility of the accountant not wishing to undermine the advice he has given by taking a prudent view of the issues' treatment in the accounts.

Familiarity

Mr Patel **highlights his friendships** with his clients. Although he would claim that this made it more likely that clients would listen to his advice, critics could suggest the friendships meant that he placed **excessive trust** in what he was told and would be **unwilling to raise awkward issues** that could jeopardise the friendships. The **provision of other services** may mean that accountants are less rigorous in auditing information with which their firm has been involved.

Intimidation

Mr Patel comments that he got to know his clients very well and presumably they got to know him very well. This could mean that if they wished to **intimidate him** into giving advice that they wanted to hear, they would have a good idea of how to do so by, for example, threatening to replace his firm as auditors.

6 Absconditum

This question tests content found in Chapters 3 and 4.

(a) **Confidentiality**

Confidentiality is an **implied term** of an auditor's contract with the client. It is also a requirement of the IESBA *Code of Ethics for Professional Accountants*. Confidentiality is essential to the auditor-client relationship because in order to form an opinion, the auditor must work closely with those who have prepared the financial statements and have their **trust**. If this is lacking, the client will not be open with the auditor fearing that matters may be reported to competitors, other third parties or regulatory authorities.

The duty of confidentiality owed by the auditor is not absolute. There are **circumstances** in which auditors have a **right or duty to disclose** matters to third parties without the client's knowledge or consent. Duties are mainly **legal duties** to report matters such as any suspicions of money laundering, drug trafficking or terrorist offences. A right to report matters also exists in these circumstances but the duty to report is more important. The auditor will also need to consider whether a report should be made in the public interest, which superseded the duty of confidentiality in certain situations. An auditor may also disclose matters to **defend himself** in disciplinary proceedings.

It is not uncommon for regulatory authorities such as the tax authorities or the police to ask 'informally' for details of confidential matters. Only when the persons requesting the information have obtained the appropriate statutory or other authorities to demand such information should the request be granted.

Auditors are under no general duty to report illegal acts (except money laundering) to the authorities; however, it is not appropriate for an auditor to continue a relationship with a client that engages in such activities, not least because the auditor may be implicated in the crime.

Confidentiality is one of the fundamental principles of professional ethics as set out in the IESBA *Code*. This imposes an obligation on accountants to refrain from disclosing confidential information acquired as a result of professional and business relationships without proper and specific authority or unless there is a legal or professional right or duty to disclose, and from using confidential information acquired as a result of professional and business relationships to their personal advantage or the advantage of third parties.

(b) **Absconditum**

Auditors should avoid **conflicts of interest** where possible. One example of a conflict of interest is where two parties in dispute request advice from the same firm. There is no absolute rule that says that a firm cannot act for both parties in these circumstances, but there have to be stringent controls to ensure that the interests of one client do not adversely affect the interests of another, and of course permission of both parties is required, which may not be forthcoming. This can be difficult with small firms because there are often insufficient staff to have two different 'teams' acting on behalf of the parties. It is crucial that the situation is disclosed to both parties, and that the firm only acts for both parties if they both agree to this.

Request - remuneration package

Some information on directors' remuneration packages should be available by inspection of the financial statements filed on public record, although this information will be historical rather than current. There are also requirements for companies to make details of service contracts available for inspection by members of companies, such as Natalia, although these often constitute a very incomplete picture of the total remuneration package.

It is clear that as existing auditor and advisor to Absconditum, it would be **inappropriate** to disclose any such information to Natalia, or even to help her find the information that is available on the public record, without the **permission** of Absconditum which is unlikely to be forthcoming.

Personal advisor

It would only be possible to act as personal advisor to Natalia if the remaining directors of Absconditum **agreed** (which seems unlikely) because the current 'negotiations' may well turn into a dispute over the valuation of the shareholding. The existing company might well wish to understate profits and assets in order to reduce the valuation, and Natalia may wish to see the amounts increased. It may be possible to act as personal tax advisor, although there are unlikely to be complicated tax implications to the buy-out.

Auditor to Apsconditum

There are potentially serious problems associated with becoming auditor to the new company because it is both in competition with the existing client and has a very similar name. Absconditum may well have a **legal case** against Natalia and the new company for attempting to pass itself off as the existing company, and thereby damaging the existing company's goodwill. The fact that Natalia has done this, together with her request for information, which she should know is confidential (in relation to remuneration), may cast doubt on her **personal integrity** which is a further reason not to act for her.

Alternatively, if the information presented in the question is incomplete, it may be possible to take the view that the firm would prefer to act as auditor and advisor to Natalia and the new company, rather than to the existing company, particularly if the terms of the engagement are attractive. There is no specific 'rule' which prohibits this course of action, however, the requirement to behave with **integrity** in all professional and business relationships suggests that this would not be an appropriate course of action.

(c) The following are important components for a strategy to address potential conflicts of interest and maintaining professional integrity when providing advisory and audit services at ABC LLP.

Ethical framework: Establish an ethical framework for guiding decision-making and behaviour in situations where conflicting interests may arise. Emphasise the importance of upholding professional ethics, maintaining independence, and preserving the confidentiality of sensitive information.

Engagement risk assessment and mitigation: Conduct a comprehensive risk assessment to identify potential risks associated with providing services to both Absconditum Co and Apsconditum. Develop risk mitigation strategies to minimise the impact of these risks on the integrity and quality of ABC LLP's services.

Conflict management: Develop strategies for managing conflicts of interest resulting in threats to independence which may arise from the dual role of advising both Absconditum Co and Apsconditum. This may include establishing clear boundaries between the two engagements, ensuring separate teams work on each engagement, implementing independent review and robust conflict of interest resolution procedures.

Ensuring client consent: Determine the necessity of obtaining informed consent from all relevant parties, including Absconditum Co, its directors, and Natalia, regarding the provision of services to Apsconditum. Outline the process for obtaining consent and ensuring transparency about the potential implications and risks involved.

Regular review: Implement a process for regular review and monitoring of the quality and independence of engagements provided by ABC LLP to Absconditum Co and Apsconditum to ensure compliance with ethical standards, legal requirements, and client expectations. This may involve periodic reviews of the engagement terms, client relationships, and any emerging conflicts or issues.

Continuing Professional Development (CPD): Provide ongoing training and development opportunities for staff involved in both engagements to enhance their understanding of professional ethics, conflict management, and regulatory requirements. Emphasise the importance of maintaining competence and integrity in delivering services to clients.

By addressing these aspects, ABC LLP can navigate the complexities of providing advisory and audit services to both Absconditum Co and Apsconditum while upholding professional standards, managing conflicts of interest, and maintaining the trust and confidence of all stakeholders involved.

7 Orange Cucumber

This question tests content found in Chapter 5.

(a) **Creative accounting**

Award up to 1 mark for each point made to a maximum of 4 marks, recognising that there may be other valid points.

Creative accounting refers to the practice of manipulating the financial statements of an organisation to present performance and/or position which is not true or fair (ie factually correct and free from bias respectively). **[1]**

It may involve improving this position by making assets appear more valuable than they should be, or by reducing liabilities to a level below what the organisation actually owes. It may also include the practice of overstating profits to make the organisation appear more successful than it really is. In some cases, a worse position or performance may be presented to avoid certain obligations, such as reducing a tax charge or to stay under an accounting threshold. **[1]**

Creative accounting may occur for many reasons, but they are most likely to include one or more of the following:

- Manipulating amounts in order to hit certain targets which would lead to the payment of a performance-related incentive (such as profit-related bonuses payable to directors) **[1]**
- Manipulating amounts in order to avoid certain conditions from occurring (such as bank loans that would need to be repaid early if the borrower breached accounting ratios relating to debt or cash flow) **[1]**
- Inflating the value of a business that is looking to float on the stock market, creating a greater demand for shares and a higher offer price (often seen in cases of owner-managed businesses where the owner wants to maximise their income from selling their stake) **[1]**
- Falsifying accounting records in order to maintain the organisation's survival (in other words, pretending that the organisation is more successful than it really is, buying more time to hopefully improve its financial position and performance) **[1]**

(b) **Fraud**

Award up to 1 mark for each point made to a maximum of 4 marks, recognising that there may be other valid points.

Fraud can be described as an intentional act where one or more individuals use some form of deception to create a financial advantage that they will benefit from. It can occur either as a loss of assets (such as cash or other valuable items) or by manipulating financial statements to show a different view of an entity. **[1]**

Fraud will usually occur when a combination of three conditions exist:

- Pressure or motivation - this often manifests itself as a need to get money, perhaps to repay debts that cannot be paid any other way, or to achieve a desirable lifestyle **[1]**
- Opportunity - the absence of anything stopping a fraud from occurring will also make fraud more likely to occur **[1]**
- Rationalisation - the third condition that forces motivated people to take advantage of a situation is being able to rationalise the fraud: in other words, convincing themselves that it is acceptable to commit this fraud because of their circumstances **[1]**

(c) **Ethical dimensions**

Award up to 1 mark for each point made to a maximum of 11 marks, recognising that there may be other valid points.

Creative accounting has occurred here because the owner has decided to manipulate the forecast financial statements **[1]**. The estimated receipts from contracts have been inflated beyond what is realistic and will present a more profitable and cash-rich business than is actually the case **[1]**. Consequently, these assumptions are more than just ambitious, they are fraudulent.

Fraud has occurred here because it is a deliberate decision **[1]** by the owner to falsify the prospects of the company as opposed to something that has happened by accident. Fraud has also occurred here because the three conditions necessary for fraud apply:

(1) Pressure to commit this fraud **[1]** as it is the only way to keep the company going and the owner will lose his company and his retirement arrangements if he does not get funding. **[1]**

(2) Opportunity to perpetrate this **[1]** as there are no other controls in place to stop this fraud **[1]** (ie there are no other board members or anyone else to challenge the owner and there are no auditors).

(3) Rationalisation of the fraud **[1]** may be easier for the owner if he believes that he is doing it for the right reasons: to secure the employment of his staff. **[1]** (However, this might be disingenuous as the owner may simply wish to maintain the value of the business until it can be sold to fund his retirement. **[1]**)

The fraud is therefore unethical because it is designed to disadvantage the bank by falsifying the company's future prospects and puts their funds at risk **[1]**. However, a further ethical dimension exists here: the employees will be re-employed without a legitimate business plan and could therefore face redundancy again **[1]** and the future owners of the company may be acquiring a business that is not a viable going concern **[1]**. The lack of transparency displayed by the owner may therefore adversely affect these stakeholders too and the only person who benefits from this is the owner. While not a professional accountant, the owner's lack of integrity **[1]** falls short of the ethical standards that would be expected by someone in a profession such as accountancy.

[Tutor note: Economies will regularly swing from boom to bust, with every generation experiencing variations in their national prosperity. Global conditions, such as the financial crisis of 2008, the COVID-19 pandemic or even ecological or political instability across the world, could also affect the global economy in ways that could never have been imagined, leading to reduced demand for goods and services and higher levels of anxiety among both consumers and companies as people become more desperate to maintain their prosperity. This desperation creates pressure and opportunity, allowing fraudsters to rationalise their actions as legitimate under the circumstances.

(d) **Ethical plan to improve performance**

Award up to 1 mark for each point made to a maximum of 6 marks, recognising that there may be other valid points.

Negotiate honestly with the bank: The board should present accurate and realistic financial forecasts to the bank without fabricating contracts. This is ethical because it maintains honesty and transparency, ensuring trust and integrity in financial dealings. **[1]**

Diversify customer base: By exploring new markets, including local community partnerships and online platforms, the company can stabilise demand. This measure is ethical because it seeks legitimate business opportunities without misleading stakeholders about the company's prospects. **[1]**

Implement cost-saving measures: The company can reduce energy consumption, optimise supply chain management, and negotiate better terms with suppliers. These actions are ethical because they improve efficiency and sustainability without compromising business integrity or employee welfare and by improving profitability, will safeguard some jobs which are at risk. **[1]**

Open communication with employees. Keeping employees informed about the company's financial situation and involving them in cost-saving strategies is ethical as it respects their right to know and participate in decisions affecting their livelihood. **[1]**

Develop a business continuity plan: Creating a robust plan that includes risk management ensures the company can adapt to economic changes. This is ethical because it demonstrates foresight and responsibility, protecting the interests of employees, customers, and other stakeholders. **[1]**

Invest in staff training and development: Enhancing employees' skills and productivity is ethical because it values their personal growth and contribution, helping them adapt to new roles and improving job security in the long term. **[1]**

Explore government grants and aid programs: Utilising available financial aid ethically supports business continuity without resorting to dishonest practices. This measure is ethical because it uses legitimate resources designed to aid businesses in hardship. **[1]**

Establish a sustainability plan to improve sustainability performance and financial performance: Implementing environmentally friendly practices, such as reducing waste and sourcing sustainable ingredients, is ethical because it demonstrates a commitment to environmental stewardship and corporate social responsibility, benefiting society and the planet. **[1]**

PRACTICE ANSWER BANK

8 Tax and public and private sector ethics

This question tests content found in Chapter 4 and Chapter 6.

(a) **Reasons**

Award up to 1 mark for each point made to a maximum of 6 marks, recognising that there may be other valid points.

Like any other engagement to provide professional services, when an accountant is asked to provide some form of tax advice to a client, there is an expectation that they will get paid for this work. All professional accountants face an ethical dilemma whenever they enter into any form of commercial arrangement with a client, as they are getting paid for a service but various codes of ethics exist to make sure the accountant has acted in the right way [1].

Ethical codes can help the client address problems such as the following:

- Does the client understand what they are asking for? If not, it is possible that on completion of the work, there could be a dispute which could harm the accountant's reputation. That is why the terms of any engagement need to be agreed in advance [1].

- Does the engagement create any form of ethical threat, such as a conflict of interests with an existing client or a new threat that could cause the accountant's integrity, objectivity, and independence to be called into question [1]?

A further dynamic that tax engagements often present is the legality of the work involved - tax planning is frequently provided to clients as they may not be experts in this complex field and a professional accountant can usually recommend suitable approaches to managing various tax arrangements. This does not usually create any ethical threats (it is within both the spirit and letter of the law) as it is advisory and does not deviate from the mainstream tax legislation currently in force [1].

Tax avoidance schemes are still technically legal but engagements to advise clients on such arrangements have become less popular among professional accountants in recent years [1]. It is not felt to be in the public interest, and therefore ethically acceptable to society, if a professional accountant finds a loophole or technicality that allows their client to avoid tax in some way and which leads to the professional accountant getting paid for it. Guidance, therefore, tends to remind professional accountants that although it may be lucrative, there is a risk of losing one's social licence to operate if found to be acting in this way [1].

Tax evasion is illegal and so should not create an ethical problem for professional accountants because they should not be involved in it [1]. However, the reason this is considered in an ethical context is that in order to enjoy the benefits of evading tax altogether, the perpetrator would most likely pay the professional accountant very well for such advice (which would, by definition, probably not be declared for tax purposes either, making the whole proposition unacceptable) [1].

(b) **Chidgey Council**

Award up to 1 mark for each point made to a maximum of 8 marks, recognising that there may be other valid points.

It is probably quite straightforward to provide a simple answer to this question - it does not sound as though doing this would be the right thing to do, so the firm should probably decline this offer [1]. However, you have been asked to evaluate this request and consider the ethical dimensions of this offer, so you will also need to explain the reasoning behind your answer.

Firstly, we need to consider whether this is merely a tax planning activity or whether it represents a form of tax avoidance [1]. The scenario tells us that this does not seem like a straightforward case of advice and might require something bespoke. As the overall aim is to reduce tax, it sounds more like tax avoidance and as such we should probably decline this offer [1].

It is also important to consider whether it would be appropriate to receive a proportion of any tax saved as part of our fee **[1]**. This sounds like a contingent fee which is not prohibited but may still not be considered ethical, so should probably not be accepted **[1]**.

The work would support an initiative that would result in the resettlement of potentially vulnerable members of society and affect their domestic lives **[1]**. It is questionable whether the firm would be comfortable profiting from such a morally dubious act, especially given that a professional accountant's duty is to act in the public interest **[1]**.

The work would also support an initiative that is likely to result in ecological damage **[1]** which may be contrary to the values held by some of the firm's other clients. This may have an adverse impact on the firm's reputation **[1]** and compromise it from undertaking future engagements.

It must be stated that the work would support an initiative that could boost the Council's financial resources, allowing all of the members of society under its care to benefit **[1]**. However, as there are questionable ethics attached to this project, it is unlikely that this financial boost would outweigh the other social costs. We should therefore politely decline this offer of work **[1]**.

(c) **Panther plc**

Identify the ethical dilemma

The first matter revolves around the potential misrepresentation of financial and operating performance data for executive director performance bonuses. A member of Panther's finance department claimed in a meeting that forecasted financial information, approximately 12% higher than the actual financial performance so overstated performance was used to determine executive director bonuses meaning these were higher than they should have been. **[1]**

While these claims require further verification, the use of forecasted data instead of actual data raises concerns about the appropriateness of the bonuses paid, should these indeed be higher than warranted. This situation may be unintentional, indicating a serious failure in internal controls and governance, or it could be intentional, necessitating the identification of responsible parties for any confirmed dishonest behaviour. **[1]**

1. **Consider if existing safeguards or other mitigations are in place**

It remains unclear from the information provided whether existing safeguards or mitigations were in place to prevent such discrepancies. Standard audit processes and governance mechanisms, including the role of the Panther Remuneration Committee in approving bonuses and the oversight of the finance department, audit committee, and internal audit, should ideally have detected such errors or misrepresentations. **[1]**

It is essential to assess the effectiveness of internal control safeguards and whether the Panther Remuneration Committee fulfilled its oversight role effectively. **[1]**

2. **Evaluate the ethical dilemma**

The use of forecasted data to overstate performance for the determination of executive director bonuses raises ethical concerns. It may lead to undeserved financial rewards, create misalignment of incentives, and breach trust with shareholders and other stakeholders. **[1]**

Additionally, it may also violate regulatory and ethical standards concerning financial reporting and compensation. **[1]**

If this situation is corroborated through an investigation, the payment of higher bonuses than allowed by the nomination committee based on executive director performance conditions would unfairly reward directors at the expense of Panther shareholders. If there is evidence suggesting that forecasted performance data was intentionally applied instead of actual performance data, resulting in higher bonus payments, those responsible would have acted dishonestly, falling below the standards expected by shareholders of the company. **[1]**

3. **Recommend a solution**

- **Immediate investigation:** The Panther Board should initiate an immediate and comprehensive investigation into the matter. This investigation should encompass a review of the process employed to determine executive director bonuses, confirming, and quantifying the amount of overpayment, an audit of the financial and operating data, and interviews with relevant personnel involved in the bonus determination process, including the finance team, the Chief Finance Officer, and Panther Nomination Committee members. **[1]**

- **Corrective actions:** Corrective actions should be taken if the investigation confirms the use of incorrect data. This includes adjusting the bonus amounts based on accurate performance data. The Panther Board should request Directors who received overpayments to return the excess amount. The Board should also evaluate the performance evaluation process to prevent such errors in the future. **[1]**

- **Temporary bonus hold:** Pending the outcome of the investigation, the Panther Board of Directors should consider suspending further payment of executive director bonuses until newly established processes are confirmed to be in place. This will ensure no further incorrect compensation is disbursed and demonstrate the commitment to transparency. **[1]**

- **Communication to investors:** Given Panther is a listed company and the gravity of this governance matter, the Board should issue a press release to the market. The release should provide a summary of the facts and reasons for the situation, explain corrective actions to prevent a recurrence and confirm that the affected directors will return overpayments. **[1]**

4. **Justify your solution**

This proposed solution is justified as it upholds ethical standards by rectifying the misrepresentation of data and ensuring fairness in executive director compensation. Conducting an investigation demonstrates the commitment to transparency and accountability. Suspending bonuses temporarily prevents additional incorrect compensation. **[1]**

Also, explaining the errors to investors is paramount for stakeholder transparency as part of the good governance system. Corrective actions rectify the issue and prevent its recurrence, thus aligning Panther with ethical and governance principles. **[1]**

9 Douglas Drinks

This question tests content found in Chapter 8.

(a) **International corporate governance codes**

Several different issues triggered moves towards systematised corporate governance.

Global investment

The trend towards global investment has meant that large investment institutions in the US in particular, but also in other countries such as the UK, have been seeking to invest large amounts of capital in companies in other countries. US investors, expecting **similar treatment** from foreign companies that they received from US companies, expressed concern about the inadequacy of corporate governance in many countries. Many of their concerns focused on the **lack of shareholder rights**, or the disregard for minority shareholder rights shown by major shareholders or the boards of foreign companies.

The move towards systematised corporate governance still has a long way to go in many countries. However, in issuing its principles of corporate governance, the OECD recognised that the demands and expectations of global investors would have to be met if the trend towards global investment (and efficient capital allocation) is to continue.

Financial reporting and auditing

There were serious concerns about the standards of financial reporting. In the late 1980s, there were a number of well-publicised corporate failures, which were unexpected because the financial statements of those companies had not given any indication of their financial problems. This also raised questions about the **quality of external auditing** and the **effectiveness of professional auditing standards**.

Executive directors

There were also concerns that many large companies were being run for the benefit of their executive directors and senior managers, and not in the interests of shareholders. For example, there were concerns that acquisitions were sometimes made to **increase the size of a company** and the power of its chief executive, rather than as a means of adding shareholder value. These concerns raised the question of the conflict of interest between the directors and shareholders.

A particular concern was the **powerful position of individuals** holding the positions of both chairman and chief executive officer in their company, and the lack of 'balance' in boards.

Directors' remuneration

Directors' remuneration also became an issue. There is a widely held view that executive directors are paid **excessive amounts**, in terms of basic salary, 'perks' and incentives. Some directors appeared to receive high rewards even when the company **performed badly** or no differently from the 'average' of other companies. Although investment institutions did not object to high pay for talented executives, they believed that incentive schemes were often badly conceived, and that executives were being rewarded for performance that was not necessarily linked to the benefits provided to shareholders, for example in terms of a higher share price.

Insider dealings

Although convictions for insider dealing have been rare, there was a suspicion that some directors might be **using their inside knowledge** about their company to make a personal gain by dealing in shares in the company. For example, directors might sell a large number of shares just ahead of a profits warning by their company or buy shares just ahead of a public announcement that might be expected to boost the share price.

Risks and controls

Again poor controls have been a symptom of poor corporate governance with, for example, **inadequate management control of individuals** such as Nick Leeson at Barings. In addition, the development of risk management frameworks, such as the COSO guidance, has impacted on regulations.

Internationalisation

More investors, in particular institutional investors, have begun to **invest outside their home countries**. In order to limit the risks of their investments, they seek to promote a common **international governance framework**.

(b) **Purpose**

The main purpose of the Sarbanes-Oxley Act was to **tackle various problems** that had been brought to light by Enron and other corporate scandals. These included poor internal controls, misleading financial statements and ineffectiveness of non-executive directors and auditor monitoring of companies. They relate to the situation in **America**, although foreign companies with a listing on the US stock market have to comply as well.

The OECD principles have been designed to establish a credible international framework that **promotes global investment**. Investors who are investing in different countries can have confidence in the corporate governance of companies that adopt the OECD principles or regimes that base their own governance codes on the OECD. The ICGN report is designed to enhance the

OECD principles by providing practical guidance for boards wishing to **enhance their reputation** for **good corporate governance** and to establish better dialogue with their investors.

Board roles

Sarbanes-Oxley aims to reinforce the **monitoring role of the board and the responsibility of the board** for producing true and fair financial statements. It lays stress on the role of the audit committee, which is compulsory for all listed companies. The audit committee should oversee the role of external auditors and establish mechanisms for dealing with complaints. Board responsibility is enforced by the chief executive officer and the chief financial officer being required to certify the financial statements, and having to forfeit their bonuses if the financial statements subsequently have to be restated.

The OECD/ICGN guidelines provide rather more general guidance on the role and responsibilities of the board. They aim to promote **board effectiveness**. The OECD principles do this by stressing the board's **overall role in strategic development**, that board members should exercise **care and good faith** as well as **independent judgement** and assigning non-executive directors to appropriate roles. The ICGN code gives some specific guidelines on how to achieve the OECD guidelines. These include listing **strategic matters** that would normally be considered by the board, recommending that certain **board committees** (nomination, remuneration and audit) be established, suggesting that the **chairman and chief executive** should be **different people** and stating that **scrutiny of director performance** would be enhanced by yearly appraisal and regular re-election.

Accounts

A major aim of the Sarbanes-Oxley legislation is to tighten up accounting rules that were perceived as too lax, allowing Enron to produce accounts that may have complied with existing standards but were misleading. Hence the Act targets the kinds of **off-balance sheet arrangements** that Enron employed. Sarbanes-Oxley also seeks to **promote effective internal controls** by requiring disclosure of management responsibility for control system maintenance, and an audited **assessment of the effectiveness of the internal control structure and the procedures for financial reporting**.

The OECD/ICGN guidelines contain **various recommendations for disclosure** based on good practice in major jurisdictions. The disclosures reflect the important areas highlighted in the guidelines including governance structures and policies, and relationships with shareholders and stakeholders. They aim to **promote disclosure** that aids investors by recommending the provision of analysis or advice that is relevant to investors. The guidelines also stress the importance of the company **excelling in the returns it achieves** in comparison with its equity-sector peer group.

Audit

Sarbanes-Oxley responded to concerns about external auditing practice by stiffening the requirements relating to auditor independence. The **enhanced role of the audit committee** was part of this, but the Act also includes **provisions limiting the non-audit services** auditors can provide and **requiring the regular rotation of lead audit partners**. The Act also includes a number of provisions relating to the **conduct of audits** and **audit firm procedures**, including retention of working papers and quality control requirements, and the requirement for auditors to review internal control systems.

The OECD/ICGN guidelines place less stress than Sarbanes-Oxley on the role of the auditor, although they do stress the importance of the auditor providing **external and objective assurance** and audit committee-auditor links. The issue of non-audit services affecting **independence is raised**, the guidance noting the various methods different regimes have used to deal with this potential problem.

Shareholders

Sarbanes-Oxley does not contain significant provisions enhancing the role of shareholders. The OECD and ICGN guidelines do contain provisions promoting shareholder interests, in line with their key objective of enhancing investor confidence. The OECD principles stress the importance of **treating all shareholders equitably** and **eliminating cross-border impediments to shareholding**. The ICGN report seeks to reinforce these general aims with some specific guidance on how **shareholder voting rights** can be **protected** and also **promoting the role of institutional shareholders,** with the idea that their active involvement can encourage better corporate governance.

Stakeholders and ethics

The provisions relating to ethics in Sarbanes-Oxley were mainly inspired by the examples of unacceptable behaviour at Enron. They are designed to reduce the chances of **poor ethical behaviour occurring** and **remaining undetected**. Hence companies are required to state whether they have **adopted a code of conduct for senior financial officers** and the **contents** of that code. The Act also contains strong provisions protecting the position of auditors, employees, and lawyers who **whistleblow** on unethical behaviour.

The OECD/ICGN guidance also stresses the importance of companies establishing an ethical code and protecting whistleblowers. However, these requirements are set in the rather wider context of encouraging companies to act in an **economically, socially, and environmentally friendly manner** and the board promoting a **culture of integrity**. The guidance also emphasises the **importance of successful and productive relationships** with stakeholders, particularly employees, and suggests various methods of enhancing employee participation.

Enforcement

Sarbanes-Oxley has passed into US law and thus companies listed on the US Stock Exchange **have to comply** with its provisions. The OECD/ICGN principles have no legislative power. However, countries are using the OECD principles as a basis for developing or judging their own regimes.

(c) **Benefits of a CSR policy**

Marketing advantage

CSR offers marketing advantages and is a differentiator, appealing to certain types of customer. It produces a **'feel good' factor**.

Publicity

CSR neutralises poor publicity from **high interest, low power stakeholders** such as pressure groups. For example using Fair Trade suppliers would mean that Douglas Drinks cannot be criticised for exploiting coffee growers. In other words, CSR can provide some assistance in **managing reputation risk**.

Staff turnover

If CSR extends to the management of employees, and Douglas Drinks is known as a good employer, the **costs of staff turnover** might be **contained**. High staff turnover means high recruitment costs, high training costs and, perhaps, an adverse impact on customer service. However, a high level of staff turnover is perhaps inevitable in a business such as this.

Impact on other stakeholders

CSR makes a **good impression on other stakeholders** (eg the Government or local community). CSR can influence a company's reputation. Being known to be a good corporate citizen may help the company if it has business dealings with other significant stakeholders.

Drawbacks of a CSR policy

Failure to maximise shareholder value

Managers in charge of corporations are responsible to the owners of the business. CSR may be a distraction from **maximising shareholder wealth**. If Douglas Drinks has a statutory duty to maximise shareholder wealth, the scope of CSR may be restricted.

Costs of compliance

There may be costs in complying. This could include **direct costs** (eg paying premium prices or higher salaries) and **indirect costs**, such as management time.

10 Imago BPO

This question tests content found in Chapter 1.

(a) **Carol's view**

Carol's view is based on a **normative view of ethics**, that the company should behave in an **ethical way as an end in itself**, and not a means to another end. Hence, Imago BPO should not hesitate to adopt the code because it signifies that ethical behaviour is at the core of what it does. Her motivation is **altruistic** rather than **business strategic**.

The moral framework that supports this view is derived from **Kant's** notion of civic duties. Kant argued that these duties are required in maintaining good in society. Amongst these duties is the **moral duty to take account of others' concerns** and opinions; not to do so will result in a failure of social cohesion and everyone being worse off.

Extending the normative view to stakeholder theory, Carol's view is that Imago BPO should accommodate stakeholder views because of its **moral duties** to its stakeholders, not because accommodating stakeholder concerns will help it achieve its own economic or other concerns.

Cosmo's view

Cosmo's view is based on an **instrumental view of ethics**. This sees the company taking ethical positions into account only when they are consistent with the overriding economic objective of **maximising shareholder value**. Hence Cosmo is concerned with the **strategic implications** of the code (will not adopting it place Imago BPO at a competitive disadvantage) and the **costs of drawing it up and implementing it**.

The instrumental view in relation to stakeholders suggests that shareholder concerns should be accommodated if not doing so threatens its ability to maximise shareholder value. Thus taking account of shareholder opinions is a **means to the end of maximising economic value**, not an end. Thus stakeholders are judged not in terms of whether it is ethically right to respond to their concerns, but how powerful they are in terms of how much influence they can have on Imago BPO achieving its economic objectives.

(b) **Conventional viewpoint**

Kohlberg identified the conventional viewpoint as one of the levels of moral reasoning. Using this perspective, individuals judge ethical decisions in terms of what is **expected of them** in terms of the norms of society or organisation. In this example, Carol would take into account what would be considered **good practice** in the industry - would other companies use similar images even if they did cause offence? She would also consider society's viewpoint as expressed in the law - would the images possibly break laws relating to good taste? Another viewpoint would be whether **members of society other than those belonging to the religious group** would find the image offensive.

Pre-conventional viewpoint

The pre-conventional reasoning viewpoint sees reasoning in terms of the **rewards or punishments** that will result from a particular act. The factors influencing the decision would be whether Imago BPO would suffer a **legal penalty** through its association with the advert, whether it would **lose business** because of the offence taken by potential client or whether (as Cosmo argues) it would **gain business** through the **free advertising**.

(c) **Variety of factors**

The board will take into account a number of different considerations, some of which are not easily comparable. However one means of aiding the decision would be to consider the various stakeholders affected, and to analyse their viewpoints in terms of **Mendelow's stakeholder influence**, considering their **relative degree of power and influence**.

Relationship with customer

One obvious stakeholder with a strong economic relationship to Imago BPO is the **customer**. The board would need to consider whether business with the customer would be **threatened** if the advertisement was withdrawn and what the consequences would be in terms of **lost sales**. Another viewpoint would be that the customer's interests, that have been secured by paying the advertisement, should take precedence over the religious group's interest, as the religious group has **no economic relationship**. Of course the customer might prefer the advertisement to be withdrawn because it was damaging its interests. Imago BPO would presumably have to comply with the request, although then the issue would be whether there should be an apology.

Negative reputation consequences

The offence caused by the advertisement is an example of a reputation risk materialising, and the board therefore has to assess the consequences in terms of what stakeholders will do. Firstly would a **boycott by members of the religious group be significant**. More widely would actions taken by the **religious group and adverse press coverage** generated lead to other organisations **being unwilling to use Imago BPO** with further lost sales. The board will need to judge the **balance and strength of the coverage**.

Positive reputation consequences

However there may be an **upside to the reputation risk**. Imago BPO may **gain business** as a result of the advertisement with more clients being willing to use the company because it is seen as **forward-looking and daring**. Cosmo Kraepelin believes that the advertisement will be good for business. This may be jeopardised if the advert is withdrawn and an apology issued.

Organisational field

The board's decision may be affected by the organisational field of the advertising industry, the common **business environment**, **norms**, and **values** within the industry. These appear to work in different directions however in this situation. On the one hand, a lot of large companies are emphasising their **ethical commitment**; however there may be pressures within the industry to be **challenging and innovative**.

National culture

The board may also consider the **place of religion in the national culture**, how strongly religious ideas affect people's beliefs and actions.

Strategic considerations

Important strategic considerations include Imago BPO's positioning relative to its competitors. Does it wish to gain a **competitive advantage** through being seen as more ethical, or through being seen as more innovative or perhaps more subversive.

Company objectives

One particularly significant aspect of strategy is whether the objective of **profit maximisation** should be given precedence over everything else or whether Imago BPO exists to fulfil other significant considerations. This could be a very important decision for Imago BPO as there is evidently a dispute between the **purely capitalist, revenue-driven view** of Cosmo Kraepelin and the view of Carol Changstein that Imago BPO should express **ethical values through what it does**. The decision may end up having a significant influence on the company's future direction.

(d) **Narrow stakeholders**

The religious group's viewpoint would be that they are **narrow stakeholders**, meaning that Imago BPO's activities seriously affected their own interests. They argue that the content and design undermines their system of beliefs and threatens the promotion of their faith.

Accountability to shareholders

How legitimate this claim is viewed as being depends on **how widely corporate accountability is defined**. **Society's views** will be a significant factor. The legitimacy of the claim would differ greatly in a **theocracy** compared with a society where the religious group represents a **minority view** and is seeking to impose its views outside the law or outside social norms. There is also the issue of whether the religious group needs to have a direct **economic claim** on Imago BPO, or whether the company is seen as having a **social contract** with society that implies a need for sensitivity on religious issues that groups in society believe to be important.

10 ChemXL

This question tests content found in Chapters 2, 8 and 9.

(a) **Award 1 mark per sensible point to a maximum of 9 marks overall**

Implementing sustainable business practices is crucial for ChemXL as it not only helps to mitigate environmental impacts but also enhances social responsibility and governance standards. By integrating sustainability into its operations, ChemXL can reduce its carbon footprint, minimise waste generation, and conserve natural resources, thereby contributing to environmental preservation and combatting climate change. **[1]**

Also adopting sustainable practices can enhance ChemXL's reputation, attract environmentally conscious customers, and mitigate regulatory risks associated with non-compliance. Furthermore, by prioritising sustainability, ChemXL can foster a positive corporate culture, attract top talent, and improve employee morale and retention rates. **[1]**

Implementing the following specific sustainable business practices at ChemXL plc will improve its environmental, social and governance sustainability performance.

Inclusive decision-making

By involving a wide range of stakeholders in decision-making processes, ChemXL can ensure that diverse perspectives are considered, leading to more balanced and sustainable business strategies. **[1]** This inclusivity helps identify potential ESG issues early and devise more comprehensive solutions, ultimately enhancing the company's environmental, social, and governance performance. **[1]**

Transparency and reporting

Adopting comprehensive reporting standards such as the Global Reporting Initiative (GRI) will enable ChemXL to transparently disclose its sustainability efforts and impacts. **[1]** By providing detailed information on environmental performance, social initiatives, and governance practices, ChemXL can build trust with stakeholders and demonstrate its commitment to accountability. This transparency is crucial for maintaining strong stakeholder relationships and improving ESG performance. **[1]**

Implementing ethical practices

Implementing ethical practices is essential for enhancing ChemXL's ESG performance. By reducing its environmental footprint, ensuring fair labour practices, and contributing to community development, ChemXL can demonstrate its commitment to sustainability. **[1]** For instance, reducing greenhouse gas emissions and improving worker safety protocols will show the company's dedication to ethical operations, which positively impacts its ESG ratings. **[1]**

Responsiveness and responsibility

Being responsive to stakeholder concerns is vital for demonstrating ChemXL's commitment to accountability. For example, if environmental groups raise concerns about plastic waste, ChemXL could

pledge to increase the use of recycled materials in its packaging. [1] This responsiveness shows stakeholders that the company values their input and is willing to make changes based on their feedback, leading to improved ESG performance. [1]

(b) **Award 1 mark per sensible point to a maximum of 10 marks overall**

Improving shareholder engagement is important for ChemXL as it fosters trust, transparency, and accountability, which are essential for maintaining investor confidence and driving long-term value creation. [1]

Actively engaging with shareholders enables ChemXL to understand their perspectives, concerns, and expectations regarding sustainability performance and governance practices. By soliciting feedback and addressing shareholder concerns, ChemXL can enhance its decision-making processes, strengthen stakeholder relationships, and mitigate the risk of shareholder activism or disinvestment. [1]

Implementing the following steps will improve stakeholder engagement at ChemXL.

Identify key stakeholders [1]

ChemXL must recognise the diverse groups affected by its actions, including employees, customers, suppliers, local communities, and investors. By identifying these key stakeholders, ChemXL can tailor its engagement strategies to address their specific needs and concerns, ensuring more effective communication and collaboration. [1]

Deploy stakeholder engagement strategies [1]

To improve shareholder engagement, ChemXL should implement various methods such as surveys, public consultations, and social media platforms to engage with its stakeholders. These strategies enable the company to gather valuable feedback and insights, which can inform its sustainability practices and align them with stakeholder expectations. [1]

Integrate stakeholder feedback into strategic and operational objectives [1]

ChemXL should evaluate and incorporate feedback from stakeholders into its strategic planning and operational practices. By integrating stakeholder input, ChemXL can ensure that its sustainability initiatives are relevant and effective, leading to improved ESG performance and stronger stakeholder relationships. [1]

Regular and transparent communication [1]

ChemXL should establish regular and transparent communication channels with its shareholders. Providing frequent updates on sustainability initiatives, progress towards goals, and any challenges faced will keep shareholders informed and engaged. This transparency demonstrates ChemXL's commitment to accountability and fosters trust and support from shareholders. [1]

Incorporate shareholder feedback into decision-making [1]

ChemXL should actively seek and incorporate shareholder feedback into its decision-making processes. This can be achieved through regular shareholder meetings, feedback surveys, and direct consultations. By valuing and acting upon shareholder input, ChemXL can enhance its sustainability practices and align them with shareholder expectations, improving overall ESG performance. [1]

(c) **Award 1 mark per sensible point to a maximum of 6 marks overall**

Cognitivism

Cognitivism asserts that moral statements can be true or false based on objective facts. [1]

From a cognitivist perspective, ChemXL's actions can be assessed based on factual evidence of harm. While it is scientifically proven that the contaminated water is harmless to humans, the immediate harm to river life, evidenced by dead fish, is an objective fact. Therefore, ChemXL's actions can be considered unethical because they result in observable harm to the environment. [1]

Non-cognitivism

Non-cognitivism holds that moral statements express emotional attitudes or prescriptions rather than objective truths. **[1]**

Non-cognitivism would focus on the attitudes and feelings about the harm caused. If the local community and stakeholders express strong negative emotions or disapproval towards the harm to river life, ChemXL's actions would be deemed unethical based on these attitudes. The ethical judgment here is subjective and relies on the community's emotional response to the environmental damage. **[1]**

Consequentialism

Consequentialism evaluates the morality of an action based on its outcomes or consequences. **[1]**

Under consequentialism, ChemXL's behaviour is evaluated by weighing the positive and negative consequences of their actions. Although the water is safe for human consumption, the negative consequences for river life are significant. The death of fish in the affected area suggests a detrimental impact on the ecosystem, which can have broader ecological repercussions. Therefore, from a consequentialist standpoint, ChemXL's actions are unethical because the harm to the river ecosystem outweighs the benefits of legal compliance and human safety assurances. **[1]**

Exam question bank

1 Chemico PLC

You have recently been appointed as the Chief Financial Officer (CFO) of Chemico PLC (Chemico), a multi-national manufacturer of chemicals, petrochemicals, and related products. You previously worked as Financial Controller for Dairy Foods and were delighted to obtain your first board position. You are keen to make a good impression.

The company continues to remain extremely profitable due to innovative products and a successful marketing campaign. However, the company has been experiencing falling profit margins.

Jamilla, the operating director has suggested the board consider moving the production of one of its main products, pesticides, away from its long established Eastern European manufacturing site in a small town in Romania to a Zarican manufacturing site. This will reduce costs and gain a competitive advantage in the market. Zarica is an emerging country in economic development. Zarica could provide lower-cost labour, easier connection with the growing market in emerging countries, and transaction costs would be reduced. However, this will lead to job losses in the Romanian town and have an associated knock-on effect in the local community where unemployment is high and many workers are now migrating to other parts of Europe to seek a better life.

The Zarican government is particularly keen for Chemico to establish a pesticide manufacturing site in their country to realise self-sufficiency in the production of crops as part of its "Sustainable Development Initiative" and has offered a grant towards the building costs of the site on the basis of a quick decision being made. The use of pesticides is increasing in Zarica and they are regarded as an essential factor in improving its agricultural productivity.

Several of the directors have shared with you that they are worried that Zarica lacks the adequate skills and technology to maintain the production of lethal chemicals such as pesticides. They are also concerned as they have heard of instances where the Zarican government have prioritised economic growth in attracting manufacturing to the area but ignored the need for adequate working conditions and health and safety procedures. Fines for health and safety breaches in Zarica are rare and there is a concern by some directors that there will be limited incentives to reduce environmental and human risks associated with pesticide production.

Of further concern was that several years ago, a competitor of Chemico, AllChem, set up a pesticide manufacturing site in another emerging economy, Radlands. Due to inadequate health and safety procedures and poor working conditions, toxic chemicals were leaked into the atmosphere from this site resulting in deaths and injuries to thousands of local residents as well as environmental damage. This cost AllChem millions of pounds in terms of fines and loss of reputation and they are still recovering financially from the aftermath. Robert Goodall, the Chief Executive Officer (CEO) of Chemico is however keen that the relocation of the manufacturing plant to Zarica should go ahead.

While the company is compliant with governance requirements, you are concerned about the way the company is managed. Robert was appointed as the CEO by the Chairman a year ago and he is keen to make his mark in the company by increasing profits. Robert had previously worked for several years with the Chairman in a smaller manufacturing company where they both served as board directors. Robert's opinion carries a lot of weight in board meetings and you have heard several of the Chemico directors' remark that 'the Chairman always agrees with Robert, so what's the point of having a chairman.'

You have also heard through the grapevine that the CFO before you was asked to resign because he was one of very few individuals who challenged the CEO's opinions, although the official line was that he was suspected of fraudulent activity. You have observed in the board meetings that they lack debate and appear to be more of a 'rubber stamping' exercise, rather than a collective meeting of minds for strategic decision making. It appears that Robert's opinion always prevails.

EXAM QUESTION BANK

You noted in the last board meeting that, in a presentation that Robert gave on a risky project that he was keen to progress, benefits seemed to be overstated and risks downplayed. As usual, this project was given the go ahead as Robert was keen on it.

The next board meeting takes place in a few days and you only received the board papers yesterday. From looking at the 500 pages of board papers, you can see that the Zarican Manufacturing Site Relocation has many pages on the significant cost savings that can be achieved for Chemico, but risks have been kept to the bare minimum.

You feel that going ahead with this project without fully considering the risks could seriously damage the reputation of the company, but you are worried about keeping your job. In a previous board meeting, where you had challenged one of Robert's proposals, you were called into Robert's office afterwards. He informed you that he was disappointed with you challenging his proposal and suggested that if you were not supportive of him, he may need to consider your future position within the company.

You have discussed your concerns about the current project with two other directors and they agree with you that further investigation into the risks of this relocation is required in light of the experience of AllChem that resulted in deaths and injuries and subsequent loss of reputation and significant financial loss. You are not looking forward to this board meeting.

Required

(a) Critically analyse, using utilitarian and Kantian theoretical perspectives, the viewpoint of the CEO and contrast with your own stance. **(10 marks)**

(b) (i) Critically evaluate the conflicts of interest around your position in the company and assess how the application of the key aspects of the 2018 IFAC Code of Ethics would inform your decision making. **(9 marks)**

(ii) Identify and critically evaluate two threats to effective corporate governance within the above scenario and suggest what safeguards could be adopted to reduce these threats.
(6 marks)

(Total 25 marks)

2 Chocco

Integrity is a fundamental principle of ethics which requires that members of the Association of International Accountants must be straightforward and honest in all professional and business relationships.

Required

(a) Appraise ONE fundamental principle (other than integrity) in the IFAC Codes of Ethics in an audit context, giving an example. **(2 marks)**

(b) Your firm has acted as the external auditor of Chocco Co (Chocco) for fifteen years and also provides a range of non-audit services including consultancy work in respect of Chocco's management accountancy systems.

Chocco manufactures chocolate biscuits and sweets and has recently decided to diversify by acquiring a small theme park. Earlier this year, the finance director of Chocco retired and was succeeded by a former member of your firm's staff who had managed the audit of Chocco for the preceding three years.

Sabbir Shafique, the engagement partner, met with Chocco's new finance director, Jilly Blue, last week. During the meeting Jilly offered Sabbir and his family unlimited access to the Chocco World theme park, once the current year audit is complete. Jilly also confirmed she would continue to be offering all the members of the audit team access to free chocolates and biscuits as with previous

years. However, Jilly also stated that, as she is still settling into her new role, she will take a dim view of interruptions and excessive questions from the audit team. To avoid too much disruption to her work demands, she has requested that Sabbir should have a catch-up meeting with her once a week and that under no circumstances should anyone other than Sabbir ask her any questions.

Jilly also asked Sabbir to request a meeting with the firm's tax manager as he needs advice on how to challenge the local tax authority in respect of Chocco's recent tax assessment. Jilly also wants the audit firm to assist in any challenge.

Required

(i) Critically analyse the above scenario and discuss SIX ethical threats which may affect the independence of your firm in respect of the audit of Chocco Co. **(9 marks)**

(ii) For each of the SIX threats discussed, recommend what action could be taken to reduce the threat to an acceptable level. **(9 marks)**

(c) ISA 240 *The Auditor's Responsibilities Relating to Fraud in an Audit of Financial Statements* describes the responsibilities of both management and the auditor with regard to preventing and detecting fraud.

Required

Evaluate the responsibilities of both management and auditors with regard to the prevention and detection of fraud. **(5 marks)**

(Total 25 marks)

3 Racer

Racer PLC (Racer) is a UK car manufacturer which builds trucks, vans and passenger cars. It sells to geographic locations across Europe, America, Asia and Zarica. In 2015, Racer became one of the largest vehicle makers in the world. However, it is struggling financially due to increased competition, rising costs and uncertainty regarding the future of diesel and petrol cars. The government plans to ban sales of petrol, diesel, and many hybrid cars in 2040 to cut air pollution and boost the UK'S electric car industry. It is therefore becoming increasingly important that the vehicles currently manufactured pass certain emission tests to ensure the company complies with the Clean Air Act and the Kyoto Protocol on global warming.

Jonathan Peters, as the Financial Director of Racer for 6 years, has been told by the Chief Executive, Sujana Ahmed, that a significant part of his job is to identify where cost savings can be made to ensure Racer's survival in the longer term. When speaking to the production team about processes and costs, Jonathan became aware that the production manager has manipulated the emission tests for Racer's new passenger vehicles.

The production manager ensured these vehicles passed the emission test by installing a 'defeat device' which reduces the toxic fumes during testing. While driving the car at normal conditions, the device will be stopped, and the car will generate NOx (Nitrogen oxide) – a hazardous gas, which is highly injurious to health, and which is 40 times higher than the permitted limit under the Clean Air Act.

On further investigation, Jonathan estimates that at least five million cars worldwide are affected. He raises this with Sujana Ahmed, who tells him that he must keep quiet about this if he wants to have a job in the future. She tells Jonathan that the costs to recall the cars and correct the emission problem will be too high a burden for Racer and it would have to close down, putting a loyal workforce out of work. In any case, she says, no one will notice and there are a lot of other companies polluting the atmosphere on a wider scale. Jonathan is a qualified accountant with the Association of International Accountants. He is concerned that he will be violating their ethical code. He is also concerned about his future job prospects,

as he relies on his salary to pay a large mortgage and support his wife and young family. He is not aware of any company policies on how to deal with this issue.

Required

(a) Critically analyse what you understand by the term whistleblowing and whether it would be an appropriate course of action for Jonathan, and how he might apply that course of action, particularly in light of the ethical dilemmas he faces and threats to his job security. **(15 marks)**

(b) If the manipulation of the emissions testing had been discovered by the external auditors, rather than Jonathan, assess what additional issues they would face. **(10 marks)**

(Total 25 marks)

4 Albian

Albian Ltd (Albian) is a technology company planning to list on a stock exchange within the next six months, and management has been advised by the company's external auditors about the need for compliance with corporate governance initiatives. The Finance Director, David Harvey, is not entirely sure exactly what is required in this area, but he is aware of the need for an Audit Committee.

In this respect, David Harvey is looking to recruit non-executive directors to establish an audit committee. The finance director has two potential non-executive directors whom he is considering approaching to join the board of Albian.

Moade Nasir is currently an executive sales director of a listed multi-national investment company; he sits on an audit committee of another large company as a non-executive director and is agreeable to being paid a fixed salary which is not related to profits. Joanna James is currently a finance director of a small retail company, which does not compete with Albian; she has expressed an interest in a fixed eight-year contract, and she is the sister of Albian's chief executive, Andrew James.

David Harvey is also of the view that having an internal audit department may highlight any control deficiencies in Albian but is unsure whether this should be set up in house or whether it should be outsourced.

Required

(a) Appraise what corporate governance is and the rationales for its introduction. **(3 marks)**

(b) Advise Albian's Board of Directors on the main functions of an audit committee. **(5 marks)**

(c) Critically evaluate the benefits to Albian of establishing an audit committee. **(9 marks)**

(d) Evaluate the advantages and disadvantages of appointing the following as non-executive directors of Albian:

(i) Moade Nasir; **(4 marks)**
(ii) Joanna James. **(4 marks)**

(Total 25 marks)

5 Gonzales

You are a newly qualified accountant who has recently made the move from a professional firm into industry, being appointed to the finance team of Gonzales Plc ('Gonzales'), a large listed clothing manufacturer based in Western Europe. You report directly to the CFO Jillian Grant. This is your first role in industry; prior to this, you worked in the audit team of a large accounting firm.

Gonzales have been established for approximately 90 years and became particularly famous for their fashionable clothes in the 1950s and 60s, with many movie stars and celebrities wearing their designs throughout Europe and the Americas. Throughout this time the company expanded massively, opening a number of factories throughout the world.

Gonzales became known as an excellent employer who provided their staff with good wages and benefits, actively contributing to the local communities in which they were based by providing schools and leisure facilities. This has been increasingly important in many areas as the manufacturing sector in Western Europe has declined over the latter part of the twentieth century, damaging many areas which relied on manufacturing jobs.

More recently, however, Gonzales have struggled due to increased competition from overseas and have suffered from poor cashflow and declining market share. The directors and senior management team have all agreed to take considerable pay cuts; however, the possibility of factories shutting down with large-scale job losses remains high.

Gonzales have recently signed a contract with Tourcash GH ('Tourcash'). Tourcash is a state owned company in the nation of Rezastan, and the contract would involve Tourcash supplying Gonzales with cotton and silk for their clothes manufacturing. The contract would allow Gonzales to acquire this silk and cotton at a much lower price than they currently pay. Projections show that this would allow the company to financially recover and become profitable again. This would secure the factories and their employees.

Rezastan, however, has a very oppressive government with a history of human rights abuses. A recent UN report has found that there is widespread use of forced labour within the country's supply chain and that the conditions for the workers are extremely poor. This is particularly the case in the state-owned cotton and silk industries which are heavily reliant on forced labour.

Ak Malby, a university professor, who was part of the UN reporting panel stated "Using forced labour is ethically wrong. In fact, western companies should never purchase goods from companies that allow the use of forced labour."

The government of Rezastan, however, is working hard to improve its international image and would be keen to partner with such an established brand as Gonzales.

The founding family of Gonzales still hold a large stake in the company, and the current CEO is Peter Gonzales, the great-grandson of the founder. You recently spoke to Peter about the issues with Rezastan but he informed you that if Gonzales didn't take up this contract then one of their main competitors would be keen to get the opportunity to acquire raw materials at such a low price. You know that Peter has been extremely worried recently about the situation with the factories and would be extremely glad to be able to save them.

You are also concerned with an incident which is happening with Jillian in work. The company's corporation tax return for the year is due; because of the company's widespread international operations the company's tax affairs are extremely complex. You have limited tax knowledge and do not understand the tax situation of the company.

Jillian has told you that, as she is extremely busy with the Rezastan deal, you will need to complete the tax return for the year, and that she does not have any time to help you. You have asked for guidance on a few points but she has always told you that she is extremely busy and that you should complete it to the best of your ability.

The tax returns and computations were previously prepared with assistance from a local firm of accountants. However, due to cost-cutting measures as a result of the company's recent performance, this arrangement has ended and all tax work is now to be done in house.

Concerned with this situation, you have investigated the company's policies and found out that they do not currently have an internal policy on ethical conduct. You have spoken to some colleagues about this but they have informed you that the company has a long-standing set of "unwritten rules" that mean there has never been much need for formal written policies. One of your colleagues in the finance team has told you that the fact there is specific guidance for accountants means that there is no need for a company to have internal policies.

Required

(a) With reference to stakeholders impacted, critically evaluate the contract with Tourcash from both a cognitive and non-cognitive viewpoint. **(10 marks)**

(b) Critically evaluate the situation regarding the tax return, outlining a course of action with specific reference to the IESBA code of ethics. **(8 marks)**

(c) Assess the argument that there is no need for a company to have its own internal policies on ethics and conduct. **(7 marks)**

(Total 25 marks)

6 Merkland and Miah LLP

You work for the audit firm of Merkland and Miah LLP ('M&M'). You are an audit senior and have recently qualified with AIA.

M&M has offices throughout the world and you are based in Birmingham in the UK. The fees of the audit partners are primarily based on the revenue and profits that their individual office brings in.

The largest client of the Birmingham office is Stratton Plc ('Stratton'), a large IT services firm. Stratton has grown significantly in recent years and they are now by far the Birmingham office's largest client accounting for a large proportion of overall revenue.

Stratton has seen particularly strong growth over the past year, with its IT services being in strong demand due to the rise in home working during the COVID pandemic. The directors of Stratton are planning a stock market listing based on this strong growth. As many of the employees have share options, this would lead to a windfall for many of them, amounting to tens of thousands of pounds each.

You have been asked by the partner, Stephen Cheng, to take charge of the audit fieldwork after the previous audit senior, Lisa Donnelly, left two months ago to join the finance team of Stratton. Lisa had previously acted as audit senior on the job for the last three years, and had being involved in some of the audit planning for this year.

On the first day of audit fieldwork, one of the audit juniors provides you with workings showing that Stratton have been recognising the entire revenue up front on long-term contracts. You speak to Stephen about this, who appears very flustered before going into his office and telling you: "Don't do anything about this – I'll sort it!"

Required

(a) Critically analyse why Stratton may have decided to recognise revenue in this way and evaluate why there could be issues if other companies acted in this fashion. **(10 marks)**

(b) Using your knowledge of audit regulations justify the need for an auditor to be independent. **(5 marks)**

(c) Critically analyse the threats to independence posed by M&M having Stratton as a client and recommend the course of action that the partners of M&M should follow. **(10 marks)**

(Total 25 marks)

7 Angele

You have recently undertaken a role as Financial Controller (FC) of Angele Ltd ('Angele'), a large computer components manufacturer. The company employs nearly 3,000 people in the town of Newton-le-Abbots. Angele are the largest employer in the town and are a major contributor to the local economy. Angele is owned by a large number of shareholders, both local and international with no individual shareholder owning more than 5%.

You have settled in well during your first few months in the company and have found the staff very friendly. Angele has a full board including a number of independent non-executive directors and an experienced suite of executive directors. Although you do not sit on the board yourself, you report directly to the CEO.

The CEO, Natasha Sidique, was recruited from a competitor two years ago and is noted as being one of the most respected and experienced executives in the industry. You have grown very close to Natasha as she has been very supportive in your new role.

Angele uses a number of heavy metals in the manufacture of computer components. These can have a very damaging impact on the local environment and, as such, the disposal of these materials is very heavily regulated.

You are on a visit to the factory floor, where you see some heavy metal waste being loaded onto a waste lorry labelled for normal landfill waste. The paperwork is then completed by the driver and the Production Manager, Mark Andrews. After the completion of the paperwork, Mark hands the driver a large brown envelope before he drives off.

You confront Mark straight away and he tells you, "You're not in class now, this is the real world. All companies have to act this way, there's no way we could stay profitable if we had to pay high fees for everything. Would you be happy telling all these people they're going to lose their jobs? I know the board will claim they know nothing about this, but deep down they must know what I'm doing. They know this is the way this business works"

Required

(a) Evaluate the concept of integrity and how it applies to accountants in their roles. **(5 marks)**

(b) Identify the stakeholders in this situation and analyse how they may be impacted by Mark's actions. **(9 marks)**

(c) Appraise what is meant by the term whistleblowing. **(3 marks)**

(d) Using the model developed by the American Accounting Association (AAA) evaluate your current situation and recommend a course of action. **(8 marks)**

(Total 25 marks)

8 Kincaid

Kincaid Plc. ('Kincaid') is a large listed furniture manufacturer based near Belfast. The company was founded by Michael Kincaid in 1952 and was listed in 1981. Although initially concentrating on a local market, the company has expanded considerably since then and now has operations worldwide. The company is listed on the UK Alternative Investment Market (AIM) and the original Kincaid family now have no interest in the business.

You have recently been appointed CFO (Chief Financial Officer), replacing Oonagh O'Connell who is moving jobs after 21 years with the business, for 15 of which she was CFO. Oonagh is particularly close to

Devraj Kumar, who is the CEO of Kincaid. Oonagh is taking on the role as CEO of Quinn Limited, Kincaid's major competitor.

Devraj has been credited in much of the media as being behind the recent rapid growth of Kincaid. Devraj's current contract relies heavily on bonuses based on the short-term profitability of the company and share options. These share options allow Devraj to buy shares at 25% below market value in one year's time if the company meets its profitability targets for the next year.

The chairperson of Kincaid is stepping down due to ill health and Devraj feels that Oonagh would be the ideal replacement due to her knowledge of the business.

Despite his recent success, Devraj is currently facing considerable opposition from within the board itself as a result of a project in South-East Asia. This project will see Kincaid buy a large area of rainforest which can then be cut down for timber. This has proved extremely controversial as the environment in which the rainforest is located is very rare and there have been considerable protests outside Kincaid's office. You know from discussions with your colleagues that many of the board are also uncomfortable with Devraj's plan.

However, the project would lead to considerable investment within the country. Accordingly, the relevant governmental authorities in South-East Asia have approved the plan and Devraj says that it should go ahead as the sole duty of the company is to maximise profits.

Required

(a) Evaluate Oonagh's suitability as chairperson of Kincaid. **(5 marks)**

(b) With reference to this particular scenario:

(i) Assess the issues with the way that Devraj's pay package is structured and how this may motivate him to act. **(5 marks)**

(ii) Critically analyse the ethical issues surrounding Devraj's proposal to acquire timber from South East Asia and what impact this may have on Kincaid's business. **(7 marks)**

(c) Devraj states that the sole duty of a company is to make profits. Evaluate this statement with reference to Carroll's Pyramid (Carroll's Model). **(8 marks)**

(Total 25 marks)

9 Birch Energy Plc

You are the newly appointed Chief Financial Officer (CFO) of Birch Energy Plc. ('Birch'). Birch was founded eight years ago by Martin Singh, a well-known entrepreneur, as a provider of domestic gas and electricity within the UK. Martin founded Birch with the specific aim of taking an ethical approach to energy generation, in particular ensuring that lower income families had access to gas and electricity at a fair price.

In line with this ethical approach, Martin has also stated his commitment to green energy. As such, Birch has invested heavily in a number of windfarm and tide energy projects throughout the UK. These are mostly long-term projects which will take several years to complete and pay off and have required extensive use of Birch's capital.

Birch was operating very successfully until late 2021 when increases in the global energy prices began to significantly increase Birch's costs. As many of their customers are on fixed low rate tariffs, many of these plans have become loss-making. Martin has also been very insistent that Birch does not pass on the full price rise to the most vulnerable customers and instead absorbs much of the cost itself.

This, when combined with the ongoing costs of the windfarms and tidal energy projects, has left Birch with significant financial worries. Your first few months in the job has included a lot of time worrying about Birch's ability to financially survive, especially with regards to ongoing cashflow pressures.

You were initially relieved, therefore, when Martin promised you that the company's short-term problems would be over. Martin had been speaking to a contact in the South American country of Costa Luna, about the discovery of a gas field in a remote and heavily rainforested area of the country. This contact has offered Birch a preferential deal to be the first extractor of this gas, which can be liquefied and transported to the UK at well below the present market rate.

Martin then presented this idea to the board with enthusiasm showing projections of how this could ensure both that Birch could continue to offer reasonably priced energy to customers and afford to continue with the wind and tidal energy power.

One of the board members, Helen Xu, was unimpressed, however. Helen pointed out that not only would the development of a new gas field be against Birch's commitment to green energy, but the project would result in a large area of rainforest being destroyed and many indigenous tribes being displaced. Helen was particularly vocal in her criticism quoting a recent climate change report, which stated: "the destruction of the natural environment in the pursuit of corporate interests is always wrong".

Martin, however, stated that while he would have liked to have avoided this situation it was, unfortunately, a financial essential. Without this project, Birch would likely have to cease trading within the next year. Not only would this lead to job losses within Birch but it would mean that customers would be moved to much more expensive mainstream suppliers and the tidal and wind power projects would cease. Martin admitted that he "wasn't 100% comfortable" with the gas project but felt it would only be a temporary measure until the wind and tidal power projects became cash generative in the next 3-5 years. Ultimately the board failed to make an absolute decision on the project and agreed to meet again next week for a more in-depth discussion.

With such a stressful day, you've been glad to accept an invitation to join an old university friend, John O'Brien, for a drink. You haven't seen John for a while and think it would be good to catch up. John is a journalist and has recently accepted a job with a major news website, so you're interested to hear how that is going.

After a bit of initial small talk John says that he's heard many rumours about the current financial situation of Birch. He says that as so many customers on lower incomes rely on Birch it's clearly in the public interest that he is able to report the full financial picture. He asks you to provide him with internal documents showing the current and projected financial position of Birch, promising that your name will be kept out of any article.

Required

(a) Develop Helen Xu's general statement that "the destruction of the natural environment in the pursuit of corporate interests is always wrong" from:

    (i) A cognitivist perspective; and **(4 marks)**
    (ii) A teleological (consequential) point of view. **(6 marks)**

(b) Assuming that Martin's financial projections are valid, evaluate Martin's justification of the project from a teleological (consequential) perspective. Ensure that your analysis encompasses an appropriate range of stakeholders, stating any issues with the approach. **(8 marks)**

(c) With reference to the IESBA fundamental principles critically appraise John's suggestions that you should pass these documents to him as it is in the public interest. **(7 marks)**

(Total 25 marks)

10 Williams and Rose LLP

You are Alison Monroe, a newly qualified AIA accountant and have just started with the audit firm of Williams and Rose LLP ('W&R') and moved to the small town of Easterness in North East Scotland. The economy of Easterness previously heavily relied on fishing and shipbuilding, but as these industries have declined, banking and the service sector have become more important to the local economy. Your first client is Connaught Holdings Plc ('Connaught'), an old and respected investment company first established in 1902.

Despite its long-established history, Connaught has faced significant challenges over the past twenty or so years and there is a general feeling that it lags behind many of its competitors. Connaught was slow to adopt online access for customers. Moreover, an attempt to expand to China and the Far East became a well-known failure with the overseas operations ceasing two years ago and these branches closing. With the recent COVID pandemic also damaging business, some financial journalists have raised doubts over whether Connaught has a future.

From discussions with the audit partner, Michelle Sanchez, you learn that Connaught is in the process of arranging a merger with the tech-based investment company Blue Wasp. The tie-up of Blue Wasp's modern app-based technology and Connaught's heritage and history would not only secure the long term future of both companies but lead to significant investment within Easterness. Michelle has previously mentioned how she is a long-standing friend of the Connaught CEO Jason Ivory and regularly has joint family holidays. You note that she is very keen that the audit goes well to secure the client's position. You have heard a lot about Jason since moving to Easterness; he is a very prominent local businessman who has twice been President of the local Chamber of Commerce and was voted "Easterness Businessman of the Year" last year.

As part of your research during audit planning you learn that the company was involved in a pensions mis-selling scandal in the late 1990s and now faces significant penalties. You are therefore surprised when no provision is setup for these amounts. When you approach Jason he initially tells you that this is fine as he's already discussed it with Michelle. When you question him further Jason angrily replies "Look, I told you this was fine, I know you're new to here so I'm going to cut you a bit of slack! But, just remember that I can have Michelle fire you in an instant. People in Easterness care what I think – I can make sure you never work in this town again!"

Taken aback, you call Michelle that afternoon. She tells you not to worry as Jason has "a bit of a temper" and asks you to not say any more about this matter. This is because Connaught still owe W&R significant audit fees from the prior year and are hoping to gain lucrative consultancy work from the merger.

Required

(a) Justify why an auditor is required to be independent and assess the threats to independence within this scenario. **(12 marks)**

(b) Evaluate the decision of Jason not to disclose the mis-selling provision. Your answer should make specific reference to the stakeholders who may be impacted. **(9 marks)**

(c) Assess the argument that an internal code of conduct would have prevented this action within Connaught. **(4 marks)**

(Total 25 marks)

11 Klingman and Krug Ltd

You are an AIA accountant of several years' standing and have recently started to act as a non-executive director (NED) of Klingman and Krug Ltd. ('K&K') a soft-drinks manufacturer based in Wales.

The company is 75% owned by a range of local and national investors (neither of whom own more than 5% individually) and 25% by the Krug family. The CEO of the company is Sir Peter Krug and the Chairperson is his older sister Ellie Krug. You were appointed to the board at the request of the local investors, who want to ensure the views of the local community are fully represented on the board of this economically significant local company.

At the most recent board meeting Peter announced that K&K were going to be making all non-management staff redundant and then re-hiring them on zero hours contracts through an employment agency. This would significantly reduce staff wages and also free K&K from commitments to holiday pay and pensions. However, Peter did not confirm that the plan had been subject to legal scrutiny, even though the relevant employment law is complex and designed to protect the legitimate rights of employees.

The plan caused concern among the board. The meeting was the first time that the board had been informed of it, and no papers or discussion documents had been circulated in advance of the meeting. When one of your fellow NEDs asked that the plan be paused while a legal review was sought, Ellie informed the board that she and Peter had already agreed the plan and begun implementation, informing the board was "only a courtesy".

In anticipation of planned cost savings, Peter suggests a substantial increase in board member salaries and fees. However, you are aware that many people in the local area are reliant on the K&K factory for employment and any reduction in employee wages will be hard on the local community.

Peter also proposes a considerable new investment in developing and selling a new premium range of soft drinks for the adult market. Peter feels that this will lead to a significant increase in profitability and the value of the company.

With your knowledge of the drinks industry, a local entrepreneur Joanne Jones has approached you for assistance in setting up a local drinks manufacturer which will primarily concentrate on producing high quality tonic waters and adult soft drinks and will be a major competitor to K&K. Joanne has offered you a seat on the board of her company.

Required

(a) Critically analyse the behaviour of Peter and Ellie from both the view of pristine capitalists and socialists. **(6 marks)**

(b) Justify the importance of good corporate governance within an organisation and report on the current corporate governance issues within K&K. **(9 marks)**

(c) Evaluate the stakeholders impacted by Peter's recommendation, and how they could be impacted. **(5 marks)**

(d) Appraise Joanne's suggestion and recommend an appropriate course of action. **(5 marks)**

(Total 25 marks)

12 Kubrick and Co

Aaron Tang works in the finance department of Kubrick and Co ('Kubrick') a manufacturer of Personal Protective Equipment ('PPE'), based in South-East Asia. Due to increased requirements for PPE during the COVID pandemic, the company has expanded significantly and Aaron was hired six months ago to assist the Chief Financial Officer (CFO).

EXAM QUESTION BANK

While reviewing company records Aaron has found that the company buys raw rubber used in the production of PPE from a company owned by the sister of the CFO, David Lai. It appears that the rubber is purchased at a rate significantly above the current market value. Further inspection of this supply contract finds that the agreement was signed off by David himself.

Concerned, Aaron reviews further documents and finds that Kubrick is also paying for the school fees for the children of the CEO and has recently paid for expensive holidays and car rentals for both the CEO and the Chairman. All of this was signed off by David.

Aaron is naturally concerned about the situation, but doesn't want to cause too many problems in his new role. He has a young family and his wife is unable to work due to ill health. Losing his job would therefore cause significant hardship for both him and his family. He has approached you as a friend for advice on what to do.

Required

(a) Critically analyse the ethical issues described in the Kubrick case-study and recommend measures which could have prevented the unethical behaviour at Kubrick. **(12 marks)**

(b) Using the AAA model critically assess Aaron's situation and recommend a course of action for Aaron. **(10 marks)**

(c) Report on what is meant by the term 'situational influences'. You may wish to make reference to the situation faced by Aaron in your answer. **(3 marks)**

(Total 25 marks)

13 Surrey Systems

You are Sam, a recently qualified AIA accountant. After qualifying with a small, local accountancy firm you have recently moved to work as an audit senior in the London office for Forres and Castle LLP ('F&C'), a large multi-national accountancy firm with practices all over the world.

The first client you have been allocated is Surrey Systems Plc. ('Surrey'), a large, listed electronics manufacturer who make components for a number of uses including domestic appliances, aircraft components and weapons systems.

During routine audit testing you have found that Surrey supplies components used in weapons systems for countries with very poor human rights records. All legal permissions have been received for the exports. You are aware that one of the countries which receives supplies from Surrey recently carried out a missile attack on a neighbouring country, which resulted in severe civilian casualties. You and some of the audit team are somewhat concerned to act for a client of this nature.

With this concern you speak to the engagement partner for Surrey. She understands your concern but points out that Surrey is one of F&C's largest clients and that F&C's London office is largely reliant on Surrey for its continued operations. Losing this client would lead to a significant decrease in the staff employed by F&C in their London office and significant redundancies and layoffs. While she appreciates why you and some of your team may feel uncomfortable with the nature of the client, she points out that:

> "Look, I'm not massively comfortable myself but I've consulted with the client and our own legal team several times and what they're doing is entirely legal and above board. Us resigning from Surrey wouldn't achieve anything: they wouldn't stop what they were doing; they would just find another auditor and we would lose out. Face it, this is a difficult and complicated world, so let's just do the job and at least then some good can come of it".

Separately, you become aware of circumstances that took place around the Newcastle office of Surrey. As part of the audit fieldwork, two members of F&C staff, Helen and Niket, were sent to visit and conduct testing at Surrey's Newcastle branch. The work was scheduled to take from Wednesday to Friday and, due to the distance from London, required Helen and Niket to stay in a hotel. On the Friday morning Niket

contacted the engagement partner to inform her that the audit work had taken longer than expected and he and Helen would have to stay the weekend in Newcastle to complete the work.

One of your other team members has told you this morning that Helen and Niket are in a relationship and has shown you pictures from social media Helen posted of their "short vacation" in Newcastle, including pictures of them sightseeing and eating at expensive restaurants.

Required

(a) (i) From a teleological viewpoint, develop the argument that the fact that someone else would do the audit job anyway means that F&C should continue with the role. **(8 marks)**

(ii) By application of Kantian philosophy to the decision to continue with this client, evaluate the idea that an action can be wrong even if it is legal. **(5 marks)**

(b) Report on the potential issues with Surrey being such a large client for the F&C audit firm.
(5 marks)

(c) With reference to the IESBA code of ethics, evaluate the situation with Niket and Helen and suggest a course of action. **(7 marks)**

(Total 25 marks)

14 Rossberg

You work as a management accountant in the finance department of Rossberg Ltd. ('Rossberg'), a distributor and wholesaler of high-quality foods. Rossberg has distribution hubs throughout Europe and North America. The company was founded 130 years ago by Johann Rossberg and is still owned by the Rossberg family. The company has prided itself on its long history of both quality and customer service and has a very traditional attitude. The current CEO, Robert Rossberg, has very openly avoided written internal policies and guidelines, stating that "I only employ ladies and gentlemen of quality and I expect their word to be their bond. That is worth more than any written code. My employees are people who unfailingly show goodwill to customers, always tell the truth, never conceal wrongdoing, and never seek to further their own interests to the detriment of the company".

Charles Carli is the head of the Estonian division of the company. Although a small division, it has generally been fairly successful, and Charles has historically been one of the company's best salespeople. Preparing a report of recent financial performance, you found that the profitability and performance of the Estonian division has decreased substantially, and your team lead has asked you to investigate this.

Your investigations have found that Charles has actually founded a fine food import company in Estonia in direct competition to Rossberg. He had used the contacts and links he had made while managing Rossberg to gain both suppliers and customers and apparently was running his new business from the premises owned and paid for by Rossberg, using staff and facilities paid for by Rossberg, while drawing a salary from Rossberg.

Upon hearing this, Robert flew out to Estonia to meet with Charles and reported that Charles has now resigned from Rossberg, that no further action will be taken, and that the matter is now considered to be closed. Your colleague Wunmi has been very against this move and states that it is "clearly in the public interest that we take strong further action against Charles".

Required

(a) From both a legal perspective and from the perspective of virtue ethics, appraise the issues with Charles's actions. **(9 marks)**

(b) Develop the idea that a formal internal code of conduct would have prevented these issues.
(7 marks)

(c) Critically analyse why Rossberg may not wish to pursue this further, contrasting this with Wunmi's argument that it is in the public interest that Charles faces further action. **(9 marks)**

(Total 25 marks)

15 Ethics and whistleblowing

You are Michael, a newly qualified AIA accountant from the UK. Three months ago, you gained a job with a large London-headquartered oil company and were moved to one of their West African facilities. Recently married, you brought your wife, Maryanne, to live with you on the site.

Although you are currently based in West Africa, you are classed as a UK employee and are subject to UK employment law including the UK Public Interest Disclosure Act (1998).

The West African facility has on-site accommodation for overseas workers from a variety of countries, including you. The facility is one of the oil company's oldest sites and is regarded as something of a "legacy facility" by many in the company. Much of the equipment and facilities on the site are older and somewhat worn out and there are rumours among your colleagues that the site is coming to the end of its useful life. Nevertheless, you have heard from many colleagues that the site is regarded as a "proving ground" for young managers and that a good performance here could lead to a transfer to a far more prestigious posting in London or the United States. Your colleagues have also told you that the facility manager, Thomas Price, has noted your potential and has sent several good reports on your performance back to headquarters in London.

The facility is in a remote part of the country; as well as the overseas employees, it is by far the largest employer of local people and the company operates a medical clinic, subsidised shop and school for local people – whether they are employees or not. This is of great value to the local population as the nearest city is nearly a day's drive away and both facilities and opportunities in the immediate area are very limited. Public sector finances in the country are very stretched and they would not be able to provide these facilities from public funds, and the facility has a large impact upon the local community. You have heard several times that the local government are keen not to upset the oil company.

Although there are facilities such as a swimming pool and golf club for overseas staff living on site, Maryanne has found the atmosphere very claustrophobic and dislikes being away from her family and friends. She has openly been talking about how much she wants to move back to the UK at the first opportunity.

One day you are at work earlier than normal to complete some tasks when you overhear two of your colleagues, Sun and Alan, talking about the plant discharging waste into the local river considerably above safe levels. Apparently, the equipment is very much out of date, but you hear Alan say, "the government inspector only visits once a year, and he never checks anything; just plays a round of golf with Thomas then signs everything off".

Concerned about this, you speak to Thomas, who tells you he is aware of the issue but that there is no way the company would pay to have the equipment replaced so it would probably lead to the site being shut down. He then asks why you are so concerned, saying "if the government don't care, why do you?"

Required

(a) Evaluate the parties who would be impacted by your decision on whether to report the excess discharge. **(10 marks)**

(b) With reference to both utilitarian and egoism theories, recommend whether you should report the discharge of the waste. **(10 marks)**

(c) Develop the concept of whistleblowing in an accounting context and recommend the steps which would be required to whistleblow in this case. **(5 marks)**

(Total 25 marks)

16 Harrow

Harrow Plc. ('Harrow') is a large agricultural holding company with operations throughout the world. Although listed on the London Stock Exchange, the company is headquartered in the island of Jorlan, a small Caribbean nation considered by some to be a "tax haven". Harrow's business involves holding a large amount of agricultural land. Some of this land is farmed directly by Harrow while other parts are leased to tenants.

Recently an unexpected landslip in part of Harrow's property in the Southern African nation of Brambadar led to the discovery of a seam of rare earth minerals, which could raise a large amount of money due to their rarity. You are a junior board member and have thus been privy to initial discussions about this.

The first problem is that the land is currently tenanted to three families each farming a section of the land. While it could be legally difficult to terminate the lease, the lease agreement does allow for increases. The CEO therefore thinks the easiest way to resolve the situation is to institute extremely large rent increases with the aim of making the tenancy unaffordable to the families. The current tenants are unaware of the rare earth minerals and, even if they were, they would have no practical or legal ability to extract the minerals themselves.

Brambadar currently has a very high tax rate, and the CEO is looking to avoid paying this. He therefore has designed a solution where a Brambadarian subsidiary will be set up to carry out the actual mining operation, but the minerals will then be sold considerably below market value to the parent company in Jorlan, who will then sell them on. The tax arrangements mean that very little tax will be paid in either Jorlan or Brambadar upon selling these minerals. Lawyers in both Brambadar and Jorlan have confirmed that this arrangement is currently legal.

The discovery of the minerals has been noted by a number of mining companies and a large mining company, Sherbourne Plc., has offered you a role as a senior board member on a significantly higher salary than you currently enjoy. The CEO of Sherbourne has said that she expects you to bring your commercial knowledge of Harrow to your new role.

Required

(a) Using a range of ethical theories, critically analyse the ethical actions of the CEO of Harrow with regards to:

    (i)   The increases in the rent price. **(7 marks)**

    (iii)   The tax arrangements. **(5 marks)**

(b) Assess the organisational culture of Harrow and consider what impact this may have on the future of the organisation. **(8 marks)**

(c) With reference to the professional standards and responsibilities of accountants, evaluate the proposal of Sherbourne's CEO. **(5 marks)**

(Total 25 marks)

17 Grapeman Group

You are Sara. You have recently qualified with AIA and have moved to Moore & Wheetman LLP ('M&W'), a mid-sized audit registered firm with offices worldwide. You are currently based in the London office.

M&W's largest client is the Grapeman Group ('Grapeman') a large energy conglomerate which has a worldwide presence but is more concentrated in Northwest Europe and the Middle East. Due to the large size of the conglomerate, M&W have divided the audit of group companies among the staff members. You are working on the audit of Grapeman UK Ltd. based in London, and Grapeman UAE PY based in Dubai.

Your main colleague on these two companies is Michael, who has been qualified for two years. At the planning meeting, Michael has let you know privately that he has deliberately overbudgeted for time in Dubai but underbudgeted for time in London. He tells you that this means that the audit team will be able to take some time off in Dubai and make it a "mini-vacation". Michael tells you that M&W staff have done this the last few years and that everyone ignores it as a minor matter – he tells you that it doesn't really matter as "the same people pay the audit bill anyway, who cares what company the cost goes to?".

Yesterday you were working on the audit of Grapeman UK. As a UK registered company they are required to have certain environmental disclosures. From your review of the accounting records, you know that during the year a very large amount of money was spent repairing a malfunctioning chimney in an oil refinery in Eastern England. A crucial piece of equipment in the chimney had broken and the chimney was emitting dangerous gasses well above legal limits. In line with Grapeman's declared adoption of environmental reporting standards, any breaches of environmental regulations should be clearly and prominently disclosed within the annual report.

You are surprised, therefore, to see no mention of these dangerous emissions in the environmental report. Believing it to be a simple oversight, you go to speak to the CFO of Grapeman UK, Helena Chu. Helena tells you that she believes that, as the malfunctioning chimney was an accident rather than a deliberate policy, there is no need to disclose this in the financial statements. Helena is keen to point out that the policy of all Grapeman companies is to have the highest levels of environmental standards.

You attempt to question Helena about this further, but she quickly cuts you off and says that it is vital that Grapeman UK has no issues in the current year. The company is due to receive a large government grant which will build a carbon capture centre in an area of England with high unemployment. In particular, the plant will allow for the employment of a large number of local young people who will be trained in well-paid and skilled jobs. Helena asks if you want to jeopardise that opportunity for the young people and the area in general.

Helena finishes by saying that, if there is a delay in signing off the accounts, she will be forced to go straight to the leadpartner on the job – and mention your name specifically as having caused problems on the job.

Concerned, you go to speak to Michael, who says that it would be best just to leave this issue as "it's above our paygrade" and "is really the partner's problem". Arriving earlier than usual at the client premises today, you overhear Michael and Helena talking. It appears that Helena has offered Michael a well-paid role in Grapeman once the audit is complete and Michael is keen to take this.

Required

(a) With reference to the principles set out in the IESBA code of ethics, evaluate the issue with the plan to change the billing allocations. **(6 marks)**

(b) Report on the specific issues and ethical threats facing you in your decision regarding the report of the breach. **(7 marks)**

(c) Using a range of ethical theories, critically analyse Helena's view that not reporting the environmental breach is the best outcome. **(8 marks)**

(d) Report on the ethical concerns which may arise from Michael going to work at an audit client. **(4 marks)**

(Total 25 marks)

18 Dragon

You are working for the local government office in the small city of Port Martha in Western England. You work in the finance function of the local government and your boss is the finance manager for the city, Sue Alliston. Your financial reports primarily go to the City Council.

You were very happy to get this job since, although the pay is not very high, it has allowed you to move back to Port Martha, where you grew up. Your father still lives in Port Martha and is currently very ill. Moving to Port Martha has allowed you to look after him yourself and spend more time with him during his illness. Although you could get a higher-paid job in the nearest large city of Manderton, this would be a three-hour drive and it would be very difficult to manage your father's care with this. Sue has been very understanding of your current situation and has allowed you time off to deal with your caring responsibilities and to work from home at times to help with your father's care.

Recently, a company called Dragon Technologies Ltd. ('Dragon') has set up a factory in the town. This has been a great benefit to the employment of the city and has also brought in considerable tax revenues to the local government. As such, the City Council are very keen that Dragon maintain their presence within the city.

You recently received a batch of payment receipts for road repairs and upgrades, which you were due to process. While processing you noted that many of the invoices have had details deliberately covered with black ink. Confused by this you ask Sue, who tells you that the work actually relates to private land on the Dragon factory site rather than public roads. This is against public spending rules, but the councillors feel that it is a small price to pay to keep Dragon happy. The councillors have therefore opted to disguise these roadworks as general council expenditure. As Dragon is by far the largest employer in the local area and contributes heavily to the city through paying taxes, the councillors feel that although disguising the expenditure in this way is against the rules it is of benefit to the city and its inhabitants.

Separately, an old school friend, John Zuma, has offered you work doing management accounting for his businesses in town. John has a range of small business in the local area including garages, restaurants and rental properties. Your current employment contract with Port Martha City Council would not exclude you from undertaking this role, but you are worried that you wouldn't have enough time to properly dedicate to the role. However, the money would come in very useful with your father being so ill.

Required

(a) With reference to stakeholder theory and transparency, evaluate the decision of the city councillors to pay for this private work. **(10 marks)**

(b) With specific reference to the current situation:

    (i) With reference to this particular scenario, report on what is meant by whistleblowing from an accounting point of view. **(3 marks)**

    (ii) Evaluate the specific issues in the scenario and the impact on you in making the decision whether or not to whistle blow. **(6 marks)**

(c) With reference to the IESBA code, critically analyse whether you should undertake doing this work for John. **(6 marks)**

(Total 25 marks)

19 Lars

Tove-Holland AG (TH) is a large, listed company operating in the mining and engineering sector in the country of Oleland. With a large number of employees they decided 55 years ago to setup a pension fund to provide for retired employees. The pension fund is a separate entity governed by trustees who are appointed by TH management, trade union representatives and retired employees. Due to recent changes in legislation the pension fund is undergoing its first external audit.

For many years the pension fund has been managed by Lars Nielsen, an independent fund manager. Lars has been a well-respected figure in the local investing and fund managing community for many years. He is particularly well noted for giving many young fund managers their first employment opportunity, especially those from more deprived backgrounds. Lars and his wife have raised large amounts of money for charity in recent years and Lars received a Royal Award two years ago for his efforts in charity fundraising.

Lars is principally paid based on the performance of the fund. Recent correspondence shows that the trustees were constantly pressuring Lars to obtain higher returns and, in several cases, threatened to move advisor if these returns were not obtained.

Initial audit work found that the model used by Lars to value the TH pension fund had been modified by Lars to be more optimistic than standard pension fund models. This appears to suggest that the assets are recognised at considerably higher than their fair value. The auditor is unsure how to react to this situation and have not yet signed the audit report.

While on a recent vacation Lars remarked to his wife that "It's funny, the longer I've been in business the more I've realised that you can't always do the right thing. – sometimes you have to think of the best outcome. Have I ever told a white lie to a client to keep work? Sure, but if nobody's really hurt and I can help those that need it, what's the harm?"

Required

(a) Evaluate which parties may have been impacted by the asset valuation issue and how. **(8 marks)**

(b) Critically analyse how Lars' actions shows the difference between individual and situational ethics. **(5 marks)**

(c) Report on the Kohlberg model of ethical levels and which level you think Lars operates at. **(8 marks)**

(d) Critically evaluate the proposition that the pension scheme trustees are partially responsible for the outcome in this instance. **(4 marks)**

(Total 25 marks)

20 Kilmar & Clark

You are Sam Patel, an AIA of many years standing. After a successful career in practice, you retired as a partner in a major firm last year and have embarked on a number of other opportunities such as consulting.

You have recently accepted a role as a Non-Executive Director (NED) on the board of Kilmar & Clark Plc ('K&C'), a large chemical manufacturing company. The company itself is a product of several mergers and has a complicated accounting and reporting system for that reason.

Before a recent board meeting, you requested financial information to back up the information within the board report. The Chief Financial Officer (CFO), Leslie Montieth, informed you that this information was not currently available due to issues with the reporting system. When you asked about this further Leslie stated clearly:

"Look, stop causing problems here. You know we're trying our best and nit-picking from some retired accountant isn't going to help anyone. There's no room on the board for people who cause problems".

Separately, the board has become aware that a number of employees at two plants are in the habit of clocking in for work on Saturdays but then immediately leaving to go to a local sports club or pub. An informal arrangement is in place that, if any emergency happens, they will be phoned to let them know of the issue.

This arrangement has been in place for many years and originated as a way of giving a bonus to staff when government tax rules made this difficult. This is against both tax rules and K&C policies, which explicitly state that all working staff should remain on site. Management have, however, previously ignored this behaviour to ensure good relations with staff. K&C now wish to stop this practice but have concerns over the best way to do this.

Required

(a) Accountants often act as non-executive directors. With specific reference to K&C and your own professional background, evaluate the ethical qualities which an accountant could bring to the role of non-executive director. **(10 marks)**

(b) Following your discussion with Leslie and with reference to professional standards, evaluate your position on the board of K&C. **(6 marks)**

(c) Report on the effectiveness of K&C's internal policies with regards to the staff leaving early. Your answer should contrast the different roles of internal policies and external law. **(9 marks)**

(Total 25 marks)

Exam answer bank

EXAM ANSWER BANK

1 Chemico PLC

This question aims to address 'explain different ethical theories and apply them to practical aspects of business and accounting decision-making' (LO1) AND 'apply appropriate and relevant ethical guidance and standards' (LO3).

Learning Outcomes: LO1 and LO3

(a) **Utilitarian perspective**

From a utilitarian perspective, the ultimate justifying reason for an action is that the action brings about more good for more people than it does harm. Utilitarianism gives priority to concern for everybody's good, including the individual's, which is factored into the total overall good. If self-interest conflicts with the overall good, self-interest is set aside. Thus, utilitarianism recommends actions that bring about the greatest good for the greatest number of people.

In the case of the CEO, Robert Goodall, he is keen to go ahead with the relocation of the manufacturing plant to Zarica. His motives are to make his mark on the company by increasing profits and the relocation of the plant will provide lower-cost labour, easier connection with the growing market in emerging countries, and reduce costs of transacting business in these Zarican counties. This will certainly be likely to increase profits, but it will also lead to job losses in the Romanian town where production currently takes place and have an associated knock-on effect in the local community in the Romanian town. Robert Goodall has also not fully considered the risks of this relocation, based on the experiences of AllChem, where a similar decision led to deaths and injuries which cost AllChem millions in terms of fines and loss of reputation. You feel that further investigation into the risks of this relocation is required in light of the experience of AllChem that resulted in deaths and injuries and subsequent loss of reputation and significant financial loss, which would allow an assessment into whether the actions brings more good for more people than it does harm. To be ethical under a utilitarian perspective, therefore, you may have to set aside your self-interest by challenging the CEO's opinion at the risk of losing your job. Robert Goodall's view may benefit the company in terms of profitability and may enhance his own reputation, but it also carries risks not only to Chemico in terms of potential fines and reputation, and also to the Romanian town (in terms of job losses and the economic prosperity of the community), but also to the potential Zarican workforce and communities based on the experiences of AllChem. Therefore from a utilitarian perspective, to fulfil his moral obligations, Robert Goodall should set aside self-interest (making his mark by increasing profit) and ensure the risks related to the Zarican relocation are fully explored and if they can't be mitigated to the greater good of more people than in does harm, then morally the relocation should not go ahead.

Kantian Perspective

If we say that we should be ethical in business because it accomplishes what we want, then we are saying it is prudent to be ethical. But that gives us only a hypothetical imperative, which to Kant is not an ethical imperative. Thus, for Kant, if we are being ethical because it's good business, we don't have the proper ethical concern.

According to Kant, therefore, if we're doing something simply to fulfil a desire, we are not acting out of a moral motive. It follows, then, that if we are doing the right things in business simply because it will improve business, we may not be doing anything wrong, but we are certainly not acting from an ethical motive. To act morally, we do something simply because it is the moral thing to do. It is our duty, a categorical imperative to do "X." This insight is usually expressed by those who say, "It's the right thing to do." But doing "X" because it is our duty is not very informative. What is our duty? Kant presents several formulas for the categorical imperative to help us decide. We will look at two of them:

- Act so that you can 'will' the maxim of your action to become a universal law.

    A maxim is your reason for acting. In the case of Robert Goodall, he is acting in self-interest to increase his reputation by putting profitability before the potential risks of harm to the Romanian town in terms of job losses and impacts on the community and the potential harm to future Zarican workers and their community. In your case, if you don't challenge the CEOs opinion to keep your job, you are acting in self-interest. By applying the universal law test, if everyone universally acted in terms of self-interest in business despite the consequences, it would reduce trust in business and create greater risks to communities and the environment in which each business operates. This could have serious consequences for the businesses as well as society and the environment.

- Act so as never to treat another rational being merely as a means.

    Under this view, everyone is morally equal and ought to be treated with respect and dignity. Everyone's rights ought to be respected; no one ought to be used merely as a means or instrument to bring about consequences that benefit the user. In this case, Robert Goodall is treating the Zarican relocation as a means to making his mark by increasing profitability of Chemico despite the risks involved.

    From the above critical analysis, It can therefore be seen that under Utilitarian and Kantian perspectives, Robert Goodall is not acting morally and if you don't speak up and challenge his opinion for fear of losing your job, neither are you.

(b) A distinguishing mark of the accountancy profession is its acceptance of the responsibility to act in the public interest. A professional accountant's responsibility is not exclusively to satisfy the needs of an individual client or employing organisation. Directors have a fiduciary duty to their shareholders to safeguard the company by appropriate risk management and to avoid reckless pursuit of profit or market dominance. While the project will likely lead to higher short term profitability, the longer term damage to the company reputation due to the risks involved and impacts on other key stakeholders could significantly impact the company sustainability. You should consider the implications of not raising your concerns about the project on the public interest.

You appear unhappy with the performance of the chairman and the lack of independence between the chairman and the CEO. Good governance practice should ensure that effective decision-making takes place, which requires robust debate and challenge to ensure all aspects of a decision are adequately addressed. This does not appear to be happening in Chemico. You should consider raising your concerns with senior independent directors. The annual board appraisal process will also provide you with the opportunity to raise your concerns you may have regarding the manner in which the board is run.

If the board decides to go ahead with the project without further due diligence you should ensure the reservations are minuted and consider your position in the company if the board decides to go ahead with the project.

Regarding the IFAC fundamental principles:

Integrity – can you allow the proposed project to go ahead without raising your concerns and asking for additional time to consider the project in more detail?

Objectivity – you are fairly new to the company. Whilst you are obviously pleased to get the role you must ensure that you properly challenge the board as and when necessary.

Professional behaviour – can you satisfy the criteria as to why you were appointed to this role if you do not voice your concerns and encourage the board to have a full and proper debate and advocate that all board members are given sufficient time to properly assess the information?

Threat	Safeguard
Overfamiliarity between CEO and Chairman is compromising the independence of the board. Non-executive directors (NEDs) are appointed by shareholders in order to represent their interests on company boards. The primary fiduciary duty that NEDs owe is, therefore, to the company's shareholders. This means that they mustn't allow themselves to be captured or unduly influenced by the vested interests of other members of the company such as executive directors, trade unions or middle management. In this scenario, the chairman is perceived to be unduly influenced by the CEO.	Recruitment processes should be put in place to ensure all board appointments do not compromise the independence between executive and non-executive directors. Therefore, recruitment processes should be in place to highlight prior relationships with board members that may compromise this independence.
Directors have a duty to keep themselves informed about the matters put before them for decision-making. It's not possible to comply with this duty unless they have relevant briefing material upon which to base decisions. In this scenario, board papers were only received the day before the board meeting and contained 500 pages of information to absorb making it difficult for directors to meet their duties.	The Company secretary should ensure that all board papers are issued on a timely basis to ensure the directors have a chance to absorb the information. This information should clearly and concisely present all key information and facts and indicate any actions required. Board papers that don't include all the necessary information in a form which is easy to read and understand can result in poor decision making.

Additional areas where credit might be given, note this is not an exhaustive list:

- Specific real-life examples that demonstrate points made

2 Chocco

This subject is taken from 'Demonstrate awareness and application of ethical guidance and Standards' (LO3) AND 'Critically evaluate alternative courses of action and make choices consistent with ethical professional behaviour' (LO4).

Learning Outcomes: LO3 and LO4

This question focuses on demonstrating an awareness of the relevant ethical guidance and standards for auditors. Students are also required to identify threats and safeguards in an audit environment, and make recommendations consistent with ethical and professional standards.

(a) **Professional behaviour**: Auditors should ensure that the company they are auditing is complying with relevant laws and regulations and ensure they and the company avoid any action that discredits the profession, eg **auditors should inform management where they discover non-compliance with relevant laws and regulations and require that the matter be resolved to ensure compliance with the law. If management fails to do this the auditor must consider their position as acting as auditor and consider whether further action is required in the public interest.**

Professional competence and due care: Auditors have a continuing duty to maintain professional knowledge and skill at a level required to ensure that a client receives competent professional

service based on current developments in practice, legislation and techniques. Members should act diligently and in accordance with applicable technical and professional standards when providing professional services, eg **auditors should attain and maintain professional knowledge and skill at the level required to ensure that a client receives competent professional service, based on current technical and professional standards and relevant legislation. Auditors should act diligently and in accordance with applicable technical and professional standards.**

Objectivity: Auditors should not allow bias, conflicts of interest or undue influence of others to override professional or business judgements, eg **relationships that bias or unduly influence professional judgement should be avoided (students may offer specific examples of such relationships** such as having a professional interest in the firm auditing, over-reliance on audit fees, over-familiarity with clients).

Confidentiality: Auditors should respect the confidentiality of information acquired as a result of professional and business relationships and should not disclose any such information to third parties without proper and specific authority or unless there is a legal or professional right or duty to disclose. Confidential information acquired as a result of professional and business relationships should not be used for the personal advantage of members or third parties, eg **auditors should avoid conflicts of interest that may breach confidentiality such as advising two clients at the same time who are competing to acquire the same company or who are in legal dispute with each other. Similarly, maintaining confidentiality means avoiding inadvertent disclosure as much as intentional disclosure (IESBA *Code*: para. R114.1). For instance, information must not be disclosed unintentionally when socialising. The *Code* also notes that the duty of confidentiality continues even after the end of the relationship with the client (IESBA *Code*: para. R114.2).**

(b) **Key answer tips**

Part (i) of this question is a typical ethics requirement. In order to score well, you must identify the threat by name and discuss how it is a threat to independence/objectivity or name the fundamental principle that is threatened. You should suggest for part (ii) the most practical safeguard to manage the situation. Note that withdrawing from the engagement should only be suggested when no other safeguards can reduce the threat to an acceptable level. Use the tabular approach shown in the model answer to structure your answer.

Threat (i)	Safeguards (ii)
Acting as auditors for 15 years	
Acting for a client for 15 years increases the risk of familiarity threat to objectivity. If, at any point, the relationship between auditor and client crosses professional boundaries then the objectivity of the auditor must be questioned.	The engagement partner should carry out an ongoing review of any matters that may affect the integrity, objectivity or independence of themselves and their staff and document the results of their ongoing review.
The auditor may become too trusting of, and reliant upon, written representations rather than more reliable forms of evidence.	Senior staff should be periodically rotated to bring in new, independent staff.

Threat (i)	Safeguards (ii)
Former employee As the FD is a former employee of the audit firm a familiarity threat arises. The audit team may be too trusting of Jilly's ability given her seniority within the audit firm before leaving. The team may not exercise sufficient professional scepticism when performing the audit and assessing Sabbir's judgements.	The composition of the audit team needs to be considered and any team members that may be friendly with Jilly or have worked closely with her in the past should be removed from the team.
Intimidation The attitude of the FD appears to raise concerns of intimidation as well as creating practical issues for the audit. The auditor may feel that they cannot disturb the FD for information which may mean sufficient appropriate evidence is not obtained to form the basis of the audit opinion.	The audit manager should discuss with the FD whether the audit senior can also request information or if information can be emailed through to the manager at the end of each day to prevent such delays occurring.
Provision of non-audit services The provision of non-audit services to an external audit client can create a self-review threat. The non-audit work would be evaluated by the external audit team who may assume that the internal audit work is competently performed and sufficient to rely on without properly testing it to confirm this is the case.	Provision of non-audit services to audit clients is not prohibited by the Code of ethics provided the threats are not significant and effective safeguards can be applied. As Chocco Co. is not listed, separate teams should be used for each service to reduce any threats to an acceptable level.
For listed clients, fees from recurring services should be monitored and not allowed to exceed 15% of the firm's total fee income. The FRC Ethical Standard suggests that 15% would be appropriate in the case of a non-listed client. This should be monitored to ensure this limit is not exceeded. An independent partner could be brought in to ensure that objectivity has not been impaired.	
Tax Advice Work If the firm were to accept the engagement to assist Chocco Co in challenging the tax authority a self-review threat could be created. If the outcome of the challenge or advisory work has a material impact on the financial statements, the audit team may be reluctant to identify any misstatements in the amounts included.	Separate teams should be used for the audit work and tax engagements, with separate reporting lines. Independent partner review of audit work relating to taxation.

EXAM ANSWER BANK

Threat (i)	Safeguards (ii)
Tax Challenge The tax work may also create an advocacy threat. Assisting with the challenge could be seen as promoting the position of the client.	If Chocco requires the firm to act on its behalf/represent Chocco during the challenge the engagement should be declined as no safeguard could reduce the threat to an acceptable level.

(c) ISA 240 *The Auditor's Responsibilities Relating to Fraud in an Audit of Financial Statements* describes the responsibilities of both management and the auditor with regard to preventing and detecting fraud.

The primary responsibility for the prevention and detection of fraud rests with those charged with governance and management as they are responsible for running the company on a day to day basis in an effective manner.

They must place a strong emphasis on fraud prevention and reduce the opportunities for this to take place. This involves a commitment to creating a culture of honesty and ethical behaviour and the implementation and maintenance of strong internal controls.

An auditor has a responsibility to obtain reasonable assurance that the financial statements taken as a whole are free from material misstatement, whether caused by fraud or error.

In order to satisfy this responsibility an auditor must carefully consider the risk of fraud when planning an audit. This includes assessing and testing systems of internal control to identify opportunities for fraud to take place. In response to this risk assessment the auditor then designs appropriate audit procedures to gather evidence to be able to conclude upon the financial statements.

Auditors must always remain professionally sceptical throughout the audit, considering the potential for management override of controls and recognising the fact that audit procedures that are effective for detecting error may not be effective for detecting fraud.

Overall, the risk of non-detection of fraud is higher than that of detecting error because of the likelihood of sophisticated fraud mechanisms and the inherent limitations of audit procedures. To this end the auditor is considered to have only a secondary responsibility when it comes to detecting fraud.

> **Additional areas where credit might be given, note this is not an exhaustive list:**
> - Reference to specific areas of the IESBA *Code*
> - Real life examples

3 Racer

This subject is taken from 'The Professional Accountant' (LO2) and 'critically evaluate alternative courses of action and make choices consistent with ethical professional behaviour' (LO4).

Learning Outcomes: LO2 and LO4

This question focuses on the identification and analysis of the ethical dimensions that arise in connection with aspects of business and public duty, specifically whistleblowing. The question also requires students to consider the role of auditors in terms of ethical breaches, public duty, and disclosure.

(a) Whistleblowing means informing the proper authorities of some significant breach of law or regulation.

In the context of business ethics, whistle blowing is the practice in which employees who know that their company or a colleague is engaged in activities that:

(1) Cause unnecessary harm;
(2) Violate human rights;
(3) Are illegal;
(4) Run counter to the defined purpose of the institution or the profession; or
(5) Are otherwise immoral.

Whistleblowers inform superiors, professional organisations, the public, or some governmental agency of those activities.

When faced with significant ethical issues, accounting practitioners such as Jonathan should follow the established policies of the organisation bearing on the resolution of such conflict.

Except in special circumstances, the whistle blower should exhaust all internal channels before informing the public. In this case Jonathan is not aware of any such policies so he should establish firstly if such a policy exists and if so, should follow it.

If no such policies exist Jonathan should consider the following courses of action:

- Discuss such problems with the immediate superior, except when it appears that the superior is involved, in which case the problem should be presented initially to the next higher managerial level. If a satisfactory resolution cannot be achieved when the problem is initially presented, submit the issues to the next higher managerial level. Except where legally prescribed, communication of such problems to authorities or individuals not employed or engaged by Racer is not considered appropriate. Jonathan has discussed this matter with his immediate superior, the Chief Executive and the matter has not been resolved. He should now consider raising this issue with the Chairman of Racer.

- Clarify relevant ethical issues by confidential discussion with an objective advisor (eg AIA, IFAC) to obtain a better understanding of possible courses of action.

- Consult with a legal representative as to legal obligations and rights concerning the ethical conflict.

- If the ethical conflict still exists after exhausting all levels of internal review, there may be no other recourse on significant matters than to resign from Racer and to submit an informative memorandum to an appropriate representative of the organisation. After resignation, depending on the nature of the ethical conflict, it may also be appropriate to notify other parties.

However, it is an issue for employees like Jonathan, who are dependent on their employment, who feel compelled to tell the proper authorities of some wrongdoing by their employers, but fear being dismissed if they do. In this case Jonathan is protected under the Enterprise and Regulatory Reform Act 2013.

Legal Protections under the Enterprise and Regulatory Reform Act 2013 are available if reports are made:

- In the public interest
- To the proper authority
- Without malice

The key issue here is the 'public interest' test – the whistle blower must 'reasonably believe that their disclosure is in the public interest'. What constitutes the public interest is not defined in legislation, however it would cover things like:

- Criminal offences
- Threats to public safety
- Environmental threats
- Terrorist activity

In this case, damage to human health and the environment is a matter of public interest and Jonathan has no malicious intent. In addition, there is a legal breach of the Clean Air Act.

A professional should not allow unprofessional acts to bring shame on the profession, and therefore there may be a time when he or she is obliged to set aside loyalty to a fellow practitioner or company and blow the whistle. Employees of companies, who are also members of professional accountancy bodies, may be required by their ethical code, particularly the aspects relating to integrity and objectivity, to make reports.

Reports to an outside body such as a regulatory authority, by professional accountants such as Jonathan, can be defended against any accusation of breaching client confidentiality, as the matter would be in the public interest.

Additional issues for auditors would be:

If auditors become aware of a significant non-compliance with the law and the potential impact on human health and on the environment regarding the emissions testing, they should report it to the directors in the first instance, with a recommendation that it be disclosed to the proper authority.

If the directors don't do that then the auditors should report it, relying on the public interest defence to guard them from accusations of breach of client confidence.

Breaches of law or regulation may have an impact on the financial statements and the auditors should assess what the effect might be and the disclosures that may be required.

This may have an influence on their audit report if suitable disclosures are not made in the financial statements.

In the case of Racer, the auditors would need to assess the likely financial implications of recalling the vehicles and correcting the emission breaches. The likelihood of any legal proceeding would also need to be assessed from car owners and others impacted by the emissions breach. The auditors may need to consult with lawyers to assist in determining the likelihood of any lawsuits and their chance of success to determine the disclosure requirements regarding liabilities and their impact on the financial statements. Consideration should also be given to the potential damage to reputation and loss of customers which will also impact the value of the company and its future prospects.

Once these investigations have taken place, the auditors have to consider their obligations under ISA 570 – Going Concern. While Racers Board of Directors have the prime responsibility for determining the appropriateness of preparing financial statements using the going concern basis, the auditor's responsibility is to satisfy themselves that the use of the going concern basis by the company is appropriate and its use has been adequately addressed in the financial statements. The definition of ISA 570 refers to a material uncertainty where this is defined in terms of the 'magnitude of its potential impact and likelihood of occurrence 'of an event or condition such that the financial statements would not give a fair representation or be misleading'. The emission issue would be a material uncertainty.

> **Additional areas where credit might be given, note this is not an exhaustive list:**
> - Discussion and application of relevant case law
> - Specific real life examples

4 Albian

This subject is taken from 'Governance and Self-Regulation' (LO4) and 'Codes, Guidance and Standards' (LO3).

Learning Outcomes: LO3 and LO4

(a) Corporate Governance is the means by which a company is operated and controlled. The aim of corporate governance initiatives is to ensure that companies are well run in the interest of their shareholders and the wider community. In response to major accounting scandals (eg Enron), regulators sought to change the rules surrounding the governance of companies, particularly publicly owned ones. In the US The Sarbanes Oxley Act (2002) introduced a set of rigorous corporate governance laws and at the same time the UK Corporate Governance Code introduced a set of best practice corporate governance initiatives in the UK.

(b) An audit committee's main functions are:

- To monitor the integrity of the financial statements of the company, and any formal announcements relating to the company's financial performance, reviewing significant financial reporting judgements contained in them

- To review the company's internal financial controls, and (unless otherwise addressed) review the company's internal control and risk management systems

- To monitor and review the effectiveness of the company's internal audit function

- To make recommendations to the board, for it to put to the shareholders, in relation to the appointment, re-appointment and removal of the external auditor; and to approve the remuneration and terms of engagement of the external auditor

- To review and monitor the external auditor's independence and objectivity and the effectiveness of the audit process, taking into account relevant UK professional and regulatory requirements

- To develop and implement policy on the engagement of the external auditor to supply non-audit services

(c) Benefits of audit committee for Albian Ltd

Appointing an audit committee will benefit Albian in the following ways:

- The finance director will benefit in that he will be able to raise concerns and discuss accounting issues with the audit committee.

- An audit committee will facilitate better communication between the directors, external audit and management.

- It will strengthen the independence of external audit as their appointment will now not be made by the board

- An audit committee will provide actionable insights to oversee and improve financial practices and reporting. This will help to improve the quality of the financial reporting of Albian; whilst the company already has a finance director, the audit committee will assist by reviewing the financial statements.

- The establishment of an audit committee can help to improve the internal control environment of the company. The audit committee is able to devote more time and attention to areas such as internal controls.

- If Albian has an internal audit (IA) department, then establishing an audit committee will also improve the independence of IA.

- The audit committee can also provide advice on risk management to the executive directors. They can create a climate of discipline and control and reduce the opportunity for fraud, as was alluded to in the scenario and increase public confidence in the credibility and objectivity of the financial statements.

- The audit committee will assume responsibility for appointing and liaising with the external audit firm, thus ensuring the independence of the external auditor especially in cases of dispute with management.

- An audit committee will ensure that corporate governance requirements are brought to attention of the board so current issues re independence of the non-executive directors and lack of timely board information will be raised.

(d) **Advantages**

- Moade Nasir already has experience of being a NED for another company and he has sat on an audit committee, hence he will be familiar with what the role entails and will be able to bring experience of being a NED to Albian. In addition, he has indicated he is agreeable to being paid a fixed fee which is not profit related; this is important as an independent NED's remuneration should be unrelated to the performance of the company.

- Joanna James is currently a finance director and so she possesses recent and relevant financial experience which is required for at least one member of the audit committee. In addition, she operates in the retail industry and so would be aware of key issues facing companies like Albian and so would have an appropriate mix of experience and knowledge.

Disadvantages

- Appointing Moade Nasir as a NED has disadvantages as he works for an investment company and so would not have relevant experience of companies such as Albian; hence he could lack the critical skills and relevant experience needed to provide meaningful advice to the executive directors. In addition, he is already an executive director for a large multinational company and a NED for another large company; it might be difficult for him to devote sufficient time to his role at Albian.

- Joanna James is the sister of the chief executive and therefore she is not an independent NED. She might be inclined to agree with the chief executive as she is his sister rather than providing the level of objective judgement required from a NED. Also, she wants a contract as a NED for a period of eight years; all directors including NEDs must be subject to re-election at regular intervals not exceeding three years.

> **Additional areas where credit might be given, note this is not an exhaustive list:**
> - Specific real-life examples

EXAM ANSWER BANK

5 Gonzales

This question aims to address 'explain different ethical theories and apply them to practical aspects of business and accounting decision-making' (LO1) AND 'apply appropriate and relevant ethical guidance and standards' (LO3).

Learning outcomes: LO1 and LO3

(a) **Chapter 1 – section 2**

From a cognitive point of view this action is clearly wrong Rezastan is in essence engaged in modern slavery and Gonzales would essentially be supporting them through their actions Rezastan is the subject of UN sanctions and supporting them would be clearly wrong. It also appears that Rezastan wants to use the long and established history of Gonzales to improve their reputation on the world stage.

This aligns with an absolutist point of view that an action is either right or wrong, therefore from a cognitive point of view this contract is clearly wrong and should not be undertaken.

From a non-cognitive point of view, however, the answer is much more complex. Peter clearly has a great deal of concern for the company and were this contract not to go ahead it is likely that the company would collapse. While this certainly would have an impact on the company itself the impact on wider stakeholders would also be considerable. Many people would lose their jobs especially in deprived communities as well as there being a considerable impact on communities supported by the charitable trust. Not accepting this contract is therefore far from free from consequences.

It also appears that if Gonzales did not accept this contract then one of their competitors would this suggests that Gonzales could have no impact on these human rights abuses, therefore why should they not accept the contract if it protects the jobs and has no impact on the human rights.

A non-cognitive view is therefore not as clear, and it largely depends on whether there is a feeling that a company should carry out this contract for the benefit of their staff and communities even in the knowledge that it means involvement with human rights abuses.

(b) **Chapter 3 – section 2**

This clearly links in with the IASB principle of professional competence and due care it is clear that you have neither the required knowledge nor experience to adequately carry out this tax return.

The principle of professional competence and due care outlines that accountants are required to act with a reasonable level of skill and competence in carrying out their role. In this case you have no experience of carrying out corporate tax work or knowledge so you should not carry out work of this nature. This applies to accountants in all roles, those working in industry and those in practice.

Furthermore, the fact that this work was previously carried out by an external accounting firm suggests that the required level of skill and experience does not exist within Gonzales.

You are, however, under a considerable amount of pressure from your immediate manager to carry out this work due to cost pressures within the organisation. You therefore face the dilemma between meeting your employer's expectations or complying with the IASB code.

The fact that you have no experience in this area suggests you would not be able to carry out the work to the required standard and there would be likely to be mistakes, thus costing your employer in the longer run and suggesting that this would be a false economy. Your first course of action would therefore be to explain this to your manager, you could also suggest that you could undertake this work with the accountant to improve your knowledge and potentially take over in coming years.

Were your manager to not accept this it would be appropriate to contact AIA to seek advice as to how you could protect your position and comply with your professional obligations.

(c) **Chapter 3 – section 1**

It is certainly true that all professional accountants are bound by codes of conduct regardless of the organisation which they work for it could be argued therefore that there is no need for a specific code of conduct.

Each organisation, however, is unique and it is unlikely that an overall code of conduct would reasonably be able to apply to every organisation each organisation therefore requires its own code of conduct to deal with the specific issues that that organisation may face in its particular industry, economy etc. It is therefore required that every organisation has a code of conduct and ethics dealing with the specific concerns it may face.

Gonzales feels that it already has an appropriate policy in place, although it is unwritten, this is, unfortunately unlikely to be sufficient. The whole point of such a policy is not to deal with the areas that everyone knows well, but communicate the areas that have ambiguity or which are not clear.

Ultimately every organisation has certain values and principles that it aims to comply with a code of ethics and conduct is the way in which the organisation communicates to its staff the way in which they should act and behave, without this being written and communicated it is unclear how the employees of an organisation would be able to understand and comply with the way in which they were expected to act.

A company-specific code of conduct is therefore necessary as professional codes for accountants will not be able to deal with the specific nature of the organisation. Similarly an unwritten code will be unable to communicate to staff the expectations and values of the organisation.

> **Additional areas where credit might be given, note this is not an exhaustive list:**
> - Specific real-life examples of these situations
> - Clear alternative routes and suggestions
> - Reference to specific sections of relevant professional codes

6 Merkland and Miah LLP

This question aims to address 'The Professional Accountant' (LO2) and 'critically evaluate alternative courses of action and make choices consistent with ethical professional behaviour' (LO4).

Learning Outcomes: LO2 and LO4

(a) **Chapter 5 – section 2, Chapter 7 – section 1**

Stratton appear to have recognised income in this way in order to encourage profitability growth. Stratton are currently in the process of planning a listing and it appears as if strong profitability would greatly aid the listing. While it is clear that individual directors would like the company to be highly profitable (and would likely receive remuneration on this fact) the issues may be more engrained within the company as many members of staff would likely receive high benefits in the case of a successful listing as a result of their share options.

Therefore although the directors may themselves benefit it is possible that the directors and those involved in the financial reporting process may also feel strongly about their staff and wish to benefit them. Their motives, therefore, might not be entirely selfish.

In this particular case Stratton have forward recognised revenue in direct contravention of accounting standards, while this is a particular issue within Stratton we must also consider what would happen if other companies acted in this way.

Were it to become widespread practice to ignore accounting standards most companies would make the decision to prepare financial statements in a manner which would benefit them the most even companies which initially aimed to act in a fair manner would be impacted by their competitors acting in an unfair manner and would be pressurised by investors to likewise disregard accounting standards. If some companies, therefore acted without regard to accounting standards would quickly lead to a "race to the bottom" in terms of compliance.

If companies didn't follow accounting standards it would very quickly become difficult to compare company financial statements and thus determine the true financial position of a company. It is thus important that companies maintain compliance with financial reporting standards.

(b) **Chapter 3 – section 4**

The role of an auditor is to provide an independent third parties opinion on the truth and fairness of the financial statements. A fundamental part of this is, therefore that the auditor is actually independent.

While the directors are responsible from preparing the financial statements many other parties rely on them. The directors could also have an incentive to manipulate financial statements to make the company appearing to be performing better than it actually was and thus benefit themselves. How therefore are users of the financial statements able to rely on them?

An audit solves this problem by having an independent third party review the financial statements this ensures that the users are not just relying on the directors but also have another party involved.

Were the auditor to not be independent and to be close to the directors or other interested parties this situation would not be solved as the users would essentially be relying on this party. It is thus of vital importance that the auditors are independent from the company being audited.

(c) **Chapter 3 – section 4**

There are a considerable number of threats to independence posed by this client:

There is a considerable familiarity risk posed by the fact that Lisa used to be the audit lead on this engagement, Lisa is therefore familiar with the audit processes undertaken by M&M. Furthermore, Lisa worked with M&M until recently meaning that many of the audit staff will be familiar with her and will be used to following her direction. This could mean that there is also an intimidation threat in acting for this client.

It is also the case that Lisa did some of the audit planning work as she only left recently this could potentially give rise to a self-review threat as the audit of Lisa's company would be based on work which Lisa had herself done.

Lisa, therefore, appears to pose a considerable independence threat to this audit, and it would not normally be possible to continue to act for the client in these circumstances. It may be possible to continue to act for the client if the audit work is now done by staff from a different office who have no involvement with Lisa and any work previously done by Lisa is removed and disregarded.

Perhaps an even bigger threat though is the size of the client – the fact that this client represents a large proportion of total fee income from the office represents both a large self-interest and intimidation threat.

The fact that this client is so big for the office, and that the partners are paid on the basis of office results means that if the client was to be lost they would lose a large amount of money. This means that the partners have a clear interest in ensuring that the client is retained and would perhaps be willing to overlook certain actions to ensure this.

Similarly the client will be fully aware of the power which they hold and will thus be willing to threaten M&M if they do not get their way knowing that the partners of M&M are unlikely to stand up to Stratton as this would cost them a significant amount of money. This is a clear intimidation threat.

Both of these can be evidenced by the fact that the partner in charge Stephen appears unwilling to confront the client directly when presented with evidence of manipulation in the financial statements. This clearly demonstrates that these independence threats are real and the partners have indeed been influenced in their decisions by the size of this client.

It would therefore appear inappropriate that this client should be maintained in the current structure, the client could be moved to a different office where they would not have such a large potential impact or alternatively a review could be carried out by an independent partner from another office to ensure that the audit was carried out correctly and that decisions were not influenced by the independence threats.

There are, therefore, severe independence threats with this client and the engagement should only be undertaken if these threats can be safely removed.

> **Additional areas where credit might be given, note this is not an exhaustive list:**
> - Clear suggestions of appropriate individual actions or alternatives
> - References to specific section(s) of relevant professional codes or audit regulation
> - Appreciation of the candidate's own views or opinions

7 Angele

This question aims to address 'The Professional Accountant' (LO2) and 'critically evaluate alternative courses of action and make choices consistent with ethical professional behaviour' (LO4).

Learning Outcomes: LO2 and LO4

(a) **Chapter 3 – section 2**

Integrity means to be straightforward and honest in all business dealings. Ultimately an accountant, whether they work in industry or in practice, is relied upon to provide information.

If an accountant knowingly provided information which was false or misled another party it would have a considerable impact not just on that accountant but on the profession as a whole. Similarly if an accountant was not honest (including by omission it would have a considerable impact on the trust placed upon the profession.

For this reason accountants are required to be straightforward and honest in all their business dealings.

(b) **Chapter 2 – section 1.4**

There are a considerable number of parties who could be impacted through Mark's actions.

You yourself are an impacted party, you are relatively new in this job and the decision you make could impact your future career considerably. If you chose to report this it could cause the failure of the company and you get blamed by your colleagues this ill feeling could cause you considerable problems in your future career.

Conversely should you choose not to report and this is later found out you could be implicated in this yourself. Being implicated in such a serious breach of environmental regulations could have a significant impact on your future career and could even lead to you being struck off as an accountant.

Mark could also clearly be impacted as he appears to be the primary instigator of this action.

Should this action be uncovered Mark would likely face criminal or civil proceedings – likely his career as a director would be over. On the other hand he is currently the main beneficiary of the current dishonest acts in keeping the company and his current position going.

The employees of the company are also a main stakeholder if the company had to pay full market rates to dispose of these products it is likely to significantly damage the company, causing either the collapse of the company or a significant loss of jobs. It may, therefore, appear obvious that it is in the interests of staff for this to continue.

This action, however, does not appear to be sustainable in the long term and it does not appear workable that a company could continue based on breaches of environmental standards in this way it therefore appears likely that failure to resolve this situation would lead to the failure of the company in any case.

The waste disposal company could be considered a stakeholder. Their whole business model is around the safe disposal of materials and were they found to have taken bribes to dispose of material incorrectly it could lead to severe criminal or civil penalties and the possible failure of the business through reputational damage.

The local community would also be a main stakeholder from one point of view they are likely to support this action as it would lead to the continuation of the company. This company is a very large local employer and is a major customer for a number of local businesses its failure would therefore be likely to have devastating impact on the local economy.

The dangerous heavy metals, however, also appear to be being disposed of incorrectly within the local area – this could potentially cause health impacts among the local community as well as severe environmental damage. It is therefore clearly in the interests of the local community that this gets resolved.

Finally, the environment more generally and the wider public could be considered stakeholders. Having the widespread dumping of such damaging material could clearly have a big impact on the environment and the health of anyone who comes in contact. For example, were this material to enter the water table it could have an impact far beyond the local community.

(c) **Chapter 6 – section 3**

Whistleblowing is the disclosure of an organisations' illegal or unethical actions by an employee.

Although the term whistleblowing can be used to describe an internal report with an organisation in practice it almost always means the disclosure of these acts to some form of external body this could include a law enforcement agency, regulatory body or similar.

As whistleblowing could reveal extremely serious issues most jurisdictions have protection for employees who "blow the whistle" in good faith.

(d) **Chapter 2 – section 2**

The AAA model for ethical decision making follows five steps.

The first step is to identify the facts within the case. In this particular case Mark appears to have arranged for another company to improperly dispose of hazardous waste in return for a bribe. You have become aware of this fact.

Step 2 is to identify the moral or ethical issues within the particular case. In this particular case the moral or ethical issue relies on two main options – do you personally take any action and report Mark's activities or do you ignore it?

Step 3 is to identify the norms, principles and values related to the case. We are a professional accountant and senior board member and therefore have a duty to act with honesty and integrity, we also cannot be seen to promote illegal actions. On the other hand as a senior employee we have the duty to act in the in the best interests of our company and promote its success. We may also want to consider the personal impact on us and our career.

Step 4 is to identify the particular courses of action in the specific case. In this case the decisions are do we report it and if so to who?

Step 5 involves taking the options identified in step 4 and laying over the principles identified in step 3. Step 6 extends this further by asking us to examine the consequences.

Choosing to do nothing is, in a sense, the easiest option from a step 5 viewpoint; the company will maintain its operations and there will be no negative impact on you for choosing to report or act on this behaviour.

When we consider this from step 6, however, it is unlikely, however, to be a good long-term option – the chances of this environmental damage being sustained in the long term is very low and its discovery at a later date could have an even larger impact upon the company. Should this come out later you could also, personally, be seen as complicit which could have a huge future impact on your career possibly including losing your qualification as an accountant.

Ignoring it would also mean that this environmental damage would continue, as professional accountants we have a duty to act with honesty and integrity and not to allow illegal acts to take place.

Reporting, however, could have severe consequences – if the company was to see a considerable increase in costs it is likely that they could become uncompetitive thus seeing numerous job losses or even closure. Step 5 would therefore suggest that we should avoid this.

Even if we extend this from a step 6 point of view, rom a personal perspective if it was found out that we were the one to have whistleblown this could have considerable consequences for us – including being bullied or otherwise discriminated against by colleagues or management possibly considerably impacting upon our private lives or wider career.

It is important to remember that we have no evidence that senior management/the directors are aware of this scheme let alone approve of it. The company could therefore be damaged simply by the actions of Mark, one individual.

Were this matter to be dealt with internally it is likely that many of the problems which the company would face through an external report would be avoided, including reputational damage. It is also a generally accepted policy of whistleblowing that an organisation should be given the opportunity to deal with this internally in the first instance. From a step 6 point of view, it therefore appears that although there is not a single desirable outcome this poses the least damaging one.

Step 7 allows us to make a final decision, in this case reporting internally in the first instance would therefore appear to be the best option as it would resolve the matter with the minimum cost to either us or the company.

Were the company not to be willing to act on it after an internal report, we would be justified in reporting this action to an external body.

Additional areas where credit might be given, note this is not an exhaustive list:
- References to real-life examples of whistleblowing
- References to whistleblowing legislation
- An appreciation of the *personal* impact of whistleblowing

8 Kincaid

This question aims to address 'explain different ethical theories and apply them to practical aspects of business and accounting decision-making' (LO1), AND 'The Professional Accountant' (LO2) AND 'apply appropriate and relevant ethical guidance and standards' (LO3).

Learning Outcomes: LO1, LO2, LO3

(a) **Chapter 8, section 1**

Oonagh could be considered a very suitable candidate as chairperson from one point of view. She is an extremely experienced accountant with a great deal of knowledge and experience of the company. She would therefore be able to bring this experience and knowledge to the company and would thus make an extremely effective and knowledgeable chairperson.

A chairperson is, however, recommended to be independent on appointment. Oonagh is clearly not independent having worked for the company for many years. Oonagh also has a considerable conflict of interest in that she is the CEO of a major competitor suggesting that she would not be able to act in the interests of the shareholders of Kincaid.

Therefore although Oonagh has some good skills and experience that she could bring to the organisation her lack of independence means that she is not suitable as a chairperson.

> **Additional areas where credit might be given, note this is not an exhaustive list:**
> - Whether the skills required to be a professional accountant necessarily translate into those required for a good chair

(b) **Chapter 8 section 2, Chapter 2 section 1**

(i) Devraj's pay package is problematic as the way it is currently structured could lead to issues with "short termism".

The role of a company director is to act in the best long term interests of a company with that aim in mind a directors' remuneration package should be structured in such a way as to encourage them to act in the best long term interests on the company.

Devraj's pay, however, is structured in a way that encourages short term benefits – for example his pay package is largely made up of bonuses and share options to be exercised over the next year this does not encourage good long term behaviour but rather actions which will lead to short term gains.

The particular concern for Kincaid is that it is possible for a company to engage in behaviour which can be very beneficial in the short term but lead to longer term damage for the company. For example, a director could make the decision to dramatically cut a company's R&D budget – in the short term this would be beneficial for the company. R&D is very expensive so cutting it back would considerably reduce costs and thus increase profits. In the longer term, however, the company would be very damaged if it had no new products or services to provide.

It is possible that this is currently happening in Kincaid as Devraj appears to be engaged in a very controversial proposal which will increase profit (and thus his bonus) although it could also cause long term reputational damage to the company.

For this reason it would be more beneficial if the pay structure for Devraj was more focused on longer term goals and aims.

(ii) The proposal to acquire timber from South-East Asia has a number of elements to it.

From one element this makes very good business sense, this will lead to a considerable increase in profits as the cost will be much lower. This would ensure the continued operation of the company and employment security for those who work there.

This work would also lead to large scale investment within the country, benefitting local people. It can certainly be argued, therefore, that this is an extremely beneficial project for the country.

Furthermore, although some might find Kincaid's actions distasteful, they are acting entirely within the law. The national government has allowed this plan to go ahead, and it can therefore be argued that it is not correct for others to determine what is and is not correct behaviour. Kincaid could also be seen to supporting this country by contributing to the prosperity of the population.

Alternatively, an ethical argument could be made that this decision is wrong regardless of the law. Causing habitat loss for numerous animal species and indigenous peoples would always be regarded as wrong regardless of the aim of the organisation involved. It may also be considered that the government do not have the best interests of the local people or the environment at heart and may be prioritising economic concerns over this.

Even aside from the ethical argument there is also an argument that this makes poor business sense. Although it certainly leads to an increase in short term profitability a number of campaigners and other interested parties have shown strong beliefs against this project. There has been increasing public interest in companies' ethical activities in recent years and a company acting in such a way, even if legal, is likely to meet with strong public condemnation.

Practically this could lead to a loss in customers, as customers no longer wish to be associated with this company, as well as losing suppliers or associates who also no longer wish to be associated with a company carrying out these actions.

(c) **Chapter 8 section 3**

The economic facet of Carroll's pyramid means that it is necessarily true that it is the duty of a company to make a profit (how, after all, could a non-profitable company survive long term?). The other facets, however, state that it is not necessarily the case that it is the sole duty of a company to make profits and it can certainly be argued that the duty of making a profit does not give a company the absolute right to act in any way.

Firstly, the legal facet states that a company could clearly not actively break the law in the result of profit. It is therefore not true that a company should seek to make as high a profit as possible if it would be an active breach of the law.

Also, under the UK Companies Act and similar legislation in other countries, it is the duty of a company to take in to account various stakeholders such as suppliers, employees etc. Therefore increasing profit while endangering employees would appear to be a breach of the companies act.

The ethical facet also argues that a company has an ethical duty to act in a way which does not damage the environment in which it operates. To this end many companies have begun to undertake CSR activities to ensure that they are having a beneficial impact on the environment they operate in.

Finally, the philanthropic facet suggests that a company has a duty to contribute to the society that it operates in. Some have argued, however, that this is also beneficial for the company itself, for example good conditions for staff could lead to short term profit decreases, but improve the company's reputation and thus profits as people become more willing to work with them. A natural conclusion from Carroll is that a company should therefore make its decisions based on their long term future as well as short term profitability.

> **Additional areas where credit might be given, note this is not an exhaustive list:**
>
> - Real life examples that demonstrate the points made

9 Birch Energy Plc

This question aims to address LO1 'explain different ethical theories and apply them to practical aspects of business and accounting decision-making' AND LO3 'apply appropriate and relevant ethical guidance and standards, such as the International Federation of Accountants Code of Ethics (adopted by AIA) and the Ethical Standard for Auditors issued by the Financial Reporting Council'.

Chapter 1 section 4
Chapter 1 section 3
Chapter 3 section 4

(a) (i) From a cognitivist view it is clear that the creation of these new gas developments would be wrong. The creation of a new gas field would therefore clearly be wrong, as a cognitivist point of view very much separates the world into clear categories of right and wrong [1]. It is very much a black and white view of the world with no shades of grey.

A cognitivist point of view would therefore accept this viewpoint that the development of the oil field is wrong regardless of the consequences. That corporate or financial interests cannot be developed at the expense of environmental damage.

Indeed it is easy to see how this argument can be advanced, the development of this gas field would undoubtedly cause widespread environmental damage in a vulnerable area as well as displacing vulnerable indigenous peoples.

From a cognitivist point of view this is clearly a wrong action and should not be pursued.

(ii) A consequentialist (teleological) viewpoint, however, would consider more the broader consequences of the actions, and considers the viewpoint that even "bad" action may be justified if it leads to a positive outcome – in essence that the ends justify the means.

In this case a consequentialist viewpoint would argue that it is entirely possible to accept that the development of the gas field in the rainforest is a bad action while still believing it is the best action to take in the circumstances.

Exploiting the gas field means that the company can continue, protecting the position of the poorer people in the UK, protecting the employees of Birch – who may lose their job if the company collapses and perhaps most importantly preserving the wind power and tidal-power projects which ensure the sustainability of long-term green energy supplies within the UK.

It is also not the case that Birch not being involved in the gas field project would mean it would not progress. Due to the high energy prices it is likely that if Birch did not progress with this project another company would. This other company may, of course, not have as progressive and socially progressive a viewpoint as Birch.

A worst-case scenario would therefore involve Birch collapsing damaging the energy security of vulnerable people, leading to job losses and preventing the continuation of these green energy projects. At the same time another company could take over the project thus meaning essentially the worst of both worlds for all involved.

From a consequentialist point of view, embarking on the gas field project, could be the best possible outcome even though the gas field project is itself a negative action.

> **Additional areas where credit might be given, note this is not an exhaustive list:**
> - Links to real-life examples of ethical dilemmas.
> - Consideration of the broader issues surrounding sustainability

(b) Utilitarianism is essentially a subset of consequentialism that argues that we should aim for the best outcome for the greatest number of people. In this particular example we can identify the following impacted parties:

- The employees of Birch
- The customers of Birch (especially the more vulnerable customers)
- The green energy projects and those that will benefit from them (especially the broader impact of environmental and green energy)
- The inhabitants of the rainforest

If we take a purely utilitarian viewpoint, therefore, it is clear that the gas field project should go ahead as it benefits the maximum number of people.

The current employees of Birch maintain their jobs and therefore secure their personal positions. The failure of the company would likely have caused many entirely innocent people to lose their livelihoods.

The vulnerable customers will continue to receive energy at a low price, for many this could be the difference between "eating and heating" some months and would therefore have a massive impact on the lives of those in deprived areas.

The green energy projects will go ahead – this will be greater energy security and sustainability in the future. It must also be remembered that the collapse of these projects could have a considerable impact on the local economy of the areas where they are being built – meaning many local suppliers and their employees could lose their jobs.

It can also be argued that the development of these green energy projects would mean that future gas exploration is unnecessary meaning that in the long term environmental damage and interference to local communities can be avoided. The damage to this community and environment, while regrettable, seems a small long term price to pay.

A purely utilitarian view, therefore suggests that the price paid by the natural environment and the local community is a small one to benefit all these people.

A major problem with utilitarianism, however, is that it often ignores individual rights. While it is easy to argue that others should make sacrifices it becomes very different in considering that you should be the one having to give up your livelihood and home for the "greater good".

Indeed it is possible to take utilitarianism to extreme levels, arguing even that an individual life is less valuable than the greater good. For this reason even many proponents of utilitarianism feel that there are certain innate lines which should not be crossed.

> **Additional areas where credit might be given, note this is not an exhaustive list:**
> - Additional consideration of how human rights interact with utilitarianism
> - Consideration of egoism as a consequential perspective
> - Use of real world examples

(c) This question is essentially one of balancing the public interest against an accountant's duty of confidentiality.

The fundamental principles is very clear that an accountant has a duty of confidentiality to their clients or (in this case) their employers. It is therefore not ordinarily permissible to release confidential documents such as internal management projections, board minutes or proposal papers without the consent of the employer.

It is John's argument that the public interest trumps this – in other words that the need of the public to know about the financial position of Birch exceeds their need for privacy. This would allow you to release this information to John.

It is correct that there is a whistleblowing exemption which allows an employee to release information if the company is breaching laws or safety regulations. There is therefore precedent for the release of confidential information.

However, there is no evidence (or even accusations) that Birch has done anything illegal or against any safety legislation. While some may find the proposals distasteful they are in no way illegal and are only at a discussion stage in any case. There is nothing here that would justify the release of these documents.

Although these documents may be of interest to John's readers that does not make it "in the public interest". There is nothing here that justifies the breaching of our duty of confidentiality and we should not provide John with these documents.

10 Williams and Rose LLP

This question aims to address LO2 'Identify and analyse, using different ethical perspectives, the ethical dimensions that arise in connection with aspects of business and public practice particularly relevant to accounting and auditing' and LO4 'Identify threats and safeguards when evaluating alternative courses of action and make choices and recommendations that are consistent with relevant guidance and that reflect standards of ethical behaviour that are appropriate for a professional accountant'.

Chapter 7 section 2
Chapter 5 section 2 and chapter 2 section 1
Chapter 8 section 2

(a) An auditor's role is ultimately to be an independent external party providing an opinion on the truth and fairness of the financial statements. A fundamental part of this is therefore that the auditor is actually independent. An opinion on the financial statements from someone who was close to the company would have limited value, there would be no independent confirmation that the financial statements were actually accurate.

The presence of an audit report allows users of financial statements to be able to trust and rely on the information within them. Without this it would be extremely difficult for users of financial statements to trust these financial statements and rely on the information within them [1]. If this was the case it would lead to a lack of trust in financial statements generally which would mean a massive decrease in investment and widespread economic damage and people and institutions simply stopped investing.

For this reason it is important that auditors are not only independent but are seen to be independent, in order to maintain general confidence in financial statements.

There are, however, a number of issues which mean that W&R may in fact not be independent of their client:

Close personal relationship: It appears as if the engagement partner, Michelle, is in fact a close personal friend of the CEO, having known him since university and regularly going on holiday with him and his family. With such a close personal relationship it appears unlikely that Michelle would have the ability to remain independent and objective of the client.

Intimidation: The CEO appears to be attempting to use his prominent position within the local business community to threaten you into not acting in the correct way with regards to this audit. Suggesting that if you do not drop your investigation and review into a certain area you will no longer be able to continue to work in the local area, let alone your current job.

Self-interest – outstanding fees: W&R currently have significant outstanding fees with the client. This could give them the incentive to ensure that the current audit continues without further issue, in order to ensure that the merger goes ahead and they are able to recover all their fees.

Self-interest – contingent fees: W&R appear to be in line for significant consultancy work fees with the client based on a successful merger. This gives them a clear incentive for the audit to be completed without issue in order that the merger goes ahead and they can collect these fees.

There would therefore appear to be several issues which would suggest that W&R are, in fact, not fully independent of the client with both the firm as a whole and individuals within the firm having clear motivations in ensuring a successful and issue free audit.

Additional areas where credit might be given, note this is not an exhaustive list:
- Further and detailed description of the independence risks
- Real-life examples of how an auditor not being independent could be problematic

---

(b) Jason clearly does not want to disclose the mis-selling provision as it would impact upon the chances of a successful merger with Blue Wasp. Connaught is currently not in a good financial position and further evidence of financial problems may lead to the merger collapsing.

There is clearly a large self-interest motivation to this; as current CEO it is likely that Jason would lose a significant amount of money if Connaught collapsed. It is also likely that this would cause a considerable amount of damage to Jason's personal reputation which could lead to Jason being unable to find alternative employment elsewhere. It is therefore very much in Jason's personal interests that the merger goes ahead and anything which may prevent this is avoided.

There are, however, a significant number of other parties who are impacted by this decision:

The employees of Connaught, would definitely be impacted. A failure of the merger may lead to the collapse of the business and accordingly them losing their jobs. They probably, wish, therefore, that this merger goes ahead successfully. It may in fact be considered that this financial reporting issue is a relatively minor price to pay to ensure the job security of a large number of people.

It could also be argued that not disclosing the provision is in fact in the interests of the former pensioners. If the company fails it is unlikely that compensation (or at least full compensation) will be paid, therefore the merger offers the best chance of a full settlement of these claims.

Similarly the merger going ahead is in the best interests of the people of Easterness. A successful and large financial company based in the town could likely lead to considerable increases in employment for local people, while conversely the collapse of the company could lead to a considerable impact on the local economy.

It is possible to argue, therefore, that not disclosing this provision is, in fact, in the overall best interests of many.

However, a number of parties could be negatively impacted. In particular Blue Wasp and its investors could take a considerable financial hit by arranging for a merger which would never have taken place had they actually known the full position. It seems clearly both unfair and improper to induce someone to act against their interests by the production of false financial information.

This may also have a negative consequence on Jason, other members of the board and W&R in future. As the provisions will likely come to light at some point, the concealment of this could lead to serious legal and financial problems for those involved in the concealment.

The concealment, therefore, has short term benefits but could lead to severe negative long term consequences. For this reason it is not recommended that Jason's plan is followed.

> **Additional areas where credit might be given, note this is not an exhaustive list:**
> - Further details on the longer-term consequences of Jason's proposal.

(c) As well as external laws many organisations are governed by internal codes of conduct which seek to lead to correct and fair behaviour by employees. Would an internal code of conduct have prevented Jason from acting in this way?

It is unlikely that a code of conduct would have directly prevented Jason. He clearly believes that what he is doing is in the best interests of himself and others, and would likely have acted in the same way regardless. It seems unlikely that Jason is unaware that his actions are against accounting and corporate governance regulations and that he is acting out of ignorance. Jason is a senior member of staff who is likely very aware of his actions and is acting in this way regardless. It is highly unlikely that an internal code of conduct would have made him view this differently.

An internal code of conduct could, however, have empowered those around Jason. Jason appears to have a powerful position within the company. Challenging him and his actions is therefore likely to be difficult for his colleagues to do. A formal code of conduct could set expectations over behaviour as well as giving a mechanism for others to challenge bad behaviour within an organisation. [1]

An internal code of conduct would, therefore, be unlikely to prevent Jason directly from having acted in this way. It may have empowered others to prevent this behaviour.

11 Klingman and Krug Ltd

This question aims to address LO1 'explain different ethical theories and apply them to practical aspects of business and accounting decision making' and LO2 'Identify and analyse, using different ethical perspectives, the ethical dimensions that arise in connection with aspects of business and public practice particularly relevant to accounting and auditing'.

Chapter 2 section 2
Chapter 8 section 1
Chapter 2 section 1 and 2
Chapter 3 section 2

(a) From the viewpoint of a pristine capitalist Peter and Ellie are acting in a correct way. Pristine capitalists view labour as a resource like any other [1]. Peter and Ellie and therefore acting correctly in looking to minimise the cost of the business's resources and therefore maximise profits for the business. A pristine capitalist, therefore, considers this much as any other expense (purchases, rent etc.) that a business should aim to gain the maximum benefit from for the available price.

Socialists, however, would view this action as reflecting Peter and Ellie's superior economic power. The area has high unemployment and few other opportunities for workers. Peter and Ellie are therefore taking advantage of this by reducing worker pay in the knowledge that these workers have few other opportunities. Socialists would believe that this is not a correct course of action and that all employees should have a share in the business's decision making.

> **Additional areas where credit might be given, note this is not an exhaustive list:**
> - Real-life examples of capitalist or socialist viewpoints

(b) Good corporate governance is essential for the success of a business. It is not simply about an ethical issue or that it is somehow inherently "good" to have strong corporate governance. It is, in fact, necessary for the success of the business, good corporate governance ensures:

- Good risk assessment and good risk control
- Good decision making
- Good compliance with laws and regulations

These help to ensure that the business is more likely to be successful and profitable and thus be attractive for new investment.

There are, however, several apparent issues with corporate governance in this business:

The chairperson is not independent of the company and is in fact the sister of the CEO.

Some of the board members, and certainly the chair should be independent in order to ensure appropriate oversight. There does not appear to be any appropriate oversight of the executive directors in this case.

The board appears to be ineffective – decisions are made by the chair and CEO without any reference to the board. There appears to be no ability for the board to change company policy or to have any impact on the decision-making process of the company. A board without these abilities is largely a pointless organisation.

Furthermore the board is not receiving the adequate material in order to carry out their role, it is essential that a board is provided with the material it requires in order to correctly carry out review and oversight of the company. As essential documents are not being provided (or being provided extremely late) the board is unable to carry out this role with any degree of skill or accuracy.

Overall it appears that the current chair and CEO have no regard for the process of corporate governance and indeed went as far as to call consulting the board "a courtesy". While the elements of a board structure may appear to be in place there is absolutely no process of oversight and joint decision making and, in fact, the current management aim to avoid this as far as possible.

> **Additional areas where credit might be given, note this is not an exhaustive list:**
> - Greater consideration of the impact of these failings
> - Discussion of the impact on you as an AIA accountant and member of the board

(c) There are a number of groups that could be impacted by Peter's recommendation:

The employees themselves would definitely be impacted by a large reduction in wages alongside the loss of additional benefits such as holiday pay and pensions. It is natural to assume this would also have an impact on the family members of these employees.

The local community: K&K are one of the largest local employers, a large-scale reduction in wages would therefore have a considerable impact on the local community and the local economy.

K&K and their investors: The reduction in the wages bill would certainly improve the short-term profitability of the company. The investment in the new adult drinks would also likely lead to greater future profits and opportunities if it were to become successful.

However, the change in the conditions of the workers may face a backlash among the wider public, similar to the circumstances impacting on P&O in the UK. This could lead to consumers boycotting the company's products and damaging the company.

In a similar way it is not entirely clear that the actions of the company are entirely legal. Potentially this could lead to them being hit with considerable fines or legal settlements.

> **Additional areas where credit might be given, note this is not an exhaustive list:**
> - As it is impossible to identify every potentially impacted party in a marking scheme any valid discussion of a stakeholder will receive credit.

(d) As an AIA-qualified accountant Joanne's suggestion would not appear to be suitable, a major part of an accountant's role is to avoid conflicts of interests as shown by the commitment to integrity in the IFAC code of ethics.

Being a non-executive director of one company while sitting on the board of a major competitor would appear to be a major conflict of interest. Even unintentionally and inadvertently it would be possible for you to share confidential information from one company to another.

It would therefore appear that Joanne's suggestion is inappropriate and should not be pursued further.

If, however, the recent events at K&K meant that you no longer wanted to continue with your role as a non-executive director it may be possible for you to resign and undertake the role with Joanne's company. If, however, you did opt to do this you would again have to ensure that no confidential or sensitive information material obtained in your role as a non-executive director would be passed to Joanne.

12 Kubrick and Co

This question aims to address LO1 'Explain different ethical theories and apply them to practical aspects of business and accounting decision making' and LO4 'Identify threats and safeguards when evaluating alternative courses of action and make choices and recommendations that are consistent with relevant guidance and that reflect standards of ethical behaviour that are appropriate for a professional accountant'.

Chapter 1 section 6
Chapter 5 section 5
Chapter 2 section 2
Chapter 1 section 6

(a) There are a number of significant issues within Kubrick:

Initially it appears the case that the primary raw material (the rubber) is being purchased at considerably above market rate from a close relative of the CFO. This would appear to be an abuse of position – essentially the CFO is using their position in the company to move money from the company to a close family member. While there is not necessarily an issue with trading with a related party (in some cases it is unavoidable) the transactions should take place at the fair, market price.

This poses a clear ethical issue as by paying above this price the costs of the company are increasing and the profit is decreasing. This naturally reduces the value that the shareholders are receiving from their investment in Kubrick. David is essentially using his position within the company to pass money to family members at the expense of the shareholders and investors of

Kubrick. As well as being arguably morally wrong this is also against his duties as a company director to act in the best interests of the company.

David is clearly aware of this as he signed off the contract.

Similarly a large amount of senior board member personal expenses is being paid by the company. While there may be some agreement reached it appears highly unusual that personal expenses of such a nature would be paid by the company. Similarly the fact that all these expenses have been approved by David appears worrying.

It is unclear from the question whether the shareholders are aware of this although once again it does appear that by paying these expenses on behalf of the senior directors the company is reducing the value which shareholders receive.

Overall there is a strong suggestion that senior members of the company are largely treating it as a source of personal funding and acting in their own interests rather than that of the directors. This is clearly an ethical issue with regards to the duties and role of a director.

Much of this situation appears to be due to the power held by individual directors. There appears to be very limited oversight or control of the directors' activities. In particular the ability of David to authorise large purchases and contracts on his own appears worrying.

This situation could have, therefore, been avoided by a process of stronger controls and oversight within Kubrick, in particular:

- There should be oversight from independent directors of the executive directors' actions. It should not be the case the executive directors are allowed to act without a process of oversight.

- No single director should be allowed to authorise large purchases or contracts without the counter signature of another director or senior member of staff.

- There should be clear company policies on non-transactions with related parties and personal expenses. No single employee should have the ability to authorise large personal expenses on their own behalf.

> **Additional areas where credit might be given, note this is not an exhaustive list:**
> - The potential controls that could be put in place is not an extensive list, as such any other valid point should gain credit.

(b) The AAA model would look at the facts surrounding the case to allow Aaron to make a decision. The model would analyse the situation as follows:

What are the facts of this case? Aaron has discovered that a number of the directors appear to be abusing their position within the company for their own benefit.

What are the ethical issues within the case? The senior directors appear to be enriching themselves and their families at the expense of the shareholders and investors of Kubrick. This represents an ethical and legal issue in a number of ways. From a legal standpoint this could be interpreted as a form of fraud or misappropriation of assets, ethically it would also appear to be a breach of the trust placed in directors.

What are the norms, principles and values related to the case? There is a clear expectation that the directors should act in the best interest of the owners of the company (the shareholders). In this sense Aaron clearly owes a duty of care to the shareholders as his ultimate employers. However Aaron clearly also owes a duty to follow the legitimate instructions of his senior managers. Aaron is also almost certainly worried about his personal position.

What are the alternative courses of action?

The alternative courses of action would appear to be:

(1) Do nothing
(2) Report to the board or other level of senior management
(3) Report externally
(4) Gain legal advice

What is the best course of action which is consistent with the norms and principles and values above: Reporting internally at first, to give a chance to resolve and then reporting externally if this has no impact.

What are the consequences of each of these courses of action?

(1) Do nothing – the easiest and safest for Aaron but ultimately it does nothing to resolve the situation. Also if the situation later emerges Aaron could be in considerable trouble for taking no action.

(2) Report to the board or other level of senior management – this may be in line with best practice but there is no guarantee that the board will act in the correct manner and Aaron may, in fact, lose his position and struggle to support his family if the board go against him.

(3) Report externally – this largely guarantees that the issue will be resolved, but at considerable personal expense to Aaron who may be sacked for reporting confidential information without the approval of his employer. Even if he was later vindicated and found to have acted correctly it is likely that he would spend a considerable amount of time unemployed and unable to provide correctly for his family.

(4) Gain legal advice – gaining advice on how to protect himself while being in this situation.

What is the decision?

The best decision would appear to be to gain advice from the AIA or other professional body on how to protect himself in this situation and how to make a disclosure.

> **Additional areas where credit might be given, note this is not an exhaustive list:**
>
> - Alternative suggestions of how to resolve the issue (this single answer is not prescriptive).

(c) Situational ethics simply refers to the fact that ethics can be affected by the situation or context surrounding the ethical issue. This may also mean that a response which would be appropriate and correct in one situation would not be correct in another – the situation can change what the response should be. For example here, Aaron may react in a different way due to the family pressures than if he had no family.

13 Surrey Systems

This question aims to address LO1 'Explain different ethical theories and apply them to practical aspects of business and accounting decision making', LO3 'Apply appropriate and relevant ethical guidance and standards, such as the International Federation of Accountants Code of Ethics (adopted by AIA) and the Ethical Standard for Auditors issued by the Financial Reporting Council' and LO4 'Identify threats and safeguards when evaluating alternative courses of action and make choices and recommendations that are consistent with relevant guidance and that reflect standards of ethical behaviour that are appropriate for a professional accountant'.

Chapter 1 sections 1 to 3
Chapter 3 sections 2 and 4

Chapter 5 section 1
Chapter 7 section 2

(a) (i) Teleological ethics is about considering the consequences of actions before making a decision in essence rather than following a particular set of rules it aims to achieve the best outcome.

In this situation the issue is that the client, Surrey, is involved in a very unpleasant and disreputable line of business, an ethical assessment could therefore suggest that F&C should not be involved with this client – this appears to be a particular concern of yours and you feel uncomfortable with the client operating in this line of business. The partner openly agrees with your assessment suggesting that there is an understanding that the nature of this client's work is unpalatable.

The partner, however, has rejected any calls to drop the client on the grounds that if we don't do the job then someone else will. In essence dropping Surrey would lead to no change in their activities. Furthermore, as Surrey are such a key client of F&C dropping them would lead to F&C losing large amounts of revenue and probably therefore considerable numbers of staff who depend on F&C for an income losing their jobs. The partner has therefore taken a very teleological view that stopping the work would do nothing to prevent the original wrong (the arms dealing and export of weapons) while causing a considerable amount of harm for those working for F&C. Harm would be caused with no resulting benefit.

While this view could be attractive teleologically – a teleological view might also consider the longer-term consequences of the actions. Although keeping this client would probably be beneficial in the short term it could cause longer term reputational damage. if F&C is seen to be happy to work with arms manufacturers other clients and suppliers may be unhappy to work with them. A full teleological assessment should therefore look at the long term as well as short term outcomes.

(ii) Kantian philosophy is the idea that universal moral principles apply regardless of the situation from a Kantian point of view, therefore, the outcomes discussed in part (a) (i) do not matter – the action is either right or wrong regardless of the outcome.

It is therefore possible to argue that if the action of delivering these military parts is inherently wrong (for example if the act of weapons dealing is considered to be against human dignity) then the action is wrong regardless. This also fits with Kant's principle of autonomy – an individual is subject only to the laws they make for themselves – again suggesting if this action is wrong, then it is unconditionally wrong.

This can be contrasted, however, with a deontological duty to follow legitimate laws and regulations – if the government has allowed the export of these materials why is there a moral imperative on us to object? Similarly the Kantian ideal does not recognise that we do not operate in a vacuum and are not necessarily able to act without considering consequences.

> **Additional areas where credit might be given, note this is not an exhaustive list:**
> - Use of external examples to explain the theories.
> - Greater expansion on Kantian thought
> - Development of the student's own personal opinions

(b) Having an audit client of a very large size poses a particular ethical risk to the audit firm the particular risk is that this causes over-dependence on a single client.

If an auditor is particularly dependent on a single client, either for the firm as a whole or for an individual office/branch it makes it very difficult for them to stand up to the client. For example, if the client attempted to apply accounting standards in an inappropriate way it would be difficult to reject the client's suggested treatment due to the knowledge that it would cause considerable damage to the firm such as staff losing their jobs. For this reason, there are restrictions on the proportion of revenue an individual client should account for in any firm.

Although Surrey are not undertaking any illegal activity it is clear from the partner's discussions that their relative size is having a considerable impact on the decisions made by the firm which appear to be made primarily for commercial reasons – suggesting a self-interest risk has already emerged.

(c) The primary issue here is that Niket and Helen appear to have undertaken a personal leisure trip to Newcastle at the client's expense from the information given it appears that there was no required reason for the trip due to the leisure activities they were able to undertake.

On the face of it this would appear to be a breach of the IESBA principle of integrity this requires fair dealing and honesty towards clients and deliberately charging unnecessary expenses to clients would appear to be a clear breach of this. It could also be argued that there could be a concern if Helen and Niket had somehow aimed to conceal their relationship in order to gain this opportunity to work away together.

However, it is not entirely certain from the evidence that Niket and Helen have done something wrong – they may have planned their time to make use of opportunities while not working (for example in evenings). The social media explanation may have also been a means of legitimately protecting client security.

Nevertheless, this evidence here seems to suggest some element of inappropriate behaviour that cannot be ignored even if there is later found to be no wrongdoing for this reason it is recommended that you report this to a higher level within the firm. It would not be appropriate for you to attempt to deal with a serious HR issue such as this alone, were Niket and Helen found to have been in the wrong the client should not be charged for their time and expenses. Regardless of the outcome in this particular case it may be valuable to remind staff of correct behaviour when charging time and expenses to clients.

> **Additional areas where credit might be given, note this is not an exhaustive list:**
> - Additional exploration of possible actions.
> - Alternative courses of action which could be taken.

14 Rossberg

This question aims to address LO1 'Explain different ethical theories and apply them to practical aspects of business and accounting decision making' and LO2 'Identify and analyse, using different ethical perspectives, the ethical dimensions that arise in connection with aspects of business and public practice particularly relevant to accounting and auditing'.

Chapter 2 section 2
Chapter 3 section 1
Chapter 3 section 2
Chapter 5 section 4

(a) Legally it appears as if Charles may have committed an act of fraud he has used his employer's resources and property for his own personal gain. It also appears as if he has used his subordinates in the division to benefit himself rather than ensure the profits of Rossberg overall. The fact that he appears to have used his position and used Rossberg's staff in this way appears to be particularly serious, furthermore he has clearly benefitted personally from this action using his position to gain lucrative sales in the country without disclosing this to his current employer, Rossberg. In not reporting his actions he could also have been argued to have deceived his current employer.

Charles may also face some form of civil penalties for breaching his contract with his employer and trading on his own behalf.

A legal point of view would therefore suggest that this action is completely wrong and inappropriate.

Considering the situation from virtue ethics it is also clear that Charles's actions are clearly wrong. Virtue ethics would suggest a duty to act with goodwill and honesty, this would appear to particularly apply towards employees acting towards their employers. Charles has clearly not acted in this way actively exploiting his employer to his own personal benefit, it is also clear that in acting this way he is being deceptive – it is not conceivable that he believed his actions were correct he was employed to carry out a particular role for an employer and instead acted to benefit himself with his employer's resources. In not disclosing this until it was found out Charles has clearly acted to deceive his employer.

> **Additional areas where credit might be given, note this is not an exhaustive list:**
> - Consideration for Charles's motivations in acting in this manner.

(b) Many organisations have a formal code of conduct setting out expectations for behaviour and conduct within the organisation. Rossberg has no such as code of conduct instead relying on the ethics and behaviour of its employees.

It is unlikely that a code of conduct would have prevented Charles's individual behaviour. As discussed above Charles clearly understood that his behaviour was against the interests and aims and did not believe it to be "right" on any inherent level, Charles's actions therefore did not come from a position of ignorance but rather a disconcerted attempt of self-interest. It is therefore highly unlikely that any internal code would have changed Charles's motivations or actions.

An internal code, however, doesn't just influence the behaviour of the individual but also those around them. A clear internal code would give those around Charles a clear framework to show that his behaviour was wrong, furthermore an internal code would likely give staff guidance on how they could raise concerns around another's behaviour.

As Charles used other staff members for his own business advantage against the interests of Rossberg a clear internal code would have given these staff members a means of raising these issues. Therefore, although it is unlikely that an internal code would have prevented Charles acting in this manner it may have assisted this situation by giving those around Charles a means of reporting the situation and allowing Rossberg to resolve it.

> **Additional areas where credit might be given, note this is not an exhaustive list:**
> - Further description of how those around Charles may act.

(c) While it is clear that Charles has acted improperly; Robert appears very unwilling to take any formal action instead allowing Charles to quietly resign. While it is clear that these actions have damaged Rossberg it is also clear that further action against Charles personally will not resolve this situation as these actions have already taken place.

Further than this it is likely that severe action against Charles personally would bring publicity to the matter. As any court case or prosecution would naturally be reported in the media. This would potentially be very damaging to the reputation of Rossberg as evidence of a staff member trading on their own behalf could make Rossberg appear incompetent and badly managed.

From Robert's point of view, therefore, although he may be extremely unhappy and angry with Charles and may personally wish negative consequences upon him, he is also likely to be aware that carrying out a negative act against Charles would only result in problems for Rossberg. Robert therefore believes that letting Charles quietly resign is not an ideal solution but is likely to be the best outcome in this particular scenario.

Public interest refers to accountants acting in the interest of the public as a whole rather than individual interest or the interests of their employer/organisation. From Wunmi's point of view, therefore, the correct outcome is not just the best for Rossberg but the best for the wider public and society in general.

Wunmi is aware that Charles has acted in an improper fashion in his management of the Estonian division while she can likely understand the logic behind Robert's position she is also concerned over the nature of Charles's character as demonstrated through his actions. She therefore believes that if Charles receives no negative repercussions, then it would be possible for him to carry out a similar act elsewhere.

From Wunmi's professional point of view, therefore, she feels that she has an obligation to prevent this, thus believing that some form of negative consequences are required against Charles to prevent this from reoccurring.

> **Additional areas where credit might be given, note this is not an exhaustive list:**
> - Further information on Robert's likely motivations.
> - References to professional accounting standards.

15 Ethics and whistleblowing

This question aims to address LO1 'Explain different ethical theories and apply them to practical aspects of business and accounting decision making' and LO2 'Identify and analyse, using different ethical perspectives, the ethical dimensions that arise in connection with aspects of business and public practice particularly relevant to accounting and auditing'.

Chapter 1 sections 1 and 2
Chapter 2 section 1
Chapter 8 sections 2 and 3
Chapter 6 sections 3 and 4

(a) There are a number of parties who could be potentially impacted by your decision:

Yourself: the decision you make could have a considerable impact on your future career and position carrying out some form of reporting would probably end your career with this current company and may give you a reputation as a "troublemaker" making it difficult to get a job elsewhere.

From an alternative point of view, however, if the contamination was to continue and come out later on, your involvement in this could have a considerably negative impact on your remaining career.

You also have personal pressures, whistleblowing could remove you from this current location pleasing your wife, however it could also anger her if you lost your job and could not get a prestigious future appointment.

Sun, Alan and Thomas: As the company officials responsible for the contamination, it is likely that the revelation of this contamination would end their career, and potentially also lead to civil or criminal penalties.

The Government Inspector: With the contamination to be revealed it is possible that the inspector would lose their job.

The local community: The impact on the local community could be considered differently from opposing viewpoints.

The community is clearly very dependent on the company for a range of facilities such as schools and clinics and as it is not economically viable to repair or replace the equipment then the disclosure of the contamination would lead to the closure of the plant and these facilities being withdrawn.

From an alternative point of view, however, the contamination is having a severe impact on the environment of the local community and therefore damaging it in the very long term, An argument could be made that this long-term damage does not justify the preservation of these local facilities in the short to medium term.

> **Additional areas where credit might be given, note this is not an exhaustive list:**
> - Identification of other potentially impacted parties.
> - Reference to real world cases bearing a similarity.

(b) An egoist point of view analyses the situation from the point of view of the individual. From your own point of view you are not responsible for the pollution nor does anyone know you are aware (the conversation was overheard) therefore it is unlikely you would ever face any punishment if it did come to light.

From an individual point of view (egoism) there is also limited benefit from reporting. Carrying out an act of whistleblowing would damage your career both with your current employer and potentially damaging your reputation with longer term employment and career options.

A utilitarian reading would instead consider the greatest good for the greatest number of people, this could change the interpretation of the situation. In this case it is possible to make an assessment that although the contamination is a bad thing the large numbers of people losing their job as the plant itself and the supporting facilities close and the considerable impact on the local community as the clinics and schools close would be a worse outcome and it is therefore in the best interests of the greatest number of people. This is particularly the case as the government is unable to run these services independently and is thus reliant on company support, the government may themselves feel that turning a "blind eye" to this pollution is in the greater good.

This, however, is quite a short-term consideration of the greater good, although the jobs, clinics and hospitals naturally benefit the community the site is already old and increasingly unsustainable – these facilities may not last for a considerably longer amount of time anyway. Environmental contamination, however, can last for a considerable period of time and cause considerable damage to the land and therefore the livelihood of those in the local community. A more long-term utilitarian view would therefore consider the impact on the people in the region over a longer period of time.

> **Additional areas where credit might be given, note this is not an exhaustive list:**
> - Detailed consideration of potential courses of action.
> - Contrast with other ethical theories.

(c) Whistleblowing is the act of an employee disclosing illegal or unethical acts by their employer to an external party. In this particular case it would refer to you disclosing the contamination which has been carried out by your employer.

Employees whistleblowing have a degree of legal protection but to enjoy this protection certain steps have to be followed – in particular there must be an attempt to disclose this to senior levels of management. In this particular case it appears that senior management are unaware of the current situation and the contamination issue is only known of by local staff. Before you reported externally, therefore, you would need to take sufficient steps to inform senior management (head office) of the issue.

16 Harrow

This question aims to address LO1 'Explain different ethical theories and apply them to practical aspects of business and accounting decision making' and LO3 'Apply appropriate and relevant ethical guidance and standards, such as the International Federation of Accountants Code of Ethics (adopted by AIA) and the Ethical Standard for Auditors issued by the Financial Reporting Council'.

Chapter 1 sections 1 and 2
Chapter 2 section 2
Chapter 3 section 1
Chapter 3 section 3
Chapter 4 section 2

(a) *Answer can be structured as two distinct parts or one combined answer:*

    (i) From a strictly absolutist or legalist point of view raising the rent could be regarded as acceptable. Absolutism or legalism considers any action to be either right or wrong in line with national or international laws. Legally the contract allows these increases to take place therefore this is an acceptable action.

    (ii) From a deontological point of view however this would consider the action from a virtues point of view. In this particular scenario the rent is being raised not as a business decision due to an increase in costs but rather as a way of removing them from the land. In this case it can be argued that the company has not acted with integrity in disguising their intentions. In not acting with integrity, they are enacting a high cost against the three families who are losing their livelihoods of the family farms. A deontological point of view would therefore argue that even though the action may not be illegal it is still wrong in that by disguising their intentions it is causing harm to others for individual gain.

(b) From an egoist point of view the company has a duty to act in its own best interests and that of its owners (the shareholders) in this case the company has therefore acted correctly in seeking to minimise their tax liability. Furthermore, there is no evidence to suggest that the arrangements are illegal therefore the company is correct to follow this course of action.

A more pluralist point of view would consider a wider group of parties in this case it would take the view that it would be unfair for the company to benefit to such an extent while the country receives virtually no benefit. This point of view often considers an element of social contract in a company's proposed actions.

> **Additional areas where credit might be given, note this is not an exhaustive list:**
> - Use of real-world examples to help illustrate key points.

(c) Organisational culture is the shared beliefs, values and assumptions within an organisation which determine how the organisation operates on a day-to-day basis.

Harrow appears to have a strong culture that the pursuit of profit is the key aim and this is held above any other duty, requirement or goal within the organisation. This can be seen in the acceptance within the organisation of strong measures to increase profits and decrease tax even though this damages the communities and countries they operate in as well as their existing clients.

While it is, of course, a primary duty of a company to make profit it is unlikely that a company which has such a strong short-term focus on profit will be successful in the longer term. For this reason, a culture which encourages consideration of a broader view of stakeholders is more likely to be in the company's long-term interests. For example, in this case although the company's actions appear to be legal, they could be viewed as distasteful by some, this could lead to customers, suppliers or other stakeholders to no longer do business with Harrow damaging their longer-term success.

> **Additional areas where credit might be given, note this is not an exhaustive list:**
> - Use of real-world examples.

(d) In this case the issue appears to be the breach of confidentiality – it is clear that Sherbourne is aiming to hire you, not due to the skills you can bring, but due to the confidential information you could bring from Harrow.

As a professional accountant this causes you two main issues. Under the IESBA code you have a duty of confidentiality to your current employer unless there is a strong reason to release the information – no such reason exists here, and it would be entirely for your own benefit only.

Furthermore, there is the principle of integrity which would include acting in your employer's best interests and not seeking to benefit unfairly from them. This course of action would clearly be against this general principle.

17 Grapeman Group

This question aims to address LO1 'Explain different ethical theories and apply them to practical aspects of business and accounting decision making', LO2 'Identify and analyse, using different ethical perspectives, the ethical dimensions that arise in connection with aspects of business and public practice particularly relevant to accounting and auditing' and LO3 'Apply appropriate and relevant ethical guidance and standards, such as the International Federation of Accountants Code of Ethics (adopted by AIA) and the Ethical Standard for Auditors issued by the Financial Reporting Council'.

Chapter 1 sections 2 to 5
Chapter 3 section 1
Chapter 3 section 4
Chapter 5 section 5
Chapter 7 sections 1 and 2.

(a) One of the key IESAB principles is that of integrity in other words honest and fair dealing towards clients and in all professional relationships.

In this particular case it appears that Michael is acting in a dishonest fashion by deliberately changing the billing structures between the clients for personal benefit – allowing staff to effectively have a holiday in Dubai subsidised by the client. Michael argues that this is acceptable as the total bill to the client is unaffected (they are both part of the same group) and it is fair that the staff benefit from this hard work.

However, it is likely that were this to be accepted in this case even though the impact on this particular company was pretty low this form of behaviour could be seen as being acceptable in the firm overall, in instances where it may have a more serious impact. For this reason, it is important that professional standards are held universally and not just where it is considered to be a particular risk.

(b) There are a large number of factors both professional and broader which could impact on your decision on whether or not to report the breach.

Professional competence: It is clear that an event like the malfunctioning chimney should be reported under ESG disclosures. If you fail to act, then you are clearly not taking on board your professional duty to ensure that the financial statements give a true and fair view.

Personal pressures in the workplace: You are still a relatively new employee and could therefore very much be worried about your position within the firm. Helena has made it very clear that if there is a delay in the sign off of the audit she will complain to the firm and blame you in particular, this could be particularly problematic as Grapeman is such a key client. You are therefore likely to be concerned that a delay while you complete additional audit work could lead to problems with your employment and future career. This is further compounded by the fact that your colleague, Michael, does not appear at all supportive of your position and in fact feels that more senior individuals in the firm should deal with this.

This could very much lead you to the feeling that it is much easier personally to do nothing.

Broader society and investment: You are aware that a delay in the sign off of the audit could lead to the investment opportunity falling through. You could thus feel a personal belief that you do not want the project to fail, and this again could be a pressure to do nothing.

> **Additional areas where credit might be given, note this is not an exhaustive list:**
> - Alternative factors or consideration of the relevant importance of these factors

(c) A number of potential ethical viewpoints are possible – all have different considerations but are centred around the idea that disclosing the chimney malfunction would lead to the carbon capture investment falling through. It must therefore be considered if failing to disclose would therefore be appropriate.

Helena is currently promoting a highly consequentialist viewpoint, a viewpoint such as this is often argued as effectively being "the end justifies the means". Helena is effectively saying that non-disclosure would lead to strong benefits to a deprived area and job opportunities for many young people. The ESG disclosures in the accounts are relatively minor and from Helena's view the benefits of failing to disclose outweigh the costs – it is thus a moral action to fail to disclose.

A subset of consequentialism, utilitarianism, could justify Helen's actions by the view that it was ensuring the greatest good for the greatest number of people by ensuring the project went ahead.

A cognitivist, however, would disagree with this viewpoint as cognitivists hold a view that an action could be either right or wrong by its nature and not just from its outcome. Cognitivists believe that a very consequentialist viewpoint, or relativism, could lead to an "anything goes" view where individuals can justify any action they feel if they believe it leads to a good outcome.

Cognitivists further criticise consequentialists by stating that often not all the outcomes of a particular decision can be predicted, and it would therefore be incorrect to make a decision based on them.

A cognitivist's viewpoint would therefore state that certain actions were wrong even if done for apparently "good" reasons and there is a certain level of actions being right or wrong. A cognitivist could therefore argue that in being dishonest Helena was acting immorally even if she was doing it for the "right" reasons.

> **Additional areas where credit might be given, note this is not an exhaustive list:**
> - Use of alternative ethical theories to assess the scenario

(d) An auditor's role is ultimately to provide an independent, third party's view on the truth and fairness of the financial statements. It is therefore vital that the auditor is actually independent.

In this particular case it appears as if Michael, a key member of the audit team, is not independent. In being offered an important and well-paid role by the client he clearly has an interest in ensuring that the audit goes well. Were Michael to cause issues with the audit or raise a large number of questions it is possible that the job offer would be withdrawn.

Michael therefore has a strong interest in ensuring that there are no issues with the audit and is thus clearly not independent. For this reason, someone with such a degree of personal interest in an activity should not be involved in the audit.

18 Dragon

This question aims to address LO3 Apply appropriate and relevant ethical guidance and standards, such as the International Federation of Accountants Code of Ethics (adopted by AIA) and the Ethical Standard for Auditors issued by the Financial Reporting Council and LO4 Identify threats and safeguards when evaluating alternative courses of action and make choices and recommendations that are consistent with relevant guidance and that reflect standards of ethical behaviour that are appropriate for a professional accountant.

Chapter 2 part 2
Chapter 2 parts 6 and 7
Chapter 6 part 5
Chapter 8 part 1 and 2

(a) Stakeholder theory refers to the rights of those who are impacted by the decisions made (or those that fail to be made by an organisation. In the case of a commercial organisation this would generally refer to the shareholders, customers, employees etc. of an organisation, however in the public sector this could be broader.

The stakeholders in this scenario are broader being the entirety of the population of Port Martha as well as associated businesses, organisations and similar based within the city [1]. It is clear that the City Council is responsible to these parties – they select the councillors, and the council should act in their best interests. It is particularly important to remember that in the case of a public body such as a local council they do not exist for their own benefit but for that of the stakeholders – the public.

This, however, does not necessarily mean that the decision of the local council is necessarily wrong, Dragon contributes a large amount to the local area both in employment and in local tax revenue. A small amount of public expenditure to support a local employer would therefore appear to be entirely justifiable.

What is perhaps more concerning in this situation is the issue of transparency – organisations should be transparent, that is open and honest to their stakeholders regarding the decision-making process and how and why decisions are made.

The City Council are, however, being anything but transparent. Rather than being honest about the decision-making process they have attempted to disguise this expenditure. This is clearly showing a lack of transparency – the council are not being open and honest about their decision-making process. Even though the decision may be entirely justifiable and correct the decision to hide it in this way shows a lack of openness and honesty on the part of the City Council.

This is particularly important in the case of a public body such as the council as it is ultimately public money that has been spent – a duty is therefore owed to ensure this money is spent properly.

> **Additional areas where credit might be given, note this is not an exhaustive list:**
> - Expansion of ideas surrounding the duties of a public body

(b) (i) Whistleblowing is the decision to report externally any breaches of law, regulations or standards by an organisation. From the point of view of an accountant this would usually refer to information or evidence that they came across in the course of their normal employment opportunities or dealing with a client.

In this particular scenario whistleblowing would refer to whether or not to report the actions of the City Council to some external body such as law enforcement.

(ii) There are a number of professional and personal pressures surrounding your decision to report or not.

Professional: It is clear that it is not normal behaviour to post heavily redacted invoices. Posting these invoices could suggest approval of these actions or at least a degree of agreement with them. This would be an incorrect action as accountants have a duty to act in the interest of public by ensuring that financial statements give a true and fair view.

From a professional point of view if this information was ever to be revealed (for example in an audit) it is likely that you could face severe professional sanctions such as a fine or being removed from your professional body.

Duty to employers: A professional accountant has a duty to their employers; it is therefore arguable that you should support their decisions and ideas.

Personal pressures: Employment opportunities in Port Martha are limited, were you to whistleblow it is likely that you would lose your current role. Although you could easily gain another role (and even a better paid one) you would not be able to care for your father. There is thus an extremely strong personal pressure for you to keep your current role, even though this may be professionally incorrect.

> **Additional areas where credit might be given, note this is not an exhaustive list:**
> - Further discussion on potential ethical pressures

(c) One of the fundamental IESBA/IFAC principles is professional competence and due care, in essence the professional accountant is required to have the requisite level of professional skill and ability to carry out an engagement properly.

In this case the concern is not that you don't have the knowledge to carry out the engagement for John (you are a very qualified and experienced accountant) but you don't have the ability to give it sufficient time.

The due care element means that an engagement should be approached with a level of seriousness, care and attention. In your individual case you are already extremely highly burdened with issues at your current employment and your personal life. It is therefore currently unlikely that you would have the necessary time to undertake this work for John with the level of care and attention which is required.

You should, therefore, currently not act for John unless your circumstances change to a degree where you could focus a reasonable degree of care and attention on John's financial statements.

> **Additional areas where credit might be given, note this is not an exhaustive list:**
> - Consideration of your personal circumstances

EXAM ANSWER BANK

19 Lars

This question aims to address LO1 'Explain different ethical theories and apply them to practical aspects of business and accounting decision making' and LO2 'Identify and analyse, using different ethical perspectives, the ethical dimensions that arise in connection with aspects of business and public practice particularly relevant to accounting and auditing'.

Chapter 1 part 5
Chapter 3 part 6
Chapter 5 part 9

(a) A number of parties could be potentially impacted by the over valuation of the fund:

Pensioners/former employees: Pensioners and former employees could see that the reduction in the fund's value could lead to reduced future pay-outs and/or the pension failing to keep up with future inflation rates. This could impact on the living standards of some who had potentially worked with the company for many years.

Current employees: The reduction in the pension fund value could mean that current employees could receive a reduced pay out or have to work longer to receive the level of pension required. Again, this could impact on the plans of these individuals.

Trustees/Management: Trustees could face a high degree of hostility for these actions having taken place "on their watch". Although not directly responsible for the actions of the fund manager it is likely that many would question their decision to engage this individual.

Lars himself: It is likely that Lars will see an effective end to his career after these discoveries. Even though this may be a relatively minor part of his overall career it is likely he will find it extremely difficult to find future clients.

Importantly these are all real individuals/groups who will be impacted by the asset valuation – showing these losses are not a theoretical thing.

> **Additional areas where credit might be given, note this is not an exhaustive list:**
> - Other parties who may have been impacted by this valuation issue

(b) Individual ethics refers to an individual's knowledge or inherent beliefs. Situational ethics refers to the fact that ethics can very much be impacted by the situation an individual is in – in other words it is also important to recognise pressures as well as simply having a knowledge of ethics. This can also be used to understand why "good people do bad things".

In this particular scenario it appears as if Lars is very much aware of professional ethics and good practice – he has a long background in providing services and indeed has shown himself to be a very generous and responsible individual. The issue does not appear to be that he was unaware but rather that he chose to act in such a manner, this may mean he acted in quite a different way than he usually does.

Situational ethics would therefore consider the pressures facing Lars in considering why he apparently acted in this way looking at the relationship with the pension fund and how he felt his actions were justified.

(c) Kohlberg's theory is an attempt to explain the moral development of individuals – in other words the stages that individuals go through when making moral decisions or judgements. Kohlberg separates human decision making into three levels, it is important to understand that Kohlberg is not a means of reaching a correct decision but rather a way of understanding how decisions are made.

In this case it appears that Lars has been operating at quite a low Kohlberg level. An argument can be made that he is operating at stage 1 – punishment avoidance. Lars has been under heavy pressure from the pension fund trustees to achieve results with regular threats to remove their custom if this isn't achieved, it can therefore clearly be argued that he wished to avoid this "punishment" and retain the business.

Alternatively, it could be argued that Lars was operating under stage 2 – instrumental-relativist or "acting in his own interest". Lars received a large bonus for meeting certain targets so it could be that personal greed of receiving a large bonus motivated him into this particular course of action.

It is important to note that all people are capable of operating at different levels on the Kohlberg scale – there isn't a sense that an individual constantly operates at the same level all of the time. Kohlberg's theory may therefore explain why Lars thought in a particular way during his decision-making process.

Additional areas where credit might be given, note this is not an exhaustive list:
- Alternative perspectives on Kohlberg
- Discussion of other Kohlberg levels

(d) It is clear that the trustees are not wholly responsible for the decrease in valuation of assets – after all they are not the ones who produced the flawed methodology. However, developing the idea of situation ethics, it may be considered that they created the situation that encouraged Lars to act in this way.

By constantly pressurising Lars to obtain high levels of growth, perhaps at unreasonable levels, and simultaneously giving high cash rewards it can be argued that the trustees created an environment where Lars felt he had no choice but to meet these aims.

Organisations should therefore consider not just the direct impact of their actions but the situations their assets may create and how people might react.

20 Kilmar & Clark

This question aims to address LO2 'Identify and analyse, using different ethical perspectives, the ethical dimensions that arise in connection with aspects of business and public practice particularly relevant to accounting and auditing' and LO3 'Apply appropriate and relevant ethical guidance and standards, such as the International Federation of Accountants Code of Ethics (adopted by AIA) and the Ethical Standard for Auditors issued by the Financial Reporting Council'.

Chapter 3 part 4
Chapter 7 parts 1 and 3
Chapter 8 parts 1 to 3

(a) An accountant is expected to act at all times with a professional attitude and showing the relevant skills and attention to the role.

From the point of view of recruiting to a company board a professional accountant is usually recruited to bring their specialist knowledge of financial matters to the company, the following would therefore would normally be expected to bring the following:

An independent voice: As a non-executive, accountant director on a company board it is expected that you would not have existing relations with the company of the board members. In this capacity the account board member is expected to offer an independent viewpoint separate to that of the executive board members.

Represent shareholders and other stakeholders: A non-executive director ultimately exists to provide representation to shareholders and other key stakeholders on the board. They should not simply be "yes-men" or go along with the aims of company management. In line with stakeholder theory their aim is to provide effective questioning and representation of these parties on the board.

Provide appropriate technical guidance: A primary reason for having an accountant as a non-executive director is to provide technical advice and guidance to the board in the particular case of K&C there appears to have been technical and system errors within this company which have not been fully addressed and which you could assist with.

Provide scrutiny: A key part of the role of a non-executive director is to ensure that proper scrutiny of the executive board decisions takes place this will normally involve a combination of all the skills mentioned above.

Courage: Ensuring that the accountant can properly act with scrutiny and independence can be difficult – particularly if other board members with strong interests want to put forward a particular point of view. It is therefore particularly important that accountants act with moral courage with regards to their role.

> **Additional areas where credit might be given, note this is not an exhaustive list:**
> - Use of real-world examples
> - Further examples of accountant or director roles within an organisation

(b) The issue here primarily relates to the ability of the accountant to carry out their role correctly. It is an important part of a non-executive director's role or an accountant's role that they are able to scrutinise the financial position of the company and advise accordingly.

In this scenario it does not appear that the correct information is being provided to you, you would therefore be unable to provide the required level of advice and guidance. Furthermore, it would appear likely that the company are using your position and background as an accountant to support their own position and make it appear to external parties as if everything is going well.

Therefore, by not investigating further and agreeing with the board reports you could in fact be contributing to a false view that the company is performing well when you do not have evidence of this fact – you could therefore be contributing to an overall misleading view of the company's position.

Furthermore, the actions of the company and its management are very unusual in restricting information from you and placing so much pressure on you to agree to these unusual arrangements. Surely if the company was performing as expected and accounting for issues normally there would be no reason why this relatively normal information could not be disclosed?

As this would be against your fundamental duty and role as a professional accountant to continue with these unusual arrangements you should make your position clear that you require this information in order to carry out your role or you will resign.

> **Additional areas where credit might be given, note this is not an exhaustive list:**
> - Expansion of the ethical issues within the company
> - Linkage to real-life scenarios on directors' actions

(c) There has been a long culture of staff members leaving early on weekends but still receiving a full day's pay. This can be examined from a number of different perspectives:

From the point of view of external regulations, it could be argued that this behaviour is entirely acceptable, government regulations on pay and taxation led to the creation of this situation and the

decision of the company is thus a natural result of this. However it is arguable that poor regulations give a company the right to act badly.

It could also be argued, however, that these actions represent a form of theft from the company, workers are getting paid without working.

These actions appear to be against the company's own internal policies; therefore, it is arguable that the workers should not be acting in such a way. In particular the fact that staff members may return to an emergency situation having been in a bar (and presumably consuming alcohol) seems incredibly risky behaviour.

Policies, as well as being written, also need proper enforcement and interpretation. In this particular scenario it is clear that regardless of what workers were told in a policy it was made very clear that their actions in leaving work early while still getting paid were entirely accepted by the company. It is therefore extremely difficult to argue that the workers have done anything wrong in acting in a way that appears to have been fully accepted and potentially even encouraged by the employer.

It is, however, not generally considered to be a good idea to have policies that are in place but disobeyed or ambiguous as this reduces the effectiveness of internal policies overall. The company should therefore look to have clear policies on what is and isn't acceptable on weekend working this may include a formal on call system which allows employees to leave the premises but remain in contact. It may also be necessary to compensate existing employees for perceived loss of benefits.

Additional areas where credit might be given, note this is not an exhaustive list:
- Additional consideration of issues with the company's culture
- Alternative points of view on the company's decision
- Additional consideration of the health and safety issues

EXAM ANSWER BANK

Mock exam 1
questions and answers

Mock Exam

Question 1

Douglas Dunn is a junior partner and training manager at Lorca & Co, a medium sized firm of auditors. He oversees the progress of the firm's student accountants. One of those under Douglas' supervision, Hedda Gabler, recently wrote in her progress and achievement log about a situation in an audit that had disturbed her.

On the recent audit of Sassoon Company, a medium sized, family-run business and longstanding client of Lorca & Co, Hedda was checking non-current asset purchases when she noticed what she thought might be an irregularity. There was an entry of £50,000 for a security system for an address in a well-known holiday resort with no obvious link to the company. On questioning this with Christina Risotto, the financial controller, Hedda was told that the system was for Mr Martin Sassoon's holiday cottage (Martin Sassoon is managing director and a minority shareholder in the Sassoon Company). She was told that Martin Sassoon often took confidential company documents with him to his holiday home and so needed the security system on the property to protect them. It was because of this, Christina said, that it was reasonable to charge the security system to the company.

Christina Risotto expressed surprise at Hedda's concerns and said that auditors had not previously been concerned about the company being charged for non-current assets and operational expenses for Mr Sassoon's personal properties.

Hedda told the engagement partner, David Hair, what she had found and David simply said that the charge could probably be ignored. He did agree, however, to ask for a formal explanation from Martin Sassoon before he signed off on the audit. Hedda was not at the final clearance meeting but later read the following in the notes from the meeting: 'discussed other matter with client, happy with explanation'. When Hedda discussed the matter with David afterwards she was told that the matter was now closed and that she should concentrate on her next audit and her important accounting studies.

When Douglas Dunn read about Hedda's concerns and spoke to her directly, he realised he was in an ethical dilemma. Not only should there be a disclosure requirement of Mr Sassoon's transaction, but the situation was made more complicated by the fact that David Hair was senior to Douglas Dunn in Lorca & Co and also by the fact that the two men were good friends.

Required

(a) Explain the meaning of 'integrity' and its importance in professional relationships such as those described in the case. **(5 marks)**

(b) Criticise David Hair's ethical and professional behaviour in the case. **(10 marks)**

(c) Critically analyse the alternatives that Douglas Dunn has in his ethical dilemma. **(10 marks)**

(Total = 25 marks)

Question 2

It was the final day of a two-week-long audit of Gunn Co, a long-standing client of Armitage & Co. In the afternoon, Paola Giraldo, a recently qualified AIA accountant and member of the audit team, was following an audit trail on some cash payments when she discovered what she described to the audit partner, Seamus Seedy, as an 'irregularity'. A large and material cash payment had been recorded with no recipient named. The corresponding invoice was handwritten on a scrap of paper and the signature was illegible.

Seamus, the audit partner, was under pressure to finish the audit that afternoon. He advised Paola to seek an explanation from Edward Hughes, the client's finance director. Seamus told her that Gunn Co was a longstanding client of Armitage & Co and he would be surprised if there was anything unethical or illegal about the payment. He said that he had personally been involved in the Gunn Co audit for the last eight years and that it had always been without incident. He also said that Edward Hughes was an old friend of his from university days and that he was certain that he would not approve anything unethical or illegal. Seamus said that Armitage & Co had also done some consultancy for Gunn Co so it was a very important client that he didn't want Paola to upset with unwelcome and uncomfortable questioning.

When Paola sought an explanation from Mr Monroe, she was told that nobody could remember what the payment was for but that she had to recognise that 'real' audits were sometimes a bit messy and that not all audit trails would end as she might like them to. He also reminded her that it was the final day and both he and the audit firm were under time pressure to conclude business and get the audit signed off.

When Paola told Seamus what Frank had said, Seamus agreed not to get the audit signed off without Paola's support, but warned her that she should be very certain that the irregularity was worth delaying the signoff for. It was therefore now Paola's decision whether to extend the audit or have it signed off by the end of Friday afternoon.

Required

(a) Explain why 'auditor independence' is necessary in auditor-client relationships and describe THREE threats to auditor independence in the case. **(9 marks)**

Paola is experiencing some tension due to the conflict between her duties and responsibilities as an employee of Armitage & Co and as a qualified professional accountant.

Required

(b) (i) Compare and contrast her duties and responsibilities in the two roles of employee and professional accountant. **(6 marks)**

(ii) Explain the ethical tensions between these roles that Paola is now experiencing. **(4 marks)**

(c) Explain how absolutist and relativist ethical assumptions would affect the outcome of Paola's decision. **(6 marks)**

(Total = 25 marks)

Question 3

(a) The audit of the financial statements of East Creech Co for the year ended 30 June 2019 is nearing completion and the company's annual general meeting is to be held next week.

The current audit firm, Cruz & Co, has not sought to be reappointed as it is East Creech Co's policy to change auditors periodically. Lopez & Co, a firm of chartered accountants, has accepted nomination as auditor for the year ending 30 June 2020.

It has just come to light that the financial statements for the year ended 30 June 2019 are materially misstated as a provision which should have been made has been omitted in error. This is of such significance that the financial statements which are soon to be issued cannot be considered to be reliable. However, the financial statements have been approved through the company's internal processes and the directors do not propose to amend them at this late stage but will not agree to a modified audit opinion. Cruz & Co has discussed the matter with Lopez & Co and obtained verbal assurances that if Cruz & Co were to express an unmodified opinion, the comparative information in the financial statements for the year ending 30 June 2020 would not be restated.

The company outsourced all legal and company secretarial work to Adam Flysch, a qualified legal practitioner, who worked from home using his own computer. Adam died suddenly in September 2020. East Creech Co does not routinely keep copies of minutes and legal documentation.

Required

Identify and discuss the ethical and other professional issues relating to the above matters.

(13 marks)

(b) You are an audit manager in Vonnegut & Co, a firm of chartered accountants. You have specific responsibility for undertaking annual reviews of existing clients and advising whether an engagement can be properly continued. The following matters have arisen in connection with recent assignments:

(i) Charles Plath is the senior in charge of the audit of the financial statements of Perry Ltd for the year ending 31 December 2019. Perry Ltd's managing director, Terry Eliot, has just sent you an e-mail to advise you that Charles has been short-listed for the position of Finance Director. You were not previously aware that Charles had applied for the position.

(4 marks)

(ii) Kimmeridge Ltd is a long-standing client. One of its subsidiaries, Durdle Ltd, has made losses for several years. At your firm's request, Kimmeridge Ltd's management has made a written representation that goodwill arising on the acquisition of Durdle Ltd is not impaired. Your firm's audit opinion in the auditor's report on the consolidated financial statements of Kimmeridge Ltd for the year ended 30 September 2019 is unmodified. Your firm's audit opinion on the financial statements of Durdle Ltd is similarly unmodified. Kimmeridge Ltd's managing director, Leslie Stripe, is due to retire in 2020 when her share options mature.

(5 marks)

(iii) Chesil Ltd is threatening to sue your firm in respect of audit fees charged for the year ended 30 June 2018. Chesil Ltd is alleging that Vonnegut & Co billed the full rate on air fares for audit staff when substantial discounts had been obtained by Vonnegut & Co. **(3 marks)**

Required

Comment on the ethical and other professional issues raised by each of the above matters and their implications, if any, for the continuation of each assignment. The division of marks for each sub-question is above. **(12 marks)**

(Total = 25 marks)

Question 4

(a) You work in a professional services firm. Discuss the ethical dimensions relating to how a professional accountant should respond when one of their clients is suspected of being involved in money laundering. **(5 marks)**

(b) Compost, Present and Future Ltd (CPF) has created an innovative process that transforms garden waste into a product that can be used instead of coal but which creates no harmful emissions. CPF anticipates that once granted a licence to operate by its government, it will provide a genuine alternative to the existing garden waste recycling services offered to councils throughout England. One of the final stages in being granted this licence is to demonstrate the viability of its process outside its own test conditions. In order to do this, it needs to collect representative amounts of real garden waste, which will only occur if a large local council awards CPF a garden waste recycling contract. Without the government licence, it is unlikely that CPF will be able to operate in the long term due to the experimental nature of its process.

You are an accountant in the finance department at CPF. You have received an email from the finance director, announcing that Bigshire Council has just awarded CPF a contract to collect its garden waste for the next five years. The email explains that the anticipated volumes of waste would be more than adequate to prove CPF's operating capability to the government and that the licence would therefore be a formality. The finance director has congratulated everyone involved in the successful tendering process with Bigshire Council, stating that: "CPF made the Council an offer they couldn't refuse!" and has concluded by asking staff to keep this information confidential until it is formally announced by Bigshire Council at its annual meeting in seven days' time.

You telephoned one of your friends who works at Bigshire Council, eager to discuss this news. She refused to talk over the phone and instead suggested that you should meet in person after work. When you met her, she explained that a week ago, while walking back to her car after work, she overheard a conversation between the finance director of CPF and the chief executive of Bigshire

MOCK EXAM QUESTIONS

Council which strongly implied that Bigshire Council had been offered a significant amount of money by CPF in return for the award of the garden waste contract.

Required

Consider the ethical dimensions of all these events. As a professional accountant, discuss how you should respond and justify your answer with reference to your duty to act in the public interest.

(11 marks)

(c) While considering how you should respond to these events, you remember that the finance director recently asked you for some information to be used as part of the Bigshire garden waste contract tender. This information was a confidential request to recommend a suitable tax structure for a company that would be set up in a country where rates of corporate taxation are much lower than in the UK. The business plan provided by the finance director seems to suggest the transfer of a sum of money each month to this company. You notice that the ownership structure indicates only one director who has the same name as Bigshire Council's chief executive.

Required

From the additional information presented, discuss the ethical dimensions and suggest a suitable response. **(9 marks)**

(Total = 25 marks)

MOCK EXAM ANSWERS

Question 1

Marking scheme

			Marks
(a)	Explanation and meaning		2
	1 mark for each explanation of importance max		3
			5
(b)	1 mark for each criticism identified in the context of the case.		
	1 mark for the development of the criticism with reference to practise or		
	application max		10
(c)	1 mark for recognition of each option max	2	
	2 marks for each relevant argument for or against either alternative max	8	
			10
			25

(a) **Integrity**

The Cadbury report defined integrity as meaning **straightforward dealing** and **completeness**. The IESBA's fundamental principles define integrity as being **straightforward and honest** in all business and professional relationships. Integrity means resisting any pressure to act unethically.

Importance in professional relationships

Reliability

Integrity should mean that colleagues should be able to **rely on a professional's word** and be sure that his **intentions are ethical.**

Promotion of ethical environment

As a partner, and hence being someone who is in charge of management, at Lorca & Co, David should be particularly concerned to promote integrity. Not only is his own integrity more important because of his position of power, but also he should set an example to other staff in order to **promote an ethical environment** at the firm on which clients and others can rely.

Efficiency and effectiveness

Integrity means that time does not have to be spent checking the statements of a professional colleague against other evidence. Instead, it should mean that other partners or staff who are unsure of an issue should feel they can obtain unbiased advice from David.

(b) **Agreeing to corruption**

It appears that David could be implicated in a **misappropriation of company funds** for Martin Sassoon's personal use. He has either agreed to this or accepted a weak explanation, raising issues about his **integrity or professional competence**.

Duty to shareholders

David seems to have allowed his relationship with Martin to override his duty to the rest of the shareholders. David is reporting to the shareholders to give them assurance of Martin's **stewardship** of the company and that he has acted reliably as their agent. He should therefore have taken an **objective** view of Martin's conduct and he has failed to do this.

Duty to tax authorities

As well as a duty to shareholders, David has a **duty to stakeholders** who have a legal or other right to rely on the reliability and completeness of information in the financial statements. This particularly applies to the tax authorities in any regime and, in many regimes, David could be charged with **colluding in tax evasion.**

Duty to professional colleagues

David has let down his partners and staff in a number of ways. Hedda's query was justified and David's initial response would have given the impression that he was **not taking the query seriously**. David then accepted what appeared to be an inadequate explanation and **did not provide any reason** for his decision. Not only was this **poor conduct of professional relationships**, it was also a partner setting a **poor example** to a student.

Failure to act in accordance with applicable technical and professional standards

David has breached auditing standards by allowing an **unmodified opinion** to be expressed on the financial statements without the required disclosure of Mr Sassoon's transaction. IAS 24 requires all related party transactions to be disclosed regardless of value.

(c) **The alternatives are:**

(i) **Take no further action**

Douglas could decide not to raise the issue with David. Possible arguments in favour of this are as follows:

Respect for David's judgement

Although David has failed to explain himself well, that may not mean that his decision was wrong. As a senior partner, David has **experience and knowledge of the client** that Hedda and Douglas lack.

Destruction of working relationships

A confrontation with David without sufficient evidence is likely to destroy not only David and Douglas's friendship, but also mean they **cannot work together in future**. It undermines the basis of trust that underpins the partnership in which they and others participate. Because of David's seniority, a dispute would also damage Douglas's position in the firm. However, if Douglas allows these considerations to be the main influence in his decision, he would clearly appear to **lack objectivity** and have yielded to the threat of **intimidation**.

(ii) **Confront David**

Douglas's other alternative is to confront David and **demand an adequate explanation**. If David does not provide one, Douglas would have to raise the matter with the other partners. Arguments in favour of this include:

Complicity in David's actions

The strength of the evidence suggests that at least Douglas should seek an explanation from David, even if he accepts it in the end. At present it seems that if Douglas takes no further action, then he, like David, is **complicit** in possible fraud, tax evasion and breaches of accounting, auditing and ethical standards.

Duty to other partners

If the transaction is found to be wrong, then sanctions may be taken not only against Martin and Sassoon Co, but also against David and Lorca & Co for failing to report the transaction and incorrectly expressing an unmodified opinion in the auditor's report. The firm may suffer **financial penalties** and a **loss of reputation** that would affect all partners. Douglas therefore has a **duty to other partners** to deal with a potentially serious problem as soon as possible.

Duty to Hedda

As a training partner, Douglas has a duty to Hedda to take her concerns seriously and make sure that they are **adequately addressed**. This is particularly important here as David has already set such a poor example. If Douglas takes no action, Hedda may take the issue further herself; reporting her concerns to other partners or seeking advice from her professional body. Douglas's position in the partnership and reputation may be damaged if he is found to have failed to investigate Hedda's concerns adequately.

Conclusion

Douglas has a clear duty to seek an **adequate explanation** from David and take the matter further if David does not provide one.

Question 2

Marking scheme

				Marks
(a)		1 mark for each relevant point on importance of independence made and briefly described. Half mark for mention only	max	3
		1 mark for each threat to independence identified	max	3
		1 mark for each threat briefly described	max	3
				9
(b)	(i)	1 mark for each organisational duty identified and briefly described		3
		1 mark for each professional duty identified and briefly described		3
		1 mark for each contrast or comparison drawn up		2
			max	6
	(ii)	1 mark for each point made on inclination towards role as employee	max	2
		1 mark for each point made on inclination towards professional duty	max	2
				4
(c)		4 marks for evidence of understanding the two positions (whether as a definition or in the other parts of the answer)		4
		2 marks for explanation of how the positions affect outcome		2
		Cross marks between these two to reflect adequacy of overall answer		
				6
				25

(a) **Reliability of financial information**

Corporate governance reports have highlighted **reliability of financial information** as a key aspect of corporate governance. Shareholders and other stakeholders need a trustworthy record of **directors' stewardship** to be able to take decisions about the company. Assurance provided by independent auditors is a key quality control on the reliability of information.

Credibility of financial information

An unmodified opinion in an independent auditor's report on the financial statements should give them more **credibility**, enhancing the appeal of the company to investors. It should represent the views of independent experts, who are not motivated by personal interests to give a favourable opinion on the annual financial statements.

Value for money of audit work

Audit fees should be set on the basis of charging for the work **necessary to gain sufficient audit assurance**. A lack of independence here seems to mean important audit work may not be done, and thus the shareholders are not receiving value for the audit fees.

Threats to professional standards

A lack of independence may lead to a failure to **fulfil professional requirements** to obtain enough evidence to form the basis of an audit opinion, here to obtain details of a questionable material item. Failure by auditors to do this **undermines the credibility of the accountancy profession** and the standards it enforces.

Threats to independence

Familiarity with client

Seamus Seedy has been partner in charge of the audit for **longer than the period recommended by most governance reports** (between five and seven years). His familiarity appears to have influenced his judgement, leading him to make the dubious assumption that because there has been no problem on this audit in the past, there cannot be a problem now.

Personal friendship – self interest

Seamus Seedy appears to be **allowing his personal friendship** with Edward Hughes to **bias his judgement** on whether to investigate the questionable payment. There is a **self interest threat** involved in Seamus Taylor's wish to maintain the friendship, and also a **lack of objectivity**.

Non-audit services – self interest

Governance codes identify **provision of non-audit services** as a potentially significant threat to auditor independence. This scenario illustrates why; a **modified opinion** on Gunn Co's financial statements may mean that the company stops using Armitage & Co to provide consultancy services. Thus, it is clearly in Armitage & Co's **self interest to give an unmodified audit opinion**, and therefore it seems doubtful that the firm is truly independent.

(b) (i) **Obedience**

As an employee, Paola owes the duty of **obedience** to her **managers** and should comply with reasonable orders provided they do not breach her professional duties.

As a professional accountant Paola should comply with the **technical and ethical standards established by her professional body**, even if these conflict with what she is being required to do in the workplace.

Interests of employer and profession

As an employee, Paola has a responsibility to **promote the interests of her employer**. These include the **commercial, fee-earning, interests**, making efforts to obtain new work and keep existing clients happy.

As a professional accountant, Paola has a responsibility to maintain the good name of her accountancy body. This includes acting **honestly and objectively**, and not allowing herself to be associated with misleading information or a misleading report.

Obligations of employment and membership

As an employee, Paola owes a general duty to '**fit in**', be part of a team and behave in ways that are in accordance with the **organisational culture** of her employer.

As a member of a professional accounting body, Paola owes the duty to act in accordance with the **norms** of that body, including its stress on **professional behaviour**.

(ii) **Acting non-commercially**

The main tension between the roles that Paola is experiencing is that if she acts in accordance with professional standards, and pursues a full explanation for the payment, she will not be acting in her employer's **commercial interests**. The audit will go on longer than budgeted, meaning that the assignment is **less profitable**. She also risks upsetting the client and **putting future income at risk**.

Paola's own interests

There is also the issue of whether Paola should take into account her own interests and if so how she should do this. She may feel that in order to make her life **easier as an employee** of Armitage & Co, she should allow the report to be signed. Against this is the **possibility of suffering disciplinary action** by her professional body if she allows the audit report to be signed, and it later turns out to be misleading.

(c) **Absolutist assumptions**

Definition

Absolutist dogmatic assumptions are based on the idea that there are **rules** which should be followed in all circumstances, **whatever the consequences**. This means that if an individual is facing an ethical dilemma, there should be a **'right' solution** to that dilemma.

Gunn Co situation

Absolutist assumptions would indicate that an audit provides **independent assurance** on a business. Because of this, all material audit queries need to be resolved if an **unmodified audit opinion** is to be given.

Conclusion using absolutist assumptions

Resolving the query is the right course of action to take and thus should be pursued, even if it means a longer audit and problems with the client.

Relativist assumptions

Definition

A relativist position would be that there are a variety of ethical beliefs and practices, and that the ethics that are most appropriate in a given situation will depend on the conditions at that time. A **pragmatic consequentialist** position would consider the **consequences** of the various options available, and choose the option that on balance **produced the greatest benefits** or the **least degree of harm**. This may be benefits or lack of harm in general, or it may be defined more narrowly to mean benefits or lack of harm to Armitage & Co or even just to Paola herself (which would be egoism).

Gunn Co situation

Using relativist assumptions would mean that Paola needs to assess the **consequences** of pursuing this point. The relativist viewpoint would take into account the argument that **not all audit trails** can **end neatly**. It would also consider the **other circumstances** surrounding the audit, including **previous experience of the client** and **personal knowledge of Edward Hughes**. That said, the relativist view would also consider the possible **adverse consequences to the reputation of Paola Giraldo and Armitage & Co** if the firm gives an unmodified opinion when it later turns out it should not have done.

Conclusion using relativist assumptions

The decision using relativist assumptions therefore requires the weighing up of **different possible consequences**. Because of this, the outcome of the decision cannot be predicted easily.

Question 3

Marking scheme

		Marks

(a) 1 mark per point up to a maximum 3 marks for any single issue
Issues ideas
Re: Change in appointment
Audit firm rotation – an independence safeguard
- Inference on communication ('professional etiquette')
- Engagement letter (responsibilities)

Re: Omission of provision
- Fundamental error
- Error vs fraud
- Competence, integrity & objectivity (Cruz & Co and Lopez & Co)
- (IAS 8 non-compliance)
- Confidentiality (communication with Lopez & Co)
- Duty of care/users
- Negligence/liability
- Misconduct

Re: Legal documentation, etc
- Audit scope
- Report to management
- Transfer books/papers/information
- Other services opportunity

                                                                             13

(b) Ethical and other professional issues
Generally 1 mark each ethical/professional issue/implication
  (i) Senior audit staff leaving for employment with client
- Objectivity (Lean)/self-interest threat
- Integrity (James and/or Charles)
- Professional courtesy
- Implications for staffing final audit
- Review of interim audit working paper

  (ii) Unmodified audit opinion
- Sufficiency of evidence (Durdle Ltd and Kimmeridge Ltd)
- Reliance on written representations (and wider implications)
- Familiarity threat
- Self-interest threat
- Undue influence

  (iii) Threatened legal action
- Advocacy threat
- Integrity of Vonnegut & Co
- Industry practice?
- Legal obligation?
- Terms of engagement

                                                     12

(i) Max 4
(ii) Max 5
(iii) Max 3
      25

(a) **Change of auditors**

East Creech Co's policy to change auditors on a periodic basis is good practice. This type of rotation is seen as a safeguard to protect independence.

As Lopez & Co has accepted nomination there were no matters brought to their attention by Cruz & Co, or if matters were raised they have been dealt with.

Due to the current circumstances (ie the directors not wishing to change the financial statements and not agreeing to a modified opinion), this may be an opportunity for Lopez & Co to remind the directors of their responsibilities for the financial statements and the accounting policies adopted. If not yet finalised this could be included in the engagement letter.

Error

Impact on 2019 accounts

As the financial statements have not been issued there is an opportunity to **correct the error**. This should be done even if this means delaying the issue of the financial statements.

If the directors refuse to correct the accounts, they are deliberately misleading the shareholders. (The error is so significant that the accounts are unreliable unless corrected.)

Cruz & Co should issue an **adverse audit opinion** irrespective of the directors' willingness or otherwise to accept it as their prime responsibility is to the shareholders and not to the directors.

Impact on 2020 accounts

In the accounts for June 2020 the omission should be treated as a fundamental error in accordance with IAS 8. This would also result in the restatement of the comparatives.

Ethical considerations

The fact that the error has only been identified at this late stage calls into question the professionalism with which the audit has been conducted and the **quality of the work performed**.

The fact that Cruz & Co is willing to issue an unmodified opinion, knowing that the accounts are materially misstated, shows a **lack of integrity**. This could result in negligence claims being made against the firm and disciplinary action being taken by the firm's regulatory body.

It also demonstrates a **lack of independence** as the auditors are clearly being influenced by the directors.

The fact that Lopez & Co has also agreed not to restate the comparatives also shows a **lack of judgement and integrity** on their part. Their independence is being affected by both the directors and the previous auditors. It also shows a lack of appreciation of respective responsibilities as it would be the directors who would prepare the accounts.

Cruz & Co and Lopez & Co have obviously had discussions regarding this issue. Unless Cruz & Co obtained permission from East Creech Co to communicate with the prospective auditors they will have breached **client confidentiality**.

Outsourced work

Outsourcing of legal and company secretarial work is common practice. The situation offers an opportunity to Lopez & Co to offer additional services.

Lopez & Co may experience difficulties in obtaining certain key documents. Even if Adam had made contingency plans it is likely that there will be some time delay in obtaining information. If the problem is significant it may constitute an inability to obtain sufficient appropriate audit evidence.

East Creech Co does not keep copies of key documents. This should be raised in Lopez & Co's management letter as it would be good practice to keep adequate documentation regarding outsourced activities.

It may be that Cruz & Co has legal documents and board minutes on their audit files which would be of ongoing use to the new auditors. Once formally appointed Cruz & Co would be expected to provide Lopez & Co with all the books and papers in their possession free of charge. If requested to do so, other information may also be provided at the request of East Creech Co (or Lopez & Co's request with the agreement of East Creech Co). Depending on the amount of work involved a fee could be charged.

(b) (i) **Perry Ltd**

Independence

In being shortlisted for a position at Perry Ltd, Charles is no longer independent with regard to the audit of Perry Ltd. There is too great a risk that he will want to impress his potential future employer and this will affect the audit that he carries out.

Quality control procedures

The IESBA *Code of Ethics* states that a firm should have quality control policies setting out that if a senior member of audit staff is potentially going to be employed by an audit client, then that member of staff should disclose that fact to the audit firm.

In this case, either Vonnegut & Co does not have such a policy, which is a failing in its own quality control, or, it does have such a policy and Charles has breached this policy in not telling the audit firm he had applied for a job at Perry Ltd.

Regardless of whether Vonnegut & Co has such a policy, it is a matter of Charles's personal integrity that he should have made the disclosure, as he should have been aware that he was not sufficiently independent of Perry Ltd to carry out the audit.

Charles should receive a warning from his employer about his conduct.

Implications for continuing the engagement

Charles should be removed from the audit immediately and a different senior appointed in his place.

Any work that Charles has already carried out, such as the planning of the audit, should be reviewed, and amended if this is felt to be necessary.

(ii) **Kimmeridge**

Audit evidence

Auditors should obtain written representations on "matters material to the financial statements when other sufficient appropriate audit evidence cannot reasonably be expected to exist. However, these representations cannot be a substitute for other audit evidence that the auditor could reasonably expect to be available".

An auditor would expect there to be sources of evidence other than management opinion about whether an asset is impaired. For example, management should have carried out an impairment review of the asset, which the auditors could have used as audit evidence, carrying out verifications on the assumptions and facts used in the impairment review.

If this evidence had been available, Vonnegut & Co should not have needed to obtain written representations about the goodwill. If the evidence had not been available, this would have constituted an inability to obtain sufficient appropriate audit evidence, as the auditors cannot just accept representations in lieu of audit evidence they expect to be available.

In addition, if the evidence was not available, then this would be a misstatement in respect of the accounting treatment, because Chatham would not have been fulfilling the requirements of IFRS 3 *Business Combinations*.

Fraudulent financial reporting

Given that due to persistent losses, the goodwill in Durdle Ltd appears to be impaired and the requirements of IFRS may not have been followed, there is a suspicion that in not recognising the impairment in Durdle Ltd, there has been fraudulent financial reporting in this situation, particularly since the managing director stands to benefit from the company doing well in the short term when she is likely to exercise her share options.

Lack of independence due to long association

It is possible that the auditors have overlooked the problems outlined above due to a lack of independence arising from the fact that Vonnegut & Co has had a long association with this client. Audit staff may have a personal relationship with Leslie Stripe to the extent that they believe her to be honest and do not suspect any wrongdoing on her part, to the point where their professional scepticism has been affected.

Implications for audit evidence

Insufficient audit evidence appears to have been obtained about the goodwill in Durdle Ltd and therefore the going concern basis of the financial statements. It is possible that there is insufficient audit evidence for other areas of the audit.

Implications for continuing the engagement

This problem does not give rise to a need for the audit firm to divest this audit client, but it does suggest that it might be necessary to rotate the senior staff associated with the audit so that the danger of long association is averted. The audit opinion for 2019 should be subject to a post-issuance review to ensure that sufficient evidence was obtained on which to base the audit opinion.

(iii) **Chesil Ltd**

Advocacy threat

An advocacy threat to independence has arisen as Chesil Ltd is threatening legal action against Vonnegut & Co.

Lack of integrity

If the allegation is true and Vonnegut & Co has recharged excessive expenses to Chesil Ltd, this does appear to indicate a lack of integrity on the part of Vonnegut & Co. However, it could have been a simple error, or it could be because Vonnegut & Co believes this to be accepted industry practice or it was an agreed policy in the engagement letter between the parties.

As legal proceedings are expensive and Vonnegut & Co does not appear to have acted illegally, Chesil Ltd might be better advised to take this matter up with the AIA than in a court of law. The audit engagement partner could advise Chesil Ltd of this, although it is unlikely that client staff will accept his advice if they believe the audit firm to be guilty.

Action to take

Vonnegut & Co should issue a credit note for the difference to attempt to solve the breach.

Implications for continuing with the assignment

Unless the dispute is settled very quickly, Vonnegut & Co is no longer independent with regard to the Chesil Ltd audit and should resign for the audit of the year-end 31 December 2019 (assuming they had previously been elected).

Question 4

Marking scheme

		Marks
(a)	Reward suitable responses with 1 mark per reasonable point made. Only ethical responses should be recognised: the actual responses to money laundering are more to do with best practice so do not directly present ethical dimensions.	5
(b)	Marks should be awarded as suggested – additional comments can be rewarded if appropriate – key areas: • Bribery and the FD • Acting in the public interest • Pragmatic stakeholder views • Ethical judgement displayed • Confidentiality	11
(c)	Marks should be awarded as suggested – additional comments can be rewarded if appropriate – key areas: • Bribery issues • Money laundering issues • Tax avoidance issues	9
		25

(a) Money laundering

When faced with suspicions of money laundering by a client, a professional accountant should respond in the following manner:

- Act on these suspicions: they cannot ignore them as that would be illegal.

- Attempt to collect as much evidence as they can to support their suspicions, albeit mindful of the risk of tipping off.

- Report their suspicions to their firm's money laundering reporting officer (MLRO) as soon as possible.

- Avoid tipping off the potential money laundered.

Although these are predominantly legal requirements, a professional accountant's response could also be framed in terms of the fundamental ethical principles:

- Professional competence and due care are required, because the professional accountant should respond appropriately in line with the training they have received on money laundering [1].

- Confidentiality is also required when dealing with any suspicious activities, by ensuring that there is no tipping off [1]. This also requires an element of professional behaviour to still be able to communicate with clients in such cases without tipping them off [1].

- There is a conflict in the application of ethical principles between the objectivity required when considering the potential loss of future client income by reporting this suspicious activity [1] and the necessary integrity to tell the truth regardless, once you have these suspicions [1]. This does present an ethical dilemma [1] - is it worth sacrificing your integrity just to preserve the fees earned from such a client?

(b) **CPF**

When considered in isolation, bribery is illegal and so as a professional accountant, you cannot allow yourself to be a part of this scheme **[1]**. You would therefore be expected to establish the facts of this matter and then confront the finance director with this evidence **[1]**. You may have to consider taking your concerns to a higher level of authority if you feel they would not be acted upon by the finance director **[1]**.

However, when we consider the ethical dimensions of these events, the facts do not tell the whole story and our duty to act in the public interest presents a number of ethical challenges that we cannot ignore **[1]** even if we ultimately reach the same conclusion that this bribery should not go unnoticed or unpunished **[1]**.

As well as their legal duty to maintain business continuity, directors of private companies also face a moral obligation to secure longer-term financial security for all their stakeholders, including employees, suppliers and shareholders **[1]**.

There will have been considerable pressure from the board of CPF to secure the company's long-term future. As a professional accountant, the finance director may have taken a pragmatic approach to this situation and concluded that committing bribery would mean only one person at CPF is affected: the finance director themselves, because he alone would shoulder the guilt of acting in an unethical (not to mention illegal) manner **[1]**. Failure to do this could lead to the end of the company which would mean that everyone employed by CPF would be affected **[1]**. The finance director is therefore likely to have concluded that it is better to bribe the Council and win the contract that way, as it has a far better social outcome than acting legally and potentially seeing the company fail **[1]**.

There are other ethical dimensions in play here. Significant amounts of money moving from private to public sector is unusual and such sums often tend to go in the opposite direction (eg paying a private company to build a public sector hospital with taxpayers' money). From an ethical perspective, passing money to help Bigshire Council could be a good thing **[1]**.

However, the Council has displayed poor ethical judgement by accepting this bribe and should change this decision **[1]**, awarding the garden waste contract on the basis of commercial and other service-related factors only **[1]**.

If we consider the bigger picture, awarding CPF the government licence to operate could lead to dramatic change in the energy industry and, ultimately, a reduction in harmful emissions of greenhouse gases if coal is no longer required to be burned. Surely that would be ethically acceptable **[1]**?

Finally, on a personal level, as a professional accountant you have neglected your duty to maintain the confidentiality of sensitive information supplied to you in good faith by calling your friend to discuss the contract **[1]**. You would normally be expected to disclose this to your employer **[1]**: however, given the ethically ambiguous nature of these circumstances, you may no longer feel you can trust CPF and seek some form of professional advice from your professional body instead **[1]**.

(c) **Bigshire**

There would appear to be two separate issues here, each connected to the Bigshire Council bribery allegations. Firstly, a regular payment is expected to be made to a company whose only beneficiary appears to be Bigshire Council's chief executive **[1]**. Secondly, this appears to be in a jurisdiction with a lower rate of corporate taxation than in the UK**[1]**.

The source of these payments is not known. If from CPF, they would appear to be a bribe to the chief executive in return for the award of the contract **[1]**. It is possible that your friend may have only heard about the payments between CPF and Bigshire Council or instead she might have misinterpreted the situation and the bribe is actually only between CPF and the chief executive **[1]**.

Alternatively, the payments may be legitimate sums from an as yet unidentified party and the finance director is simply assisting the chief executive with a vehicle for managing his tax liabilities

[1]. However, you could still question the wisdom of the finance director providing this service to the chief executive at the exact same time as the garden waste contract was being decided [1].

Each of these situations creates an ethical problem. Should this be a bribe, the payments would be illegal and represent the proceeds of crime and consequently money laundering [1]. You would therefore need to adopt extreme caution, not only regarding the bribery allegations but also the risk that you may be accused of tipping off if you confront the finance director without having first informed CPF's money laundering reporting officer (MLRO) and been cleared to proceed [1]. It is entirely possible that CPF's MLRO might actually be the finance director, so you should seek some higher authority if possible or consult your professional body for advice on your next steps [1].

Even if this is not a bribe, it appears as though you are assisting the finance director in some form of tax planning that may have strayed into the territory of tax avoidance, which is not illegal but is not entirely ethical [1]. Given the beneficiary of this arrangement works in the same public sector that such tax avoidance ultimately punishes, it adds a further ethical dimension to your consideration of these events [1].

In response, you need to tread very carefully here: tipping off is the real threat, so you need to find some way of raising this issue with the MLRO at CPF before you decide whether to confront the finance director about the bribery allegations [1]. You should probably also obtain some form of professional advice, whether from your professional body or from an independent legal source [1].

Bibliography

BIBLIOGRAPHY

Australian Bureau of Statistics in Morgan, N. (2016) *6 Personality types of accountants according to Carl Jung* [Online]. Available at: https://www.linkedin.com/pulse/6-personality-types-accountants-according-carl-jung-nicole-morgan/ [Accessed 01/2020].

BBC News, 2011: https://www.bbc.co.uk/news/business-15330870

BBC News (2012) *Starbucks, Google and Amazon grilled over tax avoidance* [Online]. Available at: https://www.bbc.co.uk/news/business-20288077 [Accessed 01/2020].

BBC News (2018) *Tesco directors acquitted in fraud trial* [Online]. Available at: https://www.bbc.co.uk/news/business-46459884 [Accessed 01/2020].

BIS (2018) *Annual Economic Report June 2018* [Online]. Available at: https://www.bis.org/publ/arpdf/ar2018e.pdf [Accessed 01/2020].

Chapman, B. (2016) SFO charges three former Tesco executives over £326m black hole in accounts [Online]. Available at: https://www.independent.co.uk/news/business/news/tesco-former-executives-charged-sfo-fraud-300m-accounts-philip-clarke-a7233766.html [Accessed 01/2020].

CIPFA (2020) *Telling the story, improving the presentation of local authority financial statements* [Online]. Available at: https://www.cipfa.org/policy-and-guidance/technical-panels-and-boards/cipfa-lasaac-local-authority-code-board/simplification-and-streamlining-the-presentation-of-local-authority-financial-statements [Accessed 01/2020].

Clark, A. (2010) *Lehman Brothers: Repo 105 and other accounting tricks* [Online]. Available at: https://www.theguardian.com/business/2010/mar/12/lehman-brothers-repo-105-enron [Accessed 01/2020].

Cox, J. (2017) *Tesco fined £129m by Serious Fraud Office for overstating profits* [Online]. Available at: https://www.independent.co.uk/news/business/news/tesco-fined-129-million-by-serious-fraud-office-overstating-profits-a7653166.html [Accessed 01/2020].

Cressey, D.R. (1973) *Other People's Money* (Montclair: Patterson Smith).

Crockett, Z. (2020) *The economics of unused gift cards* [Online]. Available at: https://thehustle.co/what-happens-to-unused-gift-cards/ [Accessed 01/2020].

Davis, A. & Rothstein, H. (2006) *The Effects of the Perceived Behavioral Integrity of Managers on Employee Attitudes: A Meta-analysis* [Online]. Available at: https://www.researchgate.net/publication/5148834_The_Effects_of_the_Perceived_Behavioral_Integrity_of_Managers_on_Employee_Attitudes_A_Meta-analysis [Accessed 10/2020].

Deloitte (2020) *International Public Sector Accounting Standards Board (IPSASB)* [Online]. Available at: https://www.iasplus.com/en/resources/global-organisations/ipsasb [Accessed 01/2020].

European Union (2019) *The EU list of non-cooperative jurisdictions for tax purposes — Report by the Code of Conduct Group (Business Taxation) suggesting amendments to the Annexes of the Council conclusions of 12 March 2019, including the de-listing of one jurisdiction2019/C 386/02 ST/13401/2019/REV/1* [Online]. Available at: https://eur-lex.europa.eu/legal-content/en/ALL/?uri=uriserv:OJ.C_.2019.386.01.0002.01.ENG [Accessed 01/2020].

FBI (2016) *History: Al Capone* [Online]. https://www.fbi.gov/history/famous-cases/al-capone [Accessed 01/2020].

Financial Reporting Council (2016) *Investigations into the preparation, approval and audit of the financial statements of Sports Direct International plc* [Online]. Available at: https://www.frc.org.uk/news/november-2016/investigations-into-the-preparation,-approval-and [Accessed 01/2020].

Financial Reporting Council (2016) Findings of the Financial Reporting Review Panel in respect of the accounts of Sports Direct International plc for the year ended 26 April 2015 [Online]. Available at: https://www.frc.org.uk/news/december-2016/findings-of-the-financial-reporting-review-panel-i [Accessed 01/2020].

BIBLIOGRAPHY

Financial Reporting Council (2016) ISA (UK) 315 (revised June 2016) Identifying and Assessing the Risks of Material Misstatement Through Understanding of the Entity and Its Environment [Online]. Available at: https://www.frc.org.uk/getattachment/0737b946-b24a-441d-a313-54e0a90f9e7d/ISA-(UK)-315_Revised-June-2016.pdf [Accessed 01/2020].

Financial Reporting Council (2017) ISA (UK) 240 (revised June 2016) The auditor's responsibilities relating to fraud in an audit of financial statements [Online]. Available at: https://www.frc.org.uk/getattachment/5dc29cef-bb77-40f9-88f5-4c1cec215f5c/ISA-(UK)-240_Revised-June-2016_Updated-July-2017.pdf [Accessed 01/2020].

Financial Reporting Council (2017) *ISA (UK) 330 (revised July 2017) The auditor's responses to assessed risks* [Online]. Available at: https://www.frc.org.uk/getattachment/809bc664-12ea-402b-ab8e-632c9bd4cd41/ISA-(UK)-330_Revised-July-2017.pdf [Accessed 01/2020].

Financial Times (2019) *Shell reveals it paid no UK corporate income tax in 2018* [Online]. Available at: https://www.ft.com/content/933fe2b8-20ee-11ea-92da-f0c92e957a96 [Accessed 01/2020].

Gowthorpe, C., and Blake, J. (1998) *Ethical issues in accounting.* Oxon: Routledge.

IESBA (2019) *Exposure Draft - Proposed Revisions to the Code to Promote the Role and Mindset Expected of Professional Accountants* [Online]. Available at: https://www.ifac.org/system/files/publications/files/IESBA-Exposure-Draft-Role-and-Mindset.pdf [Accessed 01/2020].

IFAC *Accounting basis by country* [Online]. Available at: https://www.ifac.org/system/files/Accounting-Basis-by-Country.pdf [Accessed 01/2020].

Jensen, M. (2002) *Value Maximization, Stakeholder Theory, and the Corporate Objective Function* [Online]. Available at: https://www.jstor.org/stable/3857812?seq=1 [Accessed 10/2020].

Johnson, G and Scholes, K. (2002) *Exploring Corporate Strategy*, 6th Edition. Essex: Pearson Education.

Kerr, S. (2014) *Do Your Company's Incentives Reward Bad Behavior?* [Online]. Available at: https://hbr.org/2014/08/do-your-companys-incentives-reward-bad-behavior [Accessed 10/2020]

Crane, A. & Matten, M. (2005) *Corporate Citizenship: Toward an Extended Theoretical Conceptualization* [Online]. Available at: https://www.jstor.org/stable/20159101?seq=1 [Accessed 10/2020].

Mitchell, R., Agle, B. and Wood, D. (1997) *Toward a Theory of Stakeholder Identification and Salience: Defining the Principle of Who and What Really Counts* [Online]. Available at: https://links.jstor.org/sici?sici=03637425%28199710%2922%3A4%3C853%3ATATOSI%3E2.0.CO%3B2-0 [Accessed 10/2020].

The Myers & Briggs Foundation (2020) *MBTI Basics* [Online]. Available at: https://www.myersbriggs.org/my-mbti-personality-type/mbti-basics/ [Accessed 01/2020].

North Wales Live (2013) *Slate quarry executives jailed for fraud* [Online]. Available at: http://www.eifrs.ifrs.org [Accessed 01/2020].

Ocean's Eleven. (2001) [Film] Directed by Steven Soderbergh. USA, Warner Brothers.

Protiviti and Covington (2011) *Staying out of the headlines: strategies to combat corruption risk* [Online]. Available at: https://www.protiviti.com/sites/default/files/united_states/insights/strategies-to-combat-corruption-risk-protiviti.pdf [Accessed 02/2020].

Sports Direct plc (2015) *2015 Annual Report* [Online]. Available at: https://www.sportsdirectplc.com/~/media/Files/S/Sports-Direct/annual-report/Annual%20Report%202015%20-%20FINAL.pdf [Accessed 01/2020].

Sports Direct International plc (2017) *Annual report and accounts 2017* [Online]. Available at: https://www.sportsdirectplc.com/~/media/Files/S/Sports-Direct/annual-report/Annual%20Report%202017%20-%20v3.pdf [Accessed 01/2020].

Stevens, B. (2017) Sports Direct cancels controversial deal with Mike Ashley's brother [Online]. Available at: https://www.retailgazette.co.uk/blog/2017/06/sports-direct-cancels-controversial-deal-ashleys-brother/ [Accessed 01/2020].

United States Department of Justice (2017) *Foreign Corrupt Practices Act* [Online]. Available at: https://www.justice.gov/criminal-fraud/foreign-corrupt-practices-act [Accessed 02/2020]

United States Securities and Exchange Commission (2018) *SEC Enforcement Actions: FCPA Cases* [Online]. Available at: https://www.sec.gov/spotlight/fcpa/fcpa-cases.shtml [Accessed 02/2020]

World Commission on Environment and Development (1987) *Our common future* [Online]. Available at: https://sustainabledevelopment.un.org/content/documents/5987our-common-future.pdf [Accessed 01/2020].

FRC Audit and Assurance Standards and Guidance

FRC (2020) Standards and guidance [Online]. Available at:

https://www.frc.org.uk/auditors/audit-assurance/standards-and-guidance [Accessed 02/2020].

International Ethics Standards Board for Accountants guidance

IESBA (2018) Publications [Online]. Available at:

http://www.ethicsboard.org/system/files/publications/files/IESBA-Handbook-Code-of-Ethics-2018.pdf [Accessed 02/2020].

International Financial Reporting Standards

IFRS Foundation (2016) IFRS [Online]. Available at: http://eifrs.ifrs.org [Accessed 02/2020].

Index

> Note. **Key Terms** and their page references are given in **bold**.

A
Absolutism, **6**
Accountancy as a value-laden profession, 214
Accountancy profession, 213
    criticisms, 215
    value-laden, 214
Accountancy profession in society, 213
Active stakeholders, 40
Aggressive earnings management, 151
American Accounting Association (AAA) model, 60
Application of ethical codes, 122
Aristotle, 17
Assertions, 162
Asset valuation, 169

B
Badaracco and Webb, 79
Behavioural studies, 216
Behaviours, 29
Beliefs, 29
Best value, 200
Bribery, 5, **187**
Bribery Act 2011, 187
Bureaucracy, **28**

C
Cash, 171
Close family, **116**
Coalition for Environmentally Responsible Economics, 255
Codes of conduct, 77
Cognitivism, **8**, 10, 11
Collectivism, 23
Collusion, 153
Committee of European Auditing Oversight Bodies (CEAOB), 220
Common sense, 216
Company code of conduct, 75
Competence, 85
Concealed liabilities and expenses, 165
Confidentiality, 85, **98**
Conflict of interest, 67, 90
Conflicts between clients interests, 221
Consequentialism, 11
Consumer groups, 47
Consumerism, **47**
Contingent fee, **106**
Corporate citizenship, **249**
Corporate codes, 74
Corporate codes of ethics, 74
Corporate culture, 74
Corporate finance, 111
Corporate governance, **228**
    accountability, 233
    fairness, 230
    integrity, 234
    judgment, 234
    probity, 232
    reputation, 233
    responsibility, 232
Corporate governance independence, 231
Corporate governance innovation, 231
Corporate governance scepticism, 231
Corporate governance transparency, 230
Corporate social reporting, 258
Corporate social responsibility (CSR), 43, 249, 252
Correct compartment principle, 216
Corruption, **190**
Courtesy, 85
Crane and Matten, 236, 253
Creative accounting, 146
Cressey's Fraud Triangle, 154
CSR, **253**
CSR Strategy, 256
Customer due diligence (CDD), 194
Customers, 43

D
Dealing with ethical dilemmas, 125
Deontological ethics, 4, 6, 14
Deontology, **14**
Direct stakeholders, 39
Due care, 85
Dysfunctional behaviour, 216

E
Ecological Footprint, 244
Economic responsibilities, 252
Efficient body principle, 216
Egoism, **12**
Employees, 43
Enclosure principle, 216
Enlightened long-term value maximisation, 53
Enron, 168
Environmental costs, 247
Environmental footprint, **246**
Environmental impacts, 259
Environmental problems, 215
Environmental risk screening, 255
Equivalent view, 250
Ethical codes of conduct, 257
Ethical Issues in Accounting, 213
Ethical relativism, 6, 7, 8
Ethical responsibilities, 252
Ethical safeguards, 45
Ethical stance, **236**, **253**
Ethical stance of an organisation, 236

Ethical theory, 5
Ethical threats, 85
Ethics, 74
EU audit regulation, 107, 220
Executive Share Options Plans (ESOPs), 57
Extended view, 250
External stakeholders, 39
Extortion, 5
Exxon Valdez, 255

Fairness, 230
Familiarity, 113
Fees – relative size, 107
Femininity, 23
Financial interest, 104
Foucault, 216
Fraud, 153
Fraud prevention, 155
Fraudulent disclosures in accounts, 157
FRC Ethical standard Part B6: Provisions available for audits of small entities, 118
Fundamental principles, 85

GAAP, 210
Ghost employees, 153
Gifts, 5
Gifts and hospitality, 106
Going Concern, 161
Golden rule, 15
Government, 47
Gray, Owen and Adams, 238, 239, 241, 243
Grease money, 5

Hobbes, 216
Honesty, 232
How much to disclose to the finance director, 152

IAASB Preface to International Standards on Quality Control, Auditing, Assurance and Related Services, 219
IAS 16 *Property, Plant and Equipment*, 169
IAS 37 *Provisions, Contingent Liabilities and Contingent Assets*, 166
IAS 38 *Intangible Assets*, 169
Identity and values guidance, 78
IESBA Code, 79, 211
    Financial interests (public practice), 104
    Acting with sufficient expertise, 92
    Advertising, 102
    Conflicts of interest, 90
    Conflicts of interest (public practice), 98
    Custody of client assets (public practice), 101
    Fees (public practice), 100
    Financial interests linked to financial reporting and decision-making, 92
    Inducements, gifts and hospitality (public practice), 101
    Inducements, including gifts and hospitality, 92, 93
    Non-compliance with laws and regulations, 93
    Non-compliance with laws and regulations (public practice), 101
    Pressure to breach the fundamental principles, 96
    Professional appointments (public practice), 99, 103
    Second opinions (public practice), 100
    Loans and guarantees (public practice), 104
    Business relationships (public practice), 105
    Serving as director of audit client (public practice), 105
    Compensation and evaluation policies (public practice), 105
    Overdue fees (public practice), 106
    Contingent fees (public practice), 106
    Fees - relative size (public practice), 107
    Lowballing (public practice), 108
    Recruitment services (public practice), 108
    Preparing accounts (public practice), 109, 110
    Taxation services (public practice), 110
    Loan staff (public practice), 112
    General other services (public practice), 112
    Long association (public practice), 113
    Recent service with audit client (public practice), 115
    Employment with audit client (public practice), 115
    Family and personal relationships (public practice), 116
    Litigation (public practice), 117
IESBA Exposure Draft – Proposed Revisions to the Code to Promote the Role and Mindset Expected of Professional Accountants (2019), 147
IFRS 15 Revenue from Contracts with Customers, 149
Immediate family, 116
Independence, 84, 97, 214, **231**
Independence in appearance, 84
Independence of mind, 84
Indirect stakeholders, 39
Individualism, 23
Insider dealing, 197
Institutional shareholders, 46
Institutions, 214
Instrumental view, 38
Instrumental view of stakeholders, 38

Integrated reporting, 260
Integrity, 85, **234**
Intergovernmental Panel, 244
Internal stakeholders, 39
International Auditing and Assurance Standards Board (IAASB), 219
International Financial Reporting Standards (IFRS), 210
International Monetary Fund, 12
International standard setting (audit), 219
Intimidation, 117
Inventory, 170
Involuntary stakeholders, 41
ISA 330 *The Auditor's Responses to Assessed Risks*, 162

Jensen, 53
Johnson and Scholes, 236, 253
Jones, Thomas, 27
Judgement, 234
Judgemental issues, 214
Jung, 146
Jung's personality types, 146

Kant, 14
Key audit partner, **106**
Know your client (KYC), 194
Known stakeholders, 41
Kohlberg, 4, 22, 24, 124, 213

Lack of equality, 214
Legal responsibilities, 252
Lehman Brothers, 164
Liberal democracy, 214
Liberal economic democracy, 214
Limited view, 250
Living Planet Index, 244
Lobby groups, 200
Locke, 216
Long-term creditors, 57
Long-term shareholder interest, 237, 253
Lowballing, 108

Macintosh, 216
MacIntyre, Alisdair, 16
Masculinity, 23
Mechanistic issues, 213
Mendelow, 48
Mendelow's matrix, 48
Mission statements, 257
Money laundering, **191**
Money laundering reporting officer (MLRO), 194
Monsanto, 248
Moral courage, 185

Multiple stakeholder obligations, 237, 254
Myers-Briggs Type Indicator, 146

Narrow stakeholders, 40
Negative stakeholder power, 49
Nolan Principles, 201
Non-cognitivism, 6, 7, **9**
Non-current assets, 169
Non-departmental public bodies (NDPBs), 199
Non-governmental organisations (NGOs), 199
Normative view, 38
Normative view of stakeholders, 38

Objectivity, 85
OECD principles, 229
Olympus, 185
Omission of financial records, 162
Organisation for Economic Co-operation and Development (OECD), 229
Organisational culture, **29**
Organisational field, **28**

Parmalat, 171
Passive stakeholders, 40
Personality traits, 146
Philanthropic responsibilities, 252
Pluralism, **13**
Power distance, 23
Pressure from management, 159
Primary stakeholders, 40
Principles-based approach, 127
Principles-based guidance, 82, 83
Private sector, 198
Probity/honesty, 232
Proceeds of Crime Act 2002, 192
Profession, **122**
Professional behaviour, 85
Professional codes of ethics, 79
Professional scepticism, **84,** 147, 166
Professionalism, 211
Professions, 211
Profit-making organisations, 46
Profit-related pay, 57
Public interest, 123, 211, **212**, 217
Public Interest Disclosure Act (1998), **185**
Public Interest Oversight Board (PIOB), 220
Public oversight, 220
Public sector, 198
Puxty, 215

Quasi-autonomous non-governmental organisations (QUANGOs), 199

R

Receivables, 171
Recognised stakeholders, 40
Recognised Supervisory Bodies, 218
Recruitment services, 108
Relativism, **7**
Reputation, 233
Reputation risk, 248, 257
Responsibility, 232
Revenue recognition, 148
Revised Ethical Standard, 177

S

Safeguards, 87
Safeguards created by the firm, 87, 88
Safeguards created by the profession, 87
Safeguards for accountants in business, 88
Scepticism, 84
Scottish Power, 251
Secondary stakeholders, 40
Security, 57
Self regulation, 58
Self-review, 108
Shaper of society, 237
Share option scheme, 57
Shareholder theory, 37
Shareholders, 43, 46
Short-term shareholder interest, 237, 253
Smith, Adam, 12, 17
Social accounts, 258
Social cost, 249
Social footprint, **247**
Social impacts, 247
Social responsibility, 249
Social responsibility accounting, 238
Social responsibility stances, 238
Social welfare, 214
Sports Direct, 159
Stakeholder, **36**
Stakeholder bargaining strength, 44, 45
Stakeholder influence, 49
Stakeholder mapping, 48, 49
Stakeholder risks, 44
Stakeholder theory, 36, 37
Stakeholders, 36, 56, 237, 248, 257
Stern report, 244
Stockholder theory, 37
Strategic CSR, 256
Structural adjustment programmes, 12

Substantive testing, 162
Suppliers, 43, **47**
Sustainability, **184**

T

Taken for granted assumptions, 29
Taking a big bath, **166**
Tax avoidance, **178**, 179
Tax codes of conduct, 183
Tax evasion, **179**
Tax planning, **176**
Tax planning, 176, 178
Teleological ethics, 4
Teleological or consequentialist ethics: utilitarianism, 11
Terrorism Act 2000, 192
Terrorist financing, **195**
The seven principles of public life, 201
Timing differences, 163
Tipping off, 194
Traidcraft, 238
Trainee expectations, 222
Transparency, **230**
Tucker's five question model, 61

U

UK Bribery Act (2010), 187
UK regulatory framework, 218
Uncertainty avoidance, 23
Unknown stakeholders, 41
Unprofessional behaviour, 67
Unrecognised stakeholders, 40
Utilitarianism, **11**

V

Valdez, 255
Value for money, 200
Value-laden profession, 214
Values, 29
Virtue ethics, **16**
Voluntary code of conduct, **58**
Voluntary stakeholders, 41

W

Whistleblowing, 152, **184**
Wide stakeholders, 40
World Wildlife Fund, 245